Frommer's®

P9-CEY-236

CARIBBEAN
CRUISES
AND PORTS OF CALL

Here's what the critics say about Frommer's:

"Amazingly easy to use. Very portable, very complete."
—*Booklist*

♦

"The only mainstream guide to list specific prices. The Walter Cronkite of guidebooks—with all that implies."
—*Travel & Leisure*

♦

"Complete, concise, and filled with useful information."
—*New York Daily News*

♦

"The best series for travelers who want one easy-to-use guidebook."

—*U.S. Air Magazine*

Frommer's® 2000

CARIBBEAN CRUISES
AND PORTS OF CALL

by Heidi Sarna

with Online Directory by Michael Shapiro

MACMILLAN • USA

ABOUT THE AUTHOR

Heidi Sarna has cruised on some 50 ships of all shapes and sizes, from 100-passenger sailing ships to 3,000-passenger megas, and she loves them all (well, OK, some more than others). Over the past 10 years, she has contributed articles on cruising and travel to *Travel Holiday, Bride's, New Choices, Cigar Aficionado, Travel Weekly, Travel Agent,* and *Porthole* magazines, as well as other major guidebooks and the *Boston Herald, Star Ledger,* and *Washington Times* newspapers. When she's not cruising, you're bound to find her at Manhattan's West Side docks, touring and inspecting the many ships that pass through New York.

MACMILLAN TRAVEL

Macmillan General Reference USA, Inc.
1633 Broadway
New York, NY 10019

Find us online at **www.frommers.com**.

ISBN 0-02-862891-8
ISSN 1090-2600

Editor: Matt Hannafin
Production Editor: Carol Sheehan
Photo Editor: Richard Fox
Design by Michele Laseau
Staff cartographers: John Decamillis, Roberta Stockwell
Additional Cartography by Raffaele DeGennaro, Peter Bogaty
Front cover photo: Harvey Lloyd/The Stock Market
Page creation by Melissa Auciello-Brogan, Ellen Considine, and Sean Monkhouse

SPECIAL SALES

Bulk purchases (10+ copies) of Frommer's and selected Macmillan travel guides are available to corporations, organizations, mail-order catalogs, institutions, and charities at special discounts, and can be customized to suit individual needs. For more information, write to Special Sales, Macmillan General Reference, 1633 Broadway, New York, NY 10019.

Manufactured in the United States of America

5 4 3 2 1

Contents

Part 1: Planning, Booking & Preparing for Your Cruise

7   Cheap Cruises, Older Ships: The Budget Lines   194

8   The Ultra-Luxury Lines   236

9 Soft-Adventure Lines & Sailing Ships   281

Part 3: The Ports

10 The Ports of Embarkation   333

11 Caribbean Ports of Call   366

Part 4: Appendixes

List of Maps

ACKNOWLEDGMENTS

A select group of experienced travel journalists and experts contributed to this book.

Ted Scull, a well-respected ship authority and travel writer, contributed not only his endless east side/west side humor and support, but parts of the Cunard, Seabourn, Premier, and Royal Olympic reviews.

Jonathan Siskin, seasoned travel writer, broadcaster, and poet-artist, contributed to the ACCL, Costa, Windstar, and Royal Olympic reviews.

Mark Chapman, travel editor at the *Boston Herald* and cabaret star in the making, lent his sharp eye and matching wit to the Royal Caribbean, Princess, and Norwegian reviews.

Ronald I. Framson, Certified Travel Counselor (CTC) and travel industry consultant, along with his wife, **Dee L. Framson,** CTC, Master Cruise Counsellor (MCC), and active agent, were endlessly helpful and contributed their fine-hewn experience to the "Booking Your Cruise & Getting the Best Price" chapter.

Alan Zamchick, ship lover since the age of 7 and Steamship Historical Society and World Ship Society member, dug up the facts for the history section in chapter 4.

Arline and Sam Bleecker, travel-writing team extraordinaire, contributed their valuable two cents to the Radisson review.

Robbie Peterson, freelance writer and former magazine editor, contributed her thoughts to the Clipper review.

Many thanks to all the helpful public relations staff at the cruise lines, especially Aly Bello of Carnival, Gauri Pandya of Costa, Kristin Carlson of Crystal, Kiersten Murnane of Disney, Janis Goller of Holland America, Denise Seomin of Princess, Rich Steck of Royal Caribbean/Celebrity, and Mary Schimmelman of Windstar.

Also, special thanks to Joe Romans, market research analyst at the Travel Company, for his invaluable help in obtaining the discounted cruise prices presented for the first time in this edition.

Special thanks to **Matt Hannafin,** the most thorough, patient, and good-hearted editor in New York. And most importantly, to my wonderful husband **Arun,** for his support, insight, and much-appreciated daily dose of "go do your work."

An Invitation to the Reader

In researching this book, we discovered many wonderful places—hotels, restaurants, shops, and more. We're sure you'll find others. Please tell us about them, so we can share the information with your fellow travelers in upcoming editions. If you were disappointed with a recommendation, we'd love to know that, too. Please write to:

Frommer's Caribbean Cruises and Ports of Call 2000
Macmillan Travel
1633 Broadway
New York, NY 10019

An Additional Note

Please be advised that travel information is subject to change at any time—and this is especially true of prices. We therefore suggest that you write or call ahead for confirmation when making your travel plans. The authors, editors, and publisher cannot be held responsible for the experiences of readers while traveling. Your safety is important to us, however, so we encourage you to stay alert and be aware of your surroundings. Keep a close eye on cameras, purses, and wallets, all favorite targets of thieves and pickpockets.

What the Symbols Mean

✪ Frommer's Favorites

Our favorite places and experiences—outstanding for quality, value, or both.

The following abbreviations are used for credit cards:

AE	American Express	EC	Eurocard
CB	Carte Blanche	JCB	Japan Credit Bank
DC	Diners Club	MC	MasterCard
DISC	Discover	V	Visa
ER	EnRoute		

Find Frommer's Online

Arthur Frommer's Budget Travel Online (**www.frommers.com**) offers more than 6,000 pages of up-to-the-minute travel information—including the latest bargains and candid, personal articles updated daily by Arthur Frommer himself. No other Web site offers such comprehensive and timely coverage of the world of travel.

The Gulf of Mexico & the Caribbean

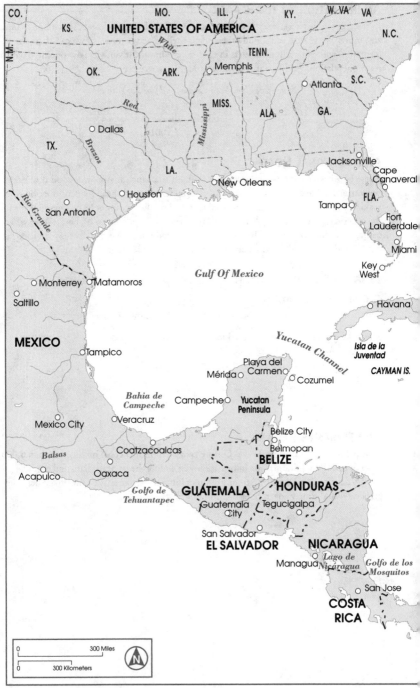

CO.
KS.
MO.
ILL.
KY.
W. VA.
VA.
N.C.
UNITED STATES OF AMERICA
N.M.
OK.
ARK.
White
TENN.
○ Memphis
○ Atlanta
S.C.
MISS.
ALA.
GA.
Red
○ Dallas
TX.
Brazos
LA.
Jacksonville
Cape
Canaveral
Rio Grande
○ Houston
○New Orleans
FLA.
San Antonio
Tampa ○
Fort
Lauderdale
○ Miami
○ Monterrey ○ Matamoros
Gulf Of Mexico
Key ○
West
○
Saltillo
○ Havana
MEXICO
Yucatan Channel
Isla de la
Juventad
CAYMAN IS.
○ Tampico
Playa del
Carmen
Mérida ○
○ Cozumel
Bahia de
Campeche
Campeche ○
Yucatan
Peninsula
○ Veracruz
Mexico City ○
Belize City
Balsas
Coatzacoalcas
○ Belmopan
BELIZE
○ Oaxaca
Acapulco ○
Golfo de
Tehuantepec
GUATEMALA
HONDURAS
Guatemala
City
Tegucigalpa
○
○ San Salvador
EL SALVADOR
NICARAGUA
Managua ○
Lago de
Nicaragua
Golfo de los
Mosquitos
○ San Jose
COSTA
RICA

0   300 Miles
0   300 Kilometers

N

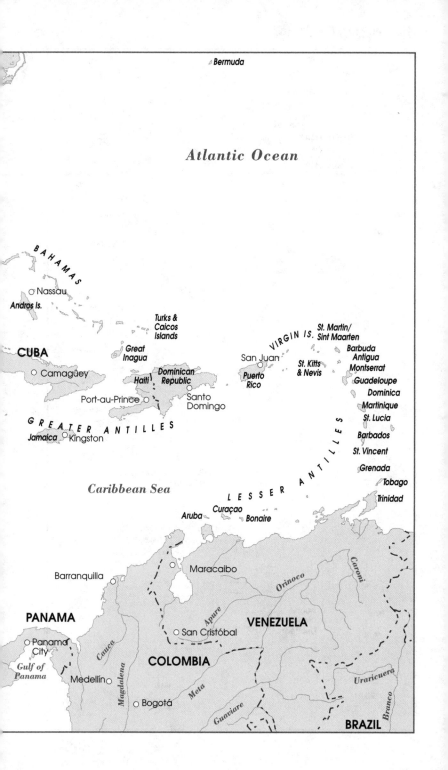

Bermuda

Atlantic Ocean

BAHAMAS

Nassau

Andros Is.

Turks &
Caicos
Islands

Great
Inagua

VIRGIN IS.

St. Martin/
Sint Maarten

CUBA

San Juan

Barbuda
Antigua

Camagüey

Haiti

Dominican
Republic

Puerto
Rico

St. Kitts
& Nevis

Montserrat
Guadeloupe

Port-au-Prince

Santo
Domingo

Dominica

Martinique
St. Lucia

GREATER ANTILLES

Jamaica   Kingston

Barbados

St. Vincent

LESSER ANTILLES

Grenada

Caribbean Sea

Tobago

Trinidad

Aruba

Curaçao

Bonaire

Barranquilla

Maracaibo

Orinoco

Caroni

PANAMA

Apure

VENEZUELA

Panama
City

San Cristóbal

*Gulf of
Panama*

Medellín

Cauca

COLOMBIA

Magdalena

Meta

Uraricuera

Bogotá

Guaviare

Branco

BRAZIL

xiii

The Eastern Caribbean

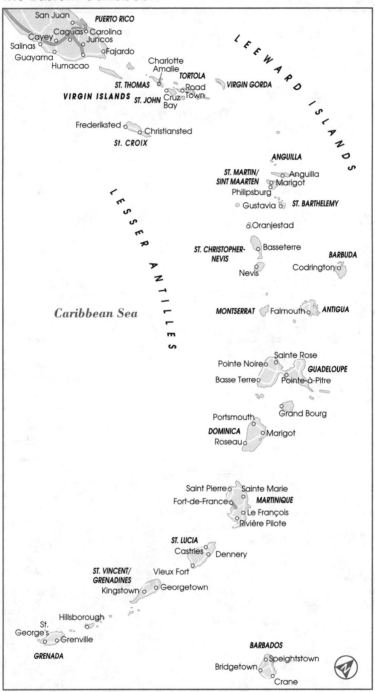

San Juan

PUERTO RICO

Caguas Carolina
Cayey Juncos
Salinas
Guayama Fajardo
Humacao

Charlotte
Amalie

TORTOLA

ST. THOMAS Road
Town **VIRGIN GORDA**

VIRGIN ISLANDS Cruz
ST. JOHN Bay

L E E W A R D

I S L A N D S

Frederiksted Christiansted

ST. CROIX

ANGUILLA

Anguilla

ST. MARTIN/
SINT MAARTEN Marigot
Philipsburg

Gustavia **ST. BARTHELEMY**

L E S S E R

Oranjestad

ST. CHRISTOPHER- Basseterre
NEVIS **BARBUDA**

Nevis Codrington

A N T I L L E S

Caribbean Sea

MONTSERRAT Falmouth **ANTIGUA**

Sainte Rose

Pointe Noire **GUADELOUPE**

Basse Terre Pointe-à-Pitre

Grand Bourg

Portsmouth

DOMINICA Marigot
Roseau

Saint Pierre Sainte Marie

Fort-de-France **MARTINIQUE**

Le François
Rivière Pilote

ST. LUCIA
Castries
Dennery

ST. VINCENT/ Vieux Fort
GRENADINES
Kingstown Georgetown

Hillsborough

St.
George's
Grenville

GRENADA

BARBADOS
Speightstown

Bridgetown
Crane

Cruising into the 21st Century

I didn't always love cruising. In fact, before I took my first one nearly a decade ago, I assumed cruises were pretty much all the same and not something I'd like. As a (then) 20-something know-it-all, I assumed they were either weigh stations for the nursing home set or cheesy floating frat parties.

Boy, was I wrong. After cruising on more ships than I can count, I have a different attitude. There's so much choice, so much variety, and so much to love. I love socializing with people of all ages and walks of life, the ritual of dining, and the chance to explore the islands. And who knew that the romance and nostalgia of being at sea, even on the newest, flashiest megaships, is so alluring? If you can break away from the disco and the conga lines long enough to wander out to some quiet corner of the deck, you'll see what I mean. The sea is a mesmerizing, powerful, and magical place to call home for a week. Just you and your shipmates alone at sea, with not another thing in sight.

HELPING YOU FIND YOUR IDEAL CRUISE

With this guide, my goal is to show you that all cruises are not created equal and that you've got boatloads of choices. I'll help you wade through the options and illustrate the vast differences between ships and cruise experiences. To do this, I've done something no other guidebook has attempted: I've divided the cruise lines into four categories—ultra-luxury lines, mainstream lines, soft-adventure and sailing-ship lines, and budget/older-ship lines—and developed a **new rating system** that judges the lines on a curve, so as to offer comparisons between comparable lines and ships. It's important to compare apples with apples, and not draw irrelevant comparisons between wildly different cruises (say, between ultra-luxurious Seabourn and adventurous Star Clippers, or mainstream Carnival and luxurious Cunard). You wouldn't compare a two-seater sports car with a hulking sports utility vehicle, would you? Same idea applies here.

HELPING YOU REALISTICALLY BUDGET YOUR TRIP

In this edition of *Caribbean Cruises,* for the very first time, you'll be able to see how much you can realistically expect to pay for your cruise.

Just like new car prices, cruise line brochure prices are notoriously misleading. It's a matter of supply and demand: Cruise lines may ask $2,000 for a cabin, but they're more than willing to book you into that same cabin for a fraction of that amount if it looks like they won't be able to get the asking price. Cruises hardly ever sell for the brochure price, but other guidebooks print those prices anyway, leaving it up to you to take a guess at what the real price might be.

I took a different approach, partnering with travel agency giant The Travel Company to provide you with the **actual prices** consumers are paying for cruises aboard all the ships reviewed in this book. Each review shows you approximately how much you can expect to pay for an inside cabin (without windows), an outside cabin (with windows), and a suite, and in Appendix A I've provided a chart that shows how these prices compare with the published brochure rates. How much of a difference could it be, you ask? Think about this: The published rate for a 7-night January 2000 booking of a low-end outside cabin on Celebrity's *Mercury* is $1,795, but at press time (June 1999) that same cabin was selling for $899. If that ain't a big difference, I don't know what is.

CRUISING TODAY

The word of the day is *choice,* as never before. There's a head-spinning variety of Caribbean-bound ships to choose from and lots more on the way, as the building spree several years in the making continues to gain momentum and cruises continue to attract millions of devotees every year. Six new Caribbean-bound ships were launched in 1999 alone, joining the nearly 100 ships already plying Caribbean routes, including the biggest and boldest in the world, Royal Caribbean's 3,100-passenger, 142,000-ton **Voyager of the Seas.** Disney's second ship, the **Disney Wonder,** debuted along with Holland America's 1,440-passenger **Volendam** and Carnival's 2,740-passenger **Triumph,** the first sister to the *Destiny.* Norwegian Cruise Lines' first new build in over 5 years, the 1,800-passenger **Norwegian Sky,** was launched along with Princess Cruises' 1,950-passenger **Ocean Princess.**

No less prodigious, 2000 will see another seven ships launched, including the first of Celebrity's Millennium series, a 1,950-passenger vessel named (what else?) the **Millennium,** and another **Carnival Destiny** sister, the 2,628-passenger **Victory.** The 2,100-passenger **CostaAtlantica,** Costa's first new build since the **Victoria** in '96, will have verandas in over 75% of the cabins, and Star Clippers' 228-passenger five-masted, fully-rigged **Royal Clipper** will be one of the biggest sailing ships ever built. And don't look for the building frenzy to slow down anytime soon—with over 40 ships on order as of early 1999, the next few years will be just as busy.

TODAY'S ACCESSORIES

So what's one of these hot new $300 to $500 million cruise ships come loaded with these days? The must-have accessories on ships large and small are private balconies, casual dining venues, specialty coffee cafes, well-equipped spas, and even cigar bars, giving passengers more onboard choices than ever. E-mail access is another emerging trend. Crystal, Norwegian, and Princess's newest ships already provide passengers with the ability to send and receive e-mail while on board, and no doubt other lines will soon jump on this sure-to-please bandwagon.

Although there are a handful of new small ships, the majority of new builds are massive, carrying upward of 2,500 passengers (plus about half that in crew) and weighing from 80,000 to 142,000 gross registered tons. The biggest cruise ship in the world (at least for now), Royal Caribbean's new *Voyager of the Seas,* is nearly as long as the Empire State Building is tall. The *Norway, QE2, Disney Magic* and *Wonder,* and *Grand Princess* are about the length of two Washington Monuments stacked on top of each other. Get the picture? Floating hotels, floating cities, floating galaxies—whatever you want to call them—these babies are *big.*

Like the race to build the tallest skyscraper, lines are forever trying to outdo each other in the size and gimmick department. Not only do their megaships have two or three sprawling dining rooms, easily a dozen bars and entertainment lounges, several pools,

Tell Us About Your Cruise!

While I, my editor, and my cronies can cover the cruise waterfront pretty well, we aren't privy to *every* great cruise moment. Let us know about your cruise! What did you like best? What did you like least? What nice little touch really made your trip? And what was your favorite experience in port? Let us know! The more opinions we hear, the better. And we may even include your impressions in future editions of this book. E-mail your thoughts to **CRUZHMS@aol.com,** or snail-mail them to Heidi Sarna, *Frommer's Caribbean Cruises,* Macmillan Travel, 1633 Broadway, New York, NY 10019.

cavernous gyms and spas, and a mall-like string of shops, they have things you'd never imagine finding on a ship, much less at some resort or hotel. The *Voyager of the Seas* has—no kidding—a rock-climbing wall and an ice-skating rink (you know, in case the four pools and regulation-sized basketball court aren't enough for you). The Carnival *Triumph, Paradise,* and *Elation* have sushi bars. The *Grand Princess,* the second biggest ship in the world, sports a nine-hole miniature golf course and a sprawling virtual-reality video arcade with dozens of machines you can climb onto and do things like hang gliding, fly-fishing, and skiing. So whatever happened to deck chairs, piña coladas, and afternoon naps? Well, for you Luddites out there, you can still choose to do nothing more than laze by the pool all day with a cold beer and a best-seller. It's up to you.

While the mondo-megas attract most of the attention these days, they're not the only fish in the sea. Just like there are five-star hotels, cozy B&Bs, and roadside motels, cruise ships come in all shapes and sizes to please all different walks of life. There are **adventurous sailing ships** and **small expedition-like vessels** navigating off-the-beaten-track ports, 40-year-old **ocean liners** reeking of the past, and **ultra-deluxe ships** serving oceans of caviar and champagne. You can sail on ships that require you pack nothing more than flip-flops, bathing suits, T-shirts, and a pass-me-another-cup-of-that-rum-punch attitude. Or you can fill your suitcase with sequins and silk and enough dinner conversation for a week's worth of elegant soirées. Depends on what you like, how much you want to spend, and where you want to go.

I COVER THE WATERFRONT: THE PORTS OF CALL TODAY

The Caribbean is a time-tested favorite, your classic picture-perfect island vacation destination. It's warm and sunny all year-round and the major ports of embarkation are easily accessible (and relatively cheap by air, when you compare it to flying to Europe or Asia). Better yet, it's hassle-free because American, Canadian, and British citizens don't need visas to go there.

Even as cruise destinations continue to expand into the far corners of the world, the Caribbean has never been more popular. With all the new ships coming on the scene, lines like Princess, Carnival, Royal Caribbean, Norwegian, Holland America, and Star Clippers are increasing their presence in the Caribbean, deploying more and bigger ships there. It's an exciting time. **Shore excursions,** too, are getting more interesting and more active, with biking, horseback riding, golfing, and river tubing trips exposing cruisers to the more natural parts of the islands.

While the Caribbean remains hot, hot, hot (and increasingly packed, packed, packed), you may notice that some of the huge ships in the Carnival, Princess, Royal Caribbean, and Norwegian fleets are visiting only three ports during a typical week-long western or eastern Caribbean cruise instead of four or five ports. Ships too big? Ports too crowded? Cruise lines wanting to keep passengers on board to spend more money in the shops, bars, and casinos? It's hard to be sure. First-timer cruisers who want to see as many islands as possible may be disappointed, but if you've been there, done that, the big ships have so much happening on board, you'll barely have time to think about going ashore.

That said, there are ships that really pack in the ports of call, visiting a different island nearly every single day, like the small-ship lines Windstar, Star Clippers, Club Med, Windjammer, Clipper, American Canadian Caribbean, and Tall Ship Adventures. Even some of the big ships, like Celebrity's *Galaxy* and NCL's *Norwegian Sea* and *Norwegian Dream,* visit five ports on their seven-night southern Caribbean itineraries.

To give you an even more well-rounded look at Caribbean cruises, in this edition I've added coverage of **Panama Canal itineraries** and also added **Bermuda** to the list of ports we cover. Sure, I know it's not in the Caribbean, but the British-flavored island is a unique cruise destination; unlike other ports where visits rarely exceed one day, the five ships that do regularly scheduled weeklong cruises to Bermuda spend three of those days tied up at Hamilton or St. George.

THE PORTS OF EMBARKATION

Like the Caribbean islands, the ports in Florida and other southern states are sprucing up their facilities big-time.

The most dramatic change on land is occurring at the **port of Miami,** which is the largest and busiest cruise ship port in the world. To accommodate the influx of new cruise ships, like the massive *Voyager of the Seas* (both Carnival and Royal Caribbean have recently signed long-term, multimillion-dollar agreements with the port), the port of Miami has spent $76 million on major improvements to terminals 3, 4, and 5, and added a 750-space parking facility. Completed in late 1999, the renovated terminals offer enhanced facilities, like a combined 4,000 additional passenger seats and a new departure area in each. Down the road, the port is even hoping to have facilities at the cruise terminals to issue airline boarding passes to departing passengers.

Still on the drawing board are plans for a **Maritime Park,** to be built on a tract of downtown waterfront on Biscayne Bay near the port. Although still in the early planning stages, the complex would likely include new ship berths as well as entertainment facilities for passengers.

Likewise, look for continuing improvements in such vibrant ports as **Tampa,** which will probably boom if and when ports open up in Cuba, and **Port Canaveral,** which has gotten a massive boost of vitality thanks to its selection by Disney as home port to its two new mega-vessels.

BON VOYAGE!

Just the fact that you've bought this book means you've got a hankering to cruise; now it's our job to find the cruise that's just right for you from among the huge selection of ships and cruise experiences in the market. I've made the reviews candid and provided lots of tips and firsthand experience to help you navigate the vast sea of choices. Together, we'll get you hooked up with the vacation of your dreams.

Bon Voyage!

Frommer's Favorites

To make it easier for you to select your cruise, I've compiled these "Frommer's Favorites," my picks of the best lines, ships, and ports of call for different types of cruise experiences. You'll find detailed reviews of all the lines and ships in part 2, "The Cruise Lines & Their Ships," and all the ports in part 3, "The Ports."

1 Best Luxury Cruises

Here's the very best for the Caribbean cruiser who's used to traveling deluxe and who doesn't mind paying for the privilege. These ships have the best cuisine, accommodations, and service at sea.

- **Seabourn:** Best overall high-brow, small-ship cruise line. With their cuisine, service, and luxurious suites, the 200-passenger *Pride* and *Legend* and the 116-passenger *Seabourn Goddesses* are the crème de la crème of cruises.
- **Cunard:** Cunard's 30-year-old *QE2* wins in the best traditional, old-time ocean liner category.
- **Celebrity Cruises:** The 1,880-passenger *Galaxy* and *Mercury* are the best luxury megaships, featuring wonderful spas, cigar bars, and entertainment lounges, and prices that are far lower than you'd expect.
- **Crystal Cruises:** The 960-passenger *Crystal Harmony* and *Crystal Symphony* are the best mid-sized ships out there, big enough to offer lots of dining, entertainment, and fitness options and small enough to bath passengers in luxury.
- **Windstar Cruises:** The *Wind Spirit* and its larger sibling *Wind Surf* are the best casual luxury ships at sea. No need for a jacket and tie; these casually elegant sailing ships offer a pampered adventure.

2 Best Cruises for First-Timers

Short 3- and 4-night cruises are one of the best ways to test the waters. Here are my favorite shorties as well as a few week-long cruises that are good choices for first-timers.

- **Carnival Cruise Lines:** The 3- and 4-night Bahamas cruises on the *Ecstasy*, sailing from Miami, or *Fantasy*, sailing from Port Canaveral, are great choices. These flashy megas offers lots to do all day long, and their standard cabins are among the largest at sea.

- **Premier Cruises:** The *Big Red Boat's* 3- and 4-night Bahamas cruises out of Port Canaveral are a good, affordable choice for families, with extensive kids' programs and facilities and lots to do for adults, too.
- **Norwegian Cruise Line:** If you like jazz, country, or big band music, the line's many 7-night music theme cruises on the *Norwegian Sea* and *Norway* will keep you occupied while you figure out whether you like cruising or not. Likewise, the *Sea's* popular "Sports Afloat" cruises are also a good choice; professional players and Hall-of-Famers from pro basketball, football, hockey, and baseball leagues sail on board select cruises, signing autographs, conducting demonstrations and contests, and mingling with passengers
- **Radisson Seven Seas Cruises:** Because of its stable twin-hull design, *Radisson Diamond* is the best ship for those who suffer—or suspect they might suffer—from motion sickness. In addition to stability, the *Diamond* offers excellent itineraries (many are a short 4 nights), one of the grandest dining rooms afloat (with superb service), all outside cabins, and first-class amenities.
- **Regal Cruises:** The *Regal Empress* may be nearly 50 years old and not so regal, but its 1-, 2-, and 3-night cruises to nowhere from New York City and its 4- and 5-night western Caribbean cruises from Port Manatee, Florida are a cheap and fun way to test the waters.
- **Royal Caribbean International:** Its ships offer a healthy dose of razzle dazzle, but they don't go overboard. The *Nordic Empress,* although not one of Royal Caribbean's newest megas, is a great ship with lots to do on board and a great 3- and 4-night itinerary round-trip from San Juan, visiting St. Thomas and Sint Maarten, and also St. Croix on the 4-nighter.
- **Crystal Cruises:** If you're a glutton for the best of everything, unlike the other high-end ships, the 960-passenger *Crystal Harmony* and *Symphony* are big enough to keep first-timers busy (even considering the typical Crystal itinerary is 10 nights) with lots of outdoor deck space, generous fitness facilities, and over a half dozen bars and entertainment venues as well as pampering service and scrumptious cuisine.
- **Disney Cruise Line:** For Disney fanatics, a 3- or 4-night Bahamas cruise on the *Disney Magic* or *Wonder* is the closest you'll get to a Disney park at sea. Half cruise, half theme park, the Disney ships are a great segue into cruising for first-timers.
- **Commodore Cruise Line:** The line's *Enchanted Capri* offers fun, 2-night "cruises to nowhere" that depart from New Orleans and head down the Mississippi into the Gulf of Mexico. Prices are ridiculously low, the casino is open 24 hours, food and entertainment are decent, and the ship's staff goes all out to make sure everyone has a good time.

3 The Most Romantic Cruises

The majority of all cruise passengers are couples, romantic or otherwise, and more of those romantic couples than ever are getting married on board or in port, renewing their vows, or celebrating anniversaries. (For how to get married on board, see chapter 1, "Choosing Your Ideal Cruise.")

- **Carnival Cruise Lines:** Any line that names its vessels after moments of high passion has to take romance seriously—how could the *Paradise, Ecstasy,* or *Fantasy* not conjure up naughty thoughts? If your idea of a romance is a date with Vegas-style glamour and excitement, Carnival is a sure thing.
- **Windstar Cruises:** Pure romance. Spend the day with your loved one in a private cove with the *Wind Surf* or *Wind Spirit* anchored offshore, bobbing calmly on the waves, their sails furled. Windstar offers a truly unique cruise experience, giving

passengers the delicious illusion of adventure and the ever-pleasant reality of first-class cuisine, service, and itineraries.

- **Holland America Line:** This line attracts lots of 50+ couples celebrating anniversaries and/or renewing vows (HAL has several goodie packages you can buy to sweeten the moment). The mid-sized **Statendam-class** ships will put you in the mood with their elegant Crow's Nest observation lounges/nightclubs, with floor-to-ceiling windows, dim lighting, and cozy seating. The private cabin balconies and glamorous two-story dining rooms will help, too.
- **Seabourn Cruise Line:** If you crave small and intimate, the *Seabourn Goddess I* and *II* are good choices and are nothing short of pampering private yachts. Of course, the champagne and caviar served to you poolside whenever you want it is a nice touch.

4 Best Cruises for Singles

A cruise can be a great social vacation for solo travelers, *if* you choose the right one.

- **Windjammer Barefoot Cruises:** If you're under 40 and have an informal attitude, these cruises—especially those aboard the *Mandalay* and *Polynesia*—are your best romantic bet. Extremely dress-down and casual, things can get very, very intimate aboard these small wind-driven ships. It's amazing what a little wind, waves, stars, and moonlight can do.
- **Club Med:** The *Club Med II,* a vessel powered to some degree by sails, is a good bet for singles, but single passengers don't necessarily find love among the passenger list—usually they're more attracted to the lovely young women or handsome men serving as social hosts.
- **Carnival Cruise Lines:** Single women under 35 seek out Carnival's fun and casual ships, in part because they attract more men under 40 than just about any other cruise line. The ships are big, offering many places to meet and mingle. Who knows who you might meet in that aerobics class, on that shore excursion, or even at your dining table?
- **Premier Cruises:** Aboard its *Big Red Boat,* reasonable single-parent rates attract single moms and dads and their children. Cartoon characters like Bugs Bunny and Sylvester can entertain the offspring while unattached moms and dads enjoy the company of other single parents.
- **Royal Caribbean International:** This line draws a good cross section of men and women from all walks of life. Like Carnival, a decent number of passengers are singles in their 20s, 30s, and 40s. Hey, you never know!
- **Crystal Cruises:** This line's pair of elegant 960-passenger ships, the *Harmony* and *Symphony,* are good choices for single ladies and men over 50. Since there tend to be more older single women cruising than older single men, "gentleman hosts"—men in their 50s and 60s, semi-employed by the line (at least for one trip)—sail on board all Panama Canal cruises and act as dancing and dinner hosts for unattached ladies.

5 Best Cruises for Families with Kids

More families are cruising than ever before and lines are beefing up their families' programs to keep the kids happy and content. All the lines included here offer supervised activities for three to five age groups for kids between ages 3 and 17, have well-stocked playrooms, wading pools, kids' menus, and cabins that can accommodate three to five people. See "Family Cruising Tips" in chapter 1 and the cruise line reviews in chapters 6 through 9, which describe children's activities in detail.

- **Disney Cruise Lines:** This family magnet offers a seagoing children's program that's the most sophisticated and high-tech in the world. Huge play areas, family-friendly cabins, and of course the ubiquitous Mickey spell success. Plus, its 3- and 4-night Bahamas cruises are marketed in tandem with stays at Disney World, so you can have your ocean voyage and your Space Mountain, too.
- **Premier Cruises:** On Premier's old but still lively *Big Red Boat,* children can be entertained by such Looney-Tunes characters as Tweety, Sylvester, Bugs Bunny, and the Tasmanian Devil. The ship's 3- and 4-day cruises to the Bahamas are particularly good for families on their first cruise, and although they're a bit less well-accessorized than the Disney vessels, they make up for it by being cheaper.
- **Carnival Cruise Lines:** Despite a let-the-good-times-roll allure that appeals to adults, Carnival goes out of its way to amuse people of all ages, and does a particularly fine job with kids 2 to 15 years old. In 1998, some 200,000 kids sailed with Carnival— a few hundred per cruise is pretty normal, and there's as many as 700 to 800 on Christmas and New Year's cruises. On Carnival's post-1990 ships, the kids' facilities are the most extensive, with the *Triumph, Destiny, Elation,* and *Paradise* offering the biggest and brightest playrooms in the fleet, stocked with computer stations, a climbing maze, a 16-monitor video wall showing movies and cartoons, arts and crafts, and oodles of toys and games.
- **Princess Cruises:** The Grand-class ships—the *Grand, Ocean, Sea, Sun,* and *Dawn Princess*—each have a spacious children's playroom and a sizable piece of outside fenced-in deck dedicated to kids only, with a shallow pool and tricycles. Teen centers have computers, video games, and a sound system (and the one on the *Grand* even has a teen's hot tub and private sunbathing deck). Children and their activities are kept separate from adults and theirs, which suits both groups just fine.
- **Celebrity Cruises:** A tie-in with the Sony Corporation means a wonderland of electronic bliss for the kids. The computer stations and games in the playrooms aboard the *Galaxy* and *Mercury* keep children happy as clams for hours.
- **Royal Caribbean International:** Sports-oriented teens will love the brand-new and just-plain-huge *Voyager of the Seas.* Believe it or not, the mammoth 3,114-passenger, 142,000-ton ship has a full-scale ice-skating rink, a rock-climbing wall, an in-line skating track (skates can be rented or you can bring your own), a pottery studio, a nine-hole miniature golf course, and regulation-sized basketball, paddleball, and volleyball courts.

6 Best Party Cruises

With the right mix of passengers, nights aboard any ship can be a party, but many passengers still appreciate the efforts of cruise ship directors to make partying come alive. Some hard-partying fans opt for a cruise set up around a specific theme, such as country-western or big band music. Others like to book shorter 3- or 4-day cruises, where some passengers come on board dead-set on packing as much party into a half week as possible.

- **Carnival Cruise Lines:** Carnival calls them "fun ships" for good reason, and their names—*Celebration, Fantasy, Imagination,* et al—couldn't be more appropriate. By day, the Pool Deck is bustling, with music playing so loud you'll have to go back to your cabin to think. And the fun keeps going after the sun goes down, with some of the best entertainment afloat. Usually three different live bands and orchestras play aboard a Carnival ship, and the discos rock until the early morning hours. Casino action is big on Carnival ships, as are Las Vegas–style revues.

- **Princess Cruises:** The *Grand-class ships,* while not as wild and crazy as Carnival, can throw a good party with their flashy discos (the multilevel, observatory-like one on *Grand Princess* is the best) and endless activities.
- **Club Med:** Aboard *Club Med II,* the social hosts (GOs) keep the ships rocking. This freewheeling abandon makes the line popular with honeymooners, singles, and loving couples. The ships are informal, Francophilic, and very, very social. The GOs display their talents every evening in song and dance, but the biggest blast occurs one night a week on every cruise: Carnival Night, when anything goes!
- **Norwegian Cruise Line:** This line is a heavy contender in the party and entertainment sweepstakes. The ships also provide the best and most elaborate theme cruises in the industry, with options that include big bands, country music, jazz, blues, and sports. When the sun goes down, NCL's ships shine with outstanding entertainment. Fully equipped theaters have stages big enough to present Broadway hits, or you could opt for NCL's own extravagant cabaret production, *Sea Legs Review.*
- **Royal Caribbean International:** You'll definitely find a party aboard any of the vessels whose names end with the phrase **"of the Seas."** From dancing to singing to comedy to elaborately costumed revues and glittery casinos, Royal Caribbean's got it all. For an exciting Saturday-night-out-on-the-town kind of thing, the new *Voyager of the Seas* features a truly unique multideck boulevard-like promenade running down the center of the ship, anchored on either end by multistory atria, with its ground floor lined with shops, bars, restaurants, and entertainment outlets.
- **Windjammer Barefoot Cruises:** Yo ho ho and a barrel of rum—no kidding, a real barrel, from which the bartenders siphon off the fixings for free Rum Swizzles as the sun goes down. On these sailing ships you get to pretend you're a freewheeling pirate sailing over the bounding main, grog in hand. Ships often anchor late in port, allowing you to enjoy some of the Caribbean's legendary nightspots, like Foxy's on Jost Van Dyke.

7 Best Adventure Cruises

If you want to explore more remote areas of the Caribbean where the megaships can't venture or be aboard a vessel that recalls the sailing days of yore, here are your best bets:

- **Royal Olympic Cruises:** The line's *Stella Solaris* does a limited number of cruises including Caribbean ports of call, but when she does, you're assured they'll be fascinating stops, and a staff of experts on board will fill your head with all kinds of interesting facts. For instance, a "Land of the Maya" cruise in March includes visits to Mexico's Yucatán Peninsula and Central America, and a panel of onboard archaeologists, anthropologists, and astronomers will help you understand the Mayan civilization.
- **American Canadian Caribbean Line:** One or more of this line's small-scale, shallow-draft, no-frills vessels heads every winter for the remote waters of the Caribbean, especially offshore Panama, Belize, and Honduras. This fascinating and relatively untouched part of Central America opens onto one of the world's greatest barrier reefs, which you may glimpse on a ride in the glass-bottomed boats ACCL carries aboard ship. The *Grande Caribe, Grande Mariner,* and *Niagara Prince* are tiny and spartan, but they are your vessels if you want to visit parts of the Caribbean that few other travelers see.
- **Windstar Cruises:** *Wind Spirit* and its larger sibling *Wind Surf* are the most high-end of the motorized sailing ships, and make stops in some of the most intriguing off-the-beaten-path ports in the Caribbean, such as Dominica or Bequia, one of the jewels of the Grenadines but a place where the megaships don't go. Other stops

include the remote, little-visited Carriacou and, in some cases, the Tobago Cays. The ships don't just "do" Guadeloupe, but take you to the even more exotic Ile des Saintes.

- **Tall Ship Adventures:** Being aboard the *Sir Francis Drake* is one of the great sailing adventures still left in the Caribbean. This authentic 1917 three-masted, 30-passenger ship makes 7-day voyages through the remotest waters of the British Virgin Islands, visiting the likes of Peter Island, Cooper Island, Marina Cay, and Long Bay, the old sailing grounds of Sir Francis himself. The ship doesn't have many of the standard cruise ship comforts, but if you choose this ship you probably aren't looking for them anyway. Instead, you'll experience the true adventure of Caribbean sailing.

- **Clipper Cruise Line:** The *Nantucket Clipper* and *Yorktown Clipper* retain the spirit of adventure now lost on all the megaships. Despite their names, these twin clippers don't have sails, but they can tie up in remote, out-of-the-way ports that most other ships have to avoid. Some cruises will introduce you to history and culture, but others are oriented toward pure adventure, concentrating on ports of call with rugged scenic beauty and opportunities for wildlife viewing. The company's ships call at remote islands in the British Virgins, such as Jost Van Dyke, Salt Island, and Norman Island, which, according to legend, inspired Robert Louis Stevenson's *Treasure Island*.

- **Windjammer Barefoot Cruises:** This eclectic fleet of piratelike sailing ships feels more adventurous than any of the others (except the *Sir Francis Drake*) and the ships will take you to some of the Caribbean's lesser frequented islands. The typical itinerary round-trip from Grenada is Carriacou, Palm Island, Bequia, St. Vincent, and Mayreau. Two of the line's ships—the passenger/cargo ship *Amazing Grace* and the sailing ship *Mandalay*—sail 13-day itineraries that stop at a whole bundle of off-the-beaten-track islands.

8   Best Theme Cruises

Theme cruises combine a Caribbean cruise with a particular entertainment-related interest—everything from solar-eclipse viewing to an Oktoberfest celebration, from a jazz festival to golfing, from basketball legends to Elvis. Check with a travel agent or cruise specialist for current offerings and options.

- **Norwegian Cruise Line:** When it comes to theme cruises, NCL, which pioneered the concept of theme cruises in the early 1980s, is the tops. The *Norway* hosts about seven or eight music cruises a year, from country to blues and big band, including its annual 2-week Jazz Festival cruise. The *Norwegian Sea* also does music cruises, celebrating '50s and '60s and country music. On the *Sea's* popular "Sports Afloat" cruises, professional players and Hall-of-Famers from pro basketball, football, hockey, and baseball sail on board, signing autographs, conducting demonstrations and contests, and mingling with passengers.

- **Holland America Line:** Big band cruises with the Glenn Miller Orchestra, Guy Lombardo's Royal Canadians, and the Tommy Dorsey Orchestra are always a hit on board the 1,494-passenger *Westerdam* in the eastern Caribbean. Other themes include some 1950s "Sock Hop" cruises featuring performers like the Platters and the Shirelles; a series of Broadway theme sailings, featuring greats like Joel Grey (from *Cabaret* and *Chicago*); and a cruise paying tribute to Frank Sinatra.

- **Disney Cruise Line:** Disney is basically a theme in and of itself, and the company's cruise ships are no different. The Disney theme is woven through virtually every aspect of shipboard life—restaurants, entertainment, cabins, the Pool Deck, even the artwork that hangs on the wall.

• **Royal Olympic Cruises:** Believing that cruising can be both fun and educational, this line has offered special cruises to view Halley's Comet, the May Equinox at Chichén Itzá, and the Perseid meteor shower, and brought guest lecturers aboard its *Stella Solaris* who are among the best in the industry. After visiting major ports in the Caribbean, the ship often heads for the Amazon on its "Sail with the Stars" program, which celebrates theater at sea with theatrical icons such as Anne Jackson and Eli Wallach.

9 Best Cuisine

Here's where you'll find the best floating restaurants, rivaling what you'd find at the best restaurants in the world's major cities.

• **Seabourn Cruise Line:** The sophisticated and contemporary cuisine on board this line's fleet of 100- to 200-passenger ships is flavorful and artfully presented, and if there's anything you want specially prepared, just ask. The dining room service is the finest of any vessel afloat.

• **Windstar Cruises:** While the fare aboard the *Wind Spirit* and *Wind Surf* doesn't equal that aboard Seabourn, it's still darn good. In 1995, this fleet upgraded its cuisine by hiring renowned Los Angeles–based restaurateur Joachim Splichal as consultant. Mealtime is a definite highlight of a Windstar cruise.

• **Radisson Seven Seas Cruises:** *Radisson Diamond's* award-winning chefs produce artful culinary presentations that compare favorably to those of New York or San Francisco's top restaurants, and the waiters are some of the industry's best. An excellent selection of vintage wines is also available.

• **Celebrity Cruise Line:** You'll find the best megaship cuisine and service on the *Century, Galaxy,* and *Mercury.* Designed by Michel Roux, Britain's most famous and celebrated French chef, who sometimes cooks for Queen Elizabeth when she "drops in" to his place on the Thames, seagoing menus are to die for. (The line's mid-sized ships, *Horizon* and *Zenith,* have the same cuisine and service.)

• **Crystal Cruises:** While all the food you'll get on these ships is first-class, the ships' reservations-only Asian specialty restaurants are the best at sea. The one on the *Harmony,* for instance, serves up utterly delicious authentic, fresh Japanese food, including sushi. The accoutrements help set the tone, too—chopsticks (and little chopstick rests), sake served in tiny sake cups and decanters, and sushi served on thick blocky square glass platters. An Asian-theme buffet lunch, offered at least once per cruise, gives passengers an awesome spread, from jumbo shrimp to chicken and beef satays to stir dry dishes.

• **Carnival Cruise Line:** Although nowhere near the league of the other lines in this category, the cuisine aboard Carnival has been upgraded in recent years, and is tasty and plentiful. And its 24-hour pizza and Caesar salad service a big hit fleetwide, as is the sushi bar (open for a few hours every afternoon) on the *Paradise.*

10 Best Port-Packed Itineraries

If you want to see as much of the Caribbean as possible, consider one of the following cruises for their one-port-every-day itineraries.

• **American Canadian Caribbean Line:** The small, spartan *Grande Mariner* and *Grande Caribe* have no equal or competition in the remote Caribbean and Central American hinterlands they visit. On 12-night itineraries, you'll explore cays and islets you've never heard of, including Laughingbird Cay, Ambergris Cay, and

Man-of-War Cay, plus Mayan ruins and even remote territories in Panama, Costa Rica, and Honduras.

- **Windjammer Cruises:** In its role as supply ship for the Windjammer Fleet, *Amazing Grace* is the ultimate island hopper, with stops at more Caribbean islands within the span of its 13-day itineraries than virtually any other cruise ship afloat. Beginning in Freeport and ending in Trinidad, its port stops include St. Kitts, Nevis, Montserrat, Ile des Saintes, Guadeloupe, Dominica, Jost Van Dyke, Beef Island, Virgin Gorda, Norman Island, Peter Island, and possibly others as well. The line's *Mandalay* also sails a 13-day route, this one between Granada and Antigua, visiting Bequia, Carriacou, Canouan, Dominica, Guadeloupe, Iles des Saintes, Martinique, Mayreau, Nevis, Palm Island, St. Lucia, St. Vincent, and Tobago Cays.

11 Best Beaches

If time logged on the beach is just as important to you as days spent at sea, you'll want to consider cruises that stop in the following ports.

- **In the Western Caribbean:** Grand Cayman and Jamaica are two of the Caribbean's best. Grand Cayman's **Seven Mile Beach** is a stretch of pristine sand easily accessible via a short taxi ride from Georgetown. Jamaica's **Negril** is also accessible via taxi, and is closer to Montego Bay than to Ocho Rios.
- **In the Eastern and Southern Caribbean**: Beach bums should head to **Trunk Bay** in St. John (protected by the U.S. National Park Service), **Grand Anse Beach** in Grenada, **Shoal Bay** in Anguilla (topless and sometimes bottomless, too), **Orient Beach** in St. Martin, and Aruba's 7 miles of beach—all excellent stretches of white sand. All are easily accessible via taxi.

12 Best Cruises for Snorkelers & Scuba Divers

Virtually any cruise you take in the Caribbean will allow you an opportunity to snorkel at one of the island ports. Scuba-diving excursions are fairly common, too. Grand Cayman, Bonaire, Virgin Gorda, St. Croix, and Belize offer the best waters.

- **American Canadian Caribbean Line:** For getting to the Caribbean's most natural, unspoiled spots known for superb snorkeling and a wealth of marine life, this line is unbeatable. Few major cruise lines ever call at Belize, which has the world's second-largest barrier reef, but ACCL's *Grande Caribe* does.
- **Princess Cruises:** Princess features "New Waves," a PADI-certified diving program available aboard ships sailing the Caribbean on 7-day itineraries. Endorsed by Scuba Schools International, this program offers introductory scuba tours, dive trips, and demonstrations, and employs fully certified instructors who are some of the best in the business.
- **Windjammer Barefoot Cruises:** Windjammer's ships offer year-round diving possibilities on 6- to 13-day cruises to some 50 ports, including the rarely visited Grenadines. For divers, the best ship in this fleet is the *Flying Cloud*, which departs from Tortola, capital of the British Virgin Islands.
- **Star Clippers:** This line's owner, Mikael Krafft, is a dedicated scuba diver, and he selects his sailing ships' itineraries through the Caribbean based in part on the accessibility of superior, intriguing, and often offbeat dive sites, including small ports that many big cruise ships can't even approach. The line's *Star Clipper* is the largest sailing vessel to feature onboard PADI dive centers.

13 Best Cruises for Golfers

Many lines sell **golfing shore excursions** with tee times and transportation between the ship and the course, and on some ships a golf pro sails on board, offering onboard lessons ($60 to $70 per hour) and escorting players to the island courses. The best courses are in Bermuda, St. Thomas, Puerto Rico, and Jamaica.

Some Royal Caribbean, Princess, and Crystal ships have actual **putting greens** on board, while others, including the new, technologically advanced ships like Celebrity's *Century, Galaxy,* and *Mercury* and Princess's *Grand, Sea, Sun,* and *Dawn Princess,* have **golf simulators.** These state-of-the-art virtual-reality machines allow you to play the great courses of the world without ever leaving the ship (for about $20 per half hour). Full-sized clubs are used and a virtual-reality video screen allows players to watch the electronic path of a ball they've actually hit soar high over the greens or land flat in a sand trap.

- **Royal Caribbean International:** This line is the golfer's favorite, as three of its ships—*Legend of the Seas, Splendour of the Seas,* and *Voyager of the Seas*—feature a real live 18-hole putting green on board. The ships are so huge and well stabilized that golfers are seldom bothered by motion. The Professional Golf Association has sanctioned Royal Caribbean as its official cruise line (which really doesn't mean much, but it sounds nice!).
- **Celebrity Cruises:** On every one of its Bermuda cruises, the *Zenith* features a PGA-certified pro who gives lessons at the ship's driving net. In port, the pro takes golfers to the courses for hands-on instruction ($200 for 5-hour playing lessons). The *Century, Galaxy,* and *Mercury* have golf simulators.
- **Crystal Cruises:** Both the *Harmony* and *Symphony* have two golf driving nets and a large putting green, so golfing fanatics can hit balls virtually all day long. There's often an instructor on board giving group instruction throughout the week.
- **Carnival Cruise Line:** Fleetwide in the Caribbean and Bahamas, a golf pro sails on board providing videotaped lessons for anyone interested ($40 a half hour; $70 per hour).
- **Princess Cruises:** The *Grand Princess* has a nine-hole miniature golf course right on board. The *Grand, Ocean, Sea, Sun,* and *Dawn* also have one of those neat golf simulators.
- **Radisson Seven Seas:** As the official cruise line of the PGA of America, the *Radisson Diamond's* Caribbean itineraries offers lots of golf excursions, and the ship has a golf cage and a certified pro offering videotaped lessons.

14 Best Islands for Serious Shoppers

There are few islands that don't have at least some shops, and most have a sprawling market or complex of stores near the cruise ships docks. Even the smaller, less touristed ports have a few stores and a market. Believe me, if a ship is coming to an island, the locals will be prepared.

The following are the absolute best spots for dedicated shoppers. All offer duty-free shopping and shops bursting with jewelry, perfume and cosmetics, clothing, accessories, arts and crafts, liquor, and souvenirs—but don't necessarily expect dirt-cheap prices. Ubiquitous chains like Little Switzerland, Colombian Emeralds, and Diamonds International sell a wide variety of duty-free gold and silver jewelry with diamonds as well as precious and semiprecious gems. In outdoor markets and craft shops, look for local specialties, such as straw hats and purses, beaded necklaces, and brightly painted folk art and carved-wood boxes, as well as your typical souvenirs: T-shirts and beach towels.

- **St. Thomas:** Close to the cruise ship docks, lovely Charlotte Amalie is the island's shopping mecca.
- **St. Croix:** Christiansted has shopping galore, and since it's part of the U.S. Virgin Islands, you get a bigger customs allowance than you do coming from non-U.S. ports.
- **Puerto Rico:** The capital, San Juan, is historic and a great shopping spot, and the same customs deal applies here as at St. Croix.
- **Grand Cayman:** Georgetown has numerous shops clustered right around its port facilities.
- **St. Martin/Sint Maarten:** French Marigot and Dutch Philipsburg are particularly good for European luxury items.
- **Aruba:** Oranjestad's Caya G. F. Betico Croes offers shopping from around the world on one main, theme-park-like shopping street.
- **The Bahamas:** Nassau and Freeport are veritable shopping free-for-alls. Go wild.

15 Best Cruises for Gamblers

Gamblers are in luck. Most cruise ships, with the notable exceptions of the small ships in the Soft Adventure category (see chapter 9, "Soft-Adventure Lines & Sailing Ships"), have casinos. The megaships have sprawling Vegas-style operations with dozens of gaming tables and hundreds of slots as well as roulette and craps. Some of the mid-sized ships are more modest, with just a couple of blackjack and poker tables and a handful of slots. The following lines have the biggest and best in the size and flashiness departments.

- **Carnival Cruise Lines:** Fleetwide, Carnival's casinos are the best at sea: bold, bright, and bathed in neon.
- **Royal Caribbean International:** Fleetwide, the casinos are exciting places to play. The three-level casino on the *Nordic Empress* is particularly appealing, and the one on the new *Voyager of the Seas* is mind-blowing.
- **Princess Cruises:** All of the line's megas attract gamblers, and the huge casino on the *Grand Princess* is the best of the lot.
- **Holland America Line:** This line's casinos are more low-key and less flashy than those on Carnival, but there always seems to be a lot of action going on.
- **Celebrity Cruises:** Some of the Caribbean's best casinos are aboard Celebrity's three megas, the *Century, Galaxy,* and *Mercury.* They're large and dazzling, but in a more subdued way than their neon competition.

16 Best Islands for Gamblers

If gambling on board ship isn't enough for you, a handful of the islands have casinos to tide you over (ships' casinos must remain closed while a ship is in port).

- **Bahamas:** In Nassau, the casinos on **Cable Beach** and **Paradise Island** are dazzling and Vegas-style, and along with those in Puerto Rico are the biggest and flashiest you'll find in the Caribbean. The best in Nassau are the **Atlantis, Paradise Island Casino,** and the **Crystal Palace Casino,** both huge, glittery extravaganzas.
- **Puerto Rico:** The island's gambling strip lies along the **Condado** in San Juan, where the casinos are Vegas-style and exciting and the locals dress for a night out. In addition to cards and slots, there are entertainment lounges and restaurants in the casino complexes.

- **Aruba:** There are about 10 casinos on this island, all near Oranjestad or along the nearby hotel strip on Palm Beach. Some of the best are at the **Americana Aruba Beach Resort,** the **Aruba Palm Beach Resort and Casino,** the **Aruba Sonesta Resort & Casino at Seaport Village,** and the **Holiday Inn Aruba Beach Resort.**
- **Curaçao:** Here, too, there are about a dozen casinos, many in Willemstad. You'll find casinos in the **Sonesta Beach Hotel & Casino, Four Points Resorts,** the **Holiday Beach Hotel & Casino,** and the **Princess Beach Resort & Casino.** The atmosphere is casual.
- **Sint Maarten:** While gambling is illegal on the French side of this island, it's not on the Dutch side, where there are about six or seven casinos, mostly in the major hotels, like the **Maho Beach Hotel** and the **Pelican Resort and Casino.** Also check out the Roman-themed **Coliseum Casino** on Front Street in Philipsburg.

17 Best Fitness Facilities & Spas

If you can't bear to miss a workout, even while on a cruise, or if a massage is your idea of nirvana, you're in luck. Most ships, especially those built within the past few years, have excellent fitness and spa facilities.

- **Celebrity Cruises:** No contest: *Century, Galaxy,* and *Mercury* have the best spa and gym complexes at sea. The 10,000-square-foot AquaSpas manage to combine the best health, beauty, and fitness regimens with striking aesthetics inspired by Japanese gardens and bathhouses (on *Century* and *Galaxy*) and Moorish and Turkish spas (on *Mercury*). Facilities include saunas, mud baths, massage rooms, and Turkish baths. Each of the three also offers the Rasul, an Oriental therapy that includes applying medicinal mud, a seaweed soap shower, an herbal steam bath and massage, and a dip in the 15,000-gallon thalassotherapy pool (an oversized, souped-up hot tub). Special features include deep-cleansing facials and newfangled slimming treatments, too.
- **Norwegian Cruise Line:** Deep down in the lowest decks of the line's *Norway* you'll find the memorable Roman Spa, which features an indoor pool, 16 treatment rooms, exercise equipment, 2 steam rooms, and 2 saunas, plus body-jet showers and a whirlpool.
- **Carnival Cruise Lines:** The two-deck-high, 15,000-square-foot Nautica Spa health and fitness center on the *Destiny* and *Triumph* are awesome, with more than 40 state-of-the-art exercise machines, including virtual-reality stationary bikes. As you pedal, a peaceful landscape unfolds before you. There's a juice bar, men's and women's sauna and steam rooms, and a whirlpool-like hydrotherapy tub whose bubbling waters are loaded with extracts of seaweed and rejuvenating oils.
- **Costa Cruises:** Done with richly colored mosaic tiles and Roman columns, the attractive and soothing Pompeii Spa on the *CostaVictoria* includes a pool, therapy rooms, and a Turkish bath. The attractive but smallish workout room shares a glass wall with the spa and pool area, and features over a dozen pieces of equipment.

Part 1

Planning, Booking & Preparing for Your Cruise

With advice on choosing and booking your ideal cruise and tips on getting ready for the cruise experience.

Choosing Your Ideal Cruise

1

There are many things you should consider before plunking down a couple of thousand dollars for the perfect cruise—oh, you know, like should you pack a bikini or a one-piece? John Grisham or Ken Follett? The new Nikon or a disposable? But way before you deal with these vital decisions, you really do need to consider some important issues. What kind of itinerary are you looking for and when do you want to go? What size ship will make you most comfortable and will its age matter? Which are family-friendly or accessible to the handicapped? Is a particular cruise active enough for you? In this chapter I'll address all these issues and more.

1 When to Go

THE CARIBBEAN   With temperatures in the balmy 80s year-round, dozens of ships stay in the Caribbean the entire year, and a bunch more spend the winters there after summering in Alaska or Europe. It's great: The Caribbean is the only major cruise destination that never closes; it's the sea that never sleeps. But (there's always a but), the only caveat to this ideal climate is **hurricane season,** which officially runs June 1 through November 30, but rarely causes cruisers anything more than a few days of rain and a bit of rocking and rolling. I've taken many cruises in the Caribbean during this period and have only occasionally run into stormy weather. With today's modern navigational equipment, it's next-to-impossible to actually get caught in a hurricane, as ships change course as soon as they get wind of a storm.

Defining seasons as "low" and "high" is hardly a science, since most lines seem to come up with their own unique pricing schemes. It is generally accepted, though, that the high season in the Caribbean is **mid-December through mid-April.** During this time, weather will most likely be perfect, the islands and ships jam-packed, and prices the highest. The holiday weeks of Christmas and New Year's are the absolute busiest and most expensive, especially on the family-oriented megas—it's one of the few times in the year when brochure rates are often not discounted (in fact, prices may be several hundred dollars more).

Despite it being hurricane season, the summer months of **June, July,** and **August** are the next busiest time of the year (to many lines, these months are also considered high-season along with December through April) because families traditionally vacation summers and because many ships migrate to Alaska and Europe for the season, leaving fewer ships in the Caribbean. Temperatures may be a bit hotter in summer, but the islands' lush and colorful flowering trees are at their height and the winds the mildest.

September, October, and November are considered low-season (often referred to as "value season"), and the time when you encounter the fewest crowds on shore and on board, and some of the lowest rates—sometimes hundreds of dollars less than other times of the year. Industry insiders tell me there can also be a lull the first 2 weeks of January, just after the rush of the holidays, and sometimes in late April and May, so look for good prices then.

BERMUDA   The Bermuda cruise season extends from late April to early October, with the peak between late June and late August, when the average temperature is 80°— 10° to 15° higher than the rest of the year.

2   Choosing the Itinerary That's Best for You

If you count every little rocky outcropping or sand bar, there are hundreds of islands in the Caribbean. Of the 40 or 50 islands on the map, cruise ships regularly visit about 25 of them. Most Caribbean cruises are 7 nights long and visit anywhere from three to six different ports of call. There are a handful of 3- and 4-night cruises out of Florida visiting the Bahamas or Cozumel, and there are 10- to 14-night Caribbean cruises that transit the Panama Canal, typically sailing between Florida and Acapulco, Mexico, visiting three to seven ports.

While they're all pretty darned appealing in some way, the Caribbean islands are not all created equal. Some islands are better for shopping, others are better for beaches or scenic drives. Some are quite developed, others remain natural. Some have piers that ships can conveniently tie right up to, while others require that ships anchor a mile or so offshore and shuttle passengers back and forth in small motorized launches called *tenders*. Big ships tend to visit the more commercialized, developed islands, while the small ships are able to access off-the-beaten-track, more natural islands. Typically the big lines divide Caribbean itineraries into **eastern, western,** and **southern,** but smaller ship lines rarely adhere to such rigid labels.

MEGASHIP ITINERARIES

WESTERN CARIBBEAN   Most western Caribbean itineraries depart from Miami, Ft. Lauderdale, Port Canaveral, or Tampa, Florida—a few from New Orleans and one even from Houston, Texas—and typically visit Grand Cayman, Jamaica, and Cozumel, on Mexico's Yucatán Peninsula. This is a popular itinerary for many lines, and you'll certainly notice the throngs of other cruise passengers in each port—often a half dozen ships will be visiting at a time.

EASTERN CARIBBEAN   Eastern Caribbean itineraries also typically sail out of Florida, and may include Puerto Rico, St. Thomas, St. Croix, Sint Maarten, and the Bahamas—all very popular and busy ports of call, especially St. Thomas, Nassau, and Puerto Rico.

SOUTHERN CARIBBEAN   A southern itinerary, more times than not, is round-trip out of San Juan, Puerto Rico, which often blends with an eastern Caribbean itinerary. Southern routes are bound to visit islands including St. Thomas, Sint Maarten, Barbados, St. Lucia, Martinique, Antigua, and maybe Dominica, Guadeloupe, Aruba, and Grenada.

SMALL SHIP ITINERARIES

Most small ships cruise in the eastern and southern Caribbean, where distances between islands are shorter. Instead of Florida, they may sail out of Barbados, Grenada, or San Juan, and visit more remote islands.

EASTERN CARIBBEAN   An eastern Caribbean itinerary might include visits to St. Barts, Virgin Gorda, Jost Van Dyke, Tortola, and St. John, as well as one or two more touristy islands, like St. Thomas.

SOUTHERN CARIBBEAN   Southern Caribbean cruises may visit Guadeloupe, Dominica, Martinique, St. Lucia, St. Vincent, and Bequia, and maybe the truly un-spoiled and remote Palm, Canouan, Mayreau, and Carriacou islands.

MATCHING YOUR HABITS TO YOUR DESTINATION

Some ports are better for certain things than others. Here's a short run-down (see part 3, "The Ports," for more detailed information).

PORTS FOR SHOPPERS

Eastern Caribbean: St. Croix, St. Martin/Sint Maarten, St. Thomas, San Juan (Puerto Rico)

Western Caribbean: Grand Cayman

Southern Caribbean: Aruba, Barbados

Bermuda

PORTS FOR BEACH LOVERS

Eastern Caribbean: Anguilla, British Virgin Islands, St. John, St. Martin

Western Caribbean: Grand Cayman, Jamaica

Southern Caribbean: Aruba, Grenada

Bermuda

PORTS FOR SNORKELERS

Eastern Caribbean: St. Croix, St. John, St. Thomas

Western Caribbean: Grand Cayman

Southern Caribbean: Bonaire, Curaçao

PORTS FOR HISTORY & ARCHAEOLOGY BUFFS

Eastern Caribbean: San Juan (Puerto Rico), Dominican Republic

Western Caribbean: Cozumel/Playa del Carmen/Calica

Southern Caribbean: Barbados, Curaçao

Bermuda

PORTS FOR NATURE BUFFS

Eastern Caribbean: St. John, Puerto Rico

Southern Caribbean: Aruba, Dominica, Grenada, Trinidad

SHORE EXCURSIONS: THE WHAT, WHY & HOW

No matter what size ship you're on or what its itinerary is, you can choose from 4 to over 40 tours in any given port, ranging in price from $20 to $200 per person. The tried and true standards are walking tours, bus trips, snorkeling and diving excursions, booze cruises on catamarans, glass-bottomed boat rides, and helicopter tours. In the past few

---

Indulging Your Obsessions at Sea: Theme Cruises

Theme cruises are becoming more and more popular, as lines look for more ways to attract passengers with unique onboard activities. There are jazz, big band, opera, and country music cruises; sailings focused on French cooking and wine; and cruises focused on international affairs, history, or investing. Crystal and Windstar, for instance, feature an annual series of **food and wine cruises,** where well-known chefs and sommeliers are on board to conduct demonstrations and tastings. Holland America, Cunard, NCL, and Crystal do quite a few **music theme cruises** every year, paying tribute to jazz, big band, '50s, or Broadway, with live bands and lots of dancing.

---

years a slew of more active, unique excursions have been introduced, such as biking, hiking, horseback riding, golfing, kayaking, and river tubing.

On the megas, excursions can sell out real fast, so don't dawdle if you know what you want; sign up the first or second day of the cruise. Because of the large numbers of passengers on a megaship, be prepared for some waiting around as each jumbo-sized tour group is herded from the ship to the awaiting army of buses or minivans.

On smaller ships, tours might never get sold out because there's room to accommodate all passengers on board. The whole process is saner, and group sizes are most likely smaller. That said, big ship or small, the attraction itself, quality of the tour guide, and execution of the tour are what determine whether you have an enjoyable time.

Although many tours are wonderful compliments to your cruise and leave lasting, fond memories—especially if you're a first-time visitor or want to leave the planning to someone else—others are overcrowded, disappointing, and not worth the money. Choose wisely, and remember, sometimes it's best to skip the organized tour and go off exploring on your own. Much of Aruba, Curaçao, St. Thomas, St. Martin, Puerto Rico, Grand Cayman, and Bermuda, for instance, are easily explored independently—all you need is a good guidebook (this one!) and a sense of adventure and you'll have a great time. In the port chapters of this book, I list both the best shore excursions and the best sights you can see on your own.

3 Choosing the Ship of Your Dreams

News flash: All ships are not the same. Even before getting to the kind of experience offered by the cruise lines, physical factors such as the age and size of the ship figure into whether it can offer you the vacation experience you want.

BIG SHIP OR SMALL?

A cruise on a big ship with 2,000-plus passengers versus a small one with only 200 is like night and day—like spending a week in a cozy New England bed-and-breakfast versus a 500-room high-rise hotel in Cancún. As much as anything else, a ship's size greatly determines its personality and the kind of vacation you'll have. Big ships tend to be busy, exciting affairs, while the smaller ones are most often low-key retreats with unique personalities. Big ships normally spend 2 or 3 days at sea on a week-long cruise because they travel great distances between ports and because there's so much to do on board; small ships are more destination oriented, visiting a different port nearly every day.

BIG SHIPS

If you seek nonstop fun and games, twinkling lights and splashes of neon, flamboyant art and towering atriums, and sweeping staircases pouring into grand two-story dining rooms, then the 1,800-passenger-plus megaliners of the Carnival, Royal Caribbean, Princess, Celebrity, and Disney cruise lines will appeal to you big-time. Slightly smaller big ships, like those of the Norwegian, Holland America, Crystal, Royal Olympic, and Premier fleets, are not quite megas, but with 800 to 1,500 passengers are big enough to offer a similarly exciting and active experience. All of these ships are so large, in fact, that they are limited to where they can tie up—certain islands and ports simply cannot handle them.

The onboard atmosphere is carefree and casual by day—with passengers decked out in bathing suits, shorts, sarongs, and sandals—and more elegant by evening, when dinner on formal nights calls for a tuxedo or suit for men and a cocktail dress or fancy pantsuit for women. Granted, the megas are buzzing social meccas, but, just like living in a metropolis such as New York City, you'll be able to blend in with the crowd and become an anonymous passenger among the throngs. Chances are you won't run into the same person twice (except your dinner mates, of course). In fact, if you don't plan specific times and places to meet up with your spouse, lover, or friend, you can roam the decks for what seems like hours looking for them (I know, it's happened to me; then again, a few hours of freedom might be a blessing).

The megas have as many as 12 or 14 decks of shops, restaurants, bars, lounges, and cabins of all shapes and sizes (and there are even more decks for the crew, decks you'll never see). Most have a multistory atrium, three or four swimming pools and hot tubs, casinos with hundreds of slot machines and dozens of card tables, three or four restaurants, a jogging track, movie theater, pizzeria, and patisserie. Mammoth spas and gyms are huge, boasting dozens of exercise machines and treatment rooms. Vast areas dedicated to children include splash pools, play rooms, and video arcades.

As you'd expect, the largest ships offer the greatest variety of **activities,** with an emphasis on choice. Countless activities are offered all day long, from dance lessons to wine tastings, fashion shows, art auctions, aerobics classes, bingo, bridge, ship tours, cooking demonstrations, pool games, and trivia contests. There are more entertainment options—piano bars, discos, martini bars, champagne bars, sports bars, theaters, and show lounges—than you could ever sample in one evening.

SMALL SHIPS

If you crave a calm, intimate experience in a club-like atmosphere where conversation is king, a smaller ship may be more up your alley. Like a tiny town, you'll quickly get to know your neighbors on a smaller ship, as you see the same faces at meals and on deck throughout the week.

Unlike the more homogenous, cookie-cutter megas, there is a variety of small-ship styles. The Windjammer, Star Clippers, Windstar, and Club Med fleets are **sailing ships** relying on both sail and engine power, and attracting passengers in their 30s through 70s. Windstar is the most upscale version, emphasizing fine cuisine and plush cabin amenities like CD players and VCRs. Windjammer is the most casual and adventurous, maintaining an anything-goes onboard atmosphere where shorts and T-shirts can be worn to dinner. Star Clippers and Club Med offer an experience midway between these two.

The Clipper and American Canadian Caribbean lines have **simple, cozy, motorized ships,** with a more sedate ambience for a generally older (over 50) clientele. The **small luxury ships** of high-end lines such as Seabourn, Cunard, and Radisson Seven Seas cruise lines offer a refined, ultra-elegant ambience. Cabins are spacious with large marble bathrooms, gourmet meals are served on fine china by white-gloved waiters, and guests dress to impress in sequins and tuxedos.

A small ship might have only one restaurant and one or two bars; a pianist or duo will entertain before dinner, and perhaps there will be a crew or passenger talent show afterward. Small ships have fewer activities options, but are no less appealing. There's usually one all-purpose lounge, or maybe a bar or central patch of outdoor deck where passengers can congregate to chat, read, have a drink, or listen to a presentation about their next port destination. There's often a cozy book and video library nearby. Generally, there's a focus on learning. On Windstar, Star Clippers, Windjammer, Clipper, and ACCL, for instance, the cruise director or captain discuss the native wildlife or history of the next port of call (on the megas, port talks are mostly about shopping opportunities). Sometimes a naturalist, author, or celebrity joins the cruise to present informal lectures on a wide variety of topics. Small ships generally visit a port nearly every single day, and they're able to easily slip in and out of more off-the-beaten-track, less spoiled ports, such as Grenada and St. Barts.

OLD SHIP OR NEW?

Depending on what you like, the age of a ship can be a plus or a minus. **New ships** come stocked with all the bells and whistles many of us have come to expect in a vacation. Aside from fresh new carpeting and upholstery, the newest ships have big gyms and spas, cabin balconies, TVs and VCRs, several restaurants, pizza and ice cream, uncluttered open expanses of deck and wide promenades, and big windows everywhere.

Now, if you appreciate relics of the past—pre-war apartments over modern ones, antiques instead of IKEA—then you'll like the handful of 30-year-old-plus **classic ocean liners** still plying the Caribbean. With sweeping, long hulls and tiered decks, wood paneling, and chunky portholes, these liners offer a nostalgic glimpse back to a lost age of cruising. Decks, doors, railings, and bar tops are made of solid varnished wood. In the bridge, an oversized wooden wheel and heavy brass compasses sit alongside modern radar devices. Cabin doors may still operate with a lock and key rather than a computerized keycard, tall sills in most doorways require some high stepping to avoid tripping (old ships are not for wheelchair users), and there's no shortage of exposed cables, fire doors, pipes, ropes, winches, and all manner of hardware. These are ships that look like ships, and for ship buffs, they are charming (and for bargain hunters, they're often the best deal in town).

That said, the old-timers can't hide the wear and tear accumulated from logging thousands of miles at sea. If you're a lover of all things fresh, new, and modern, don't even consider a cruise on one of the oldies. Repeatedly refurbished and restored through the years (often haphazardly and in the least expensive ways), many are a hodge-podge of

---

Old Ships, Aging Gracefully

Like people, some older ships have aged gracefully, others have not. Premier's 42-year-old *Rembrandt,* the former Holland America *Rotterdam V,* is the most beautiful and intact relic left, with much of her original furniture, wall finishings, and artwork. The 31-year-old *QE2,* while having undergone many more facelifts, manages to hold on to the past with dignity and her long body and razor-sharp bow still turn heads. On a lesser scale, ships like the 47-year-old *Regal Empress* of Regal Cruises have managed to retain some of their original charm, although you have to look harder to find it.

design schemes and awkward spaces. Discos, spas, and gyms are often small, dark spaces in lower decks, and carpeting, wall finishes, and outside decks are often worn. You won't find two-story dining rooms, Vegas-style casinos (they do have casinos, but they're often small and plain), and long stretches of uninterrupted deck space.

The future of some of these old-timers depends on compliance with a set of international safety regulations known as the **Safety of Life at Sea (SOLAS),** which are predominately concerned with issues like fire prevention. Ships built after 1994 automatically incorporate SOLAS safety features; ships built before 1994 have been required to add them by a progressive set of deadlines. The most sweeping changes were completed by a 1997 deadline, and three further series of changes must be implemented by October of 2000, 2005, and 2010. The changes required in 2005 and 2010, especially, may prove too costly for many of these old-timers and seal their fate forever. We'll see.

4 Matching the Cruise to Your Needs

CRUISES FOR FAMILIES

The right cruise can be the perfect family vacation. Forget that nightmarish National Lampoon stuff; in reality, cruises are safe, fun, and oh-so-relaxing for the whole brood. Cruise lines have been going to great lengths to please parents and kids alike, as families continue to become a large and influential segment of the cruising public.

It's the **megaships** that cater most to families and attract the largest numbers of them, with playrooms, video arcades, and supervised activities generally provided for children from age 2 through 17, with programs broken down into several age categories (see "Best Cruises for Families with Kids" in the "Frommer's Favorites" chapter for the best family ships). The most family-friendly ships at sea are Disney's *Magic* and *Wonder* and Premier's *Big Red Boat.* Carnival's post-1990 ships do a great job, too, and ships in the Royal Caribbean, Norwegian, Celebrity, and Princess fleets built after 1993, when family cruising was becoming more mainstream, are also well equipped to cater to families.

ACTIVITIES   With dedicated camp-counselor–like supervisors, playrooms, computer stations, state-of-the-art video arcades, and pools, your kids will have so much fun you may have to drag them away kicking and screaming at the end of the cruise. Chances are, even too-cool, nonchalant teens will be worn down by the endless activities and the chance to make new friends.

The youngest frolic in toy- and game-stocked playrooms, listen to stories, and go on treasure hunts; older kids do things like arts and crafts, computer games, lip-sync competitions, pool games, and volleyball; and teenagers go snorkeling, mingle at teen parties, or hang out at the video arcade. The megas have large playrooms with computer stations and video games as well as shelves of toys. There's usually a TV showing movies throughout the day and, for the younger ones, there are ball bins and plastic jungle gyms to crawl around in. Many megaships have shallow kiddie pools, sometimes sequestered on an isolated patch of deck.

BABY-SITTING   To ensure parents have a good time, too, there are adults-only discos and lounges, and baby-sitting from about 8pm to 2am. **Group baby-sitting** is about $4 to $5 per hour per child and, if available, **private in-cabin baby-sitting** by a crewmember is a steep $8 to $10 per hour per child, plus generally a dollar or two more for a sibling. Using a private baby-sitter every night could put a serious dent in your budget.

FAMILY-FRIENDLY CABINS   Worried about spending a whole week with the family in some cramped cabin? Well, depending on your budget, you don't have to. Now,

Family Cruising Tips

Here are some suggestions for better sailing and smoother seas on your family cruise.

- **Ask about children's amenities.** Check in advance with the cruise line to make sure the ship you're sailing offers things your child might need. Are cribs available? Children's menus?

- **Pack some basic first-aid supplies** plus any medications your doctor may suggest, and even a thermometer. Cruise lines have limited supplies of these items (and charge for them, too) and can quickly run out if the ship has many families aboard. If an accident should happen aboard, virtually every ship afloat has its own infirmary staffed by doctors and/or nurses. Keep in mind, first aid can usually be summoned more readily aboard ship than in port.

- **Warn younger children about the danger of falling overboard** and make sure they know not to play on the railings.

- **When in port, prearrange a meeting spot on board.** If your child is old enough to go off on his or her own, prearrange a meeting spot (well before the ship is scheduled to depart) and meet there just after boarding to make sure no one is still ashore.

- **Make your kids know their cabin's number and what deck it's on.** The endless corridors and doors on the megas look exactly alike.

- **Prepare kids for TV letdown.** Televisions on ships just don't have 200 channels of cable—you'll be lucky to get five or eight channels. On the brighter side, your ship is likely to have nightly movies and a video arcade.

a family of four *can* share a cabin that has **bunk-style third and fourth berths,** which pull out of the walls just above the pair of regular beds (some even have a fifth berth), but there's no two ways to slice it: A standard cabin with four people in it will be cramped, and with one bathroom . . . well, you can imagine. However, when you consider how little time you'll spend in the cabin, it's do-able. The incentive to share one cabin is the price—whether children or adults, the rates for third and fourth people sharing a cabin with two full-fare passengers are usually about half of the lowest regular rates. On occasion there are special deals and further discounts. Norwegian Cruise Line, Premier Cruises, and Royal Olympic Cruises allow children under 2 to sail for free. If you're a single parent sailing with children, Premier Cruises offers a special, reduced single-person rate that's 125% of the normal per-person rate (on most lines, singles have to pay 50% to 100% more than the regular per-person rate, since rates are based on double adult occupancy of cabins).

If you can afford it, and if space equals sanity in your book, consider **booking a suite.** Many have a pull-out couch in the living room or, better yet, two separate bedrooms and accommodate up to three or four children. The Disney *Magic* and *Wonder* boast the family-friendliest cabins at sea (and you'll pay a hefty price for them). The majority of the ships' 875 cabins are equipped with two bathrooms and a sitting area and are like mini-suites, about 25% larger than the industry standard, comfortably sleeping families of three or four. The ships' bona fide suites accommodate families of five, and nearly half of all cabins have private verandas.

Families with older kids can always consider booking **two separate cabins with interconnecting doors.** Lots of ships, big and small, have them. You'll be close to each other, but separate.

TAKING THE KIDS ON SMALL SHIPS   While there's no doubting the big new ships are best prepared for families, if your children are at least 10 or 12, some of the casual, off-beat cruises (for example, Windjammer's *Legacy* and Star Clippers' *Star Clipper*) can be loads of fun and educational to boot—if you and your kids come armed with the right attitude, of course. While you won't find a kids' playroom stuffed with toys (or many other kids on board for that matter), the experience of visiting a remote port of call every day will help keep you and the kids from going stir crazy on board. If your child is inquisitive and somewhat of an extrovert, ships like the Star Clipper vessels or Windjammer's *Legacy* offer him or her a chance to talk with the crew and learn something about how a sailing ship operates. That said, if your kids are attached at the hip to video games, computers, and big-screen TVs, the megaships are the route to take.

CRUISES FOR HONEYMOONERS & ANNIVERSARY COUPLES

If you're looking for an especially romantic cruise for your honeymoon or anniversary, you're in luck: They're all romantic. All the elements are there: moonlit nights on deck, the undulating sea all around you, romantic dining, silky beaches and exotic ports of call, maybe even a private balcony for your cabin.

Of course, different ships are romantic to different kinds of people. The megas offer glamorous, Vegas-style romance; the small, casual ships, an intimate and Sunday-drive-in-the-country kind of romance; the ultra-luxury lines, epicurean romance with gourmet cuisine, fine wine and liquor, and plush surroundings; and older ships, a nostalgic brand of romance for ocean liner lovers.

Besides their inherent romantic qualities, cruises are honeymoon havens for lots of reasons—like **Sunday departures,** which mean that couples who marry on Saturday can leave on a cruise the next day (in the past, most sailings departed on Fridays or Saturdays, so newlyweds who typically marry on Saturdays had to wait almost a week to start their cruise). Other **romantic ship features** include private balconies, 24-hour room service, hot tubs, spas, and, of course, the balmy island ports of call. Most lines will serve honeymooners a special cake in the dining room one night, and some lines—Carnival, HAL, Premier, and NCL—even go one step further and invite honeymooners to a **private cocktail party** for complimentary drinks and hors d'oeuvres (couples celebrating anniversaries are often invited as well). Norwegian Cruise Line treats honeymooners to breakfast in bed, hors d'oeuvres delivered to the cabin one evening, a free photograph, and the choice of dining at a special newlyweds-only table or a private table for two.

To get your share of honeymoon and anniversary freebies, be sure to tell your travel agent or the cruise line reservation agent that you'll be celebrating your honeymoon or anniversary on the cruise.

HONEYMOON & ANNIVERSARY PACKAGES   If you want even more romantic stuff to enhance your cruise, the lines aren't shy about selling a variety of goodies and packages geared to honeymooners and couples celebrating anniversaries and vow renewals. You'll get a pamphlet describing the available packages when you receive your cruise tickets in the mail. Packages, which need to be ordered before the cruise, start at around $30 per couple and can run into the thousands of dollars, with **wedding ceremony packages** being the most costly.

Celebrity Cruises $119 package is typical; it includes breakfast in bed served with champagne, engraved champagne flutes, fresh floral arrangement, a red rose placed on the pillow, a pair of bathrobes, and a personalized honeymoon or anniversary certificate. For a more gourmet palate, Windstar offers a box of Swiss Truffles in your cabin for $26, tray of French cheeses for $24, and a bottle of Dom Perignon and caviar at $190 a pop. Other packages may include a photograph and wedding album, chocolate-

Getting Married at Sea

If you plan on having your marriage and honeymoon all in one, you can legally get hitched on board many ships (although captains are rarely qualified—much less have the time or inclination—to legally do the officiating, except aboard the *Grand Princess*).

Civil Ceremonies in U.S. Ports
Passengers can have a civil marriage ceremony performed by a local justice of the peace or church official on board the ship (out on deck or inside one of the public rooms) before a cruise departs from any U.S. port—for example, in **Florida, New York,** or **Puerto Rico.** This way, friends and family can come aboard for a few hours for a ceremony and a reception before the ship departs.

Ceremonies in Bermuda
Couples can also tie the knot while in port in Bermuda and several Caribbean islands, either on the ship or on shore. Sometimes, where permitted, you can request or arrange to have a priest, rabbi, or other official of your choice. Ceremony and reception packages include not only the services of the officiant, but also things such as floral arrangements, tuxedo/gown rental, wedding cake, photography, music, and hors d'oeuvres, and generally start at about $500 per couple, and like weddings shoreside, can run into the thousands of dollars.

In the U.S. Virgin Islands, the Bahamas & Jamaica
The U.S. Virgin Islands (USVI)—**St. Croix, St. Thomas,** and **St. John**—as well as the Bahamas, Bermuda, and Jamaica, are some of the most popular wedding spots. Carnival may be the biggest wedding factory at sea, offering packages in San Juan, St. Thomas, Ocho Rios, Jamaica, Key West, and Nassau, and on board while anchored in Grand Cayman or Barbados.

Talk About Romantic: Having the Captain Officiate
Have your heart set on the big boss performing your marriage rites at sea? If, so, you've got one choice. Princess Cruises' *Grand Princess* is the only ship to date where the captain himself performs as many as eight bona fide, 100% legal civil ceremonies a week. He performs the wedding ceremonies in the ship's charming wedding chapel. Adorned with fresh flower arrangements (there are two full-time florists on

covered strawberries, limousine service between the ship and airport, shore excursions, and even a pair of massages at the spa.

Some lines offer **vow renewal packages** for couples who'd like to celebrate their marriage all over again. On Holland America ships, for example, couples can renew their vows at a special ceremony while at sea or in port; the $95 package includes a corsage for the bride, printed invitations to send to friends on board, a photo album, music, wine or champagne, and hors d'oeuvres. For $49 per couple, you can renew vows at a casual ceremony in a chapel by the sea on Holland America's private Bahamian island, Half Moon Cay. Princess offers similar, but souped-up, vow renewal packages for $149 and $349 per couple.

To ensure a dapper appearance on formal nights, **tuxedo rentals** can even be ordered for about $75, complete with shirt and shoes. Your tux will be pressed and waiting in the cabin. All these extras are usually purchased for a couple before a cruise by the couple themselves or by parents, friends, or their travel agent.

HONEYMOON LUXURY   High-end small-ship lines, such as Windstar, Radisson Seven Seas, Seabourn, Cunard, and Crystal, don't offer special cocktail parties and the board) as well as ribbons strung along the aisle, the room is tastefully designed in warm caramel-colored wood tones and stained glass, and there is seating for a few dozen friends and family members. Assistant pursers, decked out in their handsome dress blues, are available to escort a bride down the mini-aisle. Three different ceremony packages are offered on the ship, ranging from $1,400 to $2,400 per couple, and including photography, video, music, and salon treatments for the bride. And if you've got friends and family on board, reception packages start at $70 per person, and include hors d'oeuvres, champagne, and wedding cake.

The Details
No matter where you choose to wed, U.S. or foreign port, a **wedding license** must be obtained (or an application filed) in advance of the cruise and specific arrangements must be made for the wedding ceremony itself. Policies vary from country to country, and you need to find out what the rules are well in advance of your sailing date. At the time of booking, the cruise line or your travel agent can fill you in on the rules and regulations of the ports visited and assist you with the paperwork—for example, by sending you a license application form or telling you where to get one. To help you with the details, Carnival and Princess have **wedding departments;** other lines handle wedding planning through the guest relations office or refer you to a wedding consultant.

To get married in the USVI, for example, license applications must be received by the Territorial Court in the USVI at least 8 days before your wedding day (the license application fee is $50; contact the USVI Territorial Court in St. Thomas at ☎ **340/774-6680** for an application). In Bermuda, couples are required to file a Notice of Intended Marriage with the office of the registrar in Bermuda at least 2 weeks in advance (the fee is $176 and you can get a form from the Bermuda Department of Tourism at ☎ **800/223-6106**). You must be in the Bahamas for at least 24 hours before marrying there (the fee is $40; contact the Bahamas Tourist Office at ☎ **800/422-4262** for more information).

Remember, the cruise itinerary limits where and when you can tie the knot; time spent in a given port generally ranges from 3 to 10 hours.

like, but their ultra-deluxe amenities are especially pleasing to honeymooners. From terrycloth bathrobes and slippers that await in walk-in closets, to whirlpool bathtubs, five-course dinners served in your cabin, stocked minibars, and high crew-to-passenger ratios (meaning more personalized service), extra-special touches are business as usual on these upscale lines.

CRUISES FOR GAY MEN & LESBIANS

There are a number of particularly gay-friendly cruises and special chartered sailings for gay men and lesbians. For details, contact these specialists: **RSVP Cruises,** 2800 University Ave. SE, Minneapolis, MN 55414 (☎ **800/328-7787** or 612/379-4697); **Pied Piper Travel,** 330 W. 42nd St., Suite 1804, New York, NY 10036 (☎ **800/TRIP-312** or 212/239-2412); and **Olivia Cruises and Resorts,** 4400 Market St., Oakland, CA 94608 (☎ **800/631-6277** or 510/655-0364), which caters specifically to lesbians.

You can also contact the **International Gay Travel Association,** 4331 N. Federal Hwy., Suite 304, Ft. Lauderdale, FL 33308 (☎ **800/448-8550**), which has over 1,000 travel industry members. You might want to check out the well-known **Out & About** travel newsletter ($49 a year for 10 issues; to subscribe, call ☎ **800/929-2268** or 212/645-6922) or **Our World** travel magazine ($35 a year for 10 issues; call ☎ **904/441-5367** to subscribe) for articles, tips, and listings on gay and lesbian travel.

CRUISES FOR ACTIVE PEOPLE

Sure, there are lots of activities offered on cruises—bingo, dancing lessons, wine tasting, napkin-folding, make-up demonstrations, and lots more. But what about people who like to be physically active? Well, on the megas, and even on the small ships, there's quite a bit to do to keep your heart pumping and muscles moving (see individual ship descriptions in chapters 6 through 9).

The newer megaships (built after 1990) in the Carnival, Royal Caribbean, Princess, Celebrity, and Holland America fleets have **jogging tracks** and **well-equipped gyms** that rival those on shore (the biggest exceed 10,000 square feet, and all have dozens of exercise machines). Some ships—Royal Caribbean's *Voyager of the Seas;* Princess's *Ocean, Grand, Sea, Sun,* and *Dawn Princess;* Holland America's *Maasdam, Ryndam, Veendam,* and *Volendam;* NCL's *Leeward, Norwegian Dream, Wind,* and *Sky;* the entire Carnival fleet; Disney's *Magic* and *Wonder;* and Crystal's *Symphony*—have **basketball, volleyball,** and/or **paddle tennis courts.** The Princess's *Grand Princess* and Royal Caribbean's *Voyager, Splendour,* and *Legend of the Seas* even have **miniature golf courses** on board.

Norwegian, Crystal, Princess, Radisson Seven Seas, and Cunard have **outdoor golf cages**—areas enclosed in netting where you can swing, putt, and whack at real golf balls (sometimes, though, these nets are monopolized by the golf pro and his students). A handful of smaller ships—the Windstar and Seabourn fleets, the *Radisson Diamond,* and the *Club Med II*—have **retractable water sports platforms** that unfold from the stern for easy access to the water. Weather and conditions permitting, you can swim, be taken water-skiing or on banana-boat rides, or use the kayaks, sail boats, and windsurfers provided—all free of charge, and all just a few steps from your cabin. The *Star Clipper* carries a fleet of Zodiac boats on board, so passengers can be taken water-skiing or on banana-boat rides.

On shore, there are more and more **active excursions** being offered. No need to sit on a bus for 3 hours sweating if you'd rather be working up a sweat the natural way. Along with snorkeling and diving, options like biking, hiking, and horseback riding have become popular tours in many ports. (For more details, see chapter 11, "Caribbean Ports of Call.")

CRUISES FOR PEOPLE WITH DISABILITIES

The newest ships have been built with accessibility for disabled passengers in mind, and some of the older ones have been refitted to accommodate the disabled. Like hotels, restaurants, movie theaters, and other public places, cruise ships are catering more and more to the needs of all potential passengers. Technically, though, as foreign-flagged vessels, cruise ships are not subject to U.S. laws governing construction and design, nor are they required to obey the Americans with Disabilities act.

For those ships that can accommodate handicapped passengers, most require wheelchair-bound passengers to be accompanied by a fully mobile companion. The vast majority of ships travel with a nurse on board at all times and often there is a doctor, too; I've listed which ships have medical facilities (which are wheelchair accessible) in the "Ships at a Glance" chart in chapter 5, but check with the line to see exactly what medical services are provided. It's important to ask lots of questions and explain the nature of your disabilities in detail to your travel agent. A good agent knows exactly which cabins can accommodate wheelchair users and which ships are best equipped in general. In the ship reviews I'll tell you how many cabins are accessible on each ship;

also, deck plans in brochures usually indicate which cabins are accessible and sometimes go into detail about what's offered. In general, the newest ships are best equipped, with many wide elevators and cabins created specifically for passengers with mobility problems. The newest ships in the Celebrity, Holland America, and Princess fleets, for example, have well-planned cabins and public areas. Older, 20-year-plus ships are often not accessible, and small ships like Windjammer, Star Clippers, ACCL, and Clipper have no elevators and are just a bad bet all around for wheelchair users.

ACCESSIBLE CABINS & PUBLIC ROOMS   In general, look for ships with elevators and hallways wide enough for wheelchairs, and flat flooring at doorways. Some cabins may be specifically designed for handicapped travelers, with extra-wide doorways, large bathrooms with grab bars and roll-in showers, and furniture built to a lower height. Some public rooms—dining rooms, lounges, discos, and casinos, for example—have ramps. Keep in mind that older ships especially (generally those more than 20 years old) may have raised doorways (known as *sills* or *lips,* originally created to contain water) in bathrooms, hallways, and other public rooms, which can protrude as high as 6 to 8 inches. New ships have no or very low sills; those that do may be able to install temporary ramps to accommodate wheelchair users, which must be arranged in advance.

ELEVATORS   All of today's newest megaships are built with elevators and most are wide enough to accommodate wheelchairs; however, make sure you're certain of this before booking. Sailing ships and small vessels do not have elevators. Even if a ship does have elevators, the size of today's huge megaships means your cabin could be quite a distance from the elevators and stairs, unless you specify otherwise. If you don't use a wheelchair, but have trouble walking, you'll want to choose a cabin close to an elevator to avoid a long hike down the corridor.

TENDERING INTO PORT   If a ship is too large to dock or if the port can't accommodate ships of any size, you might need to take a tender (a small boat) to get ashore at certain ports on some itineraries. In this case, cruise ships anchor a mile or two from the shore, and passengers have to climb into the shuttle boats to get ashore; some tenders are large and stable, others are not. Keep in mind, if you have trouble walking or use a wheelchair, it might be difficult or impossible to get into certain tenders; even calm seas could rock the boats enough to make climbing inside a tricky maneuver. For liability reasons, many lines forbid wheelchairs to be carried onto tenders, meaning you might have to forgo any trips to shore and stay on board when in port. Check with your travel agent to find out if itineraries you're interested in allow your ship to dock at a pier. Note, though, that once on the cruise, weather conditions and heavy traffic may necessitate last-minute changes in the way your ship reaches a port of call.

TRAVEL AGENT SPECIALISTS   A handful of experienced travel agencies specialize in booking cruises and tours for disabled travelers. **Accessible Journeys,** 35 W. Sellers Ave., Ridley Park, PA 19078 (☎ **800/846-4537**), can even provide licensed healthcare professionals to accompany those who require aid; **Flying Wheels Travel,** 143 W. Bridge St., Owatonna, MN 55060 (☎ **800/535-6790**), is another option.

2

Booking Your Cruise & Getting the Best Price

If you've never taken a cruise before, and even if you have, it's wise to use a travel agent you know and trust to help you book the right one and get the best price. Cruise prices, unfortunately, are not always the easiest things to figure out.

Except for peak-season cruises between Christmas and New Year's (plus President's week, Thanksgiving, and 4th of July week), when prices are often higher than the brochure rates, **forget the prices listed in the cruise-line brochures**—you'll always pay less (except with a tiny minority of lines, like American Canadian Caribbean Line, which do stick to their brochure rates). Overcapacity and fierce competition have ushered in the age of the discounted fare. There are early-booking discounts as well as last-minute deals. There are high-season rates and low-season rates and special offers. Point is, there are some great bargains out there, and an experienced cruise travel specialist can help you find them.

In this chapter, I'll show you how to get a good price, keep costs down, find a reputable travel agent, and then how to choose your cabin once you've hunted down the (affordable) ship of your dreams.

1 The Prices in This Guide

Cruise guides have struggled for years to adequately drive home the point that cruise line brochure prices are almost always much, much higher than you'll actually pay. Trouble is, when all was said and done, they still would generally print the brochure rates, and rely on admonitions like "See the travel specials advertised in your Sunday newspaper" to get people the scoop on how much they'll really save.

In this guide, however, I've come up with a new approach, working with The Travel Company, the largest of the large travel-booking agencies, to present to you a sample of the **actual prices** cruises aboard all the ships in this book sell for. You can see the difference for yourself. For example, the brochure rate for a 7-night Caribbean cruise aboard Celebrity's beautiful *Mercury* is $1,795 for a low-end outside cabin. In reality, however, people who booked approximately 8 months ahead of time for an early 2000 sailing got that same cabin for $899. What a difference!

For a few more quick examples, see the "7-Night Caribbean Brochure Prices vs. Sample Actual Prices" table in this chapter. In the ship review chapters, I've listed these realistic prices for *every* ship, and in

7-Night Caribbean Brochure Prices vs. Sample Actual Prices*				
Line	Ship	Lowest Inside (brochure/actual)	Lowest Outside (brochure/actual)	Lowest Suite (brochure/actual)
Carnival	Paradise	$1,329 / $899	$1,579 / $1,009	$2,379 / $1,950
Celebrity	Mercury	$1,795 / $899	$2,225 / $1,049	$3,825 / $3,210
Commodore	Enchanted Isle	$1,250 / $699	$1,500 / $819	$1,840 / $1,562
Costa	CostaVictoria	$1,020 / $720	$1,280 / $980	$2,760 / $2,460
Cunard	QE2	$1,150 / $909	$1,640 / $1,132	$3,420 / $3,133
Disney	Disney Magic	$1,199 / $949	$1,874 / $1,549	$2,925 / $2,724
Holland America	Veendam	$1,859 / $969	$2,069 / $1,174	$4,069 / $2,340
Norwegian	Norwegian Dream	$1,569 / $1,049	$1,869 / $1,149	$2,669 / $1,499
Premier	Rembrandt	$1,198 / $799	$1,498 / $917	$2,298 / $1,978
Princess	Sea Princess	$1,733 / $969	$2,273 / $1,248	$2,873 / $1,549
Royal Caribbean	Enchantment of the Seas	$1,399 / $949	$1,849 / $1,199	$2,399 / $1,878
Seabourn	Seabourn Pride	N/A	N/A	$2,990 / $2,691
Star Clippers	Star Clipper	$1,457 / $960	$1,825 / $1,170	$2,525 / $2,102
Windstar	Wind Spirit	N/A	$3,880 / $2,402	N/A

See Appendix A, "Cruise Price Comparisons," for comparison of brochure versus sample actual prices for every ship reviewed in this book. Also, see chapter 5 for an explanation of pricing methodology. Thanks to The Travel Company for pricing research.

Appendix A, "Cruise Price Comparisons," I've shown how the brochure prices for every ship stack up against what consumers actually pay. See chapter 5, "The Ratings (and How to Read Them)" for a detailed explanation of how we arrived at these prices.

2 The Cost: What's Included & What's Not

A cruise adds up to a great value (and an even bigger convenience) when you consider that most of what you need is included in the so-called **all-inclusive rate.** Accommodations, all meals and most snacks, stops at ports of call, a packed schedule of activities, and free use of resort-quality facilities like gyms and pools, as well as cabaret, jazz performances, dance bands, discos, and more, are covered in the rate.

When figuring out your budget, though, there are **additional costs** to consider that are not included in the rates. Truth is, no cruise is truly all-inclusive, although a handful of the most luxurious and expensive lines (like Radisson Seven Seas, Seabourn, and Cunard) come the closest by including some or all alcoholic beverages (and sometimes tips) in the cruise rate.

So how much should you expect to spend over and above the cruise rate? Be prepared to shell out at least another $200 per person for a 7-night cruise for tips, bar tabs, port charges, and shore excursions (and easily double that, if, for instance, you have a bottle of wine with dinner every night and go on three $60 shore excursions). Airfare can run between $100 to over $500 depending on where you're flying from and when you

Cruise Tip: Put Aside Some Money for Crew Gratuities

Almost all cruise lines have the same kind of deal with their staff that restaurants do in the United States: They pay them minimal salaries, on the assumption they'll make most of their pay in **tips.** Generally, each passenger can expect to drop about $70 in tips for a weeklong cruise. For more on tipping, see Appendix C, "Wrapping Up Your Cruise—Debarkation Concerns."

purchase your tickets. Of course, just as at a hotel, you pay extra for items like ship-to-shore phone calls or faxes, spa and salon treatments (such as massages, manicures, facials, and haircuts), shopping in ship boutiques and at the ports of call, medical treatments in the ship's infirmary, and, of course, gambling losses.

3 How to Find the Best Deals

From early-booking discounts to last-minute deals, from sharing cabins to senior-citizen and frequent-cruiser discounts, there are a lot of ways to save money on your cruise, and in this section I'll fill you in on them.

SHOULD YOU BOOK EARLY OR AT THE LAST MINUTE?

While there are no steadfast rules about pricing—policies differ from line to line, and from week to week—generally, booking 3 to 9 months ahead of when you want to cruise ensures you get the best rates, discounted as much as 50% from the brochure prices. You'll have a better pick of cabins, too. This is especially true if you want to cruise during a popular time, like January or February, when ships get booked up fast, and discounts are reduced dramatically as the ship fills up.

Once upon a time you always secured your best cruise deals by booking at the last minute, but today this is more the exception than the rule. If you do have the flexibility essential for the waiting game, you might still get a good deal at the last-minute, however. Lines may lower prices just a few days or weeks before a cruise because there's still empty space on a ship—after all, they'd rather sell a cabin for a lower fare than not sell it at all. Gone are the days, however, of just walking into a cruise-ship terminal an hour before embarkation, suitcase and passport in hand, and negotiating the killer cruise deal of a lifetime. Most cruise lines protect their pricing policies by rejecting this type of last-minute, pier-side attempt at discounting.

Keep in mind that if you wait till the last minute you'll have to be willing to settle for whatever is available with regard to cabins and ships. Second, savings are not offered on every ship, or every sailing, so you may have to settle for something that isn't the cruise of your dreams. Third, when booking at the last minute, if you have to fly to the port of embarkation, you may have to pay an airfare so high (if you can even get it) that it cancels out your savings on the cruise. If you were planning to use frequent-flier miles, you'll likely discover that frequent-flier seats are all taken on the flights you need. Moreover, most last-minute deals are completely nonrefundable.

You'll find last-minute deals advertised in the travel section of your Sunday newspaper, particularly those papers circulated within a day's drive of the cruise ship capitals of Fort Lauderdale, Miami, and New Orleans. You should also check with a travel agent or, better yet, an agency that specializes in cruises.

PRICE PROTECTION

It's a little-known fact that if the price of your cabin category goes down after you've booked it, many cruise lines will make up the difference, in effect guaranteeing you the

Average Cost of Onboard Extras

Just so you're not shocked when your shipboard account is settled at the end of your trip, here are some average onboard prices.

Laundry	50¢–$6 per item
Self-service laundry	$1–$1.50 per load
Pressing	$1–$6 per item
Massage (25-minute session)	$35 plus tip
Massage (50-minute session)	$70 plus tip
Men's shampoo and haircut	$25 plus tip
Women's shampoo and set	$30 plus tip
Spa treatments	$15–$150 plus tip
5 × 7-in. photograph purchased from ship's photographer	$6–$7
Scotch and soda at an onboard bar	$2.50–$4.50
Bottle of domestic beer	$2.50–$3
Bottle of imported beer	$3.50–$5
Bottle of wine to accompany dinner	$10–$300
Bottle of Evian water, 1.5 liters	$2.95
0.5 liters	$1.95
Ship-to-shore phone call or fax	$4–$18/minute
Shore excursions	$20–$200
Ship souvenirs (logo T-shirts, key-chains, etc.)	$3–$35
Sunscreen, 6-oz. bottle	$10
Disposable camera	$20

lowest rates up until the day of sailing (you may notice this spelled out if you read the fine print in a line's brochure). Thing is, if a line does reduce rates just before a cruise because there are some empty cabins they'd like to fill (and keep in mind, ships usually sail at full capacity and there isn't an empty cabin or a last-minute deal to be had), don't expect them to call you and the other people who booked 4 months ago at a higher rate and tell you the prices have been reduced. You and your travel agent would need to monitor the prices on a weekly basis and then call the cruise line, which of course requires more time and energy than many people want to spend.

BUDGET CRUISE LINES

Industry-wide discounting and the glut of space has blurred the distinction between the between the so-called budget cruise line prices and the mainstream cruise line prices. At certain times, ads in major newspapers promote 7-night cruises on mainstream lines like Carnival, Royal Caribbean, Celebrity, and Norwegian for nearly as low as the bargain-basement prices often offered by Premier, Commodore, Mediterranean Shipping, Regal, and Windjammer Barefoot, budget lines with classic, older, small- to mid-sized ships. Generally, though, you'll find the budget lines offering 7-night cruises about $50 to $200 lower than equivalent itineraries on the mainstream lines. These ships won't be as plush as the new megas, but if you know what to expect, they can be wonderful experiences and a great value for money. Bottom line: Compare and contrast the prices before you make your decision.

Surfing the Web to Cruise the Seas

Are you plugged into the Internet? If so, you're ahead of the cruise-booking game. Turn to the **Frommer's Online Directory** in the back of this book for a list of cruise-related Web sites. Some, such as those from the cruise lines themselves, allow you to see pictures (or virtual reality tours!) of the ships, get details on departure dates and specific itineraries, find out about special promotions, and even book your cruise, all from the comfort of your own home. Others direct you to travel agents who specialize in cruises, and still others offer comments from the general public about their recent cruise experiences.

In early 1999 **Windjammer Barefoot Cruises** became the first cruise line to offer deeply discounted last-minute rates advertised over its Web site (www.windjammer.com). If you're willing to travel with only a week or two's notice, you can sail a 6-day cruise for as little as $500. For more information, see the Windjammer review in chapter 9, "Soft-Adventure Lines & Sailing Ships."

AIRFARE ADD-ONS

To get to the port of embarkation (assuming you can't drive there), whether it be Miami, Ft. Lauderdale, or San Juan (PR), you can either purchase airfare on your own or buy it through your travel agent when booking your cruise. This is often referred to as an **air add-on.** Except during special promotions, airfare is rarely included in the cruise rates for Caribbean cruises, as it often is on Europe and Asia itineraries.

Cruise lines purchase a bulk number of seats with airlines and can sometimes offer you a good price because of it (and sometimes not). You can usually find information on these programs, called "air add-ons" or "air/sea packages," in the back of cruise line brochures, along with prices and flights from over 100 U.S. and Canadian cities to the port of embarkation.

If you choose to arrange your own air transportation, make sure the airfare is not included as part of your cruise contract (it rarely is with Caribbean itineraries). If it is, you're often granted a deduction (usually around $250 per person) off the cruise fare. Aside from the issue of price, there are benefits and disadvantages to booking your airfare through the cruise line.

BENEFITS   You usually get round-trip transfers between the airport and the ship. A uniformed cruise line employee will be in the airport to direct you to the right bus, and your luggage will be taken from the bus to the ship without you having to lift a finger. The cruise line will know your airline schedule, and in the event of delayed flights and other unavoidable snafus, will be able to do more to make sure you and the other people on your flight get on the ship; if you've booked your airfare, you're on your own.

DISADVANTAGES   Air add-ons may not be the best deal and it might be cheaper to book your own airfare. You won't be able to use any frequent-flier miles you may have accumulated. The air add-on could require a circuitous routing—with indirect legs and layovers—before you finally arrive at your port of embarkation.

MORE WAYS TO CUT CRUISE COSTS

Here are some more suggestions to save money booking a cruise:

- **Be flexible with dates and itineraries.** Repositioning (when ships leave one cruise region and sail to another—for instance, to and from summers in Alaska to a winter season in the Caribbean) and off-season cruises are often discounted, and

Cruise Now, Pay Later

Dying to go on a cruise but a little light in the pocketbook right about now? How about taking out a cruise loan? Princess Cruises offers their customers special loan programs that allow you to finance virtually all the costs of your trip, from the cruise price and air travel all the way down to shore excursions and onboard spending.

The loans, which are repayable in 24, 36, or 48 months, are approved on an instant basis after you review your credit information on the phone with a participating bank. Princess's loan program is aptly called the **Love Boat Loan,** and offers rates that can vary from 14.99% to 26.99%, depending on your credit history. To apply, call ☎ **800/PRINCESS.**

two-for-one deals are not uncommon. Keep in mind, since most repositioning cruises require crossing great stretches of ocean, they tend to have fewer stops at ports of call, and your cruise will include long stretches of time at sea.

- **Share a cabin with family or friends.** Many lines offer cabins that can house a total of three and four passengers (sometimes even five)—two in regular beds and two in bunk-style berths that pull down from the ceiling or upper part of the wall. So for families of four or groups of very good friends, if you're willing to be a bit (or a lot) crowded, you can save money by sharing your cabin. The rates for the third and fourth passengers in a cabin, adults or children, are typically half that of the normal adult fare, and sometimes less than half. Also, look into sharing a suite; most ships have some. Disney Cruise Line, for example, offers mostly family-style suites comfortably accommodating up to five people and with one and a half bathrooms.
- **Book your cruise with a group.** Many cruise lines offer reduced rates to groups occupying at least eight cabins (some as few as five cabins), with two adults in each cabin (for a total of 16 passengers), making cruise ships a good bet for family reunions and the like. (Also, travel agents are especially good at coordinating widely scattered members of a group that plan to travel together, which could save you significant time and frustration.) Based on two people per cabin, typically the 16th person in the group gets a free cruise, and the entire group can split the savings. In general, discounts for this type of group travel can be significant, but are wholly determined by the cruise line and seasonal demand at the time you're booking.

   Some high-volume cruise agencies might be able to team you up with a "group" of their own devising that they're booking aboard a certain ship; ask about the possibility of joining a group. Unlike group travel on land, shipboard groups are not herded about as a community and, of course, have individual cabins.
- **Read the fine print.** You never know what obscure special deals might apply to you. Carnival, for instance, offers really low rates on the *Carnival Destiny* if you book one of the cabins that's one deck directly above the disco (hmm, noise?). The brochure calls them "Night Owl Staterooms—if you love to party late into the night." Turns out the dozen, category 6, inside cabins located directly under the disco on the upper deck are the recipients of a lot of noise for the music above. But if you're planning on being there yourself, dancing into the wee hours of the night, you might want to consider these cabins, which are discounted at 50% or more than other, quieter cabins in the same category!
- **Book back-to-back cruises.** Depending on when you go, cruise lines offer discounts to passengers who book what's in essence a double cruise. Technically, you'll be taking two separate cruises, but you'll be on the same ship. On ships that alter their

itineraries by the week you'll be visiting different ports on the second phase of your journey, and you'll sail with a different set of passengers. Policies vary from line to line, but typically a flat discount of up to 50% on your second cruise is offered. For instance, if you combine two or more cruises for a total of 20 days or more, Seabourn offers a 10% to 50% savings on one of the cruises. Windstar offers the same deal if you book two cruises back-to-back. Most common are discounts like the one Carnival offers: a $100 per-cabin discount on the 14-night rate when two 7-night cruises are combined.

- **Take advantage of sail-and-stay promotions.** If you want to add a few more days to your vacation, cruise lines often offer good prices for hotels in the cities of embarkation. These days, cruises are departing from ports that are tourist attractions in their own right. You might want to explore Miami before you sail, drive to Disney World from Port Canaveral, or spend a few days in San Juan.

Many cruise lines negotiate group hotel discounts for passengers interested in prolonging their vacation. These packages usually include transportation from the hotel to the ship (before the cruise) or from the docks to the hotel (after a cruise).

AVOIDING THE SINGLE PENALTY

Since cruise lines base their rates on two paying passengers sharing a cabin, passengers wanting to travel alone, in their own cabin, are usually socked with something called the **single supplement.** Sounds like you're getting a deal, doesn't it? Well, you're not—it's the cruise line that gets the supplementary cost, which is usually between 25% and 100% *more than* the standard cruise fare.

The only thing you can do to avoid this penalty is to let the cruise line match you with a (same-gender) roommate, through which arrangement the cruise line gets its full fare for the cabin. Keep in mind, you won't be able to get any info about your roommate until you walk through the cabin door (although some lines, like Royal Caribbean, let you specify smoking or nonsmoking; Carnival, on the other hand, doesn't guarantee it). Some lines, including Carnival, even offer to cluster quartets of same-sex strangers (over age 21) into cabins sleeping four, charging each about half the regular adult brochure rates. That way, they can offer the same low rate that a third and fourth passenger would have paid had they bunked with a prearranged grouping of friends. You'll wave good-bye to any semblance of privacy (or sanity!), but you'll love the price.

SENIOR-CITIZEN DISCOUNTS

The cruise industry offers some discounts to seniors (usually defined as anyone 55 years or older), so don't keep your age a secret. Membership in AARP, for example, can net you substantial discounts; always ask your travel agent about these types of discounts when you're booking. Carnival, for instance, offers savings of up to $200 per cabin on certain ships and itineraries.

For discounts in general, the best organization to belong to is **AARP (American Association of Retired Persons),** the biggest outfit in the United States for seniors. For more information, contact AARP at 601 E. St. NW, Washington, DC 20049 (☎ **800/424-3410** or 202/434-AARP).

Tour operators, many of whom are experienced in selling cruise packages to senior citizens, are alert to cruise industry discounts, and often configure blocks of cabins aboard selected cruise ships that are geared to mature clients. One well-known expert is **Grand Circle Travel,** 347 Congress St., Boston, MA 02210 (☎ **800/221-2610** or 617/350-7500). Write for a free booklet called *101 Tips for the Mature Traveler.*

REPEAT PASSENGER PROGRAMS

If you've been on one cruise (or sometimes two), you're considered a "repeater" and are often rewarded for it. It's no surprise cruise lines love passengers who keep sailing with them; repeat cruisers can be a big part of a line's business, and they often show their gratitude by offering special perks and services.

You'll get not only **special mailings and newsletters** from the cruise line, but, at the least, invitations to **private cocktail parties,** 5% to 20% **discounts on future cruises, priority check-in** at the terminal, **cabin upgrades,** and maybe even a **free cruise** if you've racked up enough sailings. Carnival, Holland America, and Windstar, for instance, offer some of these goodies. For a one-time $25 membership fee, Windjammer Barefoot cruises also doles out the perks to past cruisers.

Repeater programs are the most generous and prevalent on the smaller, upscale ships, because these ships tend to attract wealthy guests with the means to cruise often, and also because the small, high-end ships have varied worldwide itineraries that appeal to cruisers interested in traveling many weeks a year.

If you sail a total of 140 days with Seabourn, you're entitled to a free 14-day cruise. After the tenth Crystal cruise, you get a complimentary bottle of wine and fresh flowers in your stateroom. After your second cruise, Cunard doles out $100 to $200 onboard credits (gift certificates).

Often a special host sails on board acting as a concierge for any repeaters on that cruise. In every way possible, guests are treated like very special, valued customers. Repeat cruisers on the upscale ships are admitted into a secret society of sorts on some ships, wearing special lapel pins and sometimes hats, and often recognizing one another from past cruises—much like a private club. Commonly, these guests are invited to dine with the captain or another officer one night.

4 Smart Shoppers Use Travel Agents

Should you brave the shark-infested waters of cruise booking alone or seek help from a professional travel agent or cruise specialist? With so much info on the Internet and in newspapers and magazines, you can try to do all the homework yourself, and you might even be successful at landing a good deal, but why take a chance? An experienced agent knows more about what discounts and special promotions are currently available, and will have sailed on or inspected a variety of ships and be knowledgeable about the industry in general. A good agent knows which cabins' views are obstructed by lifeboats, which cabins are near loud areas like discos, children's playrooms, and the engine room, and, in general, what the major differences are between cabin categories, so that you can be assigned a cabin you're happy with. In the United States, 95% of all cruise bookings are arranged through travel agents. Some lines won't even accept reservations directly from the general public.

So how do you know an agency is any good? Look for the letters after their names. Most qualified agents are members of the **Cruise Line International Association (CLIA),** an industry marketing organization. Agents who are CLIA Master Cruise Counsellors **(MCC)** or Accredited Cruise Counsellors **(ACC)** have spent many hours studying the cruise industry and inspecting ships. Agents with a **CTC** designation after their names are Certified Travel Counselors, and have taken many hours worth of travel-related courses to earn this title. It also can't hurt if an agent is a member of industry organizations, such as the **American Society of Travel Agents (ASTA), Association of Retail Travel Agents (ARTA),** or the **National Association of Cruise Oriented Agents (NACOA).**

You also can't beat word of mouth when it comes to finding a travel agent. Ask your friends who they recommend and start from there.

CHOOSING AN AGENT

The size of a travel agency tends to matter less than the experience of its staff and the degree to which they understand your likes and dislikes. Even though you're reading this book and its reviews, and so will have an informed opinion about what cruise lines and ships are right for you, it still pays to seek out a good agent with cruise experience.

A good cruise agent has first-hand experience with cruising and asks you detailed questions about your past vacations and your lifestyle to get an idea of what you expect from your trip. Never book a cruise with an agent who asks you nothing more than a few cursory questions, especially if that person immediately suggests a particular cruise line without knowing what you want—agents work on commissions from the lines and some might try to shanghai you into cruising with a company that pays them the highest rates, even though that line may not be right for you.

Think of an agent as your travel consultant, and feel free to ask him or her any questions you may have about cruising. Many travel agents who book cruises have cruised extensively, and they can probably answer any little questions you have. Furthermore, if you have a problem with the cruise line before, during, or after your cruise, they can act as an intermediary.

Out of some 40,000 travel agencies in North America, about 3,000 of them sell 75% of all travel in North America. About 40% of those 3,000 agencies are considered cruise-onlys and the rest are full-service.

As the name implies, **cruise-only agencies** specialize in selling cruises. They also usually sell airfare along with a cruise. Some of the largest cruise-only agencies work exclusively from 800 numbers and deal with clients mostly over the phone. If you know exactly what you want or don't have a specific ship or itinerary in mind, are flexible, and like the convenience of booking a cruise by phone, then one of the big cruise-only

---

Beware of Scams

If you're uneasy about the agent you're working with, call your state consumer protection agency, the Better Business Bureau, or the cruise line to check on the agent's credentials.

If you've got the time, visit the agency in person or, if it maintains only a telephone reservation center, ask them to send you some literature about their company. If you're told that a widely advertised special is sold out and the salesperson tries to switch you onto a more expensive product, beware. If you ever fail to receive a voucher or ticket on the date it's been promised, place an inquiry immediately. If you're told that your cruise reservation was canceled because of overbooking and that you must pay extra for a confirmed and rescheduled sailing, demand a full refund.

The best way to avoid a scam is to use an agent who has been referred to you by a reliable friend or acquaintance.

Cruise Tip: It Never Hurts to Ask

With a little bit of a poker face and a touch of patience, you can sometimes wrangle free stuff out of your travel agent if you imply that you can't book a cruise unless he or she sweetens the deal. So just ask for a complimentary cabin upgrade, free shore excursions, free wine with dinner on your anniversary, or free or discounted lodging at hotels before or after your cruise. It never hurts to ask.

---

firms may be your best bet. On the other hand, if you want personalized service, hand-holding, and meeting face-to-face with an agent, you probably won't get it from a huge reservation-center–type agency. For more personalized, one-on-one service, ask friends if they can refer you to a home-based agent (or look in the yellow pages); these types of agents are affiliated with the big national agencies but embrace more of a mom-and-pop style.

Full-service agencies can book all aspects of travel, including cruises. For instance, they can shop around for airfare or put together a tailor-made land-based tour to add on to your cruise vacation—maybe a hotel and sight-seeing package in the port of embarkation. Many full-service agencies have extensive knowledge of the cruise industry, just as the cruise-only agencies do, and sell large numbers of cruises.

Whether cruise-only or full-service, a competent travel agency handles all the details involved in planning a cruise, from sending you the tickets to reserving an early or late dinner seating, arranging a limousine to take you from the airport to the ship, and ordering special extras such as a bottle of champagne for your cabin when you arrive or a tuxedo rental for formal nights. Because they sell such a high volume of cruises, many agencies get **special rates** and **additional discounts** directly from the lines and pass the savings on to you.

RECOMMENDED AGENCIES

Travel agencies come in all shapes and sizes, from small neighborhood stores to huge chain operations. For example, Cruise Holidays, AAA Travel Related Services, American Express Travel Related Services, and the McDonald's of travel agencies, the mega Travel Company, are all large, reputable companies operating nationwide through numerous affiliates. You may notice an agency you've used in the past has changed its name or has become affiliated with another agency. Well, get used it to it: Like banking, telecommunications, and the auto industry, the travel industry—from the cruise lines themselves to travel agencies—is rife with consolidation.

AGENCIES SPECIALIZING IN MAINSTREAM CRUISES

To give you an idea of where to begin, here's a sampling (by no means comprehensive) of both cruise-only and full-service agencies that have solid reputations in selling mainstream cruises such as Princess, Carnival, Royal Caribbean, Celebrity, Holland America, NCL, and Premier. A few are affiliated with the big chains; most are not. The agencies listed operate from a combination of walk-in business and 800-number telephone-based business.

- **Admiral of the Fleet Cruise Center,** 12920 Bluemound Rd., Elm Grove, WI 53122 (☎ 414/784-2628; 800 number available upon request).
- **Admiral of the Fleet Cruise Center,** 3430 Pacific Avenue SE, Ste. A-5, Olympia, WA 98501 (☎ 800/877-7447 or 360/866-7447).
- **The Travel Company** and **Cruise Fairs of America,** 2920 Century Park E, Ste. 950, Los Angeles, CA 90067 (☎ 800/456-4386 or 310/556-2925).

Cruise Tip: Weigh Value Against Price

While of course you want the best price, it's important not to make price your only concern. Value—what you get for your money—is just as important as the dollar amount you pay. Keep in mind that the advertised prices you see in newspapers are usually for the lowest grade cabin on a ship; a better cabin—one with a window and maybe a private veranda—is likely to cost more.

- **The Cruise Company,** 10760 Q St., Omaha, NE 68127 (☎ 800/289-5505 or 402/339-6800).
- **Cruises By Brennco,** 508 E. 112th St., Kansas City, MO 64131 (☎ 800/955-1909 or 816/942-1000).
- **Hartford Holidays,** 129 Hillside Ave., Williston Park, NY 11596 (☎ 800/828-4813 or 516/746-6670).
- **Just Cruisin' Plus,** 417 Welshwood Dr., Ste. 310, Nashville, TN 37211 (☎ 800/888-0922 or 615/833-0922).
- **Kelly Cruises,** 1315 W. 22nd St., Ste. 105, Oak Brook, IL 60521 (☎ 800/837-7447 or 630/990-1111).
- **Mann Travel** and **Cruises American Express,** 6010 Fairview Rd., Ste. 104, Charlotte, NC 28210 (☎ 800/835-9828 or 704-556-8311).
- **National Leisure Group,** 100 Sylvan Rd., Ste. 600, Wobrun, MA 01801 (☎ 800/435-7683 or 617/424-7990).

AGENCIES SPECIALIZING IN ULTRA-LUXURY CRUISES

This sampling of reputable agencies, both cruise-only and full-service, specializes in selling ultra-luxury cruises like Cunard, Seabourn, Silversea, Crystal, Radisson Seven Seas, and Windstar.

- **Altair Travel,** 2025 S. Brentwood Blvd., St. Louis, MO 63144 (☎ 314/968-9600).
- **Bancroft Cruise and Tour,** 162 E. Wisconsin Ave., Oconomowoc, WI 53066 (☎ 800/638-7777 or 414/367-7375).
- **Bee Kalt Travel Service,** 30301 Woodword, Royal Oak, MI 48073 (☎ 800/284-5258 or 248/288-9600).
- **Byrne & Proctor Travel Services,** 935 Main St., Chatham, MA 02633 (☎ 508/945-3010).
- **CruiseMasters** (a subsidiary of The Travel Company), 300 Corporate Point, Ste. 100, Culver City, CA 90230 (☎ 800/242-9000 or 310/568-2040).
- **Cruises of Distinction,** 2750 S. Woodword Ave., Bloomfield Hills, MI 48304 (☎ 800/634-3445 or 248/332-2020).
- **Cruise Headquarters,** 4225 Executive Sq., Ste. 1600, La Jolla, CA 92037 (☎ 800/424-6111 or 619/453-1201).
- **Jean Rose Travel,** 140 Intracoastal Pointe Dr., Jupiter Fl 33477 (☎ 800/441-4846 or 561/575-2901).
- **Largay Travel,** 5 F Village St., Southbury, CT 06488 (☎ 800/955-6872 or 203/264-6581).
- **Melroy Travel,** 4434 Highland Dr., Salt Lake City, UT 84124 (☎ 800/344-5948 or 801/272-8015).

The 222 members of **Allied Percival International (API)** group, a Fort Worth, Texas–based consortium, also specialize in upscale vacation travel. For a list of their members, call ☎ **800/401-4API** or check out their Web site at **www.apitravel.com**.

The Travel Company

Merger mania hasn't overlooked the travel agency world. In 1997, Travel Services International formed The Travel Company, the megastore of travel agencies. In its first year, The Travel Company acquired several of the top-selling cruise agencies, such as CruiseWorld, Cruises, Inc., CruiseOne, Ship 'N' Shore, Gold Coast Cruises, CruiseMasters, Inc., 1-800-Cruises, and Cruise Fares of America, along with other travel-related businesses. It claims to be the largest cruise sales distribution company in the world, selling nearly 10% of all cruises. Unlike your local Mom and Pop travel agency, the Travel Company conducts almost all of its business through its toll-free telephone service. There are no offices you can just drop in to.

Though the company is still determining how it will integrate its newly acquired agencies, for the time being most continue to operate semi-independently under their own names.

What does this all mean to you and me? Well, because of its size and the volume it sells, The Travel Company should be privy to some pretty good deals. There are, in fact, many examples of those deals right in these pages, as The Travel Company kindly provided the discounted prices I've listed in this book's cruise line reviews—prices that show right there in black and white the amazing difference between the price cruise lines ask for their product and what you actually have to pay.

For more information on The Travel Company, call ☎ **800/242-9000** or see their Web site: **www.travelco.com**.

5 Choosing Your Cabin

THE MONEY QUESTION

When it comes right down to it, choosing a cabin is really a question of money. From an inside, lower-deck cabin with an upper and lower bunk to a balconied suite with a butler, cruise ships can offer a dozen or more different cabin categories, all at different prices. Location, size, amenities, and service can vary greatly.

It's traditionally been a rule of thumb that the higher up you are and the more light gets into your cabin, the more you pay; the lower you go into the bowels of the ship, the cheaper the fare. However, on some of the more modern ships, that old rule doesn't always ring true. On ships launched recently by Carnival, for instance, designers have scattered their most desirable suites on mid-level decks as well as top decks, thereby diminishing the prestige of an upper-deck cabin. For the most part, though, especially on some of the newer and smaller ships where most cabins are virtually identical, cabins on higher decks are still generally more expensive and outside cabins (with windows) are more expensive than inside cabins (without).

EVALUATING CABIN SIZE

Don't fool yourself; it's a fact of life at sea—inch for inch, cruise ship cabins are smaller than hotel rooms. Of course, having a private balcony attached to your cabin, as many do these days, will make your living space that much bigger.

A roomy **standard cabin** is about 180 square feet, although some of the smallest are about 100 square feet. Carnival has some of the more spacious standard cabins at sea, measuring about 185 square feel. Standard cabins on Celebrity and Holland America are also fairly roomy. By way of comparison, equivalent standard cabins on Norwegian and Royal Caribbean lines are quite a bit smaller and can be cramped. Cabins on the

Reading a Ship's Deck Plan

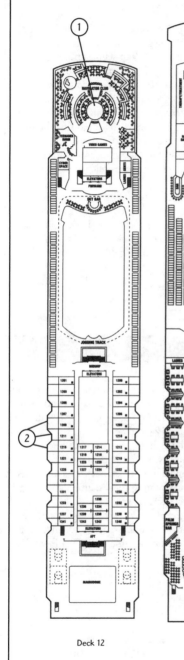

Deck 12

Deck 11

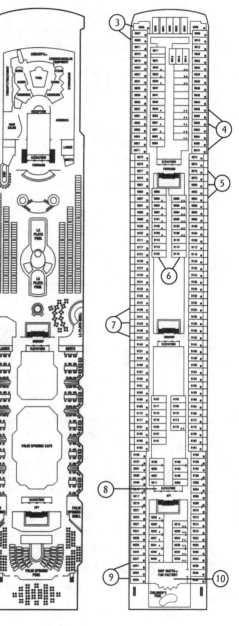

Deck 9

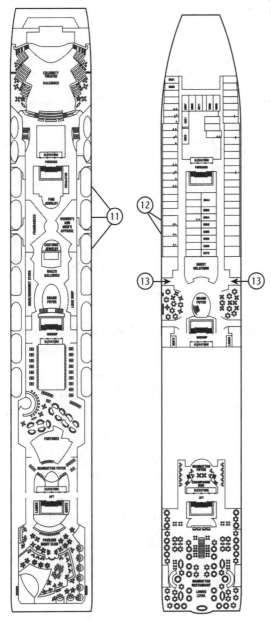

Some Cabin Choice Considerations:

1. **Note the position of the ship's disco** and other loud public areas, and try not to book a cabin that's too close or underneath. This disco is far from any cabins—a big plus.
2. **Cabins on upper decks** can be affected by the motion of the sea. If you're abnormally susceptible to seasickness, keep this in mind.
3. **Ditto for cabins in the bow.**
4. **Outside cabins without verandas** appear as solid blocks of space.
5. **Outside cabins with verandas** are shown with a line dividing the two spaces.
6. **Inside cabins** (without windows) can be a real moneysaver.
7. **Cabins amidships** are the least affected by the motion of the sea, especially if they're on a lower deck.
8. **Cabins that adjoin elevator shaftways** might be noisy. (Though proximity makes it easier to get around the ship.)
9. **Cabins in the stern** can be affected by the motion of the sea, and tend to be subject to engine vibration.
10. **Cabins near children's facilities** may not be the quietest places, at least during the day.
11. **Check that lifeboats** don't block the view from your cabin. The ones in this example adjoin public rooms, and so are out of sight.
12. **Cabins for people with disabilities** are ideally located near elevators and close to the ship's entrances (#13).

(Thanks to Celebrity Cruises for use of the Mercury's deck plan.)

Deck 7   Deck 5

small-ship lines like Windjammer and ACCL are quite snug, too. Older ships, like the *QE2* and *Regal Empress,* have cabins of extreme sizes—many standard cabins are very large (vestiges of the long cruises of ocean liner days) and some are just plain tiny (old third-class cabins and cabins for singles, or merely the result of the ships being repeatedly reconfigured and chopped up).

All the "standard" cabins on the high-end lines are roomy: Windstar's cabins are 188 square feet; Seabourn's *Legend* and *Pride* are 275 square feet, and the *Seabourn Goddess* twins are 205 square feet; and the *Radisson Diamond's* are about 250 square feet. Across the board, **suites and penthouses** are the most spacious, measuring about 250 square feet on up to over 1,000 square feet, not including private verandas.

How can you avoid size-shock when your steward shows you your cabin for the first time? Most cruise lines provide **schematic drawings,** with square footage—and in some cases, measurements of length and width—as part of the standard cruise brochures. Consider measuring off the dimensions on your bedroom floor and imagining your temporary oceangoing home, being sure to block out part of that space for the bathroom and closet. As a rough guideline, within a cabin of around 100 square feet, about a third of the floor space is gobbled up by those functional necessities.

Now, while you're sitting there within the chalk marks (or whatever) thinking "Gee, that's really not a lot of space," remember that, like a bedroom in a large house, your cabin will in all likelihood be a place you use only for sleeping, showering, and changing clothes. Out beyond the door, vast acres of public spaces await, full of every diversion imaginable. So unless you plan on holing up for most of your cruise, watching movies on your cabin TV and ordering room service, you probably don't need a palatial space.

THE SCOOP ON INSIDE CABINS VERSUS OUTSIDE CABINS

Whether you really plan to spend time in your cabin is a question that should be taken into account when deciding whether to book an inside cabin or outside cabin (that is, one without windows or one with), or whether to spend the extra money for a cabin with a veranda. If you plan on being up and out to the buffet breakfast and not stopping till the cows come home, you can probably get away with booking an inside cabin and saving yourself a bundle—heck, you'll probably be too blurry to see the cabin's amenities anyway. Inside cabins in general are not as bad or as claustrophobic as they sound. Most cruise lines today design and decorate them to provide an illusion of light and space. These are not the steerage dormitories you saw in *Titanic*. Some, in fact—such as those aboard Celebrity's *Mercury, Galaxy,* and *Century,* as well as Carnival's whole fleet—are quite nice and just as spacious as the outside cabins.

If, on the other hand, you want to lounge around and take it easy, maybe ordering breakfast from room service and eating while the sun streams in—or, better yet, eating out in the sun, on your private veranda—then an outside cabin is definitely a worthwhile investment. Remember, though, that if it's a view of the endless sea you crave, be sure when booking that your window doesn't just give you a good view of a lifeboat or some other obstruction. Some cruise line brochures tell you which cabins are obstructed, but in any case, your agent can help you determine this.

OTHER CABIN MATTERS TO CONSIDER

Many other matters come into play when booking your cabin. For instance, **cabins on the Promenade Deck** are often costly and sound just grand, but you may be distracted by passengers walking or talking outside, and particularly by those who decide to peek inside your stateroom to catch the "view."

Model Cabin Layouts

Typical Outside Cabin Configurations

- Twin beds (can often be pushed together)
- Upper berths for extra passengers fold into walls
- Bathrooms usually have showers only (no tub)
- Usually (but not always) have TVs and radios
- May have portholes or picture windows

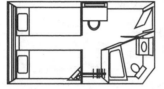 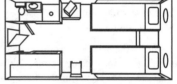

Typical Suite Configurations

- Queen-size or double beds
- Sitting areas (sometimes with sofa beds for extra passengers)
- Large bathrooms, usually with tub
- Refrigerators (sometimes stocked, sometimes not)
- Stereos and TVs with VCRs are common
- Large closets
- Large windows or outside verandas

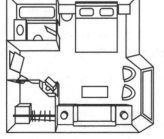 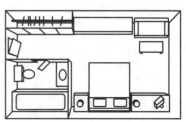

Prebooking Your Dinner Table & Arranging Special Diets

In addition to choosing your cabin when booking your cruise, you can also **choose your meal seating** for breakfast, lunch, and dinner, and sometimes even put in a request for the size table you're interested in (tables for two, four, eight, ten, etc.). Early seatings allow you to get a jump on the day and, after dinner, get first dibs on shipboard nightlife (or, conversely, promptly hit the sack); late seatings, on the other hand, allow you to sleep later in the mornings and, at dinnertime, linger a little longer over your meal. For a more detailed discussion, see "An Introduction to Shipboard Dining" in chapter 4, "The Cruise Experience."

Also, if for any reason you follow a **special diet**—whether vegetarian, low-salt, low-fat, heart-healthy, kosher, or halal—make this known to your travel agent when you book, so that the ship's chefs know you're coming. Many ships routinely offer vegetarian meals and health-conscious choices as part of their menus these days, but it can't hurt to arrange things ahead of time. Cruises are not the place to go on an involuntary starvation diet.

Then there's the matter of translating the cruise line brochures into real English. Increasingly, cruise lines use the terms "deluxe" and "standard" for their cabins. These terms can vary from line to line and are a bit meaningless, except to suggest that deluxe is larger, better located, and has more amenities.

Generally, you ask your travel agent for a specific cabin category, even a specific cabin if there's one in particular you'd like. With a few exceptions, your travel agent can tell you what your exact cabin number is when you book the cruise. (Exceptions include passengers booking as part of a group, passengers asking the cruise line to match them up with a roommate, and passengers choosing to forgo knowing the cabin they'll occupy in exchange for a lower rate—called a "guarantee," the line guarantees you a cabin, but you won't know which one until the last minute or once on board.) Before agreeing to a certain cabin, make sure it suits your particular needs. For instance, are there elevators close by (convenient, but it can also be noisy)? Is your cabin above, below, or adjacent to any noisy public rooms, such as the disco, children's playrooms, or the ship's engines? Is the view out the cabins' windows obstructed by lifeboats or other ship equipment? You can see from the deck plans included in the cruise line brochures what's where, and if some cabins in your chosen category are in a questionable spot, be sure to inquire. (See the "Reading a Ship's Deck Plan" diagram for more tips.)

Here's a few more tips:

• **Keep cabin position in mind if you suffer from seasickness.** If stability is important to you, a midship location is best because it's the area least affected by the vessel's rocking and rolling in stormy seas. In general, the best and most expensive cabins on any vessel are amidships and generally high up, and preferably include a balcony. However, the higher cabins are subject to more motion and swaying. The cheaper cabins are down below in the bow and stern; those toward the stern may suffer from engine vibrations.

Cruise Tip: Book Low-End Cabins on Luxury Ships

Rather than booking upper-end cabins on budget ships, many savvy cruisers book lower-end cabins aboard luxury cruise ships. That way they can enjoy the benefits of sailing on an upscale ship while paying less for the privilege.

- **Inquire about bed sizes if you have particular concerns.** Beds can vary in size from cabin to cabin and from ship to ship. A king-size bed at sea isn't as large as the one in your bedroom. If you're especially tall, for instance, ask your travel agent how long the beds are. Your preference for a twin or queen-size bed is another factor. Most twin-bedded cabins can be converted to make one larger bed by merely pushing the two beds together, but some, such as those with upper and lower berths, cannot.

- **Book early if you want cabins that will be in demand.** The **single-berth cabin** has almost disappeared on ships today, although they exist in older vessels. A single person can, of course, book any cabin he or she so chooses, but if you are not planning on sharing it (the cruise lines can match you with a same-sex single passenger) you'll be charged the double-occupancy rates—that is, the price of two adults, or maybe a bit less. Likewise, the older vessels are more likely to offer **triples and quads,** of particular interest to families. Try to book early if you want such a cabin, as they tend to disappear fast. Families who can afford it often book suites or book two cabins side by side, with connecting doors. This is especially desirable for those who are traveling with teenagers.

- **Pay careful attention to bathroom setups (if that's a concern of yours).** If your bathroom is important, always inquire what is offered. Many vessels offer cabins with shower only. Some others feature a shower and a tub. In some deluxe categories you even get a tub with a whirlpool. The Disney *Magic* and *Wonder* are winners in the best bathrooms award: Most of the cabins have one and a half bathrooms—one has a toilet and sink and the other a tub and shower combo.

- **Addicted to TV? Make sure your cabin has one.** Remember that not all cabins have television sets or VCRs—although the vast majority do have TVs, except for casual, small-ship lines like Windjammer and ACCL. If these amenities are important to you, always determine their availability in advance (they're listed in the ship reviews in chapters 6 through 9). Remember, too, that you generally aren't going to have the selection aboard ship that you get from your home cable system—at best, you'll have a few channels broadcasting movies, port lectures and other information of onboard interest, and maybe CNN and ESPN.

A last note: Try to book early. The cheapest and the most expensive cabins tend to sell out first.

6 Cancellations & Insurance

What should you do if the cruise you've booked is canceled before it departs? A cruise could be canceled because of shipyard delays if you've booked an inaugural cruise, or because of an impending hurricane, acts of war, the outbreak of an infectious disease, or mechanical breakdowns such as nonfunctioning air-conditioning.

In the event of a cancellation, cruise lines have in the past usually made extraordinary efforts to appease disappointed passengers, including rescheduling the cruise and offering big discounts on future cruises—after all, they don't want the bad press they'd get if they'd screwed hundreds or thousands of passengers. There are, however, no set rules on how a line will compensate you if the line cancels a cruise. And, since almost all ships are registered in foreign countries, suing the line is difficult.

If you need to cancel your cruise several months ahead of time, you'll generally get every cent back—most lines provide a full refund if you cancel at least 2 to 3 months before your departure date, although details vary from line to line. Getting closer to the cruise departure date, partial refunds are given up until anywhere from 15 to 3 days before the cruise. After that, no refund is given at all, even for medical reasons.

So what would you do if you needed to cancel a cruise at the last minute because of a sudden illness or other emergency? Or what if you've missed a flight because of bad weather and then missed the ship?

To protect yourself from any of these unpredictable occurrences, you might want to think about purchasing **travel insurance.** There are policies sold through the cruise lines (which vary from line to line) and others sold independently of the cruise lines. Both have pros and cons.

EVALUATING INSURANCE COVERAGE

Like all insurance, travel insurance comes with many optional riders that protect you against eventualities you hope you'll never encounter. Two possibilities are of major concern. The first is the potential expense of an emergency medical evacuation of the ill person from the Caribbean and, if your regular insurance doesn't cover it, the potential cost of major medical treatment while away from home. The second concern is the loss of your prepaid fare if your cruise is interrupted or if you must cancel because of a death in the family or a medical emergency, or if you missed the boat at the pier because of a flight delay.

Most insurance policies reimburse you when your trip is affected by unexpected events, such as airplane crashes or dockworkers' strikes, but not by "acts of God," such as hurricanes and earthquakes.

COVERAGE CHECKLIST

When evaluating travel insurance policies, check to see that they cover the following situations. Some may cover some, others cover others. Buy the insurance that's right for your situation.

- **Trip cancellation.** Caused by you or a member of your immediate family getting sick or dying, not limited to those who cruise. If you're traveling with a non–family member, make sure the policy covers you if you need to cancel the cruise because *that* person cannot cruise because of sickness or family death.

- **Pre-existing medical conditions.** The policy should include a pre-existing sickness exclusion rider—critical if you or any family member has a pre-existing medical condition.

Onboard Medical Care

The vast majority of cruise ships have an onboard infirmary staffed by a doctor and a nurse or two. While medical services are not free, you can visit the infirmary for seasickness and cold remedies as well as more serious ailments. Some ships, in fact, have very sophisticated equipment. Princess Cruises' *Grand Princess,* for instance, has not only a staff of one doctor and five nurses, but also high-tech medical equipment that, via special cameras and a live video system, link the ships' medical staff with the emergency department at Cedars-Sinai Medical Center in Los Angeles, in effect offering a real-time second opinion. The only ships that won't have any medical professionals on board are small-ship lines such as American Canadian Caribbean. Of course, ships big and small have the communication capabilities to contact medical assistance from the closest shore point in the event of an emergency, and in dire circumstances may even be able to have helicopters pick up and evacuate a seriously ill passenger. Although the captain does his utmost to get help or head for the nearest port, depending where the ship is during such an emergency, you can't be sure how long it might take to get reliable care.

- **Medical expenses.** Should cover medical expenses on board or in port, and should include any necessary medical evacuation from the ship or a port of call.
- **Emergency air travel home** in the event of a personal or family medical emergency or death.
- **Trip delay.** Your policy should have interruption protection should you have problems, such as weather, that prevent you getting to the cruise on time.
- **Accident coverage.** Including traveling to and from the airplane and/or ship.
- **Baggage protection.** Including loss, damage, or late arrival.
- **Bankruptcy or default of cruise line.**

Additional insurance to protect your **jewelry and valuables** on a cruise usually falls under the riders attached to your homeowner's policy. If you're in any doubt as to whether they're covered, though, check the fine print of your policy, guard your jewels carefully (confining them to your in-cabin safe or the purser's safe when not in use), or just save the aggravation and leave them at home.

Note that many policies do not reimburse you if your travel agent goes bankrupt. The bankruptcy of a travel agency poses greater risks than the bankruptcy of a cruise line. Again, using a travel agent you're very familiar with or who has been recommended to you is the safest precaution you can take.

SO WHICH INSURANCE POLICIES ARE THE BEST?

A good travel agent can tell you about policies sold through the cruise lines and ones sold independently of the lines. Although agents often get a commission for selling a cruise line policy rather than a non, most agents and industry insiders believe that non–cruise line policies are the best bet because they are much more comprehensive. Cruise line policies, for instance, do not cover medical expenses due to pre-existing conditions and often do not provide coverage if you or a family member gets sick a day or two before the cruise. Cruise-line policies also do not cover you if the cruise line goes bankrupt.

Access America, 6600 W. Broad St., Richmond, VA 23230 (☎ **800/284-8300** or 804/285-3300), and **Travel Guard International,** 1145 Clark St., Stevens Point, WI 54481 (☎ **800/826-1300** or 715/345-0505), are two reputable insurance agencies specializing in travel coverage.

7 Putting Down a Deposit & Reviewing Tickets

You've booked your cruise and now have to leave a deposit to secure the booking. Depending on the policies of the line you selected, the amount will either be fixed at a predetermined amount or represent a percentage of the ticket's total cost. More often than not, within 7 days of making a booking, a fixed $100 deposit is required on a 3- or 4-night cruise, a $250 deposit is required on a 7-night cruise, and a $350 to $400 deposit for a 10- to 14-night cruise. Upscale lines, because they cost more, may require a larger deposit or a percentage of the cruise price. For instance, Windstar requires a $500 deposit within 7 days of booking and Seabourn requires a 20% deposit within 10 days of making your reservation.

The balance of the cruise price is due anywhere from about 45 to 75 days before you depart; holiday cruises may require final payments even earlier, like 90 days before departure. The payment schedule for groups is different. Booking at the last minute usually requires payment in full at the time of booking.

Payments, whether by check or credit card, are made to your travel agent, who in turn pays the cruise line.

Carefully review your ticket, invoice, and/or vouchers to confirm that they accurately reflect the departure date, ship, and cabin category you booked. The printout usually lists a specific cabin number; if it doesn't, it designates a cabin category. Your exact cabin location is assigned to you when you board ship.

The ticket also represents a legal agreement established between you and the cruise line. The fine print should explain what happens if the cruise is canceled or you fail to show up at the pier on time. Especially if you haven't purchased travel insurance, you should check what happens if you're faced with a personal emergency and can't take the cruise or must leave before the cruise's end and fly back home on your own.

Things to Know Before You Go

3

You've bought your ticket and you're getting ready to cruise. Here's a few nuts and bolts, odds and ends, FYIs, and helpful hints to consider before you go.

1 Passports & Visas

Good news in the convenience category: Visas are not generally required for American, Canadian, and European citizens visiting the Caribbean islands (although, depending on the itinerary, you may be asked to fill out tourist cards or other forms in the airplane, airport, or cruise terminal, especially if you're flying to a non-U.S. port to start your cruise). Passports aren't necessarily required either, although it's a good idea to have one. A passport speeds your way through Customs and Immigration and you never know when entry requirements can change. Read through the documents your cruise line sends you with your tickets, and contact the line if you have any questions.

If you find you don't need a passport, you will still need **identification.** Acceptable forms of ID include an ongoing or return ticket plus an original birth certificate (or a copy that has been certified by the U.S. Department of Health) and a photo ID, such as a driver's license or an expired passport. A driver's license is not acceptable as a sole form of identification. As you would before any trip abroad, before leaving home, make two photocopies of your documents and ID. Take one set with you (keeping it in a different place from your original documents) and keep one at home.

Each particular port of embarkation has its own ritual. You may be asked to turn over your ID (for instance, your passport) and airline tickets to cruise line officials at the start of the cruise. They'll facilitate the procedures for group or individual port clearances and immigration formalities throughout the cruise and return your documents to you at the end of the cruise.

All non-U.S. and non-Canadian citizens must have valid passports, alien registration cards, and the requisite visas when boarding any cruise ship or aircraft departing from and/or returning to American soil. Noncitizens also need to present an ongoing or return ticket for an airline or cruise ship as proof that they intend to remain on local shores only for a brief stay.

No Vaccinations Required

Islands do not generally require inoculations against tropical diseases, although you might want to check out the Centers for Disease Control (CDC) Web site to see what they suggest: www.cdc.gov/travel/blusheet.htm.

2 Money Matters

Cruise ships operate as **cashless societies.** Basically, this means you keep a running tab. You sign for virtually everything you want to buy all week long—drinks at the bar, shore excursions, and gift shop purchases—and pay up at the end of the cruise with cash or a credit card. Very, very convenient, yes—and also very, very easy to spend more than you would if you were doling out wads of cash each time.

Shortly before or after embarkation, a purser or check-in clerk in the terminal or on board requests the imprint of one of your credit cards. On the last day of your cruise, an **itemized account** of all you've charged throughout the cruise is slipped beneath your cabin door. If you agree with the charges, they are automatically billed to your credit card account. If you'd rather pay in cash or if you dispute any charge, then you need to stop by the ship's cashier or purser's office, where there's usually a long line.

At embarkation, larger ships issue you an **identification card** that you show whenever you get back on the ship after spending the day in port and that you use when you sign for something. On the newest ships, this same ID card often serves as your room key. Smaller and older ships may not have either of these ID cards, and still issue regular room keys. (Some lines, such as Windjammer and American Canadian Caribbean Line, rely on the honor system and don't even use room keys.)

The cashless system works just fine on board, but you'll likely need some dough in port. Of course you can put any shore excursions you sign up for on your room tab, and credit cards are accepted at most port shops (as are traveler's checks). I do recommend having some real cash on you, ideally in small denominations, for any taxi rides or purchases you make from craft markets and streetside hawkers.

Don't worry about **exchanging money** to local currency, since the good ole U.S. dollar is widely accepted in the Caribbean (at least in the tourist-savvy ports of call you're likely to visit) and is the legal currency of the U.S. Virgin Islands, the British Virgin Islands, and Puerto Rico. If you're running low on dough, there are ATM machines in nearly every cruise port covered in this guide, in some cruise terminals, and on board many of the megaships. (Remember, though, you'll get local currency from machines in the Caribbean.) Expect a hefty fee for using ATMs on board cruise ships (like $5 in addition to what your bank charges you). Many lines, like Carnival and Royal Caribbean, cash traveler's checks (and sometimes personal checks of up to about $200 if issued in the United States); with an American Express card, you can typically cash a check for up to $250. Specific currency information is included in chapter 11, "Caribbean Ports of Call," and chapter 12, "Bermuda & the Panama Canal Route."

Cruise Tip: Don't Forget Cash When Going Ashore

It's happened to me and it's happened to my friends, so it can happen to you, too: After a few days of living cash-free aboard ship, it doesn't even cross your mind to grab the greenbacks and the plastic when you're going ashore. You get there and realize you're penniless. It's *soooo* frustrating. Don't let it happen to you.

3 Packing

The beauty of cruising, among other things, is that you need to unpack only once. Even though you'll be visiting several different countries on a typical weeklong cruise, you check into your cabin on day one, unpack, and settle in. The destinations come to you!

Just what do you need to pack? To some extent, that depends on the kind of cruise you're taking. But overall, cruise ship life mirrors that on land. Dress codes are being relaxed, and aside from the ultra-deluxe lines and formal nights on the large ships, **casual clothes** are the norm. In fact, instead of having a combination of formal, informal, and casual nights throughout the week as in the past, many lines—Carnival and Norwegian, for instance—are just going with the two formal nights and the rest of the week is considered casual.

DAYTIME CLOTHES

Across the board, casual daytime wear means shorts, T-shirts, bathing suits, and sundresses. Remember to bring a cover-up and sandals if you want to go right from your deck chair to lunch in one of the restaurants or to some activity being held in a public room. When in port, the same dress code works, but do respect local customs and err toward modesty (that is, something more than a skimpy bikini top if you're straying from the beach area). You might want to bring a pair of **aquasocks** if you plan on doing any snorkeling or water sports in port, and some good **walking shoes** to explore the islands as comfortably as possible.

If you planning on hitting the gym, don't forget sneakers and your workout clothes. And it can't hurt to bring along one pair of long casual pants and a long-sleeved sweatshirt, as well as a lightweight raincoat in case the weather turns dicey one day.

EVENING CLOTHES

When it comes to evening attire on all ships, except on the ultra-casual, small-ship lines (see chapter 9, "Soft-Adventure Lines & Sailing Ships"), you'll want to pack some dressy duds. Exceptions to this are the ultra-casual Windjammer, Star Clippers, Clipper, American Canadian Caribbean, and Tall Ship Adventures lines, where shorts, T-shirts, and sandals can take you through the day and into the evening meals (although most people tend to dress up a tad more for dinner).

Most ships have two **formal nights** on a 7-night cruise (usually the second night of the cruise, for the captain's cocktail party, and the second-to-last night of the cruise). Imagine what you'd wear to a nice wedding: Men are encouraged to wear dark suits or tuxedos and women cocktail dresses, sequined jackets or gowns, or other fancy attire (Windstar and Club Med encourage a "smart casual" look, and have a no-jackets-required rule the entire week).

The other nights are much more casual, and designated either **semi-formal** (or informal) or **casual.** Semi-formal calls for suits or sports jackets for men and stylish dresses or pantsuits for women; casual nights call for chinos or dress pants and collared shirts for men, and dresses, skirts, or pantsuits for women.

Cruise Tip: Tuxedo Rentals

If you don't own a tux or don't want to bother lugging one along, you can often arrange a rental through your travel agent for about $75. In some cases, a rental offer arrives with your cruise tickets. If you choose this option, your suit will be waiting for you in your cabin when you arrive.

Cruise Tip: Stowing the Crown Jewels

If you want to bring good jewelry, most cabins have personal safes operated by a digital code, credit card, or, once in a while, a lock and key. If your cabin doesn't have a safe, the ship's purser can keep your valuables.

In spite of the suggested dress codes, which are usually described in the back of a cruise line's brochure, you'll still find a wide variety of outfits being worn. Invariably, one person's "formal" is quite different from another's. So, like hemlines and everything else these days, to a large extent, anything goes. Passengers are asked not to wear jeans, baseball caps, shorts, and T-shirts for dinner in the formal dining rooms (although there's always a few who try). At the same time, despite the casual trend in America (read: casual Fridays and the baseball-cap, fur-coat-wearing Park Avenue set), you'll find there's a contingent of folks on board who like to get all decked out. I personally find getting dressed up for dinner a few nights a week to be part of the fun; in fact, I like to plunk myself in some heavily trafficked lounge an hour or two before dinner and do some good old fashioned people-watching. It's a veritable fashion show!

SUNDRIES

Like hotels, many ships (especially the newest and the high-end ones) come equipped with hair dryers and supply bathroom amenities such as shampoo, conditioner, lotion, and soap (although you might still want to bring your own products—except on the upscale lines, I find the ones provided often seem watered down). Some lines, like Carnival, do skimp, and provide only soap in cabins and not even hair dryers. Royal Caribbean doesn't have hair dryers on its ships either. If you bring your hair dryer, curling iron, or laptop, you might want to bring an adapter, although most ships run on 110.

No need to pack a **beach towel,** as they're almost always supplied on board (exceptions: Windjammer and ACCL). Bird watchers will want their **binoculars** and manuals, golfers their clubs (although they can always be rented), and snorkelers their gear (which can also be rented).

If you forget to pack a personal effect or two, don't despair. Even the smallest, no-frills ships have at least one small shop on board, to buy items like razor blades, toothbrushes, sunscreen, film, and other items you may need (but the stuff isn't cheap, so try to remember to bring your own).

Most ships have a **laundry service** on board and some **dry-cleaning** too, with generally about a 24-hour turnaround time; there will be a price list in your cabin. Some ships have **self-service laundry rooms** on board—Carnival, Royal Caribbean, Crystal, and Holland America, among others—so you can wash, dry, and iron your own clothes for a few dollars.

If you like reading but don't want to lug three or four hefty novels on board, there are options. Most ships of all sizes have **libraries** stocked with books and magazines. Some libraries are more extensive than others, of course; the *QE2*'s is huge, for example. Also, most ships stock paperback bestsellers in their shops.

Remember to save room in your luggage (or bring an empty duffel bag) for things you buy in port or in the ship's shops.

The Cruise Experience 4

Cruise ships are like mini societies, cities at sea, floating summer camps for adults. Evolved from the days when ships were nothing more than utilitarian modes of transport, cruise ships today are attraction-filled destinations themselves, bustling worlds at sea where there are countless things to do and so many people to meet. Good food and drink are plentiful, entertainment and activities are nonstop, and an undeniable rhythm takes hold for the duration of a cruise.

While the cruise experience varies from ship to ship, the common denominator is choice. You can run from an aerobics class to line-dancing, an art auction, and then bingo all before lunch, or choose to do nothing more than sunbathe all day on a quiet corner of deck. Whether you like to do it all or do nothing at all, cruising is a convenient and leisurely way of traveling from one exotic port to another. Unpack once, settle in, and enjoy the ride.

In the pages that follow, I'll give you a taste of cruise life, starting with a little history . . .

1 The History of Cruising

From rough-hewn dugout canoes crossing rivers to proud clipper ships carrying explorers across vast oceans to steamers transporting throngs of European immigrants to new lives in the United States, the modern-day cruise evolved from a basic and timeless need to get from point A to point B.

THE EARLY DAYS It wasn't until the late 19th century that British shipping companies realized they could make money not just by transporting travelers, cargo, and immigrants, but by selling a luxurious experience at sea. It's generally accepted that the first cruise ship was the *Ceylon,* a vessel powered by both steam and sail and owned by the **Peninsular & Oriental Steam Navigation Company** (known today as P&O). In 1881, when already 23-years-old, the small, 2,000-ton *Ceylon* was converted to a cruising yacht for carrying wealthy, adventurous guests on world cruises in lavish style. A few years later, in 1887, North of Scotland, Orkney & Shetland Steam Navigation's *St. Sunniva* was launched as the first steamer built expressly for cruising.

The Germans joined the British in the fledgling cruise trade in 1891, when the **Hamburg-American Line** sent their *Augusta Victoria* on a Mediterranean cruise from Hamburg. In 1901, the line completed its luxurious 4,400-gross-ton *Prinzessin Victoria Luise,* the first ship to offer bathrooms in every passenger cabin. These early cruise ships were luxuriously appointed with things you'd never find on a modern cruise ship—statues, frescos, ornate wooden stairways, and even plaster walls—but the onboard activities and entertainment were comparatively few. Besides lavish, very social dinners, about the only pastimes were reading, taking a good hardy walk around the deck, and sitting for musical recitals.

More and more players entered the cruise trade during the early 1900s, spending summers crossing the Atlantic and Pacific and the rest of the year doing pleasure cruises to ports in the Canary Islands, the Caribbean, Scandinavia, and the Mediterranean. Before WWI, though, cruising for pleasure still took a backseat to the more lucrative trade of transporting well-off travelers and immigrants across the Atlantic in three classes of accommodation, and there were only a handful of small ships built for cruising. The competition was fearsome between famous shipping lines such as Cunard, White Star, Hamburg America, the French Line, North German Lloyd, Holland America, Red Star Line, and a host of smaller companies, who sought to attract customers by trying to build the fastest, largest, or most luxurious new ships. It was the era of rich wood paneling, chandeliers, grand ballrooms and smoking lounges, and huge gilded suites with antiques, art, and servants' quarters. First-class became plusher, and the second and steerage classes were being upgraded (at least in name) to cabin class and tourist class, to sound more appealing. When these ships did do pleasure cruises, generally only first-class accommodations were sold and the other cabin classes were shut down until the transatlantic schedules were resumed; it wasn't until the late 1960s that the multi-class system was eliminated completely.

THE SHIP YOU ALL KNOW (AND A FEW OTHERS)   Soon after Cunard launched its popular 2,165-passenger *Mauretania* and *Lusitania* in 1906, J. Bruce Ismay, son of the White Star Cruise Line's founder, Thomas Ismay, envisioned a trio of the largest and most luxurious vessels in the transatlantic service to appeal to the rich American industrialists now crossing regularly. By 1911 the first of these three sisters, the 2,584-passenger, 46,000-ton *Olympic,* was in service, with the *Titanic* (yes, that one) scheduled for an April 1912 maiden voyage. (The third sister, originally planned as the *Gigantic,* was on the drawing boards to follow *Titanic.*)

Touted as the world's greatest ship, the *Olympic*'s maiden voyage in June 1911 was a grand, much-heralded affair. In fact, the launch of *Titanic* the following year was not nearly as anticipated; then, as we all know, tragically, the *Titanic* never made it to New York. The *Olympic* sailed on, doing time as a hospital ship in World War I, and the third of Ismay's planned trio, launched in 1914 as the *Britannic,* had a short life as a hospital ship in the Mediterranean before hitting a mine and sinking in 1916.

Right up until WWI, the Brits and Germans continued building bigger and bigger ships, exceeding 50,000 tons. During the war, practically any seaworthy ship was requisitioned to carry soldiers, supplies, and weaponry to the troops in Europe. Many grand ships were lost in the war, including Cunard's *Lusitania.*

CRUISING BETWEEN THE WARS   After the First World War, the popularity of cruising increased tremendously because far fewer immigrants were flooding to the west. During the winter months, when transatlantic travel was slow, more and more ships were rerouted to sunnier climes in the Caribbean and Mediterranean for long and expensive cruises geared to the well heeled. Cunard's *Mauretania* and her new running mate, the *Aquitania,* for instance, were yanked off the Atlantic for a millionaire's romp through the Mediterranean, carrying as few as 200 pampered passengers in the lap of luxury. In the 1920s, Cunard introduced five ships—the *Scythia, Samaria, Laconia, Franconia,* and *Carinthia*—which offered a variety of cruising options worldwide, including Bali, Bangkok, Saigon, Athens, and the Holy Land, as well as the Caribbean and Scandinavia.

Cruise Trivia

Mauretania, Berengaria, Carpathia, Britannica, Lusitania, Aquitania—for most of its history, Cunard's ships were named after provinces of the Roman empire. Today, after the company's acquisition by Carnival Corporation, it seems to be getting back to that trend, changing the name of the luxurious *Vistafjord* to *Caronia,* making it the third Cunard vessel to bear that name.

As they headed to warmer climates, the traditional black hulls of the North Atlantic trade ships were painted white to help them stay as cool as possible in these pre–air-conditioning years. This became a tradition itself, to the point that nearly all the Caribbean's ships were at one time painted a dazzling white. Today, although they're still the norm, we're seeing something of a reverse trend, with hulls being painted black or blue-black to present a more classic, dignified image and play to the public's nostalgia for the old ocean liner days.

By the 1930s, shipboard activities and amenities were becoming much more sophisticated all around, with morning concerts, horse racing, quoits, shuffleboard, bridge, Ping-Pong, motion pictures, and the first "swimming baths" (as pools were called in the early years) appearing on board. Often no more than burlap or canvas slung over wooden supports, the first permanent outdoor pools appeared in the '20s on the Italian transatlantic ships the *Roma* and the *Augustus.* In the '30s, the large outdoor pool on the *Rex* actually included a patch of sand to evoke the Lido Beach of Venice. When the great French liner *Normandie* made its maiden voyage in 1935, it boasted the cruising world's first air-conditioning system in its first-class dining room.

WORLD WAR II   When WWII began, again the great liners were called into service, and many never made it back to civilian life. The *Normandie* burned and capsized at her pier while under conversion in New York to become a troopship. Cunard's *Carinthia* and *Laconia* didn't survive either. A few, however, did complete distinguished wartime service, like the United States Line's *America,* Cunard's *Queens Elizabeth* and *Queen Mary,* and Holland America's *Nieuw Amsterdam.*

THE POSTWAR YEARS   When the war ended and with the economy in great shape, cruising boomed in the '50s and for the first time became accessible to the growing middle class. More than ever before, cruising was both transportation and a pleasurable vacation experience, with onboard life enhanced by activities like pool games, bingo, art classes, dance lessons, singles' parties, and midnight buffets—all aspects of cruising that still exist today. In the '50s, New York became one of the biggest and most important cruise ship ports in the world, offering short runs to Bermuda and serving as the home port for longer world cruises.

By the 1960s, though, the new jet airplanes replaced transatlantic ships as the public's transportation of choice, and the boom was over. Increasingly expensive to maintain, many of the great '50s liners were sent to the scrapyards. The industry seemed doomed.

But, fortunately, not for long. In the early 1960s, two Norwegian cargo and tanker ship operators, Christian and Knut Kloster, decided to get into the passenger ship business, offering Caribbean cruises aboard the 11,000-ton *Sunward* from a home port in Miami. The rest is history. The vacation cruise ships that soon began to proliferate in the Caribbean did away with the liners' multi-class system and focused solely on offering a fun-in-the-sun party at sea for all. (Cunard's *QE2,* built in 1969 for both crossings and cruising, was one of the last ships built with a multi-class system; today the ship's Queen's Grill restaurant is still reserved for only the most expensive cabins.)

Soon, the Caribbean cruise trade exploded. **Royal Caribbean Cruise Line** was formed in January 1969, and in the late '60s and early '70s, **Royal Viking, Carnival, Princess, Costa,** and **Holland America** joined the lucrative circuit as well. It was in 1968, on board Costa's *Carla C.* (at the time chartered to Princess and doing Mexican Riviera and Panama Canal cruises from Los Angeles), that American writer Jeraldine Saunders was inspired to write the novel *The Love Boat,* from which the popular television series was born. Now, millions would be introduced to cruising.

While traditionalists disdain today's cruise ships, which retain few vestiges of ocean travel's golden age, time does move on. Casual, active, and geared to the masses, today's passenger ship industry is bigger, bolder, and more successful than ever before, and with over 40 new ships scheduled to debut over the next several years, it's a safe bet that at least some of them are the classic ships of the future.

2 Checking In & Boarding

You're ready to go, packed, at the port, and even on the right pier. Do you remember the name of the ship on which you're sailing? With so many like-sounding ship names these days—dozens of Something-ations and Blah-Blah-of-the-Seas—it can get confusing. Make sure you know where you're going: You don't want to schlep your stuff to the wrong terminal.

As a safety precaution against emergencies at home, distribute your ship's **satellite phone** and fax number to people in charge of your affairs back home, but advise them to contact you only in an emergency. If they lose the ship's number, AT&T offers a service (albeit an expensive one) that connects them with the ship's operator, who in turn connects the call to the phone in your cabin or takes a message for you. The number is ☎ **800/SEA-CALL.**

After you arrive at the docks, head for the terminal; if you need a porter, tip him $1 per bag. It doesn't pay to arrive too early at the pier. Even if your ship has been berthed at port since early in the morning, new passengers are often not allowed on board until about 1pm. The cruise lines enforce this policy stringently to allow enough time for luggage and supplies to be unloaded and loaded, cabins to be vacated by former occupants and cleaned, and paperwork and customs documents to be properly completed.

When you pour out of the buses (or the car, if you drove) that have transported you from the airport to the cruise ship terminal, you'll feel like a celebrity (well, almost) making his or her way from a limo, across a red carpet, and into the Oscars ceremony at some chi-chi theater. You'll be greeted by an army of smiling cruise line employees directing you to the check-in desks, and a ship photographer just beyond check-in is ready to capture that first moment of your vacation. If you're arriving by air, the treatment begins in the airport, when uniformed ushers (often retirees) stand at the ready holding a sign with your cruise line's or ship's name on it, waiting to direct you and dozens of other giddy passengers to the buses bound for the terminal.

At the terminal, your **luggage** is whisked away from the bus or your car, never to be seen again (just kidding, but it may be a few hours before it's delivered to your cabin). Frankly, sometimes it's there by the time you've made it to your room, but sometimes it takes a few hours, depending on how big the ship is and just how much luggage needs to be delivered. Anyway, it's a good idea to keep a small bag with you containing a change of clothes, maybe a swimsuit and a pair of sunglasses, so you don't waste any time heading out on deck, grabbing a deck chair, and starting your vacation.

Before boarding, you need to check in at the terminal, hand over your cruise tickets, show some ID, and give an imprint of your credit card to establish your onboard account. On small ships, all of this is done on board. Depending on when you arrive

---

English Comes Second

Some crewmembers, especially cabin stewards, who come from all over the world, may have limited English language skills, so you might want to brush up on your sign-language. Crew members have to know a modicum of English to be hired, but sometimes it seems less rather than more, and you might run into some frustrating moments trying to communicate. Remember, these folks are very hard-working employees who are sending most of their wages home to their families, and it won't kill you to speak slower and more simply if need be.

---

and the crowd situation, you may find yourself waiting in line for as much as an hour or so; usually it's less.

For security reasons, very few cruise lines allow temporary visitors on board the ship. You'll have to say your good-byes on land.

WELCOME TO YOUR CABIN

Once on board, you may be guided to your cabin—there is no need to tip the person who leads you—or most likely you'll be on your own to find it. When you get there, your **cabin steward** will probably stop by to introduce him- or herself, inquire if the configuration of beds is appropriate (that is, do you want separate twin beds or a pushed-together double), and give you his or her extension number so you can call if you need anything. The brochures and **daily programs** in your cabin will answer many questions pertinent to your ship's social and safety rituals.

Cabins have air-conditioning and heating, usually controlled individually; hot and cold running water; life preservers for the number of people occupying the cabin (a legal requirement and essential to your safety at sea—check that they're there); extra blankets and pillows; and a safe for storing your valuables, operated either with a credit card, a combination lock, or a key.

Most ships sailing the Caribbean have **North American–style electrical outlets** (twin flat prongs, 110 AC current), although some ships have outlets for both European (220 AC) current and North American.

With a few notable exceptions, cruise liners have direct-dial **telephones** in cabins, along with instructions on how to use them, and a directory of phone numbers for the departments or services on board. From most cabin phones you can call, via satellite beams, anywhere in the world; although it's getting cheaper compared to a few years ago, this is still expensive. Charges range from around $3.95 to about $18 a minute, with $9.50 being about average. It's cheaper to call home from a public telephone in port.

3 An Introduction to Onboard Activities

If your ideal vacation is go, go, go, a cruise is the perfect playground for you. From morning till night, most 800-passenger-plus ships offer an extensive schedule of activities every day, especially during days at sea, when the ship isn't visiting a port. To keep track of the games, contests, lessons, and classes, check out the ship's **daily schedule of events,** which is placed in your cabin the previous evening, usually while you're at dinner. A **cruise director** and his or her staff are in charge of the festivities and do their best to ensure a good time is had by all. Smaller ships offer activities, too, but often with less hoopla; there may be wine tastings, trivia contests, port talks by the cruise director and captain, and maybe presentations by guest speakers on subjects from history to politics to food. The very small 50- and 100-passenger ships won't even have that.

SOMETIMES WILD, ALWAYS WACKY: ONBOARD GAMES

The ships in the Carnival, Royal Caribbean, Norwegian, Princess, Celebrity, Costa, Premier, and Commodore fleets are well known for their wacky poolside contests scheduled for an hour or two each afternoon. You might even say they sometimes go overboard (so to speak), but you'll certainly be in stitches watching the blind-folded pillow fights, belly-flop contests, the stuff-the-most-Ping-Pong-balls-or-fruit-into-your-bathing-suit contest, and the pool relay races, which require team members to pass bagels to one another with their teeth.

And it's not just the classic party ships that let their hair down. Many other lines indulge their guests in the tomfoolery, too. At its weekly deck parties, Holland America, for example, features a nearly obscene and absolutely hilarious rendition of the pass-the-balloon-from-between-my-knees-to-yours relay race. All ages participate, and you'll want to check your pride at the door before you volunteer for this one.

Game show simulations, such as the "Newlywed/Not-So-Newlywed" games, are popular. Volunteer yourself or, better yet, listen to fellow passengers blurt out the truth about their personal lives—just like on Oprah! The Carnival ships actually stage very realistic Jeopardy-like game shows, complete with buzzers, contestant podiums, and digital point keeping.

If you're a performer at heart, volunteer for the weekly passenger talent show or head to the nightclub one evening and wiggle your way into the hula-hoop or twist competitions. Cerebral types can sign up for trivia quizzes or do puzzles, or join chess, checkers, bridge, or backgammon tournaments.

Winners get more than a good time, too. Prizes like champagne, T-shirts, a couple of mugs or key chains, maybe even a massage from the spa, all make getting involved a worthwhile proposition.

HIGH ROLLERS, HIGH SEAS: SHIPBOARD CASINOS

For all you high-rollers out there, all but the smallest, adventure-oriented ships have casinos. Not surprisingly, the megas have the biggest, flashiest, Vegas-style casinos, bathed in neon, with literally hundreds of **slot machines** and dozens of **blackjack, poker,** and **craps** tables as well as **roulette.** You really will think you're in Vegas or Atlantic City when you're playing in the sprawling, glitzy casinos of Carnival, Royal Caribbean, the newer Princess ships, and Celebrity. Smaller ship lines, like Windstar, Seabourn, and Cunard, have casinos as well, albeit scaled-down ones, with maybe a dozen slots and a couple of blackjack and poker tables. Some of the budget lines, such

---

Take My Picture . . . Please

It might sound funny, but with all the pictures the **ship's photographers** are continually snapping of passengers at any vaguely interesting moment of the day—by the pool, leaning over the railing, at dinner, leaving dinner, walking down the gangway in port, you name it—I consider a daily trip to the ship's photo gallery one of my favorite cruise pastimes. While the photos are sold for a hefty $6 or $7 each, there's no obligation to buy them. The real fun is searching for your picture amid the sea of similar-looking shots—like a find-the-needle-in-the-haystack game. The wall of pictures is like wallpaper, one face after another wearing silly expressions, with closed eyes, double chins, shiny noses, or even the odd picture-perfect smile. Just don't let anyone see you laughing out loud—the next laugh could be at a picture of *you.*

What's in a Name?

So why are the names *Monrovia, Panama,* or the *Bahamas* boldly emblazoned across a ship's bow or stern? It's not where the ship was built, as you might assume, but where the ship is registered or flagged. In fact, the country where your ship is flagged or registered has nothing to do with the cruise line's home base (which is likely Florida, California, Washington, or New York). That's because most flags are based on financial considerations (read: no income tax required!) and other matters of convenience to the cruise lines. Truth is, the cruise lines save many millions of dollars a year this way. Panama and Liberia have liberal rules governing unions and so forth, so you see a lot of cruise ships registered there. Other common flags include the Bahamas, Bermuda, and the Netherlands Antilles. What does this mean to you? Chances are, not a thing. The only time it would be is in the very unlikely event that a crime or accident, for instance, is committed on board a ship; in that case, you'd have to contend with the country of registry's laws when seeking justice, restitution, etc.

as Commodore, Regal, and Premier, boast active casino scenes. Stakes aboard most ships are relatively low, with maximum bets rarely exceeding $200. Average minimum bets at blackjack and poker tables are generally $5; the minimum at roulette is typically 50¢ or $1.

Gambling is legal once a ship has sailed 12 miles from American shores, but local laws require onboard casinos to close down whenever a ship is in port. Keep this in mind when cruising to Bermuda; ships stay there for 3 whole days and there's no gambling whatsoever during that period.

Children are not allowed in onboard casinos.

Most ships also have a **card room,** which is usually filled with serious bridge or poker players and sometimes supervised by a full-time instructor. Most ships furnish cards for free, although some charge $1 or so per deck.

CLASSES, LESSONS & DEMONSTRATIONS

For the eternal student, there are volumes of learning opportunities aboard most ships. Complementary **line, country, and ballroom dancing lessons** are usually held a few times a week in the main show lounge and are taught by one of the onboard entertainers. Many cruise lines frequently put on informative **seminars** on subjects like cooking, bartending, arts and crafts, and wine tasting; there is usually a $5 to $15 charge for the wine tasting and sometimes there's a cost for arts and crafts materials. Celebrity Cruises, for instance, frequently features classes on intriguing topics such as **personal investing** or **handwriting analysis.**

The chef might do a food-decorating demonstration and share tips on how to carve flowers and animals out of fruits and vegetables. Demonstrations by the salon and spa staff on hair and skin care are common, too (and a ruse for getting passengers to sign up for the not-so-cheap spa treatments).

GOING ONCE, GOING TWICE: ART AUCTIONS

You'll either love them or find them incredibly annoying and a blatantly tacky way for the cruise lines to make more money. Truth is, art auctions on cruise ships are big business these days and lots of pieces are sold. Held three or four times a week for an hour or two at a time, the auctions are a way you can leisurely shop for art if you so choose, a luxury you may not have at home. The "auctioneer" is a salesman for the company that sells the art. From a stage, he briefly discusses a selection of the hundreds of paintings by well-known artists like Peter Max and Erté, lithographs by greats Dalí, Picasso, and Miró, and Disney animation pieces, as well as pieces by artists you've never heard of, which are displayed on the stage and all around. He starts the bidding for a piece at anywhere from $50 to $500, and sells it to the highest bidder. The art, framed or unframed, is duty-free to U.S. citizens and is packed and mailed home for you.

JUST DOING IT: ONBOARD SPORTS & FITNESS OPTIONS

If you're into sports, the megas pack the most punch. In addition to well-equipped gyms rivaling those on shore, they boast outdoor volleyball, basketball, and paddle tennis courts as well as outdoor jogging tracks and several pools for water polo, volleyball, aqua-aerobics and swimming.

See "Shipboard Gyms & Spas" later in this chapter for more information.

WATER SPORTS

For water sports enthusiasts, small ships are the best equipped. Windstar, Radisson Seven Seas, Cunard, Club Med, and Seabourn have retractable water sports platforms that, weather permitting, can be lowered from the stern into calm waters when the ship is anchored, allowing passengers to almost step right from their cabins to snorkel, windsurf, kayak, sail, water-ski, go on banana boat rides, and swim.

GOLF

If golf is your bag, more and more cruises are offering the opportunity to tee off, both on board and on shore. For the casual golfer, a few ships—Royal Caribbean's *Splendour, Legend,* and *Voyager of the Seas,* and Princess' *Grand Princess*—have **miniature golf courses** on board. For the more serious swingers, the new, technologically advanced ships like Celebrity's *Century, Galaxy,* and *Mercury* and Princess's *Grand, Sea, Sun,* and *Dawn Princess,* have **golf simulators.** These state-of-the-art virtual-reality machines allow you to play the great courses of the world without ever leaving the ship (for about $20 per half-hour). Full-sized clubs are used and a virtual-reality video screen allows players to watch the electronic path of a ball they've actually hit soar high over the greens or land flat in a sand trap.

Many more lines, including Norwegian, Crystal, Princess, Radisson Seven Seas, and Cunard, have **outdoor golf cages**—areas enclosed in netting where you can swing, putt, and whack at real golf balls any time of the day.

More and more lines are offering **golf programs** that include instruction and tips by golf pros who sail on board, videotape lessons and go over techniques with passengers; half-hour lessons are about $30 to $40, and hour-long lessons are $60 to $70. In port, even more ships have **golf excursions** to well-known courses such as Mahogany Run in the Caribbean and Mid-Ocean in Bermuda; packages typically include greens fees, cart, and transportation between the ship and course, and range from $100 to $200 per person. Celebrity, Carnival, Costa, NCL, Radisson Seven Seas (the official cruise line of the PGA of America), Seabourn, and Crystal all offer onboard instruction by golf pros on all or select cruises, as well as golfing excursions in port.

SPORTS FOR COUCH POTATOES

No need for those sports-loving couch potatoes out there to be deprived. NCL's new *Norwegian Sky* as well as the *Norwegian Wind, Norwegian Dream,* and *Norway,* Royal Caribbean's *Voyager of the Seas,* Carnival's *Destiny* and *Triumph,* Disney's *Magic* and *Wonder,* and Princess's *Grand Princess,* have dedicated **sports bars** with large-screen televisions broadcasting ESPN and live NFL games. Each of Holland America's ships has a large-screen TV in one lounge showing sports. During popular sporting events, like

Active Shore Excursions

While there's lots to do on board most ships, there's a lot you'll want to check out in port, too. With more and more active excursions being offered these days, you'll get to see the less touristy, natural parts of the islands, all the while getting a good workout. Aside from the tried and true **snorkeling** and **diving** trips, there are **biking, hiking, kayaking, horseback riding,** and **river tubing** trips, generally running about $50 to $100 per person.

the Super Bowl, many lines outfit a public area or bar with televisions for game viewing. If you want to watch the game from the comfort of your cabin, no problem. ESPN is available on cabin TVs on Royal Caribbean, Celebrity, Norwegian, Crystal, and Princess ships. For star-struck sports fans, NCL does a series of annual **sports theme cruises,** where pro basketball, football, baseball, and hockey players as well as past greats sail on board and mingle with passengers.

4 Introducing Onboard Entertainment

Cruises offer a vast repertoire of exciting entertainment. As you'd expect, the biggest ships offer the most variety. From Vegas-style cabaret to magicians, soloists, pianists, dance bands, quartets, jugglers, DJs, puppeteers, and X-rated comedians, you've got a choice.

Innovative new options are being created all the time. For example, Disney Cruise Line's *Disney Magic* has some of the most unique entertainment choices at sea. Its nostalgic Walt Disney Theatre has one of the best-equipped stages at sea—actors disappear into trap doors, fly across the stage, and go through endless exciting costume changes—for its Disney movie–inspired musicals. The *Magic* also has an innovative (and very funny) improv comedy act in the adults-only Offbeat Lounge.

To prove that not all innovative entertainment has to be big, Celebrity's ships have been featuring **roving a cappella bands** who roam around the ships in the evening, performing wherever people are gathered.

ENTERTAINMENT ON THE MEGASHIPS

Entertainment is a big part of the cruise experience on the biggest 1,200-passenger-plus megaships of Carnival, Royal Caribbean, Celebrity, Costa, Princess, NCL, and Holland America. Not surprisingly, they have an extensive variety of options throughout the day. Afternoons, you can dance the day away on deck with the **live dance band** jamming with calypso music or Bob Marley tunes. Or get your waltzing shoes on and head inside to one of the lounges for some big-band–style dancing; lines like Holland America, Cunard and NCL often feature a Glenn Miller–style group playing a set or two of 1940s dance tunes.

By about 5pm, before the first-seating dinner (and again at 7pm before the late seating begins), the entertainment choices really kick in. Head to the piano bar for a cocktail or do some pre-dinner dancing to a live jazz or big-band quartet.

About twice a week, after both the early and the late dinner seating, the main show lounge features **Vegas-style musicals,** where a flamboyant troupe of anywhere from 4 to 16 male and female dancers decked out in feather boas, sequins, and top hats slide and kick their way across the stage (and lip sync to the songs' choruses) as a soloist or two belts out show tunes. You'll hear favorites from *Phantom of the Opera, Cats, Hair, Grease, A Chorus Line,* and all the classic Gershwin and Rodgers and Hammerstein greats. Elaborate stage sets and frequent costume changes make these exciting shows the entertainment highlight of the week.

When the Broadway show stuff isn't scheduled, entertainment other nights may be a **magic show,** complete with sawing in half scantily clad assistants and pulling rabbits from hats, **acrobatic acts** (always a big hit), and **headlining soloists** (some quite good).

But if Broadway isn't your bag and magic doesn't fool you, the **disco** gets going around 9 or 10pm and goes until 2 or 3am (sometimes later). Shake your booty to the best of '70s, '80s, '90s, and Y2K pop and rock music; often a live band plays until about midnight, when a DJ takes over until the wee hours. There may be a **karaoke session** thrown in for an hour or two.

An alternative to the disco or the main show might be a **1950s sock hop** in another lounge or a **jazz trio** in yet another romantic nightspot. Night owls who love a good laugh won't want to miss the **R- and/or X-rated comedian** who does a late-night show at about 12 or 12:30am. Or for a quiet evening, many lines, like Holland America, Celebrity, and Crystal, have cinemas showing **first-run movies.**

ENTERTAINMENT ON THE SMALL SHIPS

Ships carrying 100 to 400 passengers have fewer entertainment options, but are no less appealing if you like things mellow. On the high-end lines, there may be a quartet or pianist performing before dinner and maybe afterward, a small-scale **Broadway dance revue,** and dancing in a quiet lounge. The more casual small ships might have taped music or a dude on an electric piano before and after dinner; expect a crew and a **passenger talent show** to be scheduled during the cruise, too. While in port, small-ship lines like Windstar, Star Clippers, and Windjammer Barefoot Cruises often bring on **local musicians** and/or dancers for an afternoon or evening of entertainment. The small, informal, soft-adventure–oriented vessels of American Canadian Caribbean Line, Clipper Cruises, or Tall Ship Adventures may not have any so-called entertainment at all, except perhaps a presentation about the next day's ports of call, a film, or after-dinner drinks at the bar.

5   Shipboard Gyms & Spas

If your idea of a perfect vacation starts with a run on the treadmill and a set of curls, or if a relaxing seaweed facial is more your thing, the newest ships in the Carnival, Celebrity, Royal Caribbean, Princess, and Holland America lines have the biggest and best-equipped fitness facilities. Since the early 1990s, cruise lines have prioritized their spa and fitness areas, moving them out of windowless corners of bottom decks and into prime top-deck positions with oodles of space and lots of glass for soothing views of the ocean. They offer **state-of-the art workout machines** and a host of **spa treatments** that run from the basic to the bizarre.

GYMS: AN ANTIDOTE TO THE MIDNIGHT BUFFET

The well-equipped fitness centers on the megaships may feature a dozen treadmills and just as many stationary bikes, step machines, upper- and lower-body machines, and free weights. Celebrity's *Century, Galaxy,* and *Mercury,* for instance, have **virtual-reality stationary bikes,** and the *Mercury* even has a machine that simulates in-line skating. As ships get bigger, the options just keep increasing: Royal Caribbean's *Voyager of the Seas* is currently king with its rock-climbing wall and in-line and ice-skating rinks.

The roomy **aerobics studios** on the *Grand Princess, Voyager of the Seas,* and on Holland America's and Carnival's post-1990 ships are like the kind you have at your gym back home, with mirrors and special flooring. There are at least a couple of aerobics and

Some lines dangle incentives in front of passengers to encourage and reward participation in **onboard fitness programs.** Holland America, Princess, Royal Caribbean,
and Celebrity have fitness programs that award participating passengers with points
redeemable at the end of the cruise for things like hats and T-shirts.

stretch classes per day. Certified instructors teach the classes, which usually range from
the traditional to the trendy—high- and low-impact, funk, step, body sculpting, stretch
and tone, and abdominals.

Older ships, usually those built before 1990, often do not devote nearly as much space
and resources to sports and fitness. The gyms on ships built pre-1990 are generally going
to be smaller and more spartan, but on all but the small, adventure-oriented Windjammer, Star Clippers, Clipper, ACCL, and Tall Ship Adventures cruise lines you'll find
at least a couple of treadmills and a stationary bike or step machine or two, plus some
free weights. On ships with limited gym facilities, aerobics classes tend to be held out
on deck or in a lounge.

ONBOARD SPAS: TAKING RELAXATION ONE STEP FURTHER

If your idea of a heavenly vacation is spending half of it under a towel being massaged
and kneaded with some soothing mystery oil, choose a cruise ship with a well-stocked
spa (for my picks, see "Best Fitness Facilities & Spas" in the "Frommer's Favorites"
chapter).

On ships of almost all sizes, spas are big business. On big ships built in the past 10
years, they've been given spacious quarters on top decks. The largest spas have 8 or 10
treatment rooms, a sauna and a steam room or two, and full locker rooms with showers. Like the gyms, the spas on ships built pre-1990, though, are generally going to be
small; the large spas on 30-year-old-plus *Norway* and *QE2* are exceptions. Even most
of the smaller upscale ships have some semblance of a spa and a beauty salon. For instance, Windstar Cruises' new *Wind Surf* carries only 300 passengers but boasts an impressive spa. It's only on the smallest ships—like Windjammer, ACCL, and Star
Clippers—that you won't find spas.

Some of the best spas and fitness facilities at sea are on board **Celebrity Cruises'** *Century, Galaxy,* and *Mercury.* Called the AquaSpa, these spacious health meccas are as pleasing to the eye as they are functional. The *Galaxy*'s resembles a Japanese bathhouse and
the *Mercury*'s features a Moroccan motif. The focal point in all three is a 115,000-
gallon **thalassotherapy pool,** a bubbling cauldron of warm, soothing seawater, and a
great place to relax before a massage.

The soothing ShipShape spas on **Royal Caribbean's** *Voyager, Vision, Rhapsody, Grandeur,* and *Enchantment of the Seas* are also some of the most attractive around. Adjacent
to the spas are spacious solariums with a pool, deck chairs, floor-to-ceiling windows, and
a retractable glass ceiling. These spots are a peaceful place to repose before or after a spa
treatment, or any time at all.

When it comes to big, the huge two-story Nautica Spas on the 2,642-passenger **Carnival** *Destiny, Triumph,* and *Victory* take the cake. There are dozens of exercise machines
facing floor-to-ceiling windows and an adjacent beauty salon with 18 hair-dryer chairs
(you'll think you've stumbled into the movie set of *Grease*). Other impressive spas include the 6,000 square-foot Roman Spa on **Norwegian Cruise Line's** *Norway* and the
Pompeii Spa on **Costa Cruise Lines'** *CostaVictoria,* which features accoutrements such
as tile mosaics, rattan lounge chairs, and a small plunge pool.

The Ubiquitous Steiner

The spas and hair salons on most ships (over 90 of them) are staffed and operated by a firm called Steiner, a London-based company with a hands-down corner on the market. You'll find most of the prices are steep (and this coming from a New Yorker). Rates are standardized across most ships, except on the *Seaboard Legend, Sun, Spirit,* and *Goddesses,* and the Holland America and Radisson Seven Seas fleets, where they are about 10% higher. A sampling of treatments and their standard Steiner rates at press time (they're due to increase in late 1999), not including the expected tip, are as follows:

- 55-minute full-body massage: $70
- 25-minute back and legs massage: $35
- Manicure: $20
- Pedicure: $35 (whoa!)
- 55-minute facial: $69
- Bikini wax: $17
- 55-minute Ionithermie slimming treatment: $80

The young women, mostly Brits, who do the massages, facials, manicures, pedicures, reflexology, and other services are professional, charming, and attractive in their matching white frocks. That said, while I'm one of the first in line to sign up, I've found the quality of the treatments to be inconsistent, ranging from really average (like I feel I've had big dollops of oils and creams smeared on me for no rhyme or reason) to excellent (when all I want is more, more, more). Generally, shipboard massages are very good and equivalent to what you'd get from a professional at home, but I've found some of the more exotic treatments, as well as pedicures and facials, to be disappointing. Likewise, when I ask questions about some of the more exotic treatments (like the facials or Ionithermie, a slimming/detox treatment using electrodes and mud to stimulate cells to release toxins), inquiring what is being done to my leg, head, shoulder, or whatever, the answers often seem to be nothing more than a memorized pat description of the treatment from some brochure and not always shedding much light. I expect more when I'm paying $70+ for a massage or facial.

Steiner isn't shy about pushing its extensive and expensive collection of creams, exfoliants, moisturizers, toners, and masks, either. Get a facial and you'll wind up with an itemized list of four or five products, easily adding up to over $200, that they recommend you buy to get the same effect at home (of course you can just say no). The shameless promotion of their fancy ointments, just as you're coming out of your semi-conscious post-massage trance, certainly jars you back to reality, that's for sure. (That said, I found myself raving to a friend the other day about a cream I'd bought aboard ship the week before. Can't fault the quality.)

MAKING YOUR APPOINTMENT AT THE SPA

Hurry up! Since spas are so popular these days, you'll want to head to the spa reservation desk first thing. No time to unpack or grab lunch; got to head up to that spa pronto. Appointments fill up fast, with people lining up to reserve their spots—on the megas, snaking lines 20 and 30 deep are not uncommon on the afternoon of embarkation—and if you don't sign up on the first day (second at the latest), there's a good chance the only appointment you can get will be totally undesirable (like during dinner or at some ungodly hour of the morning); worse yet, you won't get one at all.

Treatments range in price from about $15 to over $150, plus the 10% to 15% tip you're expected to give (of course, if you're unhappy with the treatment, don't tip), and are charged to your onboard account. Celebrity and Windstar allow you to **pre-book spa packages** with your travel agent, but appointment times cannot be reserved until you board the ship.

6 An Introduction to Shipboard Dining

Food, food, food everywhere. From elegant five-course meals served in grand two-story dining rooms with sea views, to massive midnight buffets, 24-hour pizza, ice-cream, pastry, and coffee shops—and even sushi bars—cruise ships big and small are offering more and more choices. The megas, of course, are nothing short of floating smorgasbords. The latest trend: dinner any way you like it. You can still go for the traditional dinner in the formal dining room, or you can now opt for a casual one in the Lido cafe or an intimate meal in a cozy reservations-only Italian restaurant. If you're feeling really unmotivated, Carnival offers pizza and Caesar salad 24 hours a day and Celebrity even delivers it to your cabin! Smaller ships have fewer choices, but even they are getting in on the pizza and alternative-restaurant bandwagon—the budget *Regal Empress* makes a mean pizza pie, and all the upscale lines are offering alternatives, too.

With such a spread to choose from, here's a blow-by-blow look at all the delicious choices.

FORMAL DINING

Dinner in the formal dining room is generally served from about 7 to 10pm, with ships carrying fewer than 400 passengers having one open-seating dinner, where guests can stroll in when they want and sit with whomever they choose. On ships carrying more than 400 or 500 passengers, there are either one or two seatings in one main dining room or, on the largest ships, two (or even three) main dining rooms with two scheduled seatings. If there are two seatings, the early or first one is about 6:30pm (early breakfast is at 7 or 7:30am and lunch about noon) and late or second is about 8:30pm (late breakfast is at 8:30am and lunch about 1:30pm). You need to reserve either the early or late seating when booking your cruise. **First seatings** are for those who prefer dining early and are ready to leave the dining room once the dishes are cleared; elderly passengers and families with children tend to choose this seating. If you choose **second seating,** you won't have to rush through predinner showering and dressing after an active day at a port of call, and the meal tends to be more leisurely, allowing you to linger over coffee and after-dinner drinks.

Generally, 7-night cruises have 2 nights per week (and 10- to 14-night cruises have 3) designated as **formal nights,** when the dress code in the main dining room calls for dark suits or tuxedos for men and cocktail dresses or fancy pantsuits for women. Other nights are designated informal and/or casual.

The *Grand Princess* has three formal dining rooms serving two seatings and *Voyager of the Seas* has a whopping three-deck-high dining room doing two seatings. Putting a unique twist on things, the *Disney Magic* and *Wonder* do two seatings in three main theme dining rooms that passengers rotate among over the course of the cruise.

From menus that offer three to six options for each course, you can choose from a wide array of international fare like escargot, vichyssoise, and veal scaloppini to American

---

Cruise Tip: Don't Worry About Missing the Show

Whether you choose an early or late seating for dinner, don't ever worry that you'll miss a cabaret revue or a planned activity: Cruise directors juggle the starting times of onboard entertainment and activities to accommodate different dining schedules.

---

favorites, such as poached salmon, prime rib, and pastas. There are also at least one or two vegetarian choices as well as healthier entrees that are lower in fat, calories, cholesterol, and sodium.

Generally, you'll be seated at a table with six or eight other guests, unless you're able to snag one of the few **tables for two** or are on one of the smaller ships that have an open-seating, sit-where-you-want policy.

The scheduled dining time you picked when booking your cruise might be confirmed at the pier during check-in or soon after you get to your cabin. If you get assigned to the first seating and you want the second one, tell your maître d', who will probably be at or near his or her station in the dining room during your initial embarkation. Most can accommodate your wishes, if not on the first night of sailing, then on the second night.

In terms of the kind of table you'll get, while it sure can't hurt to ask, don't get your hopes up if you're looking to get a deuce: Tables for two are highly coveted. If dining alone or as a couple is a major priority, the smaller, upscale ships are usually better equipped to accommodate you in this area; the megas are not. If you *do* want to meet and mingle with other passengers (hey, that's what cruises are for), I suggest trying to get a table that seats at least 6 to 10. You'll be more likely to meet pleasant dining companions and it won't be as potentially boring as a smaller grouping of four. Rotate seats every so often during the week to keep things lively and chat with new people.

Smoking is prohibited in virtually all dining rooms.

DINNER TABLE DIVORCES

Many cruisers claim their dining companions either made or ruined their cruise. If you get stuck with a couple of yahoos who seem to offend every bone in your body or there just isn't any chemistry, no need to suffer in silence. It's best to explain to the maître d' as courteously and as soon as possible that your table assignment simply won't do, and request a change. You will usually be accommodated.

THE CAPTAIN'S TABLE

If you're lucky, you might get an invitation to dine at the captain's table (but don't count on it). Seating between 8 and 10 people, the captain's table is usually positioned prominently in the dining room. The wine is flowing, compliments of the captain, and service is that much more doting. Now smile—people are watching!

So who gets a seat at this prized table? Passengers staying in the penthouse or top suites, passengers who sail the line frequently, big-time travel agents, honeymooners or other passengers celebrating special events, cruise line executives, or personal friends of the captain. It can't hurt to ask the maître d' at the beginning of the cruise if you could join the captain for dinner. Sometimes it works.

On the megas, the captain will most likely dine with passengers only once a week and the competition to join him is stiff. On smaller ships, he could be there more often and you'll have a better chance to snag a seat. On the more casual ships, like Star Clippers and Windjammer, all you need to do is ask the captain yourself when you see him on deck or on the bridge. If there's no chance of getting to the captain's table, keep in mind that other officers, like the hotel manager and chief engineer, often dine with guests, too.

If you are invited, **dress up,** not down, in relation to the formality of the ship. On all but the most casual ships, men should wear a jacket and tie. Since this is a social ritual, it's not the time to bad-mouth the line or its staff, unless something is absolutely horrendously wrong with your cruise experience.

SPECIAL DIETS

If you follow any special diet, inform the cruise line as early as possible, preferably when booking your cruise. **Vegetarian dishes** and **kosher food** are commonly available, and almost all cruise lines now feature a selection of healthier, **lighter meals,** labeled as such on the menu. On all but the most cost-conscious cruise lines, the kitchen usually tries to satisfy reasonable culinary requests.

CASUAL DINING

If you'd rather skip the formality of the main dining room, all but the tiniest ships serve breakfast and lunch (and now, even dinner—see below) in a casual **buffet-style cafe restaurant.** Usually located on the Lido Deck, with indoor and outdoor poolside seating, these restaurants serve an extensive spread of both hot and cold food items. On the megas, nearby may be a **grill** where at lunch you can get hamburgers, hot dogs, and often chicken; sometimes there are specialty stations, like a **taco bar.** On most ships, **breakfast and lunch buffets** are generally served for a 3- to 4-hour period, so guests can stroll in and out whenever they desire—although Princess Cruises has the Lido cafe open around the clock on its newest ships.

If you're not in the mood for the fuss of formal dining in the evening, either, many ships now offer dinner in the buffet-style cafe restaurant. Royal Caribbean, Carnival, Norwegian, Celebrity, Princess, Holland America, and Cunard cruise lines do. Most serve dinner buffet-style, but some do a combination of sit-down service and buffet. Wear what you want, stroll in when you please, and, in most cases, sit where you please (most are open seating). After soup and salad, two or three entrees are offered, like prime rib, salmon, or stir-fry, followed by dessert.

If you do want the fine dining and formality, but with fewer fellow diners in tow, in recent years, some lines have added intimate, **reservations-only restaurants,** seating less than 100. The *Crystal Harmony* has an Asian and an Italian restaurant; the *Radisson Diamond,* Italian; *Disney Magic* and *Wonder,* Italian (there's a $5 per person cover charge); *Grand Princess,* Tex-Mex and Italian ($3.50 per person cover charge); *Seabourn Legend, Spirit, Pride,* and *Sun,* French and Italian; Cunard's *Caronia,* Italian. Holland America Lines' new *Volendam* will also have a specialty restaurant, but its cuisine had not yet been determined at press time.

BETWEEN-MEAL SNACKING

Beyond the normal three meals a day is another full schedule of endless eating opportunities. The traditional **midnight buffet extravaganza** is still a cruise highlight on the big ships. Aside from heaps of elaborately decorated fruits, vegetables, and pastries, as well as real treats like shrimp, the nighttime feast is often focused on a culinary theme, such as Tex-Mex, Caribbean, or chocolate, and invariably features a majestic ice sculpture to top off the festive mood. In recent years, though, because of all the choices and people's healthier eating habits, more and more lines are featuring the classic midnight buffets only once or twice a week, and substituting smaller **snack stations** instead.

Throughout the day, if hunger pangs get the best of you between lunch and dinner, the megas have **pizza** available (those on Carnival's entire fleet, for example, operate 24 hours a day and serve Caesar salad, too) and self-serve **frozen yogurt** and **ice-cream** machines. The upscale lines do elegant **afternoon tea service,** offering finger sandwiches, pastries, and cookies, along with tea and coffee; and the megas, too, offer a couple of trays of cookies or sandwiches midday. Small ship lines, like Star Clippers, Windstar, and Windjammer, serve predinner snacks and hors d'oeuvres in the main lounge or bar area.

Some lines, like Princess and Carnival, also have a **patisserie** and/or **cappuccino bar** on board their ships, but they're not free. Specialty coffees and ultra-rich desserts go for about $1 to $4 each. If you'd rather not leave your cabin, most ships offer **24-hour room service** from a limited menu, or for suite guests, the same meals served in the dining room can be served in the cabin.

7 Shopping Opportunities on Ship & Shore

SHOPPING ABOARD SHIP

Even the smallest ships have at least a small shop on board selling T-shirts, sweatshirts, and baseball caps bearing the cruise line logo. The big new megaships, though, have the most extensive onboard shopping. Like mini malls, there may be as many as 10 different stores—from **toiletries and sundries** like film, toothpaste, candy, and paperback books (and even condoms) to totes, T-shirts, mugs, toys, keychains, and other **cruise line logo souvenirs.** You'll find **formalwear** like sequin dresses and jackets, silk dresses and scarves, purses, satin shoes, cummerbunds, ties, and tuxedo shirts, as well as **perfume, cosmetics, jewelry** (costume and the real stuff), and **porcelain figurines.**

A few ships have **name-brand stores.** The *Carnival Paradise* and the *Norwegian Wind,* for instance, both have Fossil boutiques on board, selling mostly watches. The Disney ships, of course, have shops selling Disney souvenirs, clothing, and toys.

All merchandise sold on board while a ship is at sea is **tax-free,** and to maintain that tax-free status, the shops are closed whenever a ship is in port. Prices can vary, though: Some items sell for less—as much as a third less than shore-side prices—and some items cost substantially more. Depends. Some of the best deals are on **alcohol.** By mid-cruise, there are often good sales on a selection of T-shirts, tote bags, jewelry, and booze. Things that usually cost you more on on board than off are disposal cameras, sunscreen, and candy and snack foods. Prices on clothing and good jewelry vary; some things are quite overpriced.

SHOPPING IN PORT

If you want to shop on shore, see "Best Islands for Serious Shoppers" in the "Frommer's Favorites" chapter, for the best shopping islands.

Before each port of call, the cruise director or shore excursion manager gives a **port talk** about that place's attractions. On the big, mass-market ships, a good 75% of the port info disseminated is about shopping (better bring along your own guidebook—this one!—if you want information on history or culture). The line often recommends a list of shops in town (it's no secret that the cruise lines have mutually beneficial deals with certain shops in every port) where they say the merchandise is guaranteed (for example, the stone falls out of your new ring once you get home, and the cruise lines say they'll try to help you get a replacement). If you're not an expert on jewelry or whatever else it is you want to buy, it might be safer to shop at these stores. That said, you won't get much of a taste for the local culture in one of the touristy chain stores. Browsing at **outdoor markets** and in smaller **craft shops** is a better way to get an idea of the island's local flavor.

Part 2

The Cruise Lines & Their Ships

Detailed, in-depth reviews of all the cruise lines in the Caribbean, with discussions of the experiences they offer and the lowdown on their ships, plus realistic info on how much your cruise will actually cost.

The Ratings (and How to Read Them)

Okay, this is it: The point where you get to decide which ship is going to whisk you off for your Caribbean getaway and be your home, entertainment center, and means of transportation for the duration of your trip. As I've said in previous chapters, all ships are not created equal, and finding the one that best matches your style is the key to getting the vacation experience you deserve.

Ship, ships, ships. Some are huge, overwhelming fortresses of activities and entertainment; others are tiny, functional, "get me from here to there" vessels with the feel of a summer camp bunkhouse. Some are high-toned country clubs that happen to float, and others are like a Texas roadhouse on a Saturday night. I've been on more ships than you could shake a stick at, and in this section I'll fill you in on what each one has to offer.

1 Cruise Line Categories

To make your selection easier (and to make sure you're not comparing apples and oranges), I've divided the cruise lines into four distinct categories, given each category a chapter of its own, and rated each line only in comparison with the other lines in its category (see more about this in "The Cruise Line Ratings & Reviews," below). The categories are as follows:

THE MAINSTREAM LINES (chapter 6)   These are the most prominent players in the industry, the jack-of-all-trades lines with the biggest ships, carrying the most passengers, and providing the most diverse cruise experiences from party-hardy to refined. (And with all the competition in the industry today, they tend to offer good prices, too.) **Lines reviewed:** Carnival, Celebrity, Costa, Disney, Holland America, Norwegian, Princess, and Royal Caribbean.

THE BUDGET/OLD SHIP LINES (chapter 7)   On a limited budget? These lines and their mid-sized ships offer some great bargains, particularly on shorter sailings of 2 to 4 days. And for the price, these lines tend to pack in plenty of good times. They don't have spiffy new ships, but for some people, that's a draw in itself: Sailing aboard some of these older vessels is like taking a trip back in time. **Lines reviewed:** Cape Canaveral, Commodore, Mediterranean Shipping Cruises, Premier, Regal, and Royal Olympic.

THE ULTRA-LUXURY LINES (chapter 8)   Got some big bucks to spend on a super-luxurious cruise? These are the ships for you. Offering elegant, refined, and doting service, extraordinary dining, spacious cabins, and high-toned entertainment aboard intimately sized, finely appointed vessels, they're the Dom Perignon of cruises. **Lines reviewed:** Crystal, Cunard, Radisson Seven Seas, Seabourn, and Windstar.

SOFT-ADVENTURE LINES & SAILING SHIPS (chapter 9)   And now for something completely different. Maybe you want the really intimate experience that a ship with only 70 to 100 passengers can offer. Or maybe you want to visit small, out-of-the-way ports that the bigger ships ignore. Maybe you prefer a good book and conversation to a large ship's roster of activities. Or maybe you want to *really* sail—on a sail-powered ship. If any of this describes you, head for this chapter, where you'll find lines that operate small, intimate ships offering unusual cruise experiences. **Lines reviewed:** American Canadian Caribbean Line, Clipper, Club Med Cruises, Star Clippers, Tall Ship Adventures, and Windjammer Barefoot Cruises.

2   The Cruise Line Ratings & Reviews

HOW TO READ THE RATINGS

The cruise industry today offers such a profusion of experiences that it makes my head spin. It also makes comparing all lines and ships by the same set of criteria completely impossible.

Think about it: Would you compare a Mercedes Benz to a sport utility vehicle? A jumbo jet to a hang-glider? A Park Avenue high-rise apartment to an A-frame in Aspen? No, you wouldn't. For the same reason, I came to the conclusion that the typical, across-the-board ratings used by most cruise guidebooks are illogical and don't give you, the reader, the kind of comparisons you need to make your decision.

For that reason, I've developed a simple system based on the classic customer satisfaction survey. In each of these "Frommer's Ratings" I judge the cruise lines on the following important considerations, rating them either *poor, fair, good, excellent,* or *outstanding.*

- Enjoyment Factor
- Dining
- Activities
- Children's Program
- Entertainment
- Service
- Overall Value

Again, though, you can't compare the experiences you'll have aboard an ultra-luxury line like Seabourn, an ultra-casual line like Windjammer Barefoot Cruises, a megaship line like Carnival, and a budget line like Cape Canaveral. They're different animals, catering to different kinds of travelers seeking different kinds of experiences. For that reason, **I've graded the cruise lines on a curve.** Remember how you used to just *love* it when the teacher did that? It works the same way here as it did in school. You should read the ratings for a line *only in relation to the other lines in the same chapter.* For example, if you see in the "Soft-Adventure Lines & Sailing Ships" chapter that Star Clippers achieves an "outstanding" rating for its dining experience, that means that among the lines in that chapter, Star Clippers has the best cuisine. It may not be up to the level of, say, the ultra-luxurious Seabourn (it's not), but if you're looking for an adventurous cruise with great food, this might be your best bet.

STRUCTURE OF THE CRUISE LINE REVIEWS

Each cruise line's review begins with **The Line in a Nutshell** (a quick word about the line in general) and **The Experience,** which—you guessed it!—is a short summation of the kind of cruise experience you can expect to have aboard that line. Following this, the **Frommer's Ratings** rate the individual elements of the cruise experience (see above),

Frommer's Cruise Line Ratings at a Glance

1 = poor **2** = fair **3** = good **4** = excellent **5** = outstanding

Cruise Line	Enjoyment Factor	Dining	Activities	Children's Program	Entertainment	Service	Overall Value
Mainstream Lines							
Carnival	5	4	4	4	4	3	4
Celebrity	5	5	5	3	4	5	5
Costa	5	4	5	3	4	4	4
Disney	5	4	4	5	5	3	3
Holland America	5	4	4	2	3	5	5
Norwegian	4	2	5	3	4	2	4
Princess	5	3	4	4*	4	4	4
Royal Caribbean	5	3	4	4	4	3	4
Budget/Old Ship Lines							
Cape Canaveral	3	3	3	3	3	3	4
Commodore	4	3	4	3*	3	4	4
Mediterranean Shipping	4	3	3	2	3	3	4
Premier	5	4	4	5*	5	4	5
Regal	4	4	4	3	3	3	4
Royal Olympic	5	5	5	N/A	4	5	4
Ultra-Luxury Lines							
Crystal	5	5	5	5	5	4	5
Cunard	5	4	4	4*	4	3	4
Radisson Seven Seas	5	5	2	N/A	3	4	4
Seabourn	5	5	2	N/A	3	5	4
Windstar	5	4	2	N/A	2	3	4
Soft-Adventure Lines & Sailing Ships							
American Canadian Caribbean	4	3	5	N/A	2	3	3
Clipper	4	4	4	N/A	3	4	4
Club Med	4	4	5	1	4	4	3
Star Clippers	5	5	4	N/A	5	5	5
Tall Ship Adventures	4	3	3	N/A	2	3	3
Windjammer	5	3	3	3*	3	3	5

NOTE: Cruise lines have been graded on a curve that compares them only with other lines within their category (i.e., Mainstream with Mainstream, Budget with Budget, etc.). See "The Cruise Line Ratings & Reviews" in this chapter for a detailed explanation of my ratings methodology.
* Does not apply to all ships in the line's fleet. See individual ship reviews for details. Lines with N/A rating for children's programs simply do not have any such program.

and the text that follows fleshes out the review, providing all the details you need to get a feel for what kind of a vacation the cruise line will give you.

RATING THE INDIVIDUAL SHIPS

The individual ship reviews that follow the general cruise line description get down into the nitty gritty, giving you all the details on the ships' accommodations, facilities, amenities, comfort level, and upkeep.

People feel very strongly about ships. For centuries, mariners have imbued their vessels with human personalities, and usually referred to them as "her." In fact, an old (really old) seafaring superstition holds that women should never be allowed aboard a ship, because the ship, being a woman herself, will get jealous. Guess that means I've made a lot of ships jealous in my time.

Be that as it may, it's a fact that people bond with the ships they sail aboard. They find themselves in the gift shop, loading up on T-shirts with the ship's name emblazoned on front. They get to port and the first question they ask other cruisers they meet is "Which ship are you sailing on?" and then engage in a friendly comparison, each walking away knowing in his heart that *his* ship is the best. I know people who have sailed the same ship a dozen times or more, and feel as warmly about it as though it were their own summer cottage. That's why, when looking at the reviews, you want to look for a ship that says "you."

In rating the ships, I've used a version of the same Frommer's Ratings system with which I reviewed the lines. It evaluates the ships' cabins, public spaces, cleanliness, decor, gyms/spas, itineraries, and a few other elements on a 1-to-5 scale, which you should read like this:

1	=	Poor	4	=	Excellent
2	=	Fair	5	=	Outstanding
3	=	Good			

In instances where the category doesn't apply to a particular ship (the Windjammer and American Canadian Caribbean ships, for instance, don't have gyms or spas), I've simply noted "not applicable" (N/A). After all, you can't rate what ain't there.

SPECIFICATIONS

I've listed some of the ships' vital statistics—ship size, year built and most recently refurbished, number of cabins, number of officers and crew—to help you compare.

Size is listed in both length of the ship, which is pretty self-explanatory, and in tons. Note that these are not actual measures of weight, but **gross register tons (GRTs)**, which is a measure of the interior space used to produce revenue on a ship. One GRT equals 100 cubic feet of enclosed, revenue-generating space.

Among the crew/officers statistics, an important one is the **passenger/crew ratio**, which tells you, in theory, how many passengers each crewmember is expected to serve.

ITINERARIES

Each cruise line review includes a chart showing itineraries for each ship the line has assigned to Caribbean, Bermuda, or Panama Canal itineraries for 2000. Often, a single ship sails on alternating itineraries—for instance, doing an eastern Caribbean route one week and a western Caribbean route the next, ad infinitum until season's end. When this is the case, I've listed both and noted that they alternate. Consult your travel agent for exact sailing dates.

For those of you who are thinking about taking a non-Caribbean cruise at some point, I've also noted other itineraries sailed by the ships. You can find more details on many of these itineraries in *Frommer's Alaska Cruises* and *Frommer's European Cruises*.

3 Evaluating & Comparing the Listed Cruise Prices

Figuring out the price of a cruise is rarely a simple task—it's like driving in some foreign place without a map. My aim, with the help of cruise agency giant The Travel Company, is to give you some direction. As I discussed in chapter 2, rates listed in the cruise line brochures are inflated and, with the exception of holidays, you can expect to pay anywhere from 10% to 50% less. The discounts come from the cruise lines when you book early (with "early" generally considered 3 to 9 months ahead) and from travel agencies, which usually offer additional savings. Because they sell so many cruises, agencies get bulk discounts from the cruise lines and pass the savings on to you.

To give you an accurate look at what you can expect to pay, I've done something new (damn smart if you ask me!). The rates listed in the ship reviews in chapters 6, 7, 8, and 9 and in Appendix A, "Cruise Price Comparisons," come straight from the experts at The Travel Company. While of course rates are always subject to the basic principles of supply and demand, the prices that appear in this book are the **actual prices** The Travel Company was offering its customers at press time (June 1999) on cruises departing in late January 2000. Remember, though, they are meant as a guide only and are in no way etched in stone—so the price you pay may be higher or even lower, depending on how far ahead you book, when you choose to travel, whether there are any special discounts being offered by the lines, and a slew of other factors. Other travel agencies may also be able to obtain similar rates.

PRICES LISTED IN THE REVIEWS

Based on what The Travel Company can offer versus brochure rates, in each ship review I've calculated **per diem prices** (the cruise price divided down to represent the rate paid per person, per day) for the following three basic types of accommodations:

• Lowest-category inside cabins (without windows)
• Lowest-category outside cabins (with windows)
• Lowest-category suites

Remember that cruise ships generally have several different categories of cabins within each of these three basic divisions, all priced differently, and that the prices I've listed represent the *lowest* categories for inside and outside cabins and suites. If you're interested in booking a roomier, higher-level cabin in any category, you'll find the price will be higher. In general, the cost of a top-level inside cabin will probably be very close to the rate for a low-level outside cabin, and the cost of a top-level outside may be very close to the rate for a low-level suite.

To contact **The Travel Company,** call ☎ **800/242-9000** or visit their Web site at **www.travelco.com**. All rates are cruise only; per person and based on double occupancy. Offers are capacity controlled and may be withdrawn by the cruise lines without notice. Fares reflected may vary depending on sailing date and are shown to provide the average level discount which can be obtained by booking through The Travel Company. Rates include port charges; government fees and taxes are additional. Other restrictions may apply.

COMPARING BROCHURE & ACTUAL PRICES

In Appendix A, "Cruise Price Comparisons," I've listed all the ships reviewed in this book, with their brochure rates noted right next to the discounted rates provided for this book by The Travel Company. Take a look—seeing how much you'll probably save can be a real eye-opener, and should entirely do away with that nasty sense of sticker shock most people get when they start looking at cruise line brochure prices.

Ship Size Comparisons

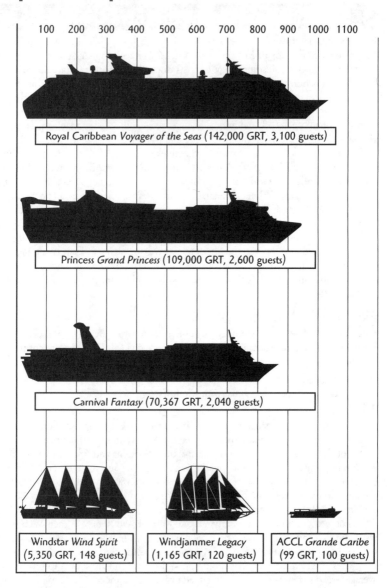

100   200   300   400   500   600   700   800   900   1000   1100

Royal Caribbean *Voyager of the Seas* (142,000 GRT, 3,100 guests)

Princess *Grand Princess* (109,000 GRT, 2,600 guests)

Carnival *Fantasy* (70,367 GRT, 2,040 guests)

Windstar *Wind Spirit*	Windjammer *Legacy*	ACCL *Grande Caribe*
(5,350 GRT, 148 guests)	(1,165 GRT, 120 guests)	(99 GRT, 100 guests)

Ships selected for this chart are representative of the various size vessels sailing in the cruise market today. See the specifications tables accompanying every ship review in chapters 6–9 to see the approximate comparative size of all the ships not shown here. (**GRT** = gross register tons, a measure that takes into account interior space used to produce revenue on a vessel. One GRT = 100 cubic feet of enclosed, revenue-generating space.)

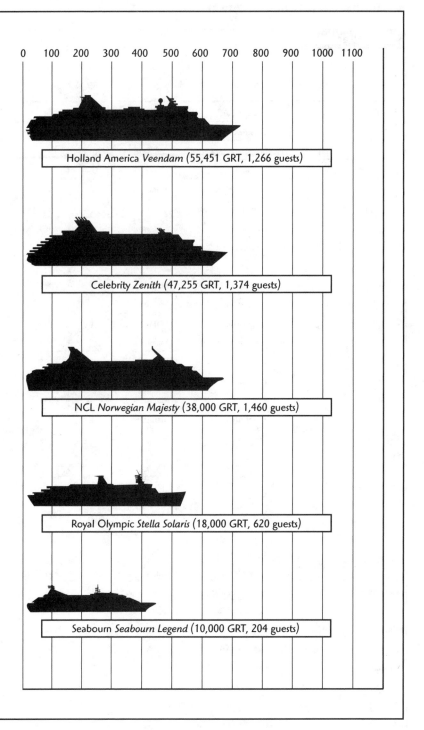

0 100 200 300 400 500 600 700 800 900 1000 1100

Holland America *Veendam* (55,451 GRT, 1,266 guests)

Celebrity *Zenith* (47,255 GRT, 1,374 guests)

NCL *Norwegian Majesty* (38,000 GRT, 1,460 guests)

Royal Olympic *Stella Solaris* (18,000 GRT, 620 guests)

Seabourn *Seabourn Legend* (10,000 GRT, 204 guests)

Cruise Line	Ship	Type of Cruise	Duration of Cruise (days)	Year Built
Ships at a Glance				
ACCL	**Grande Caribe**	Soft Adventure	11	1997
	Grande Mariner	Soft Adventure	11–14	1998
	Niagara Prince	Soft Adventure	6–10	1994
Cape Canaveral	**Dolphin IV**	Old/Budget	2–4	1956
Carnival	**Carnival Destiny**	Mainstream	7	1996
	Carnival Triumph	Mainstream	7	1999
	Carnival Victory	Mainstream	7	2000
	Celebration	Mainstream	7	1987
	Ecstasy	Mainstream	3–4	1991
	Fantasy	Mainstream	3–4	1990
	Fascination	Mainstream	7	1994
	Imagination	Mainstream	4–5	1995
	Inspiration	Mainstream	7	1996
	Jubilee	Mainstream	10–11	1986
	Paradise	Mainstream	7	1998
	Sensation	Mainstream	7	1993
	Tropicale	Mainstream	4–5	1982
Celebrity	**Century**	Mainstream	7	1995
	Galaxy	Mainstream	7	1996
	Horizon	Mainstream	10–11	1990
	Mercury	Mainstream	7	1997
	Zenith	Mainstream	7–14	1992
Clipper	**Nantucket Clipper**	Soft-Adventure	7	1984
	Yorktown Clipper	Soft-Adventure	7–10	1988
Club Med	**Club Med II**	Sailing Ship	7	1990
Commodore	**Enchanted Capri**	Old/Budget	2–5	1976
	Enchanted Isle	Old/Budget	7	1958
Costa	**CostaRomantica**	Mainstream	7	1993
	CostaVictoria	Mainstream	7	1996
Crystal	**Crystal Harmony**	Luxury	7–12	1990
	Crystal Symphony	Luxury	10–11	1995
Cunard	**Caronia**	Luxury	6–13	1973
	QE2	Luxury	7–12	1969

Gross Tonnage	Passenger Capacity (Double Occupancy)	Passenger/Crew Ratio	Alternative Dining	Casino	Children's Activities	Children's Playroom	Gym	Jogging Track	Library	Infirmary	Spa (L=limited facilities)	Swimming Pool(s)	Theater/Cinema	Wheelchair Access (P=partial)
99	100	5.5-1												
99	100	5.5-1												
99	84	5-1												
13,650	586	2.2-1		✓	✓	✓		✓	✓	✓	L	✓	✓	
101,353	2,642	2.6-1	✓	✓	✓	✓	✓	✓	✓	✓	✓	✓	✓	✓
102,000	2,758	2.6-1	✓	✓	✓	✓	✓	✓	✓	✓	✓	✓	✓	✓
102,000	2,758	2.6-1	✓	✓	✓	✓	✓	✓	✓	✓	✓	✓	✓	✓
47,262	1,486	2.2-1	✓	✓	✓	✓	✓	✓	✓	✓	✓	✓	✓	✓
70,367	2,040	2.2-1	✓	✓	✓	✓	✓	✓	✓	✓	✓	✓	✓	✓
70,367	2,040	2.2-1	✓	✓	✓	✓	✓	✓	✓	✓	✓	✓	✓	✓
70,367	2,040	2.2-1	✓	✓	✓	✓	✓	✓	✓	✓	✓	✓	✓	✓
70,367	2,040	2.2-1	✓	✓	✓	✓	✓	✓	✓	✓	✓	✓	✓	✓
70,367	2,040	2.2-1	✓	✓	✓	✓	✓	✓	✓	✓	✓	✓	✓	✓
47,262	1,486	2.2-1	✓	✓	✓	✓	✓	✓	✓	✓	✓	✓	✓	✓
70,367	2,040	2.2-1	✓	✓	✓	✓	✓	✓	✓	✓	✓	✓	✓	✓
70,367	2,040	2.2-1	✓	✓	✓	✓	✓	✓	✓	✓	✓	✓	✓	✓
36,674	1,022	1.9-1	✓	✓	✓	✓	✓	✓	✓	✓	✓	✓	✓	✓
70,606	1,750	2-1	✓	✓	✓	✓	✓	✓	✓	✓	✓	✓	✓	✓
77,713	1,896	2-1	✓	✓	✓	✓	✓	✓	✓	✓	✓	✓	✓	✓
46,811	1,354	2.1-1	✓	✓	✓	✓	✓	✓	✓	✓	✓	✓	✓	✓
77,713	1,896	2-1	✓	✓	✓	✓	✓	✓	✓	✓	✓	✓	✓	✓
47,225	1,374	2.1-1	✓	✓	✓	✓	✓	✓	✓	✓	✓	✓	✓	✓
1,471	102	3.2-1												
2,354	138	3.5-1												
14,983	386	2.1-1	✓	✓			✓	✓		✓	L	✓	✓	P
15,410	460	2.4-1		✓						✓		✓	✓	
23,395	725	2.1-1		✓	✓	✓	✓		✓	✓	L	✓	✓	P
53,000	1,356	2-1	✓	✓	✓	✓	✓	✓	✓	✓	✓	✓	✓	✓
76,000	1,928	2.4-1	✓	✓	✓	✓	✓	✓	✓	✓	✓	✓	✓	✓
49,400	960	1.7-1	✓	✓	✓	✓	✓	✓	✓	✓	✓	✓	✓	✓
51,044	960	1.7-1	✓	✓	✓	✓	✓	✓	✓	✓	✓	✓	✓	✓
24,492	679	1.6-1	✓	✓		✓			✓	✓	✓	✓	✓	✓
70,327	1,789	1.8-1	✓	✓	✓	✓	✓	✓	✓	✓	✓	✓	✓	✓

Ships at a Glance (continued)

Cruise Line	Ship	Type of Cruise	Duration of Cruise (days)	Year Built
Disney	Disney Magic	Mainstream	3–4	1998
	Disney Wonder	Mainstream	3–4	1999
Holland America	Maasdam	Mainstream	10	1993
	Nieuw Amsterdam	Mainstream	14	1983
	Noordam	Mainstream	7–10	1984
	Ryndam	Mainstream	7	1994
	Veendam	Mainstream	7	1996
	Westerdam	Mainstream	7	1986
Mediterranean Shipping	Melody	Old/Budget	11	1982
Norwegian	Norway	Mainstream	7	1961
	Norwegian Crown	Mainstream	7	1988
	Norwegian Dream	Mainstream	7	1992
	Norwegian Majesty	Mainstream	7–11	1992
	Norwegian Sea	Mainstream	7	1988
	Norwegian Wind	Mainstream	7	1993
Premier	Big Red Boat	Old/Budget	3–4	1965
	Rembrandt	Old/Budget	7	1959
	Seabreeze	Old/Budget	7	1958
Princess	Crown Princess	Mainstream	10	1991
	Dawn Princess	Mainstream	7	1995
	Grand Princess	Mainstream	7	1998
	Ocean Princess	Mainstream	7	1999
	Pacific Princess	Mainstream	7	1971
	Sea Princess	Mainstream	7	1998
	Sun Princess	Mainstream	10–11	1997
Radisson Seven Seas	Radisson Diamond	Luxury	4–10	1992
Regal	Regal Empress	Old/Budget	4–11	1953
Royal Caribbean	Enchantment of the Seas	Mainstream	7	1997
	Grandeur of the Seas	Mainstream	7	1996
	Majesty of the Seas	Mainstream	3–7	1992
	Monarch of the Seas	Mainstream	7	1991
	Nordic Empress	Mainstream	3–7	1990
	Sovereign of the Seas	Mainstream	3–4	1988

Gross Tonnage	Passenger Capacity (Double Occupancy)	Passenger/Crew Ratio	Alternative Dining	Casino	Children's Activities	Children's Playroom	Gym	Jogging Track	Library	Infirmary	Spa (L=limited facilities)	Swimming Pool(s)	Theater/Cinema	Wheelchair Access (P=partial)
83,000	1,760	1.9-1	✓		✓	✓	✓	✓		✓	✓	✓	✓	✓
83,000	1,760	1.9-1	✓		✓	✓	✓	✓		✓	✓	✓		✓
55,451	1,266	2.2-1	✓	✓	✓	✓	✓	✓	✓	✓	✓	✓	✓	✓
33,930	1,214	2.2-1	✓	✓	✓	✓	✓	✓	✓	✓	✓	✓	✓	✓
33,930	1,214	2.2-1	✓	✓	✓	✓	✓	✓	✓	✓	✓	✓	✓	✓
55,451	1,266	2.2-1	✓	✓	✓	✓	✓	✓	✓	✓	✓	✓	✓	✓
55,451	1,266	2.2-1	✓	✓	✓	✓	✓	✓	✓	✓	✓	✓	✓	✓
53,872	1,494	2.3-1	✓	✓	✓	✓	✓	✓	✓	✓	✓	✓	✓	✓
36,000	1,076	2-1		✓	✓	✓	✓	✓	✓	✓	L	✓	✓	P
76,049	2,032	2.3-1	✓	✓	✓	✓	✓	✓	✓	✓	✓	✓	✓	✓
34,250	1,052	2.2-1			✓		✓	✓	✓	✓	✓	✓	✓	✓
56,760	1,748	2.8-1	✓	✓	✓	✓	✓	✓	✓	✓	✓	✓	✓	✓
38,000	1,460	2.7-1	✓	✓	✓	✓	✓	✓	✓	✓	✓	✓	✓	✓
42,000	1,504	2.4-1	✓	✓	✓	✓	✓	✓		✓	✓	✓	✓	✓
56,760	1,748	2.8-1	✓	✓	✓	✓	✓	✓	✓	✓	✓	✓	✓	✓
38,772	1,116	2.3-1		✓	✓	✓	✓	✓		✓	L	✓	✓	P
38,645	1,074	2-1		✓	✓	✓	✓		✓	✓	✓	✓	✓	
21,010	842	2.1-1		✓	✓	✓	✓	✓	✓	✓	L	✓	✓	
70,000	1,590	2.3-1	✓	✓	✓	✓	✓	✓	✓	✓	✓	✓	✓	✓
77,000	1,950	2.2-1	✓	✓	✓	✓	✓	✓	✓	✓	✓	✓	✓	✓
109,000	2,600	2-1	✓	✓	✓	✓	✓	✓	✓	✓	✓	✓	✓	✓
77,000	1,950	2.2-1	✓	✓	✓	✓	✓	✓	✓	✓	✓	✓	✓	✓
20,000	640	1.8-1		✓			✓	✓	✓	✓	L	✓	✓	✓
77,000	1,950	2.2-1	✓	✓	✓	✓	✓	✓	✓	✓	✓	✓	✓	✓
77,000	1,950	2.2-1	✓	✓	✓	✓	✓	✓	✓	✓	✓	✓	✓	✓
20,295	350	1.8-1	✓	✓			✓	✓	✓	✓	✓	✓	✓	✓
22,000	1,068	2.8-1	✓	✓	✓	✓	✓	✓	✓	✓	L	✓	✓	✓
74,140	1,950	3-1	✓	✓	✓	✓	✓	✓	✓	✓	✓	✓	✓	✓
74,000	1,950	2.5-1	✓	✓	✓	✓	✓	✓	✓	✓	✓	✓	✓	✓
73,941	2,354	2.9-1	✓	✓	✓	✓	✓	✓	✓	✓	✓	✓	✓	✓
73,941	2,354	2.9-1	✓	✓	✓	✓	✓	✓	✓	✓	✓	✓	✓	✓
48,563	1,600	2.4-1	✓	✓	✓	✓	✓	✓		✓	✓	✓	✓	✓
73,192	2,276	2.7-1	✓	✓	✓	✓	✓	✓	✓	✓	✓	✓	✓	✓

Ships at a Glance (continued)

Cruise Line	Ship	Type of Cruise	Duration of Cruise (days)	Year Built
Royal Caribbean (cont.)	Splendour of the Seas	Mainstream	10–11	1996
	Vision of the Seas	Mainstream	10–11	1998
Royal Olympic	Stella Solaris	Old/Educational	10–56	1953
Seabourn	Seabourn Goddess I	Luxury	7	1984
	Seabourn Goddess II	Luxury	7	1985
	Seabourn Legend	Luxury	5–16	1992
	Seabourn Pride	Luxury	6–10	1988
Star Clippers	Star Clipper	Sailing Ship	7	1991
Tall Ship Adventures	Sir Francis Drake	Sailing Ship	7	1917
Windjammer	Amazing Grace	Soft-Adventure	13	1955
	Flying Cloud	Sailing Ship	6	1927
	Legacy	Sailing Ship	7	1959
	Mandalay	Sailing Ship	6–13	1923
	Polynesia	Sailing Ship	6	1938
	Yankee Clipper	Sailing Ship	6	1927
Windstar	Wind Spirit	Luxury	7	1988
	Wind Star	Luxury	7	1986
	Wind Surf	Luxury	7	1990

Gross Tonnage	Passenger Capacity (Double Occupancy)	Passenger/Crew Ratio	Alternative Dining	Casino	Children's Activities	Children's Playroom	Gym	Jogging Track	Library	Infirmary	Spa (L=limited facilities)	Swimming Pool(s)	Theater/Cinema	Wheelchair Access (P=partial)
69,130	1,804	2.5-1	✓	✓	✓	✓	✓	✓	✓	✓	✓	✓	✓	✓
78,491	2,000	3-1	✓	✓	✓	✓	✓	✓	✓	✓	✓	✓	✓	✓
18,000	620	1.9-1		✓		✓	✓	✓	✓	✓	✓	✓	✓	P
4,250	116	1.3-1		✓			✓		✓	✓	✓	✓		
4,250	116	1.3-1		✓			✓		✓	✓	✓	✓		
10,000	204	1.5-1	✓	✓			✓	✓	✓	✓	✓	✓		✓
10,000	204	1.5-1	✓	✓			✓	✓	✓	✓	✓	✓		✓
2,295	172	2.5-1							✓		L	✓		
98	28	3-1												
1,525	94	2.4-1							✓					
400	74	3-1												
1,165	120	2.8-1			✓									
420	72	2.6-1												
430	126	2.8-1												
327	64	2.2-1												
5,350	148	1.6-1		✓			✓		✓	✓	L	✓		
5,350	148	1.6-1		✓			✓		✓	✓	L	✓		
14,745	312	1.6-1	✓	✓			✓	✓	✓	✓	✓	✓		

6 The Mainstream Lines

Simply put, cruise lines with mainstream appeal fit into this category. Granted, the category covers a lot a ground, and that's the point. These ships are generalists, if you will, attempting to offer a little something for almost everyone—all ages, backgrounds, and interests.

The more elegant and refined of the lot are commonly referred to as **premium,** a notch up from **mass-market** in the sophistication department. Quality-wise, for the most part they're all on equal footing and, overall, the ships in this category are more alike than they are different.

Since this category is the most popular, it's the one that's seen the most growth, innovation, and investment in recent years, meaning the ships are, as a general rule, remarkably new—and also remarkably *big*. This is the category where the **megaships** reside, those hulking 1,200- to 3,100-passenger floating resorts that offer the widest variety of activities and entertainment. All the lines in this chapter (but particularly the "Big Three" —Carnival, Royal Caribbean, and Princess) have been pumping billions into building newer, bigger, and fancier ships, offering a wide variety of different cabins—outside (with windows), inside (no windows), suites, and cabins with private balconies and without. They'll have both formal and informal dining options, a wide array of entertainment (heavy on the Vegas-style stuff), and more activities than you can possibly squeeze into one day. Overall, the atmosphere is very social and passengers tend to enjoy mingling.

DRESS CODES   On week-long cruises aboard mass-market and premium ships there are 2 formal nights calling for dark suits or tuxedos for men and cocktail dresses, sequin numbers, or fancy pantsuits for women. The other 5 nights are some combination of semi-formal and casual, and call for casual suits or sport jackets and slacks for men, and dresses, pantsuits, or skirts and tops for women. Guests are asked not to wear shorts and T-shirts in the formal dining rooms. Daytime is casual.

Cruise Lines Reviewed in This Chapter
- Carnival Cruise Lines
- Celebrity Cruises
- Costa Cruises
- Disney Cruise Line
- Holland America Line–Westours
- Norwegian Cruise Line
- Princess Cruises
- Royal Caribbean International

Carnival Cruise Lines

SHIPS   Carnival Destiny • Carnival Triumph • Celebration • Ecstasy • Fantasy • Fascination • Imagination • Inspiration • Jubilee • Paradise • Sensation • Tropicale • Victory (preview)

3655 NW 87th Ave., Miami, FL 33178-2428. ☎ **800/327-9501** or 305/599-2200. Fax 305/406-4740. www.carnival.com.

THE LINE IN A NUTSHELL   Moderately-priced, jumbo-sized resort ships bathed in neon and glitz. If you like Las Vegas, New Orleans, and Time's Square, Carnival's brand of flamboyant fun is awesome.

THE EXPERIENCE   Nobody does it better in the party department than Carnival. This extraordinarily successful operation is the Coca-Cola of cruising, the line with the most recognized name in the biz. Since its establishment in 1972, it's the cruise experience remade into a very casual, down-to-earth, middle-American vacation getaway enjoyed by millions. The line is incredibly innovative, continually updating its onboard programs, most recently offering sushi on the *Elation* and *Paradise,* 24-hour pizza and Caesar salad fleetwide, and an entirely smoke-free ship, the *Paradise.*

The line's decor continues to evolve—each ship is a collage of textures, shapes, and images. Where else but on these floating playlands would you find a re-creation of a mogul emperor's palace complete with domed shrines and replicas of elephants, a San Francisco trolley car, or Roman columns? Aboard a Carnival cruise, the destination is the ship itself, with ports playing a secondary role. The outrageousness of the decor is part of the fun, and the point—Carnival ships provide a fantasyland you can't get at home.

Pros

- **Fun theme-park ambience** and fanciful decor is unmatched.
- **All ages.** From 20s singles and honeymoon couples to families with young kids to even grandpas and grandmas.
- **Exciting entertainment.** Ranges from some of the best head-turning Broadway-style musical reviews at sea to the classic dose of adult comedy and raging discos.

Cons

- **You're never alone.** Not in the hot tubs, on shore excursions, in the pool, while sunbathing, at the gym, at the frozen-yogurt machine . . .
- **Limited port info.** The information you'll get from port lectures and hand-outs revolves around shopping; there's next to nothing in the history and culture department.
- **Too casual.** If you like a little elegance, you'll have to grin and bear the white plastic ice/wine buckets in the cabins and the contingent of guests who insist on wearing their jeans and Birkenstocks to the dining room, disco, and bars in the evening.

Frommer's Ratings: Carnival Cruise Lines					
	Poor	Fair	Good	Excellent	Outstanding
Enjoyment Factor					✓
Dining				✓	
Activities				✓	
Children's Program				✓	
Entertainment				✓	
Service			✓		
Overall Value				✓	

CARNIVAL: BIG LINE, BIG FUN

Carnival is the Big Kahuna of the cruise world. It's got the most name recognition, the most ships, the most passengers, and those bubbly commercials with the happy music and dancing fish. The assets of its parent company, Carnival Corporation, are enormous: In addition to its own fleet of 14 ships, Carnival holds majority ownership of Cunard, 50% interest in Seabourn and Costa Cruises, full ownership of both Windstar Cruises and Holland America Line, and a 30% stake in U.K.-based tour operator Airtours.

The origins of the Miami-based company were as precarious as they were accidental. Company patriarch Ted Arison, a reclusive billionaire now living in Israel, had sold an air-freight business in New York in 1966 and intended to retire to his native Israel to enjoy the fruits of his labor. After he negotiated terms for chartering a ship in the Mediterranean, he compiled a group of paying passengers, only to discover that the ship's owner could no longer guarantee the vessel's availability. According to latter-day legend, a deal was hastily struck whereby Arison's passengers would be carried aboard an underbooked ship then owned by Knut Kloster, a prominent Norwegian shipping magnate. The combination of Arison's marketing skill and Kloster's hardware created an all-new entity that, in 1966, became the corporate forerunner of Norwegian Cruise Line.

Carnival got its start in 1972 when Arison bought the *Empress of Canada,* known for its formal and somewhat stuffy administration, and reconfigured it into Carnival's first ship, the anything-but-stuffy *Mardi Gras.* After a shaky start—the brightly painted ship, carrying hundreds of travel agents, ran aground just off the coast of Miami on its first cruise—Arison managed to pick up the pieces and create a company that, under the guidance of astute and tough-as-nails company president Robert Dickinson and chairman Micky Arison (Ted's son), eventually evolved into the most influential trendsetter in the cruise ship industry. Fourteen ships later, the rest is truly history.

THE CARNIVAL FLEET

One frequently asked question is, "Aren't all Carnival ships alike?" Yes and no.

As with many other lines, the ships in Carnival's 14-ship fleet have gotten bigger and more expensive through the years, and can easily be categorized into three groups. There are four older, 1,000- to 1,500-passenger mid-sized ships—the *Tropicale, Holiday, Celebration,* and *Jubilee*—built in the early- to mid-80s. They are cramped and less glamorous than the newer ships, yet may feel more like "real" ships to ship buffs. They cost about $100 to $170 million to build. The second group, the eight 2,000-passenger Fantasy-class ships—*Ecstasy, Elation, Fantasy, Fascination, Imagination, Inspiration, Sensation,* and *Paradise* (the last a completely smoke-free ship)—were built between 1990 and 1998 and feature wide-open decks, towering atria, large gyms and spas, and flamboyant, fanciful decor, and cost an average of $300 million each. Amazingly, in the nearly 10-year span between when the first Fantasy-class ship was built and the last one, very little of the design changed ("cookie-cutter" comes to mind). The $400-million 2,642-passenger *Destiny,* built in '96, and her $415-million sister *Triumph,* built in '99, are the largest, flashiest, and most stunning in the fleet, with super-sized versions of everything the Fantasy-class ships have and more. Called the Destiny-class ships, another three are on the drawing boards for delivery over the next 3 years.

More than any other line in its league, Carnival sticks to the Caribbean, deploying 11 of its ships there year-round and another one part of the year. The *Holiday* and *Elation* cruise round-trip from Los Angeles on year-round 3-, 4-, and 7-night cruises to the Mexican Riviera, and are not reviewed in this book.

The Day Carnival Drew the Line

In early 1997, Carnival, the party line of party lines, finally decided to draw the line somewhere, and where they chose to draw it was right at the toes of the spring-break crowd, which in past years had turned some of the line's ships into veritable frat houses. (I sailed on one of those nightmares in 1996 when 500+ graduating high-school seniors practically took over the *Celebration.* "Disaster" is an understatement.) According to Carnival's new rules, no one under 21 is allowed to sail unless sharing a cabin with an adult over 25 (with exceptions made for married couples and young people whose parents are lodged in a different cabin).

PASSENGER PROFILE

"All kinds" about sums it up. Young, old, and lots in between. Couples, singles, and families. You'll see a cross section, alright, and this trend will only grow as Carnival continues to mellow a bit from its early wild and crazy days. While it's one of the best lines to choose if you're single, Carnival's ships certainly aren't overrun by singles (in fact, you'll notice that the families on board and the couples seem to be in the majority). Carnival estimates about 30% of passengers are under age 30, another 30% are between 35 and 55, and 40% are over age 55. Half of all passengers are first-time cruisers.

Regardless of their age, passengers tend to be young at heart, ready to party, and keyed up for nonstop, round-the-clock activities. Many have visited the casinos of Atlantic City and Las Vegas and the high-rise resorts of Cancún and Jamaica, and of course are well-acquainted with the pleasures of soaks in sardine-can-like hot tubs, sunbathing, piña coladas or buckets of beer before lunch, and late-night dancing. So if you're an early-to-bed type, hate noise, hate waiting in line, and prefer tasteful jokes, subdued color schemes, and well-modulated voices, choose a different cruise line.

The typical Carnival passenger likes to dress casual, even at dinner, and a line spokesperson told me Carnival has unofficially relaxed its evening dress codes, turning a blind eye to jeans and T-shirts on all but formal nights. Even on formal nights, it's not uncommon for some passengers to run back to their cabins to change out of their dressier duds and put on their shorts or jeans before heading out to the discos and bars. On Carnival ships, you'll see the whole spectrum, from Gucci and Ralph Lauren to Mötley Crüe T-shirts and tattoos—it's a melting pot.

DINING

It's no surprise Carnival's on top of the industry's ever-evolving dining trends, offering casual alternative dining in lieu of the main restaurant fleetwide as well as 24-hour pizza, soft ice cream, and even a **sushi bar** on the *Elation* and *Paradise.* There are specialty coffee bars and patisseries on the *Elation, Paradise, Destiny,* and *Triumph,* selling highbrow goodies for about $2 to $5 a pop, and caviar and champagne combos are now available in certain bars fleetwide. There's a gala **midnight buffet** once a week, and other nights, a crêpes buffet is offered (Carnival seems to be upping the ante in the sophistication department).

Overall, it's no secret that the quality and presentation of Carnival's food has improved over the years and now is on par with Royal Caribbean, Princess, and Holland America—and, dare I say, not so far from Celebrity's. Expect all-American favorites like surf-and-turf, prime rib, and rib-eye steaks, as well as lots of pasta dishes, grilled salmon and broiled halibut, Thai pork, lamb dishes, and Thanksgiving turkey served with all the trimmings. There are also healthier **"Nautica Spa" options** on each menu as well as **vegetarian choices.**

Carnival's Vacation Guarantee

Introduced in 1996, Carnival's Vacation Guarantee program continues to make one of the boldest claims in the cruise industry: It stipulates that guests who are dissatisfied with their cruise may disembark at their first non-U.S. port of call and, subject to some restrictions, get a refund for the unused portion of their cruise contract and reimbursement for coach-class air transport back to their ship's home port. To qualify, passengers must inform the ship's purser before their first port of call.

Does this mean Carnival is confident of its product? You bet. And because the company seems poised for gathering increased market share with every mega-vessel it launches, its confidence seems fully justified.

Except for the *Tropicale,* all Carnival ships have two main dining rooms, each with two seatings for each of the day's three meals (breakfast, lunch, and dinner), with tables seating 4 to 12. Dining is a bustling, social affair, and hundreds of passengers line up early outside the doors, eager to get in (that said, the dining rooms are often not full because of all the other dining choices). Despite the hectic pace and ambience, **service** is consistently efficient and friendly, culminating in dessert time, when the lights are dimmed and the flashing neon is turned on to illuminate the waiters doing their nearly nightly song and dance routines. While the dining rooms in the post-1990 ships are especially appealing and even elegant, you still won't forget where you are. Waiter uniforms are a bit dowdy, and for you wine drinkers, don't expect a sommelier—a waiter handles the wine as well as the water. Butter is served in those little golden-wrapped pads, and cream for coffee comes on a plate of those little plastic diner-style containers. Cruise faux pas of the year goes to Carnival for making its waiters hawk the company's line of cookbooks at the table—keep the merchandise in the gift shops!

In keeping with the popular **alternative dining** trend that has swept the industry, guests aboard all Carnival ships can opt to have any meal in the **buffet-style Lido restaurants** (at no extra charge). For an unstructured and casual dinner, walk in any time between 6 and 9:30pm for tasty entrees like chicken, pasta, steaks, prime rib, swordfish steak, and stir fries when you simply don't want to face another meal in the main dining rooms. At lunch, buffets in the Lido feature the usual suspects—salads, meats, cheeses, pastas, grilled burgers, and chicken fillets, and several hot choices such as fish and chips, roast turkey and mashed potatoes, or stir fry. The buffets also feature specialty stations at lunch, serving up things like pasta or Chinese food or a Cajun fish dish. At times the buffet line gets backed up as passengers wait for bins to be restocked and servers scramble to fill them.

The most visible array of alternative options is aboard Carnival's mammoth *Destiny* and *Triumph,* which offers the attractive and dramatic two-level Galaxy and Universe dining rooms, with ocean views from both the main floor and the mezzanine level. Additionally, the *Destiny*'s casual Lido Sun and Sea restaurant and the *Triumph*'s South Beach Club restaurant each include a pair of **specialty food stations:** One features Italian and the other Chinese.

Pizza, Caesar salad, and garlic bread are available 24 hours a day, and the **self-serve soft ice cream** and frozen yogurt machine operates throughout the day.

All ships offer **24-hour room service** from a standardized menu of ho-hum staples, and kids can select from **children's menus.**

Cruise Trivia

On a typical weeklong Carnival cruise, a heck of a lot of food and drink are consumed. Here's a run-down of the gluttony: 6,000 pizzas, 2,000 steaks, 35,000 shrimp, 5,500 hamburgers, 41,660 eggs, 315 pounds of coffee, 1,800 bagels, 10,000 tomatoes, 10,080 bananas, 1,000 fresh pineapples, 18,200 soft drinks, 2,920 bottles of wine, 24,450 bottles of beer, and 600 bottles of rum. Dang!

ACTIVITIES

Never a dull moment—you can run from one activity to the next all day long if you want to. Carnival doesn't skimp in the keeping-busy department. By day, the main pool decks are the heart of the action, and between the blaring band and microphone-wielding social hosts whipping up interest in a pillow-fighting competition or belly-flop contest, you'll barely be able to hear yourself think. Lest things get too out of hand, uniformed security guards watch over the pool deck and bars to make sure things stay safe. On the megas, it's a little quieter up on the second tier of the Sun Deck and all the ships have a quieter pool and sunbathing area at the stern, sans loudspeakers.

Slot machines begin whirring and clanging at 8am in the **casinos** when the ships are at sea, and before lunch even starts waiters and waitresses in bright pink and blue uniforms are tempting passengers with trays of fruity **theme cocktails.** There are line-dancing and ballroom classes, trivia contests, facial and hairdo demonstrations, singles and newlywed parties, game shows, shuffleboard, bingo, art auctions, and movies. Fleetwide, except aboard the *Tropicale,* you can even take **golf lessons** with the onboard pro ($40 per half hour and $70 per hour). Students whack balls into a golf net while a video camera is taping their technique; the pro goes over the lesson afterward. You can spend some time in the roomy **gyms** on the Fantasy- and Destiny-class ships (gyms are tiny afterthoughts on the four oldest ships) or treat yourself to one of dozens of relaxing treatments in the Steiner-managed **spas.**

Not surprisingly with this pace, you won't find any focus on quiet times, except in the handsome-looking, subdued **libraries** on each ship. And don't expect enrichment lectures on art or history or any other cerebral topic; Carnival's breed of activities are of the hearty fun and hands-on variety.

Incidentally, Carnival vessels have based part of their success on recognizing what adults want. Each ship posts a small but obvious sign at the bottom of stairs leading to one of the sun-flooded upper decks (usually near the stack) that reads, "Adults Only, Top Optional Sunbathing." I've rarely seen many takers, though—the area is usually deserted.

CHILDREN'S PROGRAM

Carnival is right up there with the best ships for families. In 1998, some 200,000 kids sailed on board Carnival ships. A few hundred children per cruise is pretty normal and there are as many as 700 to 800 on Christmas and New Year's cruises. On Carnival's post-1990 ships, the kids' facilities are fairly extensive, with the *Triumph, Destiny, Elation,* and *Paradise* offering the biggest and brightest **playrooms** in the fleet, stocked with computer stations, a climbing maze, 16-monitor video wall showing movies and cartoons, arts and crafts, and oodles of toys and games.

The newly revamped **Camp Carnival program** offers supervised kids' activities all day long for ages 2 through 15 in four different age groups: toddlers 2 to 5, juniors 6 to 8, intermediates 9 to 12, and teens 13 to 15. Nine to 12 **counselors** organize the fun and game, which include face painting, computer games, puzzles, fun with Play-Do, picture bingo, making pirate hats, and Coketail parties for toddlers. For juniors, there's Nintendo, computer games, ice-cream parties, story time and library visits, T-shirt coloring, and swimming, while for intermediates, there are scavenger hunts, trivia and bingo, Ping-Pong, arts and crafts, computer games, dance classes, and talent shows. Separate teen discos have been phased out (seems they just weren't popular), but interested teens can join in on karaoke parties, computer games, scavenger hunts, talent shows, card and trivia games, Ping-Pong, disco parties (in the adult disco before it opens at 10pm), and of course hang out in the video arcades (the newest ships have **virtual-reality games**).

As if that's not enough, the entire fleet has a **children's wading pool** and for bigger kids, there's that great signature snaking slide at the main pool.

Mom and dad can really have the evening to themselves on the week's two formal nights, when the counselors supervise **kid's mealtime** in the Lido restaurant between 6 and 7pm. A special section is reserved for the kids, featuring the classic favorites—hot dogs, hamburgers, French fries, chicken nuggets, and Jell-O. Then, like every night, more supervised children's activities kick in between 7 and 10pm. After that, although Carnival does not offer private baby-sitting, from 10pm to 3am each evening it has **group, slumber-party–style baby-sitting** available in the playroom for $5 per hour for the first child, $3 per hour for each additional child.

Cribs are available with prior notice.

ENTERTAINMENT

Even aboard its smaller, older ships, Carnival consistently offers the most lavish entertainment extravaganzas afloat. Aboard the newer roster of megaships, the cruise line has spent millions on stage sets, choreography, and acoustical equipment that leave many other floating theaters in the dust. The show lounges on the *Destiny* and *Triumph* are spectacular three-deck extravaganzas and the casinos so large you'll think you were already in San Juan.

Carnival megaships each carry 8 to 12 flamboyantly costumed dancers, complete with feathers, sequins, and towering headdresses, for twice-weekly **Vegas-style musicals.** One or two live soloists carry the musical part of the show, while the dancers lip-synch the chorus (sometimes so well that most people don't realize the dancers aren't actually singing). A **12- to 16-piece orchestra** of traditional and digital instruments deftly accompanies the acts each night. While they may not match the most sophisticated productions on the real Broadway, Carnival shows are pretty sensational.

You'll also find comedians, jugglers, acrobatics, rock-and-roll bands, country-western bands, classical string trios, pianists, and Dorsey– or Glenn Miller–style big bands, all performing, if not simultaneously, at least during the same cruise, and sometimes on the same night. Aboard *Carnival Destiny,* there are multiple **karaoke stations**—one for every table in the Apollo Bar—and teenage dance contests.

Besides the main show lounge, most entertainment happens somewhere along the indoor Main Street–like promenade. Called the "Something-or-Other Boulevard" or

Some Special Deals

AARP Discounts: AARP members receive a $200 discount per stateroom on cruises of 10 days or more, $100 on 7-day cruises, and $50 on 3- and 4-day Bahamas cruises.

"Roommate Rates": Carnival will house up to four adults of the same gender in a cabin for $780 each on some 7-day cruises. Consult your travel agent for the most current special deals.

Carnival Fleet Itineraries

Ship	Home Ports & Season	Itinerary	Other Itineraries
Carnival Destiny	Miami, itineraries alternate weekly, year-round.	**7-night eastern Carib:** San Juan, St. Croix, and St. Thomas. **7-night western Carib:** Playa del Carmen/Cozumel, Grand Cayman, and Ocho Rios (Jamaica).	New England/ Canada
Carnival Triumph	Miami, itineraries alternate weekly, year-round.	**7-night eastern Carib:** San Juan, St. Croix, and St. Thomas. **7-night western Carib:** Playa del Carmen/Cozumel, Grand Cayman, and Ocho Rios (Jamaica).	None
Celebration	New Orleans, year-round.	**7-night western Carib:** Grand Cayman, Playa del Carmen/Cozumel, and Montego Bay (Jamaica).	None
Ecstasy	Miami, both itineraries offered each week, year-round.	**3-night:** Nassau. **4-night:** Key West, and Playa del Carmen/Cozumel.	None
Fantasy	Port Canaveral, both itineraries offered each week, year-round.	**3-night:** Nassau. **4-night:** Nassau and Freeport.	None
Fascination	San Juan, year-round.	**7-night eastern Carib:** St. Thomas, Sint Maarten, Dominica, Barbados, and Martinique.	None
Imagination	Miami, itineraries alternate weekly, year-round.	**4-night western Carib:** Key West, and Cozumel/Playa del Carmen. **5-night western Carib:** Grand Cayman, Calica/Cancún or Grand Cayman, and Ocho Rios (Jamaica).	None
Inspiration	San Juan, round-trip, itineraries alternate year-round.	**7-night southern Carib 1:** St. Thomas, Antigua, Guadeloupe, and Aruba. **7-night southern Carib 2:** St. Thomas, St. Lucia, Curaçao, and Aruba.	None
Jubilee	Miami, Nov–Mar.	**10-night eastern & southern Carib:** Tortola, Martinique, Barbados, St. Lucia, and St. Thomas. **11-night western & southern Carib:** Aruba, Cartagena, San Blas Islands (Panama), Panama Canal, Puerto Limón (Costa Rica), and Key West.	Alaska (May–Sept)
Paradise	Miami, itineraries alternate weekly, year-round.	**7-night eastern Carib:** San Juan, Tortola, and St. Thomas. **7-night western Carib:** Cozumel/ Playa del Carmen, Grand Cayman, and Ocho Rios (Jamaica).	None
Sensation	Tampa, year-round	**7-night eastern Carib:** Grand Cayman, Playa del Carmen/Cozumel, and New Orleans.	None
Tropicale	Tampa, itineraries alternate weekly, year-round.	**4-night western Carib:** Key West and Playa del Carmen/Cozumel. **5-night western Carib:** Grand Cayman and Playa del Carmen/Cozumel.	None

"Something-or-Other Way," it stretches along one entire side of each ship and is lined with just about the ships' entire repertoire of nightclubs, bars, lounges, patisseries, and the disco and casino.

By day, entertainment includes a Caribbean-style **calypso** or **steel-drum band** performing Bob Marley and other pop songs on a deck poolside, and often a pianist or string trio playing in one of the lounges.

SERVICE

Service is professional, but tends to be brisk at times. It's clear your dining room waiter and cabin stewards have a lot of work ahead of them, and there's little time for much chitchat. There always seem to be plenty of drink waiters and waitresses roaming the pool decks, though, looking to score some drink orders.

All in all, a Carnival ship is a well-oiled machine, and you'll certainly get what you need—but not much more. When you board the ship, for instance, you're welcomed by a polite and well-meaning staff at the gangway, given a diagram of the ship's layout, and then pointed in the right direction to find your cabin. Unfortunately, if you're laden with carry-on luggage and disoriented by the vessel's vast size, you might get lost looking for your cabin or have a long wait for a crowded elevator.

It's a fact of life aboard mega-liners like Carnival's that service is simply not as attentive as aboard smaller vessels. For instance, lines can get long at the breakfast and lunch buffets and, at certain times, at the pizza counter.

There is a **laundry service** on board each ship (for washing and pressing only) that charges by the piece, as well as a handful of **self-service laundry rooms** with irons and coin-operated washing machines and dryers. Dry cleaning is not available.

Celebration • Jubilee

The Verdict

Fun ships, yes, but these older Carnival ships seem outdated and frumpy compared to their slick, glamorous Fantasy-class sisters.

Jubilee *(photo: Carnival Cruise Lines)*

Specifications

Size (in tons)	47,262	Crew	670 (Internat'l)
Number of Cabins	743	Passenger/Crew Ratio	2.2 to 1
Number of Outside Cabins	453	Year Built	
Cabins with Verandas	10	*Celebration*	1987
Number of Passengers	1,486	*Jubilee*	1986
Officers	Italian/Internat'l	Last Major Refurbishment	1999

Frommer's Ratings (Scale of 1–5)

Cabin Comfort & Amenities	4	Pool, Fitness & Spa Facilities	2
Ship Cleanliness & Maintenance	4	Children's Facilities	3
Public Comfort/Space	3	Itinerary	4
Decor	4	Worth the Money	4

While this pair of mid-1980s sisters can't compare with their new post-1990 sisters in the style and amenities departments, they still successfully offer that wild and crazy brand of Carnival fun. If you like smaller ships (these are half the size of the *Destiny* and

Triumph, but they're still not *small* in any normal sense) and don't mind fewer high-tech bells and whistles, you'll find these ships more intimate and easier to explore than a megaship.

The decors of these medium-sized twins encompass all the colors of the rainbow, with healthy doses of brass and mirrors, and can be a bit jarring.

There is no atrium and the Pool Decks feel cramped at high noon and can get crowded.

Recent refurbishments on the *Jubilee* included replacing hot tubs with new models; installing new carpeting, tile, counters, and equipment for the Funnel Bar & Grill Lido restaurant; and adding a new video-game arcade and a photo gallery. At press time, the *Celebration* was scheduled for a round of refurbishments by year-end 1999.

CABINS Like the standard cabins on the entire Carnival fleet, they're big. Beige with red and black accents, decor is nothing to write home about. But the identical rooms (save the suites, of course) with their blond wood tones and accoutrements are clean and uncluttered. Like the rest of the fleet, beds can be configured as twins or doubles, according to your romantic inclinations, and each cabin has piped-in stereo music as well as a wall-mounted TV that broadcasts films through most of the day and night. The medium-sized bathrooms have showers.

The 10 suites on the Veranda Deck of each ship are as large and comfortable as those offered aboard vessels charging a lot more. Each has a whirlpool tub and shower, an L-shaped sofa that converts into a foldaway bed, a safe, minibar, walk-in closet, and sliding glass doors leading to a private balcony.

About a dozen cabins are wheelchair accessible.

Cabins & Rates						
Cabins	Per diems from	Bathtub	Fridge	Hair Dryer	Sitting Area	TV
Inside	$100	no	no	no	no	yes
Outside	$110	no	no	no	no	yes
Suite	$265	yes	yes	no	yes	yes

PUBLIC AREAS You may need to keep on your sunglasses even when you're inside the ship: Public areas explode with color in that outrageous Carnival way. We're talking lots of red, black, fuchsia, chrome, brass, glass, and neon. There's a bar designed like the inside of a trolley car and the Red Hot Piano Bar is just that—all red. In all, there are seven bars, six entertainment lounges, a casino, disco, library, card room, and video arcade. There's also a children's playroom, beauty salon, boutiques, and a small infirmary with a doctor and nurse on call. Elevators interconnect all eight decks.

POOL, FITNESS & SPA FACILITIES When the *Celebration* and *Jubilee* were built in the mid-80s, fitness wasn't the priority it is today, and—as aboard most ships of their age—it shows. The gyms are tiny afterthoughts with no more than a couple of treadmills, a stair machine or two, some free weights, and really low ceilings (I'm 5'10" and I had to hunch over a bit). There's an equally tiny spa and a sauna each for men and women. The hair salons are also small, relegated to the bowels of the ship in a windowless room not much bigger than most cabins.

There are three pools, including a small wading pool for children.

Carnival Destiny • Triumph • Victory (preview)

The Verdict

The biggest and most stunning in the fleet, these behemoths capture the classic Carnival neon and flash with mind-boggling design features.

Carnival Destiny *(photo: Carnival Cruise Lines)*

Specifications

Size (in tons)		Number of Passengers	
Destiny	101,353	*Destiny*	2,642
Triumph	102,000	*Triumph*	2,758
Victory	102,000	*Victory*	2,758
Number of Cabins		Officers	Italian/Internat'l
Destiny	1,321	Crew	1,000 (Internat'l)
Triumph	1,379	Passenger/Crew Ratio	2.6 to 1
Victory	1,379	Year Built	
Number of Outside Cabins		*Destiny*	1996
Destiny	806	*Triumph*	1999
Triumph	853	*Victory*	2000
Victory	853	Last Major Refurbishment	N/A
Cabins with Verandas			
Destiny	480		
Triumph	508		
Victory	508		

Frommer's Ratings (Scale of 1–5)

Cabin Comfort & Amenities	5	Pool, Fitness & Spa Facilities	5
Ship Cleanliness & Maintenance	4	Children's Facilities	5
Public Comfort/Space	4	Itinerary	4
Decor	5	Worth the Money	5

Late in 1996, Carnival inaugurated its largest ship to date, the 101,000-ton *Destiny,* and less than 3 years later it rolled out her 102,000-ton sister ship *Triumph,* which is scheduled to debut in July of 1999, while this book is going to press. The *Triumph* will be nearly identical to the *Destiny,* but a tad larger (with an additional deck at top) and reconfigured in a few minor ways. A third sister, *Victory,* is set to launch in late summer of 2000 and will be most similar to the *Triumph.* Taller than the Statue of Liberty, the ships cost a staggering $400 and $415 million to construct and carry 2,642 passengers based on double occupancy and 3,400 with every berth filled. The *Destiny* was the first cruise ship ever built to exceed 100,000 tons, and its sheer size and spaciousness inspired the cruise industry to build more in this league: Since its debut, Princess launched the 109,000 *Grand Princess* and Royal Caribbean is set to launch the massive 142,000 *Voyager of the Seas.*

Carnival plans on launching two more *Destiny* sisters, the *Carnival Conquest* and *Glory,* for a total of five. They're scheduled to enter the market in the fall of 2002 and summer of 2003, respectively.

Cabins & Rates						
Cabins	Per diems from	Bathtub	Fridge	Hair Dryer	Sitting Area	TV
Inside	$136	no	no	yes	no	yes
Outside	$154	no	no	yes	yes	yes
Suite	$347	yes	yes	yes	yes	yes

CABINS It would make sense that the biggest ships have the biggest cabins. Standard outside cabins are 220 square feet (and some are 260 square feet) compared to the Fantasy-class standard cabins, which are already big enough at about 190 square feet. Inside cabins on the *Destiny* and *Triumph* are a bit smaller than the outside ones, measuring 185 square feet (still quite large). More than 60% of the cabins on these ships offer ocean views, and some 60% of them have private balconies and sitting areas. Of the *Destiny*'s 806 outside cabins (and the *Triumph*'s 853), there are some 480 private verandas, and 508 on the *Triumph!* That's compared to a paltry 54 private verandas on the 618 outside cabins on the Fantasy-class ships.

Unlike the rest of Carnival's fleet, the major entertainment and recreation decks on these ships are sandwiched between accommodation decks, with, from the bottom up, two decks of staterooms followed by three public decks, then three more decks of staterooms and suites (with all the outside accommodations on these decks featuring balconies), topped by two decks that are divided between public areas, staterooms, and suites. This design centrally locates the indoor entertainment and recreation facilities for all guests (being that the ships are so dang huge), regardless of cabin location, and also allows for unobstructed views from dozens of balconied staterooms and suites.

There are two categories of suites: veranda suites measuring a mammoth 340 square feet and penthouse suites where you can live like the Sultan of Brunei with 430 square feet, which is roomy indeed. Both are located on deck 7, smack dab in the middle of the ship. Specially designed family staterooms, at a modest 230 square feet (which is comfortable, but not roomy), offer connecting cabins located convenient to children's facilities. In lieu of a private veranda, these family-friendly staterooms feature floor-to-ceiling windows for ocean views. All standard cabins have a TV, safe, hair dryer, desk, dresser, one chair and a stool, and a bath with shower. The *Destiny* and *Triumph* are the only ships in the fleet to have hair dryers in the cabins.

A total of 25 cabins on the *Destiny* and 29 on the *Triumph* (all on the Upper, Empress, Veranda, Lido, and Panorama Decks) are wheelchair accessible.

PUBLIC AREAS Carnival interior designer Joe Farcus never had so much public space to play with, and he took full advantage. The ships are dominated by staggering nine-deck atria with casual bars on the ground level, and the three-deck-high showrooms are a sight—the *Destiny* was the first of this magnitude on any cruise ship. The ships' mondo casinos span some 9,000 square feet and feature 324 slot machines and 23 table games. In addition, the Virtual World electronic game center features high-tech virtual reality that's so vivid that coming back to the real world is sometimes a disappointment. A photography studio enables passengers to make appointments for portrait taking; photographs can be digitally enhanced and a variety of photo-related souvenirs are sold. It's ideal for honeymooners.

The two-level discos are dazzling, dimly lit dens of dancing, of the likes you'd find in happening metropolises like New York City. The Sports Bar on each ship boasts multiple TV monitors projecting different sporting events simultaneously.

On the *Triumph,* a new gathering place was created by arranging the seating near the Vienna Cafe in a configuration that opens it up to both the cafe itself and the adjacent promenade, making it more like a real cafe.

There's a large number of shopping boutiques, a spacious beauty salon, library, card room, and well over a dozen bars and entertainment lounges. Both have several, self-service coin-operated laundry rooms.

Bottom line: You'll certainly get a workout making your way from room to room on these mammoth ships.

POOL, FITNESS & SPA FACILITIES   They are the most generous among the Carnival vessels, with four pools (including a kids' wading pool), seven whirlpools, and a 214-foot, two-deck-high corkscrew-shaped water slide pouring passengers in to the main pool below.

The tiered decks of the sprawling midships Lido pool area provide optimal viewing of the band and stage, pool games, and all the hubbub that happens in this busy part of the ship. Along with two whirlpools, the *Destiny* has swim-up bars at two of its main pools; the *Triumph* eliminated the swim-up bars in exchange for more deck space, larger pools, and the addition of a wading area a few inches deep surrounding the two pools. The aft pool area on both ships features two whirlpools and a retractable glass roof that covers it all, enabling deck activities and entertainment to continue even in rainy weather.

On the *Triumph,* the big stage adjacent to the main Continent pool is even bigger than the one on *Carnival Destiny,* and it has been reconfigured to allow more space for guests at deck parties, and to make the pool deck more open and visually appealing. Another modification is the placement of a small performance stage aft on Lido Deck near the New World pool.

The ships' huge health and fitness facilities are second in size only to Royal Caribbean's *Voyager of the Seas.* The 2-deck-high, 15,000-square-foot Nautica Spa health and fitness center on the *Destiny* and *Triumph* feature more than 40 state-of-the-art exercise machines, including virtual-reality stationary bikes. As you pedal, a peaceful landscape unfolds before you. There's a juice bar, men's and women's sauna and steam room, and a whirlpool-like hydrotherapy tub whose bubbling waters are loaded with extracts of seaweed and rejuvenating oils.

The adjacent children's facilities can't be topped. The 2-deck-high, 1,300-square-foot indoor and outdoor play center has its own pool and is out of the fray of the main pool deck areas. The well-stocked play area not only has toys and games, but pop-a-shot basketball, air hockey, pool, and Ping-Pong. The ships also have virtual-reality video arcades that promise hours of fun.

Ecstasy • Fantasy • Fascination • Imagination • Inspiration • Paradise • Sensation

The Verdict

These time-tested favorites are the line's original megas, and their whimsical decor and endless entertainment and activity options spell excitement from the get-go.

Fantasy *(photo: Carnival Cruise Lines)*

Specifications

Size (in tons)	70,367	Year Built	
Number of Cabins	1,020	*Ecstasy*	1991
Number of Outside Cabins	618	*Fantasy*	1990
Cabins with Verandas	26	*Fascination*	1994
Number of Passengers	2,040	*Imagination*	1995
Officers	Italian/Internat'l	*Inspiration*	1996
Crew	920 (Internat'l)	*Paradise*	1998
Passenger/Crew Ratio	2.2 to 1	*Sensation*	1993
		Last Major Refurbishment	N/A

Frommer's Ratings (Scale of 1–5)

Cabin Comfort & Amenities	5	Pool, Fitness & Spa Facilities	5
Ship Cleanliness & Maintenance	4	Children's Facilities	4
Public Comfort/Space	4	Itinerary	5
Decor	5	Worth the Money	5

These Fun Ships and their somewhat risqué names offer a successful combination of hands-on fun and a glamorous, fantasy-land decor, with acres of teak decking plus all the diversions, distractions, and entertainment options for which Carnival is famous.

Each of the eight ships was built at a cost of between $225 and $300 million at the Kvaerner Masa shipyard in Helsinki, Finland, between 1990 and 1998. Each is identical in size (70,367 tons), profile, and onboard amenities (with a few exceptions), but each ship's unique personalities shine through the combination of Carnival-style colors, decors, wall hangings, artwork, and themes created by legendary Carnival designer Joe Farcus.

From the first ship of the series, the *Fantasy,* to the last, the *Paradise,* the ships evolved to a mellower state, with muted shades of copper, teal, gold, and deep red replacing the shocking primary reds, yellows, and blues. Following the lead of the *Destiny,* the *Elation* and *Paradise* did away with hulking atria statues and instead offer a casual lobby bar in their place, making the area a more useful meeting place and hub.

The decor of the *Fantasy,* with a geometric, urban-metropolis kind of feel, is a tiny bit ragged and tired. Nevertheless, it has all the electric colors you expect from the line, and a full 15 miles of neon tubes to boot, so there's no mistaking that it's a Carnival cruise you're on.

Aboard the *Imagination,* miles of fiber-optic cable make the mythical and classical artwork glow in ways the Greek, Roman, and Assyrian designers of the originals never would have imagined. Medusas and winged Mercuries adorn the public areas, and the eclectic library contains copies of the columns Bernini added to St. Peter's Basilica in

Rome. Although the ship has miles and miles of neon, it's more muted here, the feeling more elegant.

For its inspiration, *Inspiration* turns to styles exemplified by such artists and artisans as Toulouse-Lautrec, Fabergé, Frank Lloyd Wright, and Tiffany. The most striking part of this design is in the Brasserie Café, with its twisting tubes of lavender-colored aluminum illuminated by backlit stained glass and neon. Designer Joe Farcus saw these tubes as a fanciful interpretation of the flowers and vines adorning Métro stops in Paris. Another Carnival-like touch is the guitar-shaped rock 'n' roll dance club where closed-circuit TV cameras broadcast the dance floor antics to dozens of color monitors around the room.

The *Ecstasy* features a city-scene motif, with one lounge built around an antique Rolls Royce and another around neon-bedecked skyscraper sculptures. The *Fascination* borrows heavily from Broadway and Hollywood movie-star legends and features head-turning life-sized mannequins of famous legends like John Wayne and Marilyn Monroe, whereas the *Sensation* avoids an obvious razzle-dazzle in favor of artwork enhanced with ultraviolet lighting, sound, and color. Even some of the surfaces in bars were selected to celebrate textures and the sense of touch.

The *Paradise* is just that if you're a nonsmoker. Launched in 1998, the ship, with a decor in some rooms vaguely reminiscent of the great Atlantic ocean liners, is one of the industry's only two completely smoke-free ships (Renaissance Cruises' Mediterranean-bound *R1* is the other). There is no lighting up anywhere aboard for passengers or crew, not even on the open decks, and Carnival isn't shy about pointing out the penalties dished out if you get caught trying: In addition to a $250 fine, all law-breakers will be asked to disembark the ship at the next port of call and fly home at their own expense. By early 1999, 9 passengers and 11 crew members had already been discharged. Non-smokers will absolutely love the *Paradise.* You'll notice that apparently smoking and drinking really do go hand and hand, though, because the bars and discos on the *Paradise* are noticeably less bustling and some are deserted way earlier in the evening than they would ever be on other Carnival ships. As quoted in *CruiseWeek,* an industry newsletter, Carnival president Bob Dickinson explained why, unfortunately, he thought the nonsmoking *Paradise* brings in less bar and casino revenues: "The better the education, the lower the alcohol consumption, the lower the gambling. That's just the way it is—smarter people smoke less, smarter people gamble less." Hmmm, looks like the line will think twice before ever launching a second smoke-free ship for those smarty-pants!

Anyway, despite a perceived preponderance of brainy teetotalers, the *Paradise* is actually still fun, fun, fun, in that famous Carnival way, even if it is a tad mellower than the rest of the fleet. It boasts some novelties like a complimentary sushi bar open late afternoons.

Cabins & Rates

Cabins	Per diems from	Bathtub	Fridge	Hair Dryer	Sitting Area	TV
Inside	$114*	no	no	no	no	yes
Outside	$130*	no	no	no	no	yes
Suite	$279*	yes	yes	no	yes	yes

Rates for 3- and 4-night itineraries will be cheaper. See Appendix A for details.

CABINS As with the entire fleet, standard cabins on the Fantasy Class ships are roomy at 190 square feet and are neat, tidy, and minimalist in design, with stained oak trim accents and conventional, monochromatic colors like salmon red—subdued compared to the flamboyance of the public areas. Not big on personality, the cabins are functional and well laid out.

Accommodations range from lower-deck 185-square-foot inside cabins with lower and upper berths to large suites with verandas, king-sized beds, sitting areas, and balconies. There are 26 demisuites and 28 suites, all 54 with private verandas. The 28 suites each have a whirlpool tub and shower, an L-shaped sofa that converts into a foldaway bed, a whirlpool bath, a safe, minibar, walk-in closet, and sliding glass doors leading to their private balcony, and are positioned midway between stern and bow, on a middle deck subject to the least tossing and rocking during rough weather.

All cabins, even the least expensive inside ones, have enough storage space to accommodate a reasonably diverse wardrobe and feature safes, TVs, desk and stool, chair, reading lights for each bed, bathrooms with roomy showers and generous-sized mirrored cabinets to store your toiletries.

There are about 20 cabins on each ship for disabled passengers.

PUBLIC AREAS   Each megaship in the Fantasy Class boasts the same configuration of decks, public lounges, and entertainment venues. Each ship contains a six-story atrium flanked by glass-sided elevators, plus two big-windowed dining rooms and all the options you could want for drinking, dancing, flirting, and hot-tubbing. The line's casinos are some of the largest afloat, each with a different decorative theme. Each vessel contains at least eight bars, where you might allow your emotions to go with a flow that ranges from convivial and sometimes slightly manic to subdued, soothing, reflective, and contemplative. There are at least several whirlpool tubs scattered about the ships, but good luck squeezing in—they're usually packed solid. The cluster of shops on each ship is surprisingly cramped and won't be winning any design awards.

Each has several self-service, coin-operated laundry rooms.

POOL, FITNESS & SPA FACILITIES   Although nothing special in the decor department (did Joe Farcus forget about this area?), the 12,000-square-foot Nautica Spas have everything you'll need to stay fit and healthy. Each has a roomy, separate, mirrored aerobics room and a large windowed Pepto Bismol–colored gym with (last time I counted) seven treadmills, five stationary bikes, two rowing machines, two step machines, and dozens of free weights. Each has a men's and women's locker room and sauna and steam room, as well as whirlpools and three swimming pools. The Sun Deck of each ship offers an unobstructed $^1/_8$-mile jogging track covered with a rubberized surface.

Tropicale

The Verdict

Intimate and classic but also old, small, and obviously outmoded, the *Tropicale* struggles hard to compete with the array of amenities and facilities aboard the line's larger, modern ships.

Tropicale *(photo: Carnival Cruise Lines)*

Specifications

Size (in tons)	36,674	Officers	Italian
Number of Cabins	511	Crew	550 (International)
Number of Outside Cabins	324	Passenger/Crew Ratio	1.9 to 1
Cabins with Verandas	12	Year Built	1982
Number of Passengers	1,022	Last Major Refurbishment	1998

Frommer's Ratings (Scale of 1–5)

Cabin Comfort & Amenities	4	Pool, Fitness & Spa Facilities	2
Ship Cleanliness & Maintenance	4	Children's Facilities	3
Public Comfort/Space	4	Itinerary	5
Decor	4	Worth the Money	4

In the fast-paced world of the cruise industry, a vessel that debuts as a star can quickly become yesterday's has-been—but there's always some nostalgic and loyal folks to keep carrying its banner. Such is the case with *Tropicale,* the oldest ship in Carnival's repertoire, and the one with the best-established pedigree. The first all-new ship ever commissioned by the then-fledging Carnival Cruise Lines, its construction began in 1978, and delivery to a then-skeptical marketplace occurred $3^1/2$ years later.

In many ways, its debut was a savvy reflection of the waves of things to come: In the year of its construction, its weight of nearly 37,000 tons (bulky and ponderous by cruise ship standards of the day) was considered larger than market conditions would easily bear. Soon enough, though, *Tropicale* was breaking sales records throughout the cruise ship industry, and in the '80s was the venue for hard-partying cruises whose texture and flavor eventually evolved into the mega-million-dollar Carnival image.

In 1998, the *Tropicale* underwent some substantial refurbishments, including putting in a new granite floor, seating, lighting and sound system in Dance Club disco; new chairs and carpeting in the dining room; and a new video arcade. Still, the ship has long since been surpassed in size, glamour, and stylishness by Carnival's other vessels, and observers get the definite feeling that *Tropicale*'s days with the line are numbered. Until it's finally auctioned off somewhere, though, expect a serviceable and amiable if somewhat battered ship that's seen more hard-party action than a houseful of graduating frat boys. Also look for the embryonic beginnings of design features that were later expanded and improved upon during Carnival's adolescent years, including a T-shaped (or whale-tailed) smokestack where fumes are vented high overhead and then off to either side.

Cabins & Rates

Cabins	Per diems from	Bathtub	Fridge	Hair Dryer	Sitting Area	TV
Inside	$113	no	no	no	no	yes
Outside	$128	no	no	no	no	yes
Suite	$245	yes	yes	no	yes	yes

CABINS Like the rest of the Carnival fleet, most cabins are spacious but utilitarian in design. Inside cabins aboard *Tropicale,* however, measure 170 square feet—slightly less than most of their inside equivalents aboard such Fantasy Class ships as the *Sensation* and *Inspiration.* There are a dozen suites, each with a private veranda. Most beds can be converted into either kings or twins, and a number of cabins have bunk-style third and fourth berths. All cabins have stereos, TVs, and wall safes. For obvious noise reasons, you might want to think twice about booking the cabins that abut the children's playroom, aft on the Empress Deck.

There are 23 cabins configured for disabled passengers.

PUBLIC AREAS The dining room on board this ship lies down at the water line (as opposed to more modern ships, which perch their dining rooms on one of the higher decks) and has no windows. Other than that, you'll find scaled-down versions of many of the features from other Carnival ships, including a corkscrew-shaped water slide and a piano bar whose decorative motif was inspired by the ebony and ivory keys of a piano. The Boiler Room Bar & Grill lido restaurant, for alternative dining, is brightly painted and fitted with jarringly exposed industrial-looking pipes inspired by the exterior of the Centre Pompidou in Paris. The casino is a cozy, smaller version of the mammoth gaming areas aboard larger Carnival ships. The ship's Exta-Z disco features a dance floor crafted from thick slabs of tempered glass, through which psychedelic lights shimmer and twirl as the beat goes on.

There is also a library, children's playroom, video-game room, and a volleyball court.

POOL, FITNESS & SPA FACILITIES   The *Tropicale* has scaled-down versions of the facilities aboard Carnival's larger ships. The spa, gym, and hair salon are tiny. There are men's and women's saunas and three outside swimming pools, including one kids' wading pool.

Safety at Sea?

In July of 1999, in connection with a lawsuit by a former employee, Carnival admitted that its crew members had been accused of sexually assaulting passengers or fellow workers 108 times in the five-year period between August 1993 and August 1998. Of that total, 22 of the assaults were reported as rapes, 28 were described as kisses, and the rest involved touching or other "advances." Over five years, this translates to about 1.8 accusations per month for every 120,000 passengers (Carnival's 14 ships carry approximately 2,000 passengers each on at least four cruises a month). The national media, from the *New York Times* to the *ABC Nightly News,* reported these numbers and questioned the safety of cruising. Because cruise ships are registered in foreign countries (nearly all cruise ships are, not just Carnival's) and sail in international waters, they are not required to report all accusations of crimes to the United States' authorities. As a result of this incident, however, the 16 members of the International Council of Cruise Lines changed their policies so ships sailing from U.S. ports will now report all crimes to the FBI.

Should you be worried about going on a cruise? No, but you should be as smart as you would at any resort or nightclub, especially on a more party-oriented cruise line like Carnival. It's not a good idea to ever go with a crew member or officer back to their cabin for any reason, and of course if anything inappropriate happens anywhere on ship, report it immediately to the security officer (which all the big ships have) or another top officer.

Celebrity Cruises

SHIPS   **Century • Galaxy • Horizon • Mercury • Zenith**

1050 Caribbean Way, Miami, FL 33132. ☎ **800/327-6700** or 305/539-6000. Fax 800/722-5329. www.celebrity-cruises.com.

THE LINE IN A NUTSHELL   The best of two worlds: If you like elegance without stuffiness, fun without bad taste, and pampering without a high price, Celebrity is king.

THE EXPERIENCE   With the most elegant big ships in the industry, Celebrity's entire fleet offers the best of both worlds: a refined cruise experience, yet one that is fun and active. The *Century, Galaxy,* and *Mercury,* near triplets built in the mid to late '90s, are bold, cutting-edge, and high-tech megaships, while the mid-sized *Zenith* and *Horizon,* virtual twins built in the early '90s, are more understated and traditional in their design.

Each of the ships is spacious, glamorous, and comfortable, mixing sleekly modern and vaguely art deco styles and throwing in an astoundingly cutting-edge art collection to boot. Their genteel service is exceptional: Staff members are exceedingly polite and professional, and contribute greatly to the elegant mood. Dining-wise, Celebrity shines, offering innovative cuisine that's a cut above what's offered by all the other mid-market lines.

Like all the big-ship lines, Celebrity offers lots for its passengers to do, but its focus on mellower pursuits and innovative programming set it apart. Niceties such as roving a cappella bands and magicians who sidle up to your table to entertain during pre- or after-dinner drinks lend a warmly personal touch, while seminars on personal investing and handwriting analysis offer a little more cerebral meat than the usual fare.

Celebrity gets the "best of" nod in a lot of categories: The AquaSpas on the line's megaships are the best at sea, the art collections fleetwide the most compelling, the cigar bars the most plush, and the onboard activities among the most varied. Celebrity pampers suite guests with butler service, and treats all guests to in-cabin pizza delivery.

Pros

- **Spectacular spas and gyms.** Beautiful to look at and well-stocked, the spas and gyms on the *Century, Galaxy,* and *Mercury* are the best at sea today.
- **Fabulous food.** Consistently high-rated cuisine is tops in the mass-market and premium segment of the industry.
- **Innovative everything.** Its entertainment, art, cigar bars, service, spas, and cuisine are some of the most innovative in the industry.

Cons

- **Sort-of-private verandas.** Most of the huge Sky suite verandas on the *Century, Galaxy,* and *Mercury* are exposed to the public decks above (keep that robe on!).

Frommer's Ratings: Celebrity Cruises

	Poor	Fair	Good	Excellent	Outstanding
Enjoyment Factor					✓
Dining					✓
Activities					✓
Children's Program			✓		
Entertainment				✓	
Service					✓
Overall Value					✓

CELEBRITY: THE BEST OF TWO WORLDS

Celebrity is one of those rare companies that lives up to its advertising: As the song in its commercial says, it's "simply the best" for moderately priced cruises that feel like they should cost a lot more.

Celebrity's roots go back to the powerful Greek shipping family Chandris, whose patriarch John D. Chandris founded a cargo shipping company in 1915. The family expanded into the cruise business in the 1960s with the down-market Fantasy Cruises, a line that served mostly the European market, and in 1989 pushed into the Caribbean marketplace in a big, big way by creating Celebrity Cruises. The company's rise to prominence was so rapid and so successful that in 1997 it was courted and acquired by the larger and wealthier Royal Caribbean Cruises, Ltd., which now operates Celebrity as a sister line to Royal Caribbean International. So far it's been a fortuitous marriage: Reservations, bookkeeping, maintenance, and provisioning were merged, but Celebrity has maintained its own very fine identity, offering a product that's among the best in the cruise industry.

THE FLEET

With their crisp navy-blue and white hulls and rakishly angled funnel decorated with a giant *X* (actually the Greek letter for *ch,* as in *Chandris,* the line's founding family), the profiles of Celebrity's ships rank among the industry's most distinctive. Especially striking are the design of their rear decks, tiered in dramatically rising increments upward and forward, like the terraces in a formal garden, and their bows, steeply pitched toward the water and flowing smoothly up into the ships' superstructures, suggesting both speed and grace.

As the line never tires of pointing out, it has among the youngest fleets in the industry, all of its ships having been built since 1990. It's a comment on the founding vision of the line that its oldest ships, the 1,354-guest *Horizon* and 1,375-guest *Zenith,* look practically as modern and innovative today as they did when they were introduced, and that the megaships that followed, the 1,750-guest *Century* and the 1,870-guest *Galaxy* and *Mercury,* retain many of the same design features as their younger sisters. There's no mistaking which line these ships sail for.

All of the line's ships spend at least half of each year in the Caribbean, and its *Zenith* sails Bermuda itineraries from New York in the summer and fall.

And there's more new ships on the way: Celebrity has four more ships in the works, called the **Millennium class.** The 2,000-passenger, 91,000-ton vessels (the first of which will be named—what else?—*Millennium*), unnamed at press time, are slated for delivery in June 2000, January 2001, August 2001, and April 2002, and will be very much in the Celebrity tradition, featuring large staterooms, innovative spa facilities, cigar bars, and a continued focus on fine dining, plus expanded worldwide itineraries. The ships are being built at the Chantiers de l'Atlantique shipyard in St. Nazaire, France.

PASSENGER PROFILE

Celebrity vessels attract a wide range of ages and backgrounds, although the common denominator among passengers is that they want a toned-down, elegant brand of fun cruise, with lots of activities and a glamorous, exciting atmosphere, yet not *too* wild and nutty. They're smack dab in between the Carnival crowd and the Seabourn set. The line focuses on middle- to upper-middle-income cruisers, although a handful of discreetly wealthy patrons might be on any given cruise or, conversely, a small-business owner, school teacher, police officer, or restaurant manager. Most of the clientele give the impression of being prosperous but not obscenely rich, well behaved but not above a hearty laugh at the dress-your-husband-up-in-women's-clothes act featured on one recent cruise.

Much of the clientele hails from the East Coast, and most are couples in their 30s on up, with decent numbers of honeymooners and couples celebrating anniversaries, as well as children (the line carried just over 35,000 in 1998). Many have cruised before.

DINING

Celebrity has poured lots of time and money into creating a culinary format that consistently provides well-orchestrated, well-presented, and good-tasting meals to thousands of seagoing diners.

In the mid-1990s, Celebrity signed on as its culinary consultant internationally known chef **Michel Roux,** whose most visible successes were his direction of both Le Gavroche, one of London's best restaurants, and the Waterside Inn (in Bray, Berkshire), where haute cuisine and haute grandeur have attracted the attention of well-heeled European foodies—including the Queen of England—for many years.

While Celebrity loves touting Michel Roux and its food—and it is tasty—I must say the meals served in the formal dining room are really not *that* much better than the cuisine being served these days on the newest Carnival, Royal Caribbean, Princess, and Disney ships. And this, I think, is due more to the other lines improving their cuisine over the past few years than Celebrity's slipping. It could be said that Celebrity's cuisine probably includes more exotic or international fare, like Asian and French, that more experienced palates will appreciate. Overall, though, they are pretty much in the same league now and it would be splitting hairs to argue otherwise.

A dinner menu is likely to feature something along the lines of escargots à la bourguignonne, pheasant mousseline with blueberry vinaigrette, pan-fried salmon with parslied potatoes, pad Thai (noodles and veggies in a peanut sauce), tournedos Rossini with foie gras and Madeira sauce, or a well-seasoned slab of prime rib with horseradish and baked potato. To balance such heartiness, at every meal Celebrity offers **lighter "spa" fare,** like a seafood medley in saffron sauce or oven-roasted rack of veal with steamed veggies (calories, fat, cholesterol, and sodium are listed on the back of the menu) and **vegetarian entrees** such as curried Indian vegetables or linguini with shiitake mushrooms and herbs.

Aside from the fancier stuff, Celebrity also offers the same usual suspects as its peers. An **alternative casual dining venue** is available in the Lido restaurant. Don't expect great atmosphere (it's a bit bright and spartan, especially on the *Zenith* and *Horizon*), but do expect a simple five-course meal, with a choice of main entrees like salmon, steak, pasta, and chicken. Serving dinner between 6:30 and 8:30pm by reservation only, it's a good place to bring the kids, and a good option if you want to skip the hustle and bustle (and formality) of the main restaurant. **Lunch buffets** feature all-American favorites like salads and stir fries, grilled hamburgers and hot dogs, fish and chips, cheeses and breads, omelets, pizza, smoked salmon, shrimp cocktail, and French onion soup.

A nice touch that appears on all formal nights is a late-night culinary soirée known as **Gourmet Bites,** where a series of upscale canapés and hors d'oeuvres are served by waiters in the ship's public lounges between midnight and 1am. On other nights, themed **midnight buffets** might offer up Oriental, Italian, Tex-Mex, or tropical smorgasbords, with a spread of fancifully carved fruits.

Wine-wise, Chef Roux's choices are offered in a wide price range to suit every budget. Interestingly, a few of the wines featured on board are produced by French vineyards with which Roux has a direct link and, in some cases, of which he is the owner.

ACTIVITIES

On Celebrity, there's a lot to do and a lot not to do, and the ships offer opportunities for both.

If you like to stay busy, activities during days at sea are fairly standardized across the fleet, and may include one of the fascinating **enrichment lectures** (which are complimentary) often offered by experts on topics such as personal investing, handwriting analysis, and body language. There are also the tried-and-true wine-tastings, horse racing, bingo, art auctions, trivia games, arts and crafts, spa and salon demonstrations, and line-dancing lessons. Activities are not without a dose of token cruise tomfoolery. Afternoons in the main pool area, silly pool games like the **Mr. Celebrity contest** are held, where cheeky guys strut their stuff around the pool as a panel of bathing-suit–clad female volunteers rate them. During the day, a live pop band plays a couple of sets on the Pool Deck.

If you prefer curling up with a good book in some quiet nook, you'll have no problem finding one. On the *Horizon* and *Zenith,* the aft tiered decks and the forward Marina Deck are perfect places for quiet repose, and on the *Galaxy* and *Mercury,* you can find some peace on the far corners of the Sky Deck and on the aft Penthouse Deck. Inside there are many hideaways, including Michael's Club, the edges of Rendez-Vous Square, a lounge chair at the spa's thalassotherapy pool (on the *Century, Galaxy,* and *Mercury*) and in the Fleet and America's Cup observation lounges (on the *Zenith* and *Horizon*).

CHILDREN'S PROGRAMS

Although it did not originate that way, Celebrity has evolved into a cruise line that pampers kids as well as adults, especially during the summer and holidays (with a limited program available at other times of the year). Each ship has a **playroom** (called the Fun Factory on the Century-class ships and the Children's Playroom on the *Horizon* and *Zenith*), **supervised activities** practically all day long, and **private and group babysitting.** The *Galaxy* and *Mercury* also have a wading pool.

During kid-intensive seasons, **activities** are geared toward four different age groups, between the ages of 3 and 17, with the largest facilities on the Century-class ships. Kids ages 3 to 6, dubbed "Ship Mates," can enjoy treasure hunts, clown parties, T-shirt painting, dancing, movies, ship tours, and ice-cream-sundae-making parties. "Cadets," ages 7 to 10, are amused by T-shirt painting, scavenger hunts, board games, arts and crafts, ship tours, and computer games. Your 11-to-13-year-old might want to join the "Ensign" activities, like karaoke, computer games, board games, trivia contests, arts and crafts, movies, and pizza parties. For teens ages 14 to 17 who don't think themselves too cool to participate, the "Admiral T's" group offers talent shows, karaoke, pool games, and trivia contests. On the Century-class ships there are attractive teen discos/hang-out rooms. Special activities offered in the summer include **summer-stock theater presentations,** which involve three age groups: the Ship Mates and Cadets sing, dance, and act, and the Ensigns direct and produce the plays. The Young Mariners Club

Cruise Tip

If you plan on spending quiet time in your cabins during the day, you might want to avoid booking a cabin near the children's playroom, which on all five Celebrity ships are located next to cabins. Their locations are marked on brochure deck plans.

Meeting of the Minds

The movie theaters on Celebrity's *Century, Galaxy,* and *Mercury* double as electronically sophisticated **conference/meeting rooms** (courtesy of Sony gadgetry). Conceivably, a multilingual onboard corporate sales meeting could be connected with an audiovisual presentation. The electronic features include a special interactive voting system that enables audiences to be polled for their opinions via an electronic keypad on each seat, with the results displayed on a projector screen after the poll is completed.

offers kids the chance to get a behind-the-scenes look at the cruise ship, with activities and tours related to the entertainment, food and beverage, and hotel departments. **Junior Olympics** are held poolside and the whole family is encouraged to cheer on the kids who compete in relay races, diving, and basketball hoop shooting. There are also masquerade parties, where Ship Mates and Cadets make their own masks and then parade around the ship. When a magician is onboard, he or she teaches the kids how to perform a couple of tricks.

A once-weekly, complimentary **parents' night out program** allows mom and dad to enjoy dinner alone while the kids dine with counselors. Every evening, group slumber party–style **baby-sitting** in the playroom is available from 10pm to 1am for children ages 3 to 12, for $3 per child per hour or $5 per hour for two or more children from the same family. Private in-cabin baby-sitting by a crew member is available on a limited basis for $8 per hour for up to two children.

ENTERTAINMENT

Although entertainment is not a prime reason to sail on a Celebrity ship, the line does offer a nice selection of varied, innovative performances. For instance, Celebrity Cruises fleetwide has introduced a **strolling a cappella group** as well as a wandering magician, who perform in lounges and public areas in the afternoons and before and after dinner. The four-man troupe of singers, sans instruments, delights passengers with well-known songs old and new, performed in a fun, entertaining style. Meanwhile, the tuxedo-clad magician dazzles guests with card tricks and disappearing acts.

Celebrity also offers the popular favorites, like **Broadway-style musicals** lead by a sock-it-to-'em soloist or two and a team of lip-synching dancers in full Vegas-esque regalia. On the Century-class ships, these shows are performed on some of the best-equipped, highest-tech stages at sea. They've got hydraulic orchestra pits, easily maneuverable sets (which move along tracks in the stage floor), trap doors, turntables, a video wall (showing images that coincide with the performance), and lasers. Showrooms aboard all Celebrity ships have excellent acoustics and sightlines praised as among the most panoramic and unobstructed at sea. As for the sound and light spectaculars that are so much a part of the entertainment experience these days, get this statistic: The Celebrity Showroom aboard the newest ship, *Mercury,* has no less than 152 speakers, and a typical evening show uses between 1,000 and 1,100 different lighting cues. How's that for whiz bang?

Other nights in the showroom, you'll find magicians, comedians, cabaret acts, and passenger talent shows.

When you tire of Broadway-style entertainment, you'll find all the ships have **cozy lounges** and **piano bars** where you can retreat for a romantic nightcap. In these more intimate lounges, the music of choice is often laid-back jazz or music from the Big Band era, spiced with interpretations of contemporary hits by the likes of Celine Dion or

Celebrity Art: Take a Walk on the Wild Side

Celebrity's ships—particularly the *Century, Galaxy,* and *Mercury*—contain the most impressive and striking (and sometimes downright weird) art collections at sea, featuring works by Robert Rauschenberg, Damien Hirst, Jasper Johns, David Hockney, Pablo Picasso, Andy Warhol, Sol LeWitt, and Helen Frankenthaler. Public areas in *Mercury* alone contain more than 400 works of art; some particular standouts include Christian Marclay's record-cover collages, Anish Kapoor's hallucinatory *Mirror,* Lawrence Weiner's puzzling poetic lines painted on walls throughout the ship, Lynn Davis's starkly beautiful iceberg photographs, the benignly endearing photographs of discarded flip-flops or the close-ups of smiling kids, and Art Club 2000's disturbing takeoffs of modern heroin-chic advertising trends. You'll find tapestries, cartoonish murals, and stark metal sculptures. These compelling works sometimes greet you at unexpected moments, and may even make you pause and reflect—a most rare cruise ship phenomenon.

Whitney Houston. There's also the elegant and plush **Michael's Club** for a cigar and cordial and some quiet conversation. Each ship has late-night disco dancing, usually until about 3am. You'll also find **karaoke** and **first-run movies** in the theater on the Century-class ships.

Each ship has a rather spacious **casino,** and while they may not be as hopping as the ones on Carnival, they're bustling enough to put gamblers in the mood.

You may have heard about Celebrity's connection with the Sony Corporation, the company providing the interactive video and audio systems that enhance the quality of the electronic entertainment and lighting on board. The prototypes for these systems were initially installed aboard the *Century,* the most high-tech of the three megaships, with the intention of having subsequent ships just as Sony-fied, but the hoopla has since fizzled out to a large degree, and the Sony connection has faded into the background. It's great that the equipment is there, but who needs to see Sony products screaming from shop shelves or the name bandied about at every opportunity? Of greater merit are the half dozen or so Sony personal **computers** that are available for guests to play around with on the three Century-class ships.

You'll also enjoy the **interactive system** wired to all cabin TVs. It's pretty cool and very convenient—when it's working; however, it has never functioned completely 100% on the five Celebrity cruises I've taken. When it's up to speed, you can order room service from onscreen menus, select the evening's wine in advance of dinner, play casino-style games, or browse in "virtual" shops for a wide selection of merchandise for delivery directly to your home at the end of your cruise. The systems used to allow guests to check the balance of their onboard account, but this nifty option seems to have been quietly removed (seems the cruise line execs realized that passengers checking their balance every 2 seconds is not a good thing for the ships' coffers).

SERVICE

Overall, service is polite, attentive, cheerful, and especially professional. Waiters have a poised, upscale-hotel air about them, and their manner contributes to the elegant mood. Uniforms are more distinguished looking than on some other lines (like Carnival). There are very professional sommeliers in the dining room, and in the Lido breakfast and lunch buffet restaurants, waiters are on hand to carry passengers' trays from the buffet line to a table of their choice.

Celebrity Fleet Itineraries

Ship	Home Ports & Season	Itinerary	Other Itineraries
Century	Fort Lauderdale, itineraries alternate weekly Jan–Apr.	**7-night eastern Carib:** San Juan, St. Thomas, Sint Maarten, and Nassau. **7-night western Carib:** Ocho Rios (Jamaica), Grand Cayman, Cozumel, and Key West.	Mediterranean, Europe, Russia, Baltic
Galaxy	San Juan, late Oct to late Apr.	**7-night southern Carib:** St. Lucia, Barbados, Martinique, Antigua, and St. Thomas.	Alaska Inside Passage
Horizon	Fort Lauderdale, itineraries alternate Nov–Apr (*Note:* Itineraries after April 2000 not yet set at press time).	**10-night eastern/southern Carib:** Sint Maarten, St. Lucia, Barbados, Antigua, and St. Thomas. **11-night eastern/southern Carib:** Curaçao, Guaira (Venezuela), Grenada, Barbados, La Martinique, and St. Thomas.	Europe (cruises marketed to European passengers only)
Mercury	Fort Lauderdale, late Oct to late Apr.	**7-night western Carib:** Key West, Calica, Cozumel, and Grand Cayman.	Alaska Inside Passage and Gulf
Zenith	Between San Juan and San Diego Nov–Mar; New York–Bermuda itineraries Apr–Oct.	**14-night Panama Canal:** St. Thomas, Aruba, Cartagena (Colombia), Puerto Caldera (Costa Rica), Acapulco, and Cabo San Lucas. **7-night Bermuda:** Hamilton and St. George's.	None

If you occupy a suite on any of the ships, you'll get a tuxedo-clad **personal butler** who serves afternoon tea and complimentary hors d'oeuvres from 6 to 8pm, bringing them right to your cabin. If you ask, he'll handle your laundry, shine your shoes, make sewing repairs, deliver messages, and do many other errands and favors. For instance, on a recent sailing with my mother, our butler brought her a glass of juice each night, which she needed to take with her medication. Your butler will serve you a full five-course dinner if you'd rather **dine in your cabin** one night, and if you're in the mood to compile a guest list and pay for the drinks and hors d'oeuvres everyone will consume, your butler will even organize a cocktail party for you and your private list of cruising friends, either in your suite or in any of several suitable public areas on board ship.

Other hedonistic treats bestowed upon suite guests include a bottle of champagne on arrival, personalized stationery, terry-cloth robes, a Celebrity tote bag, oversized bath towels, priority check-in and debarkation, express luggage delivery at embarkation, and, on the *Century, Galaxy,* and *Mercury,* complimentary use of the soothing thalassotherapy pool. Suite guests can even get an **in-cabin massage** daily between the hours of 7am and 8pm.

Century • Galaxy • Mercury

The Verdict

Three of the most attractive and all-around appealing megaships at sea.

Mercury *(photo: Matt Hannafin)*

Specifications

Size (in tons)		Number of Passengers	
Century	70,606	*Century*	1,750
Galaxy	77,713	*Galaxy*	1,896
Mercury	77,713	*Mercury*	1,896
Number of Cabins		Officers	Greek
Century	875	Crew	International
Galaxy	948	*Century*	843
Mercury	948	*Galaxy*	900
Number of Outside Cabins		*Mercury*	900
Century	571	Passenger/Crew Ratio	2 to 1
Galaxy	639	Year Built	
Mercury	639	*Century*	1995
Cabins with Verandas		*Galaxy*	1996
Century	61	*Mercury*	1997
Galaxy	220	Last Major Refurbishment	N/A
Mercury	220		

Frommer's Ratings (Scale of 1–5)

Cabin Comfort & Amenities	5	Pool, Fitness & Spa Facilities	5
Ship Cleanliness & Maintenance	4	Children's Facilities	4
Public Comfort/Space	5	Itinerary	4
Decor	5	Worth the Money	5

When it was launched in December 1995, the $320-million *Century* got tremendous publicity, partly because it represented Celebrity's entry into the world of megaships and partly because it was, quite simply, a particularly well-conceived and beautiful ship. The *Galaxy* was launched a year later, in December 1996, and the *Mercury* appeared a year after that. The three are more or less equivalent in size and amenities (with the primary differences being in the interior decors, arrangement of public rooms, and itineraries), and although colossal by the standards of a decade ago, none attains the mega-bulk of some of the new 100,000-ton behemoths run by such competing lines as Princess, Carnival, and Royal Caribbean.

With exteriors painted in a sharp and dazzling contrast of bright white and navy blue, all three vessels manage to be simultaneously huge and streamlined-looking, with pagoda-like sterns and rakishly angled bows designed for speed and grace. A dozen well-respected and innovative firms based in London, Athens, Las Vegas, and New York collaborated on different aspects of these ships' interior decor, investing truly enormous amounts of time and effort in their design and execution.

Of the three ships, the one that's the most dissimilar to its mates is *Century*. Although similar in many ways, it's lighter by 7,000 tons, has a capacity for 120 fewer guests, and has a brighter, glitzier feel, flaunting its high-tech-ness with video monitors and all things Sony blended into the decor. It also has a smaller children's playroom and doesn't have a wading pool. The *Galaxy* and *Mercury* are warmer and more reminiscent of classic ocean liners, but with a modern feel. The decor casts a chic and sophisticated mood, with lots of warm wood tones as well as rich, tactile textures and fabrics in deep primaries, from faux zebra-skin to buttery soft leathers, velvets, chrome, and futuristic-looking applications of glass and marble.

It's difficult to say what's most striking on these three ships. The elegant spas and their 15,000-gallon thalassotherapy pools? The twin three- and four-story atria with their serpentine staircases that seem to float without supports and the domed ceilings of painted glass? The distinguished Michael's Club cigar lounges with their leather wingbacks, velvet couches, and hand-rolled stogies? The two-story old-world dining rooms set into the stern, with grand floor to ceiling windows allowing diners to espy the glow of the wake under moonlight? An absolutely intriguing modern art collection unmatched in the industry?

Take your pick—you won't go wrong.

Cabins & Rates

Cabins	Per diems from	Bathtub	Fridge	Hair Dryer	Sitting Area	TV
Inside	$126	no	yes	yes	no	yes*
Outside	$147	no	yes	yes	some	yes*
Suite	$459	yes	yes	yes	yes	yes*

All TVs show CNN and ESPN.

CABINS   Simple yet pleasing decor is cheerful and based on light-colored furniture and monochromatic themes of muted purple-blue, green, or pinky red. Although inside cabins are about par for the industry standard, outside cabins are larger than usual, and suites (which come in four different categories) are particularly spacious and feature marble vanity/desk tops, art deco–style sconces, and rich inlaid-wood floors. Some, such as the Penthouse Suite, offer more living space (1,219 square feet, expandable to 1,433 square feet on special request) than you find in many private homes, plus such wonderful touches as a private whirlpool bath on the veranda. Royal Suites run about half that size at 637 square feet, but offer touches like French doors between the bedroom and seating area, both bathtub and shower in the bathroom, TVs in each room, and a sofa bed. The *Galaxy* and *Mercury*'s Sky Suites offer verandas that, at 179 square feet, are among the biggest aboard any ship—bigger, in fact, than those in the more expensive Penthouse and Royal suites on these ships (you might want to keep your robe on, though, as people on the deck above can see down onto part of the Sky Suite verandas). All suite bathrooms have tubs with whirlpools, hair dryers, and magnified makeup mirrors.

All cabins are outfitted with built-in vanities/desks, minibars, hair dryers, radios, and safes. Closets and drawer space are roomy and well-designed, as are the bathrooms, and all standard cabins have twin beds convertible to doubles. If you want to save money, think about booking an inside cabin, since they have all the features the outside ones do (except a window, of course).

Cabin TVs are wired with an interactive system that allows guests to order room service from onscreen menus, select wine for dinner, play casino-style games, or go shopping.

In case you're running low.

We're here to help with more than 190,000 Express Cash locations around the world. In order to enroll, just call American Express at 1 800 CASH-NOW before you start your vacation.

do more AMERICAN EXPRESS

Express Cash

And in case you'd rather be safe than sorry.

We're here with American Express® Travelers Cheques. They're the safe way to carry money on your vacation, because if they're ever lost or stolen you can get a refund, practically anywhere or anytime. To find the nearest place to buy Travelers Cheques, call 1 800 495-1153. Another way we help you do more.

do more   **AMERICAN EXPRESS**

Travelers Cheques

Eight of the cabins aboard each ship (one inside and seven outside) were specifically designed for passengers with disabilities, and include the works, from roll-in showers to wheelchair-level furniture.

PUBLIC AREAS · All three ships also are designed so well that it's never hard to find a quiet retreat when you want to be secluded but don't want to be confined in your cabin.

Dinners are served in style in the ships' gorgeous two-deck main dining rooms—the Grand Restaurant aboard the *Century,* the Orion Restaurant aboard the *Galaxy,* and the Manhattan Restaurant aboard the *Mercury,* this last featuring beautiful wooden ceilings with burnished metal joins and a number of allusions to its namesake, including a retractable screen over the aft windows printed with an image of New York's famed Flatiron Building. Raising it during meals always occasions generous oohs and ahhs.

Each vessel also boasts a cozy and rarely packed enclave, Michael's Club, that's decorated like the parlor of a London men's club and is devoted to the pleasures of fine cigars, fine cognacs, and stiff drinks. If you're a dedicated nonsmoker, don't even think of spending time here. Otherwise, puff away at some of the best cigars this side of Havana. On the *Century* and *Galaxy,* Michael's Club maintains its wood-paneled clubbiness somewhat better than aboard the *Mercury,* where it wraps around the main atrium and lets onto a very uncozy view of the shopping below. Still, you can't beat the high-backed, buttery-leather chairs and the master cigar-roller who sets up shop in the corner.

For those who don't find that smoky ambience appealing, Tastings Coffee Bar offers an alternative, with every kind of specialized upscale caffeine you can imagine. There's also the popular Rendez-Vous Square, arranged so that even large groups can achieve a level of privacy and couples can find their own nook as well. Champagne bars appear aboard the *Galaxy* and *Mercury,* and the latter also sports a nice, modern deco-looking martini bar set in the ship's aft atrium, about which our only complaint is the audible clanging of the casino's slot machines, which seems to get trapped and amplified by the atrium's drum shape. Various other bars, both indoor and outdoor, are tucked into nooks and crannies throughout all three ships.

The multitiered, glass-walled nightclubs/discos are spacious, sprawling, and elegant in a clean, modern way, yet designed with lots of cozy nooks for romantic conversation over champagne.

Each of the three ships has double-decker theaters with unobstructed views from almost every seat (avoid those at the cocktail tables at the back of the rear balcony boxes, unless you're very tall or have a really long neck) and scads of state-of-the-art equipment. Each boasts a cantilevered orchestra pit and a wall of video screens to augment the action on the stage. Libraries aboard both ships are comfortable, but not as big or well stocked as they could be. The onboard casinos are larger and more comprehensive than those aboard the line's older *Horizon* and *Zenith.*

POOL, FITNESS & SPA FACILITIES Resort decks aboard these vessels feature a pair of good-sized swimming areas rimmed with teak benches for sunning and relaxation. Even when the ships are full, these areas don't seem particularly crowded. Aboard the *Galaxy* and *Mercury,* retractable magrodomes cover one of the swimming pools with a sliding glass cupola during inclement weather.

Some of the best spas and fitness facilities at sea are on board these three ships. Called the AquaSpa, these spacious, windowed, 10,000-square-foot health meccas are a feast for the eyes as well as a sanctuary for the body and soul. The gym wraps around one side of the bow like a hook, the large spa straddles the middle, and a very modern and elegant beauty salon faces the ocean on the other side of the bow. You'll feel as though you've booked yourself into an exclusive European spa resort. The focal point of these spas is a 115,000-gallon thalassotherapy pool, a bubbling cauldron of warm, soothing seawater. After a relaxing 15- or 20-minute dip, choose a massage, Rasul treatment (a mudpack and steam bath in one), a facial, or one of the many other pampering treatments offered. As aesthetically pleasing to the eye as they are functional, each of the AquaSpas employs a design theme—a Japanese bathhouse on the *Century* and *Galaxy* and a Moroccan motif on the *Mercury*.

Although managed by Steiner like the spas on most other ships, these spas offer more exotic treatments than most—for example, mud packs, herbal steam baths, and a variety of water-based treatments involving baths, jet massages, and "aquameditation," in which you're caressed by light, whirling showers while lying on a soft mat. Certain procedures are offered in a "partner" arrangement, whereby you and your significant other can apply medicinal muds to each other and share an herbal steam bath while massaging each other with sea salt. The whole shebang ends with a warm shower and the application of an aromatic "potion" to the skin. Sound exotic? It is. There are also saunas and steam rooms (including the *Mercury's* impressive Turkish Hammam, with its uniformly heated surfaces and beautiful tilework).

In the generously sized gyms, you can get lost in the landscapes unfolding on the color monitors of the ships' high-tech virtual-reality stationary bikes. (You can even ride through the virtual water traps and make squishy sounds as you come up the other side—fun!) The Mercury even has a workout machine that simulates in-line skating. There are also aerobic classes in a separate rooms, and all three ships have an outdoor jogging track on an upper deck, a golf simulator, and one deck that's specifically designed for sports.

Horizon • Zenith

The Verdict

A casually elegant tribute to both the gentility of classic cruising and the fun and glamour of today's exciting megaships, these mid-sized ships are a very pleasing package.

Horizon *(photo: Celebrity Cruises)*

Specifications

Size (in tons)		Officers	Greek
Horizon	46,811	Crew	International
Zenith	47,225	*Horizon*	645
Number of Cabins		*Zenith*	628
Horizon	677	Passenger/Crew Ratio	2.1 to 1
Zenith	687	Year Built	
Number of Outside Cabins		*Horizon*	1990
Horizon	529	*Zenith*	1992
Zenith	541	Last Major Refurbishment	
Cabins with Verandas	0	*Horizon*	1998
Number of Passengers		*Zenith*	1999
Horizon	1,354		
Zenith	1,374		

Frommer's Ratings (Scale of 1–5)

Cabin Comfort & Amenities	4	Pool, Fitness & Spa Facilities	4
Ship Cleanliness & Maintenance	4	Children's Facilities	3
Public Comfort/Space	4	Itinerary	4
Decor	4	Worth the Money	5

The design of the twins *Horizon* and *Zenith,* with their signature sterns and bows and the immediately identifiable Chandris *X* on their funnels, ranked as one of the industry's most distinctive upon the ships' introduction, and has since become the touchstone on which all subsequent Celebrity ships have been based. Like their megaship sisters, these two smaller ships boast classy, modern interiors, fantastic service, and distinctive art collections, and after $4.5 million refurbishments in 1998 (*Horizon*) and 1999 (*Zenith*), they also offer such signature Celebrity elements as Michael's Club cigar lounges, patisseries, martini bars, art galleries, a new boutique selling upscale accessories and clothing, and enlarged spa facilities (although they lack the megas' thalassotherapy pools). Note that at press time the renovations had not yet been made to the *Zenith,* but those planned are identical to those we inspected on the *Horizon* in late 1998.

Even at peak capacity, the ships' well-designed passageways, hallways, seating arrangements, and traffic patterns create the feeling of more space than a ship of this size would ordinarily provide. An exceptionally wide indoor promenade gives passengers the feeling of strolling along a boulevard within the ship's hull. Art and sculpture decorate the ships, but the works don't equal the premier collection aboard *Century, Galaxy,* and *Mercury.*

Cabins & Rates

Cabins	Per diems from	Bathtub	Fridge	Hair Dryer	Sitting Area	TV
Inside	$138	no	no	yes	no	yes*
Outside	$155	no	no	yes	some	yes*
Suite	$341	yes	yes	yes	yes	yes*

All TVs show CNN and ESPN.

CABINS   As on the Century-class ships, accommodations offer a generous amount of space, and the muted blue, green, or red fabrics and accoutrements are tasteful, subdued, and well maintained.

All cabins on both ships have twin or double beds, with generally roomy bathrooms, and many have upper and lower berths for families or friendly foursomes. Standard cabin amenities include a glass-topped coffee table, a desk, and a nightstand with a solitary lamp that may be inadequate, especially if you're in a double. Eight cabins (*Horizon*) or six (*Zenith*) are positioned all the way aft, with windows facing the wake. Some passengers who've sailed on the line before request these rooms, preferring this classically romantic view. (Bear in mind, on the *Zenith,* the children's playroom is right in the midst of these cabins and on the *Horizon,* it's adjacent to cabins amidships on the Florida deck. So if you're planning on quiet daytimes in your cabin and will sail during school holidays, you might not want to book one of them.) Since cabins are so similar, you can book on a lower deck to save money, as long as you don't mind being in the bowels of the ship.

The 20 roomy suites on each ship measure 270 square feet and are about 25 square feet bigger than most of the suites on the Century-class ships (the only difference being that the *Horizon* and *Zenith* do not have any private verandas). Suites have a marble bathroom with whirlpool tub, a sitting area, a minibar, and butler service.

The *Horizon* has a pair of presidential suites measuring 340 square feet and the *Zenith* has two royal suites at 500 square feet, each with large sitting rooms (and on the

Zenith, a dining table and chairs), marble bathrooms, walk-in closets, as well as butler service, VCR, CD player, and minibar.

Regardless of category, all accommodations have cabin music, a personal safe, TV, glass-topped coffee table, twin or double bed, and marble-topped vanity. Cabin TVs are wired with an interactive system that allows guests to order room service from onscreen menus, select wine for dinner, play casino-style games, or go shopping. Be careful when booking if views are important to you: Some outside cabins on the Bermuda (*Horizon*) and Bahamas (*Zenith*) Decks have views blocked by lifeboats. Ask your travel agent not to book you in them—they'll know which ones you mean.

Four cabins are wheelchair accessible, with extra-large bathrooms.

PUBLIC AREAS   The decor on both is plush and modern rather than classical and conservative, with both a metallic and nautical motif working in concert. There are no multi-deck atria or flashing lights (except maybe on the dance floor of the disco). Layout differences between the two ships are minimal (*Zenith* has a larger forward observation deck, for instance).

One of the most attractive spaces is the spacious bar/observation lounge on the Marina Deck, called Fleet Bar on the *Zenith* and the America's Cup Club on the *Horizon.* Espousing a nautical motif, both have floor-to-ceiling windows, navy-blue furniture, and honey-brown wood accents. There are also humidors harboring a selection of cigars for sale; stogie smoking is permitted here, on outside decks, and in Michael's Club. The dining rooms may be the most chrome-intensive places on board (ceiling, railing, chair frames, and pillars), yet they're still pleasing, comfortable places to dine, with banquette seating for tables along the sides of the rooms.

There's never a really bad seat in the two-level Celebrity Show Lounge. Both have a modern, minimalist design. Midships on both is the Rendezvous Lounge and Rendezvous Bar, where guests, especially on formal nights, can show off their finery and relax with cocktails before heading to the adjacent dining room.

Recent refurbishments on both ships have transformed the space that was once a not very attractive or popular disco into three different rooms: a library, a card room, and an elegant Michael's Club cigar bar with wingback chairs, leather couches, and even a faux fireplace (with faux crackling fire—can you say "The Yule Log"?). Where the library and card room used to be, next to the Rendez-Vous Bar, there's now a martini bar, an art gallery offering the same kind of works you'll see at onboard art auctions, and another boutique. The disco is now part of the enlarged Zodiac Club, with lots of room for dancing and for sitting in cozy clusters. The Plaza Bar has been transformed into the COVA Café, offering specialty coffees and chocolates as well as champagne, wine, and liquors.

RECREATION & FITNESS FACILITIES   The *Horizon* and the *Zenith* have ample space dedicated to recreation, including two good-sized swimming pools that never seem to be overcrowded, even when the ships are full.

The newly renovated top-deck spa and fitness areas on both ships have floor-to-ceiling windows and resemble the spas aboard Celebrity's larger ships, and while they don't offer as many of the more exotic treatments or have the thalassotherapy pool featured on the Century-class ships, they now have expanded and enlarged spa treatment rooms and a Seraglio steam/mud room (like the Rasul on the larger ships). The gyms have more fitness equipment, and although they're larger than they were, they're still relatively small by modern standards—too small, for instance, to hold fitness classes (they're held instead in one of the nightclubs).

Other recreation facilities and options include a putting green, a golf driving net used for lessons with the pro, a jogging track, and, on the *Zenith* only, a hot tub.

Costa Cruises

SHIPS CostaRomantica • CostaVictoria

World Trade Center, 80 SW 8th St., Miami, FL 33130-3097 (mailing address: P.O. Box 01964, Miami, FL 33101-9865). ☎ **800/462-6782** or 305/358-7325. Fax 305/375-0676. www.costacruises.com.

THE LINE IN A NUTSHELL   Costa's Italian-flavored mid- and mega-sized European-styled ships offer a moderately priced, festive, international experience that you can't find on any other line.

THE EXPERIENCE   With an illustrious history stretching back almost 90 years, Costa has managed to hold onto its heritage, and that's what sets it apart. Its officers are Italian and its ships' interiors, food, and activities are still as Italian as you can find.

Costa holds a somewhat unique position in the industry. It has headquarters in both Genoa and Miami and caters heavily to the European market. Its Caribbean cruises attract mostly Americans (about 80% on any given sailing), and, conversely, its Mediterranean cruises attract mostly Europeans. That said, even in the Caribbean, the passenger mix is much more international than on most other lines.

Few other ships in the Caribbean, with the exception of Club Med, bear such an obvious national character as Costa. Costa's "Cruising Italian Style" mantra is what primarily distinguishes the fleet from the "all-American" experiences of the competition. Although on your Caribbean routing you're likely to get a less intense dose of rampant Italianism than you would aboard the line's Mediterranean sailings, and although the line employs far fewer Italian-born stewards and crew members than in years past, the line's strength in the Italian-American market means that you'll still get quite a lot.

Pros
- **Italian flavor.** Like no other line in this category, entertainment, cuisine, and service are presented with a festive Italian flair.
- **Great value for the money.** For passengers taking advantage of early booking discounts, 1-week cruise rates start at just over $100 per person per day for an inside cabin and about $150 per person for an outside cabin.
- **Large cabins on *Romantica*.** At 200 square feet, the *Romantica*'s standard cabins are by far some of the biggest at sea (wish I could say the same for the *Victoria*).

Cons
- **Very few private verandas.** The *Romantica* has only 10; the *Victoria* none.
- **Small gyms.** Although the *Victoria*'s is bigger, neither ship offers spacious gyms.
- **Few large windows.** Compared to their peers, neither of these ships has many windows or terribly much natural light in their interiors.

Frommer's Ratings: Costa Cruises

	Poor	Fair	Good	Excellent	Outstanding
Enjoyment Factor					✓
Dining			✓		
Activities					✓
Children's Program			✓		
Entertainment				✓	
Service				✓	
Overall Value				✓	

COSTA: CONTINENTAL FLAVOR IN THE CARIBBEAN

Costa's origins are as Italian as could be. In 1860, Giacomo Costa established an olive-oil refinery and packaging plant in Genoa. After his death in 1916, his sons bought a ship to transport raw materials and finished products from Sardinia through Genoa to the rest of Europe. Within 19 years, the family had acquired an additional half-dozen ships, but their fortune fell with that of their country in the years during and after World War II. At war's end, only one tiny ship remained in the family's fleet, but within 3 years they managed to acquire a dozen more, most of them carrying European passengers. Costa was the world's largest operator of passenger ships in the early 1960s, before the explosion of the U.S. cruise industry nudged it into fifth place.

In 1968, the Costa family made a major commitment to the U.S. market by establishing Costa Cruises, now a subsidiary of Genoa-based Costa Crociere. The size of both the ships and the fleet grew rapidly. In 1966, most of the line's ships weighed in at 30,000 tons; by 1993, the *CostaRomantica* topped out at 54,000 tons. Today, the line boasts two of the most modern and beautiful ships in the Caribbean, including the 76,000-ton *CostaVictoria*, the line's largest ship.

In the late '60s, Costa pioneered San Juan as a point of departure for cruises, which bolstered Puerto Rico's early attempts to restore San Juan's colonial core. Around the same time, Costa also became the first cruise line to offer air/sea packages between U.S. cities and San Juan (and soon after, to Florida also).

In 1997, Carnival Corporation and Airtours (a British tour operator in which Carnival has a 30% stake) each bought a 50% interest in Costa, vowing to keep the line just the way it is. And so they have.

Today, despite its glossy corporate veneer, the Costa organization is still very much in the family. About a dozen Costa family members work for the company. Key administrative positions affecting the North American market, however, are often filled from the ranks of Italian-born, U.S.-trained executives from outside the family. A good example is CEO Dino Schibuola, whose past experiences include stints at Celebrity Cruises and Athens-based Home Lines.

THE FLEET

The Costa fleet is diverse, from gleaming megas to old, rebuilt liners from the '60s. Of its current fleet of six, there is one megaship, the 1,928-passenger *CostaVictoria,* built in 1996; a pair of mid-sized 1,300-passenger ships, the *CostaRomantica* (built in 1993) and the *CostaClassica* (built in 1991); the 800-passenger *CostaAllegra,* built in 1969 and rebuilt in 1992; the 770-passenger *CostaMarina,* built in 1969 and rebuilt in 1990; and the 972-passenger *CostaRiviera,* built in 1963 and rebuilt in 1993. The *CostaVictoria* and *CostaRomantica* are the only two ships in the fleet deployed in the Caribbean during the winter, between November and April, and marketed to North Americans (although about 20% of passengers are Europeans). Summers and the rest of the year, the entire fleet is in the Mediterranean, Northern Europe, and the Baltic. On these sailings, about 80% of cruisers are European.

Costa's first new build since the launch of the *CostaVictoria* in 1996, the 2,112-passenger, 80,000-ton *CostaAtlantica,* is scheduled to debut in spring of 2000. In many ways, the ship represents a new chapter for Costa. The *Atlantica* will be the first Costa ship to have a substantial number of private verandas—a whopping 75% of cabins will be outfitted with them. The ship will have a retractable glass roof over its main pool deck and have a children's pool as well. A Venetian-style cafe modeled on the famous 18th-century Caffe Florian in Venice's St. Mark's Square will serve specialty coffees and drinks. The ship is being built at the Kvaerner Masa shipyard in Helsinki, Finland, to

Life on Costa's Private Island

On all eastern Caribbean itineraries, passengers spend 1 day at Costa's private beach, **Serena Cay,** on a deserted island off the coast of the Dominican Republic. This relaxing patch of paradise not only offers palm tree–fringed beaches and sunbathing, but activities like volleyball, beach Olympics, and snorkeling. There's a band and a beach barbecue to round out the day. A local island vendor rents Jet Skis and banana boat rides.

the tune of $400 million. Like the *Victoria* and *Romantica,* the *Atlantica* will summer in Europe and spend the fall and winter in the Caribbean.

PASSENGER PROFILE

This line attracts passengers of all ages who want to pay a reasonable price and who deliberately avoid all-American megaships like those of Carnival. Costa passengers are impressed with Italian style, appreciate a sense of cultural adventure and fun, and like the atmosphere of casual, sophisticated elegance and a sense of romance at which the Italians excel—for these reasons the line is a favorite of honeymooners (between the *Victoria* and *Romantica,* 17 onboard weddings were performed during the 1997/98 Caribbean season).

Costa ships capture the fancy of any travelers who have ever gotten a lump in their throat during *La Strada* or sipped espresso in a Rome cafe. Italian-Americans are heavily represented aboard every Caribbean cruise.

Costa appeals to retirees and young couples alike, although there are more passengers over 50 than under. There are children on board, but not in overwhelming numbers—typically 5% to 10% of passengers are traveling as families (expect more families on cruises during holidays). While about 80% percent are from North America, there's usually a contingent of passengers from Europe and South America. You'll also find a substantial number of repeaters as well as passengers celebrating birthdays, anniversaries, or renewed wedding vows.

DINING

Food is well prepared, heavily Italian (and at least continental), and hearty—not exactly memorable, but rather decent, flavorful cuisine.

Lovers of **Italian food** never lack for choices at the six-course dinners, which feature cuisine from a region of Italy. Appetizers might include fried calamari and Parma ham and melon along with soup, salad, and a choice of pasta dishes such as fettuccini, cannelloni, and manicotti. Among the main courses are roast rack of lamb with an herb crust, salmon with dill sauce, and beef tenderloin in puff pastry. Also available on every menu are selections from the **spa menu** such as heart-healthy lasagna, grilled sea bass, and curried vegetables and lentils. And everyone's eyes light up in anticipation of the arrival of desserts with an Italian flair, such as tiramisu, cannelloni siciliani, and chocolate soufflé.

The fare is also appreciated as much for its entertainment as for its gastronomic value: Much emphasis and a few theatrics are placed on tossing a pasta or energetically seasoning a salad while diners look on. Menus are written in both Italian and English and always feature a **pasta of the day.**

No evening on board begins without a theme, and in keeping with the line's Italian origins, three of the seven **theme nights** in a typical cruise focus on Italian food and some aspect of Italian lore, legend, and ambience. *Festa Italiana* turns the ship into an Italian street festival at sea, where guests are encouraged to wear the colors of the Italian flag and have fun participating in bocce ball, pizza-dough tossing contests, tarantella dance lessons, Venetian-mask making, and Italian karaoke. On *Notte Mediterranean,* staff members don the native dress of cultures around the Mediterranean and present a red rose to each woman passenger during dessert. Another night is the *Notte Tropical* deck party with a Mediterranean twist, where guests can enjoy ethnic dancing and ice-carving demonstrations. The highlight of many cruises is **Roman Bacchanal Toga Night,** when at least some of the guests don costumes (usually a bedsheet fastened around the waist with a belt) along with a good sense of humor. Even the cruise director (who is usually American during Caribbean sailings aboard the *Romantica* and *Victoria*) is likely to threaten, "No sheet, no eat." So, whether you look good in a toga or not, you'll probably be wearing one at dinner. So traditional are these toga nights that some repeat passengers have actually commissioned couture versions from their tailors in anticipation of their next cruise.

The *CostaRomantica* has a single dining room, and the newer and bigger *CostaVictoria* has two. Both ships maintain the typical two-seating policy—lunch is served at noon and 1:30pm and dinner at 6:15 and 8:30pm. Each also has a casual breakfast and lunch buffet restaurant where, 2 nights a week (Tuesdays and Thursdays), you can also have an **informal buffet-style dinner** instead of heading to the formal dining room.

There are, of course, plenty of places to eat between meals. Juliette's Pâtisserie serves espresso, chocolates, and pastries aboard each ship, and **Romeo's Pizzeria** offers pizza throughout the day and night. Laden with herbs and fresh mozzarella, their pies are considered by many passengers to be the most genuinely addictive food on board. **Buffets,** unfortunately, tend to lack pizzazz, focusing instead on tried-and-true hot and cold staples. Low-fat, low-salt, low-cholesterol menus are available in the dining room. Unfortunately, as on most lines, cappuccino and espresso count as bar drinks and appear on your bar tab at the end of the cruise.

ACTIVITIES

More than anything else, Costa is known for its lineup of festive activities reflecting its Italian heritage. Nights are given over to Italian and Mediterranean theme nights (see "Dining," above); daytime activities include **Italian language and cooking classes** as well as such traditional cruise staples as jackpot bingo, bridge, arts and crafts, dance classes, shuffleboard, art auctions, horse racing, Ping-Pong, and fun poolside competitions (like who looks most like Al Pacino or sings like Pavarotti). Each ship also has a library and a card room.

Avid duffers can take part in the Costa's "Golf Academy at Sea" program, featuring private 15-, 30- and 60-minute golf lessons and videotaped golf swing analysis by a PGA member golf instructor (for a fee, of course). There is also a putting cage and daily putting tournaments, and the pro will accompany guests who sign up for golfing shore excursions to some of the best course in the Caribbean, like Mahogany Run in St. Thomas and The Links at Safe Haven in Grand Cayman.

Some Special Deals

Senior Discounts: "Super Senior Discounts" are sometimes available, allowing passengers over age 60 to deduct an additional $50 from fares booked 120 days before sailing. **Children's Discounts:** Children under 17 sharing a cabin with two adults can sometimes cruise for as little as $199 per person, excluding port charges. Kids under age 2 generally sail for free. Consult your travel agent for the most current deals.

Costa Fleet Itineraries

Ship	Home Ports & Season	Itinerary	Other Itineraries
Costa-Romantica	Fort Lauderdale, itineraries alternate weekly Nov–Apr.	**7-night western Carib:** Key West, Playa del Carmen/Cozumel, Montego Bay (Jamaica), and Grand Cayman. **7-night eastern Carib:** San Juan, St. Thomas, Serena Cay, and Nassau.	Mediterranean
CostaVictoria	Fort Lauderdale, itineraries alternate weekly Nov–Apr.	**7-night western Carib:** Key West, Playa del Carmen/Cozumel, Ocho Rios (Jamaica), and Grand Cayman. **7-night eastern Carib:** San Juan, St. Thomas, Serena Cay, and Nassau.	Mediterranean

A full-time Catholic priest—usually, an Italian officer doing double duty—conducts mass almost every day in the ships' chapel. For married couples, vow-renewal ceremonies are conducted onboard in Port Everglades and St. Thomas.

CHILDREN'S PROGRAM

Compared to other cruise lines, Costa places less emphasis on separating children from adult passengers. Only 5% to 10% of passengers are traveling with their families, so there are not throngs of children on board, and the kids' programs and facilities are not nearly as extensive as those available on other lines such as Disney or Carnival.

At least two full-time **youth counselors** are available aboard each Costa ship, with additional staff pressed into service whenever more than a dozen children are on the passenger list. Both ships offer **supervised activities** for kids 3 to 17, divided into two age groups unless enough children are aboard to divide them into three (3 to 5, 6 to 8, and 9 to 12 years). The "Costa Kids Club," for ages 3 to 12, includes such activities as Nintendo, bridge and galley tours, arts and crafts, scavenger hunts, Italian language lessons, bingo, board games, face painting, movies, kids' karaoke, and "Coketail," pizza, and ice-cream sundae parties. Both the *Victoria* and the *Romantica* have a **children's playroom.** If there are enough teens on board, the "Costa Teens Club" for ages 13 to 17 offers sports and fitness programs, movie-making sessions (using camcorders), and karaoke. The *Victoria* has a teen disco.

When ships are at sea in the Caribbean, supervised Kids Club hours are from 9:30 to 11:30am, 2 to 5pm, and 8 to 10pm. The program doesn't usually operate when ships are in port unless parents specifically request it.

Two nights a week there is a complimentary **Parents Nights Out program,** when from 5 to 11pm the kids are entertained and given a special buffet or pizza party while mom and dad get a night out alone.

All other times, **group baby-sitting** for ages 3 and up is available on request every evening from 6:30pm to 11:00am, unless the vessel is in port, when hours are extended to include morning and afternoon sessions. Group baby-sitting costs $10 per child per night. There is no in-cabin private baby-sitting available.

ENTERTAINMENT

Although the passengers are international and the location is the Caribbean, the main entertainment focus aboard Costa ships is decidedly—you guessed it—Italian. Entertainment directors program amusements such as concerts, puppet or marionette shows, mime, acrobatics, or cabaret that, although produced with an Italian bent, do not require audiences to actually know the language.

If you're not looking for Las Vegas–style glitter, you'll likely find the entertainment programs amusing—and, it should be noted, completely inoffensive, a remarkable thing these days.

Both ships contain state-of-the-art **showrooms**—two-tiered affairs that evoke the half moon–shaped amphitheaters of an 18th-century opera house—as well as **casinos.** Both the theater and the casino are bigger and flashier aboard the *CostaVictoria* than aboard the *CostaRomantica*. The Broadway-style acts in the main showroom are not nearly as elaborate or professional in quality as those on other major cruise lines; however, as they do with the food, it seems passengers have a great time no matter who or what is performing. The **discos** are popular places, and there's always a coterie dancing into the wee hours.

Many passengers choose to cruise on special **Italian theme cruises** featuring popular Italian American entertainers, such as Julius La Rosa, Al Martino, and Don Cornell.

SERVICE

While far from pampering, service is more than adequate in both the dining room and cabins. The young, enthusiastic staff members are friendly, alert, hip, and quick-witted. Dining-room staff is composed of charming waiters capable of handling most culinary requests. In recent years, greater numbers of the staff hail from South America, the Philippines, and many points in between, although at least two or three in any dining room crew are likely to be the genuine Italian article.

CostaRomantica

The Verdict

Italophiles will adore this mid-sized ship that delivers an authentic, affordable slice of *la dolce vita*.

CostaRomantica *(photo: Costa Cruises)*

Specifications

Size (in tons)	53,000	Officers	Italian/International
Number of Cabins	678	Crew	600 (International)
Number of Outside Cabins	462	Passenger/Crew Ratio	2 to 1
Cabins with Verandas	10	Year Built	1993
Number of Passengers	1,356	Last Major Refurbishment	N/A

Frommer's Ratings (Scale of 1–5)

Cabin Comfort & Amenities	4	Pool, Fitness & Spa Facilities	3
Ship Cleanliness & Maintenance	4	Children's Facilities	3
Public Comfort/Space	3	Itinerary	4
Decor	4	Worth the Money	5

Designed by Gregotti Associati, creators of the Musée d'Orsay in Paris, and completed in 1993 at a cost of $325 million, the *CostaRomantica,* a stylish, austere-looking vessel, is the second youngest member (after the flagship *CostaVictoria*) of the six-ship Costa fleet. Its cool, almost clinical modern European interior design (you'll either love it or think it lacks warmth) is in sharp contrast to the festive atmosphere aboard the ship. It is not as lavishly appointed as the *Costa Victoria.*

The *CostaRomantica* and its sister ship, the *CostaClassica,* were the largest and most stylish ships in the Costa armada until 1996, when they were supplanted by the larger *CostaVictoria.* Many passengers are repeat customers, drawn to the ship for its emphasis on comfort and a contemporary Italian design accented with the best of Italy's traditions. Its relatively small size means you'll begin to recognize your fellow passengers after a few days at sea.

CABINS   In a word: big. At 200 square feet, standard outside cabins are among the largest available on any mass-market/premium cruise line. (By comparison, Carnival's are even considered roomy at 185 square feet.) The modern cabins are attractively paneled with polished cherry wood, accented with wall murals, and bedding, carpets, and upholstery are done up in warm shades of sage, teal, and golden browns that are a nice change from the whiter, more pastel ambiences of most ship staterooms. Each cabin is furnished with twin beds (some convert to queens), two armchairs, and a small table and desk.

The ten categories of accommodations range from inside cabins (large as well at 175 square feet) on Deck 4 to generously proportioned, top-of-the-line suites and mini-suites on the Madrid and Monte Carlos decks (10 and 11). Of the 16 suites, 10 have verandas and measure 580 square feet (including the verandas); they can all accommodate up to six passengers and are furnished with a queen bed, single sofa bed, and a Murphy bed along with sitting area, minibar, double vanity, and whirlpool bath. The 18 mini-suites measure 340 square feet each.

All cabins have good-sized closets, safes, hair dryers, TV, and programmed radios, and six inside cabins are wheelchair accessible.

Cabins & Rates

Cabins	Per diems from	Bathtub	Fridge	Hair Dryer	Sitting Area	TV
Inside	$103	no	no	yes	no	yes
Outside	$140	no	no	yes	no	yes
Suite	$351	yes	yes	yes	yes	yes

PUBLIC AREAS   Public areas aboard *CostaRomantica* take their names from the heritage of Italy, and sometimes sport decors to match. Examples include the Excelsior Casino, the Via Condotti shopping arcade, the Caracalla Spa and Beauty Salon, the Piazza Italia Grand Bar (this huge space, illuminated by only a single row of windows on its starboard side, is the main gathering place during the day and is especially crowded during cocktail hour before dinner), and the Botticelli Restaurant, in which murals and window blinds evoke themes from the Renaissance. (Unfortunately, its indented ceilings and marble floors, although beautiful, seem to amplify the high noise level.) Classic Italian touches in different areas of the ship include chandeliers from Murano, intricate mosaics, pear-wood inlays, and lots and lots of brilliant white Carrara marble, while a modern Italian design esthetic shows in an abundance of steel, mirrors, and sharp, efficient edges.

There's an outdoor Alfresco Café, with access to a frequently replenished buffet that sometimes gets a bit overcrowded, as do some of the other public areas aboard the ship, the result of a somewhat awkward layout.

One of the most stunning public space is the L'Opera Showroom, which resembles a Renaissance amphitheater complete with tiered seating, that presents a much less formal repertoire than its name implies. Rising two decks high, it contains 6 miles of fiber optics, mosaics inspired by 14th-century models, and a medley of eye-catching sets.

High overhead on the topmost deck is a neat glass-walled circular observatory of sorts, the Diva Disco, where you can dance as close to the stars as nearly any ship afloat will allow. Music in the ship's Tango Ballroom nightclub includes highly danceable down-memory-lane numbers performed by a six-piece band. The nerve center of the ship is the central lobby, a five-story atrium flooded with overhead light. Throughout the public areas is a $20 million art collection that includes murals, mosaics, and futuristic sculptures.

FITNESS, POOL & SPA FACILITIES   This is definitely not a ship for fitness fanatics, as facilities consist of a small albeit pleasant gym with a wall of windows, a handful of Stairmasters and treadmills, and sauna, steam, and massage rooms. Because of a lack of exercise space, it's often necessary to conduct aerobics classes in the disco. It's obvious that working out is not a top priority for most passengers, whose only trips to the fitness area, it seems, are to weigh themselves on the scale.

The Caracalla Spa has a Turkish bath as well as treatment rooms offering a wide range of massages, wraps, facials, and hydrotherapy baths, but it pales in comparison to the *CostaVictoria*'s Roman-styled spa.

There are two outdoor pools and four hot tubs on a boxy patch of tiered deck, as well as a jogging track circling the deck above.

CostaVictoria

The Verdict

A sleek megaship with a European ambience and stunning decor, this ship is an all-around beauty for those liking an internationally flavored Caribbean cruise.

CostaVictoria *(photo: Costa Cruises)*

Specifications

Size (in tons)	76,000	Officers	Italian/International
Number of Cabins	964	Crew	800 (International)
Number of Outside Cabins	573	Passenger/Crew Ratio	2.4 to 1
Cabins with Verandas	0	Year Built	1996
Number of Passengers	1,928	Last Major Refurbishment	N/A

Frommer's Ratings (Scale of 1–5)

Cabin Comfort & Amenities	4	Pool, Fitness & Spa Facilities	4
Ship Cleanliness & Maintenance	4	Children's Facilities	3
Public Comfort/Space	4	Itinerary	4
Decor	5	Worth the Money	5

The ship that launched Costa Cruises into the megaship era was inaugurated in the summer of 1996. It's the largest and most technologically sophisticated ship ever launched by the line—a flagship for the fleet and a vision of Costa's hopes for the millennium. Sleek and stylish, its mammoth size allows for more spacious and dramatic interior features and more options for dining and after-dark diversions than any other Costa ship.

Built in Bremerhaven, Germany, with an impressive cruising speed of between 21 and 23 knots, it has a streamlined, futuristic-looking design with four tiers of glass-fronted observation decks facing the prow.

As a nod to some of its mega-competitors, the interior is splashier and more colorful than that of any previous Costa vessel. It's also more monumental, with a design that's imposing but, like a well-dressed Italian who knows how to tastefully blend patterns, fabrics, and accessories to create a look right out of fashion magazines, also compelling.

Signature design elements include an abundant use of stainless steel, teak, suede, leather, tile mosaics, and Italian marble in swirled patterns of blues and greens. For instance, brilliant royal blue suede covers the tops of card tables and deep, salmon-colored suede is used on the walls of the Concorde Plaza lounge. The Bolero Buffet features teak floors, and a wraparound tile mosaic creates eye-catching walls in the Capriccio Lounge.

The sleek, seven-story Planetarium Atrium—a Costa first—features four glass elevator banks and is punctuated by a thin string of ice-blue neon subtly spiraling toward the glass ceiling dome. Also a new concept in the Costa fleet are the *Victoria's* two dining rooms, with two seatings and an abundance of seating for couples (ideal for honeymooners).

Cabins & Rates

Cabins	Per diems from	Bathtub	Fridge	Hair Dryer	Sitting Area	TV
Inside	$103	no	yes	yes	no	yes
Outside	$140	no	yes	yes	no	yes
Suite	$351	yes	yes	yes	yes	yes

CABINS   Ironically, the cabins on this newest and biggest of Costa ships are smaller than those on the *Romantica*. At 120 to 150 square feet, standard inside and outside cabins certainly won't win any awards for their size (the smallest are like walk-in closets), but their sleek design and decor bring a delicious European touch to the cruise experience. Decorative fabric panels hang on the wall above headboards, matching the bedspreads. Bedside tables and dressers are sleek and Art Deco. Stainless steel is used for all bathroom sinks, and for dressers and mirrors in the mini-suites. All cabins have TVs, radio, hair dryer, minibar, and safe. None have verandas.

Instead of opulence, Costa has decorated its regular cabins in a relatively severe, minimalist style that's short on ambience but perfectly adequate as a place to retreat between meals and bouts of activity. Some 60% of them feature oversized round portholes opening onto sea views.

Especially desirable are 14 mini-suites, which have separate living rooms, reading areas, and tubs with hydro-massage equipment. Each is outfitted with one queen-sized bed and two Pullman-style beds. What makes them a bargain is that they contain many of the same amenities and interior design features as the more expensive suites, and their space is very generous at 301 square feet. For those with imperial taste, six full-sized suites raise the beam on luxury, with one queen and two Pullman-style beds and generous 430-square-foot proportions that make them feel roomy even if they're bunking four passengers. Furnishings in these suites are made of pear wood, with fabrics by Laura Ashley, who is not even remotely Italian, and whose particular patterns in this case are relatively bold and not particularly frilly looking. Some of the suites have floor-to-ceiling windows.

Four of the ship's cabins are specifically outfitted for passengers with disabilities. Cabins on Deck 6A don't benefit from direct elevator access, and require that guests climb a half-flight of stairs from the nearest elevator bank.

PUBLIC AREAS   Public areas, especially the onboard casino, throb with color and energy. Designed to re-create an Italian Piazza, the four-story Concorde Plaza is one of the *Victoria's* signature public areas. Seating over 300 as the venue for evening dancing and music as well a perfect venue for a relaxing drink by day, the Plaza boasts a four-story-high waterfall on one end and, on the other, a wall of windows facing the sea. An elevator bank whizzes guests between floors; glass walls allow sections of cabin hallways to be privy to the attractive plaza below. A granite bar is complemented by stainless steel accoutrements. The observation lounge serves first as a grand arena for socializing and special shipboard events and second as a theater for evening entertainment.

In the Central Hall, an atrium begins in the lobby, rises seven decks, and is topped by a crystal dome that floods the interior with sunlight. Four glass-sided elevators offer passengers a quick panorama of life on board at every level.

Two main dining rooms (the Sinfonia and the Fantasia) operate on the standard two-seatings plan at both lunch and dinner. The multifunction Tavernetta Lounge features the music of a three-piece dance band and wraparound paintings of other ships in the Costa Fleet, created by marine artist Stephen Card. Buffets, a grill, a pizzeria, and an ice-cream bar ensure that no one ever goes hungry between meals.

Gamblers gravitate to the big and brassy Monte Carlo Casino, the boldest, most dramatic, and biggest of any in the Costa fleet. It's linked to the Grand Bar Orpheus, one floor below, by a curving stairway whose glass stair treads are illuminated in patterns that are almost psychedelic. This bar is the preferred spot aboard for sampling an espresso or cappuccino, or—if it's late enough and you feel a bit reckless—a selection of grappas.

Other public rooms include a play area for children, a club for teens, a chapel (not always a feature aboard today's megaships), three conference rooms, an array of boutiques, a card room, a library, and a disco.

RECREATION & FITNESS FACILITIES   The *Victoria's* Pompeii Spa is the best-accessorized and largest spa in the Costa Line and the only one that includes its own indoor pool. It's done with richly colored mosaic tiles and Roman columns. You can release your tensions in a steam bath, a sauna, or a Turkish bath, or sit and soak in the spa's Jacuzzi, which is perched artfully within the larger waters of the spa's heated swimming pool. The attractive but smallish workout room shares a glass wall with the spa and pool area and features over a dozen exercise machines.

Out on deck, there's a pair of swimming pools as well as a "misting pool" that cools off overheated sunbathers with fine jets of water. Further decks wrap around the pools and their sunbathing area, providing plenty of space for passengers to stretch out and soak up the rays, even when the ship is fully booked. It looks like a resort on the Italian Riviera with its bright yellow and blue deck chairs and its nautical blue-and-white-striped lounges. There are four Jacuzzis, a tennis court that does double-duty as a half-sized basketball court, and a jogging track, four circuits of which equal 1 mile. There's also a beauty salon aboard.

Disney Cruise Line

SHIPS   **Disney Magic • Disney Wonder**

210 Celebration Place, Suite 400, Celebration, FL 34747-1000. ☎ **800/951-3532** or 407/566-7000. Fax 407/566-7353. www.disney.com/DisneyCruise.

THE LINE IN A NUTSHELL   Highish-priced cruises on a pair of floating theme parks that are like no others in the industry. Mellow, even elegant, interiors allow the line's impressive innovations in dining, entertainment, kids' facilities, and cabin design to take center stage. If you love Disney, you'll love these ships; if not, they might not be worth their none-too-cheap price tags.

THE EXPERIENCE   The *Disney Magic* and *Disney Wonder* are the famous company's first foray into cruising, and boast a handful of truly innovative, Disney-style features, including a rotating series of restaurants on every cruise, cabins designed for families, monumental Disney entertainment, and the biggest kids' facilities at sea. It's innovations like these—along with higher prices—that set Disney's cruises far apart.

In many ways, the experience is more Disney than it is cruise, so while first-timers and Disney fanatics will just have a ball, old cruise hands may notice a few things missing (for instance, no casino or library, and fewer adult activities in general). On the other hand, the ships, designed as more-or-less identical twins, are surprisingly elegant and well-laid out, and the Disney-isms are subtly sprinkled, like fairy dust, throughout their mellow, art deco– and art nouveau–inspired interiors and grand, classic-liner-inspired exteriors. Head to toe, the ships are a class act.

In the spirit of Disney's penchant for organization, its 3- and 4-day cruises are designed to be combined with a land-based Disney theme park and hotel package to create a weeklong all-Disney vacation.

Pros

- **Kids' programs.** Two huge playrooms plus a teen cafe are the largest at sea.
- **Family entertainment.** Endearing, elaborate, family-oriented Disney musicals are performed on some of the best-equipped and most high-tech stages of any ship today.
- **Family-style cabins.** All cabins have a sitting area with a sofabed to sleep families of at least three, and the majority have a bathroom and a half.

Cons

- **Limited adult entertainment.** There is no casino or library.
- **Small gyms.** They're on the small side and border on being cramped.
- **Meager breakfast and lunch buffets.** In relation to the size of the ship, the buffet spread in the Topsider Cafe is limited.

Frommer's Ratings: Disney Cruise Line					
	Poor	Fair	Good	Excellent	Outstanding
Enjoyment Factor					✓
Dining				✓	
Activities				✓	
Children's Program					✓
Entertainment					✓
Service			✓		
Overall Value			✓		

DISNEY: THE OLD MOUSE & THE SEA

After much ballyhoo and lots of delays, the *Disney Magic* finally made its debut in the summer of 1998, and at press time its sister, the *Disney Wonder,* was scheduled to be launched in late summer 1999 after being originally slated to debut in late 1998. Disney has blamed the tardiness on the shipyard, Fincantieri of Italy, while the *Wall Street Journal* and a host of industry insiders also point to Disney's penchant for perfectionism and the ships' slew of high-tech gizmos as having had contributed to the delay. When it comes right down to it, though, it's like that old joke about the hen sleeping in the henhouse, the dog in the doghouse, and the elephant wherever the hell it wants to—Disney is a big, powerful company, and it does things when and how it chooses.

Indeed, Disney, the cruise line, does march to the beat of its own drummer and considers itself a unique species within the cruise industry. From its ships' blue-black hulls and twin funnels (one is fake) to its rotating restaurant concept, family suites with two bathrooms, and lack of a casino, Disney is different—but less so today than a year ago. Fact is, Disney has made some adjustments as a result of a spate of complaints. By trial and error, Disney has learned that it can indeed learn from the industry and from what established lines have found works. For instance, unlike most other lines operating in the Caribbean and Bahamas, Disney originally bundled its cruise and Orlando packages with airfare, thus making their prices, which are already high, seem even higher and harder to compare against similar packages offered by other lines. Disney has since changed its pricing format, and prints airfare separately in its brochures, just like everyone else. In the beginning, Disney also didn't think it needed a cruise director or hotel director. It now has both (on the *Magic,* a former cruise director with HAL and a former hotel director from the *QE2*), and attributes a smoother onboard experience to these two key individuals. Disney Cruise Line president Arthur Rodney was quoted in early 1999 as saying, "We're evolving. Those who traveled on the *Magic* in the beginning wouldn't recognize her today." There you go: You really can teach an old dog new tricks.

THE FLEET

Both **Disney Magic** and **Disney Wonder** have the same size, layout, and, for the most part, mellow decorative motifs. Inside and out, they represent Disney's attempt to re-create the grandeur of the classic transatlantic liners—an attempt at which, if we allow for their modern, Disney-fied manner, they succeed.

Both ships weigh in at 83,000 gross register tons, measure 964 feet in length (about as long as New York's famous Chrysler Building is tall), and carry 1,760 passengers at the rate of two per cabin, or up to a whopping 3,325 if every third, fourth, and fifth berth in every cabin is filled. An American staff and a crew of 945 service 875 staterooms.

The Disney touch is evident throughout the ships, although, to the designers' credit, it's not overwhelming or cloying. On the *Magic,* Mickey's big-eared head appears on the pair of giant red funnels, fanciful golden curlicues decorate the pointed blue-black bow, outlines of Mickey and the gang are quietly worked into the silver-toned grillwork and frieze in the atrium, an understated bronzy statue of Mickey as the sorcerer's apprentice in *Fantasia* appears as the focus of the three-story atrium, framed story sketches from famous 1930s and '40s Disney animated movies are blended tastefully against the generous caramel-colored wood paneling in the stairways and corridors, and a huge white-gloved Mickey hand holds up the snaking slide at the children's pool while tiny little Mickey hands quietly point to the floors above the banks of elevators.

At press time, the *Wonder* was scheduled to launch in August 1999. The layout of the ship, including cabins, pool deck, and restaurants, will be virtually identical to the

---

The Disney Cruise-Park Package: Look Ma, No Seams

In the spirit of Disney's penchant for organization, its "seamless" vacation mantra tends to leave little to chance or whim. To shuttle passengers to and from the Orlando International Airport and Disney's theme parks, Disney's got an army of special buses (with little Mickey silhouettes worked into the upholstery) at the ready. To get passengers in the mood, an orientation video about the cruise is played during the nearly hour-long trip between Orlando and the ship. At Disney's swank new cruise terminal at Port Canaveral, guests who have come from the resorts (guests doing the 7-night parks/cruise combo must do the parks portion first) already have their all-purpose, computerized "key-to-the-world" cards, which get them into their cabins, serve as the onboard charge cards, and function as their ID when getting on and off the ship in port. There's no need, then, to actually check in at the terminal. If you're just doing the cruise (as about 30% of passengers do), you get your key-to-the-world card when you arrive at the terminal.

Disney estimates that about 70% of its passengers purchase the "seamless" 7-day land/sea packages, which include either 3 or 4 days at Disney World resort and 3 or 4 days aboard ship. (Passengers wanting to book only the cruise portion can do so subject to space availability.) Costs for a 7-day package for a family of four, with airfare, could easily run about $5,000. That's roughly equivalent to a week-long holiday at Walt Disney World in Orlando, and tends to be a bit higher—as much as 25% more—than other Port Canaveral–based vessels, including those of Carnival and Royal Caribbean, each of which currently offers short sailings coordinated with vacations at or near Central Florida theme parks.

Magic. The entertainment and dining options will be a mirror image, as well. So what will the differences be? There will be different names for the public rooms and instead of the art deco motif found on the Magic, the Wonder will have an art nouveau–inspired motif in its public areas.

PASSENGER PROFILE

Just walk around Walt Disney World and you'll see exactly the kind of people Disney attracts to its ships—families, honeymooners, adults without children, and seniors. Just about everybody, actually. There are also a fair number of foreigner passengers as well—it seems like *everyone* loves Disney.

DINING

Disney's dining concept sets it apart from the big-ship crowd. While the food is average cruise fare and service varies from efficient to a bit harried and amateur, the neat catch is that there are **three restaurants** that passengers (and their servers) rotate among over the course of the cruise. Passengers dine on breast of chicken stuffed with goose liver or a beef tenderloin in a green peppercorn sauce in the elegant, 1930s-era Lumiere's on one night; enjoy the likes of roasted rum pork or grilled mahi-mahi in the tropical Parrot Cay another; and on the third eat in the signature, very Disney Animator's Palate, a bustling, high-tech eatery that starts out completely black and white and over the course of your meal gradually becomes awash in color as the walls and ceiling light up. Here, choices include rigatoni sautéed with garlic, tomatoes, and white wine, and parmesan and herb–crusted veal cutlets. For dessert, guests get to design their own creations: They're served a palette-shaped plate of ice-cream and apply their own toppings from paint-like squeeze bottles.

In all restaurants, a **vegetarian option** is offered. After its first few months, Disney also expanded its **kids' menus** to include more healthy fare in addition to the hamburger, hot dog, and macaroni-and-cheese staples.

The buffet-style breakfast and lunch spread in the Topsider Café offers items like deli meats, cheeses, and a carving station as well as rice and vegetable dishes. There's a salad bar and a dessert table. Overall, though, compared to other ships its size, it's slim pickins in the Topsider Café. Options for afternoon noshing poolside include Pinocchio's Pizzeria; Pluto's Dog House for hot dogs, hamburgers, and fries,; and Scoops ice-cream bar. There's **24-hour room service** from a limited menu, but there's no midnight buffet. If you're lucky enough to actually snag a table, the 136-passenger, **reservations-only restaurant,** Palo, is a romantic adults-only dining venue serving Italian specialties far away from the fray. If you want to dine here, be sure to book a table as soon as you get aboard the first day—and try to get aboard early, since tables go *fast.*

ACTIVITIES

Although activities for adults are limited compared to other big-ship lines, there are indeed some pastimes geared to adults and adults only. Each ship has an entertainment complex with three lounges for adults only, the cozy, reservations-only, Palo restaurant (see "Dining," above), a sprawling, casual **Jazz Lounge** (feels like an outdoor cafe in New Orleans), and the **ESPN Sky Box bar** (a smallish, brightly lit sports bar with a huge wide-screen TV showing all manner of sports on ESPN). There is not a casino of any kind, nor is there a library or a card room.

In keeping with its theme of offering a cruise experience for each member of the family, each passenger receives a personalized activities calendar every day, meaning that children's calendars advise them about playtimes and kids' activities, teens' calendars include java times in the New York–style coffee bar and are somewhat loosely structured (just the way teens like it), and adults' calendars include spa times and information on the ships' sports offerings and nightlife options.

In the first few months after the *Magic* was launched in July 1998, complaints were common about the ship not offering enough activities for adults. To Disney's credit, the company listened and responded by adding more programming. Tapping its land-based Disney Institute program, as well as its parks and hotels, it began to offer **adult workshops** on subjects like acting (taught by the actual Beast from the Broadway show), animation, photography, antiques, and topical subjects (like Jewish history) at certain times of the year. During the day at sea on the 4-night cruise itinerary, a **master chefs program** features cooking demonstrations and wine tasting by Disney resorts' top chefs and sommeliers. All these activities are complimentary except wine tasting, which is $15 per person. There are also **adult movies** (no, not *that* kind!) and a **captain's cocktail party** with complimentary drinks once per cruise.

CHILDREN'S PROGRAM

As you would expect, with as many as 500 to 800 kids on any given sailing, Disney's kids' facilities are the most extensive at sea, with as many as 50 dedicated **counselors** on hand to supervise the fun for five age groups. Nearly half a deck and two huge spaces are dedicated to kids. The Oceaneer Club, for ages 3 to 8 (with separate activities for ages 3 to 5 and 6 to 8), is a playroom themed on Captain Hook. Kids can climb and crawl on a giant pirate ship's bow as well as jumbo-sized animals and barrels, and get dressed up from a trunk full of costumes. The far-out Oceaneer Lab offers kids ages 9 to 12 (with separate activities for ages 9 to 10 and 11 to 12) a chance to work on computers, learn fun science with microscopes, and do arts and crafts.

Castaway Cay: A Well-Oiled Machine

Not surprisingly, Castaway Cay, Disney's 1,000-acre private island in the Bahamas and a port of call on both 3- and 4-night cruises, is a well-oiled machine. Disney has developed only 55 acres of the island, and guests can snorkel, feast on a buffet barbecue, ride bikes along a trail, shop, send postcards, lounge in a hammock, have a massage, or just lie on the beach. It's all sugar-white beaches, turquoise Caribbean waters, and weathered wooden huts with old-fashioned signs advertising Pop's Props & Boat Repair, Cookies BBQ, and the Conched Out Bar—all there just for the enjoyment of Disney passengers.

What's its best quality? Its accessibility. Unlike the private islands of Holland America, Royal Caribbean, Princess, Costa, and NCL, which require the ships to anchor offshore and shuttle passengers back and forth on tenders, the *Magic* and *Wonder* can pull right up to the dock, allowing guests to literally step from the ship right onto the pink cement path that leads to the island of fun. It's a 7-minute walk to the main beach area, or you can hop one of the shuttle trams, which transport passengers to the main beaches and to the adults-only beach and bar, about a mile away.

The ships arrive at the cay in the morning, and passengers are greeted by a host or hostess and given a towel, after which they scatter in all directions—families to one beach; teens to another where they can swim, lounge, or play volleyball, soccer, or tetherball; and adults 18 and older to a third, the secluded, mile-long alabaster stretch aptly called Serenity Bay, located in the north part of the island.

To make sure all members of the family are covered, parents can first head to Scuttle's Cove, a **children's activity center** for ages 3 to 12 where activities include arts and crafts, music and theater, and an excavation site where little ones (and big ones) can check out the skeletal remains of a 35-foot female whale. Kids can also go on their own dig, complete with sifting pans.

At **Serenity Bay,** the emphasis is on rest and relaxation. Guests can have a drink at the nearby Castaway Air Bar, lie on the beach, go for a swim, or head to a private ocean-view cabana for an open-air 55-minute massage.

The **family beach** is lined with lounge chairs and pastel-colored umbrellas. Families who come here can explore the island's 15-acre snorkeling course or rent a kayak, paddle boat, or banana boat. Adult- and child-sized bicycles can be rented for $5 for a ride along a 3-mile bike path around the island.

On Disney's **private island,** Castaway Cay (which each itinerary visits for a day), activities like scavenger hunts are scheduled for the kids while adults can head for the adults-only Serenity Bay. (There's also a family beach, if you're not in too dire a need of some serenity.)

For teens, the cool Common Grounds **teen coffee bar** is the place to buy a cappuccino or Virgin Margarita, plop down into the big comfy chairs, flip through one of the many magazines in the rack, or pop on one of the headphone sets hooked to a selection of over 70 music CDs. There's nothing close to this on any other ship, and even your way-too-cool teens might be enticed by the atmosphere.

Kids can eat **dinner with counselors** in the Topsiders Café; if mom and dad want more time alone, private **baby-sitting** can be arranged on a first-come, first-served basis for $11 an hour for one child or $12 for two—steep compared to the $8 charged

Disney Fleet Itineraries			
Ship	Home Ports & Season	Itinerary	Other Itineraries
Disney Magic	Port Canaveral, weekly year-round.	**3- and 4-night Bahamas:** Nassau and Castaway Cay.	None
Disney Wonder	Port Canaveral, weekly year-round.	**3- and 4-night Bahamas:** Nassau and Castaway Cay.	None

by most ships. Also, parents and kids each get a **tuned beeper** when they first check into the kids' program so that they can keep in touch even if junior is blazing through the virtual universe at the Oceaneer Lab and Mom and Dad are relaxing in the spa's thermal bath.

ENTERTAINMENT

The ships' fresh, family-oriented entertainment is a stand-out and unparalleled at sea. On one of the best-equipped stages at sea in the nostalgic Walt Disney Theatre, actors disappear into trap doors, fly across the stage, and go through endless exciting costume changes. After-dinner performances by **Broadway-caliber entertainers** in this show lounge include "Disney Dreams," a sweet musical medley of Disney classics, taking the audience from *Peter Pan* to *The Lion King;* "Voyage of the Ghost Ship," an adventurous musical with a piratey theme; and "Hercules, A Muse-ical Comedy," a salute to the popular Disney film. The *Disney Wonder* will have this exact same repertoire.

So what else is there, after the show is over and the kids are in bed? On the *Magic,* there's an adults-only entertainment area called Beat Street (on the *Wonder,* it's called Route 66). Offering entertainment for those 18 and older, these isolated sections of the forward part of Deck 3 each boast three themed nightclubs: an elegant and plush venue for **romantic music,** jazz, and blues; a 1970s-style bright and whimsical **comedy club** featuring really funny improv skits; and a room styled after an American **roadhouse** and featuring—what else?—rock 'n' roll and a large dance floor. These areas can get crowded when the ship is carrying a full load, and there won't be a quiet nook to be found—besides this area (and an adults-only pool up on Deck 9), there's not a whole lot geared to adults.

While adults traveling without children should think twice about booking with Disney during the peak kid season, for Disney fanatics and families not afraid of crowds, the ships offer the classic Disney brand of wholesome fun in an elegant, seafaring setting.

SERVICE

Some 40 nationalities come together to serve you. Many are young Americans, just as at the parks. Expect service in the dining rooms to be roughly equivalent to the top-level Disney World restaurants in Orlando—friendly and efficient, but at times amateurish to a certain degree. Cabin service isn't always the most efficient (for instance, finished food, drinks, and used towels are not always removed within a reasonable amount of time) and chances are, you'll never see or meet your steward.

Services include **laundry** and **dry cleaning** (the ships also have **self-service laundry rooms**), and 1-hour photo processing. Strollers are available at no extra cost. On Castaway Cay, cargo carts (to carry your beach stuff) and bicycles for kids and adults can be rented for $5 apiece.

Disney Magic •
Disney Wonder

The Verdict

The only ships on the planet that successfully re-create the grandeur of the classic transatlantic liners, albeit in a modern, Disney-fied way.

Disney Magic *(photo: Disney Cruise Line)*

Specifications

Size (in tons)	83,000	Crew	945 (International)
Number of Cabins	880	Passenger/Crew Ratio	1.9 to 1
Number of Outside Cabins	640	Year Built	
Cabins with Verandas	280	*Magic*	1998
Number of Passengers	1,760*	*Wonder*	1999
Officers	European/ Norwegian	Last Major Refurbishment	N/A

* Note: Double-occupancy figure. With children's berths filled, capacity can go as high as 3,325.

Frommer's Ratings (Scale of 1–5)

Cabin Comfort & Amenities	5	Pool, Fitness & Spa Facilities	3
Ship Cleanliness & Maintenance	4	Children's Facilities	5
Public Comfort/Space	4	Itinerary	4
Decor	5	Worth the Money	4

These long, proud-looking ships carry 1,760 passengers at the rate of two per cabin, but, since Disney is a family company and its ships were built expressly to carry three, four, and five people in virtually every cabin, the ship could theoretically carry a whopping 3,325 passengers. Zowie! Typically, though, every single bed will not be filled (the ship would be pretty darned crowded if it were!), and getting up past about 2,600 passengers is not common.

CABINS   The Disney ships offer the family-friendliest cabins at sea, with standard cabins equivalent to the suites or demi-suites on most ships. All of the 875 cabins have at least a sitting area with a sofabed to sleep families of three, a bunch also have a pull-down wall-bunk to comfortably sleep four, and nearly half have private verandas. At 220 square feet, the ships' standard cabins are about 25% larger than the industry standard (but—guess what?—a cruise on the *Magic* or *Wonder* costs nearly that much more than one on Carnival or Royal Caribbean). Family suites, at 304 square feet, have private verandas and sleep four or five comfortably. Outside cabins that don't have verandas have jumbo-sized porthole windows.

The decor of each cabin is virtually identical, with warm wood-tone paneling and furniture, a framed black-and-white 1930s shot of Mr. and Mrs. Walt Disney aboard the fabled ocean liner *Rex,* and over the beds an enlarged piece of sheet music with the notes and lyrics to "When You Wish Upon a Star."

Their best feature? Look no further than the bathrooms to find the pièce de résistance of the ships' staterooms and something found on no other ship today: The majority of cabins are equipped with *two bathrooms*—a sink and toilet in one and a shower/tub combo and a sink in the other, and both with ample shelf space.

All cabins have a mini-fridge, hair dryer, safe, TV, shower-tub combo, and sitting area.

Cabins & Rates						
Cabins	Per diems from	Bathtub	Fridge	Hair Dryer	Sitting Area	TV
Inside	$136*	yes	yes	yes	yes	yes
Outside	$228*	yes	yes	yes	yes	yes
Suite	$389*	yes	yes	yes	yes	yes

Prices based on a 7-night cruise/land package.

PUBLIC AREAS   The ships' three-story atria are more understated than you might expect, so much so that when I first entered the *Magic*'s, I wasn't sure I was even in the main hub of the ship. It's more like a pleasant, upscale hotel lobby than your typical flashy megaship atrium.

The adults-only area includes a comedy club, elegant piano lounge, and a large disco. There's also a family-oriented entertainment lounge called Studio Sea for karaoke, game shows, and dancing for the whole family, and a sports bar, the ESPN Sky Box, located near the ship's forward funnel and featuring worldwide sports television coverage. A really neat observation area above the bridge—unfortunately open only while the ship is in port—allows passengers to look down into the bridge and get some idea of how a ship is operated. A 270-seat cinema shows first-run or classic Disney movies. The children's facilities, as you'd expect, are the largest on any ship at sea (see "Children's Program," above, for details).

POOL, FITNESS & SPA FACILITIES   The Pool Deck of each ship pretty well sums up the segregated-yet-integrated adults/children scheme of the Disney experience: Toward the stern is Mickey's Kids' Pool, with a great big white-gloved Mickey hand holding up the snaking yellow sliding board; then, separated by a rest room area and Pinocchio's Pizza, comes Goofy's Family Pool, where adults and children can mingle. Moving forward past this family area, past the stage and the teen cafe and video arcade, you enter the Quiet Cove Adult Pool, with its whirlpools and poolside Signals Bar.

The surprisingly drab fitness centers aboard both ships are on the small side, as they often are on ships built for the 3- and 4-day cruise market, although there are a pair of virtual-reality step machines that are pretty cool and a separate aerobics area. The 8,500-square-foot, Steiner-managed Vista Spa & Salon is perched at the bow end of the deck, and has attractive tiled treatment rooms, a sauna, and a steam room. The ships have an outdoor sports deck with basketball and paddle tennis. There's also a jogging track, shuffleboard, and Ping-Pong.

Holland America Line–Westours

SHIPS   Maasdam • Nieuw Amsterdam • Noordam • Ryndam • Veendam • Volendam (preview) • Westerdam • Zaandam (preview)

300 Elliott Ave. W., Seattle, WA 98119. ☎ **800/426-0327** or 206/281-3535. Fax 800/628-4855. www.hollandamerica.com.

THE LINE IN A NUTSHELL   More than any other line today (except Cunard), HAL has managed to hang on to some of its seafaring history and tradition, offering a moderately priced, classic, casual yet refined ocean-liner-like cruise experience.

THE EXPERIENCE   HAL consistently delivers a worthy and solid product for a fair price, and is unique for offering mid-sized to large ships with an old-world elegance that remains low-key and not stuffy. These ships aren't boring, but they're sedate, so it's no surprise that the line attracts predominantly older passengers (but the age range is widening).

The line's clean and well-maintained ships are mostly mid-sized, creating a cozy atmosphere; the decor of the Statendam-class ships and the *Rotterdam* and *Volendam* is stylish, sleek, and, for the most part, understated, and their excellent layouts ease passenger movement. HAL's three older ships, the *Westerdam, Noordam,* and *Nieuw Amsterdam,* are the most humble, with pleasing but simple, public rooms.

Holland America emphasizes tradition, and that's what sets it apart. In the public areas you'll see trophies and memorabilia, and the very names of the vessels hark back to ships in the line's past. For example, the line's new flagship, the 62,000-ton *Rotterdam,* is the sixth HAL ship to bear that name.

Pros

- **History and tradition.** The impressive collection of artifacts and artwork on the ships reflect Holland America's important place in seafaring history and lend the ships more of a traditional ocean liner ambience than can be found on nearly any other line.
- **Private verandas.** Over 25% of all cabins on the Statendam-class ships and the *Volendam* boast private cabin balconies.
- **Great gyms.** For their size, the Statendam-class ships on up offer some of the most attractive, roomy, and well-stocked gyms and aerobics areas at sea.

Cons

- **Sleepy nightlife.** While there's always a few stalwarts and a couple of busy-ish nights, if you're big on late-night dancing and bar hopping, you may find yourself partying mostly with the entertainment staff.
- **Homogenous passenger profile.** Although this is changing to a certain degree, passengers tend to be 50+, low-key North American couples.

Frommer's Ratings: Holland America Line					
	Poor	Fair	Good	Excellent	Outstanding
Enjoyment Factor					✓
Dining				✓	
Activities				✓	
Children's Program		✓			
Entertainment			✓		
Service					✓
Overall Value					✓

HOLLAND AMERICA: GOING DUTCH

One of the most famous shipping companies in the world, Holland America Line was founded in 1873 as the Nederlandsch Amerikaansche StoomvAart Maatschappij (Netherlands-American Steamship Company), and because the line provided service between New York City and Rotterdam, Holland, it soon became known as Holland America Line. The company's first ocean liner was the original *Rotterdam,* which took its maiden, 15-day voyage from the Netherlands to New York City in 1872.

By the turn of the century, Holland America owned a fleet of six passenger-cargo ships, and traveled between Holland and Asia (the Dutch East Indies) via the Suez Canal. In the early 1900s, Holland America was one of the major lines transporting thousands of hopeful immigrants from Europe to the United States, and continued a regular schedule of transatlantic crossings up until 1971, when the line turned to offering cruises full time.

During World War II, the company's headquarters moved from Nazi-occupied Holland to Dutch-owned Curaçao, then the site of a strategic oil refinery. Strong links were forged with North American interests after the war when Westours, a Seattle-based company, began booking large blocks of Holland America cabins. In 1973, Holland America Line changed its name to Holland America Cruises to promote its new focus on cruising; then, in 1974, Westours and HAL were linked to give the line a presence in Alaska, where it has remained one of the two biggest cruisetour players today.

The line changed its name back to Holland America Line in 1983, seeking to capitalize on its history and seafaring traditions, and began building the fleet of mid-sized ships that exists now. The *Nieuw Amsterdam* was launched in 1983, followed by the *Noordam* in 1984, the *Westerdam* in 1986, the *Statendam, Maasdam, Ryndam,* and *Veendam* between 1993 and 1996, the *Rotterdam VI* in 1997, and the new *Volendam,* at press time scheduled to be launched in August. Two *Volendam* sister ships are due out in early and late 2000.

In the midst of this building spree, in 1988, HAL acquired Windstar Cruises, expanding its midlevel services into the upper echelons of the cruise experience. To everyone's surprise, both companies were acquired a year later by Carnival Corporation. Many industry observers predicted the company's demise, yet the opposite occurred. Carnival improved entertainment quality and quantity (the line needed both), upgraded HAL's cuisine, and provided the cash and credit to commission four additional vessels, with more to come.

THE FLEET

Of its nine ships, the 1,214-passenger **Noordam** and **Nieuw Amsterdam** (launched in 1984 and 1983, respectively) and the 1,494-passenger **Westerdam** (built in 1986 for Home Lines and purchased by HAL in 1988) are the older, plainer ships of the HAL fleet. Built in the pre-Carnival days, they lack any of the frills you'll see on the later ships. The company's four 1,266-passenger Statendam-class ships—the **Statendam** and **Maasdam** (both inaugurated in 1993), **Ryndam** (1994), and **Veendam** (1996)—are carbon copies of the same attractive, well-crafted design (with a dash of glitz here and there). They were all built at the Fincantieri shipyard in Monfalcone, Italy, as were all of the newer HAL ships.

In 1997, HAL launched its most sophisticated ship, **Rotterdam VI,** which replaces the 1957-vintage *Rotterdam V* (sold to Premier Cruises and rechristened the *Rembrandt*). The line's new flagship, it spends most of its year outside the Caribbean, and therefore isn't reviewed in this book. I've also not reviewed the **Statendam,** which spends its year in Mexico, Hawaii, and Alaska.

HAL: The Generous Line

Holland America is generous with its complimentary treats (a rarity in today's nickle-and-diming industry), serving hot canapés in some of the bar/lounges during the cocktail hour, offering freshly popped popcorn in the movie theater, doling out espresso and cappuccino at no charge in the Java Cafes, and serving lemonade on deck on all warm-weather cruises. Unlike other lines, there's no cover charge in the small, alternative restaurants on the *Volendam, Zaandam,* and *Rotterdam.* Stewards replenish a bowl of fruit in your cabin daily, and each guest is given a Holland America canvas tote bag.

At press time, two additional members of HAL's fleet, the **Volendam** and **Zaandam,** were in the latest stages of their construction. The *Volendam* is scheduled to debut in late October 1999 and the *Zaandam* in late March 2000. Meanwhile, the new sister ship to the *Rotterdam VI,* the **Amsterdam,** is scheduled to launch in late 2000. (Does this name choice portend the demise of the Nieuw Amsterdam? The cruise line says no. Hmmm . . .) The *Volendam* and *Zaandam* will combine features of the Statendam-class ships with innovations currently being seen on the new *Rotterdam,* and will be slightly larger than the latter in size (63,000 tons, as opposed to 59,652), and carry more passengers (1,440, against the *Rotterdam's* 1,316 and the Statendam class's 1,266). Harking back to HAL's Dutch roots, the *Volendam's* decorative theme will be flowers while the *Zaandam's* theme will be music—exemplified by one of the more unusual and inspired atrium decorations we know of: a huge, working pipe organ with mechanical figures of dancing musicians.

PASSENGER PROFILE

In sum, HAL stands for good, solid quality with its well-rounded onboard experience. Shipboard ambience is characterized by an unstuffy lack of pretension, relaxed friendliness, and good value for the money.

Before its acquisition by Carnival in 1989, HAL passengers tended overwhelmingly to be older people in their 60s and 70s, but Carnival's influence has moved the demographics toward a somewhat younger market, although any kind of real transformation is slow as molasses in coming and far from complete (if indeed it ever will be). HAL's passenger rosters typically include some graying, 50-ish members of the baby-boom generation, mixed in with many passengers of their parents' age.

Passengers tend to be better educated than their equivalents aboard a Carnival ship, but a lot less affluent than those aboard a luxury line like Seabourn. Passengers tend to be hospitable and amiable, and sensible with their money. They tend to be fairly set in their ways and not adventurous.

The line attracts many groups traveling together, from incentive groups to social clubs on a lark together. If you're a 40-something member of such a group and are worried about finding company aboard, don't abandon hope, particularly if you happen to be a divorcée, widow, or widower: You won't be alone.

DINING

Joining the trend, Holland America recently began offering an **alternative dinner option** in its casual buffet-style breakfast and lunch Lido restaurant. On a typical 7-day cruise, for example, the Lido dinner option will be offered on 3 nights (not on the formal nights or on the last night of the cruise), and feature open seating from 7pm through 8:30pm, so guests can dine when they choose. A pianist will entertain guests, and tables will be set with linens. The set menu features the basics: Caesar salad, shrimp cocktail, or fresh fruit cup appetizer, French onion soup, freshly baked dinner rolls, and four entree choices, including salmon, sirloin steak, roast chicken, and lasagna, served with a vegetable of the day and a baked potato or rice pilaf. Two dessert choices are cheesecake or chocolate cake. As in the formal dining room, complimentary beverages include iced tea, milk, coffee, or hot tea, and a bar steward offers additional beverages, including wine, for purchase.

Of course, an elegant dinner in the main dining room is still the preferred venue. As its executive chef, HAL employs the renowned Reiner Greubel, formerly of Westin Hotels, New York's Plaza Hotel, and his own Reiner's Restaurant in Seattle. Instead of daring experimentation, he recognizes that some of the world's finest cuisine comes from classics prepared with fresh and high-quality ingredients, and that some sophisticated palates still prefer traditional favorites: osso buco, cassoulet, Alaskan king crab, and Caribbean snapper, for instance. Dinner items might be as straightforward as roast prime rib of beef with baked Idaho potatoes and horseradish cream, or as esoteric as warm hazelnut-crusted brie with a compote of apples and onions. Children can enjoy tried-and-true staples like pizza, hot dogs, burgers with fries, chicken fingers, and tacos. These dishes are supplemented with chef's specials, such as pasta or fish and chips.

Greubel has also expanded the line's **light and healthy cuisine** with more fresh fish, such as pompano and grouper, and more pasta dishes with vegetable-based sauces. He also serves what he calls **fun foods,** meaning spring rolls and sushi, and has increased emphasis on offering the fare of the Caribbean, particularly at **theme buffets.**

A major improvement in the cuisine is the **desserts.** Greubel has moved away from grandmother's favorite cakes and heavy, cream-laden desserts in favor of newer, more sophisticated creations with more flavorful, delicate sauces, including many desserts based on tropical fruit. His crème brûlée with fresh cherries is a delight, as is his tropical trifle with salmon berries, raspberries, pineapple, kiwi, and coconut cream.

Buffets with the inevitable queues are bountiful and frequent. At lunch, they are supplemented by stations where you can make your own tacos, lavish salad bars, a different pasta every day, stir-fried dishes made to order, and an ice-cream station where you can get a scoop or two and add your own toppings. **Indonesian dishes** are the theme of at least one buffet a week, and Indonesian satay (beef or chicken grilled on a wooden skewer and served with peanut sauce) appears at buffets almost as regularly as potato salad and coleslaw.

Breakfasts contain some vestiges of Dutch cuisine, such as Gouda cheese, and Dutch influences also prevail at least once during each cruise in a **Dutch Chocolate Extravaganza,** a Holland-themed midnight buffet where the calories stack up so fast you might as well give up trying to count them.

Room service is available 24 hours a day. Midmorning bouillon and **afternoon teas** are well-attended events. Hot canapés are served in some of the bar/lounges during the cocktail hour. During warm-weather cruises, lemonade is served on deck, one of many

---

A Rose by Any Other Name Would Cost as Much

In addition to nautical memorabilia from Holland America's long history, decoration aboard all the line's ships contains a bow to the Dutch love of horticulture: HAL has a weekly budget for flowers that, according to company spokespersons, runs up to $20,000 a week for the fleet.

Holland America's Theme Cruises

Holland America Line is big on special cruises and had 14 scheduled in 1999, and a series scheduled for 2000 as well, all on board the 1,494-passenger *Westerdam* in the eastern Caribbean. Holland America will continue its extremely popular series of **Big Band cruises,** which feature the smooth sounds of the Glenn Miller Orchestra, Guy Lombardo's Royal Canadians, and the Tommy Dorsey Orchestra. Also on the schedule are a series of 1950s **Sock Hop cruises** featuring performers like The Platters and the Shirelles; a series of **Broadway theme** sailings featuring greats like Joel Grey (from *Cabaret* and *Chicago*); and a cruise paying tribute to **Frank Sinatra,** hosted by Sid Mark of the nationally syndicated radio show "Sounds of Sinatra."

thoughtful touches provided at frequent intervals by the well-trained staff. All ships but *Westerdam, Noordam,* and *Nieuw Amsterdam* have **Java Cafes,** a comfy cluster of seating around a small coffee bar serving complimentary espresso and cappuccinos—a rare freebie—mornings and afternoons.

ACTIVITIES

Activities are varied, relatively nontaxing, and fun. Seminars on upcoming ports of call are popular, as are deck games. You can learn how to dance cheek-to-cheek, be taught the fine art of vegetable carving or creative napkin folding, or play bingo or bridge. There are trivia games and Pictionary tournaments. A member of the cruise will take interested passengers on **art tours,** discussing the ship's impressive art collection and giving passengers a hand-out about the collections. Of course, you can also just relax all day in a lounge chair with a good book.

Activities pick up a bit at night, when pre-dinner cocktails and **dancing** are a major event of the day. Afterward, you might visit the show lounge and/or the **casino,** attend a "Fabulous 50s" party or a country-western night, take part in the "Champagne Slot Tournament" or "Night Owl Pajama Bingo," indulge yourself at the "Dutch Chocolate Extravaganza," or take in a **midnight movie** or the ever-popular **crew show,** in which Indonesian and/or Filipino crew members present songs and dances from their homelands.

On cruises 14 nights and longer and on transatlantic sailings, women traveling alone or those whose escorts have two left feet need not fear for lack of dance partners: A complement of "gentlemen hosts" sail on board and are available for a whirl or two around the dance floor.

CHILDREN'S PROGRAM

Whenever demand warrants it, HAL offers supervised programs for children, called **Club HAL.** The menu of activities is not anywhere as extensive as on lines like Disney, Carnival, Celebrity, Royal Caribbean, and Princess, and HAL never pretends it is. When enough kids are on board, programs are designated for three different age brackets: 5- to 8-year-olds, 9- to 12-year-olds, and teens. However, based on the number of young people aboard, these barriers sometimes blur.

Regardless of the age of the attendees, young people are diverted with pizza and soda parties, as well as tours of the bridge, the galley, and other areas below deck. There might also be movies, ice-cream parties, arts and crafts, storytelling sessions, games, karaoke, golf lessons, disco parties, charades, bingo, and Ping-Pong. On the first night of each cruise, parents meet and mingle with staff responsible for the care, counseling, and feeding of their children. Activities are not scheduled while a ship is in port.

There are **playrooms** on all ships (on the *Nieuw Amsterdam, Noordam,* and *Westerdam,* the rooms do double duty as meeting or card rooms when there aren't many kids on board); those on the Statendam-class and newer ships are the most child-friendly, by far.

Baby-sitting is sometimes (but not always) available from volunteers among a ship's staff. If a staff member is available—and be warned, their availability is never guaranteed—the cost is usually around $5 per child per hour.

ENTERTAINMENT

Onboard entertainment has improved since HAL's acquisition by Carnival, which really understands how cabaret shows should be presented. For instance, in late 1998, Holland America augmented its entertainment lineup with the introduction of *Barry Manilow's Copacabana.* This 60-minute, Vegas-style show, which is the biggest and most lavish production ever staged on a Holland America ship, is set in 1948 at the famous Copacabana night club, and is being performed on the *Ryndam, Statendam,* and *Volendam.*

Copa aside, each ship features small-scale glittery and shimmery **Broadway-style shows** with live music and laser lights. There are also trios and quartets playing big band–style oldies as well as pianists performing in the lounges.

First-run movies are shown an average of three times a day in an onboard cinema, and there's even hot, freshly made popcorn dispensed from a machine near the entrance, for those who can't watch a movie without it. There's always a **crew talent show** once per week, as well as an outdoor Caribbean-themed deck party where all sorts of silly games and contests are held. At one of these parties, I once watched dozens of passengers whooping it up in a relay-race contest that had something to do with balloons and blindfolds. It was a riot for participants and voyeurs alike.

On the Statendam-class and newer ships, the **disco** is part of the spacious Crow's Nest observation lounge. Generally a live four-piece band plays from about 9pm to midnight and a DJ takes over for the next few hours. These are attractive areas, and often a few nights a week there's a small coterie of late-night types dancing up a storm; invariably, some of the young dancers from the show troop hang out as well. On the *Noordam* and *Nieuw Amsterdam,* the disco is also in a larger lounge and sees more action than you might expect a few nights a week. There's usually a '50s sock hop theme one night in the disco to get people in the mood, with twist and hula-hoop contests, for instance.

SERVICE

Onboard service is permeated with nostalgia for the Netherlands's past and its genteel traditions. During lunch, a uniformed employee might hold open the door of a buffet, and a steward ringing a chime will formally announce the two dinner seatings.

Holland America is one of the few cruise lines that maintains a training school (a land-based facility in Indonesia known within HAL circles as the SS Jakarta) for the selection and training of its staff. On the ships, the soft-spoken staff smiles more often than not as they labor to offer reasonably attentive service. You won't find a staff member rushing toward you every time you raise an eyebrow, but if you're only moderately demanding, you'll certainly get what you want. Beginning in the mid-1990s, HAL hired more multilingual staff members (usually Dutch, German, Spanish, and English) to ensure that its guests enjoy their cruise experience unhampered by language barriers.

Holland America Fleet Itineraries

Ship	Caribbean Home Port & Season	Caribbean Itinerary	Other Itineraries
Maasdam	Fort Lauderdale and Puerto Caldera (Costa Rica), Jan–Apr.	**10-night Panama Canal:** Half Moon Cay, St. Thomas, St. John, Aruba, and San Juan del Sur (Nicaragua)	Eastern Canada/New England, Mediterranean, Europe
Nieuw Amsterdam	Tampa, round-trip, Oct–Mar.	**14-night southern Carib:** San Juan, St. Thomas, St. John, Guadeloupe, Barbados, St. Lucia, Margarita Island (Venezuela), Bonaire, Grand Cayman	Alaska
Noordam	Between Fort Lauderdale and Acapulco, Oct–Dec.	**10-night Panama Canal:** Half Moon Cay, Cartagena (Colombia), Puerto Caldera (Costa Rica), and Huatulco (Mexico)	South America, the Mediterranean, Europe
Ryndam	Fort Lauderdale, Oct–Apr.	**7-night western Carib:** Half Moon Cay, Grand Cayman, Playa del Carmen/Cozumel, and Key West.	Alaska
Veendam	Fort Lauderdale, Nov–Apr.	**7-night western Carib:** Playa del Carmen/ Cozumel, Grand Cayman, Ocho Rios (Jamaica), and Half Moon Cay. **7-night eastern Carib:** St. Kitts, St. John/St. Thomas, and Half Moon Cay.	Alaska
Volendam	Fort Lauderdale, Nov–Apr, alternating	**10-night southern Carib 1:** Antigua, St. Lucia, Barbados, Guadeloupe, St. John/St. Thomas, and Nassau. **10-night southern Carib 2:** St. Kitts, Martinique, Trinidad, Dominica, St. Thomas/St. John, and Half Moon Cay.	Alaska
Westerdam	Fort Lauderdale, Oct–Apr.	**7-night eastern Carib:** Nassau, San Juan, St. John/St. Thomas, and Half Moon Cay.	Alaska
Zaandam	Fort Lauderdale, Feb–Apr alternating 10-night itinerary; Apr–July alternating 7-night itinerary	**10-night southern Carib:** Antigua, St. Lucia, Barbados, Guadeloupe, St. John/St. Thomas, Nassau or St. Kitts, Martinique, Trinidad, Dominica, St. Thomas, and Half Moon Cay. **7-night western Carib:** Playa del Carmen/ Cozumel, Grand Cayman, Ocho Rios (Jamaica), and Half Moon Cay. **7-night eastern Carib:** Nassau, Puerto Rico, St. John/St. Thomas, and Half Moon Cay.	Eastern Canada

Although Holland America proudly touts its no-tipping-required policy, it's more diplomacy than anything else. In fact, like most other ships, tips are expected; it's just that on Holland America ships you won't be bombarded by guidelines and reminders— you can feel as though you're tipping because you truly enjoyed the service. HAL's no-tipping-required policy includes bar tabs, which, unlike on most lines, do not automatically include a 15% gratuity (if you want, you can tip a bar waiter in cash or handwrite one onto your tab).

Onboard services aboard every ship in the fleet include **laundry** and **dry cleaning.** Each ship also maintains a **self-service laundry.**

Maasdam • Ryndam • Veendam

The Verdict

Some of the most attractive mid-sized ships out there. Functional, appealing public areas are enlivened with just a dash of glitz and collections of mostly European and Oriental art and artifacts and shipping memorabilia.

Ryndam *(photo: Holland America Line)*

Specifications

Size (in tons)	55,451	Passenger/Crew Ratio	2.2 to 1
Number of Cabins	633	Year Built	
Number of Outside Cabins	502	*Maasdam*	1993
Cabins with Verandas	150	*Ryndam*	1994
Number of Passengers	1,266	*Veendam*	1996
Officers	Dutch	Last Major Refurbishment	N/A
Crew	588 (Indonesian/ Filipino)		

Frommer's Ratings (Scale of 1–5)

Cabin Comfort & Amenities	4	Pool, Fitness & Spa Facilities	5
Ship Cleanliness & Maintenance	4	Children's Facilities	3
Public Comfort/Space	5	Itinerary	4
Decor	4	Worth the Money	5

These three nearly identical vessels (plus the *Statendam,* which sails in Hawaii, Mexico, and Alaska) represent the most massive investment in hardware Holland America has ever made. Weighing in at 55,000 tons each, they were built within a 3-year span at the Fincantieri shipyard in Monfalcone, Italy, and fall somewhere between mid-sized and megaships.

The design kinks in this quartet were fine-tuned long before the first of the four was ever launched, resulting in an extremely good use of space that pays attention to traffic flows. The ships have unusual squared-off sterns surrounded by windows, and interiors designed with practicality, cost-efficiency, and easy maintenance in mind. Each has eight elevators connecting each deck.

Interior components include leather, glass, cabinets, textiles, and furniture from around the world. Touches of marble, teakwood, polished brass, and around $2 million worth of artwork for each vessel evoke the era of the classic ocean liners. Decorative themes usually emphasize the Netherlands' seafaring traditions, and the role of Holland America in opening commerce and trade between Holland and the rest of the world.

CABINS   Cabins are roomy, unfussy, uncomplicated, and comfortable. Mini-suites are 284 square feet, larger than those aboard some of the most expensive ships afloat, such as the *Seabourn Goddess I.* Full suites are 565 square feet, and culminate at 1,126 square feet in a sprawling penthouse suite. (All square footage measurements include the cabin's veranda.)

Cabins are outfitted with light-grained furniture, and, in some cases, floral-patterned curtains that separate the sleeping area from the sitting area. Accommodations may also contain Indonesian batik and floral prints and artwork that reflect some aspects of Holland's history and aesthetic. Closets and storage space are larger than the norm. Bathrooms are well designed and well lit.

All cabins have twin beds that can be converted to a queen and, in some cases, a king. About 200 cabins can accommodate a third and fourth passenger on a fold-away sofabed and/or an upper berth.

Outside cabins have picture windows and none are blocked by dangling rows of life-boats, although those on the Navigation Decks have pedestrian walkways (and, conse-quently, pedestrians) between you and your view of the sea. Special reflective glass prevents outsiders from spying in during daylight hours. To guarantee privacy at night-time, you have to close the curtains.

Fresh flowers, white-gloved stewards, and bowls of fresh fruit in the cabins add a warm, hospitable touch.

On each ship, six cabins are wheelchair accessible and specially outfitted for passen-gers with disabilities. That, plus spacious corridors, wide elevators, and wheelchair-ac-cessible toilets, makes these ships popular with people with disabilities.

Cabins & Rates

Cabins	Per diems from	Bathtub	Fridge	Hair Dryer	Sitting Area	TV
Inside	$126	some	no*	yes	yes	yes
Outside	$141	yes	no*	yes	yes	yes
Suite	$334	yes	yes	yes	yes	yes

Fridges can be requested through your travel agent and placed in cabins for a nominal fee.

PUBLIC AREAS   Joe Farcus, the brilliant designer who launched Carnival Cruise Lines' "Fun Ship" theme, played a role in the interior design of these ships, albeit with considerably more reserve and subtlety than he used at Carnival.

For the most part, public areas are subdued, consciously tasteful, and soothing. Some of the most appealing areas are the Sky Decks, which offer a 360-degree panorama where the only drawback is the roaring wind. One floor below that, almost equivalent views are available from the gorgeous Crow's Nest nightclubs. With floor-to-ceiling windows, this romantic venue, with its cozy clusters of seating, is perfect for pre-dinner cocktails and then becomes the ships' disco and after-dinner nightclub. Each ship contains an excit-ing (relatively speaking) three-story atrium—small compared to those aboard Carnival ships, but pleasingly designed with a dose of brass and flash generally centered on an imaginative (sometimes bizarre) sculpture based on some aspect of marine mythology.

Showrooms aboard each are stylish, modern tributes to Holland's great artists: Aboard *Maasdam* it's Rembrandt; *Ryndam* is Vermeer (with references to Holland's national flower, the tulip); and *Veendam* is Rubens. Unlike most ships, which have rows of ban-quettes or theater-like seats, the showrooms on these ships are uniquely configured with cozy groupings of cushy chairs and banquettes.

Each vessel's large library also pays homage to some aspect of North European cul-ture. The one aboard *Maasdam* honors Leyden, *Ryndam*'s honors Delft, and *Veendam*'s commemorates Hugo de Groot. Onboard libraries are tranquil and oft-visited retreats. There is also a spacious card room and video arcade. Nice-sized casinos are designed with enough glamour and flashing lights to get gamblers in the mood. Each ship also has a cozy piano bar nestled in a quiet nook.

POOL, FITNESS & SPA FACILITIES   The quartet of ships each has a sprawling expanse of teak-covered aft deck surrounding a swimming pool that's always exposed to the sun and air. One deck above that is a second swimming pool plus a wading pool and spacious deck area that can be sheltered from inclement weather with a sliding glass magrodome roof. Both areas are well planned and wide open. In the enclosed pool area, there is a dolphin sculpture at one end of the pool and some imaginative, colorful tile designs to spice up the area a bit. Also in this area is the attractive Dolphin Bar, with umbrellas and wicker chairs, and two hot tubs.

These ships have practice tennis courts and an unobstructed track on an upper deck for walking or jogging. The ships' roomy, windowed Ocean Spa gyms are some of most attractive and functional at sea, with a couple of dozen exercise machines, a large separate aerobics area, a juice bar, steam rooms, and saunas. The Steiner-managed spas offer the typical menu of treatments (see chapter 4, "The Cruise Experience," for a discussion of spa options). In good weather, aerobics classes are held on deck and sometimes in the pool. HAL has an incentive-based fitness program in which passengers are awarded points every time they take an aerobics class or do some other fitness activity. Points can be redeemed at cruise end for T-shirts, souvenirs, and so on.

Nieuw Amsterdam • Noordam

The Verdict

This pair of mid-sized '80s ships are the oldest and coziest in the fleet, offering a comfortable, calm, glitz-free cruise experience and a slice of the past.

Noordam *(photo: Holland America Line)*

Specifications

Size (in tons)	33,930	Crew	542/530
Number of Cabins	607		(Indonesian/
Number of Outside Cabins	413		Filipino)
Cabins with Verandas	0	Passenger/Crew Ratio	2.2 to 1
Number of Passengers	1,214	Year Built	
Officers	Dutch	*Nieuw Amsterdam*	1983
		Noordam	1984
		Last Major Refurbishment	N/A

Frommer's Ratings (Scale of 1–5)

Cabin Comfort & Amenities	4	Pool, Fitness & Spa Facilities	3
Ship Cleanliness & Maintenance	4	Children's Facilities	2
Public Comfort/Space	3	Itinerary	4
Decor	4	Worth the Money	5

The *Noordam* and the *Nieuw Amsterdam* provide the amenities most passengers associate with a classic ocean liner. Tiered aft decks offer lots of nooks for sunbathing and recall a traditional ship style. In general, outside deck space and interior public rooms are not wide-open, sprawling, flowing spaces as on most newer ships, but are more like clusters attached to one another, creating cozy, intimate areas. Compared to the newer ships, the *Noordam* and *Nieuw Amsterdam* are pared down in scope and scale, with cabins going at a commensurately pared-down price.

These vessels were built at the Chantiers de l'Atlantique shipyard in St-Nazaire, France, and are the oldest and most "classic" vessels in Holland America's fleet, smaller and more idiosyncratic than the Statendam-class quartet, and almost nostalgically

It's a big world.

And we've got the network to cover it.

Global connection with the AT&T Network | **AT&T direct service**

Enjoy going to the corners of the earth? We're with you. With the world's most powerful network, **AT&T Direct**® Service gives you fast, clear connections from more countries than anyone,* and the option of an English-speaking operator. All it takes is your AT&T Calling Card or credit card.† And the planet is yours. FOR A LIST OF **AT&T ACCESS NUMBERS**, TAKE THE ATTACHED WALLET GUIDE.

www.att.com/traveler

For Travelers
who want more than
the Official Line

Macmillan Publishing USA

Also Available:

- The Unofficial Guide to Branson
- The Unofficial Guide to California with Kids
- The Unofficial Guide to Chicago
- The Unofficial Guide to Cruises
- The Unofficial Disney Companion
- The Unofficial Guide to Disneyland
- The Unofficial Guide to the Great Smoky
  & Blue Ridge Region
- The Unofficial Guide to Miami & the Keys
- Mini-Mickey: The Pocket-Sized Unofficial
  Guide to Walt Disney World
- The Unofficial Guide to New Orleans
- The Unofficial Guide to New York City
- The Unofficial Guide to San Francisco
- The Unofficial Guide to Skiing in the West
- The Unofficial Guide to Washington, D.C.

evocative of the pre-megaship age of cruising. They were trendsetters when they were inaugurated, although the technical innovations that set them apart have long since been eclipsed.

Overall, passengers aboard these ships tend to be more sedate and low-key than those aboard the line's larger ships, and more conscious than usual of getting value for their dollars. That said, HAL guests are certainly not opposed to a good time. When I spent a week on the *Noordam,* I nearly passed out one evening from laughing so hard watching two teams of volunteers participating in a pass-the-balloon-from-my-knees-to-yours relay race at the weekly deck party. It was a big hit!

If you're planning on traveling with children, it's wiser to opt for the larger, newer HAL ships, although the *Nieuw Amsterdam* and *Noordam* have children's programs during holidays and on sailings that have a lot of kids on board. At these times, an all-purpose room is converted to a children's playroom.

Cabins & Rates

Cabins	Per diems from	Bathtub	Fridge	Hair Dryer	Sitting Area	TV
Inside	$114	no	no*	no	no	yes
Outside	$129	some	no*	no	some	yes
Suite	$215	yes	yes	no	yes	yes

Fridges can be requested through your travel agent and placed in cabins for a nominal fee.

CABINS   Each cabin is a decent size and is representative of Holland America's comfortable, low-key style. Standard outside cabins measure 177 square feet and inside cabins 148 square feet (smaller, for instance, that Carnival's standard 185- to 190-square-foot cabins). Bedding, upholstery, and carpeting are done in earth tones (bordering on drab) and furniture looks vaguely art deco. Mirrors make the space seem larger than it is, and storage space is more than adequate. Bathrooms are compact and well designed.

Most cabins on the Boat and Navigation Decks have views obstructed by lifeboats, and those on the Upper Promenade Deck overlook an unending stream of joggers, walkers, and passersby. Cabins near the stern are subject to more than their share of engine noise and vibration. Many cabins have bathtubs and all have TVs, music channels, and a fruit bowl. (There are no in-cabin safes, but valuables can be kept at the purser's desk).

Four cabins in the B category—deluxe outside double rooms on the Boat Deck—are suitable for people with disabilities. Elevators are wheelchair accessible.

PUBLIC AREAS   The decor sports teakwood, polished rosewood, and discreet colors. Bouquets of fresh flowers are liberally scattered through public areas. A 15-foot-wide teak-covered promenade allows deck chairs, strollers, joggers, and voyeurs to mingle under the open sky. Some passengers consider it the ship's most endearing feature and it's a lovely reminiscence of the classic ocean liner.

The ships have movie theaters, libraries, and card rooms.

There are some unfortunate design flaws. For example, show lounges aren't large enough to seat all passengers, so there's standing room only in the cabaret theater, with some sightlines blocked. And, in general, the ship's choppy clusters of public areas and decks can leave you disoriented at times. The one-story main-dining rooms, while pleasant, are dull compared to the more glamorous ones on the line's newer ships.

POOL, FITNESS & SPA FACILITIES   The ships have two outside pools on the decks, a wading pool, and one hot tub. You can walk or jog on the broad, unobstructed Promenade Deck. The gym and spa are small, as they are most ships built in the '80s and earlier. The gym, located on one of the topmost decks, has windows and is equipped with rowing machines, weight machines, and stationary bicycles. The spa is really just a couple of treatment rooms for massages and facials, plus a steam room and sauna. Aerobics classes are held on the decks or in a public room. A sports deck up top features a pair of practice tennis courts and shuffleboard. There's also a beauty salon/barber shop.

Westerdam

The Verdict

An appealing ship with an ocean-liner-like feel, the *Westerdam* is solid, spacious, and modestly elegant, though an odd layout makes it tricky to find some public rooms.

Westerdam *(photo: Holland America Line)*

Specifications

Size (in tons)	53,872	Crew	642 (Indonesian/
Number of Cabins	747		Filipino)
Number of Outside Cabins	495	Passenger/Crew Ratio	2.3 to 1
Cabins with Verandas	0	Year Built	1986
Number of Passengers	1,494	Last Major Refurbishment	1989
Officers	Dutch		

Frommer's Ratings (Scale of 1–5)

Cabin Comfort & Amenities	4	Pool, Fitness & Spa Facilities	3
Ship Cleanliness & Maintenance	4	Children's Facilities	2
Public Comfort/Space	4	Itinerary	4
Decor	4	Worth the Money	5

Launched in 1986 as the Home Lines' *Homeric* and bought by HAL two years later, the ship was literally sawed in half at a German shipyard in 1989 to allow for the insertion of a 140-foot midsection of cabins and public rooms. The result is a very long ship reminiscent of an old-time ocean liner, with portholes on some decks, a wide wraparound promenade, a truly lovely showroom, and spacious cabins and lounges. Unfortunately, the stretching also produced a traffic problem: Since the dining room and the gym/spa sit basically alone on their respective decks, they can only be accessed from certain elevators and stairs—it can get confusing. That complaint aside, the *Westerdam* is a comfortable, stately vessel that boasts the same great service for which HAL is known.

An added perk? Because it's an older ship, HAL generally sells *Westerdam* cruises at a lower price than cruises on its newer vessels.

Cabins & Rates

Cabins	Per diems from	Bathtub	Fridge	Hair Dryer	Sitting Area	TV
Inside	$120	yes	no*	no	no	yes
Outside	$143	some	no*	no	some	yes
Suite	$313	yes	yes	no	yes	yes

Fridges can be requested through your travel agent and placed in cabins for a nominal fee.

CABINS   Many ship cabins employ light woods and fabrics to make them seem bigger than they are, but cabins aboard the *Westerdam* are large enough to risk the dignified dark woods with which many are appointed: Standard outside cabins are a roomy 189 square feet, among the larger in the industry, while inside cabins are 153 square feet. None have verandas. Some cabins have sofa-beds and/or upper berths to accommodate additional guests; all have TVs and music channels. There are no in-cabin safes. Though clean and spacious enough, bathrooms feel old, with tiled showers that show some wear. Try to avoid cabins in the stern on the Lower Promenade Deck, which are right below the disco and casino and can be noisy.

Four cabins, plus all elevators, are wheelchair accessible.

PUBLIC AREAS   Most public rooms are located on the spacious Promenade Deck, including several lounges/bars, a low-key disco, shops, a library, casino, and the Admiral's Lounge showroom, a truly lovely space which, with the lights dimmed, takes on a rich, dark, burgundy glow. Throughout the ship, artwork reflects the theme of Dutch exploration, with large-scale antique ship models and salvaged cannon being standout display items.

The main dining room, divided into two sections and located four decks down, is sometimes difficult to find, but rewards persistence with a feeling that's both cozy and spacious. Unlike modern ships, the room is located near the waterline and so has portholes instead of large viewing windows, but as curtains are drawn during dinner on pretty much every ship, it's an inconsequential difference. The ship has two separate buffet areas.

The small children's center is basically a near-empty room, with only the "Club HAL" logo on the door clueing you in that it's a room for kids. Honestly, it seems like an afterthought.

POOL, FITNESS & SPA FACILITIES   The ship has two outside pools, one at the stern and the other up top, with a retractable dome for bad weather. Walkers and runners will enjoy the broad Upper Promenade Deck, while tennis players can use the courts on the Sports Deck. The Ocean Spa health club has windows and offers a handful of machines and weights, but is small and unfancy. Aerobics classes are offered in one of the lounges, on deck, or in the pool. There's a steam room, sauna, and a couple of massage rooms, plus a beauty salon/barber shop.

Holland America's *Volendam* & *Zaandam* (a Preview)

The 1,440-passenger, 63,000-ton *Volendam,* scheduled to debut in August 1999, just as this book hits the stores, is a new generation of Holland America ship, merging the best features from the Statendam-class ships and the line's flagship, the *Rotterdam.* The *Zaandam,* scheduled to debut in spring 2000, will be identical in size and passenger capacity, but with a different decorative theme.

The biggest ships in the fleet (the next largest is the *Rotterdam* at 59,000 tons and 1,320 passengers), the *Volendam* will be awash in all things floral, with an overall theme of flowers worked into the art, fabrics, doors, and others parts of the ship's elegant decor. The *Zaandam,* meanwhile, will be themed on music. Both will feature an Italian-themed reservations-only alternative restaurant for intimate dining, a well-stocked children's playroom, a three-story atrium, a two-story dining room at the ship's stern, a large spa and gym, two pools, and 197 deluxe veranda cabins (out of a total 710 cabins)—more than any other ships in the fleet. Generally, the layout of the public rooms will be very similar to *Rotterdam*'s. At its debut, the *Volendam* will begin 10-day southern Caribbean itineraries. The *Zaandam* will sail 7-night eastern and western Caribbean and 10-night southern Caribbean itineraries.

Norwegian Cruise Line

SHIPS   Norway • Norwegian Dream • Norwegian Majesty • Norwegian Sea • Norwegian Sky (preview) • Norwegian Wind

7665 Corporate Center Dr., Miami, FL 33126. ☎ **800/327-7030** or 305/436-4000. Fax 305/436-4126. www.ncl.com.

THE LINE IN A NUTSHELL   NCL offers affordable (sometimes downright cheap), down-to-earth cruises on its diverse fleet of mid-sized and mega-sized ships.

THE EXPERIENCE   NCL has a varied fleet, from new to old, mid-size to mega, and unlike many lines that offer a similar product across the board, it's not easy to generalize about NCL's hodgepodge fleet. Its two largest ships—the brand new *Norwegian Sky* and the classic liner *Norway*—carry about 2,000 passengers each, and it's four other vessels, the *Norwegian Wind, Sea, Majesty,* and *Dream,* carry about 1,500 each.

While the line strives to lure more upmarket travelers, truth is, their product is very mid-market and the experience not as fine-tuned and sharp as it could be. The new *Norwegian Sky,* however, scheduled to debut in August 1999, just as this book hits the stores, could be just the shot in the arm the line needs to push itself up a notch. In general, the ships attract a wide variety of passengers, with some drawn by the line's popular music or sports theme cruises, some by its cruises out of Houston, some by the nostalgia of the *Norway,* and others simply by low prices—when NCL has empty berths to fill, it's never too proud to offer some outrageous discounts to anyone interested.

Despite its shortcomings, the line is very innovative in certain areas. NCL justifiably touts its music and sports theme cruises, which in 1999 included the first "Sports Illustrated Afloat" cruise, an Elvis Cruise that featured a skydiving show by the Flying Elvi, and a blues cruise that featured Bo Diddly, Son Seals, and Johnny Johnson. Sports bars are also a big draw, as are alternative dining choices (a concept popular aboard megaships but much less common aboard small and medium-sized vessels) and the line's "Texasaribbean" itineraries, sailing year-round from Houston, Texas.

Pros

- **Theme cruises.** NCL offers more music and sports theme cruises than any other line.
- **Activities.** There's a wider range of activities on NCL ships than on most.

Cons

- **Inconsistent service.** Across the board, service isn't always as sharp as it could be and often seems lackadaisical.
- **Unmemorable food.** Don't expect miracles in the food department. As long as you don't crave sophisticated cuisine, you'll be fine.

Frommer's Ratings: Norwegian Cruise Line

	Poor	Fair	Good	Excellent	Outstanding
Enjoyment Factor				✓	
Dining		✓			
Activities					✓
Children's Program			✓		
Entertainment				✓	
Service		✓			
Overall Value				✓	

THE NORWEGIAN WAY

Norwegian Cruise Line, which today prides itself on its theme cruises, sports and activities offerings, and diverse fleet, was one of the pioneers of the North American cruise market. Its earliest roots were as the now-defunct Kloster Cruises. In 1966, Knut Knutson, the Norwegian owner of Kloster, had a cruise ship but no marketing system, and Ted Arison, an Israeli, had a great North American marketing system but no ships. Together, they formed Norwegian Caribbean Line, launching 3- and 4-day cruises from Miami to the Bahamas. In 1972, Arison and his entourage split from the company to form Carnival Cruise Lines, now the giant of the industry.

Over the years that followed, NCL had its difficulties, financial and otherwise, but by 1997 the hardest times seemed to be past, and a major program of expansion and marketing was put in place. In 1996, NCL acquired the former Cunard *Crown* (renamed the *Norwegian Crown*, and scheduled to be transferred to Norwegian's sister-line, Orient Lines, in April 2000), and in 1997, the line acquired two ships, the former Majesty Cruise Line *Royal Majesty* (renamed *Norwegian Majesty*) and the former Cunard *Crown Dynasty* (renamed *Norwegian Dynasty*, which at press time, had entered into a long-term charter agreement with Commodore Holdings). Over the past year and a half, NCL "stretched" three of its ships, cutting them in two and inserting a newly constructed midsection. The *Norwegian Dream* and *Norwegian Wind* increased their passenger capacity from around 1,200 to around 1,700, and *Norwegian Majesty* increasing its from just over 1,000 to 1,462. NCL also changed the name of almost all its ships to include the word *Norwegian*, and, in May 1998, purchased Orient Lines and its 800-passenger M/V *Marco Polo*.

Today, facing the challenges of surviving in a very competitive marketplace overrun with new megaships, NCL is making a valiant effort in marketing and promotion to create an appealing and lasting image for its fleet.

THE FLEET

While at times it's hard to keep track, at press time Norwegian had seven ships in its all-over-the-map fleet. The brand-new 2,000-passenger **Norwegian Sky** was scheduled to launch in August 1999; the 1,750-passenger **Norwegian Wind** and **Norwegian Dream** were built in 1993 and 1992, respectively; the 1,462-passenger **Norwegian Majesty** (formerly Majesty Cruise Line's *Royal Majesty*) was built in 1992 and acquired by NCL in 1997; and the 1,052-passenger **Norwegian Crown** (formerly the Cunard *Crown*, acquired by NCL in 1996 and to be transferred to Orient Lines in 2000) and the 1,504-passenger **Norwegian Sea** were built in 1988. The classic 2,032-passenger *Norway* was built in 1962 and extensively refurbished over the years, and is in a class by itself.

Over the past year NCL has divested itself of some ships as well. The 950-passenger *Leeward*, which joined NCL in 1995, left the fleet in late 1999 when its charter agreement ended. Likewise, the 800-passenger *Norwegian Dynasty* left the fleet in late 1999 when it entered into a long-term charter with Commodore Holdings.

NCL is looking to the future, too, and has signed letters of intent to build a second 2,000-passenger ship along the lines of the *Norwegian Sky*.

PASSENGER PROFILE

NCL as a rule attracts a diverse lot, and in general a younger, more price-conscious, and more active crowd than lines such as Holland America, Celebrity, and Princess. Typical NCL passengers are ages 25 to 50, and include a fair number of honeymooners and families with kids. The atmosphere aboard all NCL vessels is informal and well-suited to the serious party maker taking a first or second cruise. There are a good number of Europeans on board as well.

NCL has pioneered more theme cruises than any other line, so its passenger list is often composed of special-interest groups, including sports fans, older passengers who book big band cruises to relive the days of Glenn Miller and Benny Goodman, and young professionals attracted to the jazz, Dixieland, or blues theme cruises.

Active vacationers particularly like the line because of its enhanced **sports programs.** For instance, snorkeling and scuba lessons are often held in the ships' pools. Scuba programs, run by independent concessionaires, are aggressively promoted when they're offered. For the more sedentary sports fan, all major weekend games, including NFL playoffs, are broadcast via ESPN and CNN into passenger's cabins and onto the video monitors of each vessel's high-tech sports bar, sometimes with multiple screens broadcasting different games in different areas of the bar.

DINING

None of the Norwegian Cruise Line vessels is distinguished for its cuisine, but onboard portions are exceedingly generous. Meals are often focused on specific cuisines, such as French, Italian, Caribbean, Viking (as in Norwegian), or Tex-Mex, and you can usually count on choices like broiled mahimahi, salmon or fillet of flounder, beef Wellington, broiled lobster tail, chicken parmesan, fettuccine Alfredo, or perhaps a Jamaican jerk pork roast or roast prime rib. The wine lists appeal to standard mid-American tastes, and aren't offensively expensive.

Recent improvements have included greater emphasis on **alternative dining rooms.** All ships have the reservations-only Le Bistro restaurants, which are smaller and more intimate than the main dining rooms and serve Italian specialties at no extra cost (except a suggested $5 tip). The food here is better than in the main dining rooms, and includes items like a yummy Caesar salad made for you right at your table, a juicy beef tenderloin, and a marvelously decadent chocolate fondue. Be sure to make your reservations as soon as you get aboard.

There is a **light spa cuisine** choice as well as a **vegetarian entree** at lunch and dinner. Fresh fruit is often offered throughout the day. There are also **children's menus,** featuring the popular standards: burgers, hot dogs, spaghetti and meatballs, and ice cream sundaes.

It's generally agreed that the best cuisine on the fleet is served aboard the *Norway,* which has two main dining rooms, the domed-ceiling Windward and the balconied Leeward. There are only a few tables for two.

The *Norwegian Dream* and *Norwegian Wind* each have smaller, more intimate dining areas (three for dinner), with seating ranging from 76 in the smallest bistrolike areas to 256 in the main dining rooms. All have two seatings nightly. Both ships have a state-of-the-art **Sports Bar and Grill,** with indoor/outdoor snacking and drinking, room

Cruise Tip

NCL offers convenient (and cost-saving) **soft drink packages** for kids if yours like to fill up on Cokes. For those under age 17, Kids Soda packages offer a personalized soda cup, special straw, and unlimited fountain sodas, and can be purchased once you board ship for $16 on a 7-day cruise, $10 on a 4-day cruise, and $8 on a 3-day cruise. Deluxe "backpack packages" include the soda deal and a backpack full of fun stuff like a baseball cap, T-shirt, sunglasses ($39.50 for a 7-night cruise, $33 for 4-night cruises and $28 for 3-night cruises.

for almost 150 people, and the almost constant background noise from at least one (and sometimes several) TVs.

The *Norwegian Sea* has two main dining rooms, the 280-passenger Four Seasons and the larger, 476-passenger Seven Seas. Both are located on the Main Deck, and each features two dinner seatings. Its Lido restaurant is best for its panoramic views and informal buffets.

All NCL vessels offer **midnight buffets** and each also has an ice-cream bar open a few hours a day. Aboard the *Norway, Norwegian Dream, Norwegian Wind,* and *Norwegian Sea,* you'll find the ultra popular Chocoholic Extravaganza midnight buffet, offering everything from tortes to brownies in a format that's appealing and very fattening. On 7-night cruises fleetwide, the *Norway, Norwegian Dream,* and *Norwegian Wind* offer **English high tea.**

There is a **coffee bar** on the *Norwegian Wind, Dream,* and *Sky* serving specialty coffees as well as other beverages; all the ships serve pizza. **Room service** is available 24 hours a day.

ACTIVITIES

Adult activities are one of the line's strongest points. You'll find the most action aboard the *Norway,* but all the ships offer impressive rosters. You can take cha-cha lessons; play bingo, shuffleboard, or basketball; attend an art auction or spa or beauty demonstration; or listen to the live poolside calypso band. There are galley and bridge tours, snorkeling demonstrations in the pool, trapshooting, makeovers, talent shows, wine tasting, and trivia contests.

There are silly **poolside competitions** to keep you laughing all afternoon long. NCL also has an **incentive fitness program** that rewards cruise passengers with things like T-shirts for participation in volleyball, aerobics classes, or other fitness activities.

In port, the shore excursion menu is heavy with active tours, such as snorkeling and diving, mountain biking, and kayaking.

CHILDREN'S PROGRAM

Although the programs are not nearly as extensive or playrooms as well stocked as many other lines, NCL has expanded its Kids Crew program to offer year-round **supervised**

Private Island Paradise, Norwegian Style

Early in its corporate history, NCL became the first cruise line to develop a private island for the use of its guests when it acquired **Great Stirrup Cay,** a virtually unknown stretch of palm-studded beachfront in the southern Bahamas. Since then, as part of a land rush for hideaway islands with deepwater access, such competitors as Royal Caribbean, Princess, Holland America, and, most recently and expensively of all, Disney, have each acquired private islands or beachfronts of their own. In the case of NCL, sleepy Great Stirrup Cay suddenly comes alive when an NCL vessel docks. The site becomes an instant party loaded with lunch, bar, and water-sports facilities. Music is either broadcast or performed live, barbecues are fired up, hammocks are strung between palms, and rum punches are spiced and served. Passengers can ride paddleboats, sail Sunfish, go snorkeling, or do nothing more than sunbathe all day long. Pleasingly, the island is not overdeveloped and manages to retain more of a natural feel than some of the other major lines' islands.

NCL Fleet Itineraries

Ship	Home Ports & Season	Itinerary	Other Itineraries
Norway	Round-trip from Miami, year-round.	**7-night eastern Carib:** Sint Maarten, St. John's/ St. Thomas, and Great Stirrup Cay (Bahamas).	None
Norwegian Dream	San Juan, round-trip from Dec–Mar.	**7-night southern Carib:** Aruba, Curaçao, Tortola, and St. Thomas.	Europe, Mediterranean
Norwegian Majesty	Bermuda round-trip from Boston, Apr–Oct; Panama Canal between San Juan and Acapulco, Nov–Jan; Bahamas from Miami, Jan–Mar.	**7-night Bermuda:** St. George's. **10-night Panama Canal:** Puerto Quetzal (Guatemala), Puerto Caldera (Costa Rica), and Curaçao. **11-night Panama Canal:** Aruba, San Blas Islands (Panama), Puerto Caldera (Costa Rica), and Puerto Quetzal (Guatemala). **3-4-night Bahamas:** Nassau and Great Stirrup Cay.	None
Norwegian Sea	Round-trip from Houston, year-round.	**7-night western Carib:** Cancún, Cozumel, and Roatan (Honduras).	None
Norwegian Wind	Round-trip from Miami, Nov–Mar.	**7-night western Carib:** Grand Cayman, Roatan (Honduras), Belize, Cozumel, and Key West.	Alaska, Hawaii

activities for children ages 3 to 17. The program divides children into four age groups: junior sailors, ages 3 to 5; first mates, ages 6 to 8; navigators, ages 9 to 12; and teens, ages 13 to 17. During the off-season, activities are offered for three age groups (3 to 5, 6 to 12, and 13 to 17 years). **Activities** vary across the fleet, but may include sports competitions, dances, face painting, treasure hunts, magic shows, arts and crafts, and even a Circus at Sea. Children get their own "Cruise News" detailing the day's events.

Norwegian Dream, Norwegian Wind, Norwegian Majesty, and *Norwegian Sky* have a **playroom** called "Kids Korner," the *Norway's* is called "Trolland," and the *Norwegian Sea's* playroom is called "Porthole." Besides the new *Sky,* which promises to boast the best children's facilities, the *Norway's* facilities are probably NCL's next best (or at least biggest).

Group baby-sitting is offered for $4 per hour per child and $2 for each additional child. **Private, in-cabin baby-sitting** by a member of the crew is available from noon to 2am aboard all NCL's ships for $8 per hour for the first child and $2 per hour for each additional child.

ENTERTAINMENT

NCL has found a nice balance between theme-related events and general entertainment that keeps everyone happy. The **Vegas-style productions** are expensive, surprisingly lavish, and artistically ambitious, especially on the *Norway* and *Sky,* the biggest ships in the fleet. All the ships contain a fully equipped theater where abridged productions of such shows as *Crazy for You, Grease, 42nd Street, Will Rogers Follies,* and *Dreamgirls* have been presented. NCL also produces its own Vegas-inspired extravaganzas, *Sea Legs Express, Broadway Tonight,* and *Sea Legs Goes Hollywood,* all in the glitzy and glamorous tradition. The shows, however, lack the originality, nuance, talent level, and

A Special Deal

Children's Discounts: Children under 2 sail free with Norwegian Cruise Line.

polish of shows found on other lines, particularly Royal Caribbean, Carnival, Princess, Celebrity, and Crystal. On some nights, the showrooms also feature comedians and juggling acts.

The *Norway* boasts the fleet's biggest and splashiest **casino,** the Monte Carlo, whose art deco style includes lots of spangles and mirrored walls. Serious gamblers should sail the *Norway* only, since they may find the smaller and less comprehensive casinos of NCL's other vessels inadequate.

All the ships have bars where you can slip away for a quiet rendezvous, and small tucked-away corners for more intimate entertainment, like **pianists** and **cabaret acts.** Music for dancing is popular aboard all the ships and takes place before or after shows, and each ship has a late-night disco.

NCL pioneered the concept of **theme cruises,** and its program today includes jazz cruises, blues cruises, Dixieland cruises, '50s- and '60s-era music cruises, big band cruises, and country-western cruises. Sometimes well-known headliners are brought on for certain theme cruises. On NCL's popular **"Sports Afloat" cruises** (offered mostly on the *Norway* and *Norwegian Sea*), professional players and Hall-of-Famers from pro basketball, football, hockey, and baseball sail aboard, signing autographs, conducting demonstrations and contests, and mingling with passengers. On select itineraries on the *Norwegian Wind* and *Majesty,* **golf pros** sail on board and provide instruction. Golf excursions in port are offered as well.

SERVICE

"Uneven" is the word that keeps cropping up to describe service aboard NCL vessels. However, some passengers, especially first-timers, find the service excellent. Generally, room service and bar service fleetwide is speedy and efficient

While service isn't bad aboard the other vessels, it's better on the *Norway,* whose staff seems more seasoned and conscious of their ship's long tradition of elegance. If problems occur with service, it's usually in the main dining rooms, where the stress of feeding hundreds of passengers at the same time under cramped conditions sometimes takes its toll. The breakfast and lunch buffet restaurants often seem understaffed and hectic, especially if you're there at prime times. Cabin attendants generally win more passenger approval than the dining-room waitstaff.

Norway

The Verdict

Cruising on this ship is like going to a latter-day Frank Sinatra concert: He wasn't what he used to be, but there was enough left to make the experience refreshingly nostalgic and rewarding.

Norway *(photo: NCL)*

Specifications

Size (in tons)	76,049	Officers	Norwegian
Number of Cabins	1,016	Crew	900 (International)
Number of Outside Cabins	656	Passenger/Crew Ratio	2.3 to 1
Cabins with Verandas	56	Year Built	1961
Number of Passengers	2,032	Last Major Refurbishment	1998

Frommer's Ratings (Scale of 1–5)

Cabin Comfort & Amenities	3	Pool, Fitness & Spa Facilities	4
Ship Cleanliness & Maintenance	4	Children's Facilities	3
Public Comfort/Space	4	Itinerary	4
Decor	3	Worth the Money	5

The last of the 1,035-foot luxury liners, this ever-enduring legend, with its long, sleek hull, is the only vessel of its kind sailing today. Built in 1962 as the SS *France* and stretching the length of 3¹/₂ football fields, *Norway* was enormous by the standards of the time, and although many megaships rival it in size today, it projects an aura of nostalgia they simply cannot match. The *Norway's* only true peer in size and age is the *QE2*, which is a more luxurious, formal ship. As a classic liner in the mid-market range plying the Caribbean, the *Norway* is a singularly unique ship.

Sadly, after many facelifts over the decades (including a $65 million refurbishment begun in 1990 and a 1996 refit that brought the ship into compliance with international Safety of Life at Sea standards), the ship's interior hardware retains very little of its original grandeur, and it has become a misfit of sorts. New carpeting, fabrics, and signs were recently installed in the ship's public areas, and in late 1998 a fire sprinkler system and a new sports bar were added. Even though so much of its grand history has been stripped away, the ship's classic profile will still please ship buffs, who can revel in being there and knowing what the ship once was. For all others, the *Norway's* variety of activities and affordable price are what's most alluring.

The *Norway* today is famous for its theme cruises, and the ship is credited with pioneering such jaunts to fill the cabins during off-peak periods. Whatever the subject—country music or jazz, basketball or fitness and beauty—these theme cruises, offered throughout the year, appeal to a wide variety of tastes. Owing to its many commodious public rooms and easy flow of traffic, the *Norway* is an ideal venue for these kinds of special cruises. The focal point of activities is the International Deck, with the Great Outdoor Restaurant at the stern.

The ship's huge size limits its access to certain smaller ports, so if your interest is in visiting more remote islands, this isn't the vessel for you. When you do stop at a port of call, the passenger count causes monstrous lines upon disembarkation, which can severely limit your time ashore. Lines can also be long at buffets.

In terms of food, although menus are similar throughout the fleet, the food preparation and presentation is better on the *Norway*. On most NCL ships, the alternative Le Bistro Restaurant is head and shoulders above the main dining rooms. Not so on the *Norway*, where the meals and service in the main restaurants are quite good. The buffet at the ship's Great Outdoor Restaurant is pretty average, except for the paella cooked up on the grill. The delectably spicy dish, which includes some marvelous jumbo shrimp, sends many passengers scrambling back for seconds.

Cabins & Rates

Cabins	Per diems from	Bathtub	Fridge	Hair Dryer	Sitting Area	TV
Inside	$96	no	no	no	no	yes*
Outside	$160	some	some	no	some	yes*
Suite	$235	yes	yes	some	yes	yes*

TVs show ESPN and CNN.

CABINS As aboard all old ships, there's a vast array of jigsaw-puzzle–like cabin sizes and configurations, some of them quirkily charming because of floor plans that were designed before cruise lines came up with the idea of standardization. The good news is that since the *Norway* is an older ship built for transatlantic journeys, cabins are bigger than average and offer better drawer and closet space. You can choose from 20 cabin categories, ranging from spacious Owner's Suites with private balconies to minuscule inside cells with upper and lower berths. Cabins are spread across 10 decks, and the farther down you go, the cheaper the price.

Cabins are furnished traditionally and plainly, with some art deco touches. Since the cabin plans are so intricate, you might seek the advice of a good travel agent familiar with the ship in selecting one. Bathroom size and amenities tend to be consistent regardless of your cabin's size. Plumbing fixtures are a bit more solid than the cheaper plastic models installed aboard many newer ships. All cabins have TVs showing ESPN and CNN.

Usually the first cabins to sell out are the new 100 or so luxury cabins and suites on the two uppermost glass-enclosed decks. Half have verandas, but the veranda partitions aren't solid and don't ensure privacy. Views from cabins on the Olympic or Fjord Decks are obstructed completely or partially by lifeboats.

Travelers with disabilities should book on the International Deck, near the major public rooms, where 10 cabins are wheelchair accessible.

PUBLIC AREAS   There are 12 passenger decks, and their public areas are the most generously sized of almost any ship. The wide International Deck, where many of the lounges and public rooms are located, makes it easy to move from end to end of the ship, and, in general, the expansive public rooms give everyone plenty of elbow room, something that doesn't exist on the newer ships in NCL's fleet.

The two best public rooms on the ship are the Sports Illustrated Cafe, decorated with memorabilia from sports superstars and dedicated to the late Florence Griffith-Joyner, who died shortly before she was supposed to help celebrate the room's opening; and the Windjammer Bar, an intimate, nautically themed bar where a pianist holds forth with nightly melodies and memories, and the occasional guest singer from the audience.

If you want company, the North Cape Lounge on the pool deck accommodates 750 passengers. Two very large, very busy dining rooms keep passengers fed and happy during two separate seatings.

The vast Monte Carlo Room is a gambler's heaven, with a couple of hundred slot machines and seven blackjack tables. The balconied, two-story Saga Theater has some bad seats, but its sound, lighting, and audiovisual facilities are state of the art. This is not a conference ship, and the meeting rooms are severely limited. The library is good for reading, escaping from the crowd, and wave watching.

There are no grand ballrooms; the closest you'll come to that is Club Internationale, a high-ceilinged, boxy lounge with lots of original fixtures from the days when the ship was the SS *France*. Unfortunately, it's much too big and bright for evenings of dancing and sipping cocktails. Indeed, the afternoon teas are taken in this room, but they are not exactly elegant.

The *Norway* is not an ideal ship for children, given its complex layout and lack of modern kids' activities, but a solid children's program is in place and families shouldn't write this ship off.

POOL, FITNESS & SPA FACILITIES   The *Norway* has two large outdoor pools, the one near the Lido Bar being the larger, with ample room for sunning. There's also a cushioned, quarter-mile circuit for jogging, and games include paddleball, table tennis, skeet shooting, shuffleboard, and basketball. Snorkeling and diving classes are often available aboard in the pool and offshore during excursions.

The fitness center and separate Roman Spa are excellent, roomy facilities, the former with floor-to-ceiling windows, an indoor pool, exercise equipment, two steam rooms, and two saunas, plus body-jet showers and a whirlpool. There are also golf tees and nets for golf practice, basketball and volleyball courts, facilities for trapshooting, and the most appealing and best-stocked library of any ship in NCL's fleet.

It may be a bit of a hassle to reach the Roman Spa, located deep within the ship, as only two elevators go there from the top decks (you may want to take the stairs rather than wait what seems like a lifetime for the elevators). Once there, however, you'll find one of the best spas at sea, with 16 treatment rooms and the first hydrotherapy baths on any cruise ship.

Norwegian Dream • Norwegian Wind

The Verdict

These two vessels have most of the amenities and facilities of their giant seagoing peers, but are still small enough to offer a more intimate cruise experience and somewhat more personal service than a megaship.

Norwegian Wind *(photo: NCL)*

Specifications

Size (in tons)	56,760	Crew	614 (International)
Number of Cabins	874	Passenger/Crew Ratio	2.8 to 1
Number of Outside Cabins	716	Year Built	
Cabins with Verandas	48	*Norwegian Dream*	1992
Number of Passengers	1,748	*Norwegian Wind*	1993
Officers	Norwegian	Last Major Refurbishment	1998

Frommer's Ratings (Scale of 1–5)

Cabin Comfort & Amenities	4	Pool, Fitness & Spa Facilities	4
Ship Cleanliness & Maintenance	4	Children's Facilities	3
Public Comfort/Space	3	Itinerary	4
Decor	4	Worth the Money	4

If your heart isn't dead set on a cruise aboard a brand-new megaship, you may find NCL's modern, mid-sized twin ships, the *Dream* or *Wind*, very appealing. Both are market leaders among quality, mid-size, moderate-cost ships, and are known for their innovative designs by the Scandinavian designer who set the tone for *Royal Viking Queen* and the Seabourn twins. In 1998, both the *Wind* and *Dream* were "stretched" by grafting a 130-foot midsection into each, an operation that raised the ships' tonnage from 41,000 to 46,000 and increased their capacity from the 1,200-passenger range to over 1,700. Other improvements made possible by the stretch included the addition of a casual restaurant, a gift shop, lounges, a library, card room, cigar bar, and improved spas, health clubs, and children's facilities.

Even after the stretch, both ships remain mid-sized, but good design makes them appear to be more spacious than they are. Both forward and aft, the ships' upper decks cascade down in evenly spaced tiers, resulting in panoramic views both ahead and behind the moving ship, and walls of glass line the length of both vessels. In an attempt to save money, however, low-grade materials were used in the passageways and stairways, so you know you're not on a luxury yacht (or even any Carnival, Celebrity, Holland America or Princess ship).

Both vessels draw greater percentages of upmarket clients than any others in the NCL fleet. First-time cruisers like these two vessels. An informal style permeates both vessels, and the Norwegian officers are very smooth and charming. Unfortunately, this grace isn't always apparent in other staff members.

Note: On August 24, 1999, the *Norwegian Dream* collided with a cargo ship in the English Channel. Approximately 20 passengers reported minor injuries, but the ship was able to continue on to Dover despite suffering dramatic damage to its bow. At press time, NCL expected to have the *Dream* back in operation by October 1999.

Cabins & Rates						
Cabins	**Per diems from**	**Bathtub**	**Fridge**	**Hair Dryer**	**Sitting Area**	**TV**
Inside	$150	no	no	yes	no	yes*
Outside	$164	no	no	yes	some	yes*
Suite	$214	yes	yes	yes	yes	yes*

TVs have ESPN and CNN.

CABINS   The big draw is that nearly all cabins are outside, and about 80% of them have picture windows. Standard outside cabins measure 160 square feet, which is fairly roomy, but not large. The inside cabins are smallish, from 130 to 150 square feet.

The accommodations have a breezy decor with wood accents and pastels evocative of the West Indies. Unfortunately, storage space is minimal. Two people can just barely manage, but when a third or fourth person shares a cabin, it can get truly cramped. Bathrooms are also tiny. Most cabins have a separate sitting and sleeping area, but to accommodate this feature, the area around the beds was made smaller and is now rather cramped. Most cabins have twin beds that can be converted to queen size. Cabins on the port side are for nonsmokers. Note that lifeboats block the views of the Category 4 cabins at midships on the Norway Deck, and early-morning joggers might disturb late sleepers who have cabins on the Promenade Deck.

Suites are rather luxurious and decent-sized, with floor-to-ceiling windows, and many open onto private balconies. All suites have mini-fridges. The dozen-plus Owner's Suites are the most dramatic, followed by penthouse suites with private balconies. The 10 Superior Deluxe Penthouse suites amidships on Norway Deck have partially obstructed views because of the overhang from the restaurant above. Avoid them.

All cabins have TVs showing ESPN and CNN. Nearly a dozen cabins are wheelchair accessible, and an additional dozen or so are equipped for those with hearing impairments, an innovation aboard cruise ships.

PUBLIC AREAS   Both vessels have a terraced design, making for roomier lower-level public areas, generous amounts of deck space on upper levels, and good passenger flow.

The four onboard restaurants function with a variety of seating systems, offering passengers lots of choice. The most appealing are the dining areas facing aft over the stern. The Terraces restaurant is cozy and attractive, rising three levels and evoking a supper club in a 1930s movie. The Four Seasons restaurant is also an attractive venue with great views; it's got tiered seating and curved walls of glass that bubble out over the edges of both the port and starboard sides of the ship.

The casinos are of the glitzy variety, as they're meant to be, but are on the small side. Some lounges offer music and dancing, while in others you can find lounges with soft music (or no music at all), where you can engage in conversation. Lucky's Bar and the Dazzles disco on the Star Deck see the most late-night action. The sports bars, with giant-screen TVs, are the most popular bars on the ships.

POOL, FITNESS & SPA FACILITIES   The Pool Decks are gorgeous, with their dark wooden decks and crisp blue-and-white striped canvas umbrellas having you feeling like you're at some stylish beach resort on the French Riviera. They're one of the ships' most attractive public spaces, bringing to mind a chic European resort. Each ship has two pools. The more theatrical on each is on the International Deck, where semicircular rows of lounges and deck chairs surround a small and almost purely decorative keyhole-shaped pool at the ships' stern. The view—whether of the ocean or of your fellow passengers—is panoramic. A larger pool lies two decks above on the Sun Deck. Great pool bars allow you sip a drink while bobbing happily in the shallow pool. Each ship has two hot tubs.

Both vessels have a fitness center with state-of-the-art exercise equipment. Aerobics and exercise classes are part of the activity-filled agenda, and a small spa offers massages and a sauna along with a whirlpool. Each ship also has a jogging track, a combination basketball and volleyball court, a golf driving range, and trapshooting.

Sports fans gravitate to the Sports Deck, with its Ping-Pong tables, bar, and golf driving range. Snorkeling and water-sports lessons and programs are often available.

Norwegian Majesty

The Verdict

Everything old is new again. Recently stretched, the ship has more cabins, more restaurants, and a new lease on life.

Norwegian Majesty *(photo: NCL)*

Specifications

Size (in tons)	38,000	Officers	Norwegian
Number of Cabins	730	Crew	550 (International)
Number of Outside Cabins	481	Passenger/Crew Ratio	2.7 to 1
Cabins with Verandas	0	Year Built	1992
Number of Passengers	1,460	Last Major Refurbishment	1999

Frommer's Ratings (Scale of 1–5)

Cabin Comfort & Amenities	3	Pool, Fitness & Spa Facilities	3
Ship Cleanliness & Maintenance	4	Children's Facilities	3
Public Comfort/Space	4	Itinerary	5
Decor	4	Worth the Money	4

By normal standards, the *Norwegian Majesty* would be classified as a fairly new ship. As NCL executive vice president Art Sbarsky rightly pointed out, "Just five years ago, a seven-year-old ship would be considered quite new." But that was 5 years ago, and the explosive growth in the cruise business has made some ships seem dated before their time.

By early 1999, the *Majesty* was beginning to show its age, both in its condition and its lack of pizzazz, so NCL pulled the ship out of service for just over 100 days, sending it to the Lloyd Werft Shipyard in Bremerhaven, Germany, to be stretched, much like fleetmates *Dream* and *Wind.* In what's become a relatively routine operation in the cruise industry, the ship was literally sawed in half, like a magician's assistant, and a pre-constructed midsection was grafted into its middle, measuring just over 100 feet and containing 220 additional cabins; a new, second dining room; more pool and deck space; and the alternative Le Bistro restaurant, a signature room on NCL's ships these days. The *Majesty* is now 680 feet long and carries 1,460 people at double occupancy.

In addition to increasing the ship's size, NCL also redid all outside decking, replaced carpets, and redecorated the existing cabins. In short, the old girl got a facelift, and she's looking great!

Great is not sparkly, though, and the *Norwegian Majesty* is not going to excite fans of the Royal Caribbean, Celebrity, or Princess megaships. Nor will *Majesty* make any-one forget Holland America's or Celebrity's mid-sized vessels. But it doesn't try. NCL isn't selling *Majesty* as a floating art museum, a Las Vegas at sea, or a night at the Ritz. *Majesty* is what it is: A classy, understated, informal mid-sized ship with good food, good service, and enough entertainment and activity options to keep everyone occupied.

Cabins & Rates

Cabins	Per diems from	Bathtub	Fridge	Hair Dryer	Sitting Area	TV
Inside	$132*	no	no	yes	no	yes**
Outside	$233*	no	some	yes	no	yes**
Suite	$261*	yes	yes	yes	yes	yes**

Rates for Bermuda itineraries are higher on average.
**TVs show CNN and ESPN.*

CABINS   *Norwegian Majesty* was originally built as a Baltic ferry, but was transformed into a cruise ship—the *Royal Majesty,* for Majesty Cruise Line—before it ever left the shipyard. It was intended for short, 3- and 4-day jaunts from Miami to the Bahamas, Key West, and Cozumel and also worked in the Boston-Bermuda market—itineraries that didn't really require large cabins.

Today, though, *Majesty* is entering the 10- and 11-night Panama Canal market (along with Bermuda), and some folks may find the accommodations to be a bit, shall we say, intimate. The ship has 10 price categories, although the Penthouse Suite category has just two cabins. The Superior Deluxe Suites (18) are more than adequate, with bath-tubs and tile bathrooms, sitting areas, and enough room to move. Most Category A outside staterooms are a barely adequate 145 square feet, but in lower categories it gets even tighter at 106 square feet. All cabins have hair dryers, televisions (with ESPN, CNN, two movie channels, and an in-house station—but you probably won't want to lie around these small cabins watching TV for very long), and safes, and some rooms have refrigerators. Many cabins can accommodate a third and fourth passenger.

Some cabins on Norway and Viking Decks have views that are obstructed by life-boats. On Promenade Deck, you are likely to open your curtain in the morning and come face-to-face with a jogger. The best cabins (other than suites) may be Category A rooms on Majesty Deck, especially the ones in the bow that have windows offering sweeping vistas of the sea ahead.

PUBLIC AREAS   *Norwegian Majesty* is among the easiest ships to find your way around, and you are never far from something to do. Public areas aren't glitzy, deco-rated instead with a pleasant mixture of blues, lavenders, ivories, and lots of teak and brass.

There are two bars and the informal buffet restaurant, Cafe Royale, on Sun Deck. Although many ships put their buffet restaurant in the stern, this ship's cozy cafe is in the bow, with panoramic windows to see what's ahead. The room isn't huge, and can be crowded at mealtime, with long lines. There is another munching option in the stern: Piazza San Marco, where you can get pizza, hot dogs, and burgers.

There are outdoor tables on Sun Deck, but if you want to stay inside and the Cafe Royale tables are taken, slip down the stairs into the Royal Observatory Lounge. This is another bow-facing room with great views. It's also the scene of live entertainment nightly, including karaoke. This room is easy to miss, tucked away in the bow on a deck with no other public rooms except the Kids Corner all the way back in the stern.

The rest of the ship's nightlife is on Decks 5 and 6, except for the Frame 52 Disco on Deck 7 aft. The disco is small and not as technically advanced as some, but it serves its purpose and hops until about 3am nightly.

The Palace Theater could be described as intimate; it could also be described as claustrophobic. Either way, the sightlines are not good, with support columns all around the room. The low ceiling prevents dancers from getting too energetic. The ship offers standard NCL entertainment consisting of variety acts and song-and-dance revues that fall short of the standard being set by the Big Three (Carnival, Princess, and Royal Caribbean).

The Polo Club just outside the theater is a good place to have a drink before the show or before (or after) dinner. It usually features a pianist/vocalist. On the opposite end of the long, narrow room is the Monte Carlo Casino, which was totally redone when the ship was stretched. The casino no longer overlooks the main lobby, nor does it have a stairway to the lobby. It has been redecorated and seems darker and moodier, a perfect setting for you and your money to have a parting of the ways.

Down on Deck 5 you can eat, drink, and be merry. The Seven Seas dining room in the stern has been refurbished; it's attractive, but both it and the new Four Seasons dining room near the midships lobby seem quite crowded. Le Bistro, the line's signature alternative restaurant, is a small, intimate room off the corridor that links the two main dining rooms, and it should be a popular venue. Le Bistro serves made-at-your-table Caesar salads, cheese and chocolate fondues, and an array of continental entrees. Reservations are a good idea, although sometimes you might be able to walk in and get a table. A $5 per person tip is expected in this room.

Next door to Le Bistro is a new coffee bar. Sit on a stool at the bar or carry your drink to a nearby windowside table and watch the world go by inside and out. Shops are forward from the lobby, and there's a new card room, a small video arcade, a library, and a meeting room.

The Rendezvous Lounge and Royal Fireworks Lounge abut each other in the bow. Fireworks offers up a dance band performing adult contemporary sounds; Rendezvous is a piano bar. Both rooms tend to be underused by passengers who have no other reason to find themselves in that end of the ship.

POOL & FITNESS FACILITIES   When *Majesty* got a new midsection it got a second swimming pool (there's also a splash pool for kids on Deck 8), which should relieve some of the overcrowding the original pool used to experience. It also got a whole lot of new deck space on Decks 10 and 11. You can also catch some rays in relative peace and quiet at the stern of Viking Deck (8).

Joggers and walkers can circle the ship on the wraparound Promenade Deck 7. Deck 7 also is home to the Bodywave spa and fitness center. These facilities are not extensive by any means. The workout room is basic and has several weight stations and cardiovascular stations, and there's a separate aerobics room across the hall.

Norwegian Sea

The Verdict

While the *Sea* seems tired and dated in many ways, this mid-sized, middle-aged ship offers an ultra-casual cruise and a great itinerary at a very affordable price.

Norwegian Sea *(photo: NCL)*

Specifications

Size (in tons)	42,000	Officers	Norwegian
Number of Cabins	752	Crew	616 (International)
Number of Outside Cabins	519	Passenger/Crew Ratio	2.4 to 1
Cabins with Verandas	0	Year Built	1988
Number of Passengers	1,504	Last Major Refurbishment	1991

Frommer's Ratings (Scale of 1–5)

Cabin Comfort & Amenities	3	Pool, Fitness & Spa Facilities	2
Ship Cleanliness & Maintenance	3	Children's Facilities	1
Public Comfort/Space	3	Itinerary	5
Decor	3	Worth the Money	4

"A cruise out of Houston? Houston's not on the water! Is it?" And this came from a bright, well-traveled co-worker who had actually been to Houston. Yes, indeed, Houston is a port city, although they keep the port hidden way out yonder (technically, it's in a place called "LaPorte"). The approach isn't pretty, with refineries and freighters everywhere (then again, a lot of ports look like that). So why Houston? Why not? NCL is the only cruise line basing a ship there, and it's quite popular. Once you get to the terminal, there's no mad rush, the people are friendly and efficient, and, next to the freighters, the *Norwegian Sea* looks positively gorgeous.

This is a good thing. Whereas in a popular port like Miami or Fort Lauderdale you might get to the port, pull up alongside a newer, bigger, sleeker ship, and think, "Dang, why couldn't my travel agent have put me on *that* one?" Well, this doesn't happen in Houston, nor in Cancún, Cozumel, or Roatan, the ports on the ship's itinerary. Cozumel is the only place the *Sea* comes close to other ships, and they are way down at the other dock, so you don't get to compare much, which is good news for NCL because the *Sea* wouldn't fare too well against most of the competition. It's not a bad ship, but it's an aging ship, a relic at 12 years old. Too young to be a classic, too old to be contemporary, the ship is just right for an inexpensive cruise for a casual, laid-back crowd.

Truthfully, the highlight of any *Norwegian Sea* cruise has to be the itinerary. In addition to visiting popular Cozumel, it's the only ship that visits Cancún every week, and one of the few that docks in Roatan, a Honduran island known for its great diving and snorkeling. While Cozumel and Cancún are commercial resorts, Roatan is an unmistakably third-world island. The port is a ways away from the luxurious resorts of Fantasy Island and the West End, and getting there means seeing life as it really is in this underprivileged nation. It can be a bit disturbing, but the people are friendly and it is refreshing to experience a bit of reality after spending time in the tourist-intensive Mexican ports.

Cabins & Rates						
Cabins	Per diems from	Bathtub	Fridge	Hair Dryer	Sitting Area	TV
Inside	$127	no	no	yes	no	yes*
Outside	$153	some	some	yes	some	yes*
Suite	$253	yes	yes	yes	yes	yes*

TVs show ESPN and CNN.

CABINS   When NCL built the ship in 1988, it didn't waste space on the cabins. The rooms are small by any measure, although they do provide adequate drawer and hanging space for two people in most cases. Their decor is pleasant, and their soundproofing is great—I heard the couple next door only once. Things get cozy—that's real-estate language for "cramped"—in the standard cabins, especially the inside ones, the cheapest of the bunch. With two fold-down bunk beds and two regular berths, they allow you to cram four people into a space that's adequate for one. But if the choice is going as an anchovy or not going at all, then break out the capers. In general, bathrooms are tiny: I found a new way to turn off the shower without using my hands. It was strictly inadvertent, but it illustrates just how little room there is to maneuver.

There are four owner's suites and three deluxe suites, and these are the best and most spacious accommodations, if you can afford them. They have sitting areas, bathtubs, and mini-refrigerators. Note that many cabins on both the Star and Norway Decks have their views either obstructed or partially obstructed by lifeboats.

All cabins have hair dryers and TVs showing ESPN and CNN. In theory, all cabins have personal safes (although I was told mine would, it didn't).

The *Sea* has four cabins equipped for disabled passengers.

PUBLIC AREAS   This is not a glitzy ship, and some parts of it look the most spartan of anything in the NCL fleet. Nevertheless, the *Norwegian Sea* is seaworthy in every way and sleek in design, and it's been a hit for NCL, especially among Americans, who make up a good percentage of its passenger list and its crew.

Its Scandinavian designers, Petter Yran and Robert Tillberg, exercised restraint throughout its nine decks, trying for a modern but not ostentatious look that would attract a more discriminating clientele. A striking two-deck-high lobby has a water-and-crystal sculpture, along with a cascading fountain splashing into a marble-lined pool. I found lots of quiet little nooks in the wide, bright elevator lobbies (not to be confused with the tiny, dark elevators). On some decks there are chairs and tables near the windows in these spaces. You can sit outside Oscar's, the smoky little piano bar off the atrium, retreat to the not-very-well-stocked library, or play a game in the card room just off the large, roomy casino (with its 178 slot machines). Card games are accompanied by the quaint sounds of a Western-themed slot machine that exhorts anyone within 50 yards to "Round 'em up—it's a stampede!" How very Houston!

There's another little bar tucked away on Deck 10 aft. Gatsby's can be a bit drafty, and the chairs, while attractive, aren't conducive to long stays. But it's an intimate little wine and cigar bar with soft piano music. Right across the deck is Le Bistro, the ship's alternative restaurant, which you have to try at least once (love that chocolate fondue!). The two main restaurants are unremarkable, and the casual dining restaurant, with the most convoluted, exasperating buffet line I've ever seen, can be a pain. The food is better than it looks, though, and the specialty station outside the main buffet—pick-your-own-ingredients omelets for breakfast and soup for lunch—are delightful.

The Cabaret Lounge is the main showroom, and you'd better get there early for a seat without an obstructed view. The Stardust Lounge is a cabaret-style room that offers some alternative entertainment. There's also a disco that heats up late at night; it may be small, but it works.

RECREATION & FITNESS FACILITIES   It's not always easy to find a deck chair near the pool. Go up one flight to the Sun Deck and it gets easier—the farther from the pool and band, the less crowded it gets. And you are never too far from one of the outdoor bars. If it gets too hot, just ask one of the waiters to spritz you with his water bottle. Squirting passengers makes their day. There are two nice pools on deck (one is quite large) and a couple of whirlpools.

There are many ships to choose from when it comes to fitness and spa programs. This is not one of them. The fitness room is on the small side and has your basic equipment, and the "full-service" spa has two treatment rooms, one each for men and women. There are also his-and-hers saunas. The Promenade Deck features a quarter-mile jogging and walking track. Adjacent to the spa and gym is a golf driving net. There's also Ping-Pong and shuffleboard, and snorkeling lessons can be arranged.

Preview: *Norwegian Sky*

The 2,002-passenger, 80,000-ton *Norwegian Sky* will be the line's biggest and snazziest cruise ship to date. At press time, the ship was scheduled to launch in August 1999, just as this book hits the stores. In addition to all the exciting onboard activities NCL is so well known for, it will have the industry's first Internet Cafe, and modem access in each cabin; also, all of the *Sky*'s 257 suites will have private verandas. The ship will have a grand eight-deck atrium and lots of great public rooms, including two formal dining rooms, two 84-seat alternative restaurants, a large indoor/outdoor casual buffet restaurant, and nearly a dozen bars, including a cigar club, a sports bar, a coffee bar, and a wine bar. For kids, the *Sky* will have a children's playroom, a teen center, and a video arcade, while a large fitness and spa area will be located on the Pool Deck and feature lots of windows for ocean views. There will be two pools plus a kid's wading pool and four hot tubs. A well-stocked Sports Deck features a basketball/volleyball court, golf driving net, and a batting cage, as well as shuffleboard.

Princess Cruises

SHIPS   Crown Princess • Dawn Princess • Grand Princess • Ocean Princess (preview) • Pacific Princess • Sea Princess • Sun Princess

10100 Santa Monica Blvd., Los Angeles, CA 90067-4189. ☎ **800/421-0522** or 310/553-1770. Fax 310/284-2845. www.princesscruises.com.

THE LINE IN A NUTSHELL   Princess's mostly-mega fleet offers a quality, mainstream cruise experience. Its newest ships are stylish, floating resorts with just the right combination of fun, glamour, and gentility for an all-around pleasant and relaxing cruise.

THE EXPERIENCE   Although Princess does not position its ships in the Caribbean year-round (they spend their summers plying the waters of Alaska and the Mediterranean), those ships it does bring in for the Caribbean season are its newest and largest. If you were to put Carnival, Royal Caribbean, Celebrity, and Holland America in a big bowl and mix them all together, you'd come up with the Princess's megas. The *Grand, Sea, Sun, Dawn,* and *Ocean Princess* are less glitzy and frenzied than Carnival and Royal Caribbean, not quite as cutting edge or witty as Celebrity's *Century, Galaxy,* and *Mercury,* and more exciting, youthful, and entertaining than Holland America's near-megas, and appeal to a wide cross section of cruisers by offering lots of choice, activities, and touches of big-ship glamour, along with lots of private balconies and plenty of the quiet nooks and calm spaces of smaller, more intimate-sized vessels.

Overall, the Princess ships are one notch above mass-market ships and their most aggressive competitors, Carnival and Royal Caribbean. You certainly won't get anything near the luxury of a Seabourn or Cunard here; what you will get is a well-functioning, semiformal product delivered on a mass scale. Aboard Princess, you get a lot of bang for your buck, attractively packaged and well executed.

Pros

- **Balconies.** Nearly half of all the cabins on the *Ocean, Sea, Sun,* and *Dawn* have private balconies; on the *Grand Princess,* over half do!
- **Lots of dining choices.** The Grand-class ships have two or three main dining rooms, two intimate alternative dining restaurants, a sprawling Lido buffet open 24-hours a day, pizza poolside, and a Haagen-Dazs ice-cream parlor.

Cons

- **No free ice cream.** It may sound petty, but it's irritating that Princess sells only Haagen-Dazs ice-cream—at $1.90 a scoop and $3.75 for a sundae—in lieu of the free frozen yogurt and soft ice cream most all other lines offer. (Princess serves the free stuff only in the dining room at mealtime.)

Frommer's Ratings: Princess Cruises

	Poor	Fair	Good	Excellent	Outstanding
Enjoyment Factor					✓
Dining			✓		
Activities				✓	
Children's Activities				✓	
Entertainment				✓	
Service				✓	
Overall Value				✓	

PRINCESS: MELLOW MEGAS

Few other cruise lines (except Carnival) have managed to start so small and grow so rapidly in such a short time, starting as an obscure West Coast cruise outfit and growing into the hyper-modern upper-middle-class giant it is today.

Princess Cruises originated in 1962, when the company's founder, Stanley McDonald, chartered the long-gone *Princess Patricia* as a floating hotel for the Seattle World's Fair. He then continued to charter ships for cruises between Los Angeles, Alaska, and the Pacific coast of Mexico. Soon after, two additional ships, one of them brand-new, were leased from Costa Cruises to meet demand. In 1974, the company was snapped up by British shipping giant P&O Group, which has intensified its efforts to promote Princess vessels and Caribbean itineraries in markets on both sides of the Atlantic.

In the 1970s, Princess gained enormously by associating itself and its ships *Island Princess* and *Pacific Princess* with the TV series ***The Love Boat,*** which portrayed the cruise experience as an almost foolproof matchmaking machine. The series created a flood of paying customers anxious to experience romance on the high seas, all skippered and shepherded by tactful Gavin MacLeod and his witty crew, or some reasonable facsimile. The series gets enormous credit for promoting cruises in general and Princess in particular, so it's no wonder the company's been unwilling to let the association slip away. To this day, you'll still hear the theme song from the show sung aboard ship, and still see Gavin MacLeod pitching for the line.

THE FLEET

Princess's diverse fleet of nine ships (10 when the *Ocean Princess* is launched in early 2000) includes four Grand-class ships (the 109,000-ton super-megaship **Grand Princess** and the three mega-sisters **Dawn Princess, Sea Princess,** and **Sun Princess,** with the **Ocean Princess** coming just as this book goes to press), two near-megas (the 1,590-passenger **Crown Princess** and **Regal Princess**), the 1,200-passenger **Sky Princess** and **Royal Princess,** and the small, 640-passenger **Pacific Princess.** The *Sky* and *Royal* do not sail in the Caribbean, and so are not reviewed in this book.

The fleet first bulked up in 1988, when Princess received a massive influx of staff, equipment, and hardware through P&O's purchase of Italian-owned, Los Angeles–based Sitmar cruises. As part of this deal, Princess acquired three huge, cutting-edge ships: the *Star Princess,* whose construction was almost completed at the time of the sale (and which has since been commandeered by P&O to sail as its *Arcadia*), and the futuristic-looking *Crown Princess* and *Regal Princess,* identical 70,000-ton twins whose avant-garde design today appears somewhat dated in comparison with the line's newer ships. In 1995, Princess began a building spree that's still in high gear, with the launching of the cutting-edge Grand-class ships at a cost of no less than $300 million each.

The Grand class's *Sun Princess* and *Dawn Princess* were launched in 1995 and 1997, respectively. In May 1998 the company made giant waves throughout the travel industry with the launching of what was to date the largest cruise ship in the world, the 109,000-ton *Grand Princess.* The *Sea Princess,* a sister to the *Sun* and *Dawn,* joined the fleet later that same year, and at press time a fourth sister, *Ocean Princess,* was scheduled to debut in early 2000. Two sisters to the 109,000-ton *Grand Princess* are in the works and scheduled to enter service in the spring and fall of 2001.

For 2000, the oldest of the Princess mega lot, the nearly 10-year-old, 1,590-passenger *Crown Princess,* will spend half the year doing 10- and 11-night Panama Canal cruises, and the almost 30-year-old *Pacific Princess,* the oldest and smallest of the fleet, will spend a season in Bermuda—Princess's first ever—beginning in May.

PASSENGER PROFILE

In the past, most Princess passengers were middle-aged middle-income Americans, but the new megas are attracting younger, 30- and 40-something cruisers as well as those in their 50s and 60s, and generally a broader cross section of more active types. The *Grand Princess* and *Ocean, Sea, Sun,* and *Dawn Princess* have extensive kids' facilities and are ideal ships for families. The *Grand Princess* lures wedding parties with its wedding chapel, one of only two at sea (the other is on Royal Caribbean's new *Voyager of the Seas*) and the fact that it's the only ship where the captain conducts official marriage ceremonies on board every week. (Hey, this is the *Love Boat,* you know.) Perfect for a romantic vacation, the ships strike a balance between formal and informal, and draw a relatively affluent but not overly wealthy crowd. There's a lot going on, but plenty of opportunity to do your own thing.

Overall, the passengers are not as rowdy and boisterous as clients aboard Carnival, not as rich as those aboard Seabourn, and not as staid as those aboard Holland America. Most seem to like a bit of everything—many appreciate the traditional cruise experience offered by Princess, enjoy the treat of dressing up for dinner, and like listening to music in a cozy lounge and dabbling in the line's many onboard activities and exciting nightlife.

DINING

The newer and bigger the ship, the more dining options. Princess's food, on its newest ships especially, is on a par with that of other mass-market lines, such as Carnival, Royal Caribbean, and Norwegian, and ranges from very good to mediocre. The line doesn't seem to focus on food and beverage presentations as assiduously as, for example, Celebrity. Service is efficient, but not memorable or extraordinary in any way. At times it feels a bit harried.

On its megas, two or three **main dining rooms** have two seatings at dinner and usually two at breakfast and lunch as well. A choice of four or five entrees at dinner may include prime rib, king crab legs, turkey with all the Thanksgiving trimmings, halibut in a citrus-caper butter sauce, rack of lamb with Dijon sauce, Cornish hen, and even pan-roasted rabbit with rosemary and sage; there are always **"healthy" choices** and **vegetarian options,** too.

There's also the buffet-style Horizon Court Lido restaurant for more **casual dining** morning, noon, and night. For breakfast, you'll find everything from fresh fruit to cold cuts, from cereal to fish, and from steam-table scrambled eggs to cooked-to-order fried eggs. At lunch, you'll find several salads, fruits, hot and cold dishes, roasts, and vegetarian choices. The restaurant's multistation setup keeps lines to a minimum. Evenings, this becomes the Horizon Court Bistro, a sit-down restaurant seating about 100 guests. The food is as good as you'll get in the dining room, with a set menu all week enhanced by a few specials. Reservations aren't needed, and the only extra charge is a tip for your waiter.

The Grand-class ships have far and away the most choices beyond the typical dining rooms. Unlike any other ship in the fleet, the *Grand Princess* has two alternative, **reservations-required restaurants** specializing in Italian (with specialty pizzas, antipastos, and six kinds of pasta) and Tex-Mex (with choices like fajitas and tequila chicken). They're a great way to break up the week. Both charge a $3.50 per person cover. The *Ocean, Sea, Sun,* and *Dawn* have a **sit-down pizzeria** with a menu of pizza choices. In all these alternative venues, dining is more casual, intimate, and quiet, with tables seating mostly parties of two, four, and six. There's also **24-hour noshing**

Bye-Bye, *Island Princess*

In early 1999, Princess announced the sale of one of its original Love Boats—the *Island Princess,* built way back in 1965—to Hyundai Merchant Marine, a Korean conglomerate that once had a short-lived partnership with Carnival Corporation.

Seems like Princess is trying hard to steer its fleet as a whole toward the Grand-class philosophy of megaship cruising—balconies, lots of activities, and choices, choices, choices. As for the *Island's* sister ship, the *Pacific Princess,* senior VP of customer service and sales Rick James was quoted in industry publications saying, "She will be with us for the foreseeable future," and in fact the ship has a 3-year commitment to Bermuda itineraries, beginning in 2000.

available in the Horizon Court. Pizza and grilled burgers, chicken fillets, and French fries are served from a **poolside grill** in the afternoons, and there's a Haagen-Dazs **ice-cream parlor** serving the yummy stuff in scoops and sundaes for several dollars a pop (unfortunately, this is in lieu of the free frozen-yogurt and ice-cream machines most megas have operating most of the day).

There's **24-hour room service** in the cabins.

ACTIVITIES

The line that wants to be all things to all people is expert at programming activities to please a wide range of tastes, with the Grand-class ships offering the most elaborate and extensive repertoire and the *Crown Princess* and *Pacific Princess* being much more sedate.

Activities fleetwide include art auctions, bingo, cards, trivia games, aerobics classes, shuffleboard, Ping-Pong, golf putting, first-run movies, dancing lessons, port talks, water volleyball, beauty and spa demonstrations, and more. Additionally, the Grand-class ships offer golf via virtual-reality simulators, and the *Grand Princess* has basketball and volleyball, a virtual-reality game room, and a **miniature golf course.** And of course, you can always relax in your cabin and watch *Love Boat* reruns (of the old show or the new one).

While the pitch of activities isn't as frenzied as aboard Carnival or Royal Caribbean, the Grand-class ships aren't anywhere near sedate. They're a new breed of ship for Princess, and closer to their more party-happy competitors than ever before. The **discos** rage most nights with a fairly packed dance floor, and there are always a couple of silly **pool games** each afternoon, like a belly-flop contest or a stuff-the-most-fruit-or-Ping-Pong-balls-into-your-bathing-suit contest.

Princess's "New Waves" program offers passengers the chance to earn **PADI scuba diving certification,** a rare and worthwhile experience that's not available aboard many other ships. Sign up in advance or the moment you get aboard, as the course requires that you attend at least 15 hours of classroom and practice sessions. You can also book into the program through your travel agent when you're making your other cruise arrangements. If you opt to pursue this, approach it with the seriousness it deserves, and plan to spend some time studying.

Princess devotes a lot of attention and space to its onboard **libraries.** The *Grand Princess* also has a cozy writing area, a place to pen all those postcards you'll want to send. The Grand-class ships have a business center with fax machines and computers (for $7.50 per 15 minutes, you can even send and receive e-mail from them), open for limited hours each day.

Princess Cays: Private Island Paradise

There's an additional advantage for beach buffs aboard any of Princess's Caribbean vessels: the line's private island, Princess Cays, off the southwestern coast of Eleuthera in the Bahamas. You can swim and snorkel, and make use of Princess's fleet of Hobie Cats, Sunfish, banana boats, kayaks, and paddle wheelers. There's live music, a beach barbecue, and some great tree-shaded hammocks at the far end of the beach for anyone who wants to get away from it all or sleep off too many rum punches.

While overall the island experience is a pleasure, on a recent visit I found the service at the water sports shack to be poor. The crew in charge of the Jet Skis (which passengers were paying a nice chunk of change to rent for a half hour or hour) seemed to have no idea what was going on, and weren't apologetic about it either. Renters had to wait way past their allotted times and were left to their own devices to grab a Jet Ski when one became available. Let's hope this was an aberration.

CHILDREN'S PROGRAM

Supervised activities are offered year-round for ages 2 to 17, and are divided into two groups: "Princess Pelicans," ages 2 to 12, and teens, ages 13 to 17. Princess's newest Caribbean-bound ships, the *Grand, Ocean, Sea, Sun,* and *Dawn,* are well equipped for children. They've each got a spacious **children's playroom** and a sizable area of fenced-in outside deck dedicated for kids only, with a shallow pool and tricycles. **Teen centers** have computers, video games, and a sound system (and the one on the *Grand Princess* even has a teen's hot tub and private sunbathing deck). Smartly, these areas are places as separate as possible from the adult passengers. These ships are clearly catering to families with kids, as Princess continually seeks to broaden its appeal and distance itself from its old image as a staid, adults-only line.

While in drydock in early 1999, Princess added a playroom to the *Crown* (it doubles as a meeting room when there aren't many kids on board), but neither the children's area nor the supervised activities on this ship are anywhere near as extensive as aboard the Grand-class ships. The small *Pacific Princess* isn't especially child-friendly, although when there are at least 15 kids on board, some supervised activities are provided. There's no dedicated playroom.

Activities fleetwide include karaoke, movies, swimming and snorkeling lessons, tours of the galley and bridge, scavenger hunts, arts and crafts, coloring contests, birthday parties, dance marathons (on those ships with teen discos), hula parties complete with grass skirts, and teenage versions of "The Dating Game."

In late 1998, Princess lowered its minimum age requirement to 6 months; previously a child had to be at least a year old to sail. Princess does not offer private in-cabin baby-sitting at all, but does provide **slumber-party-style group baby-sitting** in the playroom for $4 an hour (10pm to 1am nightly, and 9am to 5pm when in port).

ENTERTAINMENT

The Grand-class ships have a lot going on, and the quality of the overall package ranks way up there. From glittering, well-conceived, and well-executed **Vegas-style production shows** to New York cabaret singers on the main stage; from a wonderfully entertaining **cabaret piano/vocalist** in the Atrium Lounge (a throwaway space for many ships) to a rocking disco, this line offers a terrific blend of musical delights, and you'll

Princess Fleet Itineraries

Ship	Home Ports & Season	Itinerary	Other Itineraries
Crown Princess	Round-trip from Fort Lauderdale, Oct–Apr.	**10-night Panama Canal:** Cozumel, Grand Cayman, Puerto Limón (Costa Rica), and Cartagena (Colombia).	Alaska
Dawn Princess	Round-trip from San Juan, itineraries alternate Oct–Apr.	**7-night southern Carib 1:** La Guaira/Caracas (Venezuela), Grenada, Dominica, and St. Thomas. **7-night southern Carib 2:** Barbados, St. Lucia, Sint Maarten, St. Kitts, and St. Thomas.	Alaska
Grand Princess	Round-trip from Fort Lauderdale, Oct–Apr.	**7-night eastern Carib:** St. Thomas, Sint Maarten, and Princess Cays.	Mediterranean
Ocean Princess	Round-trip from San Juan, itineraries alternate Oct–Apr.	**7-night southern Carib 1:** Curaçao, Isla Margarita (Venezuela), St. Vincent, St. Kitts, and St. Thomas. **7-night southern Carib 2:** Trinidad, Barbados, Antigua, Martinique, and St. Thomas.	Alaska
Pacific Princess	Round-trip from New York, Apr–Oct.	**7-night Bermuda:** Hamilton and St. George's.	Mediterranean, Europe, Africa
Sea Princess	Round-trip from Fort Lauderdale, Oct–Apr.	**7-night western Carib:** Princess Cays, Ocho Rios (Jamaica), Grand Cayman, and Cozumel.	Alaska
Sun Princess	Between San Juan and Acapulco, itineraries alternate Oct–Apr.	**10-night Panama Canal:** Puerto Caldera (Costa Rica), Cartagena (Colombia), Aruba, and St. Thomas. **11-night Panama Canal:** St. Thomas, Martinique, Grenada, and Curaçao.	Alaska

always find a cozy spot where some soft piano or jazz music is being performed. You'll also find entertainment like hypnotists, puppeteers, and comedians, plus karaoke for you audience-participation types, and, in the afternoons, a couple of sessions of that ubiquitous cruise favorite, the "Newlywed and Not-So-Newlywed Game."

Among the many bars and lounges is the clubby, old-world Wheelhouse Lounge, with its dark wood details and ship memorabilia. Plus, all Princess ships covered in this review offer a **wine bar** selling caviar by the ounce and vintage wine, champagne, and iced vodka by the glass.

The Princess **casinos** are sprawling and exciting places, too, and are bound to keep gamblers entranced (hypnotized?) with their lights and action.

SERVICE

Overall, service is efficient and lines (at least on the Grand-class ships) are short, even in the busy Lido buffet restaurants. Staff and crew aren't the friendliest nor are they the surliest; they're just well-intentioned, hard-working staff doing their jobs.

Cabin steward service is the most consistent, with dining and bar service on the slow side at times (and language barriers with bar servers can be frustrating when you're trying to get your martini just right).

All of the Princess vessels in the Caribbean offer **laundry** and **dry cleaning** services, and have their own **self-service laundromats.**

Crown Princess

The Verdict

In spite of its cramped outdoor deck space, most people will find the *Crown*'s exterior and interior design appealing and dramatic, and the cruise an overall winner.

Crown Princess *(photo: Princess Cruises)*

Specifications

Size (in tons)	70,000	Officers	Italian
Number of Cabins	795	Crew	696 (International)
Number of Outside Cabins	624	Passenger/Crew Ratio	2.3 to 1
Cabins with Verandas	184	Year Built	1991
Number of Passengers	1,590	Last Major Refurbishment	N/A

Frommer's Ratings (Scale of 1–5)

Cabin Comfort & Amenities	4	Pool, Fitness & Spa Facilities	3
Ship Cleanliness & Maintenance	4	Children's Facilities	3
Public Comfort/Space	3	Itinerary	4
Decor	4	Worth the Money	5

Between 1991 and 1995, the *Crown Princess,* along with its identical twin, the *Regal Princess,* were the company's most modern, most dramatic, and most frequently photographed vessels. Their designer, Renzo Piano, is also responsible for such high-profile designs as the Centre Pompidou in Paris and reconstruction plans for the re-united Berlin, projects that were among the most talked about in Europe since the building of the Eiffel Tower in the 1880s.

You'll either adore or dislike the configuration of the *Crown*'s exterior, which its designer has compared to the silhouette of a porpoise moving through the water. (Less generous souls say it reminds them of Darth Vader's helmet—albeit in good-guy white.) Even the smokestacks' design—jutting directly and old-fashionedly upward, as opposed to the raked stacks of most other modern vessels—has attracted criticism.

Most cruisers will find the design appealing and dramatic, but its outdoor deck space is insufficient, leading to congestion at deck buffets and around swimming pools whenever the ship is full (which is often). There's no uninterrupted Promenade Deck around the periphery of the ship, either; if you want to stroll, you'll have to walk back and forth along the ship's sides or get on a treadmill in the gym. All in all, aboard the *Crown Princess,* you'll find that there's more of an emphasis on indoor space than on outdoor.

In general, though, public areas have many pillars and columns, and a somewhat disjointed internal layout. Despite these drawbacks, the avant-garde, futuristic-looking *Crown* contains all the amenities offered by competing megaships. Its interiors are stunning and, for such a large vessel, surprisingly intimate and cozy.

Cabins & Rates

Cabins	Per diems from	Bathtub	Fridge	Hair Dryer	Sitting Area	TV
Inside	$155	no	yes	yes	no	yes*
Outside	$175	no	yes	yes	no	yes*
Suite	$237	yes	yes	yes	yes	yes*

TVs show CNN, ESPN, TNT, Nickelodeon, and BBC.

CABINS Of 795 total, 624 are outside cabins, and many have a private verandas; in fact, two whole decks of cabins have them.

Standard cabins are quite spacious at 190 square feet to 210 square feet, and suites with balconies are 587 square feet. Decor includes light-grained wood, color schemes of warm beiges and peaches, comfortably upholstered chairs and sofas, framed artwork, and rectangular windows for easy wave-gazing. Bathrooms are compact but comfortable.

If you're booking a standard cabin, opt for one of the four classified as category GG on the Plaza Deck, if they're available. These outside doubles with queen-sized beds are the ship's most convenient and the best of the standard lot. Note that views from some cabins on the Dolphin Deck are partially obstructed by lifeboats.

The lowest priced outside cabins are category G on the Fiesta Deck, with lower and upper berths (read: bunk beds) and round portholes. These cabins are good buys, especially for budget-minded friends or families traveling together.

All cabins have safes, terry-cloth robes for use during the cruise, and TVs broadcasting CNN, ESPN, Nickelodeon, BBC programming, and TNT.

About 10 cabins are wheelchair accessible.

PUBLIC AREAS An army of designers worked hard to create as many divergent decorative styles on board as possible. The plush and sleek interiors, studded with some of the most intriguing and colorful artwork afloat (and lots of pillars that wind up obstructing the flow of the rooms), feel more like a hotel than a ship, making one wonder at the logic behind a cruise ship that gives the impression you aren't at sea.

At the ship's core is the three-story Plaza Atrium, with a grand staircase. The lower level houses the lobby and reception area, as well as a bar devoted exclusively to pastries. The ship's massive casino-cum-bar-cum-observation deck is strikingly dramatic, framed by polished, rounded, bone-white "ribs" arching from ceiling to floor and glassed in by 270 degrees of panoramic curved glass windows. Situated decks above the other bars, restaurants, and public areas, it feels a million miles from everything else on the ship. In the casino, tables and slot machines lie close to a stage where a piano player or a band keeps you entertained between hands.

The Crown Court dining room boasts two-level terracing. There's also a two-level show lounge for nightly Vegas-style entertainment. At midships is Kipling's, an attractive piano bar. If you'd like to escape the hordes, though, seek out the relative calm and soothing premises of the Intermezzo Bar.

RECREATION & FITNESS FACILITIES Two pools on the Lido Deck can become crowded when the ship is completely booked. Two hot tubs are adjacent to the pools. There's shuffleboard on the Promenade Deck and Ping-Pong on the Lido Deck.

The *Crown Princess*'s health club/spa lies way down deep in the ship, so you won't have any inspiring views of the waves while you're working out. The gym is on the small side, but there is a separate aerobics rooms. You'll find a spa with several massage and treatment rooms, as well as steam rooms, saunas, and a tiny beauty salon.

Dawn Princess • Sea Princess • Sun Princess • Ocean Princess (preview)

Sun Princess *(photo: Princess Cruises)*

The Verdict

Finally, we have relaxed-yet-glitzy ships for grownups who like to enjoy the good life without pretension.

Specifications

Size (in tons)	77,000	Passenger/Crew Ratio	2.2 to 1
Number of Cabins	975	Year Built	
Number of Outside Cabins	603	*Dawn Princess*	1995
Cabins with Verandas	410	*Ocean Princess*	1999
Number of Passengers	1,950	*Sea Princess*	1998
Officers	Italian	*Sun Princess*	1997
Crew	900 (Internat'l)	Last Major Refurbishment	N/A

Frommer's Ratings (Scale of 1–5)

Cabin Comfort & Amenities	4	Pool, Fitness & Spa Facilities	4
Ship Cleanliness & Maintenance	4	Children's Facilities	4
Public Comfort/Space	5	Itinerary	5
Decor	5	Worth the Money	5

Love isn't all that's exciting and new at the Love Boat line. Anyone familiar with Princess Cruises from the old TV show or from sailing on the older ships will be thrilled with the *Ocean, Dawn, Sea,* and *Sun,* the four sisters that, along with the huge *Grand Princess,* are leading the line into the new millennium. The ships are pretty but not stunning; glitzy but not gaudy; spacious but not overwhelming. I was surprised at how easy it was to find my way around. By the end of the first day, I had the important landmarks memorized. While these ships aren't perfect, they are good enough to give Carnival, Royal Caribbean, and NCL cruisers a place to go when they want to step up but aren't interested in the slightly more chic ambience of Celebrity.

The decor of these ships is done in a style that's classic yet modern, using expensive materials such as varnished hardwoods, marble, etched glass, granite, and richly textured fabrics. Their decor doesn't sock you between the eyes with its daring; instead, it's comforting, restrained, and will probably age gracefully.

Cabins & Rates

Cabins	Per diems from	Bathtub	Fridge	Hair Dryer	Sitting Area	TV
Inside	$136	no	yes	yes	no	yes*
Outside	$178	no	yes	yes	no	yes*
Suite	$221	yes	yes	yes	yes	yes*

TVs show CNN, ESPN, TNT, Nickelodeon, and BBC.

CABINS   In general, the staterooms are clean and cozy, which is real-estate speak for "cramped." Standard outside cabins are 178 square feet including their balconies (in comparison, Carnival's standard cabins *without* balconies are nearly 190 square feet). On these ships, what you gain in balcony space you lose in room space. More than 400 cabins on each vessel boast private verandas, which help keep crowds dispersed (in other words, passengers might spend more time in their cabins/verandas instead of crowding the Pool Deck or some inside public room).

Suites can be as large as a sprawling 754 square feet, again including a veranda. In addition to the cabin stewards, all suites and mini-suites come with white-gloved butlers who will unpack for guests, deliver afternoon tea and canapés before dinner, stock your minibar (it's stocked once on a complimentary basis, including alcohol, and thereafter you're charged for what you drink), arrange shore excursions, and make spa and beauty parlor appointments.

Mini-suites are gorgeous, with a separate sitting area with pull-out sofa, chair and desk, refrigerator, two TVs (one facing the couch, the other facing the bed), desk, walk-in closet, and a separate whirlpool tub and shower in a separate room from the toilet and sink. Closets are on the small side, and hanging and drawer space are limited.

All cabins have TVs broadcasting CNN, ESPN, Nickelodeon, BBC programming, and TNT, plus refrigerators, safes, hair dryers, and terry bathrobes for use during the cruise. Some 19 cabins on each vessel are wheelchair accessible.

PUBLIC AREAS   These ships shine when it comes to communal areas. Many are bathed in marble and outfitted with light-grained wood. The ships have a decidedly unglitzy decor that relies on lavish amounts of wood, glass, and marble, and feature $2.5 million collections of original paintings and lithographs, grouped into schools and art periods. You'll also notice lots more tropical plants and flower bouquets on these ships than most, cared for by a full-time gardener.

The theater offers unobstructed viewing from every seat, and several seats in the back are reserved for passengers with mobility problems. The sound system is good, and lighting is state of the art. The smaller Vista Lounge also offers shows with good sightlines and comfortable cabaret-style seating. Dining rooms are broken up by dividers topped with frosted glass, giving the rooms an intimate feeling. There's no dramatic sweeping staircase for making an entrance, but there are also no waiters banging you in the back and squeezing by to reach other diners. The Wheelhouse Bar is a warm, elegant lounge with live entertainment, the perfect spot for pre- or post-dinner drinks. The room is done in dark, warm wood tones and has a nautical motif, including a huge model ship in a glass case. Customers sit on sofas and armchairs. It is evocative of some of the great hotel lounges, like the Oak Bar in Boston's Ritz Carlton.

There's a dark and sensuous disco; a bright, spacious, enticing casino; and lots of little lounges for an intimate rendezvous, such as the Entre Nous and the Atrium Lounge.

If you're hungry, options besides the usual main dining rooms and the buffet include an all-night sit-down restaurant (get a full dinner until 4am) and Lago's Pizzeria, a sit-down restaurant open afternoons and nights. Sorry: No take-out or delivery.

RECREATION & FITNESS FACILITIES   The center of the action for any Caribbean cruise is the pool, and these ships have plenty of space to party on the Riviera Deck. There's a lot going on, too, and if you've ever wanted to become a certified diver, this cruise will give you the chance. The New Waves program offers snorkeling and scuba lessons and rental equipment. There's also advanced lessons for divers who are already certified.

In total, there are four adult pools and one kids' wading pool, and hot tubs scattered around the Riviera deck. In all, there are three spacious decks for sunbathing.

These ships boast some of the best-designed, most appealing health clubs of any of the line's vessels. Called "The Riviera Spa Gymnasium," it offers all the requisite massage and spa treatments and is flanked with an open-air pool and a pair of whirlpools.

The gym is on the small side for a ship of this size. A teakwood deck encircles the ship for joggers and walkers, and a computerized golf center called Princess Links simulates the trickiest aspects of some of the world's best and most legendary golf courses.

Fitness classes are available throughout the day, including walks, exercise and meditation classes, and basketball.

Grand Princess

The Verdict

Second in size only to Royal Caribbean's brand-new 142,000-ton *Voyager of the Seas,* this huge, well-accoutered, and smartly laid-out ship is very easy to navigate and never feels as crowded as you'd expect; in fact, much of it feels downright intimate and cozy.

Grand Princess *(photo: Princess Cruises)*

Specifications

Size (in tons)	109,000	Officers	Italian/British
Number of Cabins	1,300	Crew	1,100 (Internat'l)
Number of Outside Cabins	928	Passenger/Crew Ratio	2 to 1
Cabins with Verandas	710	Year Built	1998
Number of Passengers	2,600	Last Major Refurbishment	N/A

Frommer's Ratings (Scale of 1–5)

Cabin Comfort & Amenities	5	Pool, Fitness & Spa Facilities	4
Ship Cleanliness & Maintenance	4	Children's Facilities	4
Public Comfort/Space	5	Itinerary	4
Decor	5	Worth the Money	5

For its first year of life, the 109,000-ton, 2,600-passenger *Grand Princess* was the world's biggest and most expensive ($450 million) cruise ship. With 18 towering decks, the ship is taller than the Statue of Liberty (from pedestal to torch) and too wide to fit through the Panama Canal. In fact, it's so big that the line's *Pacific Princess,* the original Love Boat, could easily fit inside its hull and still have lots of room to spare.

Inside and out, the *Grand Princess* is a marvel of size and design. Its massive white, boxy body with its spoilerlike aft poking up into the air cuts a bizarre, space-age profile and is like nothing else at sea. While intimidating from afar, in reality the ship's well-laid-out interior is very easy to navigate and, amazingly, the ship never feels as crowded as you'd expect; in fact, its public areas are generally less crowded than those of many smaller ships. It's rife with nooks that create a surprisingly cozy environment. This ship is truly a destination in itself, and the ports visited can't help but take a backseat to the onboard life—they're just one among many diversions and activities.

The ultra-modern ship does a good job of offering attractive, well-designed public areas and even manages a few with traditional accents. Her tiered aft decks, clubby, dimly lit lounges, and elegant three-story atrium with its classical string quartet entertaining passersby recall a grander era of sea travel.

Even the ship's medical center is grand: It boasts a high-tech "telemedicine" program that, via a live video hook-up, links the ship's doctors to the emergency room at Cedars Sinai Medical Center in Los Angeles.

Cabins & Rates

Cabins	Per diems from	Bathtub	Fridge	Hair Dryer	Sitting Area	TV
Inside	$156	no	yes	yes	no	yes*
Outside	$184	no	yes	yes	no	yes*
Suite	$228	yes	yes	yes	yes	yes*

*TVs show CNN, ESPN, TNT, Nickelodeon, and BBC.

CABINS   The *Grand Princess* has 710 cabins with verandas; only Royal Caribbean's *Voyager of the Seas* has more (757). (Be forewarned: The verandas are tiered, so passengers in levels above may be able to look down on you.) Cabins are richly decorated in light hues and earth tones and all have safes, hair dryers, refrigerators, robes for use during the cruise, and color TVs broadcasting CNN, ESPN, Nickelodeon, BBC programming, and TNT. Storage is adequate and features more closet shelves than drawer space.

A standard outside cabin (including its balcony) ranges from 215 to 255 square feet; suites are anywhere from 515 to 800 square feet, including the balconies. Cabins with balconies are larger than the equivalent on the *Ocean, Sea, Sun, and Dawn Princess* because, since the *Grand Princess* can't fit through the Panama Canal anyway, its balconies are allowed to protrude out farther rather than cutting into actual room space, as they do on the other Grand-class ships.

The suites and mini-suites (the entire Dolphin Deck is nothing but mini-suites) have tubs as well as showers (suite tubs have whirlpools), separate sitting areas with sofa beds, private balconies, and two TVs (which really seems unnecessary). A pair of Grand Suites even have fireplaces (not real wood-burning ones, of course) and hot tubs. There are two family suites that can sleep up to eight. In addition to the room stewards, all suites and mini-suites come with white-gloved butlers who will unpack for guests, deliver afternoon tea and canapés before dinner, stock your minibar (it's stocked once on a complimentary basis, including alcohol, and thereafter you're charged for what you drink), arrange shore excursions, and make spa and beauty parlor appointments.

The views from many cabins on the Emerald Deck are obstructed by lifeboats. The ship has 28 wheelchair-accessible cabins, more than any other ship afloat. (The Skywalkers disco has a wheelchair lift up to the elevated dance floor, too.)

PUBLIC AREAS   Even sailing with a full 2,600 passengers, you'll wonder where everyone is. The *Grand Princess* is a huge ship with a not-so-huge-ship feeling. Because of its smart layout, private verandas in 710 of its 1,300 cabins, six dining venues, expansive outdoor deck space divided into four main sections, and diversions like a nine-hole miniature golf course, a golf simulator, gigantic virtual-reality game room, basketball/volleyball/paddle tennis courts, four pools, nine hot tubs, and a business/computer center (where you can send and receive e-mail, among other things), passengers are dispersed rather than concentrated into one or two main areas. There's even an attractive wedding chapel where the captain himself performs about eight bona fide, legal marriages every cruise.

Coupled with this smart layout is the ship's sophisticated decor. Like the *Sea, Sun,* and *Dawn Princess,* the *Grand* offers public areas with a contemporary and upscale appeal, done up with caramel-colored wood tones and pleasing color schemes of warm blue, teal, and rust with a touch of brassy details and marble to give the place some pizzazz. Two full-time florists create and care for impressive flower arrangements and a large variety of live plants.

While the decor is soothing, the entertainment is pretty hot. Gamblers will love the sprawling and dazzling Atlantis Casino, one the largest at sea at 13,500 square feet. Three main entertainment venues include a well-equipped two-story show lounge for

Broadway-style musicals performed by 18 dancers and 4 singers, as well as a second one-level venue for smaller-scale entertainment like hypnotists and singers, and a pleasing travel-themed nightclub called the Explorer's Club, with murals of Egyptian and African scenes and a live band nightly. There's the clubby, old-world Wheelhouse Lounge as well as a woody sports bar, Snookers.

The Skywalkers disco/observation lounge, sequestered in the far aft reaches of the ship, is raised 150 feet above the ocean in a pod at the back of the ship. The unique spot offers floor-to-ceiling windows with two impressive views: forward, for a look at the ship itself from a bizarre floating-in-space perspective, or back, for a look at the sea and the giant vessel's very impressive wake. The multilevel area has lots of cozy nooks as well as the flashing lights expected from a disco. It's well positioned away from any cabins and there's a funky moving-sidewalk–like walkway that gets you there.

For kids, the two-story, indoor/outdoor Fun Zone kids' play area has tons of games and toys as well as computers and a ball bin. On the second (outdoor) level there's a splash pool, tricycles, and a mini-basketball setup, as well as a teen disco and a teens-only private patch of outdoor deck space with lounges and a hot tub.

Grand Princess's three one-story main dining rooms are named for famous artists—da Vinci, Botticelli, and Michelangelo—and decorated with murals and artwork accordingly. They are pleasant and laid out with slightly tiered levels and, by way of some strategically placed waist-high dividers, feel cozy (although the ceilings are a tad on the low side). The Horizon Terrace casual Lido restaurant is designed to feel much smaller than it actually is. With clusters of buffet stations serving a wide variety of food (stir fries, sides of beef, turkey and pork, lots of fruit, salads and cheeses, and lots more), lines are kept to a minimum and you're hardly aware of the enormity of the space. For buffet-style breakfast, lunch, and dinner, this venue is a well executed operation and is open 24 hours a day.

Besides a long list of daily diversions, the *Grand Princess* has a cavernous and truly amazing virtual-reality arcade, with dozens of machines you can climb onto and do virtual things like hang-gliding, downhill skiing, fly-fishing, and motorcycle riding. Each machine costs a couple of dollars. There's also a theme-park-like digital-photostudio where you can choose from over 40 scenes for the backdrop for your pictures.

The ship also has a library, small writing room, card room, and a business center with computers, from which e-mails can be sent and received ($7.50 for 15 minutes of use).

RECREATION & FITNESS FACILITIES   This ship has something like 1.7 acres of open deck space, so it's not hard to find a quiet place to soak in the sun. There are four great swimming pools, including one with a retractable glass roof so it can double as a sort of solarium, another touted as a swim-against-the-current pool (although truth be told, there really isn't enough room to do laps if others are in the pool, and the jets are kept at a level barely powerful enough to keep a 150-pound person in place), and a third, aft under the disco, that feels miles from the rest of the ship.

A large, almost separate part of the ship, on the forward Sun Deck, is reserved for pampering the body. Surrounding the lap pool and its tiered, amphitheater-style wooden benches is the large Plantation Spa, ocean-view beauty parlor, and the ocean-view gym, which is surprisingly small and cramped for a ship of this size (although there's an unusually large aerobics floor). Unfortunately, the sports decks are just above the spa, and if you're getting a relaxing massage when someone is playing basketball, you'll hear it.

Other recreation offerings include a Sports Deck with a jogging track, basketball, and paddle tennis, a fun nine-hole putting green, and computerized simulated golf.

Pacific Princess

The Verdict

Not for the party animals out there, this small and cozy 30-year-old classic liner offers a calm cruise in a pleasant setting.

Pacific Princess *(photo: Princess Cruises)*

Specifications

Size (in tons)	20,000	Officers	British
Number of Cabins	305	Crew	350 (International)
Number of Outside Cabins	238	Passenger/Crew Ratio	1.8 to 1
Cabins with Verandas	0	Year Built	1971
Number of Passengers	640	Last Major Refurbishment	1993

Frommer's Ratings (Scale of 1–5)

Cabin Comfort & Amenities	4	Pool, Fitness & Spa Facilities	3
Ship Cleanliness & Maintenance	4	Children's Facilities	N/A
Public Comfort/Space	4	Itinerary	5
Decor	3	Worth the Money	5

The original star of the *Love Boat* series (along with its recently sold sister, the *Island Princess*), the nearly 30-year-old *Pacific Princess* is an intimate vessel. Although in a different league than her mondo, much flashier mega sisters, the small, 640-passenger *Pacific* is novel in her own way. Public areas and the Pool Deck are well laid out and the lack of neon and glitz, towering atrium, and sprawling show lounge creates a homey, very relaxing ambience; ideal for cruises to the genteel island of Bermuda, where the ship will spend its first (and Princess's first) season the summer of 2000. Overall, the ship is well maintained, and public areas are fairly roomy for her size.

Cabins & Rates

Cabins	Per diems from	Bathtub	Fridge	Hair Dryer	Sitting Area	TV
Inside	$157	no	no	no	no	yes
Outside	$178	some	some	no	no	yes
Suite	$321	yes	yes	no	yes	yes

CABINS　Cabins are not huge and none have verandas, as is to be expected on older ships. Color schemes are based on earth tones (a bit drab) and the furniture is circa 1970s (a neat retro touch for all you sentimentalists!). All cabins have TVs, plus bathrobes for use during the cruise. There are four suites and nine mini-suites, all on the Promenade Deck (note that many cabins on this deck look out on the Promenade and some have partially obstructed views). The four suites have a sitting area, refrigerator, and bathtub. All but the suites have convertible sofa-style beds and some have third and fourth berths (a tight squeeze in the standard cabins).

There are two cabins that can accommodate wheelchair users, and all four elevators and public bathrooms are accessible.

PUBLIC AREAS　The beauty of such a small ship is its inherent coziness. There are several intimate bars to retreat to as well as a decent-sized show lounge for after-dinner cabaret and small-scale Vegas-style shows. The ship has a casino with slots and gaming tables, and there's a theater and an ocean-view library. There's a pleasant formal dining room deep down in the ship, as the Sun Deck has a casual buffet-style Lido restaurant featuring a made-to-order omelet/salad bar and lots of indoor and outdoor seating.

The ship isn't especially child-friendly, although some supervised activities are provided when there are at least 15 kids on board. There is no dedicated playroom.

There is a medical center on board.

RECREATION & FITNESS FACILITIES   Outdoor deck space is well planned and fairly spacious considering the size of the ship. There are two pools, one located aft on the Riviera Deck, with nice views of the sea and the ship's wake, and the other, on the Sun Deck adjacent to the Lido restaurant, with a retractable glass roof to ward off bad weather. Both offer ample seating and have a wide-open feel. There's a small gym, a pair of saunas, a couple of massage rooms, and a beauty salon. There's also shuffleboard, Ping-Pong, and a jogging track.

Royal Caribbean International

SHIPS   Enchantment of the Seas • Grandeur of the Seas • Legend of the Seas • Majesty of the Seas • Monarch of the Seas • Nordic Empress • Rhapsody of the Seas • Sovereign of the Seas • Splendour of the Seas • Vision of the Seas • Voyager of the Seas (preview)

1050 Caribbean Way, Miami, FL 33132. ☎ **800/327-6700** or 305/539-6000. Fax 800/722-5329. www.royalcaribbean.com.

THE LINE IN A NUTSHELL   These mostly megas provide fun, well-rounded, activity-packed cruises on attractive, glamorous, but not too over-the-top-glitzy ships.

THE EXPERIENCE   Royal Caribbean is one of the steadiest and best-conceived cruise lines, with better-than-average cruise ships appealing to a wide range of people. Lots of activities, a varied and well-executed entertainment repertoire, and enough glamour and glitz to keep things exciting, but not so much that they overwhelm the senses. These ships are a shade toned down from the Carnival brood, and while at the end of the day the onboard experience of the two fleets is similar, the Royal Caribbean ships feel and look less in-your-face than their Carnival counterparts.

Royal Caribbean's most obvious asset is its consistency. Except for two of its ships, the *Nordic Empress* and the *Viking Serenade*, the company's vessels are all megas and share such similar attributes as multistory atria and mall-like shopping complexes, two-story dining rooms and show lounges, wide-open public areas and conversely small cabins. Activities, daily programs, cuisine, bar service, and cabin service have long ago been hammered into a winning format. Prices are reasonable, too—good values for the dollar and geared to compete with the fares charged by every other megaliner afloat.

Pros

- **Entertainment.** Among the best at sea, with glamorous, well-executed, Vegas-style shows often drawing names like Marvin Hamlisch and Maureen McGovern.
- **Attractive public rooms.** Well designed, spacious, and glamorous, the lounges, restaurants, and outdoor Pool Decks are inviting: not too flashy and flamboyant and not too staid and soft.

Cons

- **Small cabins.** At just over 100 square feet, many cabins, especially on the pre-1995 ships, are downright small; with NCL, they're the smallest in the mainstream category.
- **Lines.** Hey, these are big ships, so there are going to be lines at times, especially in the buffet restaurants and getting on and off the ship in port.
- **High crew-to-passenger ratio.** The number of crew members to passengers hovers around 3 to 1 (most peers are more like 2 or 2.5 to 1).

Frommer's Ratings: Royal Caribbean International					
	Poor	Fair	Good	Excellent	Outstanding
Enjoyment Factor					✓
Dining			✓		
Activities				✓	
Children's Program				✓	
Entertainment				✓	
Service			✓		
Overall Value				✓	

ROYAL CARIBBEAN: FUN & GAMES, COOL SHIPS

Royal Caribbean was the first company to launch a fleet specializing exclusively in Caribbean ports of call—hence the company name. In the late '80s, the company expanded its horizons beyond the Caribbean, offering cruises to Europe, Alaska, and the Pacific, in the process tagging the "International" onto its name.

What began in 1969 as a consortium of Norwegian ship owners with big eyes for the North American cruise market has blossomed into an immensely profitable multinational corporation with a staggering volume and a flotilla of state-of-the-art megaships valued in the billions. In 1990, the Pritzker family (creative force behind the Hyatt empire) bought a major stake in the company, and funds from the sale, coupled with all the credit-worthiness of Hyatt, helped finance the line's massive expansion during the 1990s. In 1993, corporate coffers were enriched even further thanks to a stock offering, the company's first. Since then, shares have been traded on the New York Stock Exchange and the Oslo Stock Exchanges using the symbol **RCL.** In 1997, a corporate reorganization placed the company's assets under the supervision and control of Royal Caribbean Cruises Ltd., subdivisions of which include Royal Caribbean International (formerly known as Royal Caribbean Cruise Lines) and the smaller and somewhat fancier Celebrity Cruise Lines, whose assets and public image were acquired by Royal Caribbean during a well-publicized 1997 merger. At the time of this writing, the two lines together control 17 relatively young ships with over 30,000 berths, attracting a big chunk of the Caribbean's cruise ship passengers, a figure that will only increase as both lines add additional ships.

It was Royal Caribbean that ushered in a new generation of megaships in 1988 with the 73,192-ton *Sovereign of the Seas.* This vessel was the largest passenger ship built in the previous 50 years and was between two and four times as large as any other vessel in the fleet as it then stood. Along with its newer, improved clones, *Monarch* and *Majesty of the Seas,* the *Sovereign* tripled Royal Caribbean's cabin capacity in a mere 4 years. Beyond sheer size, though, the ships were innovative, featuring such now-standard features as soaring, multistory atria with glass-sided elevators, fountains splashing into marble pools, and an observation lounge (the Viking Crown Lounge) perched 10 or 11 stories above sea level, wrapped around the rear smokestack in a style reminiscent of big-windowed airport control towers.

THE FLEET

Counting the 142,000-ton, 3,100-passenger *Voyager of the Seas,* the first of Royal Caribbean's three Eagle-class sister ships (due to enter service in November 1999 as the world's biggest cruise ship), Royal Caribbean has 12 ships in its fleet. Six Vision-class ships, built between 1995 and 1998, are similar in design and include the 2,000-passenger *Vision of the Seas* (1998), the 1,950-passenger *Enchantment of the Seas* (1997), the 2,000-passenger *Rhapsody of the Seas* (1997), the 1,950-passenger *Grandeur of the Seas* (1996), the 1,804-passenger *Splendour of the Seas* (1996), and the 1,804-passenger *Legend of the Seas* (1995). The 2,354-passenger sister ships *Majesty of the Seas* (1992) and *Monarch of the Seas* (1991) are less exciting ships than those in the Vision class. The rest of the fleet includes the 1,600-passenger *Nordic Empress* (1990), 1,512-passenger *Viking Serenade* (1990), and 2,276-passenger *Sovereign of the Seas* (1988).

Construction is already underway on the line's next generation of ships, the pair of 85,000-ton, 2,000-passenger Project Vantage ships, called *Radiance of the Seas* and *Brilliance of the Seas,* which are to be introduced in 2001 and 2002. The second and third super-mondo-megaship Eagle-class sisters, the *Explorer of the Seas* and the *Adventure of the Seas,* are to be introduced in fall of 2000 and spring of 2002.

PASSENGER PROFILE

With its truly mass appeal, you'll find all walks of life on a Royal Caribbean cruise. The common denominator: passengers looking for fun and action in an attractive setting. You'll find passengers in their 20s through 60s, with mostly couples (a good number of them honeymooning), but also lots of families (of the nearly 1.5 million passengers who sailed with Royal Caribbean in 1998, about 100,000, or about 7%, were kids) and single friends traveling together in groups. The majority of passengers come from somewhere in North America, although in 1998 nearly 190,000 passengers (about 13%) came from Europe, South America, and elsewhere.

A shade more sophisticated than Carnival (at least in terms of ship decor), the line attracts passengers who think Carnival is a bit too glitzy and party-animal-ish. In reality, though, the differences between the two are few. Overall, passengers are active, social, and looking for a good time, no matter what their age.

The line's shorter, 3- and 4-night cruises tend to attract more of the partying crowd, as is the case with most short cruises.

DINING

The line—and by definition each of its vessels—is a member of France's Chaine des Rôtisseurs. Food aboard is good and getting better, but it's not fabulous, and falls closer to NCL than Carnival or Princess. Entrees include choices like poached Alaskan salmon, oven-roasted crispy duck served with a rhubarb sauce, prime rib served with a stuffed baked potato, and baked ziti. There's always a **light and healthy option** as well as a **vegetarian option** at lunch and dinner (spa cuisine may feature roast turkey with sweet potatoes and vegetables or a grilled chicken breast topped with spinach, prosciutto, and fresh mozzarella, and vegetarian entrees may include an eggplant parmigiana or curried vegetables served in a light cilantro-coconut sauce). Cuisine is often presented in different themes, with table settings, menus, and waiters' costumes reflecting the theme.

The **formal dining rooms** feature two seatings and the **alternative dining option,** held in the Windjammer Cafe, on the Pool Deck, offers a casual ambience and open seating for dinner between 6:30 and 9:30pm three nights a week. Decor varies from ship to ship, but is always patterned on a theme inspired by a successful Broadway play or Hollywood film. You can eat breakfast and lunch in the main dining room or in the buffet-style Windjammer Cafe. Lines, unfortunately, can grow long. **Ice cream** and a couple of toppings are available throughout the day from a station in the Windjammer. There's also a **midnight buffet** nightly, with one mondo, gala smorgasbord per week, as well as **pizza** served afternoons and late night for those after-partying munchies.

An extensive **kids' menu** (which is a fun pastime in and of itself, with word and picture games, and pictures to color in—crayons included!) features the likes of fish sticks, burritos, oven-fried lemon chicken, spaghetti and meatballs, pizza, the standard burgers, hot dogs, and fries, plus lots of yummy desserts.

Room service is available 24 hours a day from a fairly routine, limited menu. However, an especially nice feature: During normal lunch and dinner hours, a cabin steward can bring anything being served in the restaurant to your cabin.

ACTIVITIES

No problem keeping yourself occupied on a Royal Caribbean cruise. Of course, if you want to remain glued to a deck chair and do nothing, that's no problem either.

Getting the Royal Treatment on a Private Island

Royal Caribbean maintains two private beach resorts, and many of its cruises feature a day at one or the other of them. **CocoCay** (Little Stirrup Cay) in the Bahamas and **Labadee,** an isolated and sun-flooded peninsula along Haiti's north coast, are tropical retreats that the company has transformed into fun-in-the-sun playlands.

At CocoCay, an otherwise uninhabited 140-acre landfall in the Berry Islands of the Bahamas, you'll find lots of beach, hammocks, food, drink, and all the water sports you could fit into a day. The line organizes fun activities like volleyball, limbo contests, water balloon toss contests, relay races, and volleyball tournaments. Royal Caribbean even built and sank a replica of one of the pirate Bluebeard's schooners, to give snorkelers an extra thrill.

The line's other private resort, Labadee, is isolated on a scenic, carefully protected, 270-acre peninsula, and boasts five separate beaches, each with different characteristics, evoking everything from the gravel and rocks of New England to the sandy atolls and palm trees of the southern Caribbean. If it weren't for souvenir stands hawking Haitian paintings, you'd never know you were in poverty-stricken Haiti, so removed does the site seem from the problems of the rest of the country.

On both Labadee and CocoCay, children's activities include beach parties, volleyball, sea-shell collecting, and sand-castle building.

Daytime activities are typical cruise line fare: bingo, shuffleboard, horse racing, line-dancing lessons, napkin folding, spa and beauty demonstrations, art auctions, and outrageous poolside contests sure to draw laughs. The *Legend* and *Splendour of the Seas* even feature **miniature golf courses,** right on board!

One area where Royal Caribbean ("Official cruise line of the PGA Tour and Senior PGA Tour," whatever that means) really excels is in its **golf program,** "Golf, Ahoy!," which lets golfers play the best local course in any of about 10 Caribbean ports of call—courses that are usually difficult to get onto without membership privileges.

The line's **ShipShape fitness program** rewards passengers who participate in aerobics, dance classes, basketball free-throws, Ping-Pong tournaments, early-morning walk-a-thons, and any other such activity with prizes like T-shirts and baseball caps. An extensive menu of **fitness classes** includes abs, stretch, sculpting, water aerobics, and special workout classes for seniors, allowing them to sit in chairs to do light cardiovascular activities.

If **shopping** can be considered an activity, Royal Caribbean beats out Carnival with its impressive selection of boutiques (and their boutique-like storefronts) clustered around the atrium.

CHILDREN'S PROGRAM

Year-round, Royal Caribbean offers **supervised kids' programs** fleetwide for children ages 3 to 17. Though facilities on all ships are roughly comparable, those on the Vision class ships are a slight notch better, putting them on par with Carnival's *Elation* and *Paradise.* Male and female youth staff all have college degrees in education, recreation, or a related field. The "Adventure Ocean" program offers fun and games for four age groups: Aquanauts, ages 3 to 5; Explorers, ages 6 to 8; Voyagers, ages 9 to 12; and Navigators, ages 13 to 17. Each ship has a **children's playroom,** a **teen center and disco,** and a **video arcade.** There are children's menus, books, and movies, too. All day long, the fun includes talent shows, karaoke, pizza and ice cream parties, bingo, scavenger hunts, game shows, volleyball, face painting, and beach parties. The "Adventure

Preview: *Voyager of the Seas,* a REALLY BIG SHIP

At press time, Finland's Kvaerner Masa shipyard was putting the finishing touches on the world's biggest cruise ship. A marvel in size and cost (we're talking $500 million to build this baby), the 3,114-passenger, 142,000-ton *Voyager of the Seas* is slated to debut in late November 1999. The gigantic ship will have 17 decks (14 accessible to passengers) and rise over 200 feet above the sea. Over 538,000 square feet of carpet and 15,000 chairs will be installed, and a 4,100-piece, $12 million permanent art collection will be put up. The *Voyager* will have a whopping three-story dining room, a three-deck-high show lounge (five, if you count the orchestra pit and the domed ceiling), and a sprawling casino sporting the world's largest roulette wheel. (Royal Caribbean tells me that players will actually sit in this wheel. What does that *mean?!*). Believe it or not, the ship will even have a full-scale ice-skating rink, a rock-climbing wall, an in-line skating track (skates can be rented or you can bring your own), a pottery studio, a wedding chapel, and enough shops to fill the Mall of America. If that's not enough excitement for you, head over to the ship's nine-hole miniature golf course, driving range, or golf simulator; regulation-sized basketball, paddleball, and volleyball courts; or sprawling gym and spa. Another unique feature is a multideck boulevard-like promenade running down the center of the ship, anchored on either end by multistory atria, with its ground floor lined with shops, bars, restaurants, and entertainment outlets. Want more? There are inside cabins on three decks above the promenade with views from bay windows of the "street scene" below. Who needs ocean views? Did I mention there's also a bar featuring four huge aquariums, a florist shop (you never know when you'll need a dozen roses), and a "peek-a-boo" bridge that allows guests to gather above and watch the crew steering the ship? Nearly half of all staterooms will have balconies and every cabin will have a minibar, a hair dryer (a Royal Caribbean first!) and a TV. The *Voyager's* identical sisters, the *Radiance* and *Brilliance of the Seas,* are to enter service in spring of 2001 and summer of 2002.

Science" program is always a hit, and both teaches and tickles kids with scientific experiments that are loads of fun and educational.

Slumber-party-style **group baby-sitting** is available nightly between 10pm and 1am, and from noon until sailing on days the ship is in port. The charge is $4 per child. Private, **in-cabin baby-sitting** by a crew member is available and must be booked at least 24 hours in advance through the purser's desk. The charge is $8 per hour for up to two children in the same family, and $10 per hour for a maximum of three.

ENTERTAINMENT

Practically no one does entertainment as well as Royal Caribbean. There are music acts, comedy acts, sock hops, toga parties, talent shows, karaoke, and **Vegas-style shows** rife with all the razzle-dazzle passengers come to expect. There's usually a mystery "name" entertainer popping up. Don't expect Tony Bennett or Alanis Morrissette, but terrific entertainers like Marvin Hamlisch, Maureen McGovern (you've never heard "Ding Dong, the Witch Is Dead" until you've heard Miss McGovern's version), Clint Holmes, and Frankie Avalon are frequently booked to augment the ships' regular offerings. Royal Caribbean uses 12- to 16-piece bands for its main showroom, and large-cast revues are among the best you'll find on a ship. Showbands and other lounge acts keep the music playing all over the ship; all are first-rate.

Royal Caribbean Fleet Itineraries

Ship	Home Ports & Season	Itinerary	Other Itineraries
Enchantment of the Seas	Round-trip from Miami, itineraries alternate weekly year-round*.	**7-night western Carib:** Key West, Playa del Carmen/ Cozumel, Ocho Rios, and Grand Cayman. **7-night eastern Carib:** Sint Maarten, St. John's/St. Thomas, and CocoCay.	None
Grandeur of the Seas	Round-trip from Miami, year-round.	**7-night eastern Carib:** Labadee (Haiti), San Juan, St. Thomas, and CocoCay.	None
Majesty of the Seas	Round-trip western Caribbean from Miami, through Oct; round-trip southern Caribbean from San Juan from 11/99 through 5/00; 3- and 4-night Bahamas itineraries alternate weekly, round-trip from Miami, year-round from 5/00 on.	**7-night western Carib:** Ladadee (Haiti), Ocho Rios (Jamaica), Grand Cayman, Playa del Carmen/Cozumel. **7-night southern Carib:** Aruba, Curaçao, Sint Maarten, and St. Thomas. **3- and 4-night Bahamas:** Nassau, CocoCay, and Key West (on 4-nighter only).	None
Monarch of the Seas	Round-trip from San Juan, year-round.	**7-night southern Carib:** St. Thomas, Martinique, Barbados, Antigua, and Sint Maarten.	None
Nordic Empress	Itineraries alternate round-trip from San Juan, Nov–Apr; 7-night Bermuda cruises round-trip from New York.	**3- and 4-night western Carib:** St. Thomas, Sint Maarten, and St. Croix (on 4-nighter only). **7-night Bermuda:** St. George's and Hamilton.	None
Sovereign of the Seas	Alternating round-trip from Miami year-round*.	**3- and 4-night Bahamas:** Nassau, CocoCay, and Key West (on 4-nighter only).	None
Splendour of the Seas	Alternating round-trip from Miami, Nov–Apr.	**10- and 11-night Carib:** Key West (11-nighter only), Playa del Carmen/Cozumel, Grand Cayman, Ocho Rios (Jamaica), Aruba, and Curaçao.	Europe, New England/ Canada
Vision of the Seas	Alternating itineraries between San Juan and Acapulco, Nov–Apr.	**10-night Panama Canal:** St. Thomas, Curaçao, and Costa Rica. **11-night Panama Canal:** Costa Rica, Curaçao, Aruba, and St. Thomas.	Alaska, Hawaii
Voyager of the Seas	Round-trip from Miami, year-round.	**7-night western Carib:** Labadee (Haiti), Ocho Rios (Jamaica), and Cozumel.	None

Beginning in April 2000, the Enchantment and Sovereign of the Seas depart round-trip from Fort Lauderdale.

SERVICE

Overall, service in the restaurants and cabins is friendly, accommodating, and efficient, despite some language barrier problems. You're likely to be greeted with a smile by someone polishing the brass in a stairwell. That said, big, bustling ships like Royal Caribbean's are no strangers to crowds, lines, and harried servers not able to get to you exactly when you'd like them to.

Considering the vast armies required to maintain a line as large as Royal Caribbean, it's a miracle that staff members appear as motivated and enthusiastic as they do.

Laundry and **dry cleaning** services are available on all the ships, but none have self-service laundromats.

Enchantment of the Seas • Grandeur of the Seas • Legend of the Seas • Rhapsody of the Seas • Splendour of the Seas • Vision of the Seas

Rhapsody of the Seas *(photo: RCCL)*

The Verdict

This is what they had in mind when they called contemporary cruise ships "floating resort hotels." These six ships are glitzy and exciting without going overboard.

Specifications

Size (in tons)		Number of Passengers	
Enchantment	74,140	*Enchantment*	1,950
Grandeur	74,000	*Grandeur*	1,950
Legend	69,130	*Legend*	1,804
Rhapsody	78,491	*Rhapsody*	2,000
Splendour	69,130	*Splendour*	1,804
Vision	78,491	*Vision*	2,000
Number of Cabins		Officers	Norwegian/Int'l
Enchantment	975	Crew	(International)
Grandeur	975	*Enchantment*	760
Legend	902	*Grandeur*	760
Rhapsody	1,000	*Legend*	720
Splendour	902	*Rhapsody*	765
Vision	1,000	*Splendour*	720
Number of Outside Cabins		*Vision*	765
Enchantment	575	Passenger/Crew Ratio	
Grandeur	576	*Enchantment*	3 to 1
Legend	575	*Grandeur*	2.5 to 1
Rhapsody	593	*Legend*	2.5 to 1
Splendour	575	*Rhapsody*	3 to 1
Vision	593	*Splendour*	2.5 to 1
Cabins with Verandas		*Vision*	3 to 1
Enchantment	212	Year Built	
Grandeur	212	*Enchantment*	1997
Legend	231	*Grandeur*	1996
Rhapsody	229	*Legend*	1995
Splendour	231	*Rhapsody*	1997
Vision	229	*Splendour*	1996
		Vision	1998
		Last Major Refurbishment	N/A

Frommer's Ratings (Scale of 1–5)

Cabin Comfort & Amenities	4	Pool, Fitness & Spa Facilities	5
Ship Cleanliness & Maintenance	4	Children's Facilities	4
Public Comfort/Space	5	Itineraries	3
Decor	5	Worth the Money	5

There's a reason Royal Caribbean has given its Vision-class ships names like *Grandeur of the Seas* and *Enchantment of the Seas*. It's because the ships are, quite simply, grand and enchanting. From the incredible amount of glass that give the ships their light (each contains about 2 acres of glass canopies, glass windbreaks, skylights, and floor-to-ceiling windows with sweeping views) to the colorful and whimsical artwork that livens every turn, the high-tech, high-energy theater and casino to the dizzying number of entertainment options, these ships are mighty fine. The glitz and glass of the atrium, with sunlight streaming in and glinting off the chrome, the glassed-in elevators, and the white marble staircase that winds down to a landing and bandstand is a sight that stops you in your tracks. It's the first thing passengers see when coming aboard, and it sets the tone for the rest of the cruise.

Of the six Vision-class vessels, the first, *Legend of the Seas,* is the lightest, weighing in at a still-hefty 69,130 tons, with the last of the brood, *Vision of the Seas,* stepping into the ring at a heavyweight 78,491 tons. The ships evolved slightly over the 3 years between the first and latest, but for the most part they're a set of bright, cheerful siblings with similar features. The *Vision, Grandeur,* and *Rhapsody,* whose decors are newer, brighter, and classier, are simply more stunning than the older and somewhat more frayed *Legend* and *Splendour*. The *Enchantment* has more brassy-looking artwork and flashier, more metallic decorative themes than the *Vision, Grandeur,* and *Rhapsody.*

Cabins & Rates

Cabins	Per diems from	Bathtub	Fridge	Hair Dryer	Sitting Area	TV
Inside	$121	no	no	no	yes	yes
Outside	$155	no	some	no	yes	yes
Suite	$211	yes	yes	no	yes	yes

CABINS   To be polite, cabins are compact. Granted, they're noticeably larger than the cramped cubicles that were standard issue aboard the company's older ships (the *Nordic Empress*'s standard outside cabins, for instance, are a tiny 122 square feet), but they're still cramped compared to the competition. Inside cabins measure 138 square feet and outsides 153 square feet (compared to Carnival's 190 square feet for standard cabins). For big, check out the Royal Suite on each of these ships—they measure a mammoth 1,150 square feet. The *Vision*'s even has a grand piano.

In keeping up with the Joneses of today's balcony-loving industry, nearly one-fourth of the cabins aboard each ship have private verandas. About a third can accommodate third and fourth passengers, too. Regardless of the ship you opt for, your cabin will have soft color schemes of pastels that alternate with varnished hardwood trim.

All cabins have adequate storage space, safes, music channels, and TVs offering some 20 channels of video, four different music channels, three more for movies, and three more with satellite programming—tons more than competitors like Norwegian and Princess, which offer just a few channels. Bathrooms, while not the largest, have good storage space, including a multilevel built-in shelf in the shower stalls.

Each vessel has between 14 and 17 staterooms equipped for wheelchair users.

PUBLIC AREAS   Warm woods and brass, luxuriant fountains and foliage, glass and crystal, buttery leathers, and carefully chosen artwork and textures highlight the public areas. Some public areas evoke a private Roman villa; others are deliberately glitzier and flashier. Different areas of the ship were designed to evoke different places in America—for example, a wine bar in New York or a gambling hall in Las Vegas.

The layout of the Promenade and Mariner Decks—the main indoor public decks on each ship—allows for easy passage. Corridors are wide and bright, and elevators are big and fast. Focal points on the six ships are the soaring seven-story atriums known as "Centrum." Each is crowned by a sloped two-deck-high skylight. Glass elevators, à la Hyatt, take passengers up through Centrum into the stunning Viking Crown Lounge, a glass-sided aerie high above the waves. Accessorized with a superb sound and light system, it's high on everybody's list of favorite wave-watching and sight-seeing spaces, especially during transits of the Panama Canal.

The shopping arcade, Boutiques of the Centrum, is like a shipboard Fifth Avenue or Rodeo Drive, and much more appealing to look at and extensively stocked than Carnival's Fantasy-class shopping complexes, which are cramped and off the beaten track. The Schooner Bar is a casual piano bar with lots of wood and rope, befitting its nautical name, and is a great place for a pre-dinner drink or late-night unwinding. Ditto the Champagne Terrace at the foot of the atrium. Listen and dance to a trio while sipping fine wines or a glass of bubbly.

In deliberate contrast to such massive showcase spaces, each ship contains many hideaway refuges, including an array of cocktail bars, a library, and card rooms. Hundreds of potted plants and more than 3,000 original artworks aboard each ship add humanity and warmth.

The large dining rooms aboard the vessels span two decks and are interconnected with a very grand staircase and flanked with walls of glass nearly 20 feet high. Each has a decor that's contemporary and tasteful (if not reminiscent of a banquet hall), replete with lots of stainless steel, mirrors, and dramatic chandeliers. A pianist plays a massive grand piano throughout dinner service.

Full musical revues are staged in glittery, two-story show lounges, and there's not a bad seat in the house. Each has an orchestra pit that can be raised and lowered hydraulically to provide dramatic effect during cabaret shows.

The ship's casinos are Vegas-style flashy and consciously over-accessorized with hundreds of gambling stations so densely packed that it's sometimes difficult to move and always difficult to hear.

Each ship has a higher-than-expected amount of open deck areas. One of the most dramatic is the Sun Deck, which manages to incorporate two swimming pools (one covered by a retractable glass roof), whirlpools, and the Windjammer buffet-style restaurant.

The ships' conference rooms can hold up to 200 people.

Regrettably, there are no self-service laundromats.

RECREATION & FITNESS FACILITIES   The Steiner-managed ShipShape spas on these ships, especially on the *Vision, Rhapsody, Grandeur,* and *Enchantment,* are some of the most attractive around and are truly soothing respites from the hubbub of ship life. They offer a wide selection of treatments, as well as the standard steam rooms and saunas. Adjacent to the spas are spacious solariums with a pool, lounge chairs, floor-to-ceiling windows, and a retractable glass ceiling. These spots are a peaceful place to repose before or after a spa treatment, or any time at all. They're bright, comfortable, and each has an inventive design motif, like Roman, Egyptian, or Moorish. Surprisingly, the gyms are small for the ships' size and in comparison to those on Celebrity's or Carnival's megaliners.

The main pool area has four whirlpools (two on *Splendour* and *Legend*) and there are two more in the Solarium. There's usually loud music by the pool along with silly contests (of the belly-flop contest genre), which most passengers seem to love dearly.

There's a jogging track, shuffleboard, and Ping-Pong. And, if you want to swing a few clubs, the *Legend* and *Splendour of the Seas* actually sport 6,000-square-foot, 18-hole miniature golf courses.

Majesty of the Seas •
Monarch of the Seas

The Verdict

These ships are huge, and while they feel somewhat dated compared to their spiffy new Vision-class sisters, they manage to maintain an easy-going elegance, with their light color scheme and spread-out public areas.

Majesty of the Seas *(photo: RCCL)*

Specifications

Size (in tons)	73,941	Crew	825 (Int'l)
Number of Cabins	1,177	Passenger/Crew Ratio	2.9 to 1
Number of Outside Cabins	732	Year Built	
Cabins with Verandas	62	*Majesty*	1992
Number of Passengers	2,354	*Monarch*	1991
Officers	Norwegian/Int'l	Last Major Refurbishment	N/A

Frommer's Ratings (Scale of 1–5)

Cabin Comfort & Amenities	4	Pool, Fitness & Spa Facilities	3
Ship Cleanliness & Maintenance	4	Children's Facilities	4
Public Comfort/Space	4	Itinerary	3
Decor	4	Worth the Money	5

Built at the same Breton shipyard in western France for a cost of $300 million each, these mirror-image twins sport clean, distinguished profiles. Their proportions are monstrous, with a dazzling lineup of public spaces, and a roster of activities and entertainment that rivals those offered in many small cities. Decor-wise, these ships sport more brass, chrome, and neon than their newer Vision-class sisters (see review above), and seem a bit dated and dull by comparison. All in all, though, they're fine specimens.

Cabins & Rates

Cabins	Per diems from	Bathtub	Fridge	Hair Dryer	Sitting Area	TV
Inside	$128	no	no	no	no	yes
Outside	$143	some	some	no	some	yes
Suite	$268	yes	yes	no	yes	yes

CABINS The worst feature of the entire fleet—small cabins—is no less prevalent on these two ships. Standard cabins, scattered over nine decks, average a too-snug 120 square feet. In 62 of the outside cabins, some of the cramped feeling is relieved by verandas. Over 100 cabins have upper and lower berths in order to house four, albeit quite tightly. Suites are larger, of course, and moderately more comfortable than the standard cabins. The Royal Suites and the Owners' Suites are significantly larger.

All cabins have safes, music channels, and TVs with a tremendous selection (see the Vision-class ship review). Four cabins on each ship can accommodate wheelchair users.

PUBLIC AREAS Like the rest of the fleet, the glass-enclosed Viking Crown Lounge sits way up on the topmost deck, some 150 feet above sea level. This is a great place for a drink before dinner and the place to go to dance into the wee hours.

A dramatic, five-story atrium, with a color scheme that glows in a metallic shade of either bronze or champagne, is the ship's interior focal point. A sweeping staircase curves down onto the ground floor and makes for a grand scene. Public areas—including one of the largest casinos afloat—are wisely clustered aft of the atrium to minimize noise in the forward section of the ship, where most cabins are located. Broadway musicals and Hollywood films inspired the names and decor of most public areas. Each ship contains a paneled library, a massive two-story show lounge, and a host of other bars and cubbyholes scattered throughout, some with modern art nouveau decors.

Although these are monstrous ships, they're so well designed that passengers don't seem to get lost very often, and only when you find yourself standing in long lines (or taking the stairs instead of the elevators) do you realize just how big they are.

RECREATION & FITNESS FACILITIES   Two large swimming pools are located on the Sports Deck. Looking at this space when it's empty, you'd think there's all the room in the world, but when the ship is full, the rows of sunbathers resemble sardines in a tin.

The gyms aboard both ships are fairly spacious, with a wall of windows facing aft. The spas have a handful of massage and treatment rooms offering a wide range of treatments as well as separate saunas for men and women. In size and style, though, they can't hold a flame to the spas on the Vision-class ships. Other sports and fitness facilities include an unobstructed jogging track, a basketball court, shuffleboard, and Ping-Pong.

Nordic Empress

The Verdict

This mid-sized ship is an appealing, easy-to-navigate package. Public rooms are well laid out and decor is just glittery enough to keep the mood festive.

Nordic Empress *(photo: RCCL)*

Specifications

Size (in tons)	48,563	Officers	Scandinavian
Number of Cabins	800	Crew	671 (International)
Number of Outside Cabins	471	Passenger/Crew Ratio	2.4 to 1
Cabins with Verandas	69	Year Built	1990
Number of Passengers	1,600	Last Major Refurbishment	N/A

Frommer's Ratings (Scale of 1–5)

Cabin Comfort & Amenities	4	Pool, Fitness & Spa Facilities	3
Ship Cleanliness & Maintenance	4	Children's Facilities	4
Public Comfort/Space	4	Itinerary	3
Decor	4	Worth the Money	5

This hefty 48,000-ton vessel looks small when compared to the megaships forming the rest of Royal Caribbean's modern fleet. Originally part of Admiral Cruises, a now-defunct subsidiary of Royal Caribbean during its early days, the *Nordic Empress* was retained as part of a bid to capture a segment of the 3- and 4-day cruise market, and is in many ways one of the best among the vessels plying the Florida-to-Bahamas run. The ship was created for this type of cruise, where passengers tend to hurl themselves into onboard activities, knowing they don't have a languorous week to explore their surroundings, so its designers built in the most bang for the buck. It's an attractive ship, with the requisite glass, chrome, and neon, but not so much that it's overwhelming.

CABINS   Cabins are cozy at best at not more than 130 square feet (equivalent in size and amenities to those aboard the *Sovereign,* the *Majesty,* and the *Monarch*).

| Cabins & Rates | | | | | | |
Cabins	Per diems from	Bathtub	Fridge	Hair Dryer	Sitting Area	TV
Inside	$105	no	no	no	no	yes
Outside	$128	no	no	no	some	yes
Suite	$255	yes	yes	no	yes	yes

Storage space is limited, and you may find yourself just keeping some things in your suitcase.

Although small, the cabins are carefully designed, which makes them seem more livable. But a large number of them are inside and downright claustrophobic, practically guaranteeing that passengers will spend more time on deck or in public areas. Upperend cabins and suites have verandas; outside cabins without offer rectangular picture windows. Even if you upgrade for one of the smaller suites, you won't gain that much additional elbow room, although amenities are better and locations more convenient.

All cabins have safes, music channels, and TVs with a tremendous selection (see Vision-class ship review, above, for details). Four cabins are wheelchair accessible.

PUBLIC AREAS   Light floods into the atrium from above and from big windows flanking five decks on either side. So intent were the designers on creating a razzle-dazzle venue that they sacrificed space that might otherwise have gone toward cabins. Adding to the decor are a splashing fountain ringed with tropical plants and artwork based on Nordic themes. Thoughtful layout makes it easy to navigate through the *Nordic Empress*.

The Sun Deck is an important space both daytime and night. Loaded with sunbathers during the day, it's transformed into a starlit dance floor when the sun goes down. Fountains, a gazebo, and sail-like canopies create a cozy, almost clubby ambience. The *Nordic Empress* also boasts Royal Caribbean's signature Viking Crown Lounge and disco, plus a three-level casino with cozier places to play than on most ships. The two-story Strike Up the Band Showroom is very Atlantic City. In all, there are five bars, three entertainment lounges, a vibrant disco, a video game room, a playroom, and a conference center.

RECREATION & FITNESS FACILITIES   On the Sun Deck there are four hot tubs, a swimming pool, a wading pool, and shady spots to get a break from the sun. The exercise area has floor-to-ceiling windows and enough equipment to satisfy most users. There's a hot tub, sauna, plus massage, and the ship has a jogging track.

Sovereign of the Seas

The Verdict

A trendsetter in its heyday, this ship may now be somewhat dated, but it still promises and delivers an exciting cruise for the whole family.

Sovereign of the Seas *(photo: RCCL)*

Specifications

Size (in tons)	73,192	Officers	Norwegian
Number of Cabins	1,138	Crew	840 (International)
Number of Outside Cabins	722	Passenger/Crew Ratio	2.7 to 1
Cabins with Verandas	0	Year Built	1988
Number of Passengers	2,276	Last Major Refurbishment	1997

Frommer's Ratings (Scale of 1–5)

Cabin Comfort & Amenities	3	Pool, Fitness & Spa Facilities	3
Ship Cleanliness & Maintenance	4	Children's Facilities	4
Public Comfort/Space	3	Itinerary	3
Decor	4	Worth the Money	5

When it was launched in 1988, after costing $185 million to build, *Sovereign of the Seas* stopped traffic along freeways all up and down the Miami harborfront. Now, like its other '80s contemporaries, the ship seems dated in comparison to the swank newcomers. It has no cabin balconies whatsoever or decks devoted exclusively to public rooms; instead, its lounges, restaurants, kids' facilities, and spa/gym are sort of stacked along successive aft decks. Most travel agents, as well as Royal Caribbean itself, tend to lump this ship in the same category as two later models, *Monarch of the Seas* and *Majesty of the Seas;* however, the *Sovereign* has a slightly different deck layout and weighs a bit less. When launched, it was the largest passenger vessel built during the previous 50 years and the largest cruise ship in history. Enough steel went into its construction to rebuild Paris's Eiffel Tower twice.

Cabins & Rates

Cabins	Per diems from	Bathtub	Fridge	Hair Dryer	Sitting Area	TV
Inside	$92	no	no	no	yes	yes
Outside	$120	some	some	no	some	yes
Suite	$255	yes	yes	no	yes	yes

CABINS   Light, pastel colors try to make the cabins appear larger than they are, but there's no disguising their paltry 120-square-foot size. Overall, cabin decor is spartan and uninspired. All cabins have limited storage space (remember: pack light), safes, music channels, and TVs offering the same extensive programming as on the line's other ships (see Vision-class review, above, for details).

Sixteen cabins are fitted for passengers with disabilities.

PUBLIC AREAS   A five-story atrium interconnects most of the ship's many splashy and airy public areas, which are outfitted in appropriately theatrical styles.

Public areas are clustered toward the stern, with cabins mainly in the forward half of the ship, an arrangement that creates the illusion that this mighty vessel is more intimate than it is. The ship features the Royal Caribbean architectural trademark, the Viking Crown Lounge and disco encircling the smokestack 14 stories above sea level. Restaurants, show lounges, bars, and lounges are equivalent to those described above under reviews of the *Monarch* and *Majesty.*

RECREATION & FITNESS FACILITIES   Deck layout and the two good-sized swimming pools are stylish and impressive when they're empty, but the staggering number of passengers aboard this ship almost guarantees that they'll fill up. Other than that, virtually all aspects of the fitness programs aboard *Sovereign of the Seas* are equivalent to those aboard the *Majesty* and the *Monarch* (see review above).

7

Cheap Cruises, Older Ships: The Budget Lines

In this category you'll find classic ocean liners that have managed to stay around for as long as 47 years. These ships have great appeal for ship buffs and nostalgic folks, and have retained varying amounts of their former grandeur—some have aged gracefully, others not so much. For instance, Premier's *Rembrandt* (formerly Holland America's *Rotterdam V*) is the most beautiful and intact relic left, with much of her original furniture, wall finishings, and artwork still impressing passengers. The line's *SeaBreeze* and *Big Red Boat,* on the other hand, retain only their classic exterior lines, with most of their interiors stripped of any original features.

Depending on what you like, the age of a ship can be a plus or a minus. If you appreciate relics of the past—pre-war buildings over modern ones, antiques instead of IKEA—then you might like these 30-year-old-plus liners: With long, sweeping hulls, tiered decks, wood paneling, and chunky portholes, they offer a nostalgic glimpse back to a lost age of cruising. Decks, doors, railings, and bar tops are made of solid varnished wood, and cabin doors may still operate with a lock and key rather than with a computerized keycard. Tall sills in most doorways require some high stepping to avoid tripping (old ships are not for wheelchair users), and there's no shortage of exposed cables, fire doors, pipes, ropes, winches, and all manner of hardware. These are ships that look like ships, and for ship buffs, they're charming. For bargain hunters, too, they're often the best deal in town, with rates at times dipping down past $100 per person per day. (Although I must add, considering the glut of cabin space throughout the industry these days, that at times the rates for inside and low-category cabins on Carnival, Royal Caribbean, NCL, and even Celebrity and Princess can drop nearly as low).

Now, if you're a lover of all things fresh, new, and modern, you might want to pass on a cruise on one of the oldies. The old-timers can't hide the wear and tear accumulated from logging thousands of miles at sea and can't begin to compete at the same level with the flashy, state-of-the-art megas. Repeatedly refurbished and restored through the years (often haphazardly and in the least expensive ways), many are a hodgepodge of design schemes and awkward spaces. Discos, spas, and gyms are often small, dark spaces in lower decks, and carpeting, wall finishes, and outside decks are often worn. All in all, you won't be seeing a lot of flash, but you will be seeing some old ships that might not be around much longer: The future of some of them will depend on compliance with a set of international safety regulations known as the **Safety of Life at Sea (SOLAS),** predominantly concerned with issues like fire prevention. Ships built after 1994 automatically incorporate SOLAS safety features, while ships built before 1994 have been required to add them by a progressive set of deadlines. The most sweeping changes were completed by a 1997 deadline, and another series of changes must be implemented by 2000 and 2010. The changes required could prove too costly for many of these old-timers and seal their fate forever—so enjoy them while you can.

Note: There are three oldies I could have included in this section, but for various reasons decided to put elsewhere. The *QE2* is a 31-year-old classic liner that attracts a more upscale clientele than any other old-timer, so look for a review of that ship in chapter 8, "The Ultra-Luxury Lines." NCL's 38-year-old *Norway,* the former *France,* also claims a liner pedigree, but nowhere near as upscale as the *QE2;* to make things easier, I've kept the *Norway* review with the rest of the NCL fleet, in chapter 6, "The Mainstream Lines." Also, for convenience's sake, the review of Princess Cruises' 30-year-old *Pacific Princess* can be found with the rest of its fleet, also in chapter 6. On the other hand, I've included Royal Olympic Cruises and its *Stella Solaris* in this chapter primarily because of the age and wear of the ship, even though the *Stella* gets significantly higher marks than the other ships in this chapter for its fine dining and service and its enrichment program.

DRESS CODES   Like the mass-market and premium lines, weeklong cruises on these ships generally feature two formal nights, but with the exception of Premier's *Rembrandt,* you won't find too many passengers in tuxedos or fancy sequin dresses. Overall, ships in this category are somewhat more casual, with guests preferring suits or sport coats to tuxes, and pantsuits or sundresses to gowns (although it's not unheard of to see a tux and a shimmery dress). Guests are asked not to wear shorts and T-shirts in the formal dining room. Daytime is casual.

Cruise Lines Reviewed in This Chapter

- Cape Canaveral Cruise Line
- Commodore Cruise Line
- Mediterranean Shipping Cruises
- Premier Cruises
- Regal Cruises
- Royal Olympic Cruises

Cape Canaveral Cruise Line

SHIPS   Dolphin IV

7099 N. Atlantic Ave., Cape Canaveral, FL 32920. ☎ **800/910-SHIP** or 407/783-4052. Fax 407/783-2380.

THE LINE IN A NUTSHELL   This 44-year-old ship is one of the oldest classic liners sailing today, and has the bumps and bruises to show for it. But for rates often as low as $100 a day for the first passenger and $50 for the second passenger, the *Dolphin IV* delivers casual, 2- and 4-night party-cruises for people who aren't expecting plush surroundings.

THE EXPERIENCE   Canaveral Cruise Line offers good value for your cruise dollar, with 2- and 4-night quickie cruises that are an excellent opportunity for the first-time cruiser to get his or her feet wet. (From Florida, the 2-night cruises spend about 8 hours in Freeport/Lucaya, where passengers can hit the shops, casinos, and beaches, or sign up for one of the shore excursions. On the 4-night cruises, the ship visits Key West for 16 hours—one of the longest stops available here on any other ship.) Although the line offers a lot of diversions and activities, don't expect anything that even vaguely resembles the quality you'll find aboard a larger and more modern ship—though, for the price, it can be a great party if your expectations are realistic. Many people use the line as though it were a bus to the Bahamas, and many others are booked on board as part of tour packages aimed at bringing people to Freeport's casinos. Overall, it's a good choice for passengers with limited time and/or money who want to escape the midwinter doldrums.

Pros

- **Classic ocean liner.** If you long for the nostalgia of the past's great liners, you'll appreciate the ship's classically shaped hull and tiered-deck profile (although its interior is a hodgepodge of styles resulting from about a zillion refurbishments).
- **Carefree and fancyfree.** The atmosphere on these short 2- and 4-night cruises is fun, light, and convivial.

Cons

- **Small cabins.** You may want to go on a diet before you book one of the *Dolphin*'s cabins. At 80 to 120 square feet for inside cabins and about 120 to 150 for outside cabins (including suites), cramped is the operative word.
- **Crowded when full.** If the ship is carrying a full house of 700 or so passengers, the only place to hide or breathe or get a moment alone is in your cabin.

Frommer's Ratings: Cape Canaveral Cruise Line					
	Poor	Fair	Good	Excellent	Outstanding
Enjoyment Factor			✓		
Dining			✓		
Activities			✓		
Children's Program			✓		
Entertainment			✓		
Service			✓		
Overall Value				✓	

CAPE CANAVERAL: SHORT, CHEAP & FUN

Cape Canaveral is a subsidiary of the Kosmas Shipping Group, vacation timeshare marketers and operators of a dozen Florida resorts. It's one ship, the *Dolphin IV,* sails mostly 2-night cruises, with two or three 4-nighters offered per month. The drill goes like this: *Dolphin IV* sails from Port Canaveral at 4:30pm, arriving in Freeport (on Grand Bahama Island) the following morning at 8am. At 4pm that afternoon, the 2-night cruises head back to Port Canaveral for an early morning arrival the next day, and the 4-nighters sail on to Key West, arriving around noon and not departing again until 6am. A few hours later, the ship arrives back in Port Canaveral. In transit and on the islands, passengers whoop it up, and don't spend a fortune to do it. Ah, democracy!

THE FLEET

If ships, like humans, have personalities, then the 588-passenger **Dolphin IV's** is cynical, scarred, and weathered, a survivor of many corporate battles and stormy seas. Today, after many renovations—including changes that added a terrace to the ship's stern, enlarged its upper decks, and reconfigured its cabins to make more efficient use of space—it's still going strong.

PASSENGER PROFILE

Non-Floridians visiting such Orlando-area attractions as Disney World, Sea World, and Universal Studios make up a healthy percentage of all bookings, and passengers from the snowbelt often get a worthy package deal when they combine a 2-day holiday aboard the *Dolphin* with 3 days at Sea World, Universal Studios, or Wet & Wild (another Orlando-based theme park). On the other hand, Floridians use the line much like the British use their new Chunnel—as an easy way to escape the country for a weekend of fun and shopping. The cruise line itself does everything to encourage the habit with slogans like "Take a cab over to Port Lucaya."

   While there are individuals, a good number of passengers on board are there because they booked through tour companies and about 35% have been booked through an arrangement with a timeshare company. There are a fair amount of retirees, plus first-time cruisers, economy-minded honeymooners (five wedding packages are available, and ceremonies take place on board before the ship departs Port Canaveral), gamblers heading to Freeport's casinos, and families who like the family-friendly prices. Ages of travelers range from their late 20s to 70s.

   The ship isn't good for sophisticated, romantic sojourns—it lacks the comforts and sense of privacy for that—and the destination (Freeport) won't appeal much to seasoned travelers.

DINING

Don't expect anything fancy, but do expect decent cuisine and well-intentioned staff. An early and late seating for breakfast, lunch, and dinner are served in the **one dining room,** a long, narrow, L-shaped, low-ceilinged, and not particularly glamorous space. Mirrors and elaborate food displays help make the room appear larger than it really is. A pianist tickles the ivories during the two dinner seatings.

   The fare is American with a hint of continental, and is similar to what you'd be served at a decent family-style restaurant or diner. Specific **theme meals,** such as Italian, Mexican, or tropical/Caribbean, appear frequently. An evening's menu will include appetizers such as fresh fruit, melon and prosciutto ham, pâté, and escargots. In addition to a choice of three soups and three salads, main entrées may feature filet of tilapia sautéed in butter, lime juice, and green peppercorn sauce; marinated roast leg of lamb; beef tenderloin in a béarnaise sauce; and coq-au-vin (chicken braised in red wine and pearl onions). A **vegetarian option,** like a vegetable cannelloni, is offered each evening as well.

Cape Canaveral Fleet Itineraries			
Ship	Home Ports & Season	Itinerary	Other Itineraries
Dolphin IV	Port Canaveral, round-trip itineraries alternate year-round.	**2-night Bahamas:** Bahamas. **4-night Bahamas:** Bahamas, Key West.	None

Dessert choices include cheesecake, chocolate meringue cake, ice cream, sherbets, and, at the captain's welcome dinner, cherries jubilee.

Buffet-style breakfast and lunch are offered in the Lido, a well-designed casual restaurant, with the ample indoor/outdoor space divided between a barbecue and a cold buffet. Whether you want to eat there is the question, though: The buffet items look better than they taste.

Daily **midnight buffets** are showy and often have artfully arranged culinary displays. Coffee, tea, and cookies are served each afternoon at 4pm.

ACTIVITIES

The center of activity during the day revolves around the small, almost ornamental pool on the Lido Deck, which is flanked by a bar and a frequently replenished buffet. After dark, activities shift to the Monte Carlo **casino,** the **disco,** and the dance floors of the Rendezvous and Miramar Lounges. There's live music in at least one of those lounges nightly.

Daytime activities include wine tasting ($3.50 charge per person), trivia games, bridge tours, Ping-Pong tournaments, dancing lessons, horse racing, skeet shooting, scavenger hunts, a newlywed and not-so-newlywed game, and even a **"grandma's brag party,"** where grandparents share pictures of their cute grandkids.

Both itineraries visit Freeport, Bahamas, for about 8 hours, where passengers can hit the shops, casinos, and beaches or sign up for one of the shore excursions. On the 4-night cruises, the 16-hour visit to Key West is one of the longest available on any other ship, which usually move out around nightfall to other Bahamian or Caribbean sites. Partying passengers can bar-hop all through the night, and then rush back to the ship to make its 6am departure.

CHILDREN'S PROGRAM

Since the ship attracts a decent number of families, the line offers formalized programs for "Junior Cruisers" between the ages of 3 and 12 (participating kids must be out of diapers). These programs include such interactive, summer-campy pastimes as pizza parties, video presentations, arts and crafts classes, hula contests, tours of the bridge and lessons in navigation, "Coke-tail" parties, kids-only comedy hours, scavenger hunts, and pool games. There's a **supervised playroom** on board as well as a video arcade.

The line offers no baby-sitting at all.

ENTERTAINMENT

Las Vegas it's not, but there's entertainment such as comedians, magicians, and live music groups, and of course gambling is always an option.

Some Special Deals

Ask about Cape Canaveral's special discounts for seniors, as well as buy-one-get-one-at-half-price deals.

SERVICE

It's not a "snap your fingers at the waiter and he'll come running" kind of ship. Service is adequate, if hurried, and despite their occasional inexperience, the staff is friendly and tries to please. Dining-room attendants are the best of the lot.

Dolphin IV

The Verdict

Not the most luxurious ship you'll ever set foot on, this small, 586-passenger oldie offers an easygoing experience on its year-round mini-cruises.

Dolphin IV *(photo: Cape Canaveral Cruise Line)*

Specifications

Size (in tons)	13,650	Officers	Greek/International
Number of Cabins	293	Crew	300 (International)
Number of Outside Cabins	226	Passenger/Crew Ratio	2.2 to 1
Cabins with Verandas	0	Year Built	1956
Number of Passengers	586	Last Major Refurbishment	1997

Frommer's Ratings (Scale of 1–5)

Cabin Comfort & Amenities	2	Food & Beverage	3
Ship Cleanliness & Maintenance	3	Pool, Fitness & Spa Facilities	3
Public Comfort/Space	3	Children's Facilities	2
Decor	3	Itinerary	4
Service	3	Worth the Money	4

This seaworthy and solid ship has been around the block. Commissioned as the *Zion* in 1955 as a combination passenger and freight carrier, it was renamed a decade later by a Portuguese owner as the *Amelia de Mello,* and made frequent cargo and passenger runs between Lisbon and the Canary Islands. After at least 2 years in mothballs, it was sold in 1972 to a Greek line that reconfigured it into a cruise ship named *Ithaca.* Finally, in 1979, a Greek-French consortium purchased the ship, renamed it *Dolphin IV,* and poured millions into a 1981 refurbishment. In 1984, the ship was purchased by the Miami-based Dolphin Line; then, in 1995, after short-term ownership by the Royal Bank of Scotland, the aging vessel was bought by Cape Canaveral. In early 1996, after an extensive dry-docking and a series of mostly cosmetic refurbishments, it sailed its first cruise for the line.

CABINS   No beating around the bush: They're small, all right. At 80 to 120 square feet for inside cabins and about 120 to 150 for outside cabins (including suites), *cramped* is the operative word. Be forewarned: Do not bring a lot stuff (but for 2 or 4 days, you won't have to). Storage space is minimal, and bathrooms have tiny showers. If you drop the soap, it's two to one that you'll whack your head on something trying to pick it up.

Cabins come in five price categories and several configurations. Some have double beds, some have twins, others have one or two upper berths to accommodate three or four passengers (*tightly*), some come with a double bed and a sofa bed, and 13 of the smallest inside cabins have bunk beds. Decor is central Florida motel style: bland, impersonal, color coordinated, and angular. Each cabin has air-conditioning and music channels, but none—not even the suites—contain a TV. Cabins on lower decks get substantial engine noise and an occasional whiff of fumes from the ship's diesel engines.

If you want or can afford some extra space, consider booking a suite or junior suite. At 150 square feet or larger (a couple of suites on the Boat Deck are about 225 square feet), they're bigger than the barely comfortable cabins, although they're not perfect, either: five out of nine (those on the Boat Deck) are obstructed to some degree by lifeboats.

This ship is not recommended for wheelchair users. There's only one elevator and its doors are 28.5 inches wide, cabin doors are 22.75 inches wide, and bathroom doors are 21 inches wide with a nearly 6-inch riser.

Cabins & Rates						
Cabins	Per diems from	Bathtub	Fridge	Hair Dryer	Sitting Area	TV
Inside	$93	no	no	no	no	no
Outside	$127	no	no	no	no	no
Suite	$155	yes	no	no	yes	no

PUBLIC AREAS When the *Dolphin IV* is full and carrying in the neighborhood of 700 passengers, you'll know it. The ship will feel crowded. Along with bars and lounges, there's a card room, library, video-game arcade, hair salon, and, far below the waterline, a disco. Many accessories and up-to-date features were added in the late 1980s and early 1990s, including clean modern colors and a steel-and-brass wall sculpture of leaping dolphins at play, one of the first things new arrivals see when they board. Incredibly, there's only one elevator on board, an antique and unpredictable affair that interconnects only four of the six decks.

RECREATION & FITNESS FACILITIES There are three main patches of sunning space: lounge chairs surround the small Lido swimming pool, and aft and fore on the Boat Deck are two sizable stretches of deck. This ship doesn't have a gym or exercise equipment, although considering the short length of its cruises, passengers don't usually miss it. For joggers or walkers, eight laps around the unobstructed expanse of the Boat Deck equals 1 mile. Skeet shooting is usually available, too.

Commodore Cruise Line

SHIPS **Enchanted Capri • Enchanted Isle**

4000 Hollywood Blvd., South Tower 385, Hollywood, FL 33021. ☎ **800/237-5361** or 954/
967-2100. Fax 954/967-2147. www.commodorecruise.com.

THE LINE IN A NUTSHELL   These Sputnik-era vessels may show their age, but
they offer down-to-earth, fun cruises at rock-bottom rates.

THE EXPERIENCE   Commodore's *Enchanted Isle* and *Enchanted Capri* are two of
the best bargains sailing the Caribbean. The line's low rates are fantastic for first-time
cruisers on a budget. Fares are cheaper mainly because the vessels are old and lack most
of the newfangled entertainment gadgets that appear on newer ships. But what the line
lacks in technology, it makes up for in spunk, its officers and crew working hard to give
passengers what they paid for, and then some. The cruises are casual, carefree, and fun,
and the ships' small size means passengers begin to recognize each other after only a day
or so at sea—much sooner than aboard much larger ships.

Dubbed the "Happy Ship," *Enchanted Isle* pioneered theme cruises, and the *Isle* and
Capri still have sock hops and "Remember When" cruises, featuring music legends of
the 1950s. The *Capri* has an especially active casino scene—in fact, the ship's lease is
co-held by Commodore and a land-based casino concern. Today, both ships homeport
in New Orleans, and attract most of their passengers from the surrounding states: Louisiana, Mississippi, Texas, Arkansas, and Alabama. Passengers from out of this area get
a vastly different embarkation experience in New Orleans than they'd get in Florida.

Pros

- **Bargain of the century.** It's not uncommon to pay as little as $70 per day, which
  of course includes all meals and entertainment.
- **Go-get-'em spirit.** Although they don't have a lot to work with props-wise, cruise
  directors and entertainers really leap through hoops to give passengers a good time.
  I give them an A for effort.
- **Roomy cabins.** Unlike other small ships (Cape Canaveral's *Dolphin IV,* for instance),
  the majority of cabins on the *Capri* and *Isle* are spacious.

Cons

- **Rough around the edges.** These ships are old, so you'll notice some wear.
- **The low budget shows through.** Though the crew does what it can (see "Pros"),
  they aren't given a lot to work with. In the shows, a costume change means the singer
  changes her hat, and in the dining rooms, ingredients are pretty basic.

Frommer's Ratings: Commodore					
	Poor	Fair	Good	Excellent	Outstanding
Enjoyment Factor				✓	
Dining			✓		
Activities				✓	
Children's Program			✓*		
Entertainment			✓		
Service				✓	
Overall Value				✓	

Applies only to Enchanted Isle; Enchanted Capri *has no children's program.*

COMMODORE: GOOD CHEAP FUN

Formed in 1966, Commodore has been plugging along quietly ever since. The company doesn't make a lot of waves (figuratively speaking), but where some of its competitors have experienced fits of instability over the past several years, it's continued going strong, giving passengers buckets of fun at a bargain-basement price. They must be doing something right: In early 1999, Commodore Holdings Limited, the parent company of Commodore Cruise Line, announced a long-term charter of the NCL's 820-passenger *Norwegian Dynasty,* with an option to purchase the vessel. The ship will become the **Crown Dynasty** and be deployed as the first ship in Commodore's new premium cruise brand, **Crown Cruise Line.** From December 1999 to April 2000, the ship will sail 7-night round-trip cruises from Aruba, and in May 2000, in partnership with Apple Vacations, it will spend the summer cruising between Philadelphia and Bermuda and feature a program that gives passengers the option of flying one way and cruising the other, with a 3-day hotel stay in Bermuda in between. The *Dynasty* becomes the sixth ship allowed to visit Bermuda on a regular seasonal basis and, unlike the other five ships on the route, will be there on weekends only.

THE FLEET

Both of these small, elderly ships sail round-trip out of New Orleans, and have had interesting, full lives as other-named ships for other lines. The 42-year-old, 725-passenger **Enchanted Isle** started off in 1958 as the *Argentina* and over the next 30 years sailed for five different owners, including Holland America (where it was the company's *Veendam* for 11 years). Commodore bought the ship in 1990, but even then its adventures weren't over: The ship served as the "Hotel Commodore" in St. Petersburg, Russia in 1994–95. Perhaps this Russian connection got the company thinking, because in 1998 it leased a 460-passenger vessel that had spent the previous years as a cruise ship for the Soviet Union. Built in 1975 as the *Azerbaydzahn,* the **Enchanted Capri** is a small, attractive, very shippy ship with a split personality: On the one hand, it's loaded with leftovers from its Soviet past (hammers and sickles on the life jackets!), and on the other, it has some garishly decorated public spaces that scream "I'm a Caribbean cruise ship, dammit!" It's a weird mix. MTV apparently thought it was hip enough, though: It held its first MTV Spring Break cruise on the ship in 1999.

PASSENGER PROFILE

Commodore Cruises draws one of the widest spectrums of passengers in the business. Many passengers are first-time cruisers lured by the line's low per diem rates. Nearly all the passengers are American, a few hailing from the Midwest and a handful from California, but since sailings depart from New Orleans, and because so many of the line's marketing efforts are aimed directly at the regions around the Mississippi Delta, the large majority of this line's passengers come from Louisiana, Mississippi, Alabama, Texas, Arkansas, and the Florida Panhandle.

The line draws couples of all ages looking for an inexpensive, fun cruise, as well as many retirees, particularly on Caribbean winter voyages, where they account for about one in four passengers. During school vacations, Commodore draws a lot of families, plus other young professionals and blue-collar types lured by the low rates. Group travel makes up a huge percentage of Commodore's business. Budget-minded honeymooners can arrange to have their wedding ceremonies held free of charge out on deck while the ship's docked in New Orleans (a variety of extras, like a pianist or onboard reception packages, can be purchased through the line).

DINING

This isn't a cruise you choose because of its cuisine. That said, the stuff isn't bad—it's just that it's average. Entrees are the kind of thing you'd cook at home for a Sunday dinner or maybe go out to a local restaurant for: Southern fried chicken, crab cakes, linguini with seafood in a cream sauce, roast prime rib, or perhaps veal Parmesan with pasta. Ingredients and seasoning are run-of-the-mill, but if you keep in mind the low price you're paying for the cruise, you'll grab your fork, dig right in, and leave with a smile on your face.

In the **main dining room,** there are two seatings for each meal. At dinner, you're usually offered a choice of three main dishes, plus a pasta that might also serve as the **vegetarian option.** Desserts include an apple strudel, cheesecake, a cheese plate with fruit, and ice creams with your choice of sauces. More celebratory dinners (such as a final-night farewell party) are likely to include surf-and-turf and a "scallopini à la française." Menus are coordinated to theme nights, the "Remember When" shindig, or a Mexican/Caribbean deck party.

The Bistro Grill aboard the *Enchanted Isle* offers a buffet-style breakfast and lunch, but the *Enchanted Capri* has no buffet option—all meals are served in the dining room. Every Commodore cruise features a breakfast specialty from Brennan's Restaurant in New Orleans, such as eggs Sardou, a flavorful version of poached eggs with hollandaise sauce atop creamed spinach and artichoke bottoms. A continental breakfast is available from room service. The *Isle*'s Bistro also has an espresso bar, where for about $2 caffeine-loving passengers can order an espresso, cappuccino, or other specialty coffee.

An absolutely incredibly monstrously huge **midnight buffet** is offered nightly, and features every noshing option you could want, from meats and pastas through crackers and cheese to fruits, desserts, caviar on some nights, and tray upon tray of chocolates. I found the food here to be better, in general, than is offered at regular meals. Go figure. Expect long lines to get to the buffet tables, because *everybody* on board will be there.

ACTIVITIES

Routine activities include bingo, scavenger hunts, trivia games, and **silly poolside games** of the break-the-balloon-in-your-partner's-lap-with-your-butt and stuff-a-hundred-Ping-Pong-balls-into-your-bathing-suit variety. Shipboard versions of the Liar's Club, Family Feud (or in this case "Passenger Feud"), and Newlywed/Not-So-Newlywed games provide lotsa laughs, as does a first-day icebreaker game called **Afternoon Madness,** in which the passengers, broken into teams, have to produce whatever items the cruise director calls for, and then run up with their numbered team paddles to score the first point. It all starts innocently enough, with easy items such as chewing gum, lipstick, and 5-dollar bills being called out, but it's only a matter of time before the proceedings get more risqué, and before you know it, women are struggling to remove their bras (tastefully, of course) and men are struggling to put them on. Before the game winds down, normally staid gentlemen are prancing around in high heels and lipstick, telling the MC why they should be named "Queen of the Ship." (The winner's reason on my cruise? "Because I want you . . . and your brother, too.") Say what you will about the declining morals of Western civilization, but after a game like this, it's a sure bet that the passengers aboard have safely parted company with their inhibitions and are ready for the cruise ahead.

Each ship has a **disco** and **casino** that's open until the wee hours (on the *Capri*'s 2-night sailings the casino is open 24 hours).

Commodore Fleet Itineraries			
Ship	Home Ports & Season	Itinerary	Other Itineraries
Enchanted Capri	Round-trip from New Orleans, itineraries alternate weekly year-round.	**2-night Cruises to Nowhere:** At sea. **5-night western Carib:** Playa del Carmen/Cozumel, Progreso/Mérida (Mexico).	None
Enchanted Isle	Round-trip from New Orleans, year-round.	**7-night western Carib:** Playa del Carmen/ Cozumel, Grand Cayman, Montego Bay (Jamaica).	None

Commodore hosts a number of **theme cruises** each year featuring '50s rock-and-roll, rhythm and blues, country, big band music, and even Scottish music. There's dancing and lots of listening opportunities. There are also **singles cruises** from time to time, with activities, mixers, and games geared to solo passengers.

CHILDREN'S PROGRAM

Depending on the number of children on board, Commodore offers **supervised activities** for three age groups: 5 to 10, 11 to 15, and 16 to 20 (oddly enough), including parties, scavenger hunts, dancing, movies, and games. Activities are held in the kids' playroom (on the *Isle* only) or in public areas and outside decks. Baby-sitting is available.

ENTERTAINMENT

Musical acts perform throughout the day and evening, including a Caribbean dance band, a pianist, and an orchestra. Each evening offers at least one show, too, which on my recent sailing included a **comedian/impressionist** and a **"Lullabies of Broadway"** revue performed by the Commodore Showstoppers, four young, eager singers who make up with enthusiasm what they lack in costumes, sets, or props. While the comedian's material touched on adult themes, his act—like most of the activities and entertainment on board—seemed designed to cater to the ship's wide passenger demographics.

Each ship offers **karaoke** and **passenger lip-synch shows** some evenings, and has a cinema showing recent films.

SERVICE

Service generally wins nothing but favorable comments. Dining-room waitstaff manage beautifully in spite of noisy, overcrowded tables and the sometimes impossible demands made upon them—they'll even bring second helpings, and are always friendly and never reserved. Ditto for bartenders in the lounges and deckside bars. The cabin staff keep the rooms immaculate.

There is **laundry service** available as well as photo processing.

Some Special Deals

On the *Enchanted Isle,* the second passenger in a cabin pays 50% less when cruises are booked at least 120 days early.

Enchanted Capri

The Verdict

A weird mix of bright Caribbean decor and fixtures left over from the ship's Soviet days make for an offbeat and almost hip atmosphere; buckets o' fun at a dirt-cheap price make for a hell of a bargain.

Enchanted Capri *(photo: Commodore Cruise Line)*

Specifications

Size (in tons)	15,410	Officers	Ukrainian/Internat'l
Number of Cabins	230	Crew	300 (Internat'l)
Number of Outside Cabins	112	Passenger/Crew Ratio	2.4 to 1
Cabins with Verandas	0	Year Built	1976
Number of Passengers	460	Last Major Refurbishment	1998

Frommer's Ratings (Scale of 1–5)

Cabin Comfort & Amenities	3	Food & Beverage	3
Ship Cleanliness & Maintenance	3	Pool, Fitness & Spa Facilities	1
Public Comfort/Space	3	Children's Facilities	N/A
Decor	3	Itinerary	3
Service	3	Worth the Money	5

The time, the early 1990s. The place, Ukraine. Following the breakup of the Soviet Union, the Ukrainians began selling off surplus cruise ships, including a passenger-ferry-turned-cruiser named the *Azerbaydzhan,* which became, briefly, the *Island Holiday* for New SeaEscape Cruises before being leased by Commodore and a southern casino operator and rechristened the *Enchanted Capri.*

The transition makes for a bizarre experience. Aside from some garish decor Commodore added to make the ship look more Caribbean, the *Capri* is still essentially a Soviet ship. The crew is Ukrainian, most signs are in Russian with English subtitles, most of the artwork depicts Azerbaijani folk scenes, the wall-mounted crew telephones would look more at home on a nuclear submarine than on a cruise ship, and the life jackets still sport the Communist hammer and sickle. It's as if we'd said, "We won the Cold War, now give us your cruise ships."

The onboard experience, though, is 100% American. The *Capri* is a far cry even from modern mainstream ships—it's small, old, and a bit frumpy—but it's a solid vessel, and its deep draft (the amount of ship below the waterline) makes for a stable ride even on the sometimes choppy Gulf. For a bargain-basement price, passengers get good-sized cabins, passable if not remarkable meals, and almost nonstop entertainment presided over (at least when I was aboard) by identical twin cruise directors. No kidding: identical twin brothers!

Cabins & Rates

Cabins	Per diems from	Bathtub	Fridge	Hair Dryer	Sitting Area	TV
Inside	$118	no	no	no	no	no
Outside	$131	no	no	no	no	no
Suite	$213	yes	no	no	yes	no

CABINS As aboard many older ships, cabins are relatively large, particularly for the price. Almost all can comfortably accommodate a third passenger, and some can accommodate a fourth. Even the lowest-priced inside cabins are adequate for two people, although their Partridge Family–looking candy-striped bedspreads might take some getting used to. All have air-conditioning and music channels. At the high end, the two Royal Suites are decorated in more elegant colors and are bigger than my editor's apartment, with large bathrooms, enough storage space for 2 months, let alone 2 days, couches, chairs, makeup mirrors, and large, kitchen-sized refrigerators. I've been told that the ship served as a sometimes troop transport in its Soviet days. If so, this is where the admirals stayed.

Bathrooms in all cabins are spacious enough that you won't bump into the furnishings. Each has a shower; suites have bathtubs and bidets.

No cabins are designed specifically for wheelchair passengers, and because of the ship's old-fashioned layout, wheelchair users would have a tough time aboard.

PUBLIC AREAS The Capri is a real shippy ship, a classic-style oceangoer with well-trod wooden decks, machinery more in evidence than glitz, and wooden-plank rope ladders lying bound under tarps on deck—ready, it seems, should the passengers decide to stage a pirate raid on one of the oil tankers it passes heading down the Mississippi and into the Gulf.

The main hub of social activity is the pool deck and open-air bar, all the way aft. From there forward, two promenades and open areas on the top deck and just behind the bow offer considerable sunning space and wonderful observation perches. The small, mirrored disco—located on the lowest passenger deck and appropriately named The Hideaway—is reached via a stairway identified when I was aboard only with a paper sign that read "disco," stuck with masking tape to a wall near the purser's desk and pointing down.

Next door, the relatively sizable cinema is straight out of 70s/80s Moscow, with its period decor, its classic theater seats, and long balcony with only three—count em', three—comfortable swivel chairs sitting all by themselves toward the front. In the half-light, it's easy to imagine Leonid Brezhnev and his staff sitting there, playing hookey from the Kremlin. The cinema can serve as a meeting room for business groups on board.

The center of real action is the casino. Bracketed by the gaudily decorated show lounge and more restrained dining room, it opens as soon as the ship reaches the 3-mile international border and stays open all hours when the ship is at sea.

A pleasant enough piano lounge called the Rendezvous is located in the stern. A library/observation lounge, perched at the top of the ship, has few books and sees almost no visitors. A wide-open deck area just behind the bow and below the bridge offers a great wind-in-your-face observation perch.

There is one extraordinarily tiny, coffinlike elevator.

RECREATION & FITNESS FACILITIES The ship's one small pool is perched on the stern, and is a daytime hot spot even though it's just plain tiny. (An interesting side note: The pool has small windows built into its walls. On the other side of the windows is the Rendezvous Lounge. These windows would, in theory, allow a very clear underwater view of passengers frantically stuffing their bathing suits full of Ping-Pong balls during the traditional goofy pool games. The windows have other uses as well. One woman, obviously a repeat passenger, told me, "See the windows? That's where my friend Bayard mooned everybody. His wife was so mad.")

The ship has no gym or spa, and none of its decks completely encircle the ship, so joggers and walkers must deal with some stairs if they want to get in a long workout.

Enchanted Isle

The Verdict

Ship buffs and fun-seeking bargain-hunters will appreciate this matronly 42-year-old classic liner turned festive party ship.

Enchanted Isle *(photo: Commodore Cruise Line)*

Specifications

Size (in tons)	23,395	Officers	European/American
Number of Cabins	361	Crew	350 (International)
Number of Outside Cabins	289	Passenger/Crew Ratio	2.1 to 1
Cabins with Verandas	2	Year Built	1958
Number of Passengers	725	Last Major Refurbishment	1997

Frommer's Ratings (Scale of 1–5)

Cabin Comfort & Amenities	3	Food & Beverage	3
Ship Cleanliness & Maintenance	3	Pool, Fitness & Spa Facilities	2
Public Comfort/Space	3	Children's Facilities	2
Decor	3	Itinerary	4
Service	3	Worth the Money	4

This vessel, built in 1958 in the Ingalls Shipyard of Mississippi, has undergone more name changes than any other modern liner. It has been known as the *Argentina, Monarch Star, Bermuda Star,* and, in the '70s and early '80s, sailed as the *Veendam* for the Holland America Line. Commodore acquired the ship in 1989 and named it the *Enchanted Isle.* For a time in 1994, it docked in St. Petersburg, Russia, and served as a floating hotel, the Hotel Commodore, before returning to the Caribbean. In 1997, cabins were overhauled to allow greater flexibility in the configuration of beds, and verandas were added to some of the suites.

Cabins & Rates

Cabins	Per diems from	Bathtub	Fridge	Hair Dryer	Sitting Area	TV
Inside	$100	no	no	no	no	yes
Outside	$117	some	no	no	no	yes
Suite	$223	yes	no	no	yes	yes

CABINS   The ship has a large number of outside cabins with views—only 77 of the 361 cabins are insides. There are 11 cabin categories, ranging from six deluxe suites with sitting areas to a pair of deluxe outside cabins with private balconies to somewhat cramped inside cabins with upper and lower berths. Overall, though, cabins are very roomy—the smallest are 120 square feet and the largest are nearly 300 square feet.

Cabins show wear and tear, but the maintenance is top-notch, and a 1997 renovation added additional flexibility to the variety of sleeping configurations available in many of them. All cabins have TVs, telephones, air-conditioning, and music channels. There are no in-cabin safes, but passengers can check their valuables at the purser's desk. There's plenty of drawer and closet space (unless there's a fourth passenger, and then it's very tight). Many cabins have single beds that can be converted to double beds. The spotless, tiled bathrooms are large if a bit worn, and contain no hair dryers or bathrobes, but a few offer bidets. Electrical outlets are a bit scarce.

If ocean views are important to you, avoid outside cabins on the Navigation Deck, since the primary view here is of lifeboats. The views from rooms 222, 223, and 224 are not obstructed. Cabins on the Boat Deck open onto the public promenade, which cuts down on your privacy a bit.

In the lower-level cabins, passengers complain of noise, as the walls seem to be too thin; engine humming and the workings of the crew can be bothersome. There is also no elevator access to cabins on the lowest deck, but all this inconvenience might be worth it if you're on a budget.

Although the line claims to have two cabins accessible to wheelchair users, this isn't the best ship for people with mobility problems. Some public-room doorways have ledges, but they are fitted with ramps; elevators are accessible to wheelchair users.

PUBLIC AREAS   Although the rather plainly decorated, not-very-bright public rooms are polished daily, they look as though they've hosted untold thousands before you—because they have. Beyond the nicks and dents, if you look hard you can still see vestiges of the ship's early art deco design.

The oddly shaped (as is the norm on older, many-times reconfigured ships) public areas on the Promenade Deck stretch the full length aft to the main pool and buffet area. Here there's a casino, show-lounge, and a handful of bars/lounges, where you're sure to find a cozy corner.

There's also a small library (but serious readers should bring their own books), a card/writing room, and a movie theater that's also the disco at night. If you want to slip away, go to the Spyglass Lounge, an observation lounge on the Sun Deck, which most passengers don't seem to discover until near the voyage's end.

The ship has a small video-game room and a children's playroom.

RECREATION & FITNESS FACILITIES   Deck space is adequate for the number of passengers. The ship's tiered aft decks offer three levels of sunbathing spots, with the outside swimming pool on the Promenade Deck. On the Sports Deck, there's aerobics, jogging, and shuffleboard. The minuscule, windowless gym, with Nautilus, free weights, cardiovascular equipment, and not much else, can get crowded fast. Way down on the Theatre Deck is a small beauty salon and a massage room.

Mediterranean Shipping Cruises

SHIPS   Melody

420 Fifth Ave., New York, NY 10018. ☎ **800/666-9333** or 212/764-4800. Fax 212/764-8593.

THE LINE IN A NUTSHELL   While the line's one Caribbean ship, the *Melody*, isn't the fanciest afloat, it is well laid out and roomy and offers a pair of great port-packed 11-night itineraries.

THE EXPERIENCE   Once sailed as the *Star/Ship Atlantic*, a Big Red Boat for Premier Cruise Lines, and before that as the *Atlantic* for Home Lines, the 1,076-passenger *Melody* is a generally well-laid-out ship and a pretty good bargain to boot. A relative newcomer to the North American cruise market, Mediterranean Shipping Cruises is an Italian company that sails its three ships mostly in the Mediterranean.

If you and your family sailed on the *StarShip Atlantic* before, expect déjà vu the moment you step aboard. Other than painting the ship's red hull white, MSC made absolutely no changes to the ship's decor, which was last refurbished in early 1997, under Premier's ownership. Many elements of the ship's adult entertainment and activities remain in place as well, including the scuba programs operated by outside concessionaires. The big change that has occurred is that when the *Melody* operated as a Big Red Boat, it was child-oriented. That is no longer the case. This is now a ship for adults, with children's activities and supervision provided "on demand."

Unlike ships of the other Italian line, Costa, the *Melody* is older, smaller, and less plush, and its product less glossy and well rehearsed. To a point, the Italianness of the line adds a touch of European holiday to your Caribbean jaunt, but by no means should you expect grandeur or over-the-top elegance. At its worst, this ship is dowdy and a bit creaky. At its best, it can be fun. Above all, it's cheap.

Pros

- **International flair.** While not as pervasive as Costa's, the ship's Italian flavor and a more international passenger mix create a more exotic onboard experience than most Caribbean-bound ships.
- **Well-laid-out and spacious public rooms.** It's not difficult to navigate between the two decks housing the entertainment lounges, bars, casino, Lido restaurant, shops, fitness area, and pool.

Cons

- **Low-brow dining.** The Galaxy Restaurant tends to be crowded, loud, bright, and generally like a cafeteria. There's lots of chrome and flimsy, uncomfortable chairs.
- **Few windows.** Most of the public areas get very little natural light and can be a bit drab.

Frommer's Ratings: Mediterranean Shipping Cruises					
	Poor	Fair	Good	Excellent	Outstanding
Enjoyment Factor				✓	
Dining			✓		
Activities			✓		
Children's Program		✓			
Entertainment			✓		
Service			✓		
Overall Value				✓	

Mediterranean Shipping Fleet Itineraries			
Ship	Home Ports & Season	Itinerary	Other Itineraries
Melody	Fort Lauderdale, round-trip itineraries alternate between Jan and Mar.	**11-night western Carib/partial Panama Canal:** Montego Bay (Jamaica), Cartagena (Colombia), San Blas Islands (Panama), Puerto Limón (Costa Rica), Key West. **11-night eastern Carib:** St. Thomas, Antigua, Grenada, Guadeloupe, Tortola, Bahamas.	Mediterranean

MELODY: A CATCHY TUNE

In 1985, one of MSC's corporate predecessors, Flotta Lauro, became infamous as the owner of the *Achille Lauro,* whose passengers endured a much-publicized terrorist attack off the coast of Egypt. Partly because of the bad publicity that ensued, the company changed its name first to StarLauro Cruises and then, in 1996, changed it once more, to Mediterranean Shipping Cruises.

In 1998, the company expanded from its European base into the rapidly growing Caribbean market, and now offers 11-night eastern and western Caribbean itineraries from Fort Lauderdale.

THE FLEET

The 1,056-passenger, 36,500-ton *Melody,* MSC's only Caribbean ship, formerly sailed as the Big Red *StarShip Atlantic* for Premier Cruise Line. Aside from a paint job, the line has made virtually no changes to the ship since its purchase.

MSC has two other ships under its flag. The *Monterey,* built in 1952, and the *Rhapsody,* built in 1974, both offer itineraries in the Mediterranean.

PASSENGER PROFILE

Unlike most of the lines reviewed in this book, MSC is an all-Italian entity that's only recently begun marketing in North America. Consequently, you're likely to have a higher percentage of Europeans aboard, although it's safe to say about half of the passengers are from North America. Americans aboard this line tend to be older, a bit more staid, and a bit more conservative than many of the Europeans who fly into Fort Lauderdale as part of inexpensive package trips. European passengers tend to be younger, sometimes with children.

DINING

Lunch and dinner are both served in two seatings (and breakfast in one seating) in the big, well-lit Galaxy Restaurant, down close to the waterline and straddling the entire width of the ship. **Cuisine** is primarily Italian and continental, and might include rolled prosciutto in a gelatin glaze; creamed chicken in puff pastry; a Caesar salad *Palmiere; sottadito* of lamb with balsamic vinegar and "Pont-neuf" potatoes; and flambéed crêpes "Vesuvio." Appetizers often include a serving of sevruga caviar or pâté *Maison.* The wine list is mostly made up of well-chosen Italian vintages.

Buffet-style breakfast and lunch are served on the pool deck.

ACTIVITIES

This ship doesn't (and at age 18, can't) offer the range of amenities and state-of-the-art distractions you'll find on the big smack'n new megaships. There are no golf ranges, computer learning centers, water slides, or tennis and basketball courts. That said, there's still plenty going on to keep passengers busy. There's a **casino** and **disco,** plus activities like bridge, cards, jigsaw puzzles, aperitif parties before lunch, sunset cocktail parties with dance music, poolside contests, a visit to the small gym or beauty salon, a massage, stretch-and-tone aerobics classes, and movies in the theater.

CHILDREN'S PROGRAM

A low-tech, low-key indoor/outdoor **children's center** offers a modest selection of activities and a kids' wading pool, but in general, there are few efforts to segregate children into their own areas. Children's programs are formulated depending on the number of children aboard, so you'll obviously find more offered during school vacations and summer than in winter.

Baby-sitting is available at the rate of $7 per hour per child.

ENTERTAINMENT

There's at least one singer and a **musical group** that trots out danceable show tunes and favorites from both sides of the Atlantic, plus an occasional **comedian.**

You won't find any of the tongue-in-cheek "Italian-style" diversions that receive such attention at Costa, like toga parties by the pool. You're also unlikely to find such bizarre mind-benders as "stuff your bikini with Ping-Pong balls" contests, which pop up aboard some other cruise lines. Expect lots of emphasis on sunbathing, reading, mealtimes, and visits to the ports of call.

SERVICE

Overall, the *Melody* is manned by career staffers, many from Italy and benefiting from that country's superb tradition of attentive service.

Melody

The Verdict

This well-laid-out ship offers lots to do and pretty roomy spaces in which to do it.

Melody *(photo: Mediterranean Shipping Cruises)*

Specifications

Size (in tons)	36,000	Officers	Italian
Number of Cabins	538	Crew	539 (International)
Number of Outside Cabins	371	Passenger/Crew Ratio	2 to 1
Cabins with Verandas	0	Year Built	1982
Number of Passengers	1,076	Last Major Refurbishment	1997

Frommer's Ratings (Scale of 1–5)

Cabin Comfort & Amenities	3	Food & Beverage	3
Ship Cleanliness & Maintenance	4	Pool, Fitness & Spa Facilities	3
Public Comfort/Space	4	Children's Facilities	2
Decor	3	Itinerary	3
Service	4	Worth the Money	5

This medium-sized ship was built in the style of a classic ocean liner, with a layout of decks and public areas originally conceived for long-haul cruises. There's more weight and metal in this ship's design than in more modern vessels, where lighter materials and structural innovations sometimes create a cookie-cutter similarity. Teakwood decks and heavy doors with the traditional raised sill are commonplace—children often have to experiment to learn to open them. Real round portholes—an increasing rarity in these picture-window days—have been retained in many instances, and provide a nice reminder of traditional ship design.

If you opt for a cruise aboard this ship, remember that many thousands of nautical miles have washed beneath its hull, and that several previous owners used it hard and intensely—not least in its Big Red days as Premier's *Big Red Boat,* when it carried throngs of children around the Caribbean. Very few cosmetic or architectural changes have been made since the ship's acquisition by MSC in 1997.

Cabins & Rates						
Cabins	Per diems from	Bathtub	Fridge	Hair Dryer	Sitting Area	TV
Inside	$77	no	no	no	no	no
Outside	$87	some	no	no	some	no
Suite	$156	yes	yes	no	yes	yes

CABINS   Cabins aboard *Melody* come in nine different configurations, the smallest of which tends to be somewhat cramped; the others, averaging 185 square feet, are relatively comfortable. Suites are a bit more plush, with square footage of between 280 and 440 square feet. The suites can accommodate four or five people and are geared to families and to couples who want to luxuriate in a big space. Many cabins sleep between two and five occupants with upper berths and, in some cases, sofa beds. This can make shipboard density high if lots of the third, forth, and fifth berths are occupied.

Furniture in all cabins is of the durable, indestructible variety. Each cabins has music channels. Bathrooms are as family-friendly as possible, with angles rounded off to spare you any bumps and bruises. Four cabins are wheelchair accessible.

PUBLIC AREAS   The decor is cheerful, but definitely feels like vintage early '80s, with lights twinkling along shiny metallic surfaces and bright but not jarring color schemes. The only somber-looking place is the deliberately darkened and artsy-looking jazz pub space, the Blue Riband.

There are four bars aboard, and cabaret and comedy acts are presented at Club Universe. There's also an unmemorable casino that's set midships on the Lounge Deck, a photo gallery, and a video arcade. There's no library, although some books are available (err on the side of caution: pack your own). The Mercury Theater shows movies from both sides of the Atlantic.

The ship has a playroom for the kids and an infirmary for the ill.

RECREATION & FITNESS FACILITIES   *Melody* has two swimming pools, one kids' wading pool, and three whirlpools, all of which can get quite full. One of the pools is covered by a retractable magrodome roof. The ship's tiered aft decks offer lots of prime spots for sunbathing.

There's a windowless gym with a couple of massage rooms and a beauty salon. There's an unobstructed jogging track on the Sun Deck, plus setups for volleyball, aerobics classes, Ping-Pong, and shuffleboard on the ship's uppermost deck. Passengers can sign up for introductory scuba lessons, conducted in port and/or on board and operated by outside concessionaires.

Premier Cruises

SHIPS   The Big Red Boat • Rembrandt • SeaBreeze
400 Challenger Rd., Cape Canaveral, FL 32920. ☎ **800/990-7770** or 407/783-5061. Fax 407/784-0954. www.premiercruises.com.

THE LINE IN A NUTSHELL   Its ships aren't spring chickens, but Premier's low prices and fleet of diverse oldies has something to please almost everyone from families with kids, to older folks and ship lovers, to anyone looking for a cheap cruise and a unique itinerary.

THE EXPERIENCE   The ambience aboard Premier's three well-worn old ships is relaxed, upbeat, casual, and predictable. The ships range in age from 35 to 42 years old, and while they can't hide their wear and tear, they continue to offer decent cruises.

As it has been for years, the *Big Red Boat* is geared to families with kids. For ship lovers and nostalgic types, the *Rembrandt* is the best ship in the fleet, the most elegant and spacious and closest to its original grandeur. The *SeaBreeze* is the least special of the three, but recent refurbishments have improved it and actually brought back more of a nautical flavor; this ship's itinerary is its best feature.

Aboard all three, the unpretentious and undemanding style makes Premier a good choice for first-time cruisers. Don't expect glamour or anything approaching cutting-edge technology. A Premier cruise is good value for the money, but keep in mind that you may have to endure elbow-to-elbow people if your ship is full, and amenities that are acceptable but not remarkable—you won't find any frills or pretense aboard. It's all a matter of being realistic about your expectations.

Pros
- **Big Red Boat: Great for kids.** With its supervised programs for five age groups and its spacious indoor/outdoor play area, it's one of the industry's family-friendliest.
- **Rembrandt: Best preserved classic ship today.** The *Rembrandt* is the best-preserved classic ocean liner sailing today, with a wealth of art-deco and funky late-'50s/early-'60s style decor and furnishings.
- **SeaBreeze: Unique itinerary.** The ship visits Cozumel, Belize, Roatan (Honduras), and Key West on its week-long Caribbean itineraries.

Cons
- **Crowds.** When the *Big Red Boat* and *SeaBreeze* are carrying full loads, you'll notice the lines at buffets and getting on and off the ship, and you'll also be hard-pressed to find a comfortable, intimate nook that hasn't already been staked out.
- **Inconsistent service.** As Premier struggles to find its niche, the service on its ships seems to struggle at times too.

Frommer's Ratings: Premier

	Poor	Fair	Good	Excellent	Outstanding
Enjoyment Factor					✓
Dining				✓	
Activities				✓	
Children's Program		✓*			✓**
Entertainment					✓
Service				✓	
Overall Value					✓

*SeaBreeze *and* Rembrandt
**Big Red Boat

PREMIER: DIVERSE FLEET OF OLD-TIMERS

Premier Cruises was formed in 1997 after Florida-based Cruise Holdings, Inc. decided to merge its Dolphin, Seawind, and Premier Cruise Line brands into one line. The new company started with five ships, and then added a sixth, the *Rembrandt,* but by early 1999 it had signed agreements to charter its *OceanBreeze* and *Seawind Crown* through at least 2000, taking them out of the North American market. The ships that remain are old warhorses that have washed about a zillion miles of ocean beneath their bows. They're not opulent, but cruise liners don't come much tougher.

The original Premier Cruise Lines gained fame for its Big Red Boats, which, in association with Disney, spent years ferrying families on 3- and 4-day cruises between Port Canaveral and the oft-visited, heavily touristed ports in the Bahamas. The line's success no doubt influenced Disney to jump into the cruise market with both flashy, Disney-fied feet. Disney's decision, in turn, affected Premier, which sold off one of its Red Boats (the *Atlantic*) and changed its cast of cartoons from the Mickey Mouse gang to Bugs Bunny and friends while Disney was still far from launching its first ship. Now that the *Disney Magic* is up and running, the product offered aboard today's *Big Red Boat* looks downright antiquated by comparison—but, on the other hand, it's offered at a much more downmarket price.

Premier still struggles to find its niche and truly prosper. In that regard, changes seem to be imminent as a new president vows to shake things up, with plans to acquire one or two existing ships by year-end and operate at least one of them out of Port Canaveral to expand *The Big Red Boat* cruise-land package concept. Following this, Premier says it plans to market its fleet as two distinct parts: the Red Fleet (including the family-oriented *Big Red Boat* and new ships that may adopt the theme) and the Blue Fleet (comprising the other ships). A $3 to $4 million per-ship furbishment program this year will focus on renewing the fabrics used throughout the ships, and the line will begin to offer cabin amenities such as personalized bathrobes passengers can take home with them.

THE FLEET

All three ships are at least 35 years old, and each has had long and illustrious careers with various cruise lines before being bought by Premier. The ships have gone through more name changes than a struggling cabaret act looking for a lucky break. The 842-passenger, 21,010-ton *SeaBreeze* was built in 1958 as Costa's luxury flagship, *Frederico C.,* and in 1983 was bought by Premier, extensively refurbished, and renamed the *Royale*. She underwent another refit under Dolphin in 1989 and was renamed the *SeaBreeze*. The 1,116-passenger, 38,772-ton *Big Red Boat* was built in 1965 as Home Lines' *Oceanic,* then was renamed *Star/Ship Oceanic* under the original Premier. The 1,074-passenger, 38,645-ton *Rembrandt* was built in 1959 as Holland America's flagship *Rotterdam V,* and sailed in that capacity until her acquisition by Premier in 1997. Modernization on the other ships gave them a cheap though cheerful look, but *Rembrandt* maintains a solid, dignified poise and has aged quite gracefully without plastic surgery. Premier and the officers aboard the ship are proud of their *Rembrandt,* and it shows.

At press time, Premier was in negotiations to acquire the 1,010-passenger *Edinburgh Castle* (built in 1966 as Costa's *Eugenio C.* and later operated as Costa's *EugenioCosta*) and operate it as a second Big Red ship, possibly sailing out of Houston.

PASSENGER PROFILE

Because of its diverse fleet, the line attracts a somewhat diverse lot. The link between them all? They're budget seekers. All three ships (but especially *The Big Red Boat* and

Premier's Mexico Cruise/Land Packages

In April of 1999, Premier announced its new and novel Mexico cruise and land packages. Beginning in early December of 1999, Premier will deploy, under a charter arrangement, Royal Olympic's 300-passenger *Stella Oceanis* or a larger, as-yet-unnamed ship on 3- and 4-night Mexico cruises round-trip from Cancún, and the 400-passenger *Odysseus* on 3- and 4-night Mexican Riviera cruises round-trip out of Puerto Vallarta. Since there is no overlapping of ports, the 3- and 4-night cruises can be combined for a 7-night cruise, and pre- and post-cruise land packages will be available.

Scheduled to run year-round, the *Stella Oceanis* will sail alternating 3- and 4-night cruises from Cancún via the port of Calica. No other major line is doing this itinerary. It's a great idea, and depending on if and how you combine things, you have the choice of a 3-, 4-, 7-, or even 14-night package. The 3-night itinerary will visit Progreso (via Mérida) and Cozumel, and the 4-nighter will visit Roatan and Belize. Pre- and post packages offer accommodations in area five-star hotels.

the *SeaBreeze*) tend to attract a lot of first-timers; if they've sailed before, it's likely to have been aboard one of the company's corporate predecessors, *Dolphin* or *Seawind,* or aboard other budget lines such as Commodore, Regal, or Cape Canaveral. The *Rembrandt* attracts mostly an older clientele liking (and having the time for) the longer itinerary and the ship's venerated history and classic-liner ambience.

The company scoops up a good percentage of the Florida-based family and honeymoon trade. You'll find passengers of all ages, 20s and 30s to retirees. Passengers have a good time aboard these boats, but it's not the all-night party circuit you'll find on Carnival.

Passenger lists aboard *The Big Red Boat,* of course, include lots and lots of kids. The ship also attracts a fair number of international guests. Aboard *The Big Red Boat,* mid-week cruises are likely to be less crowded than weekend cruises, and with noticeably fewer children. Cruises during school holidays—Christmas, Easter, summer vacations—have the highest percentages of children and are the most crowded.

DINING

Food aboard Premier ships is of the hotel-banquet variety, and somewhat limited in selection and presentation. If you don't expect much, you won't be disappointed.

All three vessels have two seatings each for breakfast, lunch, and dinner. Dining options, especially at lunch, are supplemented with offerings from an alfresco deck-side buffet. Late-night hunger pangs can be assuaged at the **midnight buffets,** a standard feature. There are themed dinners, 24-hour room service, a poolside grill, and pizza and ice-cream counters. Afternoon tea is a regular feature, and is most elaborate on the *Rembrandt.*

Dining rooms aboard *The Big Red Boat* and *SeaBreeze* are relatively crowded and noisy. There's often piano music during dinner and special culinary theme nights. Likewise, buffets draw crowds too, and are lavish, although quantity usually wins out over quality. Relatively speaking, the dining ambience is the most elegant (although still fairly informal) aboard the *Rembrandt.*

Cuisine aboard all the line's ships is filling and sometimes savory, but isn't spectacular. Examples might include baked Alaskan salmon with a dill mousseline sauce, roast prime rib of beef with horseradish sauce, duckling à l'orange, and flaming cherries jubilee. As a change of pace, some meals might, for example, feature Greek dishes such as lamb kebabs, souvlaki, or moussaka. **Vegetarian dishes** are available, and there's always a **light and healthy option** that's lower in salt, fat, and calories.

Children's menus feature popular standards like chicken nuggets, burgers, fish sticks, pizza, spaghetti and meatballs, and, in some cases, tacos.

ACTIVITIES

Among the featured activities on the *SeaBreeze* and *The Big Red Boat* may be bingo, bridge, trivia games, horse racing, wine tastings, art auctions, movies, napkin-folding lessons, karaoke, Name That Tune, newlywed and not-so-newlywed games, and singles mixers. Many find their days at sea richly overscheduled and a lot more fun than they had expected.

On the *Rembrandt,* activities are more sedate, but include much of the above, plus things like charades, Pictionary, and spa and salon demonstrations. There are gentleman hosts on board to dance with ladies in need of a partner.

All three of Premier's vessels contain **casinos** and glittery **discos** that—with the right mix of passengers—might rock and roll till late at night. Aboard all the ships except *The Big Red Boat,* discos are far enough from cabins that they don't disturb sleeping passengers. Aboard *The Big Red Boat,* think twice before booking sternside cabins on the Continental Deck, which are directly under that ship's disco.

On the *SeaBreeze,* a new **onboard dive shack** sets up passengers with scuba-diving equipment and instruction for the interesting dive sites visited in Belize, Honduras, and Mexico.

CHILDREN'S PROGRAM

By far the family-friendliest ship in the fleet, and one of the best in the industry, is *The Big Red Boat,* which employs over a dozen full-time youth counselors, each of whom has past training in child care, education, nursing, or some related field. Children are divided into five different age categories (2 to 4, 5 to 7, 8 to 10, 11 to 13, and 14 to 17) for supervised activities that continue from early morning until 10pm. Children even have the option of heading off on their own (chaperoned) shore excursions, allowing parents to pursue their own land or sea activities.

The Big Red Boat contains an accessory-packed area aft on the Premier Deck, with a large **playroom** and outdoor-deck play space with a wading pool (all encircled with a net to keep children from falling overboard), which is the second largest children's recreation center in the short-cruise market (after Disney, of course). There's a kid-oriented ice-cream parlor, a video arcade, and teen center.

Group baby-sitting is available for kids at least 2 years of age from 10pm to 9am the following morning, for $5 per hour for the first child and $3 per hour for each additional child. For an additional fee, you can arrange to have a costumed Looney Tune character tuck your child into bed.

On the *SeaBreeze* and *Rembrandt,* there are small playrooms and limited children's activities available during the summer and holiday time for ages 3 to 13, but nothing close to what's provided on *The Big Red Boat.*

ENTERTAINMENT

Some passengers find Premier's entertainment quite cheerful and upbeat, although few consider it top tier. Most evenings, there's some kind of **cabaret act,** and a live dance band or a singer performs in one of the bars. **Karaoke** is popular across the fleet and so are theme nights (like '50s nights). Each ship has a movie theater.

Premier Fleet Itineraries			
Ship	Home Ports & Season	Itinerary	Other Itineraries
The Big Red Boat	Port Canaveral, round-trip itineraries alternate year-round.	**3- and 4-night Bahamas:** Nassau, Salt Cay.	None
Rembrandt	Fort Lauderdale, round-trip Nov–Apr.	**7-night eastern Carib:** St. John/St. Thomas, San Juan, Nassau, Salt Cay.	Mediter-ranean
SeaBreeze	Fort Lauderdale, round-trip year-round.	**7-night western Carib:** Cozumel, Roatan (Honduras), Belize, Key West.	None

Aboard *The Big Red Boat,* entertainment has a distinct and not-always-subtle theme: Families that sail together stay together. So don't expect either sophistication or raunchy humor.

On the *Rembrandt,* dancing and hobnobbing in cozy piano lounges are more the norm. The formal and theme dance nights in the ship's Ritz Carlton Lounge (with dance bands playing popular country and western, '50s favorites, and ballroom tunes) bring out the rhythm in everyone. The away-from-it-all Sky Bar is a romantic venue for a taste of caviar, pâté de foie gras, and champagne before dinner (for a charge, or course). The lovely Smoking Room has a pianist who draws good crowds late in the day and after dinner. There are thoroughly routine Vegas-style performances in the show lounge (originally built as a cinema), and some nights there may be a magician, comedian, or soloist.

SERVICE

Service aboard Premier ships lacks the polish, discretion, and finesse that higher-priced lines can afford to provide, and can be inconsistent. But for the money, the service is good, and staff morale seems to be relatively high.

The staff on *The Big Red Boat* is very patient and indulgent with children, even in difficult moments, and on the *Rembrandt,* many of the officers and crew display a palpable pride in their gracious ship.

Just like most of the mass-market and upscale lines, Premier's ships stock a nice toiletry set in each cabin bathroom, with shampoo, conditioner, lotion, and soap.

Some Special Discounts

Single-Passengers Rates: Single rates can be as low as 125% (industry standard is 150%–200%). **Senior Rates:** Senior citizens (over 55) and their spouse or guest (of whatever age group) receive discounts of 15% off their cruise when booking a category C–H cabin. **Family Discounts:** Children under 2 sail free. Seven-night packages combining a *Big Red Boat* cruise with an Orlando theme-park/hotel package are offered several times a year, and in such situations, up to two children between the ages of 2 and 12 vacation for free. **Honeymoon/Anniversary Discounts:** Honeymooners and couples celebrating their anniversary within a week of their cruise get complimentary champagne.

The Big Red Boat

The Verdict

In the family and kids department, this ship knows its stuff. While not new and glamorous like the Disney ships, this old-timer holds its own.

The Big Red Boat *(photo: Premier Cruises)*

Specifications

Size (in tons)	38,772	Officers	Greek
Number of Cabins	574	Crew	565 (International)
Number of Outside Cabins	261	Passenger/Crew Ratio	2.3 to 1
Cabins with Verandas	21	Year Built	1965
Number of Passengers	1,116	Last Major Refurbishment	1997

Frommer's Ratings (Scale of 1–5)

Cabin Comfort & Amenities	3	Pool, Fitness & Spa Facilities	3
Ship Cleanliness & Maintenance	3	Children's Facilities	5
Public Comfort/Space	4	Itinerary	4
Decor	3	Worth the Money	5

The Big Red Boat, a pioneer in family cruising, has been catering to families since the 1980s. Costumed characters like Bugs Bunny, Daffy Duck, Tweety, and other Looney Tunes sail on board, and supervised programs are offered for children in five age groups.

Aside from its fire-hydrant-red hull, *The Big Red Boat* is a dignified and stately vessel, a worthy example of the way ocean liners used to be built. Note that phrase "used to": This is by no means a modern, state-of-the-art megaship with all the newfangled gadgets. No matter how many coats of red paint get slapped on, there's no denying that it's an elderly ship whose wrinkles show. However, most passengers, both children and adults, seem more concerned with the magic of their first ocean voyage than with architectural niceties.

Rule #1 when considering *The Big Red Boat:* You've either got to have kids of your own or like being around them *a lot.* This is a parents-with-kids kind of ship.

Cabins & Rates

Cabins	Per diems from	Bathtub	Fridge	Hair Dryer	Sitting Area	TV
Inside	$97	no	no	no	no	yes
Outside	$122	some	no	no	some	yes
Suite	$229	yes	yes	yes	yes	yes

CABINS Some of the outside cabins are gratifyingly large, with suites up to 500 square feet and 21 of them with private verandas. There are more inside cabins on this ship than outside ones, and overall, quite a variety of sizes and shapes.

Configured with upper berths and sofa beds, cabins sleep between two and five. Furniture is relatively solid, and the decor is simple. To make it easier for kids to find their way home, cabin doors are color-coded. Bathrooms are family-friendly, with rounded angles.

Because of the density of cabins, compared to most other cruise lines, there's lots more activity and noise in hallways, especially during embarkation and disembarkation.

Many of the outside cabins on the Premier Deck have views that are partially blocked by lifeboats.

There is only one cabin designed for passengers with disabilities. This ship is not the best equipped for wheelchair users.

PUBLIC AREAS   The interior design is based on shiny metallic surfaces, lots of twinkling lights, and bright but not jarring colors. All told, there are five bars on board (including a couple of somewhat cozy ones, like the Heroes and Legends jazz pub, where adults can hide from the constant barrage of kiddiedom) plus a casino and several lounges where entertainment is offered.

The Big Red Boat is a sleek, bullet-shaped vessel, built before wider, sports-oriented decks came into vogue, and apparently before passengers took to migrating around the ship—some traffic flows make getting from point A to point B rather awkward. For instance, to get from one end of the Lounge Deck to the other, you have to pass through the already crowded casino.

The ship's restaurant, the Seven Continents dining room, can get mighty noisy.

RECREATION & FITNESS FACILITIES   There are two swimming pools and two whirlpools on board, plus a kids' wading pool. Both pools can be covered by a retractable glass roof.

There's a small windowless gym on the Sun Deck and an equally small beauty salon and massage room down on the Continental Deck. Aerobics classes are offered on an outside deck or an unused public lounge, and there is shuffleboard, a combo volleyball/basketball/practice tennis court, and Ping-Pong. There's an unobstructed jogging track on the Sun Deck.

Rembrandt

The Verdict

The *Rembrandt* is Premier's best ship and the most gorgeous and truest relic of a 1950s ocean liner afloat today—and a cruise on her is affordable to boot!

Rembrandt *(photo: Premier Cruises)*

Specifications

Size (in tons)	38,645	Officers	Greek
Number of Cabins	575	Crew	550 (International)
Number of Outside Cabins	307	Passenger/Crew Ratio	2 to 1
Cabins with Verandas	0	Year Built	1959
Number of Passengers	1,074	Last Major Refurbishment	1997

Frommer's Ratings (Scale of 1–5)

Cabin Comfort & Amenities	4	Pool, Fitness & Spa Facilities	3
Ship Cleanliness & Maintenance	3	Children's Facilities	2
Public Comfort/Space	4	Itinerary	3
Decor	5	Worth the Money	5

The *Rembrandt,* former Holland America's proud flagship, the *Rotterdam V,* is a treasure to savor for those who would like to be transported back to the spacious steamship era. Overall, the style is the 1950s, and both Holland America (the ship's owner until October 1997) and Premier have kept things much as they were. Now some 40 years old, the decor remains amazingly true to its period, and some rooms are simply outstanding, with fine wood and leather paneling, ceramic art work, mosaic tiles, and lacquer murals. Other rooms are more '60s funk, but all are well-maintained, museum-like specimens. Furniture is solidly made, unlike so much of what is produced these days, and screams quality. Overall, the ship boasts a truly stunning retro look, and instantly transports all who enter back in time. (That said, wear and tear can't be hidden. You'll notice worn carpeting and decks, and some cabins are musty.)

The deck spaces are roomy and varied with a wonderful teak and rubber-mat circular promenade, wooden deck chairs, and lots of tiered and semi-private deck areas. This is an ideal ship for whiling away lazy days at sea, either busy as a bee or reclusively sequestered somewhere with a good book. Never one of the 5-day transatlantic greyhounds, the ship is solid and middle-class, although whether you find that middle nostalgically luxurious or just out of date depends on you. For me, the ship has a real something—and I'm not alone. In late 1998 the hip British magazine *Wallpaper* noted that "Our ship finally [came] in—in the shape of retro-deluxe '50s ocean-liner SS *Rembrandt,* the only vessel of its kind still riding the waves. . . . To sail in the *Rembrandt* it to travel in a time machine."

CABINS   Cabins come in a motley assortment of shapes and sizes even within the same category, from spacious suites to lowly inside rooms with barely enough space to turn around in. The best-value cabins—and there are lots of them—are the larger ones on Lower Promenade, Main, and A-Deck, with a vast amount of floor space and twins beds set what seems like miles apart. The look is a bit dowdy save for the colorful batik bedspreads and curtains, but you'd need to be carrying two world cruises worth of clothes to fill the three or four illuminated closets and the several sets of drawers.

Bathrooms are definitely old, with exposed plumbing fixtures, but you also get heated towel racks (!) and the best shower pressure on the high seas.

All cabins have TVs, but do not have safes (the purser can keep an eye on your valuables). Views from cabins on the Sun Deck are partially obstructed by lifeboats.

There are no cabins officially designated for wheelchair users, and in many parts of the ship, it would be difficult to get around. Not recommended.

Cabins & Rates						
Cabins	Per diems from	Bathtub	Fridge	Hair Dryer	Sitting Area	TV
Inside	$114	no	no	no	no	yes
Outside	$131	some	no	no	some	yes
Suite	$283	yes	no	no	yes	yes

PUBLIC AREAS   Because the ship was once a two-class North Atlantic liner, the Upper Promenade and Promenade decks are completely filled with public rooms from stem to stern, with intimate bars, the large Queen's Lounge (one of the least attractive rooms) for the big functions, a beautiful wood and leather-paneled nonsmoking Smoking Room, a proper 620-seat theater with a balcony for live entertainment and movie screening, the stunning retro Ambassador Lounge, a comfy library with windows facing onto the Promenade Deck, plus a casino, card room, and several shops. The two-tiered Ritz Lounge, with its dramatic curved staircase, large windows facing aft, retro '60s furniture in plush navy and burnt orange, wood paneling, and a sweeping mural, has no equal for elegance among ships at sea today. A formal white-glove afternoon tea with music takes place in this lounge.

There's a pair of elegant, and very similar, two-deck-high dining rooms with ceramic tile ceilings and bas-relief terra-cotta figures along the walls. The Lido Terrace restaurant, serving buffet-style breakfast and lunch, has lots of indoor and outdoor seating, but seating can still be at a premium at prime times.

When demand warrants it, a children's playroom is created on the forward Promenade Deck.

There are self-service laundry rooms on board.

POOL & FITNESS AREAS   The ship has an outdoor pool located aft surrounded by lots of deck space, and true to its North Atlantic heritage, a pretty, tiled indoor pool deep down on D-Deck, adjacent to the small, Steiner-run spa. There are separate male and female saunas and massage rooms. The gym is decent, and while not the most high-tech you'll ever set eyes on, is located high up on the Sun Deck with large windows facing aft onto the open deck. The circular promenade (partially covered) is one of the best afloat and is wide enough to cater to joggers, fast-walkers, and Sunday strollers.

SeaBreeze

The Verdict

Nothing fancy (cabins are small and don't have TVs), but the Cozumel/Honduras/Belize itinerary is great and so is the price.

SeaBreeze *(photo: Premier Cruises)*

Specifications

Size (in tons)	21,010	Officers	Greek
Number of Cabins	421	Crew	400 (International)
Number of Outside Cabins	263	Passenger/Crew Ratio	2.1 to 1
Cabins with Verandas	0	Year Built	1958
Number of Passengers	842	Last Major Refurbishment	1997

Frommer's Ratings (Scale of 1–5)

Cabin Comfort & Amenities	3	Pool, Fitness & Spa Facilities	3
Ship Cleanliness & Maintenance	3	Children's Facilities	2
Public Comfort/Space	3	Itinerary	5
Decor	3	Worth the Money	4

When acquired by Dolphin in 1989, this older vessel (built in 1958 as the *Federico C.* by Costa Lines) received a $5.5 million rebuilding and reconfiguration. Additional improvements completed in 1997 greatly improved some cabins with fresh carpeting and bedding in attractive orange and blue nautical motifs. Purser's Square also got a welcome facelift, with fresh carpeting and new nautical-inspired wall treatments resembling wood paneling. Today, the ship boasts a somewhat classic ocean liner design (at least the hull is sweeping and long, although the stubby stack and twin booms cut an awkward profile), and a decor that looks a lot fresher than you'd expect from such an aged ship. However, renovations over the years have produced a somewhat labyrinthine layout, and despite its facelifts, you'll still find some tinny metal doors, dented walls, and low ceilings in places.

Cabins & Rates						
Cabins	Per diems from	Bathtub	Fridge	Hair Dryer	Sitting Area	TV
Inside	$114	no	no	no	no	no
Outside	$131	no	no	no	no	no
Suite	$283	no	no	no	yes	no

CABINS   Because of the ship's vintage, there's a jigsaw-puzzle-like layout of cabins, in all manner of shapes and sizes. There are 11 different price categories.

Cabins are small, but many have been recently outfitted in cheery navy and burnt orange nautically inspired carpeting, bedding, and drapes, which enliven the small spaces considerably. Furniture is minimal, with small space-saving writing tables that pull out from the dressers or side tables. Bathrooms are cramped. Many cabins can accommodate three and four guests (and some even five), but keep in mind, five in a cabin won't be a picnic. There are four roomy deluxe suites and three regular suites. There are tiny cabins for singles.

Cabins on the Daphne Deck look onto a busy walkway, and outside cabins on La Bohème Deck (Deck B) overlook a flotilla of hanging lifeboats.

There are no cabins specifically designed for wheelchair users, and while some public areas are accessible, overall, this ship is not recommended for passengers using wheelchairs.

All cabins have music channels. Cabins do not have TVs.

PUBLIC AREAS   Because this ship has been chopped up, renovated, refurbished, and rearranged over the decades, some public areas have assumed somewhat disjointed patterns that require circuitous walks to get from one point to another. Despite this—and despite a close configuration of chairs and tables, especially in the dining room—public areas are cheerful and bright, and mostly decorated with jazzy colors (and, unfortunately, hard-looking metallic ceilings and columns, although some renovation has created more subdued, nautical motifs).

The Agitato disco is dark and way down in the lowest depths of the ship, and transports revelers to another time and place (specifically, your favorite John Travolta *Saturday Night Fever* disco, circa 1977). The attractive Serenade Lounge is a piano bar and has nice dark wooden floors and rattan chairs, and the Prelude Lounge sports dark wooden floors and nautical signal flags decorating the walls. The Carmen show lounge is pleasant and features your classic blue and lavender upholstered seating as well as some fairly large windows letting in natural light. The Bacchanalia restaurant is one of the more attractive rooms, but it can get loud and the armless, flimsy chairs are not ideal.

RECREATION & FITNESS FACILITIES   The ship's tiered aft decks are very attractive and tend to disperse crowds and keep everyone from piling up in one place on sunny days at sea. There is one pool and three hot tubs, as well as a small, windowless gym and a tiny beauty salon and massage room down on the Fidelio Deck. There's a great unobstructed jogging track encircling the Electra Deck, as well as shuffleboard and a basketball net.

Regal Cruises

SHIPS   Regal Empress

300 Regal Cruise Way, Palmetto, FL 34221. ☎ **800/270-7425** or 941/721-7300. Fax 941/
723-0900. www.regalcruises.com.

THE LINE IN A NUTSHELL   While the line's one ship isn't exactly regal, ship buffs
will appreciate the vestiges of old-fashioned decor and bargain shoppers will love the price.

THE EXPERIENCE   Regal Cruises offers 1- to 12-night itineraries at rock-bottom
prices—like less than $70 per person per day at times. Its shorter cruises encourage a
party-hearty atmosphere, while its longer sailing are just the opposite. But if you're on
a tight budget and are looking for a Carnival-esque cruise experience, this might be a
line to consider.

The *Regal Empress*, now in its mid-40s, keeps on chugging along, but shows its age
despite dedicated efforts to keep it in shape. The most noteworthy included a $5.5 mil-
lion overhaul in 1997, which placed a TV in every cabin, added verandas to some of
the suites, and generally spiffed up the interior appearance. Still, the ship is a two-faced
blend of the best of yesterday and the worst of today. There's more wood paneling than
on most other ships in this chapter, but there's also green AstroTurf on the outside decks
and no shortage of chrome and mirrors throughout many of the public rooms. Quirks
and all, though, the *Regal Empress* offers an unpretentious cruise with decent food and
entertainment—especially considering its often bargain-basement prices. If you can afford it, book one of the suites or any of the category 3 superior outside staterooms, and
you'll have plenty of space to retire to if the crowds (and there's lots of them when the
ship is fully booked) get to you.

Pros

- **Wood paneling.** Lots of it survives—in the library, dining room, stairways and lobbies, pool bar, and Commodore Lounge—and it's incredibly charming if you appreciate the "old ocean liner" look.
- **Classic nautical lines.** The ship's long, bowed hull and tiered aft decks cut a sharp
  profile in this age of boxy lookalikes.
- **It's cheap cheap cheap.** Advertised specials commonly tout rates as low as $499 for
  a 7-night cruise. Hard to beat that.

Cons

- **Feels crowded.** There aren't that many public rooms, and the outside decks, while
  tiered, get packed on sunny days at sea. The buffet line gets backed up often.
- **Tired in places.** The green Astroturf on the outside decks, sorry-looking shops, and
  cheesy casino are reminders that this is a catch-as-catch-can ship.

Frommer's Ratings: Regal					
	Poor	Fair	Good	Excellent	Outstanding
Enjoyment Factor				✓	
Dining				✓	
Activities				✓	
Children's Activities			✓		
Entertainment			✓		
Service			✓		
Overall Value				✓	

REGAL EMPRESS: OLD & CHEAP

In 1993, the owner of two enormous travel agencies, GoGo Tours and Liberty Travel, paired up with another investor and bought the then 40-year-old *Caribe I* for a reasonable price, changing its name and marketing it through Liberty and GoGo's formidable army of sales representatives. The poor ship had its problems at first: It flunked its first two sanitation inspections and required expensive reconfigurations; then, during its first summer of operation, inexperienced crew members battled glitches in an operation schedule that demanded grueling 4-hour turnarounds between cruises. (Today, turn-around time is a reasonable 8 hours, about the equivalent of most competitors.) The company's beginnings were rocky, but some of the most obvious problems have been corrected. Those that remain? Let's just say that the cheap-as-dirt prices do a lot to alleviate complaints. Frankly, this is the perfect line for anyone who's unwilling to spend a lot of money and who doesn't particularly care about glamour. Fares are sometimes so cheap that if you happen to live within driving distance of the ship's home port (Florida's Port Manatee), you might conceivably spend less on a cruise than you would entertaining yourself back home.

Port Manatee is set in the southern boondocks of Tampa Bay, has difficulty attracting any other cruise lines to its bare-bones facilities, and usually devotes its energy to the loading of phosphates. Romantic, huh? So why does Regal dock its ship there? Remember that old saw about "In the land of the blind, the one-eyed man is king"? At Port Manatee, the *Empress* is queen of all she surveys—and port charges are less than at the nearby Port of Tampa. Another reason involves laws that say casinos can't open until ships reach international waters—it's quicker to get into the Gulf of Mexico from Port Manatee than it is from Tampa, and this means that the casino can open about an hour sooner. (Port Manatee is a 45-minute drive south of the Port of Tampa. Take exit 45 off I-75—it leads onto U.S. Highway 41—and follow the signs.)

During the summer, the *Empress* docks in New York and turns up the proverbial volume, using that city as a base for rowdy "cruises to nowhere" and more sedate excursions up and down the coast of Canada and New England (plus a handful of cruises to Bermuda).

THE FLEET

The 47-year-old, 1,068-passenger, 22,000-ton ***Regal Empress*** is Regal Cruises' only ship (see ship review for details). Its name creates some consumer confusion, similar as it is to the larger and better-accessorized *Regal Princess* operated by Princess Cruises. The similarity stops at the name, though. While the *Regal Princess* is a stylish, futuristic-looking megaship, the *Regal Empress* is older, smaller, and much less luxurious.

Built in Scotland in 1953 as a two-class ocean liner, the ship made its debut sailing from Glasgow and Liverpool to New York. In 1970, long after air travel killed the transatlantic trade, the ship switched to running cruises, but by 1974 ended up mothballed at a pier in Piraeus, Greece, where she languished until 1983. In 1984, after a major refitting, the ship sailed as the *Caribe I* ("The Happy Ship") for Commodore Cruise Lines. She was sold to Regal in 1993.

PASSENGER PROFILE

Passengers run the gamut from very young to very old, although there are many older passengers because zillions of retirees live in the Clearwater/Tampa/St. Petersburg area. You'll find hard-drinking, hard-playing passengers determined to get their money's worth aboard this vessel, but the cruises out of Port Manatee tend to be slightly more sedate than the rowdy midsummer party cruises out of New York.

Regal Fleet Itineraries

Ship	Home Ports & Season	Itinerary	Other Itineraries
Regal Empress	Port Manatee, round-trip itineraries alternate from Jan–Apr.	**4-night western Carib:** Playa del Carmen/Cozumel. **5-night western Carib:** Key West, Playa del Carmen/Cozumel. **7-night western Carib:** Grand Cayman, Roatan (Honduras), Cozumel, Key West. **11-night Panama Canal:** Grand Cayman, San Blas Islands, Puerto Limón (Costa Rica), San Andres.	South America, New England/Canada, cruises to nowhere

DINING

Regal emphasizes eating and more eating, just like the more expensive cruise lines, but with fewer of the grace notes and frills. You can enjoy early morning coffee, juices, and pastries; three square meals a day in the dining room; afternoon tea; a midnight buffet; and 24-hour room service from a limited menu.

The *Empress*'s attractive, wood-paneled Caribbean dining room still retains the grandeur of its past and outshines the food served there. There are two seatings for each meal, and the cuisine, while not gourmet in any way, shape, or form, is decent and service is professional. The main entrees, such as grilled Alaskan salmon with dill, prime rib with Yorkshire pudding, chicken marinated in lemon with rosemary, and pork scalloppine, tend to be better than the appetizers, which are mostly ultra-basic and low brow, like fried chicken fingers and bland soups, although an exception is the classic Waldorf salad with apples, celery, and walnuts. There's one **vegetarian option,** like eggplant parmigiana, and a **"calorie counter" choice,** such as a poached fish.

The buffet-style indoor-outdoor **alternative restaurant,** La Trattoria, on the Promenade Deck near the pool, serves up the basics for breakfast, lunch, and dinner, for guests not wanting to cover up their bathing suits and put on shoes to dine in the Caribbean dining room. Besides salads, cheese, fruit, and cold cuts, there are burgers, hot platters, and pizzas.

ACTIVITIES

You'll find the usual cruise ship activities, just fewer of them. Those you do find include bingo, horse racing, card parties, shuffleboard tournaments, limbo contests, skeet shooting, and live music and dancing by the pool, and there's always a movie playing. You can improve your **golf** putting skills on an AstroTurf green, or try to piece together the enormous communal jigsaw puzzles that are laid out on a prominent table. During days at sea, everyone sunbathes on deck, but the lounge chairs are rather close to one another.

Set near the stern, on the same deck as the restaurant, the ship's casino is hardly the most spectacular afloat, but it might be one of the busiest, especially when the ship is packed.

CHILDREN'S PROGRAM

This ship is not a particularly great choice for kids; however, when at least 10 kids are on board, **youth counselors** are available to supervise children's activities for several age

Some Special Deals

Regal's normal rates are often heavily discounted. Children under age 2 sail free.

groups. There is a **children's activity room** and a **video arcade,** but Regal doesn't have the awesome array of children's activities offered by Premier, Disney, Carnival, and Celebrity. Aboard Regal, activities might include arts and crafts lessons and guided tours of the ship.

Baby-sitting can be arranged with an available crew member for a fee (negotiated between the passenger and crew member).

ENTERTAINMENT

Entertainment varies according to what and who is hired to perform in the Grand Lounge showroom or the Mirage, which functions as a movie theater during the day and a disco after 10pm. There's live dance music in the Mermaid Lounge before and after dinner, and there's always **karaoke,** with the ship thoughtfully providing props. Virtually every cruise hosts a cocktail party for repeat passengers, of whom there are many.

SERVICE

Service is better than you might expect from such an inexpensive line, offering creditable amounts of guest pampering. The dining staff is professional and experienced, and the bartenders at the Pool Bar have their job down pat, pouring the drinks and offering lots of pleasant chit-chat.

There is a self-service laundry on the Sun Deck.

Regal Empress

The Verdict

However rough around the edges it may be, this old-timer retains some charming original ocean-liner features.

Regal Empress *(photo: Regal Cruises)*

Specifications

Size (in tons)	22,000	Officers	International
Number of Cabins	455	Crew	386 (International)
Number of Outside Cabins	226	Passenger/Crew Ratio	2.8 to 1
Cabins with Verandas	8	Year Built	1953
Number of Passengers	1,068	Last Major Refurbishment	1997

Frommer's Ratings (Scale of 1–5)

Cabin Comfort & Amenities	4	Pool, Fitness & Spa Facilities	2
Ship Cleanliness & Maintenance	3	Children's Facilities	2
Public Comfort/Space	3	Itinerary	4
Decor	4	Worth the Money	5

Despite years of hard use by various owners, vestiges of this ship's original elegance and good taste still remain. It boasts ample amounts of deck space, although when it's full, there won't be an inch to spare. Another appealing feature is the glass-enclosed promenade on (where else?) the Promenade Deck, whose virtues are more evident during windy weather in the North Atlantic—during hot days in the Caribbean, you'll wish it was open. Sheathed in wood paneling, the library, Caribbean dining room, Commodore lounge, and Pool Bar are the most pleasant—and original—public areas on board.

Cabins & Rates

Cabins	Per diems from	Bathtub	Fridge	Hair Dryer	Sitting Area	TV
Inside	$86	no	no	no	no	yes
Outside	$100	no	no	no	no	yes
Suite	$207	yes	yes	yes	yes	yes

CABINS As with most old ships, the 453 cabins vary widely in size, location, and configuration, with the smallest measuring a cramped 80 square feet and the largest suites a spacious 216 to 410 square feet. The majority of cabins are about 100 to 120 square feet, and a large number are inside cabins without views.

Cabins look their age for the most part. Decor is sparse, but brightly colored matching drapes and bedspreads cheer things up. The 120-square-foot category 3 superior outside cabins, for instance, are bright and cheerful and feel bigger than they are. In general, walls are white and furniture institutional looking, with touches of wood trim and, more rarely, paneling. Suites E and F, and mini-suites U90 and U91, for instance, on the Upper Deck contain quite a bit of original wood and are most distinctive, despite awkward shapes. Most doors are solid wood, and unlike the new ships (which all use computerized keycards) are all operated with lock and key, just like the old days.

In late 1997, eight suites were reconfigured to include private verandas. In all cabins, televisions and safes were added; overall, much of the carpeting, bedding, drapes, and upholsteries were replaced, and everything was freshened with renewed coats of paint.

Overall, bathrooms are small and somewhat cramped; only the largest of the ship's suites have bathtubs.

Most cabins can be configured for up to four occupants through bunk-bed arrangements. Some can be configured to accommodate five. Cabins have enough storage space, and in some cases tons of space, and a reasonable amount of elbow room, at least for a cruise of short duration. Even in the lowest category, an inside cabin might have two lower beds, two closets, and two dressers that can store most of a couple's possessions. About 10 cabins are singles.

One cabin is accessible to wheelchairs, but overall, with its awkward layout and high doorway sills, this ship is not well suited to people with mobility problems.

All cabins have TVs, music channels, and safes. Many outside cabins have portholes, and some have rectangular windows.

PUBLIC AREAS A hodgepodge of old and new, the *Regal Empress* has managed to hold onto some of its original wooden and brass fittings, but they exist side-by-side with chrome, mirrors, and other shiny surfaces. There are vestiges of the past in the rich wood paneling covering the main stairs and landings and in the purser's lobby. The library, too, is an oasis of clubbiness with its all-over wood paneling, rich carpeting, and well-upholstered chairs. The Caribbean dining room is a gem, too, retaining much of the past with its etched glass, ornate wall sconces, original murals of New York and Rio, and wooden paneling, waiters' stations, and columns. Some of the chairs are rickety rattan numbers, while others are beautiful, sturdy wooden jobs upholstered to match nicely with the deep hues in the carpeting.

The cozy Commodore Lounge is also mostly original (at least its deep wood paneling and detailing are) and on either edge of the room offers sunken seating clusters for truly private cocktails and conversation.

The slightly elevated and always bustling Pool Bar on the Sun Deck is the hub of action. It's generously done in deep caramel-colored wood (if only the decks themselves were, too!), and is surrounded by numerous sturdy bar stools.

The casino is popular, but tired and cheap-looking with its rainbow-painted walls and slots stools. A two-level disco (the Mirage, which doubles as a movie theater during the day) is dark and sultry—your classic metallic hideaway. The Mermaid bar and night-club is modern if uninspired, and pleasant with its bright blue carpeting and upholstery and sizable dance floor. The modern Grand Lounge is nothing special and is the place for cabaret acts, comedians, singing groups, and whatever other after-dinner entertainment is being featured. On the Promenade Deck near the Pool Bar, the La Trattoria buffet-style restaurant, created during the 1997 refurbishment, is nothing more than a somewhat crowded buffet line, but the colored tiles and bright canvas awnings are a nice touch. Seating is outdoors on deck or more or less inside under a patch of the covered Promenade deck.

There's also a so-called sports bar with flimsy chairs and cheap framed prints of sport stars on the wall.

At busy times, like before and after dinner, pedestrian traffic is heavy as passengers migrate from one area of the ship to another. When the ship is full, you'll know it.

RECREATION & FITNESS FACILITIES   The ship's tiered decks are very attractive and recall a classic liner. There's one small pool aboard—more a spot for sunbathers than a place to really swim—and two adjacent hot tubs, surrounded by deck chairs and tables with nice ocean-blue canvas beach umbrellas. Unfortunately, bright-green Astroturf covers virtually all of the outside decks (hiding any teak that may be underneath) and greatly detracts from the otherwise appealing areas.

There's a beauty salon and one massage room. You'll find a few exercise machines in a rather bland room on the top deck, but no sauna or showers. Two whirlpools are on deck. Stretch-and-tone classes are led by one of the showroom's dancers.

Royal Olympic Cruises

SHIPS   Stella Solaris • Olympic Voyager (preview)

1 Rockefeller Plaza, Suite 315, New York, NY 10020. ☎ **800/872-6400** or 212/397-6400. Fax 212/765-9685. www. royalolympiccruises.com.

THE LINE IN A NUTSHELL   The *Stella Solaris* is the only ship in the fleet of Greek-owned, Greek-operated Royal Olympic Cruises to spend time in the Caribbean. An older vessel, it has a no-neon, low-key atmosphere that stands in sharp contrast to the high-energy, glitzy megaships. This is not a glamour ship and will not appeal to those seeking partying fun-in-the-sun days and sequin-studded nights. The typical passenger on the *Solaris* is early to bed and early to rise, and would rather watch a PBS documentary than boogie til dawn (on this ship, the disco is a ghost town).

THE EXPERIENCE   In cruise service since 1973, the *Stella Solaris* offers a homey, friendly experience. While many cruise lines have a rapid turnover in personnel, crew members on the *Stella Solaris* have worked on the ship for an average of 14 years and some have been with the ship over 20 years, so it's not uncommon to see them greet repeat passengers like old friends—a greeting the passengers return in kind. Service aboard ship is outstanding. Waiters aboard the *Stella Solaris* take pride in both their job and their ship and are extremely attentive to individual passenger requests.

The ship's enrichment program far surpasses others in the Caribbean. First offered in 1987, it has special theme itineraries throughout the year. Especially popular are scientific theme cruises built around solar eclipses and the Mayan-themed cruises, which visit Mayan areas and have archaeologists and historians aboard to lead discussions.

Pros

- **Cultural and scientific enrichment programs.** These comprehensive programs are the major factor distinguishing the *Stella Solaris* cruise experience from the competition.
- **Swift, superb service.** Dining and cabin service are delivered with a personal touch.
- **Well-organized and diversified shore excursions.** There are from two to four excursions available at every port, some devoted to the cruise theme and others to snorkeling and/or beach excursions.

Cons

- **The ship shows its wrinkles.** While the crew works diligently to keep the decks, public spaces, and cabins clean and polished, evidence of deterioration cannot be camouflaged.
- **Small gym with little equipment.** However, this is not a negative for most passengers, who seem uninterested in exercise.
- **Lack of age diversity among passengers.** The passenger list consists primarily of retired couples (generally 65+) with some single passengers.

Frommer's Ratings: Royal Olympic					
	Poor	Fair	Good	Excellent	Outstanding
Enjoyment Factor					✓
Dining					✓
Activities					✓
Children's Program	N/A*				
Entertainment				✓	
Service					✓
Overall Value				✓	

*Royal Olympic *has no children's program in the Caribbean.*

ROYAL OLYMPIC: SPANAKOPITA, ANYBODY?

Royal Olympic offers Caribbean/Mexico cruisers something different: A little touch of Greece among the palms and white-sand beaches. Formed in 1995 from a merger of Sun Line and Epirotiki Cruises, the line's ships generally stick to the Mediterranean, but one vessel, the 47-year-old *Stella Solaris,* makes the annual trek west, offering Caribbean, Panama Canal, and Mexico/Central America cruises (the latter of which visit Mayan sites throughout the region), plus itineraries combining the Caribbean and South America.

The Sun Line was founded in 1958 by Charalambos Keusseoglou, who at the time was an executive for Homes Lines. The line's first cruise ship was a converted battleship, and the next two were converted from German excursion vessels—the first *Stella Maris* and the first *Stella Solaris.* They turned out to be good cruise ships, allowing the company to establish itself as the leading Greek/Aegean Sea cruise line for the North American market.

Holland America Line took a stake in Sun Line in 1964, but bowed out after a time, to be replaced by the Marriott Hotel group. The company became synonymous with everything Greek—Greek Island cruising and a very warm onboard Greek atmosphere. Sun Line branched out into the Western Mediterranean, the Black Sea, the Red Sea, northern Europe, and then eventually, cruises across the Atlantic, in the Caribbean, Orinoco, Amazon, and South America.

Epirotiki Lines, also a Greek family-owned company, got its start back in the 19th century, and beginning in the 1930s started operating Greek Island cruises. After World War II, they took on a number of secondhand ships from Canada and Britain, and even an ex-American yacht, and had them converted to cruising at a slightly lower level than the Sun Line standards.

Swan Hellenic, one of Britain's top cruise travel operators, chartered Epirotiki's *Orpheus* for more than two decades, and Epirotiki also branched out to other regions, with the Potamianos brothers, George and Andreas, in charge.

The two companies joined forces in 1995 as Royal Olympic Cruises, with the Keusseoglou and the Potamianos families still in charge.

THE FLEET

In service since 1953, the venerable **Stella Solaris,** originally a French cargo ship known as the *Cambodge,* was renamed after being purchased by Greek-owned Sun Line Cruises in 1973. The ship subsequently underwent a complete reconfiguration (only the hull and steam-powered engines were left intact) that transformed it into Sun Line's flagship. With the 1995 merger of Sun Line and Epirotiki, another Greek-owned line, the *Stella* became the flagship of the newly formed Royal Olympic Cruises.

The other six ships in Royal Olympic's fleet—*Olympic Countess, Stella Oceanis, Odysseus, World Renaissance, Triton,* and *Orpheus*—are based year-round in the eastern Mediterranean and specialize in cruises to ports in the Greek islands and along the Turkish coast.

Royal Olympic is in the process of upgrading its aging fleet with the construction of two sleek, high-speed, 800-passenger ships, with the first due to debut in June 2000. At press time, itineraries for the 2000–2001 season had not yet been finalized, and it has not been determined whether the new ship will spend part of its first year in the Caribbean.

PASSENGER PROFILE

Passengers are primarily senior couples who are experienced travelers and have previously cruised—either on the *Stella Solaris,* to which many are drawn back because of its enrichment programs, or aboard other ships. You'll find very few first-time cruisers aboard, as Royal Olympic is not nearly as well known in the Caribbean as the big boys (Carnival, Royal Caribbean, Princess, et al).

Younger couples may feel out of place unless they're dedicated culture vultures who enjoy hanging out with an older crowd. On my recent cruise, prizes were given to the oldest person in attendance at one of the roundtable discussions (the winner was age 87) and to the youngest (age 29). When the audience was asked how many were under the age of 50, there were only five hands raised out of approximately 300 in attendance. Honeymooners, single passengers, and families are also few and far between.

DINING

With menus designed to accommodate a wide range of tastes, from carnivorous to vegetarian, no one ever goes hungry on the *Stella Solaris*. Along with the extensive variety of choices, the quality and presentation of the **Greek cuisine** stands out.

Passengers can eat breakfast and lunch in either the Dining Room or Lido Cafe. Those who choose the Dining Room have the option of a buffet breakfast and/or ordering from a breakfast menu that includes stewed fruits; hot and cold cereals; home-baked rolls, croissants, and muffins; pancakes; French toast; several egg dishes; meats; and assorted cold cuts and cheese. Buffet-style breakfasts in the Lido feature a choice of hot and cold cereals, freshly baked croissants and muffins, eggs, pancakes, waffles, French toast, and plenty of fresh fruits and cheese. A full five-course lunch is served in the dining room, whereas the Lido has a choice of several salads, cold cuts and cheeses, a selection of sandwiches, several meat and fish dishes, and various desserts.

Dinner menus offer three **continental entrees,** plus **vegetarian, spa cuisine** (low cholesterol, reduced salt), and **Pacific Rim cuisine** (flavor and spices of the Orient and the Islands). Lunch and dinner menus usually offer a Greek specialty such as tash kebab (chunks of tender beef simmered with tomatoes and herbs served with rice pilaf), sfyrida all spetsiota (baked seabass in tomatoes with potatoes), and spanakopita (spinach pie). Following the entree is a choice of four desserts plus a sugar-free dessert and an assortment of domestic and international cheeses and fresh fruit.

The Lido is the place to go for coffee or tea 24 hours a day, an early-riser's coffee and danish from 6 to 7am, bouillon at 11am, a cocktail hour 6 to 7pm (during which all drinks except wine, champagne, and the drink of the day are half-price), and a buffet of **late-night snacks** from 11pm to midnight. An **afternoon tea** takes place every afternoon in the Solaris piano bar.

ACTIVITIES

At the top of the activity list is the provocative series of **lectures** (many with accompanying slide presentations), **roundtable discussions** (with audience participation), and **documentaries** that make up the enrichment program. Extensive reading material in the form of pamphlets, reprints of articles, maps, and diagrams provided at the beginning of the cruise supplement the lectures and discussions. Throughout the cruise, additional printed materials are distributed, and books written by the lecturers are available for sale. Passengers are encouraged to ask questions with the understanding that "there are never any dumb questions." Away from the formal presentations, lecturers are accessible and mingle with the passengers. In port, excursions are offered that compliment

Here Comes the Sun

The most recent *Stella Solaris* solar eclipse cruise in the Caribbean took place in 1998 and was the subject of a BBC documentary. It's shown on board.

Royal Olympic Fleet Itinerary			
Ship	Home Ports & Season	Itinerary	Other Itineraries
Stella Solaris	13-night southern Carib/Amazon sails between Fort Lauderdale and Manaus (Brazil), Dec–early Jan; 10-night western Carib sails round-trip from Fort Lauderdale, Mar 2000.	**13-night southern Carib/Amazon southbound:** St. Thomas, St. Lucia, Grenada, Barbados, Tobago. **13-night southern Carib/Amazon northbound:** Trinidad, Bequia, St. Vincent, Antigua, St. Thomas. **10-night western Carib/Central America:** Roatan (Honduras), Santo Tomas (Guatemala), Belize, Playa del Carmen. **56-night South American circumnavigation:** Round-trip from Fort Lauderdale, Jan–Mar 2000.	Mediterranean

the cruise theme; for example, on the Mayan regions itinerary, excursions to key Mayan sites are offered from five of the six ports.

Other **cultural and scientific-related activities** offered during the cruise included classical piano concerts, stargazing sessions at night, and gatherings at sunset "searching for the green flash" (an atmospheric phenomenon that occurs just after sunset).

In addition to its enrichment programs, the *Stella Solaris* offers such **leisure activities** as Ping-Pong and shuffleboard tournaments; dance instruction; arts and crafts classes; napkin-folding workshops; a perfume seminar and a hair, beauty, and massage demonstration; and daily (sometimes twice daily) snowball jackpot bingo. Those who want to limber up in the mornings can participate in various **exercise sessions,** including group walk-a-mile workouts around the deck, stretching classes, and low-impact aerobics. At various times throughout the cruise are also Trivial Pursuit, blackjack, bridge, and gin rummy tournaments.

Dancing in the Solaris Lounge before dinner and after the show is another popular activity. It's here that the ship's dance hosts are kept busy as partners for all the women who desire their services. On my cruise, the dapper, dashing host known as "Valentino" was in especially high demand.

CHILDREN'S PROGRAM

As a matter of course, very few children sail aboard *Stella Solaris*'s Caribbean cruises, and so there are no organized programs or activities for either children or families.

ENTERTAINMENT

The dance floor in the Solaris Lounge doubles as the stage where the ship's talented troupe of singers and dancers perform twice nightly, joined occasionally by a comedian, a magician, and/or a guest musician. Especially popular performers on a recent "Maya Equinox" cruise were the Riga Dancers, five young, lissome ladies from Latvia who lit up the stage with their colorful costumes and fancy footwork. Cruise director Dave Levesque also occasionally displayed his skill as a stand-up comedian.

Greek-flavored musical entertainment is provided at poolside during lunchtime—on my recent cruise by the Eko Trio, which also performed some evenings in the Solaris Lounge. The ship's other Greek musicians, known as the Duo Alexandru (violin and piano), played during daily afternoon tea and in the dining room at night, where they moved from table to table playing Greek tunes.

The most exciting night of entertainment on every *Stella Solaris* cruise is **Greek Night,** during which the crew and most of the passengers sport the blue and white colors of the Greek flag. Festivities begin at sunset with an ouzo party in the Lido Cafe accompanied by bouzouki music, followed by a dinner featuring a five course, all-Greek meal. The evening culminates with a gala celebration of Greek music and dance in the Solaris Lounge featuring the ship's various entertainers along with several members of the crew. At the conclusion of the show, passengers are invited to come onstage and join in several spirited Greek dances.

At some ports, **local entertainers** are invited on board to display their talents. On my early 1999 sailing, a group of schoolchildren came aboard at Puerto Cortés (Honduras) to perform folk dances, and a mariachi band enlivened the evening during the ship's stay at Cozumel.

SERVICE

As good as it gets. Dining room service is always fast and efficient, with little waiting time between courses. Many of the waiters have worked together for years and it shows in their performance, as everyone carries out his or her duties with clockwork precision. Waiters make a special effort to know passengers' names and are always willing and eager to please. In addition, there is more pampering at meal times than one would expect on a moderately priced cruise; waiters carry passenger trays to tables during buffet breakfasts in the dining room and for breakfast and lunch buffets in the Lido Cafe. Delivery of continental breakfast to cabins is always on time and room service throughout the day and night is fast and efficient. Cabin stewards also deserve kudos for making up rooms in record time.

The *Solaris* offers laundry and pressing services, but no dry cleaning or self-service laundries.

Stella Solaris

The Verdict

Calling all culture vultures! This warm, hospitable Greek ship specializes in innovative itineraries built around enrichment programs.

Stella Solaris *(photo: Royal Olympic Cruises)*

Specifications

Size (in tons)	18,000	Officers	Greek
Number of Cabins	329	Crew	320 (International)
Number of Outside Cabins	250	Passenger/Crew Ratio	1.9 to 1
Cabins with Verandas	0	Year Built	1953
Number of Passengers	620	Last Major Refurbishment	1997

Frommer's Ratings (Scale of 1–5)

Cabin Comfort & Amenities	4	Food & Beverage	4
Ship Cleanliness & Maintenance	2	Pool, Fitness & Spa Facilities	2
Public Comfort/Space	4	Children's Facilities	N/A
Decor	3	Itinerary	5
Service	5	Worth the Money	5

After almost half a century of service, the *Stella Solaris* continues to run smoothly, although it shows obvious signs of wear in both the public spaces and cabins. The teak decks are warped and uneven in many places, and wood furnishings and metal moldings in the cabins are chipped and dented. Bathroom fixtures also show signs of age (such as leaky faucets and cracks in porcelain tubs). Many of the carpets in the cabins, corridors, and public areas are stained and worn, and drab upholstery and fabrics in public areas and cabins need replacing.

However, most passengers who choose to sail on the *Stella Solaris* don't seem to mind any of this, and the ship continues to sell out many of its cruises and maintains a strong, loyal following with a repeat-passenger rate averaging around 50% per cruise. I shared a table at dinner with a couple who were warmly welcomed by several of the waiters as we sat down. It turned out they'd been on nine previous cruises aboard the ship and said they immediately felt right at home upon boarding. "This is the only ship we want to sail on anymore," they said. "It seems like family to us." Another passenger noted that "This ship has a heart and soul that you don't find on the big ships." Many passengers praised the quality of the enrichment programs and affirmed that the *Solaris* is their ship of choice because of the programs and the crew's friendly, hospitable attitude.

Cabins & Rates

Cabins	Per diems from	Bathtub	Fridge	Hair Dryer	Sitting Area	TV
Inside	$176	no	no	no	no	no
Outside	$239	yes	no	no	yes	no
Suite	$298	yes	no	yes	yes	yes

CABINS   The ship's interior design maximizes space devoted to individual staterooms, which are divided into 11 price categories. Top-of-the-line accommodations are the 34 deluxe suites located on the Boat Deck, which measure a spacious 215 square feet and look out through picture windows onto the classic promenade. The remaining 32 suites are located on Golden Deck and Ruby Deck, as are the 100 deluxe outside cabins, measuring 182 square feet. Other cabin categories range from superior outside to inside. Superior and standard cabins have two beds, and some have the option of upper berths to accommodate three or four people. (The lowest-level inside cabins have bunk beds only.) All standard cabins have showers; suites and deluxe and superior outside cabins have bathtubs. Suites have walk-in closets; other cabins have standard closets and more than ample storage space.

All suites and cabins come with four music channels featuring Greek, classical, easy-listening, and American Armed Services radio news, and are also equipped with individually controlled air-conditioning, telephone, and hair dryers, plus shampoos, sewing kits, and shower caps. All cabins have lockable drawers in which passengers can store valuables. Suites are the only category with TVs, which screen four movies daily plus national news, weather, sports, and financial reports.

No cabin or suite categories have private verandas. None are equipped for wheelchair users (and in fact, the layout of the ship would make it a bad bet all around).

PUBLIC AREAS   The user-friendly interior design of the *Solaris* provides quick and easy access from all cabins to three major public areas situated adjacent to each other midships on the Solaris Deck.

The all-purpose, 550-seat Solaris Lounge is the ship's largest public space and serves as gathering place, activity hub, and entertainment center, during the day accommodating everything from lectures to dance classes to bingo and in the evening hosting before- and after-dinner dancing and cocktails, as well as nightly cabaret-style shows. Situated at one end of the lounge is the Solaris piano bar, which along with a grand piano has three gaming tables (two blackjack, one roulette); the rest of the casino is made up of 19 slot machines located in a separate room off the Solaris Foyer, near the shore-excursion desk.

Preview: Royal Olympic's *Olympic Voyager*

Royal Olympic is celebrating the millennium with the launch of its newest ship, the 840-passenger *Olympic Voyager,* scheduled to debut in summer 2000. Built in Germany and featuring a unique mono-hull design, it will be one of the fastest ships afloat, capable of cruising at up to 28 knots. Top-of-the-line accommodations will include 48 suites highlighted by 12 penthouse suites with balconies and skylights; there will also be 16 deluxe suites with bay windows and 20 mini-suites. All 400 staterooms will have minibars, hair dryers, and interactive TV, and four cabins will be fully accessible to disabled passengers. Public rooms will include a casino, library, card room, coffee bar, piano bar, state-of-the-art spa with beauty salon, and two restaurants—a formal dining room and a smaller, alternative restaurant. There will also be a casual grill and pizza bar poolside on deck. Although at press time itineraries were not yet established, sources tell me the *Olympic Voyager* will likely cruise in the Caribbean.

Just steps away from the Solaris Lounge is the 320-seat dining room, an expansive, cheerful space surrounded by large picture windows. Just around the corner is the Grill Room, a richly appointed piano bar with leather chairs—it's the ship's favorite evening watering hole, where the incomparable Octavian, master of the electric piano, performs his scintillating repertoire.

The Lido Cafe opens directly onto the Pool Deck and, weather permitting, offers passengers the option of eating inside or at one of the tables around the pool.

Other public areas include a 275-seat cinema that hosts lectures and also screens daily movies and occasional documentaries. There is also a combination card room/library where passengers can check out books and board games. Buried deep in the bowels of the ship on Main Deck is the Taverna Disco, which opens for business every night around 11:30. Since most passengers are asleep by midnight, it's the least used of all the public areas—except for a few crew members, on my cruise it played to a nearly empty house.

RECREATION & FITNESS FACILITIES   The beauty parlor, Daphne Spa, and gym are located next to each other in a small area on Golden Deck, aft. The small gym has only a few exercise machines crammed into one room; the spa offers five massage/treatment rooms plus sauna and steam rooms.

The wide, shaded promenade encircling the Boat Deck provides plenty of space for walkers and joggers, and on days at sea is an ideal place to relax in a deck chair with a good book and immerse oneself in the balmy breezes. There is a single pool just aft of the Lido Bar, but no hot tubs.

8

The Ultra-Luxury Lines

These cruise lines are the top shelf, the best (and most expensive) of the best. Their ships, mostly small and intimate, are the sports cars of cruise ships and cater to discerning travelers who want to be pampered with fine gourmet cuisine and wines and ensconced in spacious suites with marble bathrooms, down pillows, sitting areas, minibars, and walk-in closets. Caviar is served on silver trays and chilled champagne poured into crystal glasses. Elegant dining rooms are dressed in the finest linens, stemware, and china, and guests dress in tuxedos and sparkling dresses and gowns on formal nights and suits and ties on informal nights. (An exception to this is Windstar Cruises, which, though luxurious and upscale, offers a much more casual kind of luxury and a more laid-back decor. Radisson Seven Seas also tends toward the casual, but not to Windstar's degree.) Exquisite French, Italian, and Asian cuisine rivals that of the best shoreside restaurants and is served in high style by doting, gracious waiters who know how to please. A full dinner can even be served to you in your cabin, if you like. Luxuries like these are part of the wonderfully decadent daily routine.

Entertainment and organized activities are more dignified than on other ships—you won't see any raunchy comedy routines or bordering-on-obscene pool games—and are more limited as guests tend to amuse themselves, and enjoy cocktails and conversation in a piano bar more than they would flamboyant Vegas-style stuff.

With the exception of the *QE2* and the *Crystal Harmony,* these high-end ships are small and intimate—usually carrying just a few hundred passengers—and big on service, with almost as many staff as passengers. You're not likely to feel lost in the crowd, and staff will get to know your likes and dislikes early on. The onboard atmosphere is much like a private club, with guests trading traveling tales and meeting for cocktails or dinner.

Although the high-end lines are discounting more than ever, they still can cost twice as much as your typical mass-market/premium cruise. Barring specials and low-season rates, expect to pay at least $2,000 per person for a week in the Caribbean, and easily more if you opt for the penthouse suite or choose to cruise during the busiest times of the year. Besides early-booking discounts, many high-end lines give

---

Free Stuff on the Ultra-Luxury Ships

It's a fact: The ultra-luxury ships treat passengers as though they're the Sultan of Brunei. The following shows what the lines offer their guests on a complimentary basis (or at least what they've already figured into their cruise rates).

Note: I've included Silversea Cruises in this list. While their ships don't currently sail in the Caribbean, they're a high-end line commonly compared with the lines profiled in this chapter.

Tips: Radisson, Seabourn, Silversea

Port Charges: Crystal, Silversea, Windstar

All Booze: Silversea

Wine with Lunch & Dinner: Radisson, Seabourn

One-Time Stocked Minibar: Radisson

Unlimited Stocked Minibar: Cunard (top suites only), Seabourn (upon request), Silversea

Unlimited Soda Water/Mineral Water: Radisson, Seabourn, Silversea

Some Shore Excursions: Seabourn, Silversea

---

discounts to repeat cruisers and those booking back-to-back cruises, and sometimes offer two-for-one deals and free airfare. Many extras are often included in the cruise rates (see box above).

Most people attracted to these types of cruises are sophisticated, wealthy, relatively social, and used to the finer things in life. While most are well traveled, they've most likely not done overly adventurous or exotic traveling, sticking instead to the five-star kind.

These ships are not geared to children at all, although every so often one or two show up. In this event, baby-sitting can sometimes be arranged privately with an off-duty crew member.

DRESS CODES   On Seabourn, Cunard, and Crystal, bring the tux and the sequined gown—guests dress for dinner on the two or three formal nights on these cruises. Informal nights call for suits and ties for men and fancy dresses or pantsuits for ladies, and sports jackets for men and casual dresses or pantsuits for women are the norm on casual nights. Windstar espouses a "no jackets required" policy during the entire cruise, so men, bring nothing but dress slacks, chinos, and nice collared shirts (short or long sleeves); women, leave the pantyhose at home—casual dresses and slacks are fine for evenings. Radisson is somewhere in between, so bring the suit and nice dresses, but no need to lug the tux or fancy full-length gown on board if it's not your style.

Cruise Lines Reviewed in This Chapter
- Crystal Cruises
- Cunard
- Radisson Seven Seas
- Seabourn
- Windstar

Crystal Cruises

SHIPS Crystal Harmony • Crystal Symphony

2121 Ave. of the Stars, Los Angeles, CA 90067. ☎ **800/446-6620** or 310/785-9300. Fax 310/785-3891.

THE LINE IN A NUTSHELL   Fine-tuned and fashionable, Crystal's pair of dream ships offer the best of two worlds: pampering service and scrumptious cuisine on ships large enough to offer lots of outdoor deck space, generous fitness facilities, four restaurants, and over half a dozen bars and entertainment venues.

THE EXPERIENCE   Crystal has the two largest truly upscale ships in the industry. Carrying 960 passengers, they aren't huge, but they're big enough to offer much more than their high-end peers. You won't feel hemmed in and you likely won't be twiddling your thumbs. Service is excellent, and the cuisine is very good and close to par with Seabourn, Silversea, and Radisson; the line's Asian food is tops. Unlike Seabourn, which tends to be more staid, Crystal's California ethic tends to keep things mingly and chatty. Passengers are social and active, and like dressing for dinner and being seen.

Pros
- **Four restaurants.** Only the megaships offer as many options—and none so sophisticated. There are two alternative restaurants as well as a formal dining room and a casual restaurant that puts on some of the best theme luncheon spreads at sea.
- **Best Asian food at sea.** The ships' reservations-only Asian restaurants serve up utterly delicious authentic, fresh Japanese food, including sushi. At least once per cruise, they also hold an Asian-theme buffet lunch offering an awesome spread, from jumbo shrimp to chicken and beef satays to stir-fry dishes.
- **Fitness choices.** There's a nice-sized gym, paddle-tennis court, shuffleboard, Ping-Pong, an uninterrupted jogging circuit, golf-driving nets, and a putting green.
- **Computer learning.** No other ship has such an extensive computer lab, with over 20 computer stations, complimentary training classes during sea days, and quick and easy e-mail access (both outgoing and incoming).

Cons
- **Price.** High-end lines are, well, high-priced. Crystal is no exception, so be prepared to shell out at least $2,000 per person for a 10-night Panama Canal cruise.
- **Formality.** If you're not nuts about dressing up fit to kill nearly every night, think twice about a Crystal cruise. Some passengers even get gussied up during the day.
- **Cabin size.** While certainly not tiny or uncomfortable, accommodations are smaller compared to Seabourn, Radisson, and Silversea.

Frommer's Ratings: Crystal					
	Poor	Fair	Good	Excellent	Outstanding
Enjoyment Factor					✓
Dining					✓
Activities					✓
Children's Program					✓
Entertainment					✓
Service				✓	
Overall Value					✓

CRYSTAL: SPARKLING & SPACIOUS

Established in 1990, Crystal Cruises has held its own in the high-stakes lottery of the super-upscale cruise market, establishing a unique place there. Its ships are the largest in the high-end sector of the industry, and while not quite as plush and dripping with luxury as its closest competitors—Seabourn, Radisson Seven Seas, and Silversea (a line that doesn't have either of its ships in the Caribbean, and so is not reviewed in this guide)—the Crystal sisters provide a truly refined cruise for discerning guests who appreciate superb service and top-notch cuisine.

Crystal is the North American spin-off of Japan's largest container shipping enterprises, Nippon Yusen Kaisa (NYK). Despite these origins, a passenger aboard Crystal could conceivably spend an entire week at sea and not even be aware that the ship is Japanese owned, built, and funded. More than anything else, Crystal is international, with a strong emphasis on European service. The Japanese exposure is more subtle, and you'll feel it in the excellent Asian cuisine and tasty sake served in the Kyoto alternative restaurant and in the Asian theme buffets, as well as in the handful of Japanese passengers on board many cruises. (There's a Japanese concierge on board, so don't worry about having to sit through announcements and activities being translated into Japanese.)

THE FLEET

Crystal's fleet comprises two nearly twin 960-passenger ships. The *Crystal Harmony* was built in 1990 and weighs 49,400 tons, and since 1998 has been doing a handful of Caribbean and Panama Canal itineraries each year, in addition to cruising in South America, Alaska, and the South Pacific. The *Crystal Symphony* was built in 1995 and weighs 51,044 tons. The *Symphony* is slightly bigger, with a larger atrium and some expanded public rooms (like the casino), and overall embraces a somewhat lighter color scheme. In addition to spending the year cruising in the South Pacific, Asia, the Mediterranean, and Europe, the ships are spending more time in the Caribbean and Panama Canal than ever before. Looks like a trend.

PASSENGER PROFILE

Few other cruise lines attract as loyal a crop of repeat passengers, many of whom hail from affluent regions of California and most of whom step aboard for a second, third, or fourth cruise with a definite sense of how they want to spend their time on board. There's commonly a small contingent of passengers from Japan, Australia, Europe, and South America who make up about 10% to 15% of the passenger mix. Most passengers are well-heeled couples, stylish but not particularly flamboyant, and over 55. A good number of passengers "step up" to Crystal from lines like Princess and Holland America.

Many Crystal passengers place great emphasis on the social scene before, during, and after mealtimes, and many enjoy dressing up (sometimes way up) for dinner and adorning themselves with the biggest and best diamonds they own. You'll see no shortage of big diamonds and gold Rolexes. On formal nights, the majority of men wear tuxes and many women wear floor-length gowns (although your classic black cocktail dress is just fine). Passengers tend to be well traveled, although not particularly adventurous.

The onboard jewelry and clothing boutiques do a brisk business, and it's obvious that women on board have devoted much care and attention to their wardrobes and accessories, and spent lots of time in the boutiques of Rodeo Drive and the like before their arrival on board. Although, as on most ships, dress codes are much more relaxed during the day, after 6pm, men are usually dressed as you'd expect conservative Fortune 500 board members would be. On formal nights, at least three of which occur during every 10- or 11-day cruise, virtually every male aboard opts to wear a dinner jacket or tux.

There are rarely kids on board except during the holidays, when you may see 20 to 40.

DINING

One of Crystal's best features is its diverse and high-quality cuisine. Its two themed, reservations-only **alternative restaurants**—Kyoto, a Japanese restaurant on the *Harmony,* and Jade, a pan-Asian restaurant on the *Symphony* (and Prego, an Italian restaurant on both)—are right up there with the best at sea. Personally, my favorite is Kyoto, where the Japanese food is excellent, with completely authentic sushi platters, miso soup, beef teriyaki, and pork dishes. The accoutrements help set the tone, too—chopsticks (and little chopstick rests), sake served in tiny sake cups and decanters, and sushi served on thick blocky glass platters.

Overall, the galleys aboard these ships feature a light-textured, thoughtful, **California-esque cuisine** with selections like a roasted duck with apricot-sage stuffing served with a Grand Marnier orange sauce, broiled Black Angus sirloin steak, or seared sea scallops and jumbo shrimp served with a light lobster beurre blanc over a bed of pumpkin risotto. At lunch and dinner in the dining room, there's a **low-fat selection,** such as broiled fillet of Chilean sea bass served with steamed vegetables (with calories, fat, cholesterol, sodium, carbohydrates, and protein content listed), as well as an **entree salad**—like a mixed grill salad with grilled herb-marinated chicken breast, jumbo shrimp, and filet mignon—if you'd rather skip the main course. **Vegetarian** meals are available.

In a kind of homage to the California wine industry, Crystal offers one of the most sophisticated inventories of **California wines** on the high seas. Extensive **French wines** are also offered. Prices begin at as little as $18 a bottle, with many selections in the $20 to $60 range, and as high as $800.

The main dining room is chic and stylish with white Doric columns, high-backed chairs, and mirrored ceilings with lotus-flower lighting fixtures (sources tell me, though, that the dining room will be completely refurbished in late spring of 2000). Tables are not too close together, and there are well over 20 tables for two, mostly along the side or near the ocean-view windows.

Because of the size of the ship, **dinner is served in two seatings** here. Lunches and breakfasts, however, are open seating in the dining room and the Lido buffet restaurant. Service by the team of ultra-professional, gracious European male waiters is excellent, and there seem to be more nattily attired staff than passengers. In the main dining room—and to a somewhat lesser degree in the alternative restaurants—table settings are lavish and include fine, heavy crystal and porcelain. Even in the Lido restaurant, waiters are at hand to serve you your salad from the buffet line, prepare your coffee, and then carry your tray to wherever it is you want to sit.

Themed luncheon buffets—Asian, Mediterranean, or a western barbecue, for instance—are excellent and are generously spread out at lunchtime by the pool and sometimes in the lobby/atrium, where the midnight buffet takes place. No expense or effort is spared to produce elaborate food fests, with heaps of jumbo shrimp, homemade sushi, Greek salads, shish kebabs, and more.

If you don't want to stroll much further than your deck chair or if you've slept through lunch, between 11am and 6pm daily you can order something from the Trident Grill on the Pool Deck and have a seat, in your bathing suit if you so desire, at the counter or head back to your deck chair. The Grill serves beef, chicken, and salmon burgers, pizza, tuna melts, hot dogs, fries, fruit, and a special of the day, like a Caesar salad and chicken wrap.

Yet another place for a snack or a specialty coffee is the Bistro, open from 9:30am to 11:30am for a late continental breakfast and then between 11:30am and 6:00pm for complimentary grazing at the buffet-style spread of cheeses, cold cuts, fruit, cookies, and pastries. For a few dollars, you can also sip an almond mocha, hazelnut latte, espresso, or fruit shake, or a glass of pinot grigio or a nice merlot.

Children's Specials

Children 11 and under pay 50% of the minimum fare when accompanied by two guests paying full fare.

For **afternoon tea,** it's the ultra-chic Palm Court on one of the ship's uppermost decks. A sprawling space with floor-to-ceiling windows and pale blue and white furniture in leather and rattan, the area gives off an overall light, soft, and ethereal ambience.

There is, of course, **24-hour room service.** If you've booked one of the suites, room-service attendants are likely to be of the white-gloved variety.

ACTIVITIES

While not overwhelming, Crystal offers an interesting selection of activities. Count on several **enrichment lectures** throughout a cruise, such as a historian presenting a slide show and speaking about the Panama Canal and how it was built, or a movie critic talking to guests about Hollywood and movies. Most speakers are not celebrities, but well-known personalities do occasionally show up on Crystal cruises. In the past, some notables have included TV patriarch Walter Cronkite, glitz-meister Judith Krantz, former secretary of state and Iran-contra defendant Caspar Weinberger, Hollywood gossip enthusiast Bill Harris, "Laugh-In" regular Arte Johnson, NBC news commentator Edwin Newman, biographer David McCullough, and maritime historian Bill Miller.

Crystal also offers its **Wine & Food Festival** program during many of its cruises (some 30 in 1999), where a respected wine expert conducts two complimentary tastings and a guest chef from a well-known restaurant conducts a pair of cooking demonstrations for guests and then presents those very entrees at dinner that night. Guests can ask questions and mingle with these interesting personalities.

There are often **dancing lessons** taught by guest teachers as well, popular when offered. Learn to swing, or do the rumba and merengue. Group lessons are complimentary, and sometimes private lessons can be arranged with the instructors for about $50 per hour per couple. The line is big on organizing **bridge and paddle-tennis competitions,** game-show-style contests, and trivia games, as well as providing mid-afternoon dance music with the resident dance trio or quartet, serving tea to the accompaniment of a harpist, offering interesting arts and crafts like glass etching, and even presenting guest fashion shows. Commonly, a golf expert sails on board, too, conducting complimentary **group golf lessons** by the driving nets several times per cruise (again, private lessons can be arranged for a fee).

Kudos to the line's **Computer University**—it's really something else. Each ship has a well-stocked computer lab with over 20 computer workstations. On cruises with at least 6 days at sea, complimentary classes are offered on topics like a basic introduction to using the computer, understanding the Internet and the Web, and how to buy a computer. Cruises with fewer sea days also offer guests the opportunity to learn about using e-mail. On all cruises, e-mail access is readily available, so passengers can send and receive e-mails to a special personal address they're given when they get their cruise documents. All computer use is free of charge, except a $5 fee to set up an e-mail account and a charge of $3 every time you send or receive an e-mail up to about seven to eight pages long. There's nothing else as extensive at sea.

CHILDREN'S PROGRAM

Relatively speaking, this is not a line for kids. Crystal is a sophisticated cruise line that focuses its attention on adults. That said, each ship does have a small but bright **children's**

Crystal Fleet Itineraries			
Ship	Home Ports & Season	Itinerary	Other Itineraries
Crystal Harmony	Itineraries between Acapulco and San Juan, Acapulco and New Orleans, Acapulco and Ft. Lauderdale, Acapulco and Barbados, Sept–Dec 1999, and Mar–May and Nov–Dec 2000; Eastern Caribbean itineraries round-trip from Ft. Lauderdale and Barbados Nov, Jan, and Mar.	**11- and 12-night Panama Canal:** May visit Grand Cayman, Caldera (Costa Rica), Aruba, Curaçao, St. Thomas, Barbados, St. Lucia, the Bahamas, Playa del Carmen/Cozumel, and San Blas Islands. **10- and 11-night eastern Carib:** May visit St. Thomas, St. Barts, St. Lucia, Antigua, Sint Maarten, Tortola, and Barbados. **7-night eastern Carib:** Sint Maarten, St. Thomas, Antigua, and St. Lucia.	Alaska, South America
Crystal Symphony	11-night itineraries between Barbados and Acapulco, Acapulco and Fort Lauderdale Nov–Dec 2000; 10-night itinerary round-trip from Fort Lauderdale, Dec 2000.	**11-night Panama Canal:** Curaçao, Aruba, Puerto Caldera (Costa Rica), or Bahamas. **10-night eastern Carib:** St. Thomas, St. Barts, St. Lucia, and Sint Maarten.	World cruise, Mediterranean, Europe

playroom, primarily used during holiday cruises when as many as 20 to 40 kids may be on board. At times like this, **counselors** are on hand to supervise activities for several hours in the morning and in the afternoon (on a recent Easter-time cruise, six counselors were on board to supervise about 35 kids). **Baby-sitting** can be arranged privately through the concierge, but Crystal is not shy about pointing out that they do not offer a day-care service and parents are responsible to make sure their kids are well behaved. Generally, though, you'll find few if any kids on board the majority of Crystal cruises.

ENTERTAINMENT

Any cruise line that's based in Los Angeles, the entertainment capital of the world, is bound to take its onboard cabaret and show times seriously. Shows in the horseshoe-shaped, rather plain Galaxy Lounge encompass everything from **classical concertos** by accomplished pianists to **comedy.** A troupe of spangle-covered lip-synching dancers and a pair of lead singers are likely to do a **Vegas-style performance** based on the hits of Cole Porter or a medley of the best works of Rodgers and Hammerstein. Onboard entertainment is good, but certainly not the high point of the cruise. There sure are lots of options, though.

In addition to the Galaxy show lounge, after dinner each night, a second large, attractive lounge is the venue for **ballroom style dancing** to a live band. There's also a small, separate (and usually empty) **disco** on the *Harmony,* featuring **karaoke** a couple of nights per cruise (on the *Symphony,* the disco is part of the Starlight Club), and a pianist in the dark, paneled, and romantic Avenue Saloon (my favorite room) playing popular show tunes and pop hits from "New York, New York" to "My Funny Valentine" before and after dinner. A **movie theater** shows first-run movies several times a day, and cabin TVs feature a wonderfully varied and full menu of movies each day, listed in the daily schedules under categories such as comedy, classics, arts and documentaries, concerts, and regular first-run movies.

Gamblers will have no problem feeling at home in the roomy **casinos,** which are supervised directly by Caesar's Palace Casinos at Sea (the one on the *Symphony* is nearly twice as large as the one on the *Harmony*).

SERVICE

The hallmark of a high-end cruise like Crystal is its service, so the line's staff is better-trained and more attentive than that aboard most other cruise lines, and is typically of an international cast: The dining room and restaurant staffs hail from Italy, Portugal, and other European countries, and have trained in the grand restaurants of Europe and North America; the pool attendant who brings you a fresh towel and a glass of lemonade, as well as the bartender mixing your martini, is likely to be Filipino; and the cabin stewardess who tidies your stateroom is likely to be from Scandinavia or some other European country like Hungary. Overall, the dining/bar staff is best, outshining the room stewardesses. Without a doubt, service is a high point of the Crystal cruise experience. Even the staff manning the information and concierge desks in the lobby are endlessly good-natured and very helpful—a rare find, indeed.

I might note, the Crystal ships are the only one I've come across that have both a small pool and a hot tub for their crew members (located at the bow of the ship on Deck 5). It pays to keep the crew happy, I guess!

In addition to laundry and dry cleaning services, self-serve laundry rooms are available.

Crystal Harmony • Crystal Symphony

The Verdict

These gracious ships are small enough to feel intimate and personal, yet large enough for a whole range of entertainment, dining, and fitness diversions.

Crystal Harmony *(photo: Crystal Cruises)*

Specifications

Size (in tons)		Number of Passengers	960
Harmony	49,400	Officers	Norwegian/
Symphony	51,044		Japanese/Internat'l
Number of Cabins	480	Crew	545 (Internat'l)
Number of Outside Cabins		Passenger/Crew Ratio	1.7 to 1
Harmony	461	Year Built	
Symphony	480	*Harmony*	1990
Cabins with Verandas		*Symphony*	1995
Harmony	260	Last Major Refurbishment	N/A
Symphony	276		

Frommer's Ratings (Scale of 1–5)

Cabin Comfort & Amenities	4	Pool, Fitness & Spa Facilities	4
Ship Cleanliness & Maintenance	3	Children's Facilities	2
Public Comfort/Space	5	Itinerary	4
Decor	4	Worth the Money	5

Plush, streamlined, extravagantly comfortable, and not as overwhelmingly large as the megaships being launched by less glamorous lines, these ships compete with the hyper-upscale Seabourn vessels, although Crystal's ships are almost five times as large as Seabourn's, with a broader choice of onboard diversions and distractions. *Harmony* has features (like a small casino) that were "corrected" in 1995 with the design of the ship's newer twin, the *Crystal Symphony,* a slightly bigger ship with a larger casino, no inside cabins, and a larger atrium/lobby area. Its two alternative restaurants are on the main entertainment deck with the rest of the action (the *Harmony*'s are on the Lido Deck).

The hub of both ships is the atrium. Impressive and stylish, and less overwhelming than aboard some of the larger mass-market and premium ships, it's where you'll find the concierge, information and shore excursion desk, the Crystal Cove lounge, the ship's chic shops, and the site of the much-awaited midnight buffets, which are presented with fanfare every evening.

Cabins & Rates

Cabins	Per diems from	Bathtub	Fridge	Hair Dryer	Sitting Area	TV
Inside	$201	yes	yes	yes	yes	yes
Outside	$260	yes	yes	yes	yes	yes
Suite	$459	yes	yes	yes	yes	yes

TVs show CNN and ESPN.

CABINS   The smallest, balcony-less cabins aboard *Harmony* begin at 183 square feet and on the *Symphony,* at 202 square feet, a size large enough to incorporate a sofa, coffee table, and desk. Outside staterooms without verandas measure 198 to 215 square feet; those with verandas are 246 square feet (including the veranda). Despite their high price tag, the majority of Crystal's cabins are smaller than the smallest aboard any of the Seabourn vessels (its smallest cabins measure 277 square feet), or even the space within the smallest cabins aboard either of Cunard's *Sea Goddesses* (205 square feet). About half the accommodations have small verandas, measuring about 6 by 8 feet. While drawer space is adequate, the hanging closets are smaller and tighter than you'd expect on ships of this caliber. Bathrooms are compact on the *Harmony* and don't offer a lot of storage space or convenient towel racks; those on the *Symphony* are larger and better designed. The bathrooms are mostly tiled. I found the cabins to be not entirely sound-proofed; I could hear our neighbors talking and hear their television quite easily.

Deck 10 holds the ships' spectacular, attractively styled penthouses; the four best measure nearly 1,000 square feet, including the balconies. The other two categories are about 492 and 360 square feet, including balconies. All have walk-in closets, Jacuzzi bathtubs, and bidets, and the four Crystal penthouses have a full-fledged Jacuzzi in the living room, with an ocean view to boot!

The *Harmony* has 19 inside cabins; the *Symphony* has none. Of the cabins without verandas, most have large rectangular windows; on the *Harmony,* 14 have rounded portholes instead. Each of them is positioned near the bow on Deck 5, below the show lounges, and forward of the ship's main dining room. The E category cabins located amidships on the *Harmony* on Decks 7 and 8, and on the *Symphony* on Deck 8, have views obstructed by lifeboats.

Overall, color schemes are pastels—pinks, mints, blues, and beiges—and golden-brown wood tones, and are cheerful, breezy, and light. All cabins have a sitting area, bathtub (a compact one on the lower category cabins) and shower, TVs broadcasting CNN, ESPN and other channels, VCR, minibar, hair dryer, and safe.

PUBLIC AREAS   Throughout the ship, you'll notice an intensely cultivated sense of craftsmanship, with marble features and brass, glass, and hardwood paneling mingling with flowers and potted plants (especially palms). In that classic California style, the color schemes are light and airy throughout with lots of white and very pastel furniture and walls. Passenger throughways are wide and easy to navigate. The atrium/lobby areas on these ships are miniature, more subdued versions of the glittery megaship atria, but still the most dazzling area of the ships.

Designed with curved walls and low, vaulted ceilings, the ship's main dining rooms are elegant and spacious and done up in light colors. The chunky silverware and heavy crystal glassware twinkle and shine and mirror a sophisticated land-based restaurant. The Jade and Prego alternative restaurants on the *Symphony* are much more interesting and colorful than the *Harmony*'s plainer, almost ordinary decor (although sources tell me a *Harmony* drydock in late spring 2000 will include a facelift to the ship's alternative restaurants).

There are two large entertainment lounges, one for Vegas-style material and another for ballroom dancing to a live band.

The ship has a hushed, somewhat academically charming library that's outfitted with comfortably upholstered chairs and a worthy collection of books, periodicals, and videos. There's also a large theater for movies and slide-lectures.

The ship has six-plus bar/entertainment lounges as well as a roaming staff that wanders the public areas throughout the day and much of the night, offering to bring drinks to wherever you happen to be sitting. The dark Avenue Saloon, where polished mahogany, well-maintained leather upholsteries, and a live pianist draw passengers in, is one of the prime before- and after-dinner cocktail spots (and my personal favorite, by far).

RECREATION & FITNESS FACILITIES   These ships offer a lot of outdoor activities and spacious areas in which to do them. There are two outdoor swimming pools separated by a bar, ice-cream bar, and sandwich grill, as well as two hot tubs. One of the pools is refreshingly oversized, stretching almost 40 feet across one of the sundecks. The other has a swim-up bar and can be covered with a retractable glass roof. The gym and separate aerobics area are positioned for a view over the sea and the adjacent Steiner-managed spa and beauty salon are sizeable.

There's also a pair of golf driving nets, a putting green, a large paddle-tennis court, and Ping-Pong tables. Runners and walkers, note: Just under four laps equals 1 mile on the broad, uninterrupted teak Promenade Deck.

The ships' generous tiered after-decks are gorgeous and provide quiet places for an afternoon spent dozing in a deck chair or for quiet repose leaning against the railing and allowing yourself to become entranced by the ship's wake.

Cunard

SHIPS   Caronia • Queen Elizabeth 2

6100 Blue Lagoon Dr., Miami, FL 33126. ☎ **800/5-CUNARD** or 305/463-3000. Fax 305/269-6950. www.cunardline.com.

THE LINE IN A NUTSHELL   Cunard is the biggest consumer of caviar on earth—get the picture? Catering to a wealthy, well-traveled clientele, the line offers an onboard experience that's high-brow British all the way.

THE EXPERIENCE   Can you say "history"? Can you say "God Save the Queen"? Cunard, about 160 years old at this writing, is a bona fide cultural icon, a tangible reminder of the days when Britannia really did rule the waves, and that's what sets it apart from the pack. From the formal, British-style service to the decor, which through artwork and memorabilia pays tribute to England and Cunard's long history, the experience is nostalgic and genteel. Activities are relatively mellow, featuring enrichment lectures, ship tours, reading, and movies. Likewise, entertainment features pianists, singers, live dance bands, and lots of conversation and cocktails. Passengers participate at their own pace. Dining is a formal affair, one of the day's main events, and guests dress the part.

Cunard currently has two ships in its fleet, the classic *QE2* and the *Caronia* (the former *Vistafjord,* only recently renamed). The *QE2* recalls the great ocean liner days of decades ago—among other reasons, because it was built decades ago (in 1969). Both ships are scheduled for extensive refurbishment in late 1999, and it's needed. The *QE2* just turned 30, and when I was aboard in early 1999 I couldn't help but notice some waterstained ceilings, a musty feeling on the lower decks, and a hodgepodge of cabin decor—the wrinkles and accumulated clutter of age.

Pros

- **British flavor.** If you're a fan of Britain and things British, sailing Cunard is the next best thing to being there. The onboard ambience is quiet, sedate, and ever so polite.
- **Service.** Overall, service is highly professional, efficient, and nonintrusive.
- **History.** These ships evoke the past with their decor, staff, and proud nautical histories, making for a special, comforting, nostalgic, and educational experience.

Cons

- **Ships show their age.** Although both ships are slated for multimillion-dollar facelifts in late 1999, they're older ships and can't hide their wrinkles completely.
- **Few verandas.** The *QE2* has only 33 and the *Caronia* just 25.
- **Staid.** If you're not looking for a mellow, low-key jaunt, you'll likely be bored with the slow, almost solemn pace.

Frommer's Ratings: Cunard					
	Poor	Fair	Good	Excellent	Outstanding
Enjoyment Factor					✓
Dining				✓	
Activities				✓	
Children's Program				✓*	
Entertainment				✓	
Service			✓		
Overall Value				✓	

* *QE2 only.*

CUNARD: THE OLD GUARD LIVES ON

Soon after the mid-1998 announcement that Cunard's owners had sold the company to none other than the savvy Carnival Corporation, grand plans began to be hatched, the biggest being the merging of Cunard with Carnival's ultra-luxurious Seabourn line. According to the plan (which was still being implemented as this book went to press), the smaller ships in Cunard's fleet—the two *Sea Goddesses* and the *Royal Viking Sun*—would be transferred to Seabourn and renamed the *Seabourn Goddesses* and the *Seabourn Sun,* respectively. This will leave Cunard with two ships, the famous *QE2* and the newly renamed *Caronia* (formerly *Vistafjord*). A third ship, dubbed "Project Queen Mary" (at least for now), is in the planning stages.

The point to all of this? Creating two distinct upscale brands—Cunard's *QE2* and *Caronia* offering old-world, British-style big-ship cruising and Seabourn's modern Scandinavian style of cruising on small, intimate ships.

To get ready for the rebranding and the new millennium, the *QE2* will go into a month-long drydock in November 1999 for an $18 million sprucing up. All penthouses and cabins will be redesigned, and all the restaurants will be improved. For instance, the Caronia Restaurant will have a new table layout, dumbwaiters, new music system, new chairs, new chandeliers, and a new entrance. "All designs are sensitive to the vessel's heritage and regal atmosphere," says Cunard Line Limited's president, Larry Pimentel. At year-end 1999, the *Vistafjord* will undergo a $5 million transformation into the *Caronia,* getting a new navy-blue hull as well as British-flavored carpeting, wall coverings, and a general overhaul of the furnishings throughout her public areas and cabins.

To get to this exciting time in Cunard's life, this resurrection of sorts, the line has had to go through its share of turbulence, doubt, and monumental change. Once upon a time, Cunard was the absolute king of the seas, operating ships whose names still carry the ring of luxury, grandeur, and the power of the British Empire in the fullness of its maturity: *Mauretania, Berengaria, Queen Mary.* Today, the line continues to carry formidable prestige, and its famous flagship, the *QE2,* remains the most famous passenger ship in the world, and the only ship offering transatlantic service on a regular schedule.

Things have changed, though. Once the most British of companies, Cunard has been based in the United States since 1997, first in New York, and then—shocker of shockers!—moving in 1997 to Miami. As if that were not enough to make Queen Victoria turn in her grave, there was the sale to Carnival Corporation in 1998. What at first glance seemed like an incredibly unlikely pairing (and humorous, too), has turned out to be a savvy business decision in many ways. Cunard, which had not made money for years, is now in the black, reportedly earning some $35 million in 1998. Carnival Corp. is a well-oiled machine, and remember, it also owns Holland America Line, and has managed to lend that line its considerable managerial talents while maintaining some semblance of its Dutch character. This, no doubt, is part of Carnival's astounding success: It knows when to leave a good thing alone—brand and experience-wise—all the while injecting its efficient management and operations, greater economies of scale, and mondo capital.

To understand the significance of the Cunard-Carnival marriage, a short history lesson might be valuable. In 1977, in a move widely criticized at the time as the sellout of part of Britain's national heritage, Cunard's headquarters were moved from London to New York; in the years that followed, Cunard's sometimes stuffy, sometimes haughty management style caused backlashes of resentment from scores of travel industry insiders, including such highly vocal employees as Peter Ward, who ruled the Cunard empire briefly and who publicly condemned the secretive and indecisive fiefdoms that competed within the line's corporate labyrinth. Even travel agents, a group that cruise lines tend to pamper and court, loudly criticized Cunard's clerical workers for their lack of helpfulness and clarity. Despite all this, the prestige and undeniable glamour of Cunard kept it going and helped it grow, and Cunard responded by buying a flotilla of ships from other carriers.

In 1983, Cunard bought the Norwegian American Line, in the process acquiring a pair of ships, the *Sagafjord* (which was subsequently sold in 1996) and the *Vistafjord* (to be named *Caronia* by year-end 1999). In 1986, the company obtained its most consistently luxurious and upscale vessels: the sedate and yacht-like *Sea Goddess I* and *Sea Goddess II* (which are going to Seabourn in late 1999). In 1992, Cunard added another luxury worldwide cruise ship, the *Royal Viking Sun* (also going to Seabourn).

Cunard has been no stranger to hardship. In the mid '90s streaks of bad luck involved a series of engineering, managerial, and logistical mishaps that wreaked havoc with the *QE2* and other Cunard ships, and with the line's teetering reputation. In 1995, the same year that Cunard declared a $25 million loss, the line's parent company, Trafalgar, was bought by the Kvaerner Group, a Norwegian engineering and shipbuilding concern with a strong presence in London and a controlling interest in Finland's massive Kvaerner Masa Shipyards.

Interestingly, Kvaerner had bought Trafalgar mainly for its engineering divisions, and had little interest in retaining Cunard. When it was unable to sell the line, however, Kvaerner moved to cut costs and simultaneously re-emphasize Cunard as a cruise line for the affluent and demanding, selling its most downscale ship, the *Cunard Countess,* and ending its operation of the *Cunard Dynasty.* (After a stretch with NCL, that ship is now scheduled to sail for a new venture being launched by Commodore Holdings—see the Commodore review in chapter 7, "Cheap Cruises, Older Ships: The Budget Lines," for details.) That same year Cunard downsized its staff and moved from New York to Miami. These moves apparently paid off: For the first time in 4 years, Cunard posted a profit in 1997—a fact that no doubt convinced Carnival that Cunard was ripe for the picking. On June 5, 1998, Carnival plucked. Today, Cunard's future looks bright indeed.

THE FLEET

The new Cunard includes the 1,500-passenger, 70,327-ton **QE2,** built in 1969. The 24,492-ton, 677-passenger **Caronia,** the former *Vistafjord,* was built in 1973 and will undergo an extensive refurbishment in late 1999 in preparation for quite a few Caribbean sailings in 2000. (I've included a preview at the end of this review detailing what the "new" *Caronia* will offer.)

Cunard has something new on the way, too. Dubbed **Project Queen Mary,** the buzz is that Cunard is going to build a brand-new *Queen Mary* to re-create the grandeur of the old Queen liners. Although at press time plans weren't finalized, according to Larry Pimentel, president and CEO of Cunard Line Limited, the line's objective is "nothing less than to create a new Golden Age of sea travel for those who missed the first. The ship itself will be a bit of a maritime museum." The skinny is that the ship will be similar in profile and ambience to the *QE2,* but larger and more modern. Sources say the new grand ole liner will cost a whopping $600 million to build and could be launched as soon as 2003. By early 1999, a letter of intent with a shipyard had not yet been signed, and Asian shipyards were looking increasingly attractive because the major European ones are booked up through 2003.

PASSENGER PROFILE

Cunard attracts a well-traveled, soft-spoken crowd of older passengers, many of them repeaters, generally in their 50s and on up. They're usually the type who would prefer a 4pm tea to a communal soak in a hot tub with a bottle of tequila and a gaggle of strangers. They appreciate Cunard's old-timey virtues. Passengers are typically of an Anglophile bent, and many UK folks sail this line. There are mostly couples, but also

---

Tips on Tipping: Cunard

At press time, Cunard was set to introduce a new tipping policy to go into effect by January 2000. Instead of passengers tipping in cash at the end of the cruise (as is done with most lines), gratuities will be added to each guests' shipboard account at a rate of $10 to $13 per day, depending on your accommodation. At the end of the cruise, guests can adjust the amount depending on their view of the service.

---

many widows and widowers, as well as friends and relatives traveling together. Gentlemanly hosts are on board to chat and dance with single ladies.

Cunard probably carries more clients who sail just for the pleasures of sea- and stargazing than any other line. If you crave solitude and the healing powers of a sojourn at sea, no Cunard staff member will ever disturb your quietude.

DINING

The *QE2* has its own unique dining setup, like no other ship that exists today. **Five reserved-seat restaurants** are assigned according to the cabin accommodation you've chosen. The Queen's Grill is the crème de la crème and is located high on the Boat Deck. The virtually identical Princess Grill and Britannia Grill are smaller, tiered, and facing port and starboard respectively, while the large high-ceiling Caronia Restaurant is more like a traditional ocean liner dining room. The sprawling but nicely partitioned two-sitting Mauretania Restaurant is reserved for the lowest-priced cabins.

Menu choices are basically the same across all the restaurants, although more is available at the Queen's Grill. Expect to see a traditional American roast beef and an English cut with Yorkshire pudding, grilled Dover sole, médaillons of veal in a marsala sauce, poached salmon with shallots, or sliced breast of duck with raspberry sauce.

Because they serve fewer passengers, presentation is generally more sophisticated in the grill rooms. **Special orders** are no problem in the Queen's Grill, and you can request dishes you might have seen on earlier menus or something you've dreamed up on your own. At dinnertime on its transatlantic crossings, this ship can be one of the most formal afloat, with guests dressed to the nines, especially in the grill rooms. In the Caribbean, though, formality and fanciness are a bit more toned down.

If you want to go more casual, the large Lido **buffet-style restaurant** for breakfast, lunch, and dinner has several well-laid-out stations (successfully reducing queues) with lots of variety and attractive presentation. The Pavilion, one deck below, is the venue for a light continental breakfast or a simple hamburger/hot dog grill lunch.

Vegetarian and health-conscious dishes are available.

The *Caronia*'s elegant Franconia dining room serves the ship's well-dressed passengers some of the best food afloat at one unhurried sitting. There are lots of tables for two. Tivoli, a 40-seat reservations-only restaurant with its own kitchen, offers an all-Italian dinner menu and wine list and sea views over the stern. Buffets are set up in the indoor/outdoor Lido Cafe and by the pool.

There is 24-hour **room service** aboard both ships.

ACTIVITIES

In addition to cards, trivia games, and reading, the *QE2* offers its own unique agenda of activities. The ship's popular **lecture program** features a wide range of speakers, some well known and others just very good at what they do, on diverse topics such as an author's latest book (which is available for purchase and a signing at the library, natch), producing a movie, investing in the stock market, foreign affairs, how to shop for bargains in New York, and ocean liner history. There are regular classes in the **Computer**

Ship	Home Ports & Season	Itinerary	Other Itineraries
Cunard Fleet Itineraries			
Caronia	6-, 7-, and 9-night eastern Carib between Ft. Lauderdale and Barbados, Mar–May; 13-night Carib round-trip from Ft. Lauderdale, Apr.	**6-, 7-, and 9-night eastern Carib:** May visit Bahamas, St. Croix, Antigua, St. Lucia, Dominica, St. Kitts, Puerto Rico, Guadeloupe, and Tortola. **13-night Carib:** New Orleans, Cozumel, Port Antonio (Jamaica), St. Croix, Tortola, Bahamas.	Trans-atlantic, Canary Islands, Brazil/Amazon, Europe/Africa
Queen Elizabeth 2	12-nighter from New York to Miami, Oct '99; 7-nighter round-trip from Miami, Nov '99.	**12-night eastern/southern Carib:** Miami, Nassau, Aruba, partial Panama Canal transit, Cartagena (Colombia), St. Thomas, and Miami. **7-night eastern Carib:** Sint Maarten, St. Kitts, San Juan, and St. Thomas.	Trans-atlantic, Europe, Eastern Canada/New England.

Learning Center, and the rooms are open for those who already know what they're doing. A member of the staff will take passengers on the ship's **Heritage Trail,** which details Cunard's 160-year history in original oil paintings, trophies, and collected memorabilia, including a wonderful photo display of the famous passengers who have crossed on Cunard ships.

Out on deck, activities include a **putting green** and **golf driving net,** a combo basketball and paddle tennis court, shuffleboard, and an outdoor pool.

The *QE2*'s library may very well be the biggest at sea, with a large section of books to borrow and another with books for sale.

Both Cunard vessels have a **casino,** although they're nothing like the electronic, glittering mini-Vegases you find aboard the more high-charged Carnival ships.

Given the ambience Cunard is striving to create under its new ownership, activities aboard the refurbished *Caronia* should roughly parallel those aboard the *QE2* (although changes still in the works at press time make it impossible for me to say this with certainty).

CHILDREN'S PROGRAM

While you're not likely to encounter hordes of them, it's not uncommon to see a handful of kids, mostly grandkids, on board for Cunard's Caribbean itineraries, and the Christmas cruise attracts lots of children.

On the *QE2* there are **supervised programs** and an excellent nursery and **children's playroom,** with cute tiny furniture and games, staffed by well-trained English-style nannies. Kids will enjoy visits to the pet kennels, just next door, as well as activities like a captain's Coketail party, kids' talent show, a costume party in the Grand Lounge with lots of prizes, magic shows, tea parties, and tours of the ship. The ship is large enough to keep kids entertained and busy even without a lot of organized activities.

On the *Caronia,* supervised children's programs are offered for children between 7 and 14 when there are at least 15 children on board.

Baby-sitting can be arranged privately with a staff member.

ENTERTAINMENT

The *QE2*'s Grand Lounge is not set up for big Vegas-style production shows, but the smaller acts performed there are decent. Throughout the ship are cabaret acts, singers, small bands, large bands, cocktail and classical pianists, a harpist, and even karaoke. There's a great house band for dancing the fox trot, jitterbug, tango, and waltz in the Queen's Room, a traditional ballroom. There are always gentlemanly hosts sailing on board to dance and chat with single ladies. Throughout the ship are nearly a dozen bars and entertainment lounges, and the Golden Lion Pub is always a favorite watering hole. The ship's library stocks videos for in-cabin viewing by suite passengers (and there's a large movie theater as well, if the big screen serves you better).

The *Caronia* offers the same type of elegant, understated entertainment as her bigger sister, with after-dinner concerts in the Garden Lounge and shows and big-band dancing in the spacious, high-ceilinged ballroom. Amidships is a proper movie theater for first-run films and special-interest lectures.

SERVICE

Overall, service is efficient and first-class; however, in that British way, it's quiet and not gushing. Things can get a bit harried in the *QE2*'s two-sitting Mauretania Restaurant (the truth is, the *QE2* is a hard ship to work because of the long distances to and from the galleys).

Caronia

The Verdict

As this vessel is being extensively refurbished at press time, I'll save the verdict for next year. For now, safe to say that it'll offer an experience similar to the *QE2*, but on a smaller scale.

Caronia *(photo: Cunard)*

Specifications

Size (in tons)	24,492	Officers	British/European
Number of Cabins	376	Crew	400 (mostly European)
Number of Outside Cabins	324		
Cabins with Verandas	25	Passenger/Crew Ratio	1.6 to 1
Number of Passengers	679	Year Built	1973
		Last Major Refurbishment	1999

Frommer's Ratings (Scale of 1–5)*

Cabin Comfort & Amenities	N/A	Pool, Fitness & Spa Facilities	N/A
Ship Cleanliness & Maintenance	N/A	Children's Facilities	N/A
Public Comfort/Space	N/A	Itinerary	N/A
Decor	N/A	Worth the Money	N/A

As the Caronia *is still being refurbished and re-created at this writing, ratings are not yet possible.*

Originally completed in 1973 as the *Vistafjord*, the ship is a true ocean liner known for its sophisticated long-voyage cruising, catering to older, well-heeled Americans, Germans, and British. Today, the 679-passenger, 24,492-ton ship's tradition lives on, albeit renamed and spruced up. At press time, new Cunard owners Carnival Corporation are set to give her a major $5 million refit in late 1999, transforming her into the *Caronia*, complete with British registry and a midnight-blue Cunard hull. This *Caronia* will be the third ship in Cunard's history to bear that name (the first sailed from 1905 to 1931; the second from 1948 until 1970) and is intended, like the *QE2*, to provide a traditionally British experience, with British officers (who will serve aboard the *QE2* on an alternating basis) and a 400-member, mostly European staff.

Cabins & Rates

Cabins	Per diems from	Bathtub	Fridge	Hair Dryer	Sitting Area	TV
Inside	n/a	no	yes	yes	no	yes*
Outside	$229	no	yes	yes	no	yes*
Suite	$665	some	yes	yes	yes	yes*

TVs show CNN. All cabins have VCRs.

CABINS   Most of the 376 cabins are outsides, and all are designed for longer voyages, with spacious floor plans and plentiful stowage. The detailed cabin plans are well worth studying because of the intriguing variety of arrangements. All cabins have light wood accents, TVs with VCRs, two-music channels, phones, safes, minibars, robes, fresh fruit daily, and bottles of sparkling wine upon embarkation. Many cabins on Promenade Deck overlook the open side deck, and some Sun Deck cabin views are obstructed by lifeboats. Some cabins in the top aduplex suites are among the nautical world's best, featuring glass-enclosed lounges with treadmills and indoor-outdoor hot tubs on upper levels and bedrooms with hot tubs below.

Single travelers have more accommodation options aboard this ship than any other afloat, with a choice of 73 dedicated single cabins. Most of these are outside, and half have bathtubs.

As aboard the *QE2*, suite guests have minibars stocked with two bottles of wine or liquor of their choice (and replenished on request). Otherwise, wine, liquors, beer, and soft drinks in the other cabins and throughout the ship's public rooms are available for purchase.

PUBLIC AREAS   *Caronia's* public rooms represent understated European elegance. The forward circular Garden Lounge, with its lovely semicircular bands of colored lights recessed in the ceiling, is the place for proper afternoon tea and after-dinner concerts. The spacious, high-ceilinged ballroom offers shows and big-band dancing on a large wooden floor. Gentleman hosts provide company and act as dance partners for ladies traveling alone. Side galleries provide intimate spaces for the Golden Lion Pub (replacing the North Cape Bar), mahogany-paneled library, bookshop, and casino. Amidships is a proper movie theater for first-run films and special-interest lectures, and the aft-facing Piccadilly nightclub doubles as a daytime retreat for readers, who revel in the views over the Veranda Deck pool.

RECREATION & FITNESS FACILITIES   In addition to the pool on the Veranda Deck, a second pool lies deep within the hull in a complex that includes a gym, sauna, and massage facility. Deck space is good and the favored place for outdoor reading is the wide teak promenade beneath the lifeboats (there are tucked-away spots all over the upper decks as well).

Queen Elizabeth 2

The Verdict

For the past two decades, this grand dame has been the only game in town for a traditional, regularly scheduled transatlantic crossing, and she gives passengers that same wonderful ocean liner feel and nostalgic British flavor when at sea en route to Bermuda and the Caribbean.

QE2 (photo: Cunard)

Specifications

Size (in tons)	70,327	Officers	British/European
Number of Cabins	931	Crew	1,000 (Internat'l)
Number of Outside Cabins	625	Passenger/Crew Ratio	1.8 to 1
Cabins with Verandas	33	Year Built	1969
Number of Passengers	1,789	Last Major Refurbishment	1999

Frommer's Ratings (Scale of 1–5)

Cabin Comfort & Amenities	3	Pool, Fitness & Spa Facilities	4
Ship Cleanliness & Maintenance	3	Children's Facilities	3
Public Comfort/Space	4	Itinerary	4
Decor	4	Worth the Money	5

The *Queen Elizabeth 2* turned 30 in 1999 and is still doing what she was designed for, providing a fast transatlantic crossing (she remains the only ship doing so on a regular schedule) and undertaking a series of short and long cruises to the Caribbean and Bermuda from both the U.S. and U.K. Her high speed allows her to get to the Caribbean more quickly than nearly all other ships. At press time, the ship was slated to undergo a major refurbishment to the tune of $18 million, which will include a substantial facelift to all her public areas and staterooms, which were renovated in a piecemeal fashion in the past. Happily, with these renovations and the $65 million worth of refittings made in '94 and '96, she is sailing into the millennium in terrific shape, sporting her classic ocean liner's midnight blue hull, spotless white superstructure, and the famous Cunard red-orange and black funnel.

The ship has an intensely loyal following, with passengers coming back year after year. They'll even book the same cabin and dine in the same restaurant, often even at the same table. There are also those who come once to say they have done it, and may never come again.

Cabins & Rates

Cabins	Per diems from	Bathtub	Fridge	Hair Dryer	Sitting Area	TV
Inside	$130	no	no	no	no	yes*
Outside	$162	some	some	some	some	yes*
Suite	$448	yes	yes	yes	yes	yes*

*TVs show CNN.

CABINS   Being an older ship originally designed for two classes, there's a huge range of cabin accommodations, and layout and decorative variations within a single category. The ship's year-end refit will greatly redo the cabins and the bathrooms, creating a more cohesive look.

The high-up veranda cabins were added to the ship over the years, and they are in a separate penthouse location, effectively cut off from the rest of the ship. The midships Deck One and Two Q3 Grades were the top accommodations when the ship was new, and they remain the preferred choice for traditionalists who want an authentic steamship cabin. They have wood paneling, satin padded walls, a large elliptical window or three elliptical portholes, walk-in closets/dressing rooms, a corner for a standing steamer trunk, and a large marble bathroom with full-sized tub and bidet.

The mid-priced Princess and Caronia Grade cabins are also roomy for this level, while the lowest priced are deep in the ship and relatively tight, with many inside, including some with upper and lower berths. However, they provide moderately priced accommodations for those who could otherwise not afford the ship. During rough weather conditions, the portholes on Five Deck may be sealed by metal covers called "deadlights."

All cabins have TVs showing CNN, lots of movies, and even Cunard history films, and many outside cabins have sitting rooms, bathtubs, and mini-fridges. Top suites have VCRs. Views from some of the cabins on the Sports and Boat Decks are partially obstructed by lifeboats.

Over 100 cabins are designated for singles, and four cabins are specially equipped for wheelchair users, although parts of the ship have small steps and raised doorways.

PUBLIC AREAS   Nearly all the public rooms range over two complete decks (Upper and Quarter Decks) and offer a great variety of venues for socializing, reading, and special functions. Every public room has been redone several times over, so the decor is now both traditional and up-to-date but not dated, using effects like burled wood paneling, royal blue carpets, art deco–style room dividers in the Mauretania Restaurant, a teak deck in the Yacht Club bar, and etched glass and wood partitions in the Golden Lion Pub. The Chart Room, a lovely two-part lounge bar, has a harpist alternating with a pianist playing the room's centerpiece: the grand piano from the old *Queen Mary.*

Cunard's heritage is all over the ship, fortunately. Before the 1994 refit, much of what now makes the ship so special and grand—memorabilia and art—apparently had not been deemed fashionable enough to display. Times have changed, though, and the past is in vogue again. Most notable are huge oil paintings in the central stairway of Queen Elizabeth that the Queen Mother commissioned for the former Royal Mail Ship (RMS) *Queen Elizabeth* and another of Princess Elizabeth and Prince Philip that once hung in the main lounge of the old green-hulled world cruiser *Caronia,* which sailed from 1948 until the early 1970s. The 10-foot lighted scale model of the record breaking *Mauretania,* the fastest ship on the Atlantic for over two decades, is a showstopper in the same foyer, and nearby is a large oil painting showing the same ship coming down the River Tyne near Newcastle, England, where she was built. The aft stairway is a two-deck gallery of original paintings by two artists (one being Stephen Card) showing Cunard ships from the line's 160-year history.

Cunard's history is also captured in several museum-quality display cases throughout the ship, which hold Cunard memorabilia like table settings, old tickets, brochures, and luggage tags, and a nostalgic collection of photos of VIPS—celebrities, politicians and heads of state who have sailed on the venerated Cunard ships over the course of the century. There are also trophies and posters on display, as well as historical tidbits about the *QE2's* life as a troopship during the Falkland Islands War, for instance. To explore all of it, a member of staff takes passengers on a tour called the "Heritage Trail" and hands out brief write-ups on the collections.

A medical center staffed by doctors and nurses is available.

There are self-service laundry rooms.

RECREATION & FITNESS FACILITIES The *QE2* has four hot tubs and two pools, one indoors on a lower deck with the spa and gym and the other located on the ship's classic tiered aft decks, which fill up quickly (as do the limited deck chairs) during sunny days at sea. The best location for a deck chair is on the Sun Deck because it's sheltered from the wind by a surrounding glass enclosure and is somewhat off the beaten track.

Steiner runs the spa and fitness facilities; although they're complete in the range of offerings, they are deep down in the hull, with the spa on Six Deck and the gymnasium and indoor pool (a rarity these days) on Seven Deck. The Spa offers a ten-station AquaSpa as well as treatment rooms, sauna, and massage. The gym positioned alongside the glassed-in pool has the typical range of treadmills, cycles, and stretching machines, and for active types, there are aerobics classes and daily forced-march hikes out on deck.

Deck facilities include a putting green and golf driving net, a combo basketball (don't expect this one to get much use!) and paddle tennis court, and shuffleboard.

Radisson Seven Seas Cruises

SHIPS Radisson Diamond • Seven Seas Navigator (preview)

600 Corporate Dr., Suite 410, Fort Lauderdale, FL 33334. ☎ **800/285-1835** or 954/776-6123. Fax 954/772-3763.

THE LINE IN A NUTSHELL Radisson carries passengers in style and extreme comfort. Its brand of luxury is casually elegant and somewhat subtle, its cuisine near the top.

THE EXPERIENCE These ships are spacious, and service is supreme. Unlike most of the other high-end ships these days, extras like tips, wine with dinner, stocked minibars (stocked once, at least), and unlimited soft drinks and mineral waters are included in the rates. Both the *Radisson Diamond* and the *Seven Seas Navigator* have all outside cabins, and well over half of them have private balconies. Cuisine is some of the best at sea, and in addition to their formal restaurants, both ships have alternative, reservations-only restaurants specializing in Northern Italian food. Even if what tickles your fancy isn't on the menu, the chef will prepare it for you. There isn't a staff member aboard who wouldn't go out of his or her way to ensure that you have the best time. You can hardly walk anywhere on ship without staff members asking if there's something they can do for you.

These surprisingly informal ships tend to be less stuffy, less snooty, and a bit more casual than Seabourn and Cunard. You can chuck your tux for the most part.

Pros

- **Few extra charges.** Unlike most of its peers, Radisson includes tips, wine at dinner, unlimited soft drinks and mineral water, and an initial stocked minibar in its cruise rates. The only charges are for alcoholic beverages and shore excursions.
- **Lots of private verandas.** In fact, 75% of cabins have them.
- **Great dining.** Cuisine is superb, and aboard the *Diamond,* there's just one open seating for all meals in one of the most beautiful dining rooms afloat.
- **Speedy 24-hour room service.** It's so fast, your order may be at the door before your phone's handset hits the cradle.

Cons

- **Few windows on the Diamond.** This boxy vessel has much underutilized space, and many key public rooms are somewhat cold and have no windows.
- **Few activities.** Pray for good weather on days at sea since activities are minimal.
- **Limited entertainment.** Onboard entertainment is provided mainly by the crew, along with a few pro crooners or instrumentalists. It's good, but doesn't measure up to the rest of the experience.

Frommer's Ratings: Radisson Seven Seas					
	Poor	Fair	Good	Excellent	Outstanding
Enjoyment Factor					✓
Dining					✓
Activities		✓			
Children's Program	N/A*				
Entertainment			✓		
Service				✓	
Overall Value				✓	

Radisson has no children's program.

RADISSON: INFORMAL ELEGANCE

In 1992, Minneapolis-based Radisson Hotels Worldwide began a venture that has evolved into Radisson Seven Seas Cruises, a line that markets and manages (but in many cases does not own) a mini-armada of widely different though usually luxurious ships, including the ultra-top-notch *Radisson Diamond* (the subject of this review), the globe-trotting *Song of Flower,* and the brand-new *Paul Gauguin,* which spends the whole year in Polynesia. It also markets a few Antarctica sailings on the *Hanseatic.* All of them are either mainstream luxury vessels or niche-market vessels catering to affluent travelers headed to the Amazon or Antarctica. Of them, only the *Diamond* spends significant time in the Caribbean, but it's created such a stir since its much-publicized 1992 launch that it's enabled Radisson to become a highly visible force within the Caribbean luxury cruise market. The *Seven Seas Navigator,* still under construction at this writing at the T. Mariotti shipyard in Genoa, Italy, will be sailing Panama Canal and Bermuda itineraries after its launch, which is scheduled for August 1999, just as this book hits the stores. The ship will be Italian flagged.

THE FLEET

Radisson Seven Seas operates a diverse four-ship fleet, with the 350-passenger, 20,000-ton, 1992-built **Radisson Diamond** the only ship spending any time in the Caribbean. Carrying only 350 passengers, the ship has such an unusual design that it tends to stop traffic. Designed and built by a group of Finnish investors at a price of around $125 million, and purchased outright by Radisson in 1997, it is basically a gigantic catamaran, its vast, wide shell supported by a pair of submarine-like hulls that are 28 feet in diameter and 123 feet longer than a football field. The six-deck superstructure they support rides 28 feet above the water and is 103 feet wide by 420 feet long. Compare that to Cunard's *QE2,* which is 963 feet long, but only 2 feet wider than the *Diamond.*

From its snub nose to its hydraulically lowered marina in the stern, the boxy-looking ship is a show-stopper, although more for its unusualness than for a really ship-like beauty of line. Once on board, though, passengers find some of the most carefully crafted interiors, most upscale amenities, and most superb cuisine afloat. As such, the ship has become a favorite of North America–based big-ticket spenders, many of them repeaters. It has also become a favorite choice for full charters (which must be arranged at least a year in advance) and oceangoing conventions. So many top business executives from Fortune 500 companies have conducted meetings aboard the *Diamond* that industry pundits have occasionally referred to it as "The Write-Off Boat." The vessel is intimate enough, and its staff is savvy enough, to pull off such combinations of business and pleasure with high style.

The 180-passenger, 8,282-ton **Song of Flower** sails exotic itineraries worldwide, including Europe, the Mediterranean, and the Far East. The 188-passenger, 9,000-ton **Hanseatic** is the line's luxurious expedition ship, sailing worldwide from the Arctic to Antarctica, South America, and Africa. The 320-passenger, 18,800-ton **Paul Gauguin** spends the year doing 7-night cruises in French Polynesia. At press time, a fifth ship, and the line's largest, the 490-passenger, 30,000-ton **Seven Seas Navigator,** was scheduled to enter service in late August 1999.

PASSENGER PROFILE

This line appeals primarily to well-traveled and well-heeled passengers in their 50s and 60s, but younger passengers pepper the mix. It's perfect for passengers with sophisticated tastes who appreciate a somewhat less formal ambience and don't need napkin-folding classes to entertain them during the day.

One Good Deal, One Added Cost

Solo Passenger Rates: The solo cruiser pays about $600 over the regular rates for a 5-night Caribbean cruise. **Port Charges Cost Extra:** Unlike most lines, port charges are not included in the cruise rates and will run you about $100 to $125 for a 5- or 6-night cruise aboard the vessel's Caribbean itineraries.

In the Caribbean, passengers are mainly American, although there is a contingent of foreign nationals. Honeymooners are common, but no special arrangements or programs are available for them. Most of *Diamond*'s passengers cruise frequently, and many have been on Seabourn. Many have explored larger ships like Crystal and even Princess and Carnival's *Destiny,* but most prefer small-ship experiences.

Some passengers traveling independently complain that the *Diamond* is too heavily oriented to conventioneers, as it was almost exclusively after its debut. Even so, most conventioneers are top executives or top producers for their organizations, who fit very well into the ship's passenger demographics. Nevertheless, when a sizable group is on board, the group might take over the lounge, and other passengers might feel excluded. To avoid this, Radisson tries not to book more than three corporate groups at a time onto any sailing.

DINING

Superb menus are designed for a sophisticated palate, and include some of the best cuisine in the cruise industry. The highest-quality ingredients include the freshest fish at sea, and dishes like sushi are offered.

You might start with chilled snow crab claws or a medley of California rolls, followed by a chilled cantaloupe bisque or Filipino shrimp soup, and then maybe a spinach salad. **Main courses** might include grilled sea bass with a mango chutney, double-broiled tournedos of beef with a béarnaise and peppercorn sauce, or grilled scallops on a bed of leeks. Each evening's menu on the *Radisson Diamond* includes a wok special, a **light choice,** and chef's special and sumptuous (though too rich) entrees.

The Grand Dining Room has an open seating policy for all meals. The Grill, a splendid and very popular indoor/outdoor setting, offers a variety of beautifully presented foods at breakfast and lunches, focusing on a theme such as Scandinavian, Asian, or seafood. Each evening, the Grill transforms into Don Vito's, one of the liveliest reservations-only **alternative dining venues** you're likely to encounter at sea, with singing waiters belting out "O Sole Mio" and inviting you to join in. It's perhaps the most fun experience you'll have on board. Its fixed multi-course menu changes daily, and may feature farfalle with fresh tomato, eggplant and mozzarella, risotto with pumpkin and truffle flavor, or a veal tenderloin with pine nut sauce. The room seats only about 55, so don't dawdle in making your reservations.

In addition to a fixed **24-hour room service menu,** there is a full breakfast menu (real aficionados might want to stay clear of the bagels), and during dinner hours, a full restaurant menu, delivered course by course to passengers in their cabins. Plus you can always get virtually anything on request.

Specialty coffees are complimentary any time.

ACTIVITIES

Days are basically unstructured, with most passengers lazing around the pool deck. Those bored by simple sun worship can fine-tune their golf swing under the tutelage of a **PGA pro.** However, there really are very few diversions aboard beyond bingo, cards, dance lessons, art auctions, and an occasional **enrichment lecture.**

Radisson Fleet Itineraries

Ship	Home Ports & Season	Itinerary	Other Itineraries
Radisson Diamond	6-night itineraries from San Juan, round-trip Nov; 7-night Panama Canal, San Juan to Balboa, Panama, Nov; 7-, 8-, and 10- night between Puntarenas (Costa Rica) and San Juan or Puntarenas and Aruba, Dec–Feb; 7-night eastern Carib, Feb.	**6-night eastern Carib:** Martinique, St. Kitts, Barbados, and St. Thomas. **7-night Panama Canal:** Aruba, Cartagena (Colombia), San Blas Islands (Panama), and Puntarenas (Costa Rica). **7-, 8-, and 10-night Panama Canal:** May visit San Blas Islands (Panama), Cartagena (Colombia), Aruba, Curaçao, and St. Thomas. **7-night eastern Carib:** Grenada, Barbados, Martinique, St. Kitts, and St. Thomas.	Europe, Mediter-ranean
Seven Seas Navigator	7-, 9-, and 10-night Panama Canal between Ft. Lauderdale and Puntarenas (Costa Rica) or San Juan and Puntarenas, Jan–Apr; 9-night Bermuda round-trip from Ft. Lauderdale, Oct.	**7-, 9-, and 10-night Panama Canal:** May visit Puerto Armuelles (Panama), Cartagena (Colombia), Aruba, Grand Cayman, Roatan (Honduras), Cozumel, Calica/Cancun, and Key West. **9-night Bermuda:** Charleston (SC), Hamilton, and Nassau.	Alaska, Mediterra-nean, Costa Rica

This is more of an amuse-yourself ship, where you're provided with a plush setting and a staff that brings you luxurious food and drink whenever they're needed, but after that you're on your own. Arm yourself with a good book or interesting companion and you'll be fine. Videotapes and books are available 24 hours from the library.

There's a **late-night disco** (Windows Lounge, set toward the bow on Deck 8) for anyone still up at midnight (there aren't many). There's a **small casino** as well.

CHILDREN'S PROGRAM

These ships are geared to adults, and mature ones at that. There's no child care and no special activities for children.

ENTERTAINMENT

Entertainment is very modest, and most passengers are happy with the low-key offerings such as pianists, singers, or small bands. Entertainment is mainly a few headline crooners and musicians and enrichment lecturers. Passengers are content with relaxing evenings among newly made friends.

There isn't enough entertainment to satisfy those who enjoy the facilities and activities aboard large mainstream ships or those who love a Las Vegas ambience. That isn't what this ship is about, but even if it were, the poor design of the show lounge—surely one of the most oddly configured theaters at sea—would only add to the problems: Essentially, it's a stage sunk in a well of balconies with the only good sightlines being on the immediate periphery.

SERVICE

The service is among the best at sea and the equal of Seabourn, which is the best in the business. Staff strive to fulfill every passenger request with a smile. You rarely, if ever, hear the word "no." The service is a major plus that goes a long way to overcoming this ship's physical limitations (low natural light, plain decor, and so forth).

The crew-to-passenger ratio seems so high that one staff person could pour your coffee while another stirs in your sugar. Stewardesses ably care for your cabin, although slip-ups are not unheard of. Surprisingly, at check-in on a recent cruise, I found six empty water bottles in our storage drawers and a pair of old sneakers and a chocolate wrapper under the bed. However, stateroom service and the attention generally given it are excellent.

The European waitstaff is highly trained and supremely gracious and professional. They're intimately knowledgeable about the menu, and eager to please guests at every turn.

Radisson Diamond

The Verdict

The *Radisson Diamond* offers small-ship luxury cruising for well-heeled passengers who enjoy excellent service and fine cuisine without snootiness and without an ultra-formal dress code.

Radisson Diamond *(photo: Radisson Seven Seas)*

Specifications

Size (in tons)	20,295	Officers	International
Number of Cabins	177	Crew	192 (International)
Number of Outside Cabins	177	Passenger/Crew Ratio	1.8 to 1
Cabins with Verandas	121	Year Built	1992
Number of Passengers	350	Last Major Refurbishment	N/A

Frommer's Ratings (Scale of 1–5)

Cabin Comfort & Amenities	4	Pool, Fitness & Spa Facilities	3
Ship Cleanliness & Maintenance	3	Children's Facilities	N/A
Public Comfort/Space	4	Itinerary	4
Decor	3	Worth the Money	5

The *Radisson Diamond* is surprisingly informal for a luxury vessel, and the extraordinarily low density of passengers and the high ratio of crew members to passengers makes you feel like you're on a private yacht. While the ship has its faults—most notably, it has few windows and natural light, a somewhat plain decor, and, at press time, some carpeting and wall/ceiling treatments in need of refurbishing—service and cuisine are top-notch, and the ship's unique catamaran-like design sets it apart from the pack. It's as luxurious as Silversea and Seabourn without the formality and price, and offers ample space; from the dramatic three-deck-high forward lounge to the underwater viewing room in the starboard hull, the ship gives you plenty of leg room and elbow room for stretching.

The vessel's catamaran-style SWATH (Small Waterplane Area Twin Hull) design provides extraordinary stability, embodying features that will still be novel well into the next century. Special features include two sets of stabilizers on pontoons that remain at a more or less constant depth of 5 feet below the water line. For this reason, the letters before the ship's name are not the more standard MV (motor vessel) or MS (motor ship), but rather SSC (semisubmersible craft)—the SSC *Radisson Diamond*. That's a good one to tell your friends: "I'll be sailing on a semisubmersible craft."

Because of its wide stance and unusual design, the ship wins hands-down as one of the most unflappably stable in the cruise industry, providing a platform where glasses of champagne could be stacked on tabletops with barely a spill. Consequently, the *Radisson Diamond* is a good choice for landlubbers who'd like to go on a cruise but suffer from severe motion sickness. You might still get a little green, but it won't be as bad as aboard more conventional, single-hulled ships.

However, you pay for this stability in speed. Small sailing catamarans are faster than single-hulled ones because their hulls are so slim, creating less drag in the water. Since *Diamond*'s semisubmerged hulls are relatively massive, the ship's an absolute slowpoke, with a cruising speed that rarely exceeds a maximum of around 12.5 knots—about 40% slower than many other cruise ships. Consequently, cruises tend to last longer for the number of sea miles (and ports of call) covered, and ports visited are closer together. Overall, though, considering the elegance and high quality of the service, amenities, and cuisine on board, no one seems to object.

Cabins & Rates

Cabins	Per diems from	Bathtub	Fridge	Hair Dryer	Sitting Area	TV
Inside	n/a	yes	yes	yes	yes	yes*
Outside	$299	yes	yes	yes	yes	yes*
Suite	$366	yes	yes	yes	yes	yes*

TVs show CNN.

CABINS The cabins are among the largest and most luxurious in Caribbean waters. All accommodations are outside suites measuring 243 square feet (in the case of the 121 balcony suites, this includes the balcony). The 53 cabins without balconies have big, rectangular windows. Views are wide open and unobstructed from every cabin aboard. Despite their size, many of the staterooms are deep and narrow, meaning there's very little room between the foot of the beds and the cabin's wall. About half the cabins on Deck Eight can accommodate a third person on a foldaway couch. Done in a mix of modern and art deco styling, the decor is subdued, with touches of blond woods, pastel colors, and comfortable settees.

All cabins have a TV broadcasting CNN and other channels, a VCR, minibar stocked free of charge one time, and a safe.

Stateroom bathrooms fall short of super luxury styling: While there are marble-topped vanities, bathtubs with showers, and hair dryers, they're not as opulent as you might expect given the glamour and spaciousness of the cabins. Each stateroom comes with thick terry-cloth robes for passenger use.

Two cabins are specially outfitted for people with disabilities.

PUBLIC AREAS Most public rooms are situated around a central core, making the *Diamond* a very simple ship to negotiate. The ship's most notable space is its single-seating main dining room, one of the loveliest and most romantic at sea. The vast room, buttressed by a two-deck-high wall of glass, is divided into three intimate sections and punctuated by soaring stylized acanthus-leaf columns that lend the room an art-deco feel.

Except for the dining room, the decor is not as drop-dead gorgeous as you might expect on a luxury vessel. *Diamond* has fewer of the elegant furnishings and yachtlike appointments you'd associate with luxury cruising.

Since the designers deliberately placed all the passenger accommodations along the perimeter of the ship, most public rooms (including the casino and the main show lounge) are inside, and therefore get little direct sunlight—but since these areas are busy mostly after dark, you don't always notice. Exceptions to this are the main restaurant, which has banks of windows overlooking the ship's stern, and The Grill, where sunlight floods in from the side.

One complete deck, called the Constellation Center, is almost solely devoted to a convention and meeting center. It's accessorized with in-house publishing facilities, a handful of computers, small boardrooms for gatherings of about a dozen participants each, an auditorium that seats 240, and audio and video devices to record the minutes of your meeting.

The Lounge, a three-tier room with a dramatic forward view of the sea, serves as an observation post, cocktail lounge, tea-time rendezvous, after-dinner dance floor, and late-night disco. On the deck above is "The Club," a quiet, comfortable, and commodious yet windowless lounge that features a live pianist before and sometimes after the dinner hour. Usually when passengers want privacy and quiet, they retreat to their suites, but you might also find a secluded spot on an out-of-the way deck chair, in a quiet corner of the cocktail bar, or in an unused conference room. The library has popular videotapes, films, and books. There are plans to add a pizzeria on the pool deck aft.

While the crew is everywhere polishing and painting, this ship doesn't feel quite ship-shape. Recent inspection showed that furnishings and carpeting are rather careworn and could use a facelift.

RECREATION & FITNESS FACILITIES   Passengers flock to the outdoor decks on sunny days, and there's always enough deck space and chairs to go around. There are intimate alcoves as well, but many of them are rather too oddly configured to be of much advantage. The only part of the ship that offers great sunbathing is poolside and the nearby flanks of the vessel (or on your private veranda, of course).

The ship lacks a traditional promenade deck, but the perimeter of Deck 11 has been turned into a jogging track (13 laps equal 1 mile) that encloses the ship's Steiner-managed spa and gym, which is stocked with Nautilus machines, treadmills, and stationary bicycles. In its four massage rooms (which the last time I checked needed some work, with torn leather and peeling wallpaper), the spa offers steam and massage rooms, beauty treatments, and herbal wraps. There are daily aerobics and yoga classes held in the Lounge, on its small wooden stage.

From the stern (only when the waters are dead calm, however), a floating marina can be lowered as a platform for sailing, swimming, windsurfing, and water-skiing.

Preview: Radisson's *Seven Seas Navigator*

As this book went to press, Radisson's fifth and largest ship was entering its final stages of construction at the T. Mariotti shipyard in Genoa, Italy. The smallest suite on the all-suite 490-passenger, 30,000-ton ultra-luxurious ship measures a very generous 301 square feet and the largest 1,173 square feet (including their balconies). Nearly 90% of all cabins will have private balconies. Cabins will be bathed in damasks and silks in hues of terra-cotta, sand, and taupe, creating a warm, rich ambience. All suites will have walk-in closets, a sitting area, a once-stocked minibar, TV/VCR, and bathrooms with full tub and separate shower. The ship will feature a two-level show lounge, several other bars and lounges, and a top-deck observation lounge for sweeping views of the sea, adjacent to the gym and spa.

Seabourn Cruise Line

SHIPS Seabourn Goddess I • Seabourn Goddess II • Seabourn Legend • Seabourn Pride • Seabourn Sun (preview)

55 Francisco St., Suite 710, San Francisco, CA 94133. ☎ **800/929-9595** or 415/391-7444. Fax 415/391-8518. www.seabourn.com.

THE LINE IN A NUTSHELL   Small and intimate, these sleek modern ships are floating pleasure palaces bathing all who enter in doting service and the finest cuisine at sea.

THE EXPERIENCE   This line is a genuine aristocrat, with perfect manners. Its small, luxurious ships have unprecedented amounts of onboard space and staff for each passenger, service worthy of the grand hotels of Europe, and the hushed, ever-so-polite ambience that appeals to prosperous, usually older passengers who appreciate the emphasis on their individual pleasures. If you're the type of person who responds to discretion and subdued good taste (and who has the cash to pay for it), it might be perfect for you. A travel agent faced with a "which ship is for us" query from Henry and Nancy Kissinger would definitely book them on Seabourn.

Pros

- **Top-shelf service.** Staff seem to know what you need before you ask, and there's more staff per passenger than most any other line afloat. They're professional, polished, and champing at the bit to please. On the *Goddesses,* you'll even be served champagne and caviar on the beach when in port.
- **Excellent cuisine.** Rivaling the best land-based restaurants, cuisine is as exquisite as it gets at sea, with creative, flavorful dishes served with an extensive wine list.
- **Remote ports of call.** These ships are able to visit less-touristed Caribbean ports (like the British Virgin Islands) that larger ships can't or don't visit.
- **Large cabins.** Cabins are not mere cabins, but roomy suites, with cushy features like walk-in closets, bathtubs, quality bath amenities from Neutrogena, personalized stationery, and complimentary stocked minibars.

Cons

- **Few or no private verandas.** Maybe you couldn't care less, but there are only six private balconies on the *Legend* and *Pride,* and none on the *Goddesses.*
- **Limited activities.** If you need things to do around the clock, forget about it. The Seabourn ships have limited organized activities on board (but those they do have are good). For the most part, guests are content with socializing and reading.
- **Shallow drafts, rocky seas.** While it's relatively rare to hit rough seas in the Caribbean, if you do, these small ships are tossed around more than the megas are.

Frommer's Ratings: Seabourn					
	Poor	Fair	Good	Excellent	Outstanding
Enjoyment Factor					✓
Dining					✓
Activities		✓			
Children's Activities	N/A*				
Entertainment			✓		
Service					✓
Overall Value				✓	

Seabourn has no children's program.

SEABOURN: THE CAVIAR OF CRUISE SHIPS

Seabourn was established in 1987 when luxury cruise patriarch Warren Titus and Norwegian shipping mogul Atle Brynestad commissioned a trio of ultra-upscale 10,000-ton vessels from a North German shipyard. Streamlined, with modern, yacht-inspired designs, the *Seabourn Pride, Legend,* and *Spirit* manage to look both aggressive and elegant in their bright white paint jobs, and are small enough to venture safely into exotic harbors where megaships cannot go. Seeing one of the Seabourn vessels moored at St. George's Harbour in Grenada, one of the world's most colorful ports, is an especially beautiful sight.

Although now co-owned by founder Brynestad and industry giant Carnival Corporation, the line maintains strong links with its Norwegian roots, registering each of its ships in the country and preferring to restock many of its marine supplies there.

In mid-1998, Carnival Corporation bought Cunard Line, one of Seabourn's primary competitors in the luxury cruise market. Faced with the problem of how to market the two brands, Carnival decided to go with core strengths, maintaining Seabourn's niche in the small-ship ultra-luxury market and pushing Cunard as the option for cruisers who want the traditional British ocean liner experience. As a result, three of Cunard's small ships—the *Sea Goddess I, Sea Goddess II, and Royal Viking Sun*—will be transferred to the Seabourn fleet by year-end 1999 and renamed *Seabourn Goddess I, Seabourn Goddess II,* and *Seabourn Sun.* Together, the two brands, operating under the umbrella banner of Cunard Line Limited, account for almost 50% of the worldwide luxury cruise market.

THE FLEET

Officially beginning in 2000, the Seabourn fleet comprises six ships, its three original and three former Cunarders. Of its original 204-passenger, 10,000-ton trio—the **Legend, Pride,** and **Spirit**—the *Legend,* built in 1992, and the *Pride,* built in 1988, spend part of the year in the Caribbean. (The final member of the trio, *Seabourn Spirit,* was built in 1989 and roams along the coast of Africa and Asia most of the year, rarely returning to the Western Hemisphere at all.) Seabourn's new adoptees are the 115-passenger, 4,260-ton **Seabourn Goddess I** and **II** (built in 1984 and 1985) and the 740-passenger, 37,845-ton **Seabourn Sun,** built in 1988. The *Sun* splits its time between the Mediterranean, Europe, South America, the Pacific, and the Caribbean and Panama Canal.

PASSENGER PROFILE

Most have more than comfortable household incomes, usually in excess of $250,000. Many are retired (or never worked to begin with), and many have net worths in the millions, and sometimes much higher. The majority of passengers are couples, and there are always a handful of singles as well, usually widows or widowers. Few seem to come aboard with children or grandchildren in tow.

In many ways, the passenger roster looks like the membership of a posh country club, where old money judges new money. Most passengers are North American, and dress expensively though not, of course, flashily. Many passengers are not particularly chatty, giddy, or outgoing. They are likely to have sailed aboard other luxury cruise lines and stayed in five-star hotels. Passengers expect to receive good service in an atmosphere of discreet gentility.

The line's history of repeaters is among the highest in the industry, sometimes as many as 50% aboard any given cruise.

DINING

Cuisine is one of Seabourn's strongest points, matching what you'd find in a world-class European resort hotel. The line assumes that most of its passengers are used to getting

Goddesses on the Beach

The pièce de résistance of your *Seabourn Goddess* cruise comes at midday near the end of the trip, as you lounge on a quiet beach. As you gaze out toward the anchored ship you'll see the captain, standing at the bow of a bright-red Zodiac and holding a huge Cunard flag embossed with a rampant gold lion, coming swiftly toward the beach, looking like George Washington crossing the Delaware, but in decidedly better weather and absolutely bluer water.

The captain's soldiers—20-something European stewards wearing Hawaiian shirts—hop out carrying a life ring that doubles as a floating serving tray for an open tin of Russian malossol caviar, encircled by little dishes of sour cream, chopped egg (of the chicken variety), and minced onion. Wade into the gentle surf up to your waist and spoon up a morsel. Stewards move about with bottles of Moet & Chandon champagne and Absolut vodka encased in orchid-filled cylinders of ice.

A buffet spread out under a lean-to features choices such as freshly grilled lobster tails, barbecued spare ribs, carved roast beef, baked potato, salads, and fresh fruit. Passengers feast not on beach towels spread out on the sand, but under umbrellas at tables set with proper china and hotel silver brought ashore by the staff.

It doesn't get any better than this!

what they want, usually whenever they want it, so meals are served in a manner that satisfies both appetite and the expectation of high-class service. Fleetwide, dining is open seating, allowing guests to dine whenever they choose, within a window of several hours at each mealtime.

On the *Legend, Pride,* and *Spirit,* tables seat up to 10, but you'll almost never have a problem getting a table for two if that's your wish. Also, tables are spaced far enough apart so you'll never feel crowded. There are no set seating arrangements, so passengers can dine with whomever they want, just like at a private dinner party.

Dinner service is high style and extremely formal. Men are expected to wear jackets and, on most evenings, neckties as well. Two formal evenings are held during the course of any 1-week cruise. Virtually every male present appears in a tuxedo, and the events are, indeed, very formal. Staff members almost run at a trot through the elaborate, six-course European service. It's all extremely civilized.

On the *Goddesses,* the dress code and ambience is less formal and stuffy, but the food and service is no less top-of-the-line.

Seabourn cuisine is an eclectic mix. The *Legend, Pride,* and *Spirit* feature old favorites such as beef Wellington, Dover sole, and broiled lobster; ethnic dishes reflecting the itinerary of wherever the ship happens to be at the time; and a mixture of light Pacific Rim and California cuisine. Dishes are prepared to order, **spa menus** are available at every meal, and passengers can make virtually any special request they want. On the *Goddesses,* the dinner menu includes three appetizers such as carpaccio of beef tenderloin, lobster aspic and sautéed crab cakes, three hot or cold soups, and four entrees such as a baby lamb loin or stuffed quail, plus a Golden Door Spa menu and a **vegetarian dish.** Complimentary wines are served at lunch and dinner, and every night features a flaming dessert served in individual portions or such choices as chocolate mousse with fresh berries or coconut crème brûlée.

If your mood doesn't call for the dining room, the *Legend, Pride,* and *Spirit* have an **alternative dining option,** the Veranda Café. (On the *Goddesses,* all meals are served in the dining room, and one night there's a festive dinner served out on deck by the pool.) The Veranda serves bountiful breakfasts every morning, with omelets made fresh to your specifications and rows of herring and smoked salmon reflecting the ship's Norwegian origins. At lunchtime, you'll find salads, sandwich makings, fresh pasta, and maybe jumbo shrimp, smoked salmon, and smoked oysters on the cold side and hot sliced roast beef, duck, and ham on the carving board. A **special of the day**—pizza with pineapple topping, chili, or corned beef—will also be available at the Sky Bar overlooking the Lido, for those who don't want to change out of their swimsuits. Dinner is served under the stars on the Lido Deck several evenings a week as well, offering a meal roughly equivalent to whatever's being whipped up in the main dining room. Dinners here are romantic candlelight affairs, and are often based on Italian, French, and seafood themes. In good weather it's a treat to eat at one of the arc of tables located aft overlooking the wake and under a protective canvas awning.

On the *Goddesses,* there are wonderful hors d'oeuvres, such as jumbo shrimp, smoked salmon, and the best caviar available practically around the clock in unlimited quantities.

Room service is available 24 hours a day on all ships. During normal lunch or dinner hours, your private meal can mirror the dining room service, right down to the silver, crystal, and porcelain. After hours, the menu is more limited, with burgers, salads, sandwiches, and pastas. And whenever a cruise itinerary calls for a full-day stopover on a remote island, a lavish beach barbecue might be whipped up at midday.

ACTIVITIES

These small ships don't offer much in the way of organized activities, and that's what most passengers really love about the line. With no rah-rah, in-your-face cruise directors shouting at them, passengers are just left alone to pursue their own personal peace.

You'll won't find the bingo, karaoke, and silly poolside contests featured by mass-market lines. The atmosphere is ever-tasteful and unobtrusive. Activities include card games and tournaments, trivia contests, tours of the ship's galley, visits to the cozy library, and watching movies in your cabin. You'll soon realize that many passengers are aboard to read, quietly converse with their peers, and be ushered from one stylish spot to the next.

That said, you don't have to be sedate, either. The *Legend, Pride,* and *Spirit,* and both *Goddesses,* have **retractable water sports marinas** that unfold from the ships' stern, weather and sea conditions permitting, and gracefully usher passengers into the sea for water-skiing, Jet Skiing (limited), windsurfing, sailing, snorkeling, banana-boat riding, and swimming.

There are few, if any, public announcements to disturb your solitude, which is a relief when compared to the barrage of noise broadcast aboard many other lines.

On certain cruises there are **guest lecturers,** such as noted chefs, authors, or statesmen, or maybe a wine connoisseur, composer, anthropologist, TV director, or professor, who

---

Two Good Deals, One Added Cost, & One Bit of Confusion

Solo Passenger Rates: Depending on the cruise, single supplements are as low as 110% of the per-person rate for double occupancy of the same standard suite. **Beverage Credits:** Guests can prepurchase shipboard beverage credits through their travel agents—a $100 credit pays for $150 of shipboard beverages. **Port Charges Not Included:** Seabourn is one of the few lines that does not include port charges, on average about $200, in the cruise rates. **Tips:** Gratuities are officially included in the cruise fare, but staff is not prohibited from accepting additional tips.

Seabourn Fleet Itineraries

Ship	Home Ports & Season	Itinerary	Other Itineraries
Seabourn Goddess I	Round-trip from St. Thomas and between St. Thomas and Barbados, Nov–Apr. Itineraries alternate.	**7-night eastern Carib 1:** Tobago, Grenada, St. Lucia, Guadeloupe, Antigua, and St. Martin. **7-night eastern Carib 2:** St. John, St. Martin, St. Barts, Antigua, Virgin Gorda, and Jost Van Dyke. **7-night eastern Carib 3:** St. Croix, St. Barts, Nevis, Martinique, Mayreau, Carriacou.	Mediterranean
Seabourn Goddess II	Several alternating homeports: round-trip from St. Thomas; between St. Thomas and Barbados; round-trip from Barbados; between Barbados and Puerto Rico; round-trip from Puerto Rico; between Puerto Rico and St. Thomas; Nov–Apr.	**7-night eastern Carib:** Ports on alternating itineraries may include Mayreau, Bequia, St. Lucia, Barbados, St. Croix, St. Thomas, Virgin Gorda, Antigua, Jost Van Dyke, St. Barts, St. Martin, Nevis, Dominica, and Tobago.	Mediterranean
Seabourn Legend	7- or 8-night itineraries round-trip from San Juan and from San Juan to Barbados, from Barbados to St. Thomas; 5-night itineraries between Fort Lauderdale and St. Thomas, St. Thomas to San Juan, round-trip from San Juan, and San Juan to St. Barts; Panama Canal itineraries between Fort Lauderdale and Acapulco, Nov–Mar.	**7- or 8-night eastern/southern Carib:** May visit St. Lucia, Antigua, St. Barts, St. Martin, Virgin Gorda, Grenadines, Dominica, Tobago, Barbados, and St. Croix. **5-night eastern Carib:** May include St. Barts, San Juan, St. Martin, St. Croix, Virgin Gorda, and St. Lucia. **16-night Panama Canal:** San Juan, St. John, St. Thomas, St. Barts, Virgin Gorda, Aruba, Cartagena (Colombia), San Blas Islands (Panama), Puerto Caldera (Costa Rica), and Puerto Quetzal (Guatemala).	Mediterranean, Europe
Seabourn Pride	7-night itineraries between Fort Lauderdale and St. Thomas; 6-night itineraries between St. Thomas and Barbados, and round-trip from Fort Lauderdale; Panama Canal itineraries between Fort Lauderdale and Puerto Caldera (Costa Rica), Puerto Caldera and San Juan, Nov–Mar.	**7-night eastern Carib:** Jost Van Dyke, St. Barts, Virgin Gorda, and St. John. **6-night eastern Carib:** St. Lucia, Bequia (Grenadines), Dominica, Mayreau (Grenadines) or St. Martin, St. Croix, St. Barts, and Virgin Gorda. **10-night eastern Carib:** St. John, St. Martin, Virgin Gorda, St. Barts, and Key West. **10- and 12-night Panama Canal:** May include St. John, St. Thomas, San Juan, St. Barts, Virgin Gorda, Aruba, Cartagena (Colombia), and San Blas Islands (Panama).	Europe, South America, Eastern Canada/ New England

---

Preview: The "New" *Seabourn Sun*

The last ship to carry the venerated Royal Viking name, the *Royal Viking Sun,* built in 1998 for luxurious long-distance cruising, was Cunard's most elegant ship, especially after the line spent some $11 million on a facelift in 1995 to freshen her up. The ship is scheduled to transfer to the Seabourn fleet as part of corporate reshuffling, but before it does, the ship will undergo a dramatic $15 million conversion that will completely redesign her public rooms and refurbish her cabins (as well as rename her *Seabourn Sun*). The Midnight Sun lounge will be extended aft and turned into a full-sized cabaret show lounge, and the spa/gym/pool area above will be expanded and improved and a magradome glass roof added above the pool. The Garden Cafe will be expanded, too. When completed, the *Seabourn Sun* will be virtually all new. The ship's gross tonnage is expected to increase by 5,000 to 6,000 tons.

---

present lectures and mingle with guests. From time to time, the line manages to bring on the likes of Patricia Neal, Walter Cronkite, or Art Buchwald. (Note, however, that these programs tend to be more prevalent on European/Mediterranean and Far East itineraries than on Caribbean ones.) You can generally count on port lectures from resident travel experts.

Each ship has a small-scale, staid, and rather un-casino-like **casino** with a couple of blackjack tables and a handful of slots.

CHILDREN'S PROGRAM

These ships are not geared to children. The *Goddesses* prohibit them outright, setting the minimum passenger age at 16. You may see a younger child occasionally on the *Legend, Pride,* or *Spirit*—probably a very bored child, as the line provides no special programs, no special menus, and no special concessions for children.

In a pinch, you may be able to arrange to have an available crew member provide baby-sitting.

ENTERTAINMENT

Entertainment is not Seabourn's strong suit, but if you're happy with a singer, pianist, or duo doing most of the entertaining, you'll be pleased enough. On all the ships, a resident dance band or music duo performs a roster of old favorites, while the mellow piano bar is always a good option. The *Legend* and *Pride* have small show lounges, but the *Goddesses* have none.

SERVICE

Seabourn maintains the finest service staff of any line afloat. Most are young northern Europeans, many Norwegian, who are recruited after they've gained experience at one of the grand hotels of Europe. They are, overall, universally charming, competent, sensitive, and discreet—among Seabourn's most valuable assets.

Laundry and dry cleaning are available. There are also complimentary self-service laundry rooms on the *Legend* and *Pride.*

All Seabourn ships provide Neutrogena bathroom amenities as well as designer soaps from Hermés, Chanel No. 5, and Tiffany. Cabin minibars are stocked with two bottles of wine or spirits of the guests' choice (replenished only on request). Soft drinks, beer, and mineral water are complimentary and replenished daily.

Seabourn Goddess I •
Seabourn Goddess II

The Verdict

About as good as it gets, with highest marks for the small ship atmosphere, the attentive European service, and the creative menus. Of course, the champagne and caviar served poolside whenever you want it isn't too shabby either.

Seabourn Goddess *(photo: Seabourn Cruise Line)*

Specifications

Size (in tons)	4,250	Officers	Norwegian
Number of Cabins	58	Crew	89 (European/Int'l)
Number of Outside Cabins	58	Passenger/Crew Ratio	1.3 to 1
Cabins with Verandas	0	Year Built	1984/1985
Number of Passengers	116	Last Major Refurbishment	1997

Frommer's Ratings (Scale of 1–5)

Cabin Comfort & Amenities	5	Pool, Fitness & Spa Facilities	3
Ship Cleanliness & Maintenance	4	Children's Facilities	N/A
Public Comfort/Space	5	Itinerary	4
Decor	4	Worth the Money	4

These two ships espouse a casually elegant ethos similar to Windstar, where tuxes, ties, and gowns can be left at home. For both weary workaholics or those used to doing very little, it would be hard to find a more relaxing vacation, better food, or more attentive service while enjoying a variety of small Caribbean ports. Calling at yacht harbors and anchoring off beautiful beaches, these petite ships seem to blend right in with the yachts in the harbor.

While the *Seabourn Goddesses* continue to provide the supreme service and yachtlike elegance they did in their Cunard days, they're now being targeted to a younger crowd in their 30s and 40s—people who want the service and top-notch amenities, but sans over-the-top formality. Despite the marketing, expect the ships to continue drawing a mostly middle-aged 50- to 60-something crowd for at least a while longer.

Cabins & Rates

Cabins	Per diems from	Bathtub	Fridge	Hair Dryer	Sitting Area	TV
Inside	n/a	yes	yes	yes	yes	yes
Outside	$526	yes	yes	yes	yes	yes
Suite	$1,024	yes	yes	yes	yes	yes

CABINS   Each of the 58 virtually identical one-room ocean-view suites average 205 square feet. Unlike the layouts on many ships, the bedroom is positioned alongside the cabin's large window and the sitting area is inside. They are located forward and amidships, and the soundproofing between cabins is good and engine noise minimal. While similar in design, they are less roomy than those aboard the larger Seabourn trio or the *Silversea* twins, and the bathrooms are relatively small.

The superb design features includes twin beds convertible to queens, several mirrors, remote control television and VCR, music channels, automated wake-up calls, international direct-dial phones, complimentary stocked minibar and refrigerator, fresh flowers, fresh fruit, terry-cloth robes, hair dryer, and bathrooms with full-sized tubs. The 24-hour room service provides a full-course meal setup in your suite at a proper table seating four.

If you can afford it, two units can be interconnected to provide a full 410 square feet of space.

These ships are not recommended for passengers with disabilities, as doorways leading to staterooms and toilets are not big enough to accommodate a wheelchair. Persons in wheelchairs also can't go ashore, because the wheelchairs can't be taken on the launches that shuttle passengers to shore in ports where the vessel must anchor offshore.

PUBLIC AREAS   Upon boarding, you immediately notice the elaborate flower arrangements in all public areas and the sophisticated European atmosphere and high-quality furnishings. Public areas are awash with marble, polished hardwoods, and Oriental carpets. So posh are they, and so yacht-like the feel of the vessels, that you expect an English lord to walk through the door at any moment to suggest a cocktail.

The Main Salon and its small bar alcove are the venue for indoor socializing before dinner, and a singer and musical duo often provide light entertainment. The hot and cold hors d'oeuvres may include smoked salmon, jumbo shrimp, and an open tin of malossol caviar.

There's dancing in the Main Salon after dinner, while one deck up a popular, long-serving pianist entertains at the Club Salon piano bar, located next to the diminutive two-blackjack-table casino. There's also a small book and video library, several slot machines, and a purser's foyer with a boutique.

RECREATION & FITNESS FACILITIES   The mostly open and partly shaded Lido Deck has deck chairs, a pool, hot tub, and bar (order yourself some champagne, caviar, and jumbo shrimp while you lounge!). A covered deck above has additional deck chairs with more at Sun Deck level. The gym, spa, and beauty salon are high up, looking aft on Deck 5. There's also a jogging track on this level, but it's so small-scale you're likely to get dizzy if you run it at high speeds.

Seabourn Legend • Seabourn Pride

The Verdict

Hands-down, these ships are top of the market and the cream of the crop. They're the most luxurious ships at sea, designed to let you be as social or as private as you like.

Seabourn Legend (photo: Seabourn Cruise Line)

Specifications

Size (in tons)	10,000	Crew	140 (International)
Number of Cabins	100	Passenger/Crew Ratio	1.5 to 1
Number of Outside Cabins	100	Year Built	
Cabins with Verandas	6	*Legend*	1992
Number of Passengers	204	*Pride*	1988
Officers	Norwegian	Last Major Refurbishment	N/A

Frommer's Ratings (Scale of 1–5)

Cabin Comfort & Amenities	5	Pool, Fitness & Spa Facilities	3
Ship Cleanliness & Maintenance	4	Children's Facilities	N/A
Public Comfort/Space	5	Itinerary	4
Decor	4	Worth the Money	4

These two understated, beautifully designed ships represent luxury cruising at its very best, going everywhere one would ever want to cruise. Passengers who like to be social and meet others with similar interests will find plenty of opportunities to do so at open-sitting meals, in the intimate public rooms, and out on deck. On the other hand, if you want to get away from it all, you can also be completely private in your spacious suite, at a table for two in the restaurant, or in a quiet corner of the deck.

Cabins & Rates

Cabins	Per diems from	Bathtub	Fridge	Hair Dryer	Sitting Area	TV
Inside	n/a	yes	yes	yes	yes	yes**
Outside	n/a	yes	yes	yes	yes	yes**
Suite	$384	yes*	yes	yes	yes	yes**

*The four handicapped-accessible suites have showers only.
**TVs show CNN and ESPN.

CABINS   The great majority of the accommodations are handsomely designed "Type A" 277-square-foot one-room suites (remember, an average cabin on Carnival is 190 square feet), varying only in location but priced at four different levels. Suites are popular for entertaining and dining, as the lounge area's coffee table rises to dining table height, and one can order hors d'oeuvres such as caviar and smoked salmon at no extra charge. Closet space is more than adequate for hanging clothes, but drawer space is more limited. The *Pride* has twin sinks in the all-white marble bathrooms; *Legend* has a single sink.

The two Classic Suites measure 400 square feet, and two pairs of Owner's Suites are 530 and 575 square feet. These six have the only (small) verandas on the ships. (At press time, there was talk about balconies being added to other cabins on the ships, but no firm decision or schedule had been announced.) The Owner's Suites have dining rooms and guest powder rooms. As in any cabins positioned near the bow of relatively small ships such as these, these forward-facing suites can be somewhat uncomfortable during rough seas. The dark wood furnishings of these suites make the overall feeling more like a hotel room than a ship's suite. Regal Suites, at 554 square feet, are simply two combined 277-square-foot Seabourn suites with one room given completely over to a lounge.

Everything about a Seabourn cabin has the impeccably maintained feel of an upscale Scandinavian hotel. Each cabin has a 5-foot-wide rectangular picture window with an electric blind that, with the flick of a switch, can shut out the glare of the mid-afternoon sun. Each unit contains a fully stocked bar, a walk-in closet, safe, a VCR and TV broadcasting CNN and ESPN among other channels, crystal glasses for every kind of drink, terry-cloth robes, and fresh fruit daily. Videotape movies are available from the ship's library, and the purser's office broadcasts films from the ship's own collection. Color schemes are either tastefully ice-blue or champagne-colored, with lots of bleached oak or birch wooden trim, as well as mirrors and a sophisticated bank of spotlights.

Owner's Suites 5 and 6 have obstructed views.

There are four wheelchair-accessible suites.

PUBLIC AREAS An attractive double open spiral staircase links the public areas, which are, overall, a bit duller than you'd expect on ships of this caliber. For the most part, they're spare and almost ordinary looking. Art and ornamentation are conspicuous by their absence. It's almost as if in its zeal to create conservative decors, management couldn't decide on the appropriate artwork and so omitted it completely. (There are a few exceptions: The *Legend* has an attractive curved ocean-liner-motif mural in its stair foyers.)

The forward-facing observation lounge on Sky Deck offers an attractive, quiet venue all day long for reading, a drink before meals, cards, and afternoon tea. A chart and compass will help you find out where the ship is currently positioned, and a computerized wall map lets you track future cruises.

The Club lounge and bar, with an aft-facing position, is the ship's principal social center, with music, a small band, a singer and/or pianist, and fancy hot hors d'oeuvres before and after dinner. Next door, behind glass, is the ship's casino, with gaming tables and a separate small room for slot machines. The semi-circular and tiered formal lounge on the deck below is the venue for lectures, pianists, and the captain's parties.

The formal restaurant, located on the lowest deck, is a large low-ceilinged room with an open seating policy. The Veranda Café, open for breakfast, lunch, and, except on formal nights, dinner, is an intimate, well-designed indoor/outdoor facility.

One of the best places for a romantic, moonlit moment is the isolated patch of deck at the far forward bow on the Magellan Deck.

RECREATION & FITNESS FACILITIES The outdoor pool, not much used, is awkwardly situated in a shadowy location aft of the open Lido Deck, between the twin engine uptakes, and is flanked by lifeboats that hang from both sides of the ship. A pair of whirlpools are located just forward of the pool. There's a third hot tub perched on the far forward bow deck. It's isolated and a perfect spot (as is the whole patch of deck here) from which to watch the landscape or a port come into sight or fade away.

A retractable, wood-planked water sports marina opens out from the stern of the ship so passengers can hop into sea kayaks or go windsurfing, water-skiing, or snorkeling right from the ship. An attached steel mesh net creates a saltwater pool when the marina is in use.

The gym and Steiner-managed spa are roomy for ships this small, and are located forward of the Lido. There is a separate aerobics areas, plus two saunas, massage rooms, and a beauty salon.

Windstar Cruises

SHIPS   Wind Spirit • Wind Star • Wind Surf

300 Elliott Ave. W., Seattle, WA 98119. ☎ **800/258-7245** or 206/281-3535. Fax 206/281-0627. www.windstarcruises.com.

THE LINE IN A NUTSHELL   The no-jackets-required policy onboard Windstar's four sleek vessels defines the line's casually elegant attitude. They really do feel like private yachts—they're down-to-earth and port intensive, yet service and cuisine are first-class.

THE EXPERIENCE   Windstar offers a truly unique cruise experience, giving passengers the delicious illusion of adventure on board its fleet of four- and five-masted sailing ships and the ever-pleasant reality of first-class cuisine, service, and itineraries. This is no barefoot, rigging-pulling, paper-plates-in-lap, sleep-on-the-deck kind of cruise, but a refined yet down-to-earth, yacht-like experience for a sophisticated, well-traveled crowd who despise big ships and throngs of tourists.

Onboard, fine stained teak, brass details, and lots of navy-blue fabrics and carpeting lend a traditional nautical ambiance. While the ships' proud masts and yards of white sails cut an ever-so-attractive profile, the ships are ultra-state-of-the-art and the sails can be furled or unfurled at the touch of a button. The ships are so stable, in fact, that at times the bridge may actually induce a modest tilt so passengers remember they're on a sailing ship. In the Caribbean, at least once per week if at all possible, the captain shuts off the engines and moves by sail only, to give passengers a real taste of the sea. Under full sail, the calm tranquility of the cruises is utterly blissful.

Pros

- **Cuisine.** The ambience, service, and imaginative cuisine created by renowned Los Angeles chef Joachim Splichal is superb. Dining is an event much looked forward to each day. Seating is open, and guests can usually get a table for two.
- **Informal and unregimented days.** This line offers the most casual high-end cruise out there—an approach much loved by passengers who like fine service and cuisine but don't like the formality and stuffiness of the majority of high-end lines.
- **Itineraries.** Except the *Wind Surf,* which has 1 day at sea, these small ships visit a Caribbean port every day of a weeklong cruise, and the ports visited are wonderfully less touristed than many of those visited on the megaship routes.

Cons

- **No verandas.** If they're important to you, you're out of luck.
- **Limited activities and entertainment.** This is intentional, but if you need lots of organized hoopla to keep you happy, you won't find much on these ships.

Frommer's Ratings: Windstar					
	Poor	Fair	Good	Excellent	Outstanding
Enjoyment Factor					✓
Dining				✓	
Activities		✓			
Children's Program	N/A*				
Entertainment		✓			
Service			✓		
Overall Value				✓	

Windstar has no children's program.

WINDSTAR: CASUAL ELEGANCE UNDER SAIL

Launched in 1986, Windstar Cruises combines the best of 19th-century clipper design with the best of modern yacht engineering. As you see a Windstar ship approaching port, each with four or five masts the height of 20-story buildings, you'll think the sea-faring days of Joseph Conrad or Herman Melville have returned. The ships are beautiful, and so is the experience on board—the line's ad slogan, "180 degrees from the ordinary," is right on target.

But Captain Ahab wouldn't know what to do with a Windstar ship. Million-dollar Hewlett-Packard computers control the six triangular sails with their at least 21,489 square feet of Dacron, flying from masts that tower 204 feet above deck. These computers automatically trim the sails and control fin stabilizers, rudder tab, anti-heeling devices, and much, much more. Sails can be retracted in 2 minutes to a diameter of less than a foot.

The original designs were developed by Warsila Marine Industries in Helsinki, and the ships were built at Le Havre in France. The catalyst behind the formation of the company was a flamboyant French entrepreneur, Jean Claude Potier, a native Parisian, who, in a 25-year-span, was instrumental in leading the French Line, the Sun Line, and Paquet during their transition into the modern cruise age.

In the late 1980s, Windstar was acquired by Holland America Line, which is itself wholly owned by Carnival Cruise Lines. As such, Windstar is the most adventure-oriented of Carnival's many cruise line divisions, and although not as luxurious as Carnival's most upscale branch, Seabourn, it nonetheless prides itself on a cruise experience that's much, much more upscale than the ones offered aboard any of Carnival's megaships, and is the most high-end, by far, among the competing sailing cruise ships in the Caribbean (Star Clippers and Windjammer are much less snazzy, with food and service nowhere near Windstar's, and are deliberately mid- and down-market, respectively).

THE FLEET

Today, Windstar's fleet consists of four ships, the 148-passenger **Wind Star, Wind Song,** and **Wind Spirit,** all constructed originally for Windstar and built in 1986, 1987, and 1988, and the 312-passenger **Wind Surf** built in 1990 and sailed until 1997 as the *Club Med I* for Club Med Cruises. The *Wind Surf* is the only one of the Windstar ships to have a spa and to offer a substantial number of suites (31). Of the four, only the *Surf* and *Spirit* spend significant time in the Caribbean. The *Wind Star* sails a Belize/Honduras itinerary from Cancún.

PASSENGER PROFILE

People who expect high-caliber service and very high-quality cuisine but detest the formality of the other high-end ships and the mass mentality of the megaships are thrilled with Windstar. Most passengers are couples in their 30s to early 60s (pretty evenly distributed across range, with the average about 48), with a smattering of parents with adult children and the occasional single friends traveling together.

The line is not the best choice for first-timers, since it appeals to a specific sensibility, and is definitely not a good choice for singles or families with children under 15 or 16.

Overall, passengers are sophisticated, well traveled, and more down-to-earth than passengers on the other high-end lines. Most want something different from the regular cruise experience, eschew the "bigger is better" philosophy of conventional cruising, and want a somewhat more adventurous, port-intensive Caribbean cruise. These cruises are for those seeking a romantic escape, who like to visit islands not often touched by regular cruise ships, including the Grenadines, the Tobago Cays, British Virgin Islands and relatively isolated dependencies of Guadeloupe, such as the Ile des Saints.

About a fourth of all passengers are repeaters, a figure that represents one of the best recommendations for Windstar, and about 20% are first-timers. There are often a few honeymooners on board.

DINING

A high point of the cruise, the cuisine is among the better prepared aboard ship in the Caribbean, although maybe not quite the caliber of Seabourn or the *Radisson Diamond.*

The line's cuisine was the creation of the renowned chef/restaurateur **Joachim Splichal,** winner of many culinary awards (including some from the James Beard Society) and owner of Los Angeles's Patina Restaurant and Pinot Bistro. At its best, Splichal's food is inventive and imaginative, as reflected by such appetizers as a corn risotto with wild mushrooms and basil or a "Farinetta" bread and parmesan griddle cake with roasted chicken and shallots, followed by a seafood strudel of lobster, scallops, mussels, king crab, and shrimp in a lobster sauce, or an artfully presented potato-crusted fish with braised leeks and apple-smoked bacon, or a salmon tournedo with an herb crust served with stewed tomatoes and garlicky broccoli rabe. Irresistible desserts such as banana pie with raspberry sauce and French profiteroles with hot fudge sauce are beyond tempting. A very good wine list includes California and European vintages.

Called the "Sail Light Menu," **healthy choices** and **vegetarian dishes,** designed by light-cooking expert Jeanne Jones, are available for breakfast, lunch, and dinner (fat and calorie content is listed on the menu). The light choices may feature Atlantic Salmon with couscous and fresh vegetables or a Thai country-style chicken with veggies and oriental rice. The vegetarian options may feature a fresh garden stew or a savory polenta with Italian salsa.

The once-a-week **evening barbecues** on the pool deck are wonderful parties under the stars, and an ample and beautifully designed buffet spread offers more than you could possible sample in one evening. The setting is sublime, with tables set with linens and, often, a live Caribbean-style band performing on board for the evening.

Each ship has **two dining rooms,** one casual and breezy and used during breakfast and lunch (The Veranda) and the other a more formal room (The Restaurant) that's the stage for dinner. On the *Wind Spirit,* The Veranda is a sunny, window-lined room whose tables extend from inside onto a covered deck (unfortunately, you do have to go outside on deck to get there, so if it's raining you get wet), while The Restaurant is enclosed and accented with nautical touches like teakwood trim and paneling and pillars wrapped decoratively in hemp rope.

At breakfast and lunch, meals can be ordered from a menu or selected from a buffet, so your choices are many. Made-to-taste omelets and a varied and generous spread of fruits are available at breakfast, and luncheons may feature a tasty seafood paella and a hot pasta dish of the day. There is **open seating for meals,** at tables designed for between two and eight diners. You can often get a table for two, but you might have to wait if you go during the rush.

Windstar's official dress code is "no jackets required," which is a big draw for guests. In The Restaurant, guests are asked to dress "casually elegant," which generally means trousers and a nice collared shirts for men and pantsuits or casual dresses for women.

The **24-hour room service** includes hot and cold breakfast items (cereals and breads as well as eggs and omelets) and a limited menu that includes sandwiches, fruit, pizza, salads, and other snacks.

Windstar Fleet Itineraries

Ship	Home Ports & Season	Itinerary	Other Itineraries
Wind Spirit	St. Thomas, round-trip from Dec–Apr.	**7-night eastern Carib:** St. John, St. Martin, St. Barts, Tortola, Jost Van Dyke, and Virgin Gorda.	Mediterranean
Wind Star	Cancún, round-trip from Jan–Apr and Nov–Dec, 2000.	**7-night Belize:** Roatan (Honduras), Goff's Cay (Belize), Half Moon Caye Reserve (Belize), San Pedro (Belize), and Cozumel.	Mediterranean
Wind Surf	Barbados, round-trip from Dec–Apr.	**7-night eastern Carib:** Tobago Cays, Tobago, Bequia, Martinique, St. Lucia or Nevis, St. Martin, St. Barts, Iles des Saintes, and St. Lucia.	Mediterranean

ACTIVITIES

Since these ships generally visit a port of call every single day of the cruise and guests spend the day on shore exploring, there are few organized activities offered, and the daily schedules are intentionally unregimented—the way guests prefer it. Weather and conditions permitting, the ships anchor and passengers can enjoy kayaking, sailing, windsurfing, banana boat rides, and swimming from the **water sports platform** lowered at the stern. There will be a handful of scheduled diversions, such as gaming lessons in the casino and walk-a-mile sessions and stretch classes on deck. Chances are there may be a vegetable carving or food decorating demonstration poolside, as well as clothing or jewelry sale items on display by the pool. Before ports, brief orientation talks are held.

The pool deck, with its hot tub, deck chairs, and open-air bar, is conducive to sun bathing, conversations with shipmates, or quiet repose with only the sky and surf to amuse you. There's an extensive video library and CD collection from which passengers can borrow for use in their cabins.

The company's **organized island tours** tend to be more creative than usual, and the cruise director/shore excursions manager/jack-of-all trade person or couple are knowledgeable and able to point passengers toward good spots for such independent activities as bird watching, snorkeling, or a nice meal.

CHILDREN'S PROGRAM

As children are not encouraged to sail with Windstar, there are no activities planned for them. There are often a handful of teenagers on board who spend time sunbathing or holed in their cabins watching movies.

ENTERTAINMENT

For the most part, passengers entertain themselves. There's often a duo on board (a pianist and a vocalist) performing during cocktail hour before and after dinner in the ships' one main lounge. **Local entertainment,** such as steel bands, calypso bands, or a group of limbo dancers, is sometimes brought aboard at a port of call. A very modest **casino** offers slots, blackjack, and Caribbean stud poker. After dinner, passengers often go up to the pool bar for a nightcap under the stars, and sometimes after 10 or 11pm, disco/pop music is played in the lounge if guests are in the dancing mood.

SERVICE

Windstar is a class operation, as reflected in its thoughtful service personnel. The staff smiles hello and makes every effort to learn passengers' names. Dining staff is efficient and first-rate as well, but not in that ultra-professional, military-esque, five-star-hotel, Seabourn kind of way. That's not what Windstar is all about. Officers and crew are helpful, but not gushing. It's common for several married couples to be among the crew.

The line operates under a "tipping not required" policy, although generally guests do tip staff much as on other ships; on Windstar, like Holland America, there's just less pressure to do so.

Wind Spirit • Wind Star

The Verdict

Some of the most romantic, cozy yet roomy small ships out there, these ships look chic and offer just the right combination of creature comforts and first-class cuisine, along with a casual, laid-back, unstructured ethic.

Wind Spirit *(photo: Windstar/Harvey Lloyd)*

Specifications

Size (in tons)	5,350	Officers	British/Dutch
Number of Cabins	74	Crew	89 (International)
Number of Outside Cabins	74	Passenger/Crew Ratio	1.6 to 1
Cabins with Verandas	0	Year Built	1988/1986
Number of Passengers	148	Last Major Refurbishment	N/A

Frommer's Ratings (Scale of 1–5)

Cabin Comfort & Amenities	5	Pool, Fitness & Spa Facilities	2
Ship Cleanliness & Maintenance	4	Children's Facilities	N/A
Public Comfort/Space	4	Itinerary	5
Decor	4	Worth the Money	5

Despite these ships' high-tech design and size—significantly larger than virtually any private yacht afloat—they nonetheless have some of the grace and lines of a clipper ship, with practically none of the associated discomforts. There's even a needle-shaped bowsprit jutting into the waves. Getting around is usually easy, except that there's no inside access to the breakfast and luncheon restaurant, so during high winds or rain, access via an external set of stairs can be moderately inconvenient.

Cabins & Rates

Cabins	Per diems from	Bathtub	Fridge	Hair Dryer	Sitting Area	TV
Inside	n/a	no	yes	yes	no	yes*
Outside	$343	no	yes	yes	no	yes*
Suite	n/a	no	yes	yes	yes	yes*

*TVs show CNN.

CABINS   All cabins are very similar and display a subtle nauticalness. They're roomy at 188 square feet, but nowhere near as large as your typical high-end ship suite. Beds can be adapted into either a one-queen-size or two-twin-sized format. Each cabin has a VCR and TV showing CNN and lots of movies, a CD player, a minibar, a pair of large round portholes with brass fittings, bathrobes, fresh fruit, and a compact closet.

Teakwood-decked bathrooms, largish for a ship of this size, are better laid out than those aboard many luxury cruise liners, and contain a hair dryer, plenty of towels, and more than adequate storage space. Like the ship's main public rooms, cabins are based on navy-blue fabrics and carpeting, along with wood tones—attractive, but simple, well constructed and utilitarian. The large desk/bureau is white with dark brown trim and the rest of the cabinetry is a medium wood tone.

Although all the cabins are comfortable, cabins amidships are more stable in rough seas. Note that the ship's engines, when running at full speed, can be a bit noisy.

This line is not recommended for passengers with serious disabilities or those who are wheelchair bound. There are no elevators on board, access to piers is often by tender, and there are raised doorsills.

PUBLIC AREAS   There aren't a lot of public areas on these small ships, but they're more than adequate for ships that spend most of their time in port. The four main rooms include two restaurants, a library, and the vaguely nautical-looking Lounge, with several cozy, somewhat private partitioned-off nooks and clusters of comfy caramel-colored leather chairs surrounding a slightly sunken wooden dance floor. In the corner is a bar and, in another, a piano and music equipment for the onboard entertainment duo. Here passengers congregate for port talks, pre- and post-dinner drinks, dancing, and any local dance performances. The second bar is the one out on the pool deck, which also attracts passengers before and after dinner for drinks under the stars. Here there's a piano in the corner of the deck (which doesn't get much play), but mostly this is your typical casual pool bar, and the place where cigars can be purchased and smoked.

The wood-paneled library manages to be both nautical and collegiate at the same time. Guests can read, play cards, or check out one of the hundreds of videotapes (CDs are available from the purser's office nearby).

The yachtily elegant, dimly lit main restaurant is similarly styled with navy carpeting and fabrics combined with wood details and nautical touches. The Veranda breakfast and lunch restaurant is light and airy. Throughout the ship, large glass windows, which are locked into a permanently closed position, allow in plenty of light if not air.

RECREATION & FITNESS FACILITIES   The swimming pool is tiny, as you might expect aboard such a relatively small-scale ship, and there's an adjacent hot tub. The deck chairs around the pool can get filled during sunny days, but there's always the crescent-shaped slice of deck above and more space outside of the Veranda restaurant. On Deck Four, there's an unobstructed wraparound deck for walkers.

There's a cramped gym in a cabin-sized room, and an adjacent co-ed sauna. Massages and a few other types of treatments are available out of a single massage room next to the hair salon on Deck One.

Wind Surf

The Verdict

This sleek, sexy, super-smooth sailing ship is a gem, offering an extensive spa along with an intimate yacht-like ambience.

Wind Surf *(photo: Windstar Cruises)*

Specifications

Size (in tons)	14,745	Officers	English/Dutch
Number of Cabins	156	Crew	163 (International)
Number of Outside Cabins	156	Passenger/Crew Ratio	2 to 1
Cabins with Verandas	0	Year Built	1990
Number of Passengers	312	Last Major Refurbishment	1997

Frommer's Ratings (Scale of 1–5)

Cabin Comfort & Amenities	5	Pool, Fitness & Spa Facilities	5
Ship Cleanliness & Maintenance	4	Children's Facilities	2
Public Comfort/Space	4	Itinerary	4
Decor	4	Worth the Money	5

The newest member of the Windstar fleet of deluxe motor-sailers continues the line's tradition of delivering a top-of-the line cruise experience that's as chic and sophisticated as it is easy-going and unregimented. Previously sailing under the Club Med banner (it originally entered service as the *Club Med I*), the ship was designed by the same French architect who worked on the other three Windstar vessels, and for the most part is an enlarged copy of them. Purchased for $45 million and subsequently renamed, the *Wind Surf* underwent a major $8 million renovation in early 1998, which included an overhaul of all the public areas and the addition of 30 suites, a 10,000-square-foot spa complex, an alternative restaurant, and a casino.

As part of the conversion, many areas were gutted and all the grace notes of upscale, high-end life at sea were added to make what has emerged since then as a very elegant vessel. Despite a passenger capacity more than double her sister ships (312 versus 148), the *Wind Surf* maintains the feel of a private yacht.

Cabins & Rates

Cabins	Per diems from	Bathtub	Fridge	Hair Dryer	Sitting Area	TV
Inside	n/a	no	yes	yes	no	yes*
Outside	$343	no	yes	yes	no	yes*
Suite	n/a	no	yes	yes	yes	yes*

*TVs show CNN.

CABINS Cabins are clones of those described in the *Wind Spirit/Wind Star* review, above. The interiors of both suites and standard cabins feature generous use of polished woods (burled maple and teak), bedspreads and curtains in navy blue and beige color schemes (suites are maroon and beige), white laminated cabinetwork, and plentiful storage space. All cabins have ocean views, and both standard cabins (188 square feet) and suites (376 square feet) are well supplied with creature comforts, including terry robes, hair dryers, well-stocked minibars, safes, VCRs and CD players, and satellite TVs with CNN. Bathrooms have teakwood trim, and are artfully designed and more appealing than those aboard many luxury cruise ships. Extra-spacious suites have separate sleeping and living quarters and his-and-hers bathrooms (each with a shower and a toilet).

As part of *Wind Surf*'s metamorphosis in 1998, cabins were completely reconfigured for a reduced passenger capacity of 312 instead of the *Club Med*'s 386. In addition, 30 suites were added on Deck 3 (its original layout had only one), making the vessel the most suite-heavy of the Windstar fleet.

The ship has two elevators (unlike the other ships in the Windstar fleet, which have none), but still is not recommended for people with serious mobility problems. Access to piers is often by tender, and ramps over doorsills are not adequate.

PUBLIC AREAS   Since the *Wind Surf*'s passenger-space ratio is 30% greater than its sister ships, its two main public spaces—the bright and airy Wind Surf Lounge where passengers gather in the evening for cocktails and to listen to a three- to five-person band play your favorite requests, and the Compass Rose piano bar, popular for after-dinner drinks—are also roomier than comparable public spaces on the other ships. There's also the pool bar for a drink under the stars.

As on the other Windstar ships, breakfast and lunch are served in the glass-enclosed Veranda Cafe topside, while the *Wind Surf* offers an alternative dinner option that's unique—in addition to the Restaurant, the smaller 90-seat Bistro (adjacent to the Veranda) serves dinner each night.

Also unlike the other Windstar ships, *Wind Surf* has a 2,100-square-foot conference center that lies amidships and just below the water line (a company spokesperson says about 25% of the *Wind Surf*'s total business comes from charter and corporate incentive business; sometimes the whole ship is chartered, sometimes just half or less). Suitable for between 118 and 180 occupants, depending on the arrangement of tables and chairs, it contains technical amenities such as a photocopy machine and audiovisual equipment.

Other public areas include a casino that's nestled into one edge of the Windsurf Lounge, a library (in which the line hopes to install data-port jacks for laptops by year-end 1999), and a gift shop.

RECREATION & FITNESS FACILITIES   The *Wind Surf* has the most elaborate fitness and spa facilities in the Windstar fleet (the line's three 148-passenger ships have no spa and a tiny gym) and in fact outclasses facilities on other similar-sized ships. There's a well-stocked windowed gym on the top deck, a "sports" pool for aqua-aerobics and scuba lessons (passengers can get resort certification), and an aerobics room one deck below that's also used for yoga and golf swing practice. The new Steiner-managed WindSpa offers a roster of exercise, massage, and beauty regimens that rival those available at many land-based spas. There's aromatherapy, a variety of massages and other treatments, a sauna, and a steam room. Spa packages—geared to both men and women—can be purchased in advance through your travel agent, with appointment times made once you're on board.

Besides the sports pool, there's another pool on the Main Deck as well as two hot tubs. For joggers, a full circuit teak promenade wraps around the Bridge Deck.

Soft-Adventure Lines & Sailing Ships

Whether the small, motorized coastal cruisers of American Canadian Caribbean Line and Clipper or the sailing ships of Star Clippers, Tall Ship Adventures, and Windjammer Barefoot Cruises, these ships are a far different breed from the rest. All are small and intimate, and often more adventure tour than they are "cruise" as we have come to know it. Leave the jackets, ties, pumps, and pearls at home: These vessels espouse an ultra-casual ethic and take passengers close up to the islands and the sea.

These vessels generally visit a port every day, and because they have shallow drafts (the amount of the ship that rides below the waterline), they're able to sail adventurous itineraries to small, out-of-the-way ports that the big cruise ships would run aground trying to approach. Also, since all these ships depart from one or another of the Caribbean islands rather than Florida, there's little time spent at sea getting to your first port.

Passengers are well-traveled people who like to learn and explore more than they care about plush amenities and onboard activities of the bingo and horseracing variety. Don't expect doting service, but do expect very personal attention, as crew and passengers get friendly fast.

Food will be basic, hearty, and plentiful, but don't look for room service and midnight buffets, because there aren't any. There may not be TVs in the cabins and you won't find a casino. The ships in this chapter are like private yachts or summer camps at sea. You'll have fun, make lots of new friends, and be able to let your hair down.

DRESS CODES   Dress code? What's a dress code? Aboard most of the ships in this chapter you can get away with a polo shirt and khakis (or shorts) at pretty much any hour of the day, and on some—Windjammer and Tall Ship Adventures, specifically—you could show up to dinner in your bathing suit and not feel out of place. These are monumentally casual ships.

Cruise Lines Reviewed in This Chapter
- American Canadian Caribbean Line
- Clipper Cruise Line
- Club Med Cruises
- Star Clippers
- Tall Ship Adventures
- Windjammer Barefoot Cruises

American Canadian Caribbean Line

SHIPS   Grande Caribe • Grande Mariner • Niagara Prince

461 Water St., Warren, RI 02885. ☎ **800/556-7450** or 401/247-0955. Fax 401/247-2350. www.accl-smallships.com.

THE LINE IN A NUTSHELL   Small and intimate, these three extremely no-frills, moderate-priced ships travel to offbeat places and attract a well-traveled, down-to-earth older crowd. It's a dose of real Americana—in the vessels themselves, the officers, the passengers, and the crew.

THE EXPERIENCE   This trio of innovative and extremely informal small ships offers an unusual cruising experience, focusing on encounters with indigenous peoples and navigating such hinterlands as the cays off the coast of Belize, remote out-islands in the Bahamas, and exotic islands near the Pacific mouth of the Panama Canal.

Of all the small-ship lines, ACCL offers the most bare-bones experience in terms of amenities, services, and meals. It's also the only line featuring a BYOB policy. Owing to the ships' tiny size, there are no quiet nooks besides your cabin for you to run and hide—you're in close quarters and constant contact with everyone else. Luckily, the ships attract a generally convivial crowd, many of whom have sailed with ACCL before.

Pros

- **Casual and unpretentious.** If you're looking for a do-it-yourself, cost-effective adventure at sea, these tiny yet innovative vessels are tops.
- **Imaginative itineraries.** One-of-a-kind itineraries are innovative, and the ships' exploratory technical innovations allow a close-up experience of out-of-the-way islands.
- **BYOB policy.** ACCL's BYOB policy provides substantial savings on bar bills. The bus or van that transports passengers from the airport or hotel to the ship stops at a reasonably priced liquor store en route so those interested can stock up (a bottle of rum purchased in Panama City, for example, costs less than $4).

Cons

- **No frills.** Cabins are tiny, decor is bland, towels are changed every other day, there are no beach towels (bring your own), and meals are served family-style.
- **No place to hide.** There's little privacy. When the ships are at or near full capacity, they're full. Your cabin is your only sanctuary—and the accordion-style doors and thin cabin walls will make you feel closer to your fellow passengers than you might prefer.
- **Minimal port information.** For a line that's so destination-oriented, ACCL's ships have a surprising lack of books and naturalists/historians to provide background on the islands' history, culture, and nature.

Frommer's Ratings: ACCL					
	Poor	**Fair**	**Good**	**Excellent**	**Outstanding**
Enjoyment Factor				✓	
Dining			✓		
Activities					✓
Children's Activities	N/A*				
Entertainment		✓			
Service			✓		
Overall Value			✓		

ACCL offers no children's programs.

ACCL: TINY SHIPS, BIG ADVENTURE

For more than half a century (since 1949), master ship builder and ACCL founder/builder/captain/president Luther Blount has been designing and building a variety of vessels, including cargo ferries, short-haul freighters, and tugboats in his Warren, Rhode Island shipyard. In 1966, Blount built his first cruise ship, the 20-passenger *Canyon Flyer,* which specialized in cruising New England and Canadian waters. Over the years he has refined the design of his ships, gradually increasing both size and capacity and expanding itineraries while remaining faithful to his original concept that "small is the only way to cruise." At over age 80, Blount continues to head one of the only family-owned companies in the cruise industry.

Along with building almost 300 ships over the past 50 years, Blount also holds over 20 patents for his innovative designs, which include an extendible **bow ramp** that, combined with an unusually shallow draft of about 6^1/$_2$ feet, makes it possible for the ships to nudge their bows directly onto beaches, silted riverbanks, or virtually anywhere else and disembark passengers directly onto the shore. The ships also feature **retractable pilot houses** that enable them to cruise under low bridges on inland waterways. Each also has a **sternside swimming platform,** a Blount-designed 24-passenger **glass-bottomed boat,** and Sunfish boats that are launched for short sails during Caribbean and Central American beach breaks. His ships' popular appeal is evident by the fact that several former ACCL ships have been purchased by other small cruise lines, including Alaska Sightseeing/Cruise West and Glacier Bay Tours & Cruises/Voyager.

Innovative Caribbean itineraries are designed to bypass "tourist trap" ports and islands. If you sail this line, you'll sail waters normally traveled only by private yachts and walk on pristine beaches that passengers from few, if any, mainstream cruise ships have ever explored.

All said, American Canadian Caribbean is a delightfully rare find. It's one of the few cruise entities in the business that designs, builds, maintains, and markets berths aboard its own ships. Just be sure you know what you're getting into, because these ships, with their spartan, communal, rough-and-ready lifestyle, just aren't for everyone.

THE FLEET

In operation since April 1997, the 100-passenger *Grande Caribe* is the first of ACCL's Grande Class vessels, carrying more passengers and featuring roomier lounges and dining areas than previous ACCL ships. It is identical in size to its sister Grande Class ship, the 100-passenger *Grande Mariner,* which entered service in 1998. The smaller 84-passenger *Niagara Prince,* built in 1994, rounds out the current ACCL fleet.

PASSENGER PROFILE

These ships attract mostly senior couples in their 60s, 70s, and 80s, with the average age of an ACCL passenger being 72. While some are physically fit, a good number walk with canes and use hearing aids. These casual ships appeal to an unpretentious, sensible, early-to-bed cruise crowd. Wash-and-wear fabrics, durable windbreakers, and easy-to-care-for sportswear is about as fancy as you'll get aboard this line. Passengers want to escape the overrun ports of the Caribbean (such as St. Thomas) and flee to isolated beaches and secluded havens to become quietly acquainted with regional cultures or comb the beaches. That said, passengers tend to be less adventurous than those on other small ship lines, so the line doesn't offer harder activities, such as excursions in inflatable Zodiac boats.

Since most passengers are grandparents, common topics for conversations often concern the grandkids and experiences during World War II. Besides senior couples, there may be a few mother-daughter traveling companions.

ACCL has one of the most loyal followings of any line, so it's not unusual to have upward of 50% repeaters on a particular cruise. Many passengers have been on other small ship lines, such as Windjammer, Special Expeditions, Clipper, Glacier Bay/ Voyager, and Alaska Sightseeing/Cruise West. Travel programs for seniors, such as Elderhostel, are also popular with the typical ACCL passenger.

The ships will not appeal to young couples, singles, honeymooners, or families. Children under age 14 are prohibited, and there are no children's facilities or activities.

A warning: Ceilings throughout ACCL ships are set at about 6'4", so if you're very tall, you might want to consider another line—unless you enjoy stooping, of course.

DINING

Wholesome, all-American food is well prepared and casually presented, but overall is nothing special. There are no individually printed menus; instead, the daily menu with selections for all three meals is posted every morning on the blackboard in the dining room.

Early risers will find "eye-opener" coffee available in the lounge beginning at 6:30am, and a selection of fruit juices is available here every morning before breakfast. Breakfast combines buffet and table service, with passengers having a choice from the buffet table of hot or cold cereal, yogurt, and fruit. Slices of a variety of melons are placed on tables while waiters deliver a different hot dish every morning, such as scrambled eggs with bacon, Belgian waffles, pancakes, French toast, or cheese omelets.

Lunch is the lightest meal of the day and consists of homemade soup (such as tomato basil, vegetable, or beef orzo) along with a sandwich on freshly baked bread (turkey, ham and cheese, and tuna) plus a salad, chips, fruit, and dessert.

Dinners begin with a salad and fresh bread followed by a main entree like BBQ ribs, roast beef, chicken, or fish, along with vegetables, rice, or potatoes, plus dessert. Since there is only one entree, anyone wanting an **alternative meal** (such as fish instead of beef) can be accommodated if they notify the kitchen before 10am. **Special dietary needs** can also be met with advance notice.

Since the line has a **BYOB policy**, all alcoholic beverages—which guests can buy at a liquor store en route to the ship from the airport or their hotel—are kept in the lounge; beer and wine are placed in a cooler near the bar and there are separate shelves set aside for bottles. To avoid drinking someone else's booze, all bottles and cans are labeled with the passengers' cabin number. Soft drinks, along with tonic and soda water, are provided free of charge at the bar.

Meals are served promptly at 8am, noon, and 6pm every day and are announced by one of the waitresses clanging a cowbell as she passes through the corridors and lounge. Rather than wandering in gradually, everyone typically arrives within a few minutes of hearing the bell. Dining is open-seating, communal style for all meals, as passengers group themselves around circular and rectangular tables primarily seating eight (just one or two tables are set for four). Passengers interact and get to know each other sooner rather than later. Mixing with your fellow passengers at meals is mandatory since there are no tables for two and no room service for private dining in the cabin.

Cruise Tip: Saving Your Soles on ACCL Excursions

ACCL ships don't always select beach stopovers because of their soft and glistening sands. Many expeditions to remote places incorporate stops at gravel- and/or coral-covered beaches, so it's a good idea to pack a pair of nylon or rubber sandals or shoes to wear on the beach and in the water.

Flexible Itineraries & Other Vagaries of Small-Ship Cruising

As is the case with most other small-ship lines, all ACCL itineraries are flexible and may be altered at the discretion of the captain, who might change direction and head for another island because of sea and/or wind conditions. On itineraries featuring the Panama Canal, the time of transit could take place during the day or night (exact time of crossing cannot be determined before departure). While every effort is made to transit during the day, on a recent cruise, the time was changed the day before from a morning to an evening transit, entering the first lock around 7pm and departing the last set of locks around 3am. Needless to say, passengers were disappointed. Although locks are very well lit throughout the night, the rest of the transit was in darkness.

A variety of teas as well as coffee and hot chocolate are available 'round the clock in the dining room, along with cookies and fresh fruit.

ACTIVITIES

With the exception of a few printed quizzes and an occasional arts and crafts and/or napkin folding class, daytime activities are concentrated in recreational pursuits off the ship during calls at remote islands and beaches. As some of the areas frequented by ACCL ships (especially those off the coast of Belize) are among the richest repositories of underwater life in the western hemisphere, there are frequent opportunities for **snorkeling** (with masks and fins provided free of charge) as well as swimming from the ships' **swimming platform** in the stern. The ships haul along a Sunfish (mini sailboat) for passengers to use as well as a 24-passenger **glass-bottomed boat,** which is used at some islands to view coral formations and tropical fish.

The amount of time spent at each island varies from a few hours to an entire morning or afternoon. Except for a couple overnight sailings, most of the time the ship remains anchored at night, as sailing between islands usually takes place during the day.

Some itineraries include visits to villages inhabited by indigenous tribal peoples. For example, Panama cruises include stops at several Kuna Indian villages and an optional excursion by cayuga (native boat resembling large dugout canoe) to the Embara village in the Darien Jungle. Those with puritan sensibilities are advised that Embara women wear only grass skirts, and men wear loincloths.

During calls at some of the San Blas islands on the Panama itinerary, the cruise director may bring member(s) of the community aboard ship to discuss native life and culture. With the cruise director acting as translator, Kuna women discuss their daily lives as well as the unique art of mola making, while a Kuna medicine man also comes aboard to discuss methods and techniques of treating illness.

That said, although ACCL promotes the fact that all of its cruises are accompanied by experts, on a recent Panama cruise, lectures were limited to talks by an American living in Panama who visited the ship for 1 day and discussed the past, present, and future of the Panama Canal. The only other "expert" was a young Panamanian in his 20s who had lived with some of the native Indian tribes but had a poor command of English and was an inexperienced lecturer, and was dismissed by the cruise director midway through the cruise. The line simply does not have the variety or quality of naturalists and historians you'll find on competing lines (Clipper Cruise Line, for instance, plus such non-Caribbean soft-adventure lines as Special Expeditions, Alaska Sightseeing/ Cruise West, and Glacier Bay/Voyager). The ships' libraries (a few shelves in the lounge)

ACCL Fleet Itineraries*

Ship	Home Ports & Season	Itinerary	Other Itineraries
Grand Caribe	Panama itineraries between Balboa and Colón (Panama), Dec–Mar.	**11-night Panama/Panama Canal:** Portobelo, San Blas Islands, Contadora, Isla de Rey, Darien, Contadora, Mogo Mogo, Isla Pacheque, and Taboga.	Erie Canal, St. Lawrence Seaway, Intracoastal Waterway, Nova Scotia
Grand Mariner	Virgin Islands itineraries round-trip from St. Thomas, Dec–Jan; eastern Carib itineraries between Antigua and either Sint Maarten or Grenada Jan–Mar; Panama itineraries between Balboa and Colón (Panama), Mar–Apr; other 1-time itineraries round-trip from Trinidad to Curaçao and from Balboa to Belize City.	**11-night Virgin Islands Carib:** St. John's, Tortola, Virgin Gorda, Prickley Pear, Salt Island, Andegada, Beef Island, Jost Van Dyke, and Norman Islands. **11-night eastern Carib:** Il Pineel & Tinatmarre, Anguilla, St. Barts, Saba, St. Kitts, Nevis or Guadeloupe, Dominica, Martinique, St. Lucia, and Grenadines. **12-night southern Carib/Orinoco:** Margarita Island (Venezuela), Island of Tortuga, Los Roques, and Bonaire. **14-night southern Carib:** Bocas del Toro, Bluefield's, Corn Islands, Pearl Islands, Miskitos Islands, Roatan (Honduras), Livingston (Guatemala), Punta Gorda, West Snake Cay, and Goff Cay.	Erie Canal, St. Lawrence Seaway, Intracoastal Waterway, Nova Scotia
Niagara Prince	Round-trip from Belize City, Dec–Apr.	**10-night Belize:** Goff Cay, Tobacco Range, Victoria Channel Reef, Moho Cay, Laughing Bird Cay, Placencia, Punta Gorda, Livingston (Guatemala), El Gofete, Casa Guatemala, Castilo San Felipe, West Snake Cay, Punta Icacos, Lime Cay, and Water Cay. **6-night Belize:** Goff Cay, Tobacco Cay, Victoria Channel Reef, Moho Cay, Lime Cay, Placencia, West Snake Cay, Punta Icacos, and Laughing Bird Cay.	New England, Intracoastal Waterway

Note: Itineraries can change on short notice, depending on new markets that open and unforeseen changes in conditions at ports of call—it's all part of the adventure.

have limited background material, and because no reading list is supplied before the cruise, passengers should do their own research and bring guidebooks.

There is no daily printed schedule; instead, the agenda of activities and ports of call are posted every morning on a bulletin board, and the cruise director runs through the daily schedule after breakfast.

Aside from the destination-oriented activities, the main evening event is a **movie** from the ship's video collection shown after dinner on the large-screen TV in the lounge. There may also be an occasional session of "The Not-So-Newlywed Game."

CHILDREN'S PROGRAM

The minimum age for children on board is 14 years old, and there are no special facilities even for those who clear that mark. Unless you have a particularly self-reliant teenager who enjoys the company of older passengers, leave the kids at home.

ENTERTAINMENT

Amusement is mostly of the do-it-yourself nature. The BYOB cocktail hour is a time for songfests, piano music, announcements, and an occasional lecture about an upcoming sight or experience. The cruise director might arrange some onboard activities, but

A Few Good Deals & One Extra Charge

Unlike most other cruise lines, ACCL's brochure rates are very rarely discounted. That said, they do offer a few good deals. **1999 Deals:** To celebrate its 50th anniversary, throughout 1999 ACCL is offering a $500 discount to passengers who refer new first-time passengers; both couples get the discount. **Cabin Shares:** A 15% discount is granted for anyone sharing a cabin with two other passengers. **Back-to-Back & Repeater Deals:** A 10% discount is given if you book two back-to-back cruises, and the line gives passengers an 11th cruise free after their 10th (paid) cruise. **Port Charges:** Expect to pay between $120 and $200 per person in addition to the cruise rates.

they will be low-key. Sometimes **local entertainers,** such as Garifuna dancers in Belize or soca/reggae musicians in the Virgin Islands, will be invited on board for an evening or will perform for passengers in port.

SERVICE

Most of the personable 18-member staff is made up of Americans, with a few coming from Central American countries and/or the Caribbean (depending on the itinerary). Some of the foreign members of the staff speak limited English, but this does not limit their effectiveness in getting their jobs done.

The crew is versatile by necessity, having to double on many jobs that bigger ships have segregated into separate departments. You may see your cabin attendant waiting tables at dinner, or notice one of the laundry workers clearing dishes.

Service is adequate in the dining room, although with just three or four waiters serving 70 passengers it can be slow at times; however, since the day's agenda proceeds at a leisurely pace, nobody is in a hurry to go anywhere. Cabins are made up once a day after breakfast, while towels are changed every other day.

Most of the staff come from Luther Blount country (Rhode Island) and probably won't be doing this type of work as a career. In fact, serving aboard an ACCL vessel seems like a summer job, something akin to working as a camp counselor in Maine. What they lack in experience, the staff makes up in enthusiasm and friendliness.

There is no laundry service or room service, nor is there an onboard doctor or medical facilities (ships this size are not required to provide them, as they always sail close to land).

Grande Caribe •
Grande Mariner

The Verdict

Functional and no-frills, these ships are best described as well-thought-out vehicles for transporting passengers to remote ports.

Grande Caribe *(photo: ACCL)*

Specifications

Size (in tons)	99	Officers	American
Number of Cabins	50	Crew	18 (American/Int'l)
Number of Outside Cabins	41	Passenger/Crew Ratio	5.5 to 1
Cabins with Verandas	0	Year Built	1997/1998
Number of Passengers	100	Last Major Refurbishment	N/A

Frommer's Ratings (Scale of 1–5)

Cabin Comfort & Amenities	2	Pool, Fitness & Spa Facilities	N/A
Ship Cleanliness & Maintenance	4	Children's Facilities	N/A
Public Comfort/Space	3	Itinerary	5
Decor	2	Worth the Money	4

Seaworthy, practical, and unfussy, this newest pair of ACCL ships are in many ways the culmination of 30 years of ACCL's corporate philosophy. Even better, they're the most comfortable and appealing vessels the line has ever built. Constructed at a cost of between $7.5 and $8 million each, they were conceived as state-of-the-art replacements for the dowdier and more battered *Caribbean Prince* and *Mayan Prince,* vessels that ACCL sold to Alaska-based Glacier Bay Tours and Cruises (a.k.a. Voyager Cruise Line), which jumped to bid the moment they were offered for sale and now operates the vessels in Alaska and in Mexico's Sea of Cortez.

The design of this pair of newcomers added a much-needed improvement to ACCL's basic, generic package: a lounge/bar on the upper deck that's separate from the rest of the dining room and doubles as a communal rendezvous point that can accommodate every passenger on board. The space this area opens up aboard these very small ships does a lot to relieve the claustrophobia that's been an unavoidable hallmark of ACCL vessels in the past.

The *Grand Caribe* and *Mariner's* system of cabin ventilation is also a marked improvement over earlier ACCL vessels, and they're also a lot quieter due to the use of twin-screwed, 1,400 horsepower engines that are mounted on cushioned bearings.

Cabins & Rates

Cabins	Per diems from	Bathtub	Fridge	Hair Dryer	Sitting Area	TV
Inside	$107	no	no	no	no	no
Outside	$177	no	no	no	no	no

CABINS   Spartan in design (four bare white walls) and amenities (soap and towels only; no TV or radio), the ships' 50 compact, definitely cramped cabins—measuring between about 80 and 120 square feet—are somewhere between cozy and claustrophobic. However you describe them, there is minimal room for couples to maneuver (watch out for flying elbows!) and hardly any space to stretch out in the minuscule bathroom. The cramped bathrooms get soaked whenever you bathe, thanks to a hand-held sprayer that hangs from a fixture in the wall and shoots water virtually everywhere.

Passengers 6 feet or taller, beware of the low bridge over the toilet (I banged my head twice). Most cabins also have a small table plus a second mirror with two small shelves.

The cabins on Sun Deck are the only ones equipped with sliding picture windows and regular doors that open onto an outside deck. All other cabins have sealed windows and vinyl, accordion-like partitions instead of doors and open onto an inside corridor (all cabin doors or partitions lock from the inside only). Many cabins have two lower berths that can be made up into a double bed.

Six windowless units are adjacent to staff quarters on the lowest deck and have sloping outside walls and upper and lower berths. Cabins on the Main Deck closest to the dining room and cabins on the Sun Deck closest to the lounge are susceptible to noise from these two public rooms.

It's a good idea to pack light since storage space is limited to a small rectangular hanging closet plus three drawers and the space under the beds. There are also five hooks affixed to panels on walls for hanging clothes. There's an extra cabinet for storage between beds on *Grande Mariner.*

None of the cabins are wheelchair accessible. There are no elevators, but there is a stair lift for those who may have difficulty walking between decks.

PUBLIC AREAS   Made up of three decks, both ships have larger public spaces than the *Niagara Prince,* with their lounges located on the Sun Deck and the dining room and galley situated on the Main Deck. The ships' main public area is the lounge/bar, with wraparound windows that allow it to serve as a viewing area during the day. Furnished with couches and chairs and containing a small collection of magazines and paperback books left behind by past passengers (bring your own books if you like to read), it also hosts the lively BYOB pre-dinner cocktail hour every evening and is a favorite place to escape the confines of the cabin, read, and socialize. The room also serves as an auditorium for occasional lectures and arts and crafts classes, has board games and puzzles, and hosts the screening of movies and documentaries on its large-screen TV/VCR.

The other public space is the dining room, next to the galley on the Main Deck. The public areas of the *Caribe* are made up primarily of metal; the *Mariner* has more polished woods in both the dining room and lounge, giving it a slightly warmer atmosphere.

As on the other ships in this category, there's no onboard shop, but logo items—caps, T-shirts and so on—are available for purchase from the cruise director.

During the day, many passengers view the passing scene from atop the ship's Sun Deck, which is partially covered by a large awning that offers protection from the intense tropical sun.

POOL, FITNESS & SPA FACILITIES   There are no exercise facilities, swimming pools, or spas aboard either of these ships, which seems to suit many of ACCL's older passengers just fine. You can walk around the Sun Deck for fitness (12.5 laps equals 1 mile). The top outside deck has some deck chairs, partially shaded by an awning, for anyone interested in sunbathing.

Niagara Prince

The Verdict

This bare-bones ship—even smaller and more basic than the *Caribe* and *Mariner*—offers the down-to-earth cruiser an adventurous, offbeat way to see the Caribbean.

Niagara Prince *(photo: ACCL)*

Specifications

Size (in tons)	99	Officers	American
Number of Cabins	42	Crew	17 (American/Int'l)
Number of Outside Cabins	40	Passenger/Crew Ratio	5 to 1
Cabins with Verandas	0	Year Built	1994
Number of Passengers	84	Last Major Refurbishment	N/A

Frommer's Ratings (Scale of 1–5)

Cabin Comfort & Amenities	2	Pool, Fitness & Spa Facilities	N/A
Ship Cleanliness & Maintenance	3	Children's Facilities	N/A
Public Comfort/Space	2	Itinerary	5
Decor	2	Worth the Money	4

Overall, the *Niagara Prince* is more cramped than its two fleetmates, with its lounge and dining area sharing the same public space (there are separate lounges and dining areas on the other two ships). Many of *Niagara's* remarkable engineering features were designed specifically for usually cold northern waters, not for the smooth Bahamian winter waters. Consequently, although the ship is versatile, you won't find any of the sun-worshipping options (large sun decks, etc.) that are standard issue aboard most Caribbean-bound ships.

Like its siblings, the *Niagara Prince* is equipped with a retractable pilot house, extendible bow ramp, shallow draft, retractable stern swimming platform, glass-bottomed boat, and Sunfish.

Cabins & Rates

Cabins	Per diems from	Bathtub	Fridge	Hair Dryer	Sitting Area	TV
Inside	$107	no	no	no	no	no
Outside	$177	no	no	no	no	no

CABINS   In the Luther Blount tradition, cabins aboard this vessel are even smaller and more cramped than those on the Grande Caribe and Mariner. Ranging from 72 square feet to 96 square feet, cabins are simple and spartan looking, utterly without frills and decorated in a spare style. Each has individual climate controls and all but two offer some kind of outside view. There are no cabin keys—passengers are on the honor system—but cabins can be locked from the inside.

If it's at all possible, try for a cabin in the number range of the 50s, 60s, or 70s, all of which offer sliding picture windows. There are only two inside cabins, inexpensive and a tight 80 square feet each. The 40 outside cabins are more or less equivalent, despite slight variations in their configuration of beds. Some single beds can be made up as doubles, and certain cabins can accommodate a third person (good luck!).

No cabins are wheelchair accessible. There are no elevators, but there is a stair lift for those who may have difficulty walking between decks.

PUBLIC AREAS   The *Niagara Prince* has only two decks (Sun Deck and Main Deck), with the main public area on the Sun Deck, where the lounge shares the same space with the dining room and galley. Unfortunately, this area seems full to overflowing almost all the time. Frankly, there simply aren't too many public areas aboard this ship that don't seem to bulge with passengers, regardless of the time of day or night you happen to be there. Your favorite perch—simply for lack of anything better—might be along the railing on one of the narrow side decks, or atop one of the two compact open decks sternside.

POOL, FITNESS & SPA FACILITIES   As aboard the *Caribe* and *Mariner,* there are no exercise facilities, swimming pools, or spas aboard.

Clipper Cruise Line

SHIPS   Nantucket Clipper • Yorktown Clipper

7711 Bonhomme Ave., St. Louis, MO 63105-1956. ☎ **800/325-0010** or 314/727-2929. Fax 314/727-6576. www.clippercruise.com.

THE LINE IN A NUTSHELL   These down-to-earth, comfortable small ships focus on offbeat ports of call, learning, and mingling with passengers and crew.

THE EXPERIENCE   You won't find glitter, glitz, or Las Vegas gambling aboard any of this line's ships. Instead, the mood is perky, all-American, and unpretentious (and like many of the American-crewed small ships, cruise rates are not cheap). The line it most resembles in spirit is American Canadian Caribbean Line, but the Clipper ships come with a few more amenities and are definitely a notch up in the plush department.

Clipper caters to mature, seasoned, easy-going, relatively affluent older passengers seeking a casual (but not too casual) vacation experience, enjoying firsthand the natural beauties of the Americas and the Caribbean. Being small ships, the ambience is intimate and conducive to easily making new friends. A cruise director helps organize the days, answers questions, and assists passengers on what to do and how to do on shore.

The line's two Caribbean ships, *Nantucket Clipper* and *Yorktown Clipper,* are small and maneuverable enough to access remote coral reefs of the southern Caribbean; isolated refuges in the BVIs and Central America; and remote hideaways in the Grenadines. Wet landings at isolated ports are common (you'll be fine with a pair of rubber sandals).

Pros

- **Interesting ports of call.** Their smallness enables them to visit more remote ports in the BVI and Grenadines, for instance, that most ships can't get close to.
- **Informal atmosphere.** No need to dress up at all—everything's casual and easy-going all day long.
- **Young, enthusiastic American crew.** While they may not be the most experienced or mature, they're sweet and engaging and their enthusiasm can be downright contagious.
- **Port lecturers.** Historians, naturalists, and educators often present informal talks and mingle with guests.

Cons

- **Noisy engines.** If you can help it, don't book a cabin on the lowest deck (Main Deck), where noise from the engines can get quite loud. In general, no matter where you are, when the engines are running, you can hear them.
- **No stabilizers.** If you hit some choppy waters and you're prone to seasickness, you're in for some unpleasantness.

Frommer's Ratings: Clipper Cruise Line

	Poor	Fair	Good	Excellent	Outstanding
Enjoyment Factor				✓	
Dining				✓	
Activities				✓	
Children's Program	N/A*				
Entertainment			✓		
Service				✓	
Overall Value				✓	

Clipper offers no children's programs.

CLIPPER: CASUAL, COMFORTABLE CRUISING

One of only a handful of cruise lines ever launched from the great American grain belt, Clipper's roots and marketing strategy are firmly based in St. Louis, Missouri, a city whose dependence on the navigation of rivers, rather than seas, profoundly influenced the design and vision of these ships.

Extolling the beauty of small-ship adventures, Clipper Cruise Line advertises that its ships are used for exploring the waterways of America. But Clipper explores the Caribbean as well, and the line's well-attended Caribbean sailings are taking up more of its time.

The company was founded in 1982 by Barney Ebsworth, creator of the INTRAV group of wholesale travel and travel-related companies, which he founded in 1959. In late 1996, after years of operating as independent entities, INTRAV acquired Clipper, in the process streamlining in-house operations and offering an expanded series of travel-related services. Clipper now operates officially an INTRAV subsidiary, although the two remain separate brands. Paul Duynhouwer, president of Clipper when it stood alone, is now the president and CEO of INTRAV.

Although Clipper's ports of call are more interesting than the well-trod landings favored by most larger lines, the line has only recently begun to venture into some of the wildly exotic ports that have long been favored by the more aggressively adventuresome American Canadian Caribbean Line. (Clipper's new itineraries include forays into the jungles of Central America—including excursions into Panama—and, aboard its newest ship, even excursions to the Arctic and Antarctic.) With ACCL you get to experience the Caribbean via the line's cutting-edge (but spartan) cruise technology, but here you get the spectacular views but in a somewhat more cushy environment, with a greater amount of onboard space. As a company spokesperson notes, "We provide a soft adventure for travelers who may shy away from roughing it, and we think of ourselves not as a cruise line, but as a travel company that just happens to have ships."

THE FLEET

The 102-passenger, 1,471-ton *Nantucket Clipper* entered service in 1984; the 138-passenger, 2,354-ton *Yorktown Clipper* entered service in 1988. Though of slightly different sizes, the two ships are comparable in design, decor, and amenities. Both offer itineraries in the Caribbean.

In 1998, the company bought a third vessel, the 122-passenger, 4,364-ton *Clipper Adventurer.* Built in 1976, the vessel has a hardened-steel hull that allows it to sail itineraries in rougher parts of the world than the Caribbean—amid the ice floes of the Arctic and Antarctic, for instance. At least during the lifetime of this edition, this vessel will remain outside the Caribbean throughout the year. In late 1998, the line also announced it was acquiring a fourth ship, the luxurious 120-passenger, 5,200-ton *Oceanic Odyssey* from Spice Islands Cruises of Bali, Indonesia. Built in 1989, the ship will be renamed *Clipper Odyssey* in late 1999 and be positioned year-round in the South Pacific and the Orient.

PASSENGER PROFILE

The majority of passengers are well-traveled 50-plus couples who want to cruise in a manner that's culturally and physically comfortable. They are not interested in fancy wardrobes or intricate social rituals. Many are "what you see is what you get" types: honest, unassuming, and not particularly indulgent of airs or pretensions in others. They are most interested in the cultural history and ecosystems of ports of call, not in extraneous hype, garble, marketing, or salesmanship.

There are no facilities for travelers with disabilities aboard the ships.

Clipper Fleet Itineraries

Ship	Home Ports & Season	Itinerary	Other Itineraries
Nantucket Clipper	St. Thomas, round-trip from Dec–Feb.	**7-night eastern Carib:** St. John's, Jost Van Dyke, Sopers Hole, Tortola, Virgin Gorda, Salt Island, Norman's Island, and Christmas Cove.	U.S. East coast, Eastern Canada, Great Lakes, Hudson River
Yorktown Clipper	Eastern Caribbean between Grenada and St. Kitts, Jan–Feb; Southern Caribbean between Curaçao and Trinidad, Dec–Feb.	**7-night eastern Carib:** Union Island, Bequia, St. Lucia, Dominica, and Nevis. **10-night southern Carib/Orinoco River:** Bonaire, Margarita Island (Venezuela), Tobago, and Orinoco River.	Costa Rica, Sea of Cortez, Northern California, British Columbia, Southeast Alaska

DINING

The fare is all-American, prepared by attendees of the Culinary Institute of America. A combination sit-down and buffet-style breakfast is served at 8am (waiters take orders from the menu or you can help yourself). Lunches and dinners include a limited selection of main courses (usually two) plus a pasta and vegetarian dish. Soups are hearty and wholesome. Whenever it's practical, **local ingredients** are incorporated into the daily menu. The cuisine, overall, is tasty, hearty, fairly basic fare that passengers are generally quite content with. Hors d'oeuvres before dinner in the lounge are popular and may include mushroom caps stuffed with escargot or maybe smoked salmon with petit toasts.

You'll see the world through the picture windows in each ship's one restaurant. Seating is open at tables set up for four to six diners; if you like a table for two, this category of cruising isn't for you in the first place. Waitresses are young American women who may not be the most professional attendants, but make up for it in perkiness.

While there are set times for meals, the staff can accommodate those who stroll in late. Coffee and tea are available in the lounge 24 hours a day and hors d'ouevres are served there before dinner.

If you follow any **special diets,** give the line ample warning and they should be able to accommodate you.

Like similar ships, there is no room service, unless you're too ill to attend meals.

ACTIVITIES

By design, these ships don't offer much in the way of scheduled activities of the typical cruise ship variety; unregimented days are what attracts many passengers to Clipper in the first place. What the line does offer are interesting lectures about upcoming ports of call. **Guest speakers** include historians, naturalists, and educators who present talks and mingle with guests. Besides this, passengers mostly socialize, read, maybe do some needlepoint, and enjoy the places they're going.

CHILDREN'S PROGRAM

These ships have no facilities or programs of any kind for children. If you want to bring a young niece, nephew, or grandchild, they'll be expected to behave like young adults. Most teenagers would be bored to death aboard a Clipper Cruise. Baby-sitting is not available.

ENTERTAINMENT

The "more substantive" travel experience, says Clipper, eschews casinos, professional singers and/or dance bands, and comedy and/or magic acts. However, on rare occasions, a live band might play ashore at a port of call, ending the performance at a relatively early hour.

The **onboard lectures** are well attended, delivered in an anecdotal style by experts in such fields as botany, marine life, archaeology, and social history. Being able to meet, dine with, and challenge the opinions of the resident experts is an important part of the onboard entertainment. Overall, the tone is studious, unpretentious, and easygoing.

Aboard either vessel, *the* spot for a rendezvous with fellow passengers is the Observation Lounge, where you'll find a piano, a bar, a small library, and big windows for land- and seascape-watching. Passengers socialize here or curl up quietly with a good book. Each ship has two communal TVs with VCRs for watching nature films and the like, and nearly each night a first-run popular movie is featured.

SERVICE

Staff, crew, and officers are selected as much for their abilities to relate to passengers as for their skills. They are, almost without exception, American born and bred, and quite often young. The staff wears many hats simultaneously, usually with good cheer, and seems equally adept at cleaning up a galley or cabin, tossing a salad, or distributing lifejackets during a safety instruction drill. No one is particularly servile (thank God), and seem happy about their work in a casual, friendly way.

There is no room service.

Nantucket Clipper • Yorktown Clipper

The Verdict

Like a pair of your favorite walking shoes, these low-frills yet comfortable and convivial small ships carry the well traveled to off-the-beaten-track ports in search of adventure.

Yorktown Clipper *(photo: Clipper Cruise Line)*

Specifications

Size (in tons)		Officers	American
Nantucket Clipper	1,471	Crew	
Yorktown Clipper	2,354	*Nantucket Clipper*	32 (International)
Number of Cabins		*Yorktown Clipper*	40 (International)
Nantucket Clipper	51	Passenger/Crew Ratio	
Yorktown Clipper	69	*Nantucket Clipper*	3.2 to 1
Number of Outside Cabins		*Yorktown Clipper*	3.5 to 1
Nantucket Clipper	51	Year Built	
Yorktown Clipper	69	*Nantucket Clipper*	1984
Cabins with Verandas	0	*Yorktown Clipper*	1988
Number of Passengers		Last Major Refurbishment	N/A
Nantucket Clipper	102		
Yorktown Clipper	138		

Frommer's Ratings (Scale of 1–5)

Cabin Comfort & Amenities	3	Pool, Fitness & Spa Facilities	N/A
Ship Cleanliness & Maintenance	3	Children's Facilities	N/A
Public Comfort/Space	3	Itinerary	5
Decor	3	Worth the Money	4

These two ships hold few passengers, but population density aboard is fairly high, given there are only two public rooms. The four-deck ships have no elevators. Both were built in a riverfront shipyard in Jeffersonville, Indiana, a fact that helps reinforce the all-American image of this solid, Midwestern line. Both ships boast drafts of only 8 feet, which allows access to out-of-the-way ports where larger ships can't go. Each, however, lacks some of the distinctive engineering innovations, such as bow ramps for disembarkation directly onto local beaches, that are standard features aboard the vessels of Clipper's most visible Caribbean competitor, American Canadian Caribbean Line. That said, Clipper's accommodations and public areas are a bit more plush (relatively speaking) than ACCL's. Both the *Nantucket* and *Yorktown Clipper* emphasize such resortlike activities as golf (whenever there's a suitable course nearby), art and history lectures with an emphasis on the geography of the region, and swimming and snorkeling, often directly off the sides of the ships.

Cabins & Rates

Cabins	Per diems from	Bathtub	Fridge	Hair Dryer	Sitting Area	TV
Outside	$193	no	no	no	no	no

CABINS   Although small, cabins are functional and adequate unless you bring lots of luggage (which is not the style of this cruise line and its passengers anyway).

All cabins are outside, and except for those at the lowest level, most have picture windows. Rooms have showers but no tubs. There are no phones or TVs, but each cabin does have music channels. Decor is your basic doctor's-waiting-room style: pleasant, plain, and utilitarian.

Cabins come in six different categories, based on location and their relative size. Each has two lower-level beds, permanently fixed in an L-shaped corner configuration or as two units set parallel to one another. Most passengers find this acceptable, but if moonlight and splashing waves make you romantic, you might not be pleased with the layout. Some cabins contain Murphy-type beds that unfold from the wall to accommodate a third person.

The half-dozen cabins in the stern of the Lounge Deck can be noisy, in part from socializing in the nearby public areas and in part from propeller and/or engine vibration. Note that the four cabins on *Yorktown*'s uppermost deck, which are listed among the line's top cabin category, are accessible only from the sometimes windy outside deck.

There are no special facilities aboard for travelers with disabilities and no cabins designed specifically for single occupancy.

PUBLIC AREAS   Each ship has four decks and only two public areas: the dining room and the Observation Lounge. The pleasant lounge, which has big windows, a bar, a small library, and enough space to seat everyone on board for lectures and meetings, is the main hub of activity. The dining room aboard each ship is the most charming area. Other than that, don't expect any other cozy hideaways on board other than your cabin. There is, though, plenty of outdoor deck space for those liking to linger over a sunset or watch the scenery and sea glide past.

POOL, FITNESS & SPA FACILITIES   Neither ship has a swimming pool or any workout machines. For some exercise, you can jog or walk around the deck.

Club Med Cruises

SHIPS Club Med II

Club Med Sales, Inc. 7975 N. Hayden Rd., Ste A-105, Scottsdale, AZ 85258-3246. ☎ **800/ CLUBMED.**

THE LINE IN A NUTSHELL French-style fun in the sun is what's you'll get on this floating Club Med resort, a five-masted, engine-powered sailing ship where the crowd is international and the good times are universal.

THE EXPERIENCE Club Med's one ship, the *Club Med II,* is a stable, high-tech version of an 18th-century clipper ship, with five masts, seven computer-operated sails, and a vague and sometimes far-fetched self-image as a private yacht. While the ship's sails add a lovely grace note, that's mostly all they do—in actuality, the ship relies almost entirely on its diesel engines for propulsion.

The line is often compared to Windstar, yet Windstar generally attracts a more affluent, sophisticated clientele and carries fewer passengers by half. Americans make up between 20% and 30% of the passengers on board any Caribbean itinerary, but the language on board is French and the currency is the franc. Just as at Club Med's land resorts, the ship is staffed by a cadre of *gentils organisateurs* (GOs), an army of cheerleaders who function as quasi-passengers, participating in the activities and encouraging passengers to do the same. Many guests love these GOs, but others find them irritating.

Note that the "club" in Club Med isn't just a word: You really have to join, with a one-time initiation fee of $30 per family (which includes travel insurance coverage) and an annual fee of $50 per adult and $20 for each person under 12.

Pros

- **International ambience.** Francophiles and anyone who enjoys mingling with Europeans will appreciate the *Club Med II*'s international mix of passengers.
- **Water sports.** Retractable water sports platform lowers from the ship's stern and allows guests to conveniently windsurf, kayak, water-ski, snorkel, and swim.
- **Comfortable cabins.** For a small ship, these cabins are comfy and come stocked with a TV, minibar, a couple of terry bathrobes, and a hair dryer.

Cons

- **International ambience.** Overkill. For some cruisers, the entire Club Med *savoir faire* misses the mark. Potential passengers who suspect they'd feel this way would be better off sailing with Windstar.
- **GOs with attitudes.** Casual and unpretentious yes, but sometimes you wish they'd remember who's the passenger and who's the staff.

Frommer's Ratings: Club Med Cruises					
	Poor	Fair	Good	Excellent	Outstanding
Enjoyment Factor				✓	
Dining				✓	
Activities					✓
Children's Program	✓				
Entertainment				✓	
Service				✓	
Overall Value			✓		

CLUB MED: FRENCH-STYLE FUN AT SEA

In the late 1980s, Club Med founder and CEO Gilbert Trigano heard the cruise industry's siren song and ordered up a pair of exotic-looking masted cruise ships to import his *la vie en rose* holiday experience onto the high seas. Realizing that there would be no reason for the venture if it simply siphoned off business from CM's land-based resorts, Club Med Cruises targeted as its potential passengers those people who hadn't visited its other resorts, or would not, people attracted to the more luxurious accommodations offered at sea as opposed to the stripped-down barracks of many Club Med villages.

The venture has had mixed results. Although the cruise industry is rapidly expanding, in 1997 Club Med became one of the few cruise lines to reduce the size of its fleet when it sold the *Club Med 1* to Windstar Cruises, which immediately renamed it the *Wind Surf* and initiated a radical upgrading of its interior.

THE FLEET

The 392-passenger, 14,745-passenger **Club Med II** was built in 1992 and is the sole ship of the famous vacation resort company. It's outfitted with masts and sails, but these accoutrements are just that: auxiliaries to the ship's engines, aesthetic ornaments aboard a vessel that usually diesels its way between ports. On some cruises, if the wind isn't cooperative, the sails are hoisted only occasionally, perhaps during exits and entrances from harbors, or at the beginning and end of a cruise.

Unlike actual sailing ships, the *Club Med II* heels only slightly, and then only in the strongest of winds; sometimes CM captains actually induce a slight tilt to simulate the feeling of a ship under sail. The crew seems eerily absent from the minute-to-minute deck-side trimming of sails, and that's because the lines, ropes, riggings, and sails are set and fine-tuned via computer monitors from the bridge.

Despite all this mechanization, many passengers are awed by the vessel's sheer beauty, which adds to the romance of sailing through Caribbean waters. The ship's five masts and seven sails are merely a grace note, beautiful and evocative when viewed from the decks, but oddly out of proportion to the bulk of the ship's hull when seen from afar.

PASSENGER PROFILE

Many passengers are alumni from Club Med villages; others like the company's concept of relaxed informality but prefer the ship's more luxurious accommodations to the bare-boned CM villages on land. Some two-thirds of the passengers range from 35 to 55 years old. Many are French-born. The Americans you'll meet on a CM Caribbean itinerary tend to include youngish and relatively sophisticated urban professionals from New York, New Jersey, Connecticut, Massachusetts, Pennsylvania, and, to a lesser degree, California. This affluent, professional group, ranging in age from 28 to about 55 years old, tends to be sports- and fitness-conscious, international in outlook, and appreciative of luxury without insisting on formality (like Windstar, no jackets are required ever). They like to visit exotic ports of call, are not particularly upset by any shortcomings in cuisine or in availability of onboard shopping options, and spend a lot of time playing at water sports.

Partying on board will probably not descend to the raunchiness that's the norm on some megaships. That's just not the style here.

Children under 10 are not permitted to sail aboard a Club Med vessel.

DINING

Two dining areas both sport sea views, and a single open seating at dinner lets passengers bond or break shipboard relationships at will. Officers and staff dine with the passengers, contributing to the clublike ambience. Tables for two are widely available;

conversely, if you're looking for company, one of the GOs will quickly bustle you to a communal table.

Cuisine is—you guessed it—French, with a few hints of Italian and other continental traditions showing through occasionally. Charming touches include cheese carts featuring café au lait, espresso, and a selection of cheese that is very French indeed. Food is not gastronomically superlative, but is plentiful and prepared and served with style and an occasional flourish. Meals are always accompanied by complimentary beer or red and white wine (usually one of Club Med's private-label wines). A surcharge is imposed for consumption of more esoteric vintages.

Substantial and somewhat formal fare is served during breakfast and lunch hours in an indoor-outdoor bistro called the Odyssey. At lunchtime, both à la carte sit-down service and buffet spreads à la Med are featured. On some beach days, a crew sets up a buffet, usually with lobster, on whatever beach happens to be nearby.

Dinners are more formal events capping otherwise more relatively relaxed days. As in France itself, they can last for up to 3 hours. Diners opt for meals served between 7:30 and 9:30pm in the Odyssey or the more formal Le Louisiane Restaurant. The dress code is usually casual or informal, with the exception of two gala dinners (dressy, but not necessarily black-tie) that are offered during the course of each 7-night cruise.

Room service is available 24 hours a day, although some items carry a supplemental charge and the menu is limited. Continental breakfast is always available in cabins. Upon request, **special diets**—such as low-calorie, nonfat, or vegetarian—are accommodated.

ACTIVITIES

The teakwood decks support an ongoing, cross-cultural carnival that tries to be all things to all passengers. The outdoor areas invite sunbathing, although complaints are sometimes voiced (bilingually) when the ship's sails block the rays. **Deck games** with the GOs come with unbounded enthusiasm that can be a bit much, particularly if you don't feel as youthful as the GOs.

One benefit of the ship's relatively small size is the *Hall Nautique,* a **private marina** created by opening a massive steel hatch at the ship's stern, allowing windsurfers, sailboaters, water-skiers, and snorkelers direct access to the open sea. Gear for all of these sports is provided free. A flotilla of tenders carry day-trippers to the sands of isolated beaches.

Bridge has caught on in recent years aboard ship, and a GO will organize lessons and tournaments for whoever is interested. The **casino,** offering blackjack and roulette along with the inevitable slot machines, is small but generally adequate for the number of players.

There's also a gym with his-and-hers saunas.

CHILDREN'S PROGRAM

Only children aged 10 and over are allowed on board, and even those who make the grade are not particularly welcome. Club Med does not advertise that it accepts children and does not encourage it, as the ship, in theory at least, is "for sophisticated adults." If teenagers make it aboard, GOs will supervise daytime activities for them, but otherwise there are no special activities for them. If you happen to be holidaying with a group of teenagers, adolescents, or children, you'll be much, much happier at one of Club Med's "family villages" (such as those in Eleuthera, the Bahamas; Punta Cana, in the Dominican Republic; and Sandpiper, in Florida), which are specifically designed to be child-friendly.

Club Med Fleet Itineraries			
Ship	Home Ports & Season	Itinerary	Other Itineraries
Club Med II	Martinique, round-trip from Nov–Apr.	**7-night Carib:** Itineraries include a combination of the following ports: Aruba, Barbados, Bequia, Bonaire, Dominica, Grenada, Jost Van Dyke, La Blanquilla, Les Saintes, Los Roques, Mayreau, Puerto Rico, St. Barts, St. Kitts, St. Lucia, St. Thomas, St. Martin, Tintamarre, Tobago Cays, and Virgin Gorda.	Mediter-ranean

ENTERTAINMENT

By design, it's rather amateurish. GOs entertain on every cruise, lip-synching their way through Barbra Streisand or (on one dreadful night) Wayne Newton. Some passengers feel more professional entertainment should be provided, whereas others join in the fun and have a good time. Sometimes **local bands** come aboard for the evening at various ports of call. On the do-it-yourself front, the **karaoke** microphone is a popular staple, and owing to the multinational nature of the Club Med experience, you might hear such jarring transitions as Dolly Parton segueing into Edith Piaf. On **Carnival night,** passengers masquerade in stage makeup and stylized costumes supplied by the staff.

There's a piano bar on board, and a nightclub that's staffed by GOs who may sing, dance, and tell jokes (in several languages). Later, beginning around 10:30pm, the ship's **disco** swings into action. Formally known as *Fantasia,* it's referred to by virtually everybody at Club Med as simply "le disco" or "le dansing." Sheathed in mirrors and chrome, it rocks and rolls to a Francophilic beat till everyone decides to totter off to bed. It's hidden away behind an unmarked door on the vessel's bottom deck, a little too close to the engine room for anything approaching real glamour, but far from any cabins where passengers might be sleeping.

SERVICE

Remember that Club Med really is a club in many ways, and while efforts are made to attend to your needs and wants, the staff is much more laid-back than the white-gloved, heel-clicking servants aboard Seabourn or Cunard's upscale vessels. In some ways, the army of GOs function on board as reliably energetic guests rather than as hotel staffers in the traditional sense, so service relies on cooperation and cheerful coexistence. The illusion is maintained that whoever is serving you is a *copain* (French for jolly good fellow) and is doing so as a favor rather than as a duty. In some cases, if the staff finds a request inconvenient, you may find that they deliberately forget it. More immature staff members can often be downright brusque, patronizing, or insulting.

Club Med maintains a "no tipping" policy at each of its resorts and on board its ship, a policy that's consistent with the company's all-inclusive price structures. Despite that, many staff members are pleased to discreetly accept a gratuity for exemplary service.

Special Deals & Extra Charges

Single-Passenger Deals: Single occupants of double cabins pay a 30% surcharge. **Port Charges:** For most itineraries, port charges are an additional $126 per person.

Club Med II

The Verdict

This sleek, five-masted, French-flavored ship offers an exotic international passenger mix and a truly unique Caribbean cruise experience.

Club Med II *(photo: Club Med Cruises)*

Specifications

Size (in tons)	14,983	Officers	French
Number of Cabins	191	Crew	184 (International)
Number of Outside Cabins	191	Passenger/Crew Ratio	2.1 to 1
Cabins with Verandas	0	Year Built	1990
Number of Passengers	386	Last Major Refurbishment	N/A

Frommer's Ratings (Scale of 1–5)

Cabin Comfort & Amenities	4	Pool, Fitness & Spa Facilities	3
Ship Cleanliness & Maintenance	3	Children's Facilities	N/A
Public Comfort/Space	3	Itinerary	5
Decor	3	Worth the Money	4

The decor and amenities aboard *Club Med II* are on a par with the chain's finest, most stylish, and most upscale resorts. Within the Club Med subculture, this is about as good as it gets.

Every upper deck on this vessel is affected by the very masts, riggings, and sails that make it distinct—even the curiously understated smokestacks, with funnels that pivot so as to direct smoke away from the sails.

Sunbathing, for instance, can be challenging. You'll soon get used to moving each time the sails do, so that you don't get stuck in the shade when you want to be soaking up the sun.

Cabins & Rates						
Cabins	Per diems from	Bathtub	Fridge	Hair Dryer	Sitting Area	TV
Outside	$137	no	yes	yes	no	yes

CABINS   A prime incentive for a cruise aboard the *Club Med II* is the care and attention devoted to cabin accouterments. All cabins are outside, and have their own pair of brass-trimmed portholes, climate control, music channels, minibar, safe, surprisingly generous closet, and telephone.

Significantly, regardless of the deck on which it's located, each cabin is almost exactly identical to every other one on board, with almost no variation for the height at which it sits above the waterline. None of the units has a private balcony. Most cabins contain a generous 188 square feet each. There are also five suites, each with 258 square feet and a rectangular picture window. Other than the additional space, they differ little from the cabins. Cabin decor includes high-tech detailing, mahogany trim, and white walls offset by at least one other color, often navy blue. Bathrooms come equipped with a hair dryer and a pair of terry-cloth robes. Cabins are outfitted with both 110- and 220-volt current, allowing appliances from both Europe and North America to be used without converters or adapters.

Laundry service is available for a supplemental fee, but dry cleaning is not.

Some cabins contain upper bunks for a third passenger. There are no single cabins, and no cabins are especially suited for passengers with disabilities.

PUBLIC AREAS   Various decorative details, including the use of Burmese teak as sheathing for all decks and a mixture of high-tech lines with lots of hardwoods, maintain the illusion that the vessel is, indeed, a small-scale yacht rather than a 14,000-ton ship. Scattered over its eight decks are four bars and lounges, a nightclub, a casino, and a medical center staffed by a doctor and nurse. One large lounge that serves as an all-purpose bar, lecture hall, and rendezvous point. Lounges are soothing if colorful, often done up with unusual murals and designs in a sort of postmodern interpretation of art deco. Large windows bring views of the sea indoors. Two elevators connect the eight decks.

POOL, FITNESS & SPA FACILITIES   The ship contains a pair of medium-sized saltwater pools, a small gym with ocean views, a sauna, and massage facilities. There are aerobics classes offered, and for joggers and walkers there's an uninterrupted jogging circuit around the ship.

Star Clippers

SHIPS **Star Clipper • Royal Clipper (preview)**

4101 Salzedo Ave., Coral Gables, FL 33146. ☎ **800/442-0553** or 305/442-0550. Fax 305/442-1611. www.star-clippers.com.

THE LINE IN A NUTSHELL   With the sails and rigging of classic clipper ships and some of the cushy amenities of modern megas, a cruise on this line's 170-passenger ships offers adventure with comfort.

THE EXPERIENCE   On Star Clippers, you'll have the best of two worlds. On one hand, these cruises espouse an unstructured, let-your-hair-down, hands-on ethic—you can climb the masts (with a harness, of course), pull in the sails, crawl into the bow netting, or chat with the captain on the bridge. On the other hand, the ship offers comfortable, almost cushy, public rooms and cabins.

On board, ducking under booms, stepping over coils of rope, leaning against railings just feet above the sea, and watching sailors work the winches or climb the masts and the captain and his mates navigate from the open-air bridge are constant reminders that you're on a real working ship. Further, listening to the captain's daily talk about the next port of call, the history of sailing, or some other nautical subject from his forward perch on the Sun Deck, you'll feel like you're exploring some of the Caribbean's more remote stretches in a ship that belongs there—an exotic ship for an exotic locale. In a sea of lookalike megaships, the *Star Clipper* stands out, recalling a romantic, swashbuckling era.

Pros

- **Hands-on experience.** You never have to lift a finger if you don't want to, but if you do, you're free to help out.
- **Comfortable amenities**. A pair of pools, a piano bar and deck bar, a bright and pleasant dining room serving tasty food, and a clubby, wood-paneled library balance out the swashbuckling spirit.
- **Rich in atmosphere.** On these beautiful ships, it's a treat to wallow in the ambience.
- **Off-beat itineraries.** While not as far-flung as those offered by ACCL or even Clipper, Star Clippers itineraries do take passengers to some remote ports.

Cons

- **Rolling.** Even though the ships have stabilizers and ballast tanks to reduce rolling, you'll feel the motion if you run into rough seas, as is the case with any small ship.
- **No fitness equipment.** Like most ships of this kind and size, if you like to work out, you're out of luck. You'll have to do your exercising in port.

Frommer's Ratings: Star Clippers					
	Poor	Fair	Good	Excellent	Outstanding
Enjoyment Factor					✓
Dining					✓
Activities				✓	
Children's Program	N/A*				
Entertainment					✓
Service					✓
Overall Value					✓

Star Clippers offers no children's program.

STAR CLIPPERS: COMFORTABLE ADVENTURE AROUND

Clipper ships—full-sailed, built for speed, and undeniably romantic—reigned for only a brief time on the high seas before being driven out by steam-driven engines, iron and then steel hulls, and the philosophy that bigger is better. During their heyday, however, these vessels engendered more romantic myths than any before or since. They helped open the Pacific Coast of California during the Gold Rush of 1849, carrying much-needed supplies around the tip of South America from Boston and New York. Even after the opening of the Suez Canal in 1869, names like *Cutty Sark, Ariel,* and *Flying Cloud* remained prestigious, and no sailing ship has ever surpassed the record of *Sea Witch,* a vessel that once sailed from Canton, China, to New York in 74 days.

By the early 1990s, despite the nostalgia and sense of reverence that had surrounded every aspect of the clippers' maritime history, nothing that could be technically classified as a clipper ship had been built since the *Cutty Sark* in 1869. In fact, their return to the high seas as viable commercial ventures could only have been realized by a nautical visionary with a passion for ship design and almost unlimited funds. The right combination of these factors emerged in Mikael Krafft, a Swedish-born industrialist and real-estate developer who invested vast amounts of personal energy and more than $80 million in the construction of two modern-day clippers at a Belgian shipyard in 1990 and 1991.

Before this venture, Krafft had sailed a series of high-tech yachts, including a particularly spectacular version 128 feet long. To construct his clippers, he procured the original drawings and specifications of Scottish-born Donald McKay (a leading naval architect of 19th-century clipper-ship technology) and employed his own team of naval architects to solve such engineering problems as adapting the square-rigged, four-masted clipper design to modern materials and construction.

Krafft established his wind-driven line as Clipper Cruises, and was promptly sued by the Missouri-based line of the same name (profiled earlier in this chapter). After several messy and expensive legal battles, Krafft adopted Star Clippers as the name of his line, and successfully wedged his way into a small but distinctive niche in the cruise ship market.

In its short history, the line's *Star Clipper* has assembled quite a list of firsts: the first commercial sail-driven vessel to cross the Atlantic in 90 years; the first ship ever to pass full U.S. Coast Guard certification and safety exams on the first try; and one of the only ships to ever enter the Port of Miami under full sail—a daunting feat, considering the motorized traffic barreling through on all sides. Also impressive is the fact that both ships received the highest rating available by Lloyd's Register—the "+100 A-1-A" rating, which hadn't been awarded to a sailing vessel since 1911. On Star Clippers, you'll be sailing aboard vessels where safety and nautical logistics are more visible and more all-encompassing than aboard most other lines, where operations are kept safely hidden away.

How do their prices and amenities compare to the products of Windjammer Barefoot Cruises and Windstar Cruises, two other companies that run original (if modernized) sailing ships or have replicated the sailing ships of yore? Star Clippers is smack dab in the middle—more luxurious and usually a bit more expensive than the bare-boned, no-frills Windjammer excursions and less opulent, less formal, and less expensive than Windstar. Onboard atmosphere is quite casual. During the day, shorts with polo shirts and topsiders are standard issue, and for dinner many passengers simply change into cleaner and better-pressed versions of the same, with perhaps a change from shorts to slacks for most men. Overall, the experience is salty enough to make you feel like a fisherman keeling off the coast of Maine, without the physical hardship of actually being one.

THE FLEET

The **Star Clipper,** built in 1992, spends its winters in the Caribbean, and the **Star Flyer,** built in 1991, operates entirely in the Far East and the Aegean. The twin vessels are at once traditional and radical. They're the tallest and among the fastest clipper ships ever built. With dimensions about 100 feet longer than the average 19th-century clipper, they're so beautiful that even at full stop they seem to soar.

Part of the ships' success derives from a skillful blend of traditional aesthetics and newfangled materials and technology. The configuration of the vessels' sails is not quite traditional, having been adapted to include a higher percentage of triangular sails and fewer of the square-rigged sails usually associated with clippers. Also, sails are made of lightweight Dacron rather than canvas, which rots easily and is so heavy that the amount of sail each of Krafft's ships flies (36,000 square feet) would probably have capsized an original clipper. Further innovations include masts crafted from steel and aluminum alloys instead of tree trunks and a network of electric winches that eliminates the backbreaking labor historically involved in the sails' raising and lowering. Fewer than 10 deckhands can manipulate the ships' sails, as contrasted to the 40 to 55 that were needed to control and maintain sails aboard the 19th-century ships. Concessions to modern design include a bow thruster and a single propeller that's used to navigate in and out of tricky harbors or during dead calms. When used together, they can spin each craft around on a very tight axis. Star Clippers almost never use their bow thrusters for such basic tasks as coming about into the wind—both crew and ships are simply too proud for that.

One of the great challenges owner Mikael Krafft and his designers faced was taking a type of ship originally intended to haul tea, wool, and opium and adapting it to carry vacationing passengers. The new clippers needed the amenities of a private yacht and also the space—both for provisions and passenger comfort. I'm happy to report that they got it right.

As opposed to the *Club Med 1,* a bulkier cruise ship that just happens to be outfitted with sails, Star Clipper's ships look like they should sail under wind power, and generally rely on sails for about 25% to 35% of their propulsion (the rest of the time, they rely on the engines).

Each ship performs superlatively, and can reach a speed of 17 knots. During the *Star Clipper's* maiden sail in 1992 off the coast of Corsica, it sustained speeds of 19.4 knots, thrilling its owner and designers, who had predicted maximum speeds of 17 knots. During most cruises, however, the crew tries to keep passengers comfortable and decks relatively horizontal, and so the vessels are kept to speeds of 9 to 14 knots.

At press time, the line plans to launch its newest ship, the 228-passenger, five-masted, fully rigged **Royal Clipper,** in early 2000. At 439 feet in length, the ship will be one of the largest sailing ships ever built.

PASSENGER PROFILE

While you're likely to find a handful of late-20-something honeymoon-type couples, the majority of passengers are well-traveled couples in their late 40s to 60s, all active and intellectually curious professionals such as executives, lawyers, and doctors.

With only 170 passengers aboard, each cruise seems like a triumph of individuality and intimacy. The line's unusual niche appeals to passengers who might recoil at the lethargy and/or sometimes forced enthusiasm of cruises aboard larger, more typical vessels. About 40% of any passenger roster is composed of people who have never cruised before, perhaps for this very reason.

As the line has matured and increased both its stature and its prestige, many passengers have tended to be repeaters. About half are European, the remainder North

American and a steadily growing number of Latin Americans. All tend to be active, sports-conscious, and curious—and, as you might expect, many come from boating or yachting backgrounds. Many are devoted conservationists who appreciate a vessel that relies primarily on wind power rather than diesel fuel, and many have traveled extensively.

Mikael Krafft himself may even be on board, in many cases with his wife and children, traveling as a low-key, highly accessible guest.

DINING

Overall, food is good and presented well, with breakfast and lunch buffets being the best meals of the day. Star Clippers' cuisine has evolved and improved through the years as the line has poured more time and effort into it. All meals are open seating and served in the restaurant to tables of four, six and eight, and the dress code is always casual. Catering to the European as well as the North American clientele, all buffets included a better-than-average selection of cheeses, like brie and smoked Gouda, several types of salad, cold cuts, and fish. At breakfast, in addition to a cold and hot buffet spread, there's an omelet station where a staff member will make your eggs the way you like them. Late afternoon snacks served at the Tropical Bar include items like tacos, spring rolls, or ice-cream sundaes with fresh coconut and pistachio toppings. Vegetarian dishes are offered at all meals, and the line can accommodate most *special diets* if given advance notice.

At dinner, two main entrees, appetizers, and dessert courses are offered as well as a soup and salad. Choices include, for example, lobster and shrimp with rice pilaf, beef curry, and pasta dishes. Dinners are sometimes sit-down and sometimes buffet, and can be somewhat chaotic and rushed. When the ship is at full capacity, things can feel a bit frenetic (breakfast and lunch don't get as crowded as passengers tend to eat at staggered times). The booths along the sides, seating six, are awkward when couples who don't know each are forever getting up and down to let the others in and out (sources tell me the new *Royal Clipper* will avoid this layout). The dining room has mahogany trim and a series of thin steel columns that pierce the center of many of the dining tables. While the columns were the best way to solve the structural problem inherent in such a large open space, they sometimes slightly block sightlines across the tables.

Waiters and bartenders are efficient and friendly, and dress in costume for several theme nights each week.

There's a worthwhile selection of **wines** on board, with a heavy emphasis on medium-priced selections from California. Coffee and tea are available 24 hours a day.

Room service is available only for guests who are sick and can't make it to the dining room.

ACTIVITIES

If you're looking for action, shopping, and dozens of organized tours, you won't find much on these ships and itineraries. For the most part, socializing among passengers and with the crew is the main activity (as it is on most any ship of this size). In fact, the friendliness starts the moment you board, with the captain and hotel director personally greeting passengers and inviting them to have a complimentary cocktail and some hors d'oeuvres.

You won't find the typical cruise ship onboard pastimes, and that's a big part of the line's allure. Many activities involve simply exploring these extraordinary ships. The captain gives informal talks on maritime themes, and at least once a day the cruise director speaks about the upcoming ports and shipboard events. Knot tying might be the topic of the day, or you might get to participate in a man-overboard drill. Within reason, passengers can lend a hand with deck-side duties, observe the mechanics of navigation, and have a token try at handling the wheel when circumstances and calm

Star Clippers Fleet Itineraries

Ship	Home Ports & Season	Itinerary	Other Itineraries
Star Clipper	Antigua, round-trip itineraries alternate weekly.	**7-night eastern Carib 1:** St. Barts, Tortola/Sandy Cay, Norman Island, Virgin Gorda, Sint Maarten, and St. Kitts. **7-night eastern Carib 2:** Dominica, St. Vincent/Bequia, Tobago Cays, St. Lucia, Martinique, and Iles des Saintes.	None

weather permit. Each ship maintains an **open-bridge policy,** allowing passengers to wander up to the humble-looking navigation center at any hour of the day or night.

Other activities may include a brief engine-room tour and a **scuba lesson** in the pool, and massages are available too (a great deal at $28 an hour), doled out in a spare cabin or a small cabana on deck. Of course, sunbathing is a sport in and of itself, and crawling in the bowsprit netting to do so is a thrill and an effective way to try and spot dolphins in the sea just feet below you.

Port activities are a big part of these cruises. Sailing from one island to another and tending to arrive at the day's port of call sometime after 9am (but usually before around 11am and usually after a brisk early-morning sail), the ships anchors offshore and passengers are shuttled back and forth by tender (on many landings, you'll have to walk a few feet in shallow water between the tender and the beach).

Activities in port revolve around beaches and water sports, which are all complimentary. **Snorkeling** equipment is issued at the beginning of the week for anyone who wants it, and for water-skiing and banana boat rides, the young surfer-boy sports staff operates four Zodiacs that are carried along with the ship. Being that everything is so laid back, there are no sign-up sheets, so guests merely hang out and congregate by the gangway or on the beach until it's their turn.

Ships tend to depart from their island ports of call early enough so they can be under full sail during sunset. Trust me on this one: Position yourself at the ship's rail or dawdle over a drink at the deck bar to watch the sun melt into the horizon behind the silhouette of the ships' masts and ropes. It's something you won't forget.

CHILDREN'S PROGRAM

This is not a line for young children, and there are no supervised activities. That said, an experience aboard a sailing ship can be a wonderful educational and adventurous experience, especially for children at least 10.

No baby-sitting is available, unless a well-intentioned crew member agrees to volunteer his or her off-duty hours.

ENTERTAINMENT

Some sort of featured entertainment takes place each night after dinner by the Tropical Bar, which is the main hub of activity. There's a **crew talent show** one night, and on others a trivia contest and a dance or steel band performed by **local entertainers** on board for the night. A keyboard player is on hand to sing pop songs before and after dinner, and a pianist plays jazzy tunes in the Piano Bar each evening. Some nights, disco music is put on the sound system and the deck between the deck bar and library becomes a dance floor.

A couple of movies a day are available on cabin TVs, if you feel like vegging. Besides this, it's just you, the sea, and the conversation of your fellow passengers.

Port Charges Not Included

Port charges are about $118 per person in addition to the cruise rates for 7-day Caribbean cruises with Star Clippers.

SERVICE

Service is congenial, low-key, unpretentious, cheerful, and reasonably attentive. Expect efficient but sometimes slightly distracted service in the cramped dining room, and realize that you'll have to fetch your own ice, bar drinks, and whatever else you might need during your time on deck.

The crew is international, hailing from places like Poland, Switzerland, Russia, Germany, Romania, Indonesia, and the Philippines, and their presence creates a wonderful international flavor on board. Crew members are friendly and indulgent and usually good-natured about clients who want to tie knots, raise and lower sails, and keep the deck shipshape. As English is not the mother language of some crew members, though, certain details might get lost in the translation.

Officers typically dine with guests at every meal, and if you'd like to have dinner with the captain, just go up to the bridge one day and ask him.

Star Clipper

The Verdict

With the sails and rigging of a classic clipper ship and the creature comforts of a modern mega, a cruise on the 172-passenger *Star Clipper* offers the best of two worlds and a wonderful way to do the Caribbean.

Star Clipper *(photo: Star Clippers)*

Specifications

Size (in tons)	2,298	Officers	International
Number of Cabins	84	Crew	70 (International)
Number of Outside Cabins	78	Passenger/Crew Ratio	2.5 to 1
Cabins with Verandas	0	Year Built	1991
Number of Passengers	172	Last Major Refurbishment	N/A

Frommer's Ratings (Scale of 1–5)

Cabin Comfort & Amenities	3	Pool, Fitness & Spa Facilities	3
Ship Cleanliness & Maintenance	4	Children's Facilities	N/A
Public Comfort/Space	3	Itinerary	5
Decor	3	Worth the Money	5

Life aboard the *Star Clipper* means life on deck. Since there are few other hideaways, that's where most passengers spend their days. Made from teakwood, these decks were planned with lots of passenger space, although much of it is somewhat cluttered with the winches, ropes, and other equipment of these working ships. There are lots of nooks and crannies on deck, and even with a full load the ship rarely feels overly crowded (except at dinner). More sail-trimming activity occurs amidships and near the bow, so if you're looking to avoid all bustle, take yourself off to the stern.

Cabins & Rates						
Cabins	Per diems from	Bathtub	Fridge	Hair Dryer	Sitting Area	TV
Inside	$137	no	no	yes	no	no
Outside	$167	no	no	yes	no	yes
Suite	$300	yes	yes	yes	no	yes

CABINS   Cabins feel roomy for a ship of this size and were designed with a pleasant nautical motif—blue fabrics and carpeting, portholes, brass-toned lighting fixtures, and a dark wood trim framing the off-white furniture and walls. The majority of cabins are outside and measure from about 120 to 130 square feet, have two twin beds that can be converted into doubles, a small desk/vanity with stool, and an upholstered seat fitted into the corner. Storage space is more than adequate for a 7-night casual cruise in a warm climate, with both a slim floor-to-ceiling closet and a double-width closet of shelves; there is also storage below the beds, desk, nightstand, and chair. Each cabin has a telephone, hair dryer, and safe, and all but the four smallest inside cabins (measuring a compact 95 square feet) have a color television showing news and a selection of popular movies.

Standard bathrooms are small but functional, with marble walls, a nice mirrored storage cabinet that actually stays closed, and a narrow shower divided from the rest of the bathroom by only the curtain (surprisingly, the rest of the bathroom stays dry when the shower's being used). The sink and shower are fitted with annoying push valves, which release water only when they're compressed. The only real difference between the cabins in categories two and three is about a square foot of space. The eight deluxe cabins measure about 150 square feet, open right out onto the main deck, and have minibars and whirlpool bathtubs. Because of their location near the Tropical Bar, though, noise can be a problem.

None of the units is a suite, except for one carefully guarded (and oddly configured) owner's suite in the aft of the Clipper Deck that's available to the public only when it's not being set aside for special purposes.

Take note: The ship's generator tends to drone on through the night; cabins near the stern on lower decks are the most susceptible to this.

No cabins were designed for wheelchair accessibility. These ships are not recommended for passengers with mobility problems.

PUBLIC AREAS   The handful of public rooms include the dining room, a comfy piano bar, the outside Tropical Bar (sheltered from the sun and rain by a canopy), and a cozy, paneled library with a decorative, nonfunctioning fireplace and a good stock of coffee-table books, tracts on naval history and naval architecture, and a cross section of general titles.

The roomy yet cozy piano bar has comfy banquette seating. That area and the outdoor Tropical Bar are the ship's hubs of activity.

Throughout, the interior decor is pleasant but unmemorable, mostly white with touches of brass and mahogany or teakwood trim—not as upscale looking as vessels operated by Windstar, but cozy, appealing, well designed, and shipshape.

POOL, FITNESS & SPA FACILITIES   Each ship has two small pools, meant more for dipping than swimming, one with glass portholes peering from its depths into the piano bar (and vice versa). The pool near the stern tends to be more languid, the favorite of sunbathers, whereas the one at midships is more active, with more noise and splashing and central to the action. At both, the ship's billowing and moving sails might occasionally block the sun's rays, although this happens amidships much more frequently than it does at the stern.

Preview: Star Clippers' *Royal Clipper*

Clipper's biggest and plushest ship is on the way. The fully-rigged, 439-foot, 228-passenger *Royal Clipper* will be launched in early 2000 (not in fall of 1999 as originally planned) and be one of the biggest sailing ships ever built, with five masts flying 42 sails that together stretch to 56,000 square feet. It will be able to hit 13 knots under engine power and 20 knots under sail power only. Size and power aside, the ship will also be extremely well accoutered, with a windowed disco, a three-story glass atrium, a two-deck restaurant, 14 suites with private deck patios, a retractable water sports platform, three pools, and a massage and fitness center. In the winter, the ship will do alternating 7-night Caribbean cruises round-trip from Barbados, and in summers will sail 7-night alternating Mediterranean cruises.

While there's no gym of any sort, aerobics and stretch classes are frequently held on deck between the library and Tropical Bar. Partly because Mikael Krafft is an avid scuba diver and partly because itineraries focus on waters that teem with marine life, each ship offers (for an extra charge) the option of PADI-approved scuba diving. Certified divers will find all the equipment they'll need on board. Even uncertified/inexperienced divers can pay a token fee for training that will grant them resort certification and allow them to make a number of relatively simple dives. There's also snorkeling (complimentary equipment is distributed at the start of the cruise), water-skiing, windsurfing, and banana boat rides offered by the ship's water sports team in all ports (the ships carry along Zodiac motor boasts for this purpose).

Tall Ship Adventures

SHIPS   Sir Francis Drake

1389 S. Havana St., Aurora, CO 80012. ☎ **800/662-0090** or 303/755-7983. Fax 303/755-9007. www.tallshipadventures.com.

THE LINE IN A NUTSHELL   With its one tiny, authentic sailing ship, this line offers the real thing for a freewheeling and adventurous crowd of all ages.

THE EXPERIENCE   This antidote to the megas is a refreshingly simple and back-to-the-basics kind of cruise experience where you and only 28 or 29 other passengers spend a cozy week enjoying real life at sea on a real ship.

At age 83, the *Sir Francis Drake* is the oldest ship covered in this book and the only one originally built to be powered by sail only (a diesel auxiliary engine was added in the 1930s). Even after many refits (and a few wars under its belt), the ship still reeks of the past and recalls a bygone era of ship travel, offering passengers a casual, not very frilly, but wonderfully different and adventurous journey at sea. You can easily pretend you're a character in some romantic travel adventure novel on this three-masted schooner as it nudges its way into the harbors of such remote places in the British Virgin Islands and the Grenadines as Peter Island, Guana Island, Palm Island, and Ile les Saintes. The *Sir Francis Drake* is often the only ship in sight, and you'll never encounter crowds or any monstrous megaships.

Passengers are unconventional, young-at-heart types who love the experience of just being at sea on a classic clipper ship and appreciate the small cabins and simple fare as part of the authentic experience. There are few organized activities or arranged entertainments, and that's what passengers like. Instead, they enjoy socializing and exploring the ship—you can even climb up to the crow's nest and enjoy panoramic views of the sea and islands, as though you were the captain of your own ship.

Pros

- **Ultra-casual and laid back.** Leave your pretenses at home. This is one of the most casual and unregimented cruises you could ever find.
- **Remote ports.** No shopping meccas and crowded cruise ports for this ship; it heads instead for places like the Grenadines and the nooks and crannies of the BVIs.

Cons

- **Small.** Everything's pretty tiny, including your cabins. But remember, lots of time is spent on shore, out on deck, and in the water.
- **Rocking and rolling.** If you're prone to sea sickness and the ship hits a rough patch of sea, you'll feel it, all right.

Frommer's Ratings: Tall Ship Adventures					
	Poor	Fair	Good	Excellent	Outstanding
Enjoyment Factor				✓	
Dining			✓		
Activities			✓		
Children's Activities	N/A*				
Entertainment		✓			
Service			✓		
Overall Value			✓		

Tall Ship Adventures offers no children's program.

SIR FRANCIS DRAKE: IT'S THE REAL THING

If you've always wanted to sail a true old clipper ship, here's your chance. For as long as it remains seaworthy, you can cruise aboard *Sir Francis Drake,* one of the fewer than 100 remaining tall ships originally built to navigate under sail only. Tall Ship Adventures was formed especially to administer this remarkable vessel, which carries 28 to 30 passengers on weeklong jaunts around the British Virgin Islands and Grenadines.

THE FLEET

A sturdy sailing craft, the *Sir Francis Drake* was built as the *Landkirchen* during the most violent days of World War I. Launched in 1917 from a berth beside Germany's Weser River, it boasted a riveted steel hull and a shape and dimensions that have changed little since then. Before a diesel motor was added in the 1930s, it operated exclusively under sail. The ship visited most of the Baltic ports, and made five sail-driven trips between Germany and the Pacific coast of Chile, hauling supplies outbound and copper on the return trip.

World War II did more to cramp this ship's style than the corrosive effects of sea and salt. All the records associated with its past journeys went up in flames during the Allied bombings of northern Germany early in 1945. In December of that year, the ship was sold at auction as an Allied war prize to new (German) owners. It carried cargo through the Baltic until 1979, when it was given a much-needed refitting. Rechristened as the *Godewind,* the vessel hauled day-trippers off the coast of Martinique for a few years.

Then a New Zealander, Capt. Bryan Petley, persuaded his partner, Eckart Straub, to purchase the ship. In 1988, it was refurbished and renamed *Sir Francis Drake,* since the partners planned to sail the waters of the British Virgin Islands that had so fascinated this English admiral. (The deepwater channel that bisects the British Virgin Islands is also named for Drake.) Today, Straub, a sometimes-resident of Stuttgart, is the sole owner of the line, which is the only cruise line headquartered in Colorado. In 1996, after brief stints of registry in both Honduras and Panama, the *Drake* was re-registered in Equatorial Guinea—a highly unusual legal home in the world of Caribbean cruising.

Today, the ship's figurehead, a reproduction of the ship's original added in the early 1990s, is a scantily clad mermaid whose face bears a striking similarity to the face of Kathryn Straub, the American-born wife of the ship's owner.

PASSENGER PROFILE

Passengers aboard this line tend to be less demanding and more self-reliant than those aboard more typical cruise lines. They're more interested in nautical terms and sailing techniques, too, although few actually insist on hoisting a yardarm. These passengers entertain themselves by watching waves and listening to the wind, and understand that ships with sails don't always follow a rigid itinerary. Passengers are roughly the same types who enjoy Windjammer Barefoot Cruises. Both lines attract hardy, young-at-heart, salty types who have a certain degree of earthy humor. Aboard *Sir Francis Drake* there's less focus on heavy-duty yo-ho-ho drinking.

The passenger list is mainly North American, but about 25% of the passengers hail from Europe, mostly Britain and Germany.

DINING

Because of the vessel's small size and small passenger roster, *Sir Francis Drake*'s chefs have enormous flexibility in choosing and altering their menus, supplementing provisions they have aboard with what they find fresh in port markets. Where larger lines must sock away carloads of provisions at the beginning of every trip, this small-scale contender is always on the lookout for lobster, fresh fish, and fresh vegetables, which local merchants offer whenever the ship arrives in port.

Tall Ship Adventures Fleet Itineraries*

Ship	Home Ports & Season	Itinerary	Other Itineraries
Sir Francis Drake	Tortola, round-trip from Nov–June; St. Lucia, round-trip from June–Oct.	7-night eastern Carib: May include Peter Island, Cooper Island, Marina Cay, Long Bay, and sites on or off the coast of Virgin Gorda, including the Bitter End Yacht Club, The Baths, and Norman Island. 7-night eastern Carib: May include Dominica, Martinique, Guadeloupe, Ile des Saintes, St. Vincent, and the Grenadines.	None

Although itineraries follow basically the same route weekly, port stops can vary depending on wind and weather.

This is a line with absolutely no pretensions toward fancy food or elaborate presentations. As the galley prepares the same meal for everyone aboard, there's really no choice at most dinners as to what you'll eat; instead, the waitstaff will recite the evening's menu to the assembled crowd. Don't be surprised to hear baked chicken actually called "baked chicken," grilled sirloin steaks called "grilled sirloin steaks," and lobster called "lobster"— this is a straightforward line. Relatively simple lunches might feature burgers, fried shrimp, salads, pizzas, and sandwiches. Dinners are usually more elaborate than lunches, but there's nary a hint of gourmet pretension, with the emphasis being more on simple, solid North American staples, with an overtone of Caribbean mixed in. If you're absolutely opposed to eating red meat, you should inform the reservations agent when you book, and chicken or fish can usually be prepared for you on the side, but if you're a strict vegetarian, you might quickly grow tired of the boiled vegetables you're given.

There's a single seating for both lunch and dinner. At some lunches, and during at least one dinner, burgers and meat might be barbecued atop a gas-fired grill on deck. When weather permits, beach picnics are prepared.

ACTIVITIES

The activities program is more noteworthy for what it isn't than for what it is. There are no scheduled activities of any kind. Instead, passengers read, chitchat with staff or fellow passengers, watch the waves, watch the crew manipulate the sails, or just relax.

But you won't lack for things to do. Mornings are usually spent **sailing** for periods of between 1 and 4 hours. Lunch is usually on board or on a beach somewhere, with afternoons (about 4 hours) devoted to exploring sparsely inhabited islands whose sometimes unnamed cays and islets encourage spontaneous stops for beach time and shell collecting.

After an afternoon ashore, the ship repositions itself around dusk to a new site. Dinner is served in the main lounge; recorded music is played and cocktails are served on deck. Generally, the ship ties up at night so passengers can partake of the local **island nightlife.** The ship usually does not sail at night, allowing passengers to slumber as their craft rolls gently at anchor.

Snorkeling is popular aboard every Tall Ship cruise (equipment is complimentary), with one favorite spot for exploration being the mouths of sea caves peppering the rocky

Port Charges Not Included

Depending on ports visited, port charges for a Tall Ship Adventures cruise range from $35 to $50 per person in addition to the cruise rates.

coast of Norman Island (a deserted BVI island that inspired Robert Louis Stevenson's *Treasure Island*). During afternoon stopovers at, say, The Baths at Virgin Gorda, practically everyone dons face masks and fins for views of underwater reef life.

CHILDREN'S PROGRAM

There are no special activities of any kind for children. If you're interested in bringing yours along, the line will determine, depending on their age, whether they're permitted on board. I don't recommend this line for children under 10 or 12; however, if you have a special teenager who's really curious about sailing ships and the sea, he or she might have an absolutely fabulous time.

ENTERTAINMENT

It's about as low-key and do-it-yourself as anything afloat. Recorded calypso music playing on the deck might induce some passengers to dance (briefly) during the cocktail hour, but overall, entertainment comes down to whatever party you create on your own. Occasionally a local band is brought on board for a few hours. Vaguely structured afternoon get-togethers, "promptly scheduled at five-ish," feature "snacks and swizzles" accompanied by a complimentary bowl of rum-based pirate's punch. Sometimes it clicks and sometimes it doesn't. Sometimes the good times have a theme, as when palm fronds might be shaped into a headdress or a bedsheet pressed into duty as a toga. There might even be a good-natured contest or two, to determine, say, who is the best dancer aboard.

More frequently, you'll get your entertainment off-ship. Landfalls are scheduled to coincide with the evening festivities at lively, isolated bars and marinas on the British Virgin Islands. Known mostly to the yachting crowd, they include the Bitter End Yacht Club on Virgin Gorda, Cane Garden Bay on Tortola, Foxy's on Jost Van Dyke, and Pusser's Bar and Grill on Marina Cay, near the east end of Tortola.

SERVICE

Like most very small ships, service is reasonably attentive and crew and passengers tend to become friendly fast. Cabin service is perfunctory but efficient, involving brief cleanups in the morning. Towels are changed only every other day. Unless you're deathly ill, don't expect room service (there's no phone to call for it anyway).

Sir Francis Drake

The Verdict

A true adventure at sea. You can easily forget the world you normally live in and enjoy this historied sailing ship, the intimate and carefree onboard atmosphere, and the truly remote island paradises you'll find on shore.

Sir Francis Drake *(photo: Tall Ship Adventures)*

Specifications

Size (in tons)	98	Officers	International
Number of Cabins	14	Crew	10 (International)
Number of Outside Cabins	14	Passenger/Crew Ratio	3 to 1
Cabins with Verandas	0	Year Built	1917
Number of Passengers	28–30	Last Major Refurbishment	1996

Frommer's Ratings (Scale of 1–5)

Cabin Comfort & Amenities	2	Pool, Fitness & Spa Facilities	N/A
Ship Cleanliness & Maintenance	3	Children's Facilities	N/A
Public Comfort/Space	3	Itinerary	5
Decor	3	Worth the Money	5

The vessel is tiny and as hopelessly antiquated next to modern megaships as the *Spirit of St. Louis* would be next to the space shuttle. But loyal passengers, some of whom sail almost every year, find those traits just add to the ship's charm. *Sir Francis Drake* is an authentic three-masted topsail schooner, measuring only 28 feet wide and (with the spearlike bowsprit included) 165 feet long. Its shallow draft of 9.2 feet allows it to go into bays and coves that most cruise ships can't enter.

Other than its navigational aids, in a deckhouse near the stern, few aspects of its operation are computerized. The sails of this three-masted ship (6,456 square feet of them) are furled and unfurled the way they've always been: manually (albeit with modern winches). You can always help.

Cabins & Rates

Cabins	Per diems from	Bathtub	Fridge	Hair Dryer	Sitting Area	TV
Outside	$140	no	no	no	no	no
Suite	$197	no	yes	no	yes	no

CABINS   Each cabin is a spartan, durable, no-nonsense cubbyhole that's a lot less roomy than you might hope. Standard cabins measure only a cramped 8 by 10 feet, and some smaller ones with bunk beds measure only 8 by 8 feet and are covered in "simulated mahogany" plastic panels. Even the ship's only suite, at 11 by 18 feet, is smaller than the size of standard cabins aboard some upscale conventional cruise lines. Remember not to pack much, as there's not much storage space. But hey, this is a real sailing ship—plush cabins aren't the point.

Even though the line designates its accommodations as "outside cabins," only the ship's one suite has conventional portholes. Instead, light filters down from overhead skylights, eliminating the need for artificial lighting during daylight hours. Severe claustrophobics might find the arrangement confining.

Each cabin is air-conditioned, and set more or less at the waterline, which adds the soothing sound of water splashing against the hull to your seagoing experience. Beds are bolted into position, thereby preventing configurations of twins, doubles, and bunks from ever being changed. For this reason, it's important to state your sleeping preferences in advance, at the time of your initial reservations.

The spartan nature of the cabins extends to the head-style bathrooms, tiny tile-sheathed cubicles containing a toilet, a sink, a drain in the floor, and a showerhead, all in one space.

PUBLIC AREAS   No one would call the *Sir Francis Drake* a luxurious vessel, and although it likely looks more glamorous today than it did as a cargo ship, there's absolutely nothing fancy or elaborate aboard. The vessel's small size limits public areas to a few that are used, and used, and used again.

Other than the deck area, where passengers seem to spend 80% of their waking hours in the open air (or under shade), the Main Salon is the ship's catch-all public area. It serves as an all-purpose drinking area, dining area, lecture hall, card room, and general hangout. Tastefully and durably outfitted with dark paneling and blue-and-white upholstery, it's a room you'll see plenty of, because there's really no other place to go, other than the upper decks, which you'll see plenty of as well. There are bars both on deck and in the Main Salon.

POOL, FITNESS & SPA FACILITIES   Not surprisingly, there's no state-of-the-art gym or any kind of fitness equipment. Passengers get their exercise participating in the ship's water sports program. The ship carries a motorboat for tendering passengers from anchorage to pier.

Many passengers make it a point to swim to shore from the ship's nearby anchorage, swim laps around the ship as it bobs at anchor, and dive (water depth permitting) into the water from the ship's jutting bowsprit. For insurance purposes, the ship does not have scuba gear among its playthings, preferring to point scuba enthusiasts in the direction of land-based outfitters.

One activity aboard this antique vessel is among the least widely available in the cruise industry: Each of the ship's three masts has its own crow's nest, and if you're fit enough—and are granted the captain's permission—you can climb to one of them and enjoy sweeping panoramas over land and sea.

Windjammer Barefoot Cruises, Ltd.

SHIPS   **Amazing Grace • Flying Cloud • Legacy • Mandalay • Polynesia • Yankee Clipper**

1759 Bay Rd., Miami Beach, FL 33139 (P.O. Box 190–120, Miami Beach, FL 33119). ☎ **800/327-2601** or 305/672-6453. Fax 305/674-1219. www.windjammer.com.

THE LINE IN A NUTSHELL   Ultra-casual and delightfully carefree, this eclectic fleet of cozy, rebuilt sailing ships (powered by both sails and engines) lures passengers into a fantasy world of pirates-and-rum-punch adventure.

THE EXPERIENCE   When you see that the captain is wearing shorts, shades, and sandals like the rest of the laid-back crew, you'll realize Windjammer's vessels aren't your typical cruise ships. Their yards of sails, pointy bowsprits, chunky portholes, and generous use of wood create a swashbuckling storybook look, and while passengers don't have to fish for dinner or swab the decks, they are invited to help haul the sails, crawl into the bow net, and sleep out on deck whenever they please. With few rules and lots of freedom, this is the closest thing you'll get to a real Caribbean adventure.

Making their way to off-the-beaten-track Caribbean ports of call, the ships are ultra-informal, and hokey yet endearing rituals make the trip feel like summer camp for adults. Add in the line's tremendous number of repeat passengers (and a few of its signature "rum swizzles") and you have a casual experience that's downright familial.

Pros

- **Informal and carefree.** You can wear shorts and T-shirts all day and to dinner, too.
- **Friendly and down-to-earth.** Crew and passengers mix and mingle, and in no time the ships feel like one great big happy family at sea.
- **Adventurous.** With the sails flapping and wooden decks surrounding you, it's no great leap of faith to feel like a pirate lost at sea.
- **Cheap.** Windjammer's per diem rates tend to be lower than those of Star Clipper and significantly lower than Windstar Cruises.

Cons

- **Tiny cabins.** No polite way to say it: Cabins are cramped. But who wants to stay inside, when the wide-open decks are so inviting?
- **Mal de mer.** If you're prone to seasickness, these ships may set you off and running.
- **Loose port schedule.** Sailings usually follow the routes described in the brochures, but one destination might be substituted for another if a particularly adverse wind is blowing, or if there's a storm between you and your scheduled destination.

Frommer's Ratings: Windjammer Barefoot Cruises					
	Poor	Fair	Good	Excellent	Outstanding
Enjoyment Factor					✓
Dining			✓		
Activities			✓		
Children's Program			✓*		
Entertainment			✓		
Service			✓		
Overall Value					✓

*Children's program is available on the Legacy only.

WINDJAMMER BAREFOOT CRUISES: LETTING IT ALL HANG OUT

When British poet Thomas Beddos wrote, "The anchor heaves, the ship runs free, the sails swell full, to sea, to sea," he might as well have been describing the Windjammer operation. There's no pretense here: On these authentic vessels, which have withstood the test of time and tide, you can taste the salt air as it blows among the riggings and feel the sails stretch to the wind, propelling you toward adventure.

With six sailing ships, Windjammer has the largest fleet of its kind at sea today (the runner-up is reportedly the Norwegian government). From an inspired if unintentional beginning, it has grown into one of the major lines for cruisers who want to forgo the orchestrated regimentation on the giant cruise ships.

The famous and now semi-retired **Captain Mike Burke**—Cap'n Mike, as he's been known for the past half century—founded the company in 1947 with one ship, and for years ran down-and-dirty party cruises popular with singles, purchasing ships rich in history but otherwise destined for the scrap yard and transforming them into one-of-a-kind sailing vessels.

Legend has it that Burke, released from navy submarine duty in 1947, headed for Miami with $600 in back pay, intending to paint the town red. He succeeded. The next morning, he awoke with a blinding hangover and no money, on the deck of a 19-foot sloop moored somewhere in the Bahamas. Mike Burke had apparently bought himself a boat. Using a mostly empty bottle of Scotch, he christened the boat *Hangover,* and the rest is history. The *Hangover* was followed by the *Tondeleyo,* a 70-foot ketch for which Burke traded the house he'd wound up with after a divorce. He lived aboard to save money, and then started ferrying friends out for weekends of sailing and fishing. Demand escalated, and Burke quit his full-time job to become a one-man cruise line.

After another year, Burke acquired a 150-foot schooner named *Janeen,* which had run aground and was in need of serious repairs, and thus began his life's work as a restorer of tall ships. After refurbishing *Janeen* himself, Burke rechristened her *Polynesia,* hired a crew of four, and began carrying passengers on weeklong cruises. *Polynesia* was followed by the *Brigantine Yankee* and the *Polynesia II,* and then by the ships that form the current Windjammer fleet. Some people collect antique cars; Mike Burke collects tall ships.

Burke works on a principle that anyone who's ever bought an old house will understand: Buy them cheap and decrepit, fix them up, and then stand back and admire your handiwork. His six children (including company president Susan) have assisted him in his ventures, renovating the vessels at the line's old shipyard near Miami and at a new yard in Trinidad. Burke says that the saddest thing he's ever seen is a tall ship permanently tethered to a pier, serving as a museum.

Are these cruises fun? No cruise can be all bad when it includes complimentary Bloody Marys in the morning, Rum Swizzles at sunset, and wine with dinner. Since service for each meal involves two separate seatings, passengers have plenty of time to enjoy another drink or two while waiting for (or recovering from) their feast. The bar operates on a doubloon system—a kind of debit card for drinks.

Swimming pools? There's no need, as the crystal-clear Caribbean is the swimming hole. Shuffleboard? Are you kidding? That's for those other cruise ships. Work the sails? Well, no. The crew handles that (although passengers are sometimes invited to lend a hand). This is a barefoot adventure, not a Shanghai special: Your duty is to sit back and live it up, not winch up a topsail whenever the captain barks an order.

This is a T-shirt and shorts adventure that's ultra-laid-back: There are no keys for the cabins, rum punch is served in paper cups, daily announcements are written in magic marker on a bulletin board, chances are the purser doubles as the nurse and gift shop manager, and itineraries are only partially finalized before a ship's departure and are based on wind and tides. Vessels tend to sail during the late afternoon or night, arriving each morning at landfalls, allowing passengers to enjoy the local terrain and diversions. Favored waters include the Grenadines and the Virgin Islands, mini-archipelagos that offer some of the most challenging and beautiful sailing in the hemisphere, as well as esoteric landfalls such as cone-shaped Saba, historic Statia, or mysterious Carriacou, sites almost never visited by larger ships. (The line's one sailless ship, *Amazing Grace,* serves as a supply vessel in addition to carrying passengers, and so maintains a more rigid schedule.)

Despite the fact that the company's fleet is worth millions and its clear public image is the envy of many larger operators, Windjammer continues to think of itself as a mom-and-pop cruise line—and therein lies at least part of its allure. Passengers who enjoy this line tend to have a bit of the rebel in them, and enjoy chucking convention overboard and letting it all hang out.

That said, the company is no longer quite the same wild and crazy Windjammer that used to advertise in *Hustler* and promised its passengers they'd get a "bang" out of their vacation. Windjammer still remains for the most part a let-your-hair-down, party-on scene and a great way to see some of the Caribbean's more offbeat islands, but since Mike Burke's children have taken over control of the company, they've made an effort to offer a somewhat more wholesome, mainstream experience. A few years back, Windjammer added an activities mate (a.k.a. cruise director) to organize a few more activities for passengers, and has made an effort to improve the overall quality of the dining and cabin service. It also began offering a kids' program on the flagship *Legacy* during the summer months for ages 6 to 12.

So has Windjammer gone soft? No more so than the rest of us. As one longtime captain told me, the line has just had to change its approach to keep up with what people want. After all, it's not the '70s anymore. Despite any changes, the rum swizzles still flow freely and the wind still blows through the rigging. What more could a wannabe pirate want? Yo ho ho, y'all.

THE FLEET

Not a ship younger than 40 in the bunch, the Windjammer fleet of six includes the *Mandalay*, built in 1923; the *Flying Cloud*, built in 1927; the *Yankee Clipper*, built in 1927; the *Polynesia*, built in 1938; the *Amazing Grace*, built in 1955; and the *Legacy*, built in 1959.

The **Mandalay** was once one of the most famous and luxurious ships in the world, the *Husar IV*, dream boat of financier E. F. Hutton and his wife, Marjorie Merriweather Post. Later, it was commissioned as a research vessel by Columbia University, which sailed it for 1.25 million miles trying to develop theories (since proven correct) about continental drift. It's estimated that by the early 1980s, half the knowledge of the world's ocean floor was gathered by instruments aboard this ship.

The **Flying Cloud,** built in Nantes, France, in 1935, functioned long ago as a training vessel for French cadets. During World War II, the ship served as a decoy and spy ship for the Allied Navy. Its moment of glory came when Charles de Gaulle decorated it for sinking two Japanese submarines while it was carrying nitrates from Tahiti. More than any other vessel in the Windjammer fleet, this one resembles a pirate ship of old.

The **Yankee Clipper,** once the only armor-plated sailing yacht in the world, was built by arms baron Alfred Krupp, whose armaments influenced the outcome of the Franco-Prussian War of 1870. Hitler once stepped aboard to award the Iron Cross to one of his U-boat commanders. Seized by the United States as war booty after World War II, the ship eventually became George Vanderbilt's private yacht. While the Vanderbilts

The *Fantôme* Tragedy

Tragically, Windjammer's oldest vessel, the *Fantôme,* went down with its entire crew under the fury of October 1998's Hurricane Mitch. As the storm grew, the week's scheduled cruise was aborted and all passengers were sent safely home. Thirty-one crew members then tried to outrun the storm, perishing when it shifted course, sinking the ship somewhere off the coast of Honduras. Besides a few battered pieces of wreckage, the *Fantôme* and its crew were never recovered.

owned it, the *Yankee Clipper* was the fastest two-masted sailing vessel off the California coast, once managing an almost frightening 22 knots under full sail. Burke bought the ship just before it was due to be broken down for scrap, then gutted, redesigned, and rebuilt it, stripping off the armor in the process. Renovations in 1984 added a third mast, additional deck space, and cabin modifications. Although not as light and streamlined as it was originally, it's still a fast and very exciting ship.

The *Polynesia,* built in Holland in 1938, was originally known as the *Argus,* and served as a fishing schooner in the Portuguese Grand Banks fleet. Windjammer bought it in 1975. Its original fishiness has disappeared, thanks to a good scrubbing, a complete reconfiguration of the cabins and interior spaces, and the addition of varnished wood. Less stylish-looking than many of its thoroughbred siblings, it nonetheless remains one of the fleet's most consistently popular ships.

Amazing Grace is the sailless, diligent, and dogged workhorse in the bunch, functioning as the freight-carrying diesel-driven ship that keeps the other members of the fleet supplied and provisioned. Because of its large hold, it's the most stable ship in the fleet, with no apologies for its role as a slow but reliable umbilical cord to its younger and more high-strung siblings. Its itineraries are more comprehensive than those of any other ship in the fleet, stopping at each port the others use, as well as at supply depots en route.

In 1997, the line launched its newest and largest ship, *Legacy.* Originally a motored research vessel for the French government, it was designed with a deep keel that gave it additional balance during North Atlantic and North Sea storms. At the time, it was one of several government-owned ships sending weather reports to a central agency in Paris, which used them to predict storm patterns on the French mainland. The advent of global satellites made the vessel obsolete. It was bought by Windjammer in 1988, and, over the course of a decade, over $10 million was poured into a massive reconfiguration conducted at Windjammer's family-managed shipyard in Trinidad. Four steel masts and 11 sails were added, plus accoutrements the vessel needed for 7-day barefoot jaunts through the eastern Caribbean. At 1,165 tons, it's larger than any other vessel in the Windjammer fleet, although still tiny compared to a megaship.

The *Legacy* may represent the first of a new breed for Windjammer, which has tossed the idea of adding more ships of this type over the next few years.

Which is the line's best ship? Each of them is nearly human, according to crew members, with distinctive personalities to match their distinctive lines. The *Mandalay, Yankee Clipper, Flying Cloud,* and *Polynesia* are roughly equivalent in amenities, activities, and onboard atmosphere, and since each has been extensively refurbished, they have more or less equivalent interior decors. As for their capabilities as sailing ships, Captain Stuart Larcombe, who has served aboard them all, told me that the award goes to the *Yankee Clipper,* followed by the *Mandalay* (but his favorite, all around, was the *Fantôme*).

The new *Legacy* is larger, roomier, and more comfortable than its siblings, and tends to rely heavily on its engines to augment the sails. Rather than quibble about differences

Online Last-Minute Windjammin' Discounts

In 1999 Windjammer initiated a fantastic "CyberSailors" program of last-minute deals on its Web site (www.windjammer.com). Sign up and the line will send you weekly updates of incredibly discounted cruises, some up to 50% off. The catch? They're really last-minute, with the notices sent not more than 2 weeks before sailing. Still, if you're able to pick up and go at a moment's notice, you can often get a weeklong Caribbean cruise (without airfare) for around $450.

between these ships, I'd suggest paying less attention to their minor physical differences and more to their different itineraries and varied ports of embarkation. Where exactly is it you want the wind to take you?

The *Amazing Grace* is a different bird, with a quieter onboard atmosphere, and tends to attract a much older clientele. As one bartender on the ship told me, "If we have a young person aboard, they probably made a mistake."

Sooner or later Windjammer hopes to launch the **Rogue,** a second cargo/passenger ship that—if they ever get it reconditioned—will sail itineraries much like those followed by the *Grace.*

PASSENGER PROFILE

Unlike some "all things to all people" lines, Windjammer is for a particular kind of informal, fun-loving, and down-to-earth passenger, and though some compare the experience to a continuous fraternity party, I wouldn't go that far. In fact, the passenger and age mix puts the lie to that description. From honeymooning couples in their 20s to grandparents in their 70s, the line attracts a broad range of adventurers who like to have fun and don't want anything resembling a highly regimented vacation. Passengers are pretty evenly divided between men and women, and 15% to 20% overall are single. Passengers aboard the *Amazing Grace* commissary ship, however, tend to be older (60s plus) than those aboard the wind-driven sailing ships.

Many passengers love the experience so much that they return again and again. The record is held by the late "Pappy" Gomez of Cleveland, Ohio, who sailed with Windjammer more than 160 times, but many, many people have sailed with the line 30, 40, or 50 times. The line's supply officer told me he never steps aboard one of the ships without seeing passengers he's sailed with before.

Young children should probably not go (in fact, the line doesn't accept passengers under 6), nor should anyone prone to seasickness (there's quite a bit of that the first days afloat) or anyone wanting to be pampered (there's none of that during any day afloat). These ships are not for people with disabilities, either.

DINING

When it comes to dining, "slide over and pass me the breadbasket" about sums it up. Family-style and informal, there's nothing gourmet about the food; it ranges from mediocre to delicious. All breads and pastries are homemade, and at dinner, after soup and salad are served, passengers can choose from two main entrees, like curried shrimp and roast pork with garlic sauce. Don't be surprised if the waiters ask for a show of hands to see who wants what. Unlimited cheap red and white wine are complimentary and freely poured into the plastic wineglasses. Tasty breakfasts like eggs Benedict as well as normal fare, and lunches such as lobster pizza and apple salad, are served buffet style.

Elaborate dining rituals and fussed-over food are not the reason to sail aboard this line. Food is wholesome, communal, and simple—definitely not cordon bleu. At certain

Windjammer's Theme Cruises: You're Not in Kansas Anymore

Windjammer is not what you'd call a straitlaced cruise line, so it really means something that when the ships are chartered for theme cruises, the level of permissive wackiness actually goes *up*. Don't expect the kind of tame country music or big band themes that Holland America and NCL have run through like phases of the moon for years. Besides the dozen or so **singles theme cruises** it schedules every year on the *Polynesia*, Windjammer charters its ships occasionally to groups who put together **gay cruises** (there was one in 1998 and one scheduled for '99), **nudist cruises** (there's even been a gay nudist cruise), and **"Parrothead Cruises,"** where fans of Jimmy Buffet do the Margaritaville thing (note that Buffett does not officially endorse these events). Don't worry about getting stuck on one of these cruises if you don't want to: They're special cruises put together and marketed by travel agents; if one of them appeals to you, though, inquire with Windjammer about when the next one is scheduled.

islands, the crew lugs ashore a picnic lunch for an afternoon beach party, and each sailing usually includes an on-deck barbecue one evening. There are two open seatings for dinner.

Many dishes overall are rooted in Caribbean tradition. The chef will accommodate **special diets,** including vegetarian and low-salt.

ACTIVITIES

Windjammer deliberately deemphasizes the activities that dominate shipboard life aboard larger vessels, although it might occasionally host an on-deck crab race. Otherwise, your entertainment is up to you. If the weather's fine and you want to help trim the sails, you might be allowed to help. If the weather gets dicey, however, don't even think about it.

Generally at least once per cruise, on one of the ships' beach visits—to Jost Van Dyke, perhaps—the activities mate might also organize **team games** reminiscent of mid-'60s cocktail-party movies (think Cary Grant and Audrey Hepburn in the nightclub scene in *Charade*). It's the usual embarrassing stuff: Passengers twirl hula-hoops while dressed in snorkel gear; pass cucumbers to each other, clasping them only with their thighs; flop onto slippery foam mats and try to swim out to and around a landmark. Silliness, in other words—but it does make for instant camaraderie. After all, after someone's seen you act this dumb, they've seen it all.

The line still hosts singles cruises on the *Polynesia* and the *Flying Cloud* several times a year. (See the box on theme cruises, below, for more info.)

CHILDREN'S PROGRAM

No children under 6 are allowed aboard any ship in the Windjammer fleet, and children under age 16 must be accompanied by an adult. Sales agents usually prefer that children be at least 10 years old. Aboard most of the ships, teenagers divert themselves the same way adults do, with conversation, shore excursions, reading, and watching the wide blue sea. Otherwise, few concessions are made for their amusement. Baby-sitting is not available. This situation is markedly different aboard *Legacy*, where a "Junior Jammers" program was set into place shortly after the ship's inauguration. Here, children are divided into roughly compatible age brackets and kept involved for 12 hours a day with a roster of fun, amusing, diverting, or challenging summer camp–style activities.

Windjammer Fleet Itineraries*

Ship	Home Ports & Season	Itinerary	Other Itineraries
Amazing Grace	Round-trip between the Bahamas and Trinidad year-round.	**13-night eastern/southern Carib:** Ports include Antigua, Bequia, Conception, Cooper Island, Dominica, Grand Bahama, Grand Turk, Grenada, Little Inagua, Iles des Saintes, New Providence, Nevis, Palm Island, Plana Cay, Providenciales, Puerto Plata, St. Barts, St. Kitts, St. Lucia, Sint Maarten, Tobago, Tortola, Trinidad, and Virgin Gorda.	None
Flying Cloud	Round-trip from Tortola, itineraries alternate year-round.	**6-night eastern Carib 1:** Salt Island, Cooper Island, Virgin Gorda, and Jost Van Dyke. **6-night eastern Carib 2:** Cooper Island, Peter Island, Norman Island, and Virgin Gorda.	None
Legacy	Round-trip from St. Thomas, itineraries alternate year-round.	**7-night eastern Carib:** Two alternating itineraries may include Buck Island, Vieques, St. John, Jost Van Dyke, Virgin Gorda, Tortola, Norman Island, Culebra, and Luis Peña.	None
Mandalay	Alternating 13-night itineraries between Grenada and Antigua, and 6-night itineraries round-trip from Grenada, Nov–May. 7-night itinerary between Grenada and Puerto la Cruz, June–Oct.	**13-night eastern Carib:** Antigua, Bequia, Carriacou, Canouan, Dominica, Grenada, Guadeloupe, Iles des Saintes, Martinique, Mayreau, Nevis, Palm Island, St. Lucia, St. Vincent, and Tobago Cays. **6-night eastern Carib:** Grenadines. **7-night Venezuela:** Mochima National Park, Blanquilla, Margarita Island, and Los Testigos.	None
Polynesia	Round-trip from Sint Maarten Nov–May, from St. Lucia June–Oct, itineraries alternate year-round.	**6-night eastern Carib 1:** From Sint Maarten: St. Barts, Anguilla, Tintamarre, and Saba. From St. Lucia: Martinique, Iles des Saintes, and Dominica. **6-night eastern Carib 2:** From Sint Maarten: Columbier Beach, St. Barts, St. Eustatius, Nevis, and St. Kitts. From St. Lucia: St. Vincent, Mayreau, Palm Island, and Bequia.	None
Yankee Clipper	Round-trip from Grenada, itineraries alternate year-round.	**6-night eastern Carib 1:** Carriacou, Palm Island, Bequia, St. Vincent, and Mayreau. **6-night eastern Carib 2:** Palm Island, Union Island, Bequia, Canouan, Tobago Cays, and St. Vincent.	None

Note: Windjammer Barefoot cruises often adjust their itineraries in mid-cruise to reflect changing wind and weather patterns, as well as any island event of particular interest. Each cruise itinerary is up to the ship's captain.

ENTERTAINMENT

Social interaction around the bars is emphasized. One or two nights a week a **local pop band** is brought on board for a few hours of dancing, and there's a weekly barbecue buffet dinner and a **costume party.**

Just about every day is spent in port somewhere and the occasional day at sea might feature a knot-tying demonstration and a bridge tour. The entertainment is the ship itself and the camaraderie between passengers. At about 5pm every day, gallons of complimentary **rum swizzles** are generously offered along with hors d'oeuvres like spicy meatballs, chicken fingers, and cheese and crackers. Guests gather on deck, often still in their sarongs and shorts, mingling in the fresh sea air with taped music playing in the background.

Stowaways & Other Deals (Plus One Extra Charge)

Stowaways: Rather than fork over a bundle for a hotel the night before your cruise, you can stay aboard your docked ship for a relatively modest $45 per person, double occupancy. **Past Passengers Club:** A $25 membership fee entitles clients to the Windjammer newsletter, $25 discounts when you book two cruises back-to-back, and notice of other discounts and special sailings. **Children's Rates:** A child under 12 sharing a cabin with two adults is charged 50% of the adult fare. **Port Charges:** Six- and 7-night cruises generally run $65 per person. Port charges for 13-day outings cost $135 per person.

After dinner, head up to the on-deck bar (drinks are cheap: $2 for a Red Stripe or Heineken and $2.80 for the most expensive cocktail) or grab a deck chair or mat and hit the deck. Generally, the ship stays late in one or two ports so passengers can head ashore to one of the island watering holes.

SERVICE

Service is straightforward and efficient, but not doting. Unlike more upscale cruise lines, with Windjammer there's no master/servant relationship between passengers and staff—the crew are simply fellow travelers who just happen to steer the ship or serve dinner or drinks when their schedules call for it. They're a good bunch.

The line tends to attract a staff that shares founder Mike Burke's appreciation for the wide-open sea and barely concealed scorn for corporate agendas and staid priorities. Many are from the same Caribbean islands Windjammer's ships visit.

Amazing Grace

The Verdict

If you're looking for a slow and easy (and cheap) tour of the Caribbean and like the novelty of being on a supply ship as it does its rounds, a trip on this charming tub is bound to create lasting memories.

Amazing Grace *(photo: Windjammer Barefoot)*

Specifications

Size (in tons)	1,525	Officers	British/American
Number of Cabins	47	Crew	40 (International)
Number of Outside Cabins	46	Passenger/Crew Ratio	2.4 to 1
Cabins with Verandas	0	Year Built	1955
Number of Passengers	94	Last Major Refurbishment	1995

Frommer's Ratings (Scale of 1–5)

Cabin Comfort & Amenities	2	Pool, Fitness & Spa Facilities	N/A
Ship Cleanliness & Maintenance	3	Children's Facilities	N/A
Public Comfort/Space	3	Itinerary	5
Decor	3	Worth the Money	5

The *Amazing Grace,* a dowdy but reliable sea horse, is the closest thing to a banana boat in the cruise industry. Moving its way doggedly and regularly through most of the Caribbean archipelago, it is the only vessel in the Windjammer fleet that does without sails.

Built as the *Pharos* in Dundee, Scotland, in 1955, it mostly carried supplies to isolated lighthouses and North Sea oil rigs, but once or twice it was pressed into service as a weekend cruiser for the queen of England. The vessel was acquired by Windjammer in 1988 and, despite many modernizations, still retains some vestiges of its British past. Today, it's still a freighter servicing remote outposts, albeit in the warm Caribbean rather than the chilly North Sea. If you come aboard expecting to be treated like royalty, however, you'll be sorely disappointed.

Some of the line's least dramatic (but cheapest) cruises are its languid "slow boat to China" odysseys aboard the *Grace,* and its itinerary, featuring an amazing number of offbeat ports, is top-notch. The lack of organized activities is a drawback on these long sailings, however, so you'll be forced to create your own. Guests are noticeably more sedentary, definitely older, and less party-oriented than those aboard the line's more raffish sail-powered vessels. Most tend to turn in by 10pm.

Cabins & Rates

Cabins	Per diems from	Bathtub	Fridge	Hair Dryer	Sitting Area	TV
Outside	$111	no	some	no	no	no
Suite	$235	no	yes	no	yes	yes

CABINS As you might have guessed, cabins are utterly without frills and very small, but they're a tad roomier than others in Windjammer's fleet. About half contain the varnished paneling from the ship's original construction; the others are more modern, with almost no nostalgic value. Although there's a sink in each cabin, this is the only ship in the fleet where you'll have to share shower and toilet facilities with other passengers. The honeymoon suite, near the stern, is often rented by non-honeymooners because of its somewhat larger size. There are no wheelchair-accessible cabins.

PUBLIC AREAS You can have a lot of fun aboard this ship, although there's no avoiding reminders that it is indeed a glorified freighter. A bar/lounge faces forward across the bow and another sits in open air on the stern, and there's a TV room. Some of the greatest authenticity preserved from the ship's early days is a piano room and a smoking room/library, which sports etched glass doors and mahogany walls. Because large sections of this vessel (the storage areas) are off-limits to passengers, many people tend to gravitate to the deck areas—including the lovely Promenade Deck—for reading, napping, or whatever.

The dining room has booth-type tables that seat up to eight passengers. There are two open seatings, generally at 6:30 and 8pm.

POOL, FITNESS & SPA FACILITIES There's no swimming pool, gym, or fitness facilities. Instead, you'll get your exercise during snorkeling and scuba sessions at the ports of call. Snorkeling gear (mask, fins, snorkel, and carrying bag) rents for $20 per week, and one-tank dives, as offered by an array of outside concessionaires, cost around $50 at each of the ports of call. (Novice divers pay $85 for a "resort course.") Shore outings sometimes include strenuous hiking expeditions. All excursions and scuba expeditions are conducted by outside agencies, not by Windjammer, and passengers are required to sign a liability release before participating.

Flying Cloud • Mandalay • Polynesia • Yankee Clipper

The Verdict

Bound by wood and sails, this oddball group of little ships have led fascinating and long lives and today promise adventure, good times, and offbeat ports for a bargain price.

Yankee Clipper *(photo: Windjammer Barefoot)*

Specifications

Size (in tons)		Officers	British/American/
Flying Cloud	400		Australian
Mandalay	420	Crew	
Polynesia	430	*Flying Cloud*	25 (International)
Yankee Clipper	327	*Mandalay*	28 (International)
Number of Cabins		*Polynesia*	45 (International)
Flying Cloud	33	*Yankee Clipper*	29 (International)
Mandalay	36	Passenger/Crew Ratio	2.2–3.1 to 1
Polynesia	46	Year Built	
Yankee Clipper	32	*Flying Cloud*	1927
Number of Outside Cabins		*Mandalay*	1923
Flying Cloud	33	*Polynesia*	1938
Mandalay	36	*Yankee Clipper*	1927
Polynesia	46	Last Major Refurbishment	
Yankee Clipper	32	*Flying Cloud*	1991
Cabins with Verandas	0	*Mandalay*	1982
Number of Passengers		*Polynesia*	1990
Flying Cloud	74	*Yankee Clipper*	1984
Mandalay	72		
Polynesia	126		
Yankee Clipper	64		

Frommer's Ratings (Scale of 1–5)

Cabin Comfort & Amenities	2	Pool, Fitness & Spa Facilities	N/A
Ship Cleanliness & Maintenance	3	Children's Facilities	N/A
Public Comfort/Space	3	Itinerary	5
Decor	3	Worth the Money	5

Despite different origins, different histories, and subtle differences in the way they react to the wind and weather, each of these sailing ships shares many things in common with the others, and for adventure and interesting ports of call they're all absolutely top-notch. I've opted to cluster them into one all-encompassing review because of the extent to which each has been rebuilt and reconfigured to the Windjammer ideal. For the ships' individual histories, refer to the pages above.

How to select one or another if you're a first-time Windjammer client? I advise you to select your ship based on its itinerary rather than its aesthetics, taking into account the frequent cruises for singles that are held aboard the *Polynesia* and the *Flying Cloud*. Other than that, choose the boat you want to float based on your schedule and any special promotions the line might be offering.

Cabins & Rates						
Cabins	Per diems from	Bathtub	Fridge	Hair Dryer	Sitting Area	TV
Outside	$143	no	no	no	no	no
Suite	$163	no	some	no	yes	some

CABINS   There's no getting around it: Cabins are cramped, just as they would have been on a true 19th-century clipper ship. Few retain any glamorous vestiges of their original owners, and most are about as functional as they come. Still, they're adequate enough and it's the adventurous thrill of sailing on one of these ships that you come for, not luxurious cabins.

Each cabin has a minuscule bathroom with a shower that tends to spray water everywhere, regardless of how careful you are. On many vessels, hot water is available only during certain hours of the day, whenever the ships' galleys and laundries aren't using it. Be prepared for toilets that don't always function properly, and retain your sense of humor as they're repaired.

Storage space is limited, but this isn't a serious problem because few passengers bring very much with them. Many cabins have upper and lower berths, some have lower-level twins, and a few have doubles.

Some vessels have a limited number of suites that, although not spacious by the standards of larger ships, seem to be of generous proportions when contrasted to standard cabins. There are no wheelchair-accessible cabins on any of these ships.

PUBLIC AREAS   What glamour may have been associated with these ships in the past is long gone, lost to the years or in the gutting and refitting they required before entering Windjammer service. There are patches of rosewood or mahogany, but otherwise the decors are durable, washable, and practical, and appropriate backdrops for passengers so laid-back that few bother to ever change out of their bathing suits, T-shirts, and shorts. Dining rooms are cozy and wood-paneled; overall, they've been designed with efficiency in mind. The *Mandalay*'s is open-air, and is the only dining room in the fleet that isn't air-conditioned (evenings are generally pretty cool, though). By contrast, the seemingly endless teakwood decks look positively opulent, and many passengers adopt some preferred corner of the decks as a place to hang out.

POOL, FITNESS & SPA FACILITIES   Ships are too small to offer health clubs or any of the sauna and fitness regimens so heavily promoted aboard larger ships. None of the vessels has a swimming pool. You'll get an adequate amount of exercise, however, during snorkeling and scuba sessions conducted at the ports of call. Snorkeling and diving fees/specifications are the same as aboard *Amazing Grace* (see review above).

Legacy

The Verdict

The brightest and most spacious of Windjammer's ships, the *Legacy* is a real winner in my book, with comfortable cabins, good-sized private bathrooms, a cheerful dining saloon with large round booths, and a sprawling expanse of outdoor deck space. Even when full, the ship doesn't feel crowded.

Legacy *(photo: Windjammer Barefoot)*

Specifications

Size (in tons)	1,165	Officers	American/British/Australian
Number of Cabins	60		
Number of Outside Cabins	40	Crew	43 (International)
Cabins with Verandas	0	Passenger/Crew Ratio	2.8 to 1
Number of Passengers	120	Year Built	1959
		Last Major Refurbishment	1998

Frommer's Ratings (Scale of 1–5)

Cabin Comfort & Amenities	3	Pool, Fitness & Spa Facilities	N/A
Ship Cleanliness & Maintenance	4	Children's Facilities	N/A
Public Comfort/Space	4	Itinerary	5
Decor	3	Worth the Money	5

The *Legacy* is Windjammer's newest acquisition, its biggest and most modern, and the first of a new breed. Built in 1959 as a motorized research vessel, the ship was acquired by Windjammer in 1989, converted into a traditional-style "tall ship," and relaunched in 1997.

Some hardcore Windjammer veterans consider the *Legacy* a somewhat wimpy addition to the rough and tumble venerated fleet. Equating Windjammer's signature yo-ho-ho pirate adventures with the cramped, bare-bones life aboard its smaller, older ships, stalwart Windjammer fans wondered whether the comfort available on this new vessel (and the children's program it offers—a Windjammer first) meant the old days were gone forever. It was like seeing a group of 30- or 40-somethings returning to their favorite college-era dive bar and finding it newly sheathed in wood paneling, with brass lamps in place of the neon lights and jazz on the juke box instead of "Born to Run."

With this ship, Windjammer has moved into a new era. Roomier and more stable than the rest of the sailing fleet, it sports a lovely profile that makes it the center of attention whenever it sails into port. It is indeed the most comfortable of the Windjammer lot, but it still embraces that irreverent Windjammer spirit we've come to know and love. It takes only a glance at the carved wooden figurehead on the ship's prow—which depicts none other than Cap'n Mike Burke himself, wearing a tropical-print shirt, beer in one hand and a ship's wheel in the other—to see that this is still very much a laid-back, partying vessel. It's just a cushier one.

There are tradeoffs for this comfort, to be sure: The *Legacy's* sails, for instance, are often more decorative than functional. Although crew members told me they think of the vessel as a sailing ship with auxiliary engines instead of a motor ship with sails, in practice I found that the engines were almost always in use, with the sails contributing mood more than actual propulsion. What this means is that you'll always hear a certain amount of engine noise, so if you're hoping for the silence of true sailing, you'll be disappointed. (That said, we did go under full sail at least one afternoon, and the captain told us the ship had been clocked at 10.5 knots under sail alone.)

The times they are a-changin', but, for the most part, the song remains the same. Sure, just as aboard Star Clippers and Windstar, you won't be tacking into the wind like Erroll Flynn (it's just not practical to rely on wind only to get you to your scheduled port calls), but you can still take joy in the sheer beauty of the sails, and get a thrill when they do catch the wind, stretching taut from the masts. And sure, you descend from the main deck to most of the cabins via a wide (relatively speaking) stairway rather than the kind of tiny circular stairway you'd see aboard the line's older ships, but you'll spend a lot less time tending to bumps on your noggin because of it. And no, sadly, you can't climb the masts anymore—the line dislikes being sued by passengers who've had one too many rum swizzles and fallen off—but you're still welcome, *very* welcome, to have that one rum swizzle too many. Just be sure to keep your feet on deck while you're doing it—or, if you're adventurous, sit out in the bow rigging, as a bunch of us did after late champagne one memorable night in 1998.

Cabins & Rates

Cabins	Per diems from	Bathtub	Fridge	Hair Dryer	Sitting Area	TV
Outside	$143	no	no	no	no	no
Suite	$163	no	no	no	yes	yes

CABINS   Cabins aboard the *Legacy* are somewhat larger and more comfortable than aboard the line's older ships, but if you're used to sailing aboard large cruise ships, they'll probably seem cramped. Berths are either doubles or bunk beds, and if you're in the upper portion of the latter, watch your head: More than one passenger has woken up and knocked himself silly on the metal porthole cover that projects from the wall when open. You might do well to sleep with your feet toward it.

Suites—both the Admiral Suites and Burke's Berth, which is the best in the house—offer windows instead of portholes, plus space for a third occupant. There is a triple-berth option offered as well in the Commodore class cabins, but it affords a minimum of personal space. Burke's Berth is the only cabin aboard that offers an entertainment center, bar, and vanity. Storage in all cabins is perfectly adequate for this type of T-shirt and shorts cruise, with each containing a small closet/drawer unit and having additional space under the bed.

Bathrooms offer an adequate amount of maneuvering space and small, curtained showers, some with a raised lip that contains the runoff but some not, making for a perpetually wet bathroom floor. Although these facilities are small and spartan compared to those offered on larger and glitzier ships, they're still far better than the head-style facilities aboard the other Windjammer sailing ships.

Single cabins are available. As with all the Windjammer ships, the *Legacy* is not a good option for people with disabilities.

PUBLIC AREAS   The top deck, with a large canopied area at its center, is the social focus of the cruise, the space where the rum swizzles are dispensed at sunset, where visiting bands perform at night, and where the captain gives his daily morning "Story Time," a short talk that's 20% ship business; 40% information about the day's port call, activities, or sailing route; and 40% pure humor. (*Tip:* The captain will come out and say "Good morning, everybody!" and the passengers—many of whom have taken these trips before and know the drill—respond in full voice, "Good morning, Captain SIR!" It happens every time.) The ship's bar is also located on this deck, as is the requisite barrel of rum—a real barrel, from which the bartender siphons off what he needs every day.

The Poop Deck offers the best sunbathing space, although the position of the sails—when they're raised—could force you to move quite often. Passengers lounge on patio-style white plastic recliners or on one of the many blue cushions strewn about, which many passengers also use to sleep out on deck, under the stars—something the line fully encourages.

At the bow, navigation of the ship is often from the ship's wheel mounted out in open air. When seas are calm and sailing is easy, the crew offers passengers a chance to steer. Unlike on most larger cruise ships, the *Legacy*'s bow is generally open to passengers, allowing you to do your Leonardo DiCaprio "King of the World" bit, or, even better, to climb out on the netting that projects to the tip of the bowsprit, and lounge there while the blue Caribbean Sea splashes and sprays below you. Don't miss this opportunity—trust me.

All meals are served in the comfortable aft dining room, fitted with large circular tables (a bummer if you're stuck in the middle, three or four people from freedom) and decorated with faux tropical plants. The only other interior public room is a small and not terribly appealing lounge that offers a TV/video arrangement and a smattering of books and board games. In an entire week aboard, the only person I saw using this room was a 10-year old boy watching movies. Where was everyone? Out on deck, where they belong.

POOL, FITNESS & SPA FACILITIES   As aboard the rest of the line's ships, there are none. No spa, no gym, no jogging track. Aboard ship, the most exercise you're likely to get is if you volunteer to help hoist the sails. In port, however, you'll have such options as snorkeling, scuba diving, sea kayaking, and hiking to help you work off dessert. Of course, there are silly beach relay races and other games organized by the activities mate to get your heart rate up. Snorkeling and diving fees/specifications are the same as aboard *Amazing Grace* (see review above).

Part 3

The Ports

With information on the ports of embarkation, advice on things you can see and do on your own in 21 Caribbean ports of call plus Bermuda and the Panama Canal, and tips on the best tours.

The Ports of Embarkation 10

The busiest of the ports of embarkation is Miami, followed by Port Everglades in Fort Lauderdale and Port Canaveral at Cape Canaveral. Tampa, on Florida's west coast, is also becoming a major port, especially for cruise ships visiting the eastern coast of Mexico, while New Orleans is popular for ships sailing to Mexico. San Juan, Puerto Rico, is both the major port of embarkation in the Caribbean Basin and a major port of call. (See chapter 11, "Caribbean Ports of Call," for a review.)

All these ports are tourist destinations themselves, so most cruise lines now offer special deals to extend all Caribbean/Bahamian cruise vacations in the port either before or after the cruise. These packages, for 2, 3, or 4 days, often offer hotel and car-rental discounts as well as sightseeing packages. Have your travel agent or cruise specialist check for the best deals.

In this chapter, I'll describe each port of embarkation, tell you how to get to it, and suggest things to see and do there, whether hitting the beach, sightseeing, or shopping. I'll also recommend a sampling of restaurants and places to stay. You'll find more detailed information about each destination in *Frommer's Florida, Frommer's Miami & the Keys, Frommer's New Orleans,* and *Frommer's Puerto Rico.*

1 Miami & the Port of Miami

Miami is the cruise capital of the world. More cruise ships, especially super-sized ones, berth here than anywhere else on earth, and more than 3 million cruise ship passengers pass through yearly. Not surprisingly, the city's facilities are extensive and state-of-the-art, and Miami International Airport is only 8 miles away.

Just across the bridge from the Port of Miami is **Bayside Marketplace,** downtown Miami's waterfront and restaurant shopping complex, which can be reached via regular shuttle service between each cruise terminal and Bayside's main entrance.

Industry giants Carnival and Royal Caribbean have both recently signed long-term, multimillion-dollar agreements with the port, and to accommodate the influx of new cruise ships (like Royal Caribbean's massive *Voyager of the Seas*), Miami has spent $76 million on major improvements to terminals 3, 4 and 5, and the addition of a 750-space parking facility. Slated for completion in late 1999, the renovated terminals will offer enhanced facilities, such as 4,000 additional passenger seats

Miami at a Glance

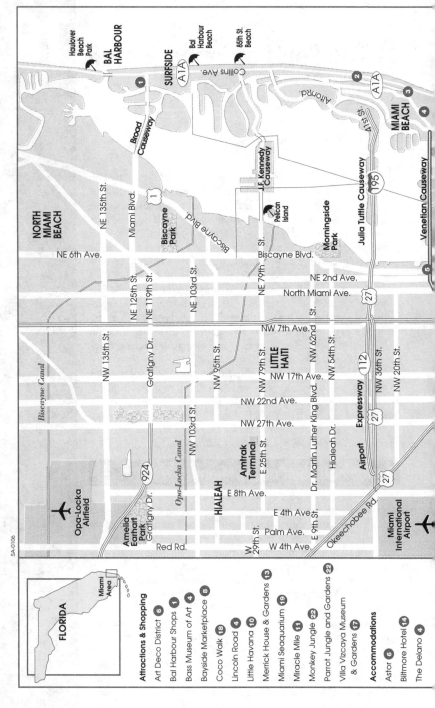

Haulover
Beach
Park

BAL
HARBOUR

Bal
Harbour
Beach

85th St.
Beach

SURFSIDE

A1A

Collins Ave.

1

Broad
Causeway

Altonpd.

2

A1A

3

4

MIAMI
BEACH

J.F. Kennedy
Causeway

NE 135th St.

Miami Blvd.

Pelican
Island

195

NORTH
MIAMI
BEACH

Biscayne
Park

Biscayne Blvd.

Morningside
Park

Julia Tuttle Causeway

Venetian Causeway

NE 6th Ave.

Biscayne Blvd.

NE 79th
St.

NE 2nd Ave.

North Miami Ave.

27

5

NE 125th St.

NE 119th St.

NE 103rd St.

NW 7th Ave.

St.

112

NW 36th St.

NW 20th St.

Biscayne Canal

NW 135th St.

Gratigny Dr.

NW 95th St.

NW 79th St.

LITTLE
HAITI

NW 62nd

NW 17th Ave.

NW 54th St.

Expressway

27

NW 22nd Ave.

NW 27th Ave.

Dr. Martin Luther King Blvd.

Hialeah Dr.

Airport

Opa-Locka Canal

NW 103rd St.

Amtrak
Terminal

E 25th St.

Opa-Locka
Airfield

924

HIALEAH

E 8th Ave.

Okeechobee Rd.

27

Amelia
Earhart
Park

Gratigny Dr.

Red Rd.

W
29th St.

Palm Ave.

W 4th Ave.

E 4th Ave.

E 9th St.

Miami
International
Airport

SA-0106

FLORIDA

Miami
Area

Attractions & Shopping

Art Deco District 6
Bal Harbour Shops 1
Bass Museum of Art 4
Bayside Marketplace 8
Coco Walk 18
Lincoln Road 4
Little Havana 10
Merrick House & Gardens 13
Miami Seaquarium 19
Miracle Mile 11
Monkey Jungle 22
Parrot Jungle and Gardens 22
Villa Vizcaya Museum
& Gardens 17

Accommodations

Astor 6
Biltmore Hotel 14
The Delano 4

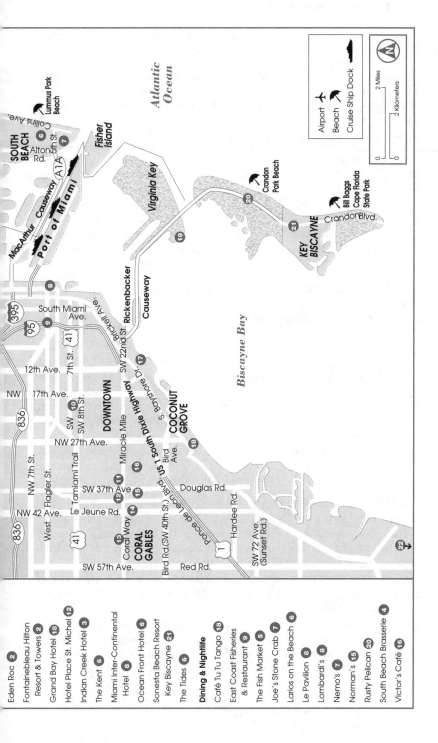

Legend

Airport ✈

Beach ⚲

Cruise Ship Dock

N

0 — 2 Miles
0 — 2 Kilometers

Atlantic Ocean

Lummus Park Beach

SOUTH BEACH

Collins Ave.

Altona Rd.

5th St.

6

7

Fisher Island

MacArthur Causeway

A1A

Port of Miami

Crandon Park Beach

20

Bill Baggs Cape Florida State Park

21

KEY BISCAYNE

Crandon Blvd.

Virginia Key

19

Rickenbacker Causeway

SW 22nd St.

Brickell Ave.

395

95

836

South Miami Ave.

8

9

41

7th St.

12th Ave.

17th Ave.

NW

SW

10

SW 8th St.

DOWNTOWN

Miracle Mile

NW 27th Ave.

11

16

12

15

Tamiami Trail

SW 37th Ave.

Douglas Rd.

17

Biscayne Bay

COCONUT GROVE

18

S. Bayshore Dr.

Bird Ave.

US 1 South Dixie Highway

Bird Rd.(SW 40th St.)

13

14

CORAL GABLES

Coral Way

Le Jeune Rd.

NW 42 Ave.

NW 7th St.

West Flagler St.

41

SW 57th Ave.

SW 72 Ave. (Sunset Rd.)

Red Rd.

1

Ponce de Leon Blvd.

Hardee Rd.

22

Eden Roc **2**

Fontainebleau Hilton Resort & Towers **2**

Grand Bay Hotel **18**

Hotel Place St. Michel **12**

Indian Creek Hotel **3**

The Kent **6**

Miami Inter-Continental Hotel **8**

Ocean Front Hotel **6**

Sonesta Beach Resort Key Biscayne **21**

The Tides **6**

Dining & Nightlife

Café Tu Tu Tango **18**

East Coast Fisheries & Restaurant **9**

The Fish Market **5**

Joe's Stone Crab **7**

Larios on the Beach **6**

Le Pavillon **8**

Lombardi's **8**

Nemo's **7**

Norman's **15**

Rusty Pelican **20**

South Beach Brasserie **4**

Victor's Café **15**

335

among the three terminals and a new departure area in each. Down the road, the port is even hoping to have facilities at the cruise terminals to issue airline boarding passes to departing passengers.

Still on the drawing board are plans for a **Maritime Park,** to be built on a tract of downtown waterfront on Biscayne Bay near the port. Although still in the early planning stages, the complex would likely include new ship berths as well as entertainment facilities for passengers.

GETTING TO MIAMI & THE PORT

The Port of Miami is at 1015 N. America Way, in central Miami. It's on Dodge Island, reached via a five-lane bridge from the downtown district. For information, call ☎ 305/371-PORT.

BY PLANE   Miami International Airport is about 8 miles west of downtown Miami and the port. If you've arranged air transportation and/or transfers through the cruise line (see chapter 2, "Booking Your Cruise & Getting the Best Price"), a representative will be at the airport and will direct you to shuttle buses that take you to the port. Taxis are also available; the fare from the airport to the Port of Miami is about $20. Some leading taxi companies include **Central Taxicab Service** (☎ 305/532-5555), **Diamond Cab Company** (☎ 305/545-5555), and **Metro Taxicab Company** (☎ 305/888-8888).

You can also take a **Metrobus** (☎ 305/770-3131) from the airport to the port for only $1.25, but you'll have to carry your luggage. **SuperShuttle** (☎ 305/871-2000) charges about $7 to $14 per person, with two pieces of luggage, for a ride within Dade County, which includes the Port of Miami. Their vans operate 24 hours a day.

BY CAR   The **Florida Turnpike,** a toll road, and **Interstate 95** are the main arteries for those arriving from the north. Coming in from the northwest, take **Interstate 75** or **U.S. 27** to reach the center of Miami. Parking lots right at street level face the cruise terminals. Parking runs $8 per day. Porters can carry your luggage to the terminals.

BY TRAIN   Amtrak (☎ 800/872-7245) offers three trains daily between New York and Miami, and daily service between Los Angeles and Miami. You'll pull into Amtrak's Miami terminal at 8303 NW 37th Ave. (☎ 305/835-1205).

EXPLORING MIAMI

Miami is no longer just a beach vacation—you'll also find high-quality hotels, distinctive restaurants, unusual attractions, and top shopping. After a relaxing day on the water, take advantage of choice theater or opera, restaurants serving exotic and delicious food, the hopping club scene, or the lively cafe culture.

VISITOR INFORMATION   Contact the **Greater Miami Convention and Visitors Bureau,** 701 Brickell Ave., Miami, FL 33131 (☎ 800/283-2707 or 305/539-3000) for the most up-to-date information.

GETTING AROUND   See "Getting to Miami & the Port," above, for taxi information. The meter starts at $1.50, and ticks up another $2 each mile and 25¢ for each additional minute, with standard flat-rate charges for frequently traveled routes.

Bus transportation in Miami is often a nightmare. Call ☎ 305/770-3131 for public transit information. Fare is $1.25.

Metromover (☎ 305/770-3131), a 4.4-mile elevated line, circles downtown, stopping near important attractions and shopping and business districts. It runs daily from about 5am to midnight. The fare is 25¢.

HITTING THE BEACH

A 300-foot-wide sand beach runs for about 10 miles from the south of Miami Beach to Haulover Beach Park in the north. Although most of this stretch is lined with a solid wall of hotels, beach access is plentiful, and you are free to frolic along the entire strip. There are lots of public beaches here, wide and well-maintained, complete with lifeguards, toilet facilities, concession stands, and metered parking (bring lots of quarters). A wooden boardwalk runs along the hotel side of the beach from 21st to 46th streets—about 1 1/2 miles.

Lifeguard-protected public beaches include **21st Street,** at the beginning of the boardwalk; **35th Street,** popular with an older crowd; **46th Street,** next to the Fontainebleau Hilton; **53rd Street,** a narrower, more sedate beach; **64th Street,** one of the quietest strips around; and **72nd Street,** a local old-timers spot. On the southern tip of the beach is family favorite **South Pointe Park,** where you can watch the cruise ships. **Lummus Park,** in the center of the Art Deco district, is the best place for people-watching and model-spotting. The beach between 11th and 13th streets is popular with the gay crowd. Senior citizens prefer the beach from 1st to 15th streets.

To escape the crowds, head up to the 40-acre **North Shore State Recreation Area,** 3400 NE 163rd St. at Collins and Biscayne (☎ **305/919-1844**).

In Key Biscayne, **Crandon Park,** 4000 Crandon Blvd. (☎ **305/361-5421**), is one of metropolitan Miami's finest white sand beaches, stretching for some 3 1/2 miles. There are lifeguards, and you can rent cabanas with a shower and chairs. Saturdays and Sundays the beach can be especially crowded. Parking nearby is $3.50.

SOUTH BEACH & THE ART DECO DISTRICT

Miami's best sight is a part of the city itself. Located at the southern end of Miami Beach, the ❂ **Art Deco district** is filled with outrageous and fanciful 1920s and 1930s architecture that shouldn't be missed. This treasure trove features more than 900 buildings in the art deco, Streamline Moderne, and Spanish Mediterranean Revival style. The district stretches from 6th to 23rd streets, and from the Atlantic Ocean to Lennox Court. Ocean Drive boasts many of the premier art deco hotels.

Also in South Beach is the ❂ **Bass Museum of Art,** 2121 Park Ave. (☎ **305/673-7533**), with a permanent collection of Old Masters, along with textiles, period furnishings, objets d'art, ecclesiastical artifacts, and sculpture.

CORAL GABLES & COCONUT GROVE

These two Miami neighborhoods are fun to visit for their architecture and ambience. In **Coral Gables,** the old world meets the new, as curving boulevards, sidewalks, plazas, fountains, and arched entrances evoke Seville. Today the area is home to the **University of Miami** and the **Miracle Mile** (it's actually half a mile), a 5-block retail mecca stretching from Douglas Road (37th Avenue) to Le Jeune Road (42nd Avenue). You can even visit the boyhood home of George Merrick, the man who originally developed Coral Gables. The **Coral Gables Merrick House & Gardens,** 907 Coral Way (☎ **305/460-5361**) has been restored to its 1920s look and is filled with Merrick memorabilia. The house and garden are open for tours on Wednesday and Saturday between 1 and 4pm.

Coconut Grove, South Florida's oldest settlement, remains a village surrounded by the urban sprawl of Miami. It dates back to the early 1800s when Bahamian seamen first sought to salvage treasure from the wrecked vessels stranded along the Great Florida Reef. Mostly people come here to shop, drink, dine, or simply walk around and explore. But don't miss the ❂ **Vizcaya Museum & Gardens,** 3251 S. Miami Ave. (☎ **305/250-9133**), a spectacular 70-room Italian Renaissance–style villa.

ANIMAL PARKS

Just minutes from the Port of Miami in Key Biscayne, the **Miami Seaquarium,** 4400 Rickenbacker Causeway (☎ **305/361-5705**) is a delight. Performing dolphins such as Flipper, TV's greatest sea mammal, perform along with "Lolita the Killer Whale." You can also see endangered manatees, sea lions, tropical theme aquariums, and the gruesome shark feeding. It's open daily from 9:30am to 6pm. Admission is $18.95 for adults, $13.95 for seniors over 55, and $16.95 for children 3 to 9.

At **Monkey Jungle,** 14805 SW 216th St., Homestead (☎ **305/235-1611**), the trick is that the visitors are caged and nearly 500 monkeys frolic in freedom and make fun of them. The most talented of these free-roaming primates perform shows daily for the amusement of their guests. The site also contains one of the richest fossil deposits—some 5,000 specimens—in South Florida. It's open daily from 9:30am to 5pm. Admission is $11.50 adults, $6 children 4 to 12, under 3 free.

In South Miami, **Parrot Jungle and Gardens,** 11000 SW 57th Ave. (☎ **305/666-7834**), is actually a botanical garden, wildlife habitat, and bird sanctuary all rolled into one. Children can enjoy a petting zoo and a playground. It's open daily from 9:30am to 6pm. Admission is $13.95 adults, $8.95 children 2 to 10, free for children under 2.

ORGANIZED TOURS

BY BOAT   **Heritage Tours of Miami II** features jaunts aboard an 85-foot schooner. Tours depart from the Bayside Marketplace at 401 Biscayne Blvd. (☎ **305/442-9697**) and are offered September through May only. The daily 2-hour cruises pass by Villa Vizcaya, Coconut Grove, and Key Biscayne and put you in sight of Miami's spectacular skyline. They leave at 1:30pm, 4pm, and 6pm. Tickets cost $12 for adults, $7 for children under 12. On Friday, Saturday, and Sunday evenings, there are 1-hour tours to see the lights of the city at 9pm, 10pm, and 11pm.

ON FOOT   An **Art Deco District Walking Tour,** sponsored by the Miami Design Preservation League (☎ **305/672-2014**), leaves every Saturday at 10:30am from the Art Deco Welcome Center at 1001 Ocean Dr., South Beach. The 90-minute tour costs $10.

SHOPPING

Most cruise ship passengers shop right near the Port of Miami at **Bayside Marketplace,** a mall with 150 specialty shops at 401 Biscayne Blvd. Some 20 eateries serve everything from Nicaraguan to Italian food; there's even a Hard Rock Cafe. You can also watch the street performers or take a boat tour from here.

A free shuttle from the Hotel Inter-Continental in downtown Miami takes you to the **Bal Harbour Shops** (9700 Collins Ave.), which houses big-names stores from Chanel to Lacoste to Neiman-Marcus and Florida's largest Saks Fifth Avenue.

In South Beach, **Lincoln Road,** an 8-block pedestrian mall, runs between Washington Avenue and Alton Road, near the northern tier of the Art Deco district. It's filled with antique shops, interior design stores, art galleries, and even vintage clothing outlets, as well as coffeehouses, restaurants, and cafes.

Just a short drive south of downtown, the **Dadeland Mall,** at the corner of U.S. Highway 1 and Southwest 88th Street (☎ **305/665-6226**), is the most popular shopping plaza in suburban Dade County. Its tenants include Burdines and Burdines Home Gallery, Lord & Taylor, and Saks Fifth Avenue. The food court offers many quick bite options from fast food to sweets.

Coconut Grove, centered on Main Highway and Grand Avenue, is the heart of the city's boutique district.

In Coral Gables, **Miracle Mile,** actually a half-mile stretch of Southwest 22nd Street between Douglas and Le Jeune roads, features more than 150 shops.

For a change of pace from the fast-paced glitz of South Beach or the serene luxury of Coral Gables, head for **Little Havana,** just west of downtown Miami on Southwest 8th Street, where there are some interesting shops.

ACCOMMODATIONS

Thanks to the network of highways that cut through Miami, you can stay virtually anywhere in Greater Miami and still be within 10 to 20 minutes of your cruise ship.

DOWNTOWN   Set across the bay from the cruise ship piers, the **Miami Inter-Continental Hotel,** 100 Chopin Plaza (☎ 800/327-3005 or 305/577-1000), is a bold triangular tower soaring 34 stories.

SOUTH BEACH   The art deco **Astor,** 956 Washington Ave. (☎ 800/270-4981 or 305/531-8081), originally built in 1936, reopened after a massive renovation in 1995. The Astor is only 2 blocks from the beach, but if that's still too far for you, try the up-scale **Ocean Front Hotel,** 1230–38 Ocean Dr. (☎ 800/783-1725 or 305/672-2579). **The Delano,** 1685 Collins Ave. (☎ 800/555-5001 or 305/672-2000), is a sleek, postmodern, and self-consciously hip celebrity hot spot. The hip **The Tides,** 1300 Ocean Dr. (☎ 800/688-7678 or 305/604-5000), is right on the beach. **The Kent,** 1131 Collins Ave. (☎ 305/531-6771), like The Tides, is part of Chris Blackwell's Island Outpost chain and also an art deco monument.

MIAMI BEACH   At the ✪ **Indian Creek Hotel,** 2727 Indian Creek Dr. at 28th Street (☎ 800/491-2772 or 305/531-2727), each room is an homage to the 1930s art deco age. The **Eden Roc,** 4525 Collins Ave. (☎ 800/327-8337 or 305/531-0000), and the **Fontainebleau Hilton Resort & Towers,** next door at 4441 Collins Ave. (☎ 800/548-8886 or 305/538-2000), are both popular, updated 1950s resorts, with spas, health clubs, outdoor swimming pools, and beach access.

COCONUT GROVE   Near Miami's City Hall and the Coconut Grove Marina, the ✪ **Grand Bay Hotel,** 2669 S. Bayshore Dr. (☎ 800/327-2788 or 305/838-9600), overlooks Biscayne Bay.

CORAL GABLES   The famous **Biltmore Hotel,** 1200 Anastasia Ave. (☎ 800/228-3000 or 305/445-1926), was restored a few years ago. There's also the **Hotel Place St. Michel,** 162 Alcazar Ave. (☎ 800/848-HOTEL or 305/444-1666), a three-story establishment that seems like an inn in provincial France.

KEY BISCAYNE   The **Sonesta Beach Resort Key Biscayne,** 350 Ocean Dr. (☎ 800/SONESTA or 305/361-2021), offers relative isolation from the rest of congested Miami.

DINING

DOWNTOWN   **Lombardi's,** in Bayside Marketplace (☎ 305/381-9580), is a moderately priced Italian restaurant. **East Coast Fisheries & Restaurant,** 360 W. Flagler at South River Drive (☎ 305/373-5516), is a no-nonsense retail market and restaurant, offering a terrific variety of the freshest fish available. Only a 5-minute taxi ride from the cruise docks, ✪ **The Fish Market,** on the fourth floor of the Wyndham Hotel, 1601 Biscayne Blvd. (☎ 305/374-0000), is one of Miami's finest and most elegant restaurants, and the prix-fixe lunch is one of the best bargains in town. In the lobby of the elegant Hotel Inter-Continental Miami, ✪ **Le Pavilion,** 100 Chopin Plaza (☎ 305/577-1000), is one of the most artful and European restaurants in town.

SOUTH BEACH   Join the celebs and models at **Nemo's,** 100 Collins Ave. (☎ 305/532-4550). Take time to stroll down the pedestrian mall on Lincoln Road, which offers art galleries, specialty shops, and one of the area's best dining establishments. **South Beach Brasserie,** 910 Lincoln Rd. (☎ 305/534-5511), is the creation of actor-restaurateur Michael Caine. At the legendary **Joe's Stone Crab,** 227 Biscayne St., between Washington and Collins avenues (☎ 305/673-0365), about a ton of stone-crab claws are served daily when in season. Even if Gloria Estefan weren't part-owner of **Larios on the Beach,** 820 Ocean Dr. (☎ 305/532-9577), the crowds would still flock to this bistro serving old-fashioned Cuban dishes, such as *masitas de puerco* (fried pork chunks).

COCONUT GROVE   If you'd like to people-watch while you eat, head for **Café Tu Tu Tango,** 3015 Grand Ave. on the second floor of Coco Walk. This second-floor restaurant is designed to look like a disheveled artist's loft, complete with original paintings (some half-finished) on easels or hanging from the walls.

CORAL GABLES   **Norman's,** 21 Almeria Ave. (☎ 305/446-6767), is run by its namesake, Norman Van Aken, a specialist in American and West Indian cuisine.

KEY BISCAYNE   The surf and turf is routine at the **Rusty Pelican,** 3201 Rickenbacker Causeway (☎ 305/361-3818), but it's worth coming for a drink and the spectacular sunset view.

LITTLE HAVANA   One reason to visit Little Havana is to enjoy its excellent Hispanic cuisine. There's none better than at **Victor's Café,** 2340 SW 32nd Ave. (☎ 305/445-1313), where the elite meet to eat black beans.

MIAMI AFTER DARK

Miami nightlife is as varied as its population. On any night, you'll find world-class opera or dance, as well as grinding rock and salsa. Restaurants and bars are open late. For clubs and live music, head for hopping South Beach, with beachfront bars, clubs, and more, many of which stay open until dawn. Biscayne Bay, Coconut Grove, and Coral Gables also have their share of pubs and clubs. Check *The Miami Herald* for listings of major cultural events.

2 Fort Lauderdale & Port Everglades

Port Everglades, in Broward County, is the second-busiest cruise port in the world. It boasts the deepest harbor south of Norfolk along the eastern seaboard, an ultramodern cruise ship terminal, and an easy access route to the Fort Lauderdale airport, less than a 5-minute drive away. The port lies some 40 miles north of Miami's center.

The port itself is fairly free of congestion. Ten modern cruise terminals offer covered loading zones, drop-off and pickup staging, and curbside baggage handlers. Terminals are comfortable and safe, with seating areas, snack bars, lots of taxis, clean restrooms, and plenty of pay phones. Two separate parking lots have a total of 4,500 parking places, priced at $8 per day.

For information about the port, call **Port Everglades Authority** at ☎ 954/523-3404.

GETTING TO FORT LAUDERDALE & THE PORT

BY AIR   The **Fort Lauderdale/Hollywood International Airport** (☎ 954/359-6100) is small, extremely user-friendly, and less than 2 miles from Port Everglades. Cruise line buses meet incoming flights when they know transfer passengers are on board, so make arrangements for pickup when you book your cruise. Taking a taxi to the port costs $9 to $12.

Fort Lauderdale at a Glance

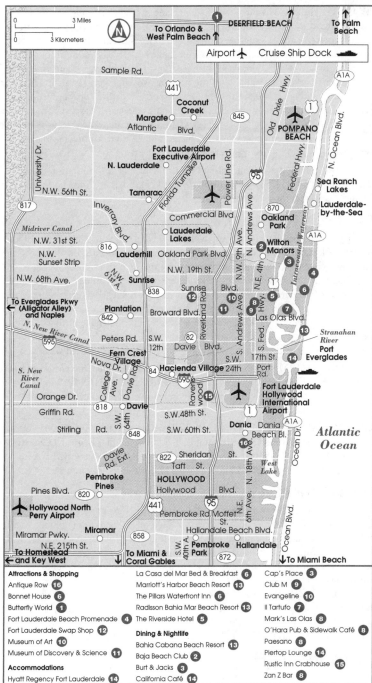

0 — 3 Miles
0 — 3 Kilometers

To Orlando & West Palm Beach ↑

DEERFIELD BEACH

To Palm Beach

Airport ✈ Cruise Ship Dock ⛴

Sample Rd.

441

Coconut Creek

Margate
Atlantic   Blvd.

845

Old Dixie Hwy.

POMPANO BEACH

1

N. Ocean Blvd.

A1A

Fort Lauderdale Executive Airport

N. Lauderdale

University Dr.

N.W. 56th St.

817

Inverrary Blvd.

Tamarac

Florida Turnpike

Power Line Rd.

Commercial Blvd.

N.W. 9th Ave.

N. Andrews Ave.

870

Oakland Park

Sea Ranch Lakes

Lauderdale-by-the-Sea

A1A

2 Wilton Manors

Midriver Canal

N.W. 31st St.

816

N.W. Sunset Strip

N.W. 68th Ave.

Lauderdale Lakes

Lauderhill Oakland Park Blvd.

N.W. 19th St.

N.E. 4th

3

4

N.W. 31st Ave.

Sunrise

838

Sunrise   Blvd.

12   10

N.E. Hwy.

5

6

To Everglades Pkwy ← (Alligator Alley) and Naples

Plantation

842

Broward Blvd.

11

9   8

S. Andrews Ave.

7

Las Olas Blvd.

N. New River Canal

595

Peters Rd.

S.W. 12th

Davie   Blvd.

82

Riverland Rd.

13

S. Fed.

Stranahan River

Port Everglades

S. New River Canal

Nova Dr.

Fern Crest Village

Hacienda Village 24th

84

595

Ravenswood

S.W. 17th St.

Port Rd.

14

Orange Dr.

College Ave.

Davie Rd.

Griffin Rd.

818   Davie

S.W. 64th

S.W.48th St.

S.W. 60th St.

15

Fort Lauderdale Hollywood International Airport

1

Dania

Dania Beach Bl.

A1A

Ocean Dr.

Atlantic Ocean

Stirling   Rd.

848

16

N. 18th Ave.

West Lake

Davie Rd. Ext.

822

Sheridan   St.

Taft   St.

Pembroke Pines

Pines Blvd.

820

HOLLYWOOD

Hollywood   Blvd.

N.E. 6th Ave.

95

Ocean Blvd.

Hollywood North Perry Airport

441

Pembroke Rd. Moffet St.

Miramar Pkwy.

Miramar

858

Hallandale Beach Blvd.

N.E. 215th St.

S.W. 40th A

Pembroke Park

872

Hallandale

To Homestead ← and Key West

To Miami & ↓ Coral Gables

↓ To Miami Beach

SA-0107

Attractions & Shopping
Antique Row 16
Bonnet House 6
Butterfly World 1
Fort Lauderdale Beach Promenade 4
Fort Lauderdale Swap Shop 12
Museum of Art 10
Museum of Discovery & Science 11

Accommodations
Hyatt Regency Fort Lauderdale 14

La Casa del Mar Bed & Breakfast 6
Marriott's Harbor Beach Resort 13
The Pillars Waterfront Inn 6
Radisson Bahia Mar Beach Resort 13
The Riverside Hotel 5

Dining & Nightlife
Bahia Cabana Beach Resort 13
Baja Beach Club 2
Burt & Jacks 3
California Café 14

Cap's Place 3
Club M 9
Evangeline 10
Il Tartufo 7
Mark's Las Olas 8
O'Hara Pub & Sidewalk Café 8
Paesano 8
Piertop Lounge 14
Rustic Inn Crabhouse 15
Zan Z Bar 8

341

BY CAR   The port has three passenger entrances: Spangler Boulevard, an extension of State Road 84 East; Eisenhower Boulevard, running south from the 17th Street Causeway (A1A); and Eller Drive, connecting directly with Interstate 595. Interstate 595 runs east-west, with connections to the Fort Lauderdale/Hollywood Airport, Interstate 95, State Road 7 (441), Florida's Turnpike, Sawgrass Expressway, and Interstate 75. Convenient parking is available at the port in two large garages. The 2,500-space Northport Parking Garage, next to the Greater Fort Lauderdale/Broward County Convention Center, serves terminals 1, 2, and 4. The 1,000-space Midport Parking Garage serves terminals 18, 19, 21, 22, 24, 25, and 26. Garages are well lit, security-patrolled, and designed to accommodate RVs and buses. The 24-hour parking fee is about $7.

BY TRAIN   Amtrak (☎ **800/USA-RAIL**) trains from New York to Miami make various stops along the way, including Fort Lauderdale. The local station is at 200 SW 21st Terrace (☎ **954/587-6692** or 305/835-1123). Taxis are lined up to deliver you to Port Everglades for a $10 to $15 fare.

EXPLORING FORT LAUDERDALE

Fort Lauderdale Beach, a 2-mile strip along Florida A1A, gained fame in the 1950s as a spring-break playground, popularized by the movie *Where the Boys Are*. But in the 1980s, partying college kids, who brought the city more mayhem than money, began to be less welcome. Fort Lauderdale tried to attract a more mainstream, affluent crowd in an effort to transform itself into the "Venice of the Americas." The city has largely been successful.

In addition to miles of beautiful wide beaches, Fort Lauderdale has more than 300 miles of navigable natural waterways, in addition to innumerable artificial canals that permit thousands of residents to anchor boats in their backyards. You too can easily get on the water by renting a boat or hailing a private, moderately priced water taxi.

VISITOR INFORMATION   The **Greater Fort Lauderdale Convention & Visitors Bureau,** 1850 Eller Dr., Suite 303, Fort Lauderdale, FL 33316 (☎ **954/765-4466**), is an excellent resource, distributing a comprehensive guide on events and sightseeing in Broward County.

GETTING AROUND   For a taxi, call **Yellow Cab** (☎ **954/565-5400**). Rates start at $2.45 for the first mile and $1.75 for each additional mile. **Broward County Mass Transit** (☎ **954/357-8400**) runs bus service throughout the county. Each ride costs $1.15 for the first transfer and 15¢ for each additional same-day transfer.

HITTING THE BEACH

Backed by an endless row of hotels and popular with visitors and locals alike, the **Fort Lauderdale Beach Promenade** underwent a $20 million renovation not long back, and it looks marvelous. It's located along Atlantic Boulevard (Fla. A1A), between SE 17th Street and Sunrise Boulevard. The fabled strip from *Where the Boys Are* is Ocean Boulevard, between Las Olas Boulevard and Sunrise Boulevard. On weekends, parking at the oceanside meters is difficult to find.

Fort Lauderdale Beach at the Howard Johnson is a perennial local favorite. A jetty bounds the beach on the south side, making it rather private, although the water gets a little choppy. High school and college students share this area with an older crowd. The beach is at 4660 N. Ocean Dr. in Lauderdale by the Sea.

SEEING THE SIGHTS

The **Museum of Discovery & Science,** 401 SW Second St. (☎ **954/467-6637**), is an excellent interactive science museum, with an IMAX theater. Check out the 52-foot-tall "Great Gravity Clock" in the museum's atrium.

The **Museum of Art,** 1 Las Olas Blvd. (☎ **954/763-6464**), is a truly terrific small museum of modern and contemporary art.

A guided tour of the **Bonnet House,** 900 N. Birch Rd. (☎ **954/563-5393**), offers a glimpse into the lives of the pioneers of the Fort Lauderdale area. This unique 35-acre plantation home and estate survives in the middle of an otherwise highly developed beachfront condominium area. Tours are offered Wednesday through Friday at 10am or 1pm, Saturday and Sunday at 1 or 2pm; arrive 15 minutes before the tour.

Butterfly World, Tradewinds Park South, 3600 W. Sample Rd., Coconut Creek, west of the Florida Turnpike (☎ **954/977-4400**), cultivates more than 150 species of these colorful and delicate insects. In the park's walkthrough, screened-in aviary, visitors can watch newborn butterflies emerge from their cocoons and flutter around as they learn to fly.

ORGANIZED TOURS

BY BOAT   The Mississippi River–style steamer *Jungle Queen,* Bahia Mar Yacht Center, Florida A1A (☎ **954/462-5596**), is one of Fort Lauderdale's best-known attractions. Dinner cruises and 3-hour sightseeing tours take visitors up the New River past Millionaires' Row, Old Fort Lauderdale, the new downtown, and the Port Everglades cruise ship port. Call for prices and departure times.

✪ **Water Taxi of Fort Lauderdale,** 651 Seabreeze Blvd. (☎ **954/467-6677**), is a fleet of old port boats that navigate this city of canals. The boats operate taxi service on demand and carry up to 48 passengers each. You can be picked up at your hotel and shuttled to the dozens of restaurants and bars on the route for the rest of the night. The service operates daily from 10am to midnight or 2am. The cost is $7 per person per trip, $13 round-trip, $15 for a full day. Opt for the all-day pass—it's worth it.

BY TROLLEY BUS   **South Florida Trolley Tours** (☎ **954/946-7320**) covers Fort Lauderdale's entire history during a 90-minute open-air trolley tour. Tours cost $12 for adults; children under 12 are free. The trolleys pick up passengers from most major hotels for three tours daily, at 9:30am, 12:05pm, and 2:10pm.

ON FOOT   The **Historical Society Museum,** 219 SW Second Ave. (☎ **954/463-4431**), offers walking tours of the city's historic center. Tours must be requested and are conducted Tuesday through Friday from 10am to 4pm. They cost $10 to $15 per person. You can also walk along **Riverwalk,** a 10-mile linear park along the New River that connects the cultural heart of Fort Lauderdale to its historic district.

SHOPPING

Not counting the discount "fashion" stores on Hallandale Beach Boulevard's "Schmatta Row," there are three places every visitor to Broward County should know about.

The first is **Antique Row,** a strip of U.S. 1 around North Dania Beach Boulevard (in Dania, about 1 mile south of Fort Lauderdale/Hollywood International Airport) that holds about 200 antique shops. Most shops are closed Sundays.

The **Fort Lauderdale Swap Shop,** 3291 W. Sunrise Blvd. (☎ **954/791-SWAP**), is one of the world's largest flea markets. In addition to endless acres of vendors, there's a mini–amusement park, a 12-screen drive-in movie theater, weekend concerts, and even a free circus complete with elephants, horse shows, high-wire acts, and clowns. It's open daily.

Sawgrass Mills, 12801 W. Sunrise Blvd., Sunrise (☎ **954/846-2300**), a behemoth mall shaped like a Florida alligator, covers nearly 2.5 million square feet, including more than 300 shops and kiosks, such as Saks Fifth Avenue, Levi's, Ann Taylor, Waterford Crystal, and hundreds more, offering prices 20% to 60% lower than in the Caribbean.

Take Interstate 95 North to 595 West until Flamingo Road, where you'll exit and turn right. Drive 2 miles to Sunrise Boulevard.

Not for bargain hunters, swanky **Las Olas Boulevard** hosts literally hundreds of unusual boutiques. Close to Fort Lauderdale Beach, the **Galleria** mall, 2414 E. Sunrise Blvd., between NE 26th Avenue and Middle River Drive (☎ **954/564-1015**), has Neiman-Marcus, Saks, Macy's, Cartier, Brooks Brothers, Lord & Taylor, and many other stores.

ACCOMMODATIONS

Fort Lauderdale Beach has a hotel or motel on nearly every block, and the selection ranges from run-down to luxurious.

✪ **Hyatt Regency Fort Lauderdale** at Pier 66 Marina, 2301 17th St. Causeway (☎ 800/233-1234 or 954/525-6666), is a circular landmark with larger rooms than some equivalently priced hotels in town. Its famous Piertop Lounge, a revolving bar on its roof, is often filled with cruise ship patrons.

Marriott's Harbor Beach Resort, 3030 Holiday Dr. (☎ 800/222-6543 or 954/525-4000), is the only resort set directly on the beach. Its modest-sized bedrooms have water views.

Radisson Bahia Mar Beach Resort, 801 Seabreeze Blvd. (☎ 800/327-8154 or 954/764-2233), is scattered over 42 acres of seacoast. A four-story row of units is adjacent to Florida's largest marina. **The Riverside Hotel,** 620 E. Las Olas Blvd. (☎ 800/325-3280 or 954/467-0671), which opened in 1936, is a local favorite. Try for a ground-floor room, which has higher ceilings and more space.

La Casa del Mar Bed & Breakfast, 3003 Grand Granada St. (☎ 800/739-0009 or 954/467-2037), a 10-room Spanish-inspired inn, appeals to the bed-and-breakfast fancier and is only a block away from Fort Lauderdale Beach. **The Pillars Waterfront Inn,** 111 N. Birch Rd. (☎ 954/467-9639), is a small, 22-room inn, the best of its size in the region. The clean and simple accommodations have very comfortable beds. For other inns, call the **Fort Lauderdale Convention and Visitors Bureau** (☎ 954/765-4466) for its *Superior Small Lodgings* guide to the area.

A number of chains operate here, including **Best Western** (☎ 800 528-1234), **Days Inn** (☎ 800/325-2525), **Doubletree Hotels** (☎ 800/222-8733), and **Holiday Inn** (☎ 800/465-4329).

DINING

The only restaurant at Port Everglades, ✪ **Burt & Jacks,** at Berth 23 (☎ 954/522-2878), is a collaboration between actor-director Burt Reynolds and restaurateur Jack Jackson. As you sit at this elegant restaurant, you can watch the cruise ships and other boats pass by. A waiter will arrive with steaks, lobster, veal, pork chops, etc.; you choose and your dish will arrive perfectly cooked.

Bahia Cabana Beach Resort, 3001 Harbor Dr. (☎ 954/524-1555), offers American-style meals three times a day in hearty portions. The hotel's bar, known for its Frozen Rumrunner, is the most charming and laid-back in town.

In the shadow of the Hyatt Pier 66 Hotel, **California Café,** Pier 66, 2301 SE 17th Causeway (☎ 954/728-8255), serves avant-garde modern cuisine at affordable prices.

Cap's Place, 2765 NE 28th Ct., in Lighthouse Point (☎ 954/941-0418), is a famous old-time seafood joint, offering good food at reasonable prices. The restaurant floats on a barge; you get a ferry ride over. Dolphin (a local saltwater fish, not the mammal) and grouper are popular, and like the other meat and pasta dishes here, can be prepared any way you want.

Evangeline, 211 Hwy. A1A at Las Olas Boulevard (☎ 954/522-7001), as the name suggests, is a Cajun-style place. At lunch, enjoy an oyster or catfish po' boy, or rabbit gumbo for dinner. You can also try the alligator.

Il Tartufo, 2400 E. Las Olas Blvd. (☎ 954/767-9190), is the most charming and fun Italian restaurant in Fort Lauderdale. It serves pizzas, oven-roasted specialties, and other Italian standards, plus a selection of fish baked in rock salt.

Mark's Las Olas, 1032 E. Las Olas Blvd. (☎ 954/463-1000), is the showcase of Miami restaurant mogul Mark Militello. The daily changing menu might include Jamaican jerk chicken with fresh coconut salad or a superb sushi-quality tuna.

Zan Z Bar, 602 E. Las Olas Blvd. (☎ 954/767-3377), serves the food and wine of South Africa, and not many places can boast that. For a taste of the country, order a sample platter for two that includes ostrich tips, cured beef strips, and savory sausages.

Paesano, 1301 E. Las Olas Blvd. (☎ 954/467-3266), is chic and elegant, with good, old-fashioned food, such as 16-ounce T-bone steaks and numerous pasta dishes.

Garlic crabs are the specialty at the **Rustic Inn Crabhouse,** 4331 Ravenswood Rd. (☎ **954/584-1637**), located west of the airport. This riverside dining choice has an open deck over the water.

FORT LAUDERDALE AFTER DARK

From the area's most famous bar, the ✪ **Piertop Lounge,** in the Hyatt Regency at Pier 66 (☎ 954/525-6666), you'll get a 360-degree panoramic view of Fort Lauderdale. The bar turns every 66 minutes. There's a dance floor and floor shows.

On weekends it's hard to get into **Club M,** 2037 Hollywood Blvd. (☎ 954/925-8396), one of the area's busiest music bars. Although the small club is primarily a local blues showcase, electric and traditional jazz bands also perform.

O'Hara Pub & Sidewalk Café, 722 E. Las Olas Blvd. (☎ 954/524-2801), is often packed with a trendy crowd, who come here to listen to live blues and jazz. Call their jazz hotline (☎ 954/524-2801) to hear the lineup.

If you want to dance, try the **Baja Beach Club,** 3200 N. Federal Hwy. (☎ 954/561-2431), perhaps the world's only dance club that anchors an entire shopping mall.

With the 1991 completion of the **Broward Center for the Performing Arts,** 201 SW Fifth Ave. (☎ 954/462-0222), Fort Lauderdale finally got itself the venue it craved for top opera, symphony, dance, and Broadway productions. Look for listings in the *Sun-Sentinel* or *The Miami Herald* for schedules and performers or call the 24-hour **Arts & Entertainment Hotline** (☎ 954/357-5700).

3 Cape Canaveral & Port Canaveral

Underrated Port Canaveral is Florida's most unusual and multifaceted port, with facilities that are the most up-to-date, stylish, and least congested of any port in Florida. After years of underutilization, the cruise industry is starting to give the port the attention it's due. With the competition between a stronger Premier, an expanded Disney product, and Carnival and a returning Royal Caribbean, Port Canaveral's 3-to-4-day cruise market is growing and really putting this port on the map. Cruise lines appreciate the port's proximity to Cape Canaveral's Kennedy Space Center and Walt Disney World at Orlando. Many lines offer pre- or post-cruise packages.

Port Canaveral has an abundance of bars and restaurants, facilities noticeably absent at many other Florida harbors. The best ones are positioned adjacent to the frequently dredged deepwater access channels used by most ships. Sitting at one of these restaurants' sundecks during happy hour, you'll feel as though you could reach out and shake the hand of a cruise ship passenger gliding into or out of the port.

The 3,300-acre port covers an area larger than the Port of Miami. Terminal no. 10, a $24 million structure completed in 1995, which was built in a modern, dramatic style, and nicknamed the *Bahnhof* because of its resemblance to a futuristic German railway station. Terminal no. 5, built in 1991, looks a bit like a glossy, downtown hotel. The new Disney terminal was built in an updated, Disney-fied art deco style. The other terminals are more industrial, like oversized Quonset huts. As you head for your cruise ship, look for shrimp and fish nets drying in the sun. This port is the home base for the region's fishing industry.

GETTING TO CAPE CANAVERAL & THE PORT

Port Canaveral is located at the Cape Canaveral side of the Bennett Causeway on the 528 Bee Line Expressway. For information about the port, call the **Canaveral Port Authority** at ☎ **407/783-7831.**

BY AIR   The nearest airport is the **Orlando International Airport** (☎ **407/ 825-2001**), a 45-mile drive from Port Canaveral via Highway 528 (the Bee Line Expressway). Cruise line representatives will meet you if you've booked air and/or transfers through the line. **Cocoa Beach Shuttle** (☎ **800/633-0427** or 407/784-3831) offers shuttle service between Orlando's airport and Port Canaveral; the trip costs $20 per person each way.

BY CAR   Port Canaveral and Cocoa Beach are about 35 miles southeast of Orlando and 190 miles north of Miami. They're accessible from virtually every interstate highway along the east coast. Most visitors arrive via Route 1, Interstate 95, or Highway 528 (the Bee Line Expressway from Orlando). At the port, park in the North Lots for north terminals nos. 5 and 10 and the South Lots for nos. 2, 3, or 4. Parking costs $7 a day.

BY TRAIN   Amtrak (☎ **800/USA-RAIL**) trains make stops at Kissimmee, Sanford, and Orlando, the closest points to the port, but still about 55 to 60 miles away. You'll have to rent a car or take a taxi to the port. The Kissimmee railway station is at 316 Pleasant St. (corner of Dakin Avenue and Thurman Street). The Orlando station is at 1400 Slight Blvd., between Columbia and Miller streets. The Sanford station is at 800 Persimmon Ave., at the corner of 8th Street.

EXPLORING CAPE CANAVERAL

Most passengers spend only a night or two in Cocoa Beach, visiting the Kennedy Space Center and going to the beach, before rushing to nearby Orlando and Walt Disney World.

VISITOR INFORMATION   Contact the **Cocoa Beach Chamber of Commerce,** 400 Fortenberry Rd., Merritt Island, FL 32952 (☎ **407/459-2200**).

GETTING AROUND   For taxis, call **Cocoa Beach Cab Co.** (☎ **407/784-8294**). Buses are run by the **Space Coast Area Transit Authority (SCAT)** (☎ **407/633-1878** for information and schedules). A ticket costs $1 for adults, 50¢ for senior citizens, free for children under 6. No buses pass close to the port.

✿ TOURING THE JOHN F. KENNEDY SPACE CENTER

Set amid many square miles of marshy wetlands favored by birds, reptiles, and amphibians, the **John F. Kennedy Space Center Visitor Complex,** Kennedy Space Center, Florida 32899 (☎ **407/452-2121**), has played an important role in the minds of people around the world as the cradle of the Space Age and a symbol of America's technological prowess. Even if you've never really considered yourself a science buff, you'll appreciate the sheer grandeur of the place and the achievements represented by the facilities here. A $79 million renovation of the site, completed in 1998, has sparked new life into the site, making it more appealing for visitors than ever. The visitor center stands with an isolated, even eerie, dignity within the municipality of the Kennedy Space Center.

The sheer scope of the site can be confusing, even baffling, without some guidance from the organization's official caretakers. Parking is free in any of the vast lots nearby. (Remember to note the location of your car!) It's best to make a stop—maps and advice are free—at a highly visible booth, Information Central, within the visitor center.

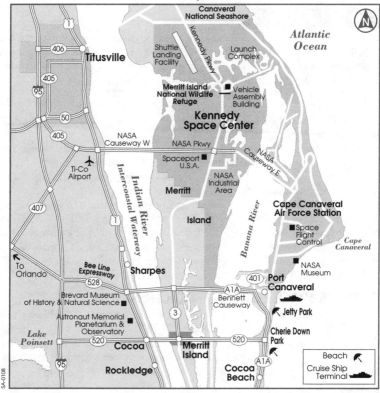

It maintains the same hours (9am to 6pm daily except Christmas and some launch days) as the complex itself. Expect to spend a full day on-site to best experience the wealth of options.

The core of the site revolves around the visitor center, site of the **Rocket Garden,** which displays the now-obsolete shells of at least eight space rockets that during their heydays were the hottest things in the world of astrophysics. There are also hundreds of exhibitions and photographs detailing humankind's exploration of space, with an emphasis on the progression of visionary developments in logical sequence since the inauguration of the space program. The visitor center is also home to two IMAX theaters that show three separate films, each about 45 minutes long.

Some visitors pressed for time opt to remain entirely within the center, which does not charge admission. But for a more complete insight into the Space Age, take a bus tour of the complicated subdivisions that rise from the hundreds of acres of marshy flatlands nearby. Self-guided and self-timed, they depart at 15-minute intervals. Each bus is equipped with video screens portraying great moments of the space program's past. Tours make stops at three pivotal points within the complex, the Apollo Saturn V Center, Launch Complex 39, and the International Space Station Center.

The most comprehensive visitor package is the **Crew Pass.** Priced at $19 for adults, and $15 for children aged 4 to 11, it includes unlimited access to any of the tour buses and entrance to any one of the ongoing IMAX movies. The tour itself, without access to any of the IMAX theaters, costs $14 for adults and $10 for children under 11. Admission to the visitor center itself is free. Individual IMAX films are $7.50 each per

---

Wanna See a Launch?

There are only about a dozen launches every year, so chances are you won't catch one. Still, you never know. Call ☎ **407/449-4343** for schedule information. During launch days, some parts of the complex, including Launch Complex 39 and its Observation Gantry, are firmly closed to everyone except NASA insiders.

---

adult, and $5.50 per child under 11. Most major credit cards are accepted throughout the complex.

There's a handful of fast-food, theme-parkish eateries adjacent to the visitors' center. Among the cheapest and least formal of the bunch is something called The Launch Pad, serving family-friendly burgers and hot dogs. Better-recommended is Mila's, a fancy diner serving American-style platters, sandwiches, and salads.

To get to the Kennedy Space Center from Cocoa Beach, take A1A north. About a mile after A1A takes a sharp jog to the left, you will see signs for S.R. 401 and the Kennedy Space Center. Turn right and follow signs over the NASA Causeway, which leads directly to the Space Center. It's about a half-hour drive. From Orlando, take the Bee Line Expressway (S.R. 528) east, and where the road divides, go left on S.R. 407, make a right on S.R. 405, and follow the signs. Parking is free.

ANOTHER SPACE-RELATED ATTRACTION

Six miles west of the Kennedy Space Center is the **U.S. Astronaut Hall of Fame,** State Rd. 405, 6225 Vectorspace Blvd., Titusville (☎ **407/269-6100**), a satellite attraction founded by the astronauts who flew the first Mercury and Gemini missions into outer space. It contains space program memorabilia, displayed with a decidedly human and anecdotal touch. Open daily 9am to 5pm.

HITTING THE BEACH

Cocoa Beach, Merritt Island, and the surrounding landscapes are known as "The Space Coast" and most of the beaches there are called "parks." Here are my favorites.

Jetty Park, 400 E. Jetty Rd., near the port, is more like a Florida version of Coney Island than the parks described below. A massive stone asphalt-topped jetty juts seaward as protection for the mouth of Port Canaveral. You'll see dozens of anglers there waiting for a bite. Parking costs $1 a car.

On the border between Cocoa Beach and Cape Canaveral, **Cherie Down Park,** 8492 Ridgewood Ave., is a relatively tranquil sunning and swimming area. You'll find a boardwalk, as well as showers, picnic shelters, and a public restroom. Parking is $1 per car.

Set in the heart of Cocoa Beach, **Lori Wilson Park,** 1500 N. Atlantic Ave., has children's playgrounds and a boardwalk that extends through about 5 acres of protected grasslands. Parking is $1 per car. Next to it is **Fischer Park,** with public rest rooms and a seasonal scattering of food kiosks. Parking is $2 a car.

The region's best surfing is at **Robert P. Murkshe Memorial Park,** SR A1A and 16th streets, Cocoa Beach, which also has a boardwalk and public rest rooms.

SHOPPING

Cocoa Beach offers a wide array of shopping, but the most unique shopping experience is **Ron Jon Surf Shop,** 4151 N. Atlantic Ave., Cocoa Beach, as you're driving down Florida A1A. The wildly original art deco building is more interesting than the merchandise, but if you're looking for a surfing souvenir, you'll find it here. The store also rents beach bikes, boogey boards, surfboards, in-line skates, and other fun stuff by the hour, day, or week.

ACCOMMODATIONS

Closest to the port and the Kennedy Space Center is the ✪ **Radisson Resort at the Port,** 8701 Astronaut Blvd. (☎ 800/333-3333 or 407/784-0000). The bedrooms are comfortable, but not as wonderful as those at the Inn at Cocoa Beach. Chain hotels in the area include the **Cocoa Beach Hilton,** 1550 N. Atlantic Ave (A1A) (☎ 800/HILTONS or 407/799-0003); the **Holiday Inn Cocoa Beach Resort,** 1300 N. Atlantic Ave. (☎ 800/2BOOKUS or 407/783-2271), more upscale and better designed than the average Holiday Inn; and the **Howard Johnson Plaza Hotel/Cocoa Beach,** 2080 N. Atlantic Ave. (☎ 800/654-2000 or 407/783-9222).

Between the sea and route SR-520 and behind Ron Jon Surf Shop, ✪ **The Inn at Cocoa Beach,** 4300 Ocean Beach Blvd. (☎ 800/343-5307 or 407/799-3460), is more of an upscale, personalized inn than a traditional hotel (it even calls itself an oversized bed-and-breakfast). A taxi from Port Canaveral to the Inn will cost around $12 to $15. Call **Comfort Taxi** at ☎ 407/799-0442.

DINING

In the heart of Cocoa Beach, **Bernard's Surf,** 2 S. Atlantic Ave. (☎ 407/783-2401), has been a Florida institution since 1948. Specializing in steaks and seafood, the name Bernard's Surf should be followed by *& Turf*—it's a carnivore's paradise. The walls are adorned with pictures of astronauts who have celebrated their safe return to Earth with a filet mignon here.

Near the port is the only five-star restaurant in town, ✪ **Flamingo's,** in the Radisson Resort at the Port, 8701 Astronaut Blvd. (☎ 407/784-0000). The fish dishes are the best around the port, made with top-notch ingredients and deftly prepared.

Lloyd's Canaveral Feast, 610 Glen Cheek Dr. (☎ 407/784-8899), is the waterfront's best-designed seafood restaurant. Outdoor tables are set on pier-like terraces over the water, and you can watch the cruise ships sail from their berths to the sea.

✪ **The Mango Tree,** 118 N. Atlantic Ave. (☎ 407/799-0513), is the most beautiful and sophisticated restaurant in Cocoa Beach. Indian River crab cakes are perfectly flavored, and the sesame-seed encrusted grouper with a tropical fruit salsa is yummy.

PORT CANAVERAL AFTER DARK

The Pier, 401 Meade Ave. (☎ 407/783-7549), is the largest and busiest entertainment complex in Cocoa Beach, crowded every afternoon and evening with diners, drinkers, and sunset-watchers. Two open-air cafes, four bars, and a pair of restaurants jut 800 feet beyond the shoreline into the waves and surf. At **Marlin's Sports Bar,** you can enjoy fish platters, drinks, or sandwiches and a view of the sea that practically engulfs you. One or sometimes two bands play live 6 nights a week.

In Cocoa Beach's Heidelberg restaurant, the smoky and noisy **Heidi's Jazz Club,** 7 N. Orlando Ave. (☎ 407/783-6806), offers jazz and classic blues.

4 Tampa & the Port of Tampa

The Port of Tampa is set amid a complicated network of channels and harbors near the historic Cuban enclave of Ybor City and its deepwater Ybor Channel. The port's position on the western (Gulf) side of Florida makes it the logical departure point for ships headed for westerly ports of call, including the beaches and Mayan ruins of the Yucatan, the aquatic reefs of Central America, and the ports of Venezuela. The port's safe harbors have kept ships secure even during devastating tropical storms.

The bulk of the port's 400,000 or so annual passengers make their way through the modern terminal no. 2, also known as the **Seaport Street Terminal,** which was doubled

Tampa & St. Petersburg at a Glance

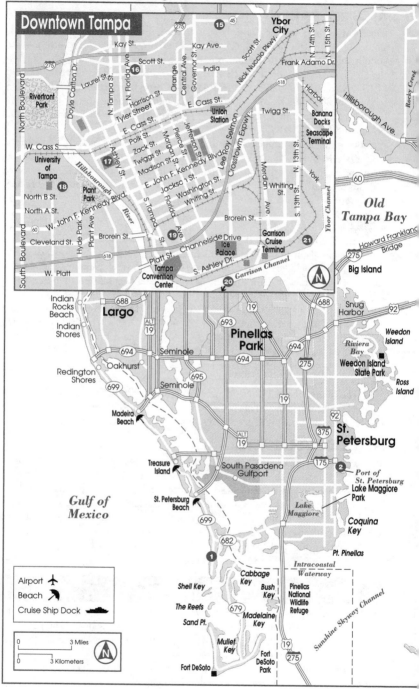

Downtown Tampa

Ybor City

Kay St.
Kay Ave.
Scott St.
Scott St.
N. Florida Ave.
N. Tampa St.
Laurel St.
Doyle Carlton Dr.
Central Ave.
Orange
Governor St.
India
Nick Nuccio Pkwy.
Frank Adamo Dr.
14th St.
15th St.

North Boulevard

Riverfront Park

Harrison St.
Tyler Street
E. Cass St.
Polk St.
Zack St.
Twiggs St.
Madison St.
Ashley St.
Pierce St.
Morgan St.
Jefferson St.
Union Station
Twigg St.
Harbor
Banana Docks
Seascape Terminal

W. Cass S.
University of Tampa
Plant Park
North B St.
North A St.
Hyde Park
Plant Ave.
W. John F. Kennedy Blvd.
E. John F. Kennedy Blvd.
Jackson St.
Washington St.
Whiting St.
Whiting St.
Meridian Ave.
S. 13th St.
S. 13th St.
York
Ybor Channel

Hillsborough River

Cleveland St.
Brorein St.
Brorein St.
Brorein St.
S. Florida Ave.
Crosstown Expwy.
LeeRoy Selmon

Old Tampa Bay

W. Platt
S. Tampa Ave.
Platt St.
Tampa Convention Center
Channelside Drive
Ice Palace
S. Ashley Dr.
Garrison Cruise Terminal
Garrison Channel

Howard Frankland Bridge
Big Island
Snug Harbor

Indian Rocks Beach
Indian Shores
Largo
688
ALT 19
693
19
Pinellas Park
694
694
688
694
275
Weedon Island
Riviera Bay
Weedon Island State Park
Ross Island

Redington Shores
694
Seminole
Oakhurst
695
Seminole
699
ALT 19
19
92
375
St. Petersburg
175
2
Port of St. Petersburg

Madeira Beach

Treasure Island
South Pasadena
Gulfport
Lake Maggiore Park
Lake Maggiore
Coquina Key

Gulf of Mexico
St. Petersburg Beach
699
682
1
Pt. Pinellas

Shell Key
Cabbage Key
Bush Key
Pinellas National Wildlife Refuge
Intracoastal Waterway

The Reefs
Sand Pt.
679
Madelaine Key
19
275
Sunshine Skyway Channel

Mullet Key
Fort DeSoto Park
Fort DeSoto

Airport ✈
Beach ↘
Cruise Ship Dock ⛴

0   3 Miles
0   3 Kilometers

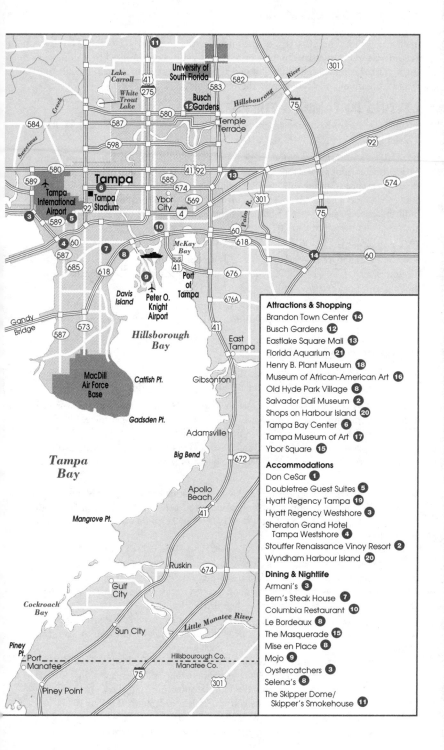

Attractions & Shopping

Brandon Town Center **14**
Busch Gardens **12**
Eastlake Square Mall **13**
Florida Aquarium **21**
Henry B. Plant Museum **18**
Museum of African-American Art **16**
Old Hyde Park Village **8**
Salvador Dalí Museum **2**
Shops on Harbour Island **20**
Tampa Bay Center **6**
Tampa Museum of Art **17**
Ybor Square **15**

Accommodations

Don CeSar **1**
Doubletree Guest Suites **5**
Hyatt Regency Tampa **19**
Hyatt Regency Westshore **3**
Sheraton Grand Hotel
  Tampa Westshore **4**
Stouffer Renaissance Vinoy Resort **2**
Wyndham Harbour Island **20**

Dining & Nightlife

Armani's **3**
Bern's Steak House **7**
Columbia Restaurant **10**
Le Bordeaux **8**
The Masquerade **15**
Mise en Place **8**
Mojo **9**
Oystercatchers **3**
Selena's **8**
The Skipper Dome/
  Skipper's Smokehouse **11**

in size in 1998. The 30-acre site also includes the constantly evolving **Garrison Seaport Center,** a massive complex of restaurants and shops inspired by Baltimore's Inner Harbor complex. This hub of waterfront activity and entertainment includes the Florida Aquarium and a multiscreen theater complex.

GETTING TO TAMPA & THE PORT

The Port of Tampa is located at 13th and Platt streets. For information, call ☎ **813/ 272-0555.**

BY AIR   Tampa International Airport (☎ **813/870-8700**) lies 5 miles northwest of downtown Tampa, near the junction of Florida 60 and Memorial Highway. If you haven't arranged transfers with the cruise line, the port is an easy 15-minute taxi ride away; the fare is $10 to $15. **Central Florida Limo** (☎ **813/396-3730**) also runs a minivan service, which costs $5.50 per person from the airport to Garrison Terminal and $7.50 per person to Pier 202.

BY CAR   Tampa lies 200 miles southwest of Jacksonville, 63 miles north of Sarasota, and 254 miles northwest of Miami. It's easily accessible from Interstate 275, Interstate 75, Interstate 4, U.S. 41, U.S. 92, U.S. 301, and many state roads. The port has ample parking with good security, and costs $8 per day.

BY TRAIN   Amtrak (☎ **800/USA-RAIL**) trains arrive at the Tampa Amtrak Station, 601 Nebraska Ave. N., Tampa (☎ **800/872-7245**). Taxi fare to the port costs $5 to $7.

EXPLORING TAMPA

Tampa is best explored by car, as only the commercial district can be covered on foot. If you want to go to the beach, you'll have to head to neighboring St. Petersburg.

VISITOR INFORMATION   Contact the **Tampa/Hillsborough Convention and Visitors Association, Inc.** (THCVA), 111 Madison St., Suite 1010, Tampa, FL 33602 (☎ **800/44-TAMPA** or 813/223-2752). You can also stop by the **Tampa Bay Visitor Information Center,** 3601 E. Busch Blvd. (☎ **813/985-3601**), north of downtown in the Busch Gardens area. The office books organized tours of Tampa and the rest of Florida.

GETTING AROUND   Taxis in Tampa do not normally cruise the streets for fares, but they do line up at public loading places. You can also call **Tampa Bay Cab** (☎ **813/251-5555**), **Yellow Cab** (☎ **813/253-0121**), or **United Cab** (☎ **813/ 253-2424**).

The **Hillsborough Area Regional Transit/HARTline** (☎ **813/254-HART**) provides regularly scheduled bus service between downtown Tampa and the suburbs. Fares are $1.15 for local services and $1.50 for express routes; correct change is required.

The **People Mover,** a motorized tram on elevated tracks, connects downtown Tampa with Harbour Island. It operates from the third level of the Fort Brooke Parking Garage, on Whiting Street between Franklin Avenue and Florida Street. Travel time is 90 seconds and service is continuous, Monday through Saturday from 7am to 2am, and Sunday from 8am to 11pm. The fare is 25¢ each way.

The **Tampa-Ybor Trolley** interconnects the city's sites in one 15-mile loop. You can board at any of 17 stops (each clearly marked with orange-and-green signs) that include Harbour Island, downtown Tampa, the Florida Aquarium, and the Garrison Cruise Ship Terminal. Service is provided daily from 7:30am to 5:30pm. The fare is 25¢.

Tampa Town Water Taxi (☎ **813/253-3076**) provides shuttle service along the Hillsborough River via a 44-passenger air-conditioned ferry, connecting downtown locations. The shuttle operates at half-hour intervals, Monday through Thursday from 2pm to 11pm, Friday from 2pm to 1am, Saturday from noon to 1am, and Sunday from noon to 11pm. Daytime round-trips cost $5 and evening round-trips (after 8pm) cost $6.

✪ BUSCH GARDENS

Yes, admission prices are high, but Busch Gardens remains Tampa Bay's most popular attraction. The 335-acre family entertainment park, at 3000 E. Busch Blvd. (☎ **813/ 987-5171**), features thrill rides, animal habitats, live entertainment, shops, restaurants, and games. The park's zoo ranks among the best in the country, with nearly 3,400 animals.

In 1996, Busch Gardens opened Montu, the world's tallest and longest inverted roller coaster. It's part of **Egypt,** the park's ninth themed area. The area includes a replica of King Tutankhamen's tomb, plus a sand-dig area for kids.

Timbuktu is a replica of an ancient desert trading center, complete with African craftspeople at work. It also features a sandstorm ride, a boat-swing ride, a roller coaster, and an electronic games arcade. **Morocco,** a walled city with exotic architecture, has Moroccan craft demonstrations, a sultan's tent with snake charmers, and the Marrakech Theaters. The **Serengeti Plain** is an open area with more than 500 African animals roaming freely in herds. This 80-acre natural grassy veldt can be viewed from the monorail, the Trans-Veldt Railway, or the skyride.

Nairobi is home to a natural habitat for various species of gorillas and chimpanzees, a baby animal nursery, a petting zoo, reptile displays, and Nocturnal Mountain, where visitors can observe animals active at night. **Stanleyville,** a prototype African village, has a shopping bazaar and live entertainment, as well as two water rides: the Tanganyika Tidal Wave and Stanley Falls. **The Congo** features white-water raft rides, as well as Kumba, the largest steel roller coaster in the southeastern United States, and Claw Island, a display of rare white Bengal tigers in a natural setting.

Bird Gardens, the original core of Busch Gardens, offers rich foliage, lagoons, and a free-flight aviary holding hundreds of exotic birds, including golden and American bald eagles, hawks, owls, and falcons. This area also features Land of the Dragons, a new children's adventure area.

Crown Colony is the home of a team of Clydesdale horses, as well as the Anheuser-Busch hospitality center. Questor, a flight simulator adventure ride, is located here.

A 1-day ticket costs $40.95 for adults, $34.95 for children ages 3 to 9; kids 2 and under are free. The park is open daily from about 9am through 7 to 9pm, with extended hours in summer and during holiday periods. To get here, take Interstate 275 northeast of downtown to Busch Boulevard (exit 33), and go east 2 miles to the entrance on 40th Street (McKinley Drive). Parking is $3.

MORE ATTRACTIONS

Only steps from the Garrison Seaport Center, the ✪ **Florida Aquarium** (☎ **813/ 224-9583**) celebrates the role of water in the development and maintenance of Florida's topography and ecosystems, with more than 4,350 specimens. One intriguing exhibit follows a drop of water as it bubbles through Florida limestone and wends its way to the sea. Another evokes a watery landscape as painted by Monet.

Thirteen silver minarets and distinctive Moorish architecture make the ✪ **Henry B. Plant Museum,** 401 W. Kennedy Blvd. (☎ **813/254-1891**), the focal point of the Tampa skyline. Modeled after the Alhambra in Spain, this National Historic Landmark, built in 1891 as the 511-room Tampa Bay Hotel, is filled with European and Oriental art and furnishings.

The **Museum of African-American Art,** 1308 N. Marion St. (☎ 813/272-2466), features visual art by and about people of African descent. The collection covers the 19th and 20th centuries and represents more than 80 artists.

The permanent collection of the **Tampa Museum of Art,** 600 N. Ashley Dr. (☎ 813/274-8130), is especially strong in ancient Greek, Etruscan, and Roman artifacts, as well as 20th-century art. The museum grounds, fronting the Hillsborough River, contain a sculpture garden and a reflecting pool.

In St. Petersburg, the ✪ **Salvador Dalí Museum,** 1003 Third St. S. (☎ 813/823-3767), contains the largest assemblage of the artist's works outside Spain. The former marine warehouse that houses this widely divergent collection is as starkly modern as the works of art displayed within.

ORGANIZED TOURS

BY BUS   Swiss Chalet Tours, 3601 E. Busch Blvd. (☎ 813/985-3601), operates guided tours of Tampa, Ybor City, and the surrounding region. Four-hour (10am to 2pm) tours run on Monday and Thursday, and cost $35 for adults, $25 for children. Eight-hour tours on Tuesday and Friday cost $45 for adults, $35 for children. You can also book full-day tours to most Orlando theme parks, including MGM Studios, Epcot/Walt Disney World, and Sea World, as well as to the Kennedy Space Center and Cypress Gardens.

HITTING THE BEACH

You have to go to St. Petersburg, across the bay, for a north-to-south string of interconnected white sandy shores. Most beaches have rest rooms, refreshment stands, and picnic areas. You can either park on the street at meters (usually 25¢ for each half hour) or at one of the four major parking lots, located from north to south at Sand Key Park, beside Gulf Blvd. (also known as Route 699), just south of the Clearwater Pass Bridge; Redington Shores Beach Park, beside Gulf Boulevard at 182nd Street; Treasure Island Park, on Gulf Boulevard just north of 108th Avenue; and St. Pete Beach Park, beside Gulf Boulevard at 46th Street.

St. Petersburg Municipal Beach lies on Treasure Island. **Clearwater Beach,** with its silky sands, is the place for beach volleyball. Water-sports rentals, lifeguards, rest rooms, showers, and concessions are available. The swimming is excellent, and there's a pier for fishing. Parking is $7 a day in gated lots.

If you want to shop as well as tan, consider **Madeira Beach,** midway between St. Petersburg and Clearwater, with a boardwalk, T-shirt emporiums, and ice-cream parlors.

Honeymoon Island isn't great for swimming, but it has its own rugged beauty and a fascinating nature trail. From here, you can catch a ferry to **Caladesi Island State Park,** a 3¹/₂-mile stretch of sand at #3 Causeway Blvd. in Dunedin (☎ 813/469-5918 for information).

You can also go south to **Fort Desoto Park,** 3500 Pinellas Bayway S. (☎ 813/866-2484), consisting of about 900 acres and 7 miles of waterfront exposed to both the Gulf of Mexico and a brackish channel. There are fishing piers, shaded picnic areas, a bird and animal sanctuary, campsites, and a partially ruined fort near the park's southwestern tip. Take Interstate 275 South to the Pinellas Bayway (exit 4) and follow the signs.

SHOPPING

In **Ybor Square,** 1901 13th St. (☎ 813/247-4497), nearly 40 shops lie within three charming brick buildings dating from 1886 that once housed the world's largest cigar factory. The shops sell everything, including, of course, cigars. More upscale stores are located in **Old Hyde Park Village,** Swann and Dakota avenues near Bayshore Boulevard

(☎ 813/251-3500). **The Shops on Harbour Island,** 601 S. Harbour Island Blvd. (☎ **813/202-1830**), are set on an island off the coast of Tampa's commercial heart.

Malls include the **Brandon Town Center,** at the intersection of State Road 60 and Interstate 75; **Eastlake Square Mall,** 56th Street at Hillsborough Avenue; and the city's largest mall, **Tampa Bay Center,** Himes Avenue and Martin Luther King, Jr. Boulevard. You'll find substantial discounts at the **Gulf Coast Factory Shops,** 5461 Factory Shops Blvd. (corner of Interstate 75 and Highway 301, ☎ **941/723-1150**).

ACCOMMODATIONS

TAMPA The **Doubletree Guest Suites,** 11310 N. 30th St. (☎ 800/222-TREE or 813/971-7690), feels like a friendly college dormitory. Each handsomely furnished accommodation contains two separate rooms, one with a wet bar and small refrigerator.

There are two Tampa Hyatts: the **Hyatt Regency Tampa,** Two Tampa City Center (☎ 800/233-1234 or 813/225-1234), which towers over Tampa's commercial center; and the ✪ **Hyatt Regency Westshore,** 6200 Courtney Campbell Causeway (☎ 800/233-1234 or 813/874-1234), at the Tampa end of the long causeway traversing Tampa Bay. At the Westshore, some Spanish-style townhouses/villas are set about a half mile from the main hotel building.

Sheraton Grand Hotel Tampa Westshore, 4860 W. Kennedy Blvd. (☎ 800/866-7177 or 813/286-4400), is Tampa's most stylish modern hotel. The 11-story building is modeled after a butterfly.

Wyndham Harbour Island, 725 S. Harbour Island Blvd. (☎ 800/822-4200 or 813/229-5000), sits on one of Tampa Bay's most elegant residential islands.

ST. PETERSBURG The ✪ **Don CeSar,** 3400 Gulf Blvd. (☎ 800/282-1116 or 813/360-1881), is the most famous landmark in town. This pink-sided Moorish/Mediterranean fantasy, listed on the National Register of Historic Places, sits on 7¹/₂ acres of beachfront. Guest rooms are first-rate, usually with water views. Also in St. Pete, ✪ **Stouffer Renaissance Vinoy Resort,** 501 Fifth Ave. NE at Bay Shore Drive (☎ 800/HOTELS1 or 813/894-1000), reigns as the *grande dame* of the region's hotels. Accommodations in the new wing ("The Tower") are slightly larger than those in the hotel's original core.

DINING

On the 14th floor of the Hyatt Regency Westshore Hotel, **Armani's,** 6200 Courtney Campbell Causeway (☎ 813/874-1234), is a Northern Italian restaurant with flair. Dishes are all prepared with fine ingredients.

The steaks at ✪ **Bern's Steak House,** 1208 S. Howard Ave. (☎ 813/251-2421), are close to perfect. You order according to thickness and weight.

Le Bordeaux, 1502 S. Howard Ave. (☎ 813/254-4387), presents competent French food at reasonable prices. The changing menu often includes bouillabaisse and filet of beef with Roquefort sauce.

In Ybor City, ✪ **Columbia Restaurant,** 2117 Seventh Ave. E., between 21st and 22nd streets (☎ 813/248-4961), occupies a tile-sheathed building that fills an entire city block, about a mile from the cruise docks. The aura is pre-Castro Cuba. The more simple your dish is, the better it's likely to be. Filet mignons, *palomillo,* roasted pork, and the black beans, yellow rice, and plantains are flavorful and well-prepared. Flamenco shows begin on the dance floor Monday through Saturday at 7:30pm.

At lunch, ✪ **Mise en Place,** 442 Kennedy Blvd. (☎ 813/254-5373), serves an array of delicious sandwiches, as well as savory pastas, risottos, and platters. More formal dinners feature free-range chicken with smoked tomato coulis, and loin of venison with asparagus, tarragon mash, and red-onion balsamic marmalade.

✪ **Mojo,** 238 E. Davis Blvd. (☎ 813/259-9949), sits on Davis Island, a residential island separated from the commercial heart of Tampa by a narrow channel. This is the most flamboyant and charming restaurant in town. At lunch, its Caribbean menu includes a roast pork sandwich with lime-flavored cumin, onions, and provolone cheese on Cuban bread.

The best fish in Tampa is served at **Oystercatchers,** in the Hyatt Regency Westshore Hotel complex, 6200 Courtney Campbell Causeway (☎ 813/874-1234). Pick the fish you want from a glass-fronted buffet or enjoy mesquite-grilled steaks, chicken rollatini, and shellfish.

Selena's, 1623 Snow, Old Hyde Park (☎ 813/251-2116), serves a mix of New Orleans Cajun and Northern Italian cuisine. An upstairs bar/lounge hosts live jazz Thursday through Saturday.

TAMPA AFTER DARK

Nightfall now transforms **Ybor City,** Tampa's century-old Latin Quarter, into a hotbed of music for all tastes, ethnic food, poetry readings, and after-midnight coffee and dessert. Thousands crowd one of its main arteries, 7th Avenue, Wednesday through Saturday evenings. **The Masquerade,** 1503 E. 7th Ave. (☎ 813/247-3319), set within a 1940s movie palace, is the first of the many nightclubs that pepper the streets here.

Elsewhere, **The Skipper Dome/Skipper's Smokehouse,** 910 Skipper Rd. (☎ 813/ 971-0666), is a favorite evening spot, with an all-purpose restaurant and bar (with oysters and fresh shellfish sold by the dozen and half dozen). For live music, head out back to the "Skipper Dome," a sprawling deck sheltered by a canopy of oak trees.

The Tampa/Hillsborough Arts Council maintains **Artsline** (☎ 813/229-ARTS), a 24-hour information service about current and upcoming cultural events.

5 New Orleans & the Port of New Orleans

There's power and majesty in this historic port, 110 miles upriver of the Gulf of Mexico. By some yardsticks, it's the busiest port in the nation, servicing many vessels much larger than the cruise ships that call New Orleans home. Although the bulk of business conducted here mainly involves the transport of grains, ores and mining byproducts, machinery, and building supplies, the city is poised for increased visibility as home port to a handful of cruise ships. Cruises from here are mainly bound for the western edge of the Caribbean, including the western "Mexican Riviera" and Cancún and Cozumel.

If you're boarding a cruise ship in New Orleans, it's almost certain your access will be through the Julia Street Cruise Ship Terminal on the Julia Street Wharf. Originally developed as part of the 1984 Louisiana World's Exposition, the cruise ship area was inaugurated in 1993, then doubled in size in 1996. It lies near the commercial heart of town, a 10-minute walk from the edge of the French Quarter, or a short and convenient trolley ride away.

GETTING TO NEW ORLEANS & ITS PORT

The port is at 1350 Port of New Orleans Place. For information, call the **Port of New Orleans** at ☎ 504/522-2551.

BY AIR New Orleans International Airport is 10 miles northwest of the port. Cruise line representatives meet all passengers who have booked transfers through the line. For those who haven't, a taxi to the port costs about $19 and takes about 20 minutes. **Airport Shuttle** (☎ 504/592-0555) runs vans at 10- to 12-minute intervals from outside the airport's baggage claim to the port and other points in town. It costs $11 per passenger each way, free for children under 6.

Greater New Orleans

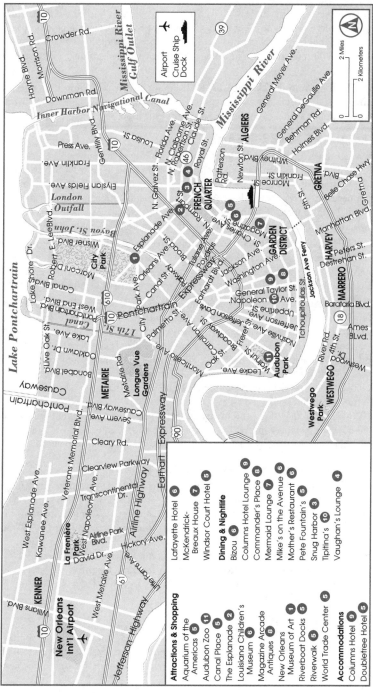

Attractions & Shopping

Aquarium of the Americas ⑤
Audubon Zoo ⑪
Canal Place ⑤
The Esplanade ②
Louisiana Children's Museum ⑥
Magazine Arcade Antiques ⑤
New Orleans Museum of Art ①
Riverboat Docks ⑤
Riverwalk ⑤
World Trade Center ⑤

Lafayette Hotel ⑥
McKendrick-Breaux House ⑦
Windsor Court Hotel ⑤

Dining & Nightlife

Bizou ⑥
Columns Hotel Lounge ⑨
Commander's Place ⑧
Mermaid Lounge ⑦
Mike's on the Avenue ⑥
Mother's Restaurant ⑤
Pete Fountain's ⑤
Snug Harbor ③
Tipitina's ⑩
Vaughan's Lounge ④

Accommodations

Columns Hotel ⑨
Doubletree Hotel ⑤

357

BY CAR   Highways I-10, U.S. 90, U.S. 61, and Louisiana 25 (the Lake Pontchartrain causeway) lead directly to New Orleans. You can park your car in long-term parking at the port, but only for blocks of 1 week. Reserve parking directly with your cruise ship operator. You must present a boarding pass or ticket before parking. The cost is $45 per week.

BY TRAIN   Amtrak (☎ 800/USA-RAIL) trains stop at the **Union Passenger Terminal** at 1001 Loyola Ave., in the central business district. Taxis are outside the passenger terminal's main entrance; the fare to the port is $6.

EXPLORING NEW ORLEANS

In many respects, the **French Quarter** *is* New Orleans, and many visitors never leave its confines. It's the oldest part of the city and still the most popular for sightseeing. But if you venture outside the French Quarter, you'll be able to feel the pulse of the city's commerce, see river activities that keep the city alive, stroll through spacious parks, drive or walk by the impressive homes of the Garden District, and get a firsthand view of the bayou/lake connection that explains why New Orleans grew up here in the first place.

VISITOR INFORMATION   Contact the **Greater New Orleans Convention and Visitors Bureau,** 1520 Sugar Bowl Dr., New Orleans, LA 70112 (☎ 504/566-5011), for brochures, pamphlets, and information. Once you arrive, stop at the **New Orleans Welcoming Center,** 529 St. Ann St. in the French Quarter (☎ 504/566-5031).

GETTING AROUND   Taxis are plentiful. If you're not near a taxi stand, call **United Cabs** (☎ 504/522-9771) and a cab will come within 5 to 10 minutes. The meter begins at $2.10, and rises 40¢ per mile thereafter.

Streetcar lines run the length of St. Charles Avenue. They operate 24 hours a day and cost $1.25 per ride (you must have exact change). A transfer from streetcar to bus costs 10¢. Board at the corner of Canal and Carondelet Streets in the French Quarter. A VisiTour Pass, which gives you unlimited rides on all streetcar and bus lines, sells for $4 for 1 day, $8 for 3 days.

Where the trolleys don't run, a **city bus** will. For route information, call ☎ 504/248-3900 or pick up a map at the Visitor Information Center (address above). Most buses charge 80¢ (plus 30¢ for a transfer) per ride, although some express buses charge $1.25.

A **Vieux Carré Minibus** takes you to French Quarter sights. The route is posted along Canal and Bourbon streets. The minibus operates daily between 5am and 7:25pm and costs $1.

From Jackson Square (at Decatur Street), you can take a 2¼-mile horse-drawn carriage ride through the French Quarter. **The Gay Nineties Carriage Tour Co.** (☎ 504/943-8820) offers fringe-topped wagons suitable for up to 10 passengers at a time, daily from 9am to midnight. A ride costs $8 per adult and $4 per child.

A free **ferryboat** departs at frequent intervals from the foot of Canal Street, carrying cars and passengers across the river to the Algiers section of town. A round-trip passage takes about 25 minutes.

SEEING THE SIGHTS

The well-designed ✪ **Aquarium of the Americas,** 1 Canal St., at the Mississippi River (☎ 504/861-2537), is a million-gallon tribute to the diversity of marine life. A 400,000-gallon tank holds a kaleidoscope of species from the deep waters of the nearby Gulf of Mexico.

You'll need at least 3 hours to visit the ✪ **Audubon Zoo,** 6500 Magazine St. (☎ 504/861-2537), home to 1,500 animals in natural habitats. In a Louisiana swamp

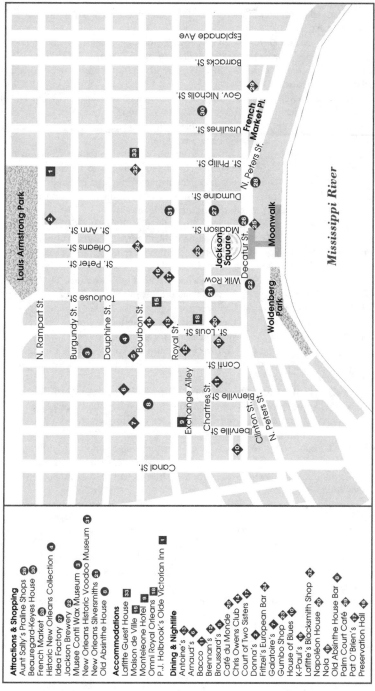

Esplanade Ave

Barracks St.

Gov. Nicholls St. ㉙

㉚ Ursulines St.

French Market Pl.

St. Philip St. ㉝

㉜

Dumaine St.

N. Peters St.

① ㉛ ㉗ ㉘

Louis Armstrong Park

② St. Ann St. ㉖ ㉕

Orleans St. ㉔ Madison St. Moonwalk

St. Peter St. ㉓ Jackson Square Decatur St.

⑯ Wilk Row

N. Rampart St. Toulouse St. ⑰ ㉒ Woldenberg Park

⑮ ㉑

Burgundy St. Dauphine St. ⑱ Mississippi River

③ ④ Bourbon St. ⑬ ⑳

⑤ ⑲

Royal St. ⑫

⑥ Conti St.

Chartres St.

⑧ Bienville St.

⑦ ⑨ Exchange Alley Iberville St.

Clinton St.

N. Peters St.

⑩

Canal St.

Attractions & Shopping

Aunt Sally's Praline Shops ㉖
Beauregard-Keyes House ㉚
French Market ㉙
Historic New Orleans Collection ④
Idea Factory
Jackson Brewery ㉒
Musée Conti Wax Museum ③
New Orleans Historic Voodoo Museum ㉛
New Orleans Silversmiths ㉑
Old Absinthe House ⑧

Accommodations

Lafitte Guest House ㉝
Maison de Ville ⑮
Monteleone Hotel ⑨
Omni Royal Orleans ⑱
P.J. Holbrook's Olde Victorian Inn ①

Dining & Nightlife

Antoine's ⑯
Arnaud's ⑥
Bacco ⑤
Brennan's ⑬
Broussard's ㉙
Café du Monde ㉕
Chris Owens Club ⑫
Court of Two Sisters ㉓
Donna's ②
Fritzel's European Bar ㉔
Galatoire's ⑦
Gumbo Shop ㉓
House of Blues ⑩
K-Paul's ⑲
Lafitte's Blacksmith Shop ㉜
Napoléon House ㉘
Nola ⑰
Old Absinthe House Bar ⑧
Palm Court Café ㉙
Pat O'Brien's ㉗
Preservation Hall ㉖

replication, alligators and other reptiles slither and hop among native birds and clusters of marsh grasses.

Despite its massive Doric columns and twin staircases, local architects nonetheless refer to **Beauregard-Keyes House,** 1113 Chartres St. (☎ **504/523-7257**), as a "Louisiana raised cottage." Built in 1826, it's one of the most impressive and socially prestigious structures in town.

Incorporating seven historic buildings connected by a brick courtyard, ✪ **The Historic New Orleans Collection,** 533 Royal St. (☎ **504/523-4662**), evokes New Orleans of 200 years ago. The oldest building in the complex escaped the tragic fire of 1794. The others hold exhibitions about Louisiana's culture and history.

Housed in a former granary 4 blocks from the river, the **Louisiana Children's Museum,** 420 Julia St. (☎ **504/523-1357**), divides its exhibits into activities for children over and under the age of 8. The Lab demonstrates principles of physics and math, motion, and inertia. Younger children play in a simulated supermarket and attend puppet workshops, cooking programs, and storytelling sessions.

Musee Conti Wax Museum, 917 Conti St. (☎ **504/525-2605**), is the bayou equivalent of Madame Tussaud's, featuring pivotal figures in Louisiana history and legend. Look for the replicas of the notorious politico Huey Long, jazzmeister Pete Fountain, Andrew Jackson, and Jean Lafitte.

The collections of the **New Orleans Historic Voodoo Museum,** 724 Dumaine St. (☎ **504/523-7685**), celebrate the occult and the mixture of African and Catholic rituals first brought to New Orleans by slaves from Hispaniola. An herb shop/apothecary is stocked with ingredients. Staff there can also put you in touch with psychics. A guided voodoo walking tour of the French Quarter departs from the museum daily at 1pm.

The collections of the **New Orleans Museum of Art (NOMA),** Lelong Avenue (☎ **504/488-2631**), span the centuries, with one floor devoted to ethnographic and non-Western art.

The ✪ **Old Absinthe House/Tony Moran's Restaurant,** 240 Bourbon St. (☎ **504/523-3181**), is the oldest bar in America, built in 1806 by two Spanish partners. Upstairs is a restaurant, Tony Moran's, open only for dinner.

The **World Trade Center of New Orleans,** 2 Canal St. (☎ **504/529-1601**), one of the tallest buildings in town, has the ✪ **Viewpoint** observation platform on its 31st floor. Check out the freighters, cruise ships, tug boats, submarines, and aircraft carriers that ply the swift-flowing waters of New Orlean's harbor. A cocktail lounge spins slowly on the 33rd floor.

ORGANIZED TOURS

ON FOOT   Friends of the Cabildo (☎ **504/523-3939**) lead 2-hour walking tours of Vieux Carré (the French Quarter). They leave from the Museum Store at 523 St. Ann St. every Tuesday through Sunday at 10am and 1:30pm, and Monday at 1:30pm, except holidays. Donations are expected: $10 per adult, and $8 for seniors over 65 and children ages 13 to 20.

Magic Walking Tours (☎ **504/588-9693**) offers theme tours associated with the city's cemeteries, its Garden District, or its voodoo traditions. Tours cost $10 per person during the day, and $14 per person at night.

You can see historic interiors on a **Hidden Treasures Tour** (☎ **504/529-4507**).

BY BOAT   The paddlewheeler *Creole Queen* departs from the Poydras Street Wharf, adjacent to the mall Riverwalk, every day at 10:30am for a 2½-hour waterborne tour. Riverwalk is at the end of Canal Street; the wharf is about 2 blocks east. There's a buffet restaurant and a cocktail lounge on board. Daytime cruises cost $14 for adults, $7 for children. Evening cruises, with live jazz, cost $39 for adults, $18 for children.

Another steam-powered stern-wheeler is the *Natchez,* departing daily from the Toulouse Street Wharf, next to the French Quarter's Jackson Street Brewery. Cruises begin at 11:30am and 2:30pm and feature live jazz and an optional Creole-style luncheon buffet. The cost is $14.75 for adults, $7.25 for children 6 to 12, free for children under 6 (food is an additional $8 for adults, $4.50 for children). Evening jazz cruises, with a buffet dinner, cost $38.75 for adults, $19.25 for children.

The riverboat *John James Audubon* departs from the Canal Street dock at Riverwalk, and travels the Mississippi as far as the Audubon Zoo and the Aquarium. The cruise costs $26.50 for adults, $15.25 for children.

The *Queen of New Orleans,* at the New Orleans Hilton Riverside (☎ **504/ 587-7777**), is a casino paddlewheeler boat with slot machines. The 90-minute cruises run 24 hours a day, departing every 3 hours.

BY BUS A 2-hour **Gray Line** bus tour, 1300 World Trade Center of New Orleans (☎ **800/535-7786** or 504/587-0861), offers a fast overview of the city. Tours cost $18 for adults and $9.50 for children, and require advance booking.

SHOPPING

Shopping here is, in a word, fun. Antique stores are especially well-stocked, and gift shops seem to sell more than just a cheap array of T-shirts and souvenir items (although there are plenty of those, too).

Major shopping venues include the triple-tiered mall **Canal Place,** where Canal Street meets the Mississippi Wharves. **The Esplanade,** 1401 W. Esplanade, boasts a constantly busy food court and more than 150 retailers. **The French Market,** whose main entrance is on Decatur Street across from Jackson Square, is big on Louisiana kitsch and cookware. The **Jackson Brewery,** adjacent to Jackson Square, is a transformed suds factory filled with more than 125 retailers. **Riverwalk** is a covered mall that runs along the wharves between Poydras Street and the Convention Center.

You'll find a row of art galleries along **Julia Street,** between the Mississippi River and Camp Street. A jumble of antiques and flea market–style emporiums sit along a 6-block stretch of **Magazine Street,** between Audubon Park and Canal Street. There's also **Magazine Arcade Antiques,** 3017 Magazine St. (☎ **504/895-5451**).

For crafts, try the **Idea Factory,** 838 Chartres St. (☎ **504/524-5195**), where woodworkers stay busy shaping and gluing letterboxes, trays, paper-towel holders, and wall brackets. You'll find new and antique silver at **New Orleans Silversmiths,** 600 Chartres St. (☎ **504/522-8333**).

You can see pralines being made at **Aunt Sally's Praline Shops, Inc.,** 810 Decatur St. (☎ **504/524-5107**). They'll ship anything home for you, and sell you items such as cookbooks, packaged Creole food, and Louisiana memorabilia.

ACCOMMODATIONS

Seekers of Southern charm and grace head for the **Columns Hotel,** 3811 St. Charles Ave. (☎ **800/445-9308** or 504/899-9308), a former private residence in 1883 now converted into a small hotel. One of the stateliest remaining examples of belle époque Italianate architecture, it's listed on the National Register of Historic Places.

Conveniently located near both the embarkation piers for cruise ship passengers and the French Quarter, the **Doubletree Hotel,** 300 Canal St. (☎ **504/581-1300**), is at the edge of the city's business district. Rooms are comfortable and clean.

The ✪ **Omni Royal Orleans,** 621 St. Louis St. (☎ **800/THE-OMNI** in the U.S. and Canada, or 504/529-5333; fax 504/529-7089), is a most elegant hotel located smack in the center of the Quarter. The lobby is a small sea of marble, and the rooms are sizeable and comfortable. Truman Capote and William Styron both stayed here.

○ **Lafayette Hotel,** 600 St. Charles Ave., at Lafayette Square (☎ 800/733-4754 or 504/524-4441), resembles an upscale turn-of-the-century hotel in London. From old-world architecture, French doors, and wrought-iron balconies to marble floors, polished mahogany, and English botanical prints, the ambience is consistently luxurious.

Lafitte Guest House, 1003 Bourbon St. (☎ 800/331-7971 or 504/581-2678), is a meticulously restored elegant French manor house furnished with splendid antiques. The three-floor brick structure in a residential section of Bourbon Street was built in 1849. Its marble ceilings, wrought-iron balconies, and Victorian antiques are as alluring as each of its individually decorated bedrooms, which come in various sizes.

In the heart of the French Quarter, one of the best small hotels in the world, the ○ **Maison de Ville,** 727 Toulouse St. (☎ 800/634-1600 or 504/561-5858), is located on its original 1742 site. It was here that Tennessee Williams "polished" *A Streetcar Named Desire.* Just steps from honky-tonk Bourbon Street, here you find an air of Southern gentility.

One of the best guesthouses for value is **The McKendrick-Breaux House,** 1474 Magazine St. (☎ 888/570-1700 or 504/586-1700), built at the end of the Civil War by a wealthy plumber and Scottish immigrant. Located in the lower Garden District, it has been completely restored to its original charm. Each room is furnished with antiques, family collectibles, and fresh flowers.

About 7 blocks from the cruise ship terminal is the *grande dame* of the French Quarter, the atmospheric **Monteleone Hotel,** 214 Royal St. (☎ 800/535-9595 or 504/ 523-2341). Decor and floor layouts are slightly different in each of the 597 rooms.

Three streets from Bourbon in the French Quarter, ○ **P.J. Holbrook's Olde Victorian Inn,** 914 N. Rampart St. (☎ 800/725-2446 or 504/522-2446), is a beautifully restored 1840s home, with antiques and reproductions. Some rooms have balconies, and most come with fireplaces. P.J. herself exemplifies Southern hospitality.

Only blocks from the French Quarter, ○ **Windsor Court Hotel,** 300 Gravier St. (☎ 800/262-2662 or 504/523-6000), rents 224 beautifully furnished bedrooms, all but 50 of which are suites. From its $8 million art collection to the harpist floating celestial music over the afternoon tea drinkers, the Windsor Court provides more of an English country house experience than a Louisiana sojourn.

DINING

Don't ask what's new at ○ **Antoine's,** 713 St. Louis St. (☎ 504/581-4422), established in 1840. Oysters Rockefeller, first served here in 1899, are still available. Tournedos of beef, ramekins of crawfish cardinal, and *pompano en papillote* remain perennial favorites, and rightly so. The only radical menu change occurred in the 1990s, when French menu terms were given English translations.

The legendary **Arnaud's,** 813 Bienville St. (☎ 504/523-5433), lies within three interconnected, once-private houses from the 1700s. The five belle-époque dining rooms here are lush with Edwardian embellishments. Menu items include Shrimp Arnaud, snails *en casserole,* oysters stewed in cream, rack of lamb diablo, roasted *duck à l'orange,* and classic bananas. The dark balcony around the main dining room is where proper New Orleans gentlemen used to dine with their mistresses (while their wives dined below, unawares).

A great New Orleans bistro, **Bacco,** 310 Charles St. (☎ 504/523-6441), stands adjacent to the De La Poste Hotel, right in the heart of the French Quarter. In an elegant setting of pink Italian marble floors and Venetian chandeliers, you can feast on wood-fired pizzas, regional seafood, and such specialties as porcini roasted duck and crabmeat and pappardelle.

Bizou, 701 St. Charles Ave. (☎ **504/524-4114**), is hardly the most glamorous place in New Orleans, but its cuisine, a rejuvenation of Creole and French traditional cookery, has the exuberance of a spring day. Try the crawfish cakes with Creole mustard and baby greens in a Tabasco-infused white butter.

Broussard's, 819 Conti St. (☎ **504/581-3866**), has thrived here since 1920. It's a quieter, more dignified version of Antoine's, less heavily patronized by out-of-towners, and more authentic to the "Nawlins" ethic. Dishes include filets of pompano Napoléon-style (with scallops and a mustard-caper sauce, served in puff pastry with a side order of shrimp).

At the corner of Washington Avenue and Coliseum Street in the Garden District, **Commander's Place,** 1403 Washington Ave. (☎ **504/899-8221**), still reigns as one of the city's finest dining choices. The cuisine is haute Creole. Try anything with shrimp or crawfish, or the Mississippi quail.

✪ **Galatoire's,** 209 Bourbon St. (☎ **504/525-2021**), feels like a bistro in turn-of-the-century Paris, and still basks in its legendary reputation. Menu items include trout (*meunière* or *amandine*), remoulade of shrimp, oysters en brochette, a savory Creole-style bouillabaisse, and a good eggplant stuffed with a puree of seafood.

Lines often stretch halfway down the block for one of the 116 seats at **K-Paul's Louisiana Kitchen,** 416 Chartres St. (☎ **504/524-7394**), one of Louisiana's most famous restaurants. Once seated, expect company—tables on the street level are communal. Try fiery gumbos, Cajun popcorn shrimp, roasted rabbit, the delicious spicy blackened fish (especially tuna), and for the rare vegetarian, the breaded, vegetable-stuffed eggplant.

Brennan's, 417 Royal St. (☎ **504/525-9711**), is the place for the legendary "Breakfast at Brennan's," a multi-course affair that's changed very little over the years. It includes traditional dishes like eggs Hussarde, eggs Sardou, and trout Nancy (fillet of fresh trout sautéed and topped with lump crabmeat, sprinkled with capers and lemon-butter sauce). Turtle soup is a famous local dish, and Brennan's makes one of the best. Desserts include bananas Foster (sautéed in liqueur, brown sugar, cinnamon, and butter; drenched in rum; set ablaze; and served over vanilla ice cream). It's a little overwhelming. My editor ate there recently, and afterward stumbled to the nearest phone, cancelled his lunch and dinner reservations, and went back to the hotel for a nap.

The ambience is more of a draw than the food at the **Court of Two Sisters,** 613 Royal St. (☎ **504/522-7261**), but what a draw it is. You enter through an arch into a huge courtyard filled with flowers, fountains, and low-hanging willows, with a wishing well at its center. You can dine outside amid the greenery or in the Royal Court Room. The daily jazz brunch buffet features more than 60 dishes (meat, fowl, fish, vegetables, fresh fruits, homemade bread, and pastries) and a strolling jazz band.

The **Gumbo Shop,** 630 St. Peter St. (☎ **504/525-1486**), is a cheap and convenient place to get solid, classic Creole food. The menu reads like a textbook list of traditional local food: red beans and rice, shrimp Creole, crawfish étouffée. The seafood gumbo with okra is a meal in itself, and do try the jambalaya. Other dishes include crawfish and penne pasta, filet mignon, salads, po' boys (from regular ham and cheese to Cajun sausage), and homemade desserts such as Southern pecan pie with ice cream.

Located in the Lafayette Hotel (see above), ✪ **Mike's on the Avenue,** 628 Charles St. (☎ **504/523-1709**), is a favorite with the discriminating palates of New Orleans locals. Chef Mike Fennelly marinates simple lamb chops in a fresh rosemary and pomegranate sauce, then covers them with a jalapeño mint glaze.

If you don't mind facing the world's toughest waitresses, head for **Mother's Restaurant,** 401 Poydras St. (☎ **504/523-9656**), at the corner of Tchoupitoulas. Customers have been flocking to this crowded place since 1938. Homemade biscuits and red bean omelets are featured at breakfast, giving way at lunch to po' boys. For dinner you can get everything from soft-shell crabs to jambalaya.

Napoléon House, 500 Chartres St. (☎ 504/524-9752), at the corner of St. Louis Street, would have been the house of the lieutenant himself if a wild plan had been achieved. A landmark 1797 building, this place is a hangout for drinking and good times, but also serves food. The specialty is Italian muffuletta, with ham, Genoa salami, pastrami, Swiss cheese, and provolone.

At **Nola,** 534 St. Louis St. (☎ 504/522-6652), Cajun New Orleans mingles gracefully with Hollywood. Try such intriguing dishes as slow-roasted duck with a sweet and spicy glaze, along with a buttermilk corn pudding.

✪ **Café du Monde,** at 813 Decatur St., right on the river (☎ 504/581-2914), is basically a coffee and donuts stop (okay, coffee and beignets—a square, French doughnut-type object, hot and covered in powdered sugar), but it's *the* place for people-watching.

NEW ORLEANS AFTER DARK

Do what most people do: Start at one end of **Bourbon Street** (say, around Iberville), walk down to the other, and then turn around and do it again. Along the way, you'll hear R&B, blues, and jazz pouring out of dozens of bars, be beckoned by touts of the numerous strip clubs, and see one tiny little storefront stall after another sporting hand-lettered signs that say "Our Beer Is Cheaper Than Next Door." It's a scene. Base and immoral? Maybe, but it's loads of fun. Grab yourself a big $2 beer or one of the famous rum-based Hurricanes (preferably in a yard-long plastic cup shaped like a Roswell alien) and join the party.

Preservation Hall, 726 St. Peter St., just off Bourbon (☎ 514/523-8939), is a deliberately shabby little hall with very few places to sit and no air-conditioning. Nonetheless, the place is usually packed with people in to see the house band, a bunch of mostly older musicians who have been at this for *eons.* Don't request "When the Saints Go Marching In" 'cause the band won't play it—even classics get to be old smelly hats when you've played them 45,000 times.

Chris Owens Club, 500 Bourbon St. (☎ 504/523-6400), is a one-woman cabaret act. New Orleans legend and mistress of ceremonies Ms. Owens sings along with whatever band happens to be accompanying her that night. Jazz legend Al Hirt performs here between 2 and 4 nights a week. On nights when Ms. Owens is indisposed, the venue becomes a dance club.

On a small stage in back of **Fritzel's European Bar & Cuisine,** 733 Bourbon St. (☎ 504/561-0432), musicians will improvise, boogie, and generally shake, rattle, and roll. It's one of the better places on Bourbon. Very late at night, musicians from other clubs might hop on stage to jam.

Not to be confused with the Old Absinthe House/Tony Moran's Restaurant, **Old Absinthe House Bar,** 400 Bourbon St. (☎ 504/525-8108), features antique bar fixtures and rock and blues music that attracts energetic fans from throughout Louisiana.

Lafitte's Blacksmith Shop, 941 Bourbon St. (☎ 504/523-0066), is a French Quarter pub housed in an 18th-century Creole house that looks like only faith keeps it standing. Tennessee Williams used to hang out here.

Established in 1933, the quite touristy **Pat O'Brien's,** 718 St. Peter St., just off Bourbon (☎ 504/525-4823), is famous for its twin piano players, raucous high jinx, live comedians and singers, and gargantuan Hurricanes. There's also an outdoor courtyard.

If you're looking to get away from the Bourbon scene and hear some real brass-band jazz, head up to **Donna's,** 800 N. Rampart St., at the top of St. Ann Street (☎ 504/596-6914). This joint is often packed, especially for the more famous acts—the Marsalis family has been known to play here from time to time—though when I was there recently to see a fella named Tuba Fats and his band, the patrons were almost outnumbered by the musicians. There's no better place to hear that authentic sound that made New Orleans famous. Cover varies, but is always reasonable. Owner Donna is often tending bar.

Elsewhere in town, Pete Fountain, the Dixieland clarinet maestro, runs **Pete Fountain's** in the plush third-floor interior of the New Orleans Hilton, 2 Poydras St. (☎ **504/561-0500**). If he's not on tour, Fountain usually performs several nights a week.

Jazz, blues, and Dixieland pour out of the nostalgia-laden bar and concert hall **Tipitina's,** 501 Napoleon Ave. (☎ **504/895-8477**).

At the **Mermaid Lounge,** 1100 Constance St. (☎ **504/524-4747**), in the Warehouse District, anything goes, and music ranges from rockabilly to jazz. It's open Wednesday through Saturday, and sometimes Tuesday night, if the mood strikes. The joint keeps going at least until 2am, but if it's jumping, the owners will keep it open later.

House of Blues, 225 Decatur St. (☎ **504/529-1421**), is one of the city's largest live music venues. You stand and move among the several bars that pepper the club. There's also a restaurant.

Follow the footsteps of Michael Jordan and U2 to the Victorian Lounge at the **Columns Hotel,** 3811 St. Charles Ave. (☎ **504/899-9308**), and try one of the staff's justly celebrated Bloody Marys. A young local crowd is attracted to this bar on the fringe of the Garden District, where a jazz trio entertains on Tuesday nights.

At **Palm Court Café,** 1204 Decatur St. (☎ **504/525-0200**), you'll find an equal appreciation of good jazz and international food.

One block beyond Esplanade, on the periphery of the French Quarter, **Snug Harbor,** 626 Frenchman St. (☎ **504/949-0696**), is a jazz bistro, a classic spot to hear modern jazz in a cozy setting. Sometimes R&B combos and blues are added to the program. There's a full dinner menu as well.

Vaughan's Lounge, 800 Lesseps St. (☎ **504/947-5562**), is a genuine New Orleans joint. Owner Kermit Ruffins will sometimes offer a barbecue out back.

6 San Juan & the Port of San Juan

In addition to being the embarkation port for a number of ships, San Juan is also a major port of call. See chapter 11, "The Caribbean Ports of Call," for all information.

11 Caribbean Ports of Call

There are two kinds of cruisers when it comes to ports of call: those who choose a certain cruise *because* of its itinerary and those who don't. But even if you've been there, done that, and cruise primarily for the onboard ship life, you'll want to know how best to spend the limited time you have in whichever port you happen to land.

Here's the good news: There are no lousy Caribbean islands! Sure, depending on your likes and dislikes, you'll appreciate some more than others. Some of the ports and islands—like Key West, St. Thomas, and Nassau—are much more overrun with tourists than others, but then again, they'll appeal to shoppers with their large variety of stores and bustling main streets. Other islands—Virgin Gorda, St. John, Jost Van Dyke, and the Grenadines, for instance—are quieter and more natural and will appeal to those of you who'd rather walk along a deserted beach or take a drive along a lonely, winding road in the midst of pristine tropical foliage. Some ports are expensive, like Bermuda, the U.S. Virgin Islands, St. Barts, St. Martin, and Aruba, while others are cheaper, like Cozumel, Jamaica, and the Grenadines.

Most of the big lines also have a **private island** or patch of island in the Bahamas that's included as a port of call on many of their Caribbean and Bahamas itineraries. Royal Caribbean, Princess, Disney, Holland America, Norwegian, and Costa all have one of these well-stocked island paradises that are off-limits to anyone but the line's passengers. While completely lacking in any true Caribbean culture, they do offer cruisers a guaranteed beach day with all the trimmings—a long stretch of beach with lounge chairs and strolling waiters selling tropical drinks, as well as water sports, shops, walking paths, hammocks, and casual picnic-style restaurants. On Disney's island, you can even rent bicycles and ride around the island.

Choosing what activities to participate in on board ship is one thing, but when the ship pulls up to a port of call, figuring out how to make the best of your limited time there is another. Should you take an organized tour or go off on your own and wing it? And just what are the best shore excursions? Where are the best beaches? Where's the shopping? Any good restaurants or bars nearby?

I'll answer all those questions, and more, as I take you to 21 ports of call, mainly in the Caribbean, but also including the Bahamas, Mexico's Yucatán Peninsula, and Key West. (See chapter 12, "Bermuda & the Panama Canal Route," for coverage of Bermuda and the ports along the Panama Canal routes.) At some ports, your best bet is to just head off **exploring on your own,** but at others, this could take too

Rental Cars

If you opt to explore an island on your own or want to rent a car in your port of embarkation or debarkation, you should make rental arrangements in advance, especially during the popular winter months. Following are the reservations numbers and Web sites for the major companies. Smaller companies that rent jeeps, motorscooters, and such are listed in the individual port sections.

Advantage: ☎ 800/777-5500, www.arac.com

Alamo: ☎ 800/327-9633, www.goalamo.com

Avis: ☎ 800/331-1212 in Continental U.S., www.avis.com

Budget: ☎ 800/527-0700, www.budgetrentacar.com

Dollar: ☎ 800/800-4000, www.dollarcar.com

Hertz: ☎ 800/654-3131, www.hertz.com

National: ☎ 800/CAR-RENT, www.nationalcar.com

Payless: ☎ 800/PAYLESS, www.paylesscar.com

Thrifty: ☎ 800/367-2277, www.thrifty.com

Value: ☎ 800/327-2501, www.go-value.com

much time, entail lots of hassles and planning, may cost more, and might not be safe (because of poor roads or driving conditions, for instance). In these cases, the **shore excursions** offered by the cruise lines are the way to go. Under each port review I'll run through a sampling of both the best excursions and the best sights and activities you can see and do on your own.

Shore excursions can be a wonderful and carefree way to get to know the islands, offering everything from **island tours** and **snorkeling and sailing excursions** (often with a rum-punch party theme) to more physically challenging pursuits, like **bicycle tours, hiking, kayaking,** and **horseback riding excursions.** Keep in mind, shore excursion prices vary from line to line, even for the exact same tour; the prices I've listed are typical and are adult rates. Also note that in some cases the excursions fill up fast, especially on the megaships, so don't dawdle in signing up. When you receive your cruise documents, or at the latest when you board the ship, you'll get a pamphlet with a listing of the excursions offered for your itinerary. Look it over, make your selections, and sign up the first or second day of your cruise. (In some cases, if a tour offered by your ship is booked up, you can try and book it independently once you get to port. The popular *Atlantis* submarine tour, for example, usually has an office/agent in the cruise terminals or nearby.)

As I said, in some cases it's a great idea to go off on your own, so I'll also advise you which islands are good for solo exploring, whether on foot or by taxi, motorscooter, ferry, or otherwise. Remember, though, if you opt to do your own independent touring, you'll be forgoing the narrative a guide gives, and may miss out on some of the historical, cultural, and other nuances of a particular island.

Cruise Tip: Yankee Dollars Accepted Here

The U.S. dollar is widely accepted throughout the islands as well as Bermuda, so even though I've listed each island's official local currency, there's rarely a need to exchange U.S. dollars. Credit cards and traveler's checks are also widely accepted.

Caribbean Port Calls at a Glance

Line	Ship	Itinerary (nights/region)*	Private Beaches & Islands	Antigua	Aruba	Barbados	British Virgin Islands	Cozumel/ Playa del Carmen	Curaçao
ACCL	Grande Caribe	11/PC							
	Grand Mariner	11/C							
		12 & 14/E							
	Niagara Prince	6 & 10/ Belize							
Cape Canaveral	Dolphin IV	2/C							
		4/C							
Carnival	Carnival Destiny	7/E							
		7/W						✓	
	Carnival Triumph	7/E							
		7/W						✓	
	Celebration	7/C						✓	
	Ecstasy	3/C							
		4/C						✓	
	Fantasy	3/C							
		4/C							
	Fascination	7/E				✓			
	Imagination	4/W						✓	
		5/W							
	Inspiration	7/S(a)	✓	✓					
		7/S(b)			✓				✓
	Jubilee	10/E & S				✓	✓		
		11/W & S			✓				
	Paradise	7/E					✓		
		7/W						✓	
	Sensation	7/E						✓	
	Tropicale	4/W						✓	
		5/W						✓	
Celebrity	Century	7/E							
		7/W						✓	
	Galaxy	7/S		✓		✓			
	Horizon	10/E & S		✓		✓			
		11/E & S				✓			✓

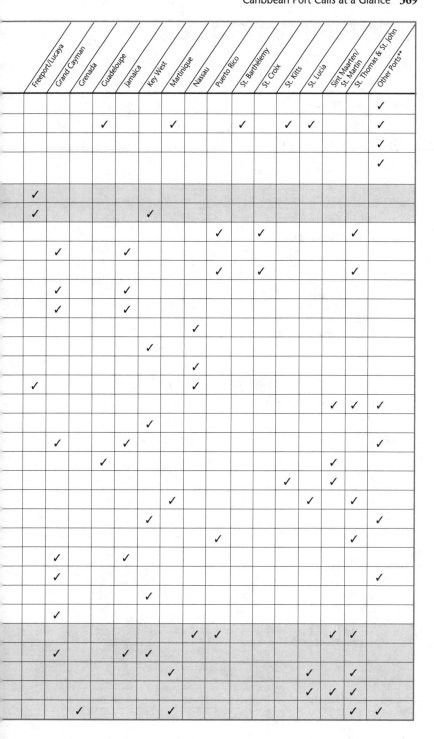

Freeport/Lucaya	Grand Cayman	Grenada	Guadeloupe	Jamaica	Key West	Martinique	Nassau	Puerto Rico	St. Barthélemy	St. Croix	St. Kitts	St. Lucia	Sint Maarten/St. Martin	St. Thomas & St. John	Other Ports**
															✓
			✓			✓			✓		✓	✓			✓
															✓
															✓
✓															
✓					✓										
								✓		✓			✓		
	✓			✓											
								✓		✓			✓		
		✓		✓											
		✓		✓											
						✓									
					✓										
						✓									
✓						✓									
													✓	✓	✓
					✓										
	✓			✓											✓
		✓											✓		
											✓		✓		
						✓						✓	✓		
					✓										✓
							✓						✓		
	✓			✓											
	✓														✓
					✓										
	✓														
						✓	✓						✓	✓	
	✓			✓	✓										
						✓						✓			✓	
												✓	✓	✓	
		✓				✓								✓	✓

Caribbean Port Calls at a Glance (continued)

Line	Ship	Itinerary (nights/region)*	Private Beaches & Islands	Antigua	Aruba	Barbados	British Virgin Islands	Cozumel/ Playa del Carmen	Curaçao
Celebrity (cont.)	Mercury	7/W						✓	
	Zenith	14/PC			✓				
Clipper	Nantucket Clipper	7/E					✓		
	Yorktown Clipper	7/E							
		10/S							
Club Med	Club Med II	7/C**			✓	✓	✓		
Commodore	Enchanted Capri	5/W						✓	
	Enchanted Isle	7/W						✓	
Costa	CostaRomantica	7/E	✓						
		7/W						✓	
	CostaVictoria	7/E	✓						
		7/W						✓	
Crystal	Crystal Harmony	7/E		✓					
		11 & 12/ PC			✓	✓		✓	✓
		10 & 11/E		✓		✓	✓		
	Crystal Symphony	10/E							
		11/PC			✓				✓
Cunard	Caronia	6, 7 & 10/E**		✓			✓		
		13/C					✓	✓	
	QE2	7/E							
		12/E & S			✓				
Disney	Disney Magic	3 & 4/B	✓						
	Disney Wonder	3 & 4/B	✓						
Holland America	Maasdam	10/PC	✓		✓				
	Nieuw Amsterdam	14/S				✓			
	Noordam	10/PC	✓						
	Ryndam	7/W	✓					✓	
	Veendam	7/E	✓						
		7/W	✓					✓	
	Westerdam	7/E	✓						
Mediterranean Shipping	Melody	11/E		✓			✓		
		11/W & PC							

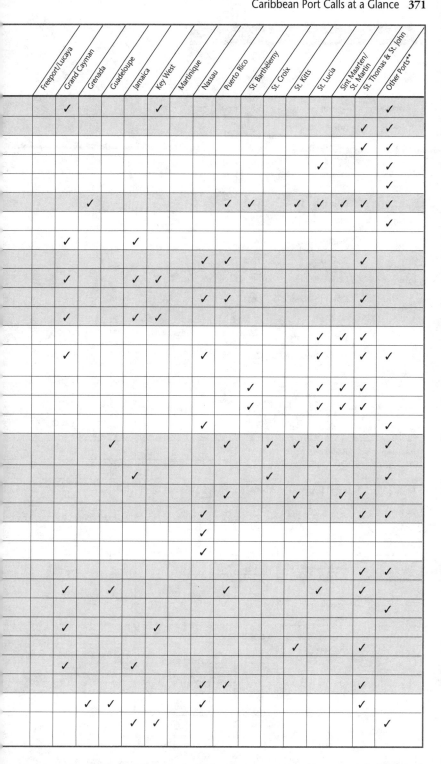

	Freeport/Lucaya	Grand Cayman	Grenada	Guadeloupe	Jamaica	Key West	Martinique	Nassau	Puerto Rico	St. Barthelemy	St. Croix	St. Kitts	St. Lucia	Sint Maarten/St. Martin	St. Thomas & St. John	Other Ports**
		✓				✓										✓
														✓	✓	
														✓	✓	
													✓		✓	
																✓
			✓						✓	✓		✓	✓	✓	✓	✓
		✓			✓											
								✓	✓						✓	
		✓			✓	✓										
								✓	✓						✓	
		✓			✓	✓										
													✓	✓	✓	
		✓						✓					✓		✓	✓
										✓			✓	✓	✓	
										✓			✓	✓	✓	
							✓									✓
			✓					✓			✓	✓	✓			✓
					✓						✓					✓
								✓				✓		✓	✓	
							✓							✓	✓	
								✓								
								✓								
														✓	✓	
		✓		✓				✓					✓	✓		
																✓
		✓			✓											
											✓			✓		
		✓		✓												
								✓	✓					✓		
			✓	✓			✓							✓		
					✓	✓										✓

Caribbean Port Calls at a Glance (continued)

Line	Ship	Itinerary (nights/region)*	Private Beaches & Islands	Antigua	Aruba	Barbados	British Virgin Islands	Cozumel/ Playa del Carmen	Curaçao
Norwegian	Norway	7/E	✓						
	Norwegian Dream	7/S			✓	✓			✓
	Norwegian Majesty	10/PC							✓
		11/PC			✓				
	Norwegian Sea	7/W						✓	
	Norwegian Wind	7/W						✓	
Premier	Big Red Boat	3 & 4/B							
	Rembrandt	7/E							
	SeaBreeze	7/W						✓	
Princess	Crown Princess	10/PC						✓	
	Dawn Princess	7/S-1							
		7/S-2				✓			
	Grand Princess	7/E	✓						
	Ocean Princess	7/S-1							✓
		7/S-2		✓		✓			
	Sea Princess	7/W	✓					✓	
	Sun Princess	10/PC			✓				
		11/PC							✓
Radisson	Radisson Diamond	4 & 5/E**					✓		
		7–10/PC							
Regal	Regal Empress	4/W						✓	
		5/W						✓	
		7/W						✓	
		11/PC							
Royal Caribbean	Enchantment of the Seas	7/E	✓						
		7/W						✓	
	Grandeur of the Seas	7/E	✓						
	Majesty of the Seas	3 & 4/B*	✓						
		7/W	✓					✓	
		7/S			✓				✓
	Monarch of the Seas	7/S		✓		✓			

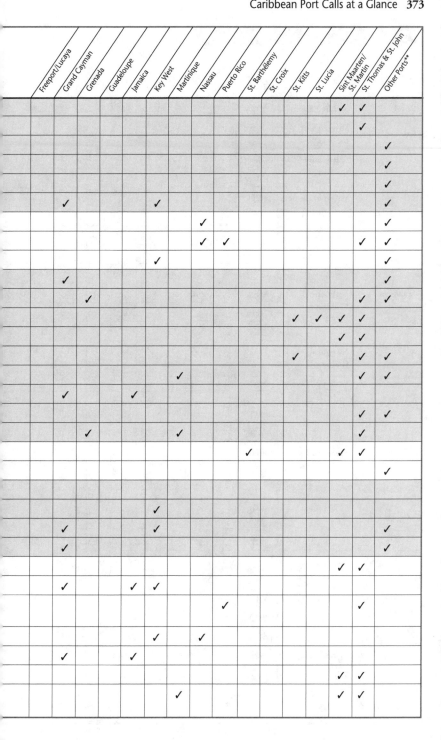

Freeport/Lucaya	Grand Cayman	Grenada	Guadeloupe	Jamaica	Key West	Martinique	Nassau	Puerto Rico	St. Barthélemy	St. Croix	St. Kitts	St. Lucia	Sint Maarten/St. Martin	St. Thomas & St. John	Other Ports**
													✓	✓	
														✓	
															✓
															✓
															✓
	✓				✓										✓
						✓									✓
						✓	✓							✓	✓
					✓										✓
	✓														✓
		✓												✓	✓
										✓	✓		✓	✓	
													✓	✓	
											✓			✓	✓
						✓								✓	✓
	✓			✓											
													✓	✓	
		✓				✓								✓	
								✓					✓	✓	
															✓
					✓										
	✓				✓										✓
	✓														✓
													✓	✓	
	✓			✓	✓										
							✓							✓	
					✓	✓									
	✓			✓											
													✓	✓	
					✓								✓	✓	

Caribbean Port Calls at a Glance (continued)

Line	Ship	Itinerary (nights/region)*	Private Beaches & Islands	Antigua	Aruba	Barbados	British Virgin Islands	Cozumel/Playa del Carmen	Curaçao
Royal Caribbean (cont.)	Nordic Empress	3 & 4/W*							
	Sovereign of the Seas	3 & 4/B*	✓						
	Splendour of the Seas	10/W & S			✓			✓	✓
		11/W & S			✓			✓	✓
	Vision of the Seas	10/PC							✓
		11/PC			✓				✓
Royal Olympic	Stella Solaris	10/W						✓	
		13/S(a)				✓			
		13/S(b)		✓					
Seabourn	Seabourn Goddess I	7/E(a)		✓					
		7/E(b)		✓			✓		
		7/E(c)							
	Seabourn Goddess II	7/E**		✓		✓	✓		
	Seabourn Legend	5/E**					✓		
		7 & 8/E & S**		✓		✓	✓		
		16/PC			✓				
	Seabourn Pride	6/E(a)							
		6/E(b)					✓		
		7/E					✓		
		10/E					✓		
		10 & 12/PC			✓		✓		
Star Clippers	Star Clipper	7/E(a)					✓		
		7/E(b)							
Tall Ship Adventures	Sir Francis Drake	7/E(a)					✓		
		7/E(b)							
Windjammer	Amazing Grace	13/E & S*	✓				✓		
	Flying Cloud	6/E					✓		
	Legacy	7/E					✓		
	Mandalay	6/E							
		13/E		✓					

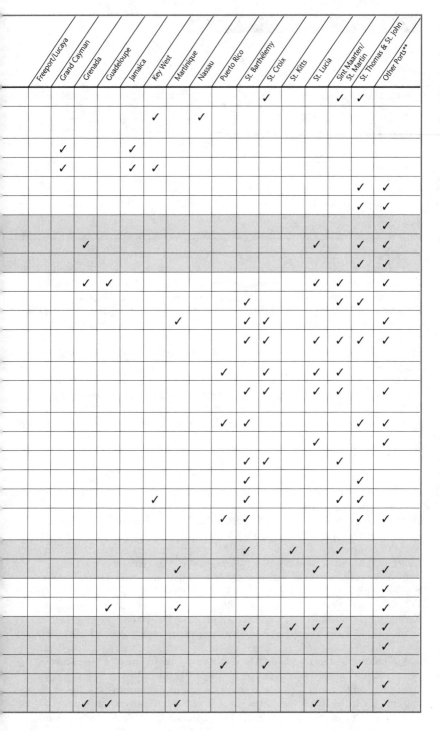

Freeport/Lucaya	Grand Cayman	Grenada	Guadeloupe	Jamaica	Key West	Martinique	Nassau	Puerto Rico	St. Barthélemy	St. Croix	St. Kitts	St. Lucia	Sint Maarten/St. Martin	St. Thomas & St. John	Other Ports**
									✓				✓	✓	
					✓		✓								
	✓		✓												
	✓			✓	✓										
														✓	✓
														✓	✓
															✓
		✓									✓			✓	✓
														✓	✓
		✓	✓								✓	✓			✓
									✓		✓	✓			
						✓			✓	✓					✓
									✓	✓	✓	✓		✓	✓
								✓		✓	✓	✓			
									✓	✓	✓	✓			✓
								✓	✓					✓	✓
											✓				✓
									✓	✓		✓			
									✓					✓	
					✓				✓				✓	✓	
								✓	✓					✓	✓
									✓		✓	✓			
						✓						✓			✓
															✓
			✓			✓									✓
									✓	✓	✓	✓			✓
															✓
								✓		✓			✓		
															✓
		✓	✓			✓					✓				✓

Caribbean Port Calls at a Glance (continued)		Itinerary (nights/region)*	Private Beaches & Islands	Antigua	Aruba	Barbados	British Virgin Islands	Cozumel/Playa del Carmen	Curaçao
Line	Ship								
Windjammer (cont.)	Polynesia	6/E							
	Yankee Clipper	6/E							
Windstar	Wind Spirit	7/E					✓		
	Wind Star	7/Belize						✓	
	Wind Surf	7/E							

See individual line reviews for exact itineraries.
*C = Caribbean, E = Eastern Caribbean, W = Western Caribbean, S = Southern Caribbean, B = Bahamas,
PC = Panama Canal.
**All ports not visited on every cruise.

It's safe to say most cruise ships arrive in port sometime before 10am, although it's difficult to generalize and will vary slightly from line to line and port to port. You rarely have to clear customs or immigration, because your ship's purser has your passport or documents and will have done all the paperwork for you. When local officials give the word, you go ashore. Sometimes you can walk down the gangplank right onto the pier, but if you're on a large cruise ship and the port isn't big enough, your ship will anchor offshore and ferry passengers to land via a small boat called a **tender.** In either case, you might have to wait in line to get ashore, but the waits can be longer if you have to tender in. Once ashore, even if you've come by tender, you aren't stuck there—you can return to the ship at any time for lunch, a nap, or whatever. Tenders run back and forth on a regular basis. Just be sure you get on the one that's heading to your ship.

All shore excursions are carefully organized to coincide with your time in port. If you're going it on your own, you can count on taxi drivers to be at the pier when your ship docks. It's a good idea to arrange with the driver to pick you up at a certain time to bring you back to the port. If you opt to explore an island on your own, you should always make car-rental arrangements in advance, especially during the popular winter months. To cut costs, form a car pool with another couple or two.

With regard to **duty-free shopping,** the savings on duty-free merchandise can range from as little as 5% to as much as 50%. Unless there's a special sale being offered, many products carry comparable price tags from island to island. If you have particular goods you're thinking of buying this way, it pays to check prices at your local discount retailer before you leave home, so you'll know whether you're really getting a bargain.

It's also a good idea to talk with your cruise director or shore excursion manager before you reach a port if you want to do something special (like take a submarine ride in St. Thomas) or pursue a sport, be it scuba, golf, tennis, horseback riding, or fishing. Keep in mind that they'll most likely just tell you to sign up for one of their organized excursions and won't have the time or ability to help you arrange personal and private tours. This is especially true on the megaships; the small, high-end lines, though, can and will help you in this way. You'll need to reserve spots for many of these activities before you land, because facilities might be filled by land-based vacationers or by passengers from other cruise ships. It goes without saying that if you arrive at a port of call and find the harbor filled with ships, expect the shops, restaurants, and beaches—everything, as a matter of fact—to be crowded. Call from the docks for a reservation.

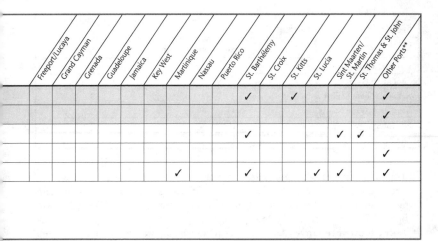

	Freeport/Lucaya	Grand Cayman	Grenada	Guadeloupe	Jamaica	Key West	Martinique	Nassau	Puerto Rico	St. Barthélemy	St. Croix	St. Kitts	St. Lucia	Sint Maarten/St. Martin	St. Thomas & St. John	Other Ports**
										✓		✓				✓
																✓
									✓				✓	✓		
																✓
							✓		✓				✓	✓		✓

Most passengers start heading back to the ship around 4pm or not much later than 5pm. By 6pm you're often sailing off to your next destination. In some cases—in Nassau, New Orleans, Key West, and the British Virgin Islands (for the smaller ships), for instance—the ship may leave after midnight so passengers can stay ashore to enjoy the nightlife on the island. In Appendix B, "Sample Daily Calendars & Menus," we've included a few sample "port day" activity calendars, which should give you an idea of how some lines structure and schedule their days at anchor.

1 Antigua

Covering about 110 square miles, rolling, rustic Antigua (An-*tee*-gah), part of the British Leewards, claims to have a different beach for every day of the year. This may be an exaggeration, but its numerous sugary-white, reef-protected beaches are reason enough to visit, even if just for a day. Antigua is also known for its **English Harbour,** home of Nelson Dockyard National Park, one of the Caribbean's major historical attractions.

Some British traditions (including a passion for cricket) linger on, although the nation became independent in 1981. The island has a population of about 80,000, mostly descended from the African slaves of plantation owners. Some 4,000 years ago, Antigua was home to a people called the Ciboney, who later disappeared completely and mysteriously from the island. When Columbus showed up in 1493, the Arawaks had already settled on the island, to be joined in the mid–17th century by the English. Many conflicts between the European settlers and Arawaks ensued and eventually the English won out.

There are isolated and conservative (but very glamorous) resorts, horribly maintained highways, and some of the most interesting historic naval sites in the British maritime world. Antigua is politically linked to the sparsely inhabited and largely underdeveloped island of Barbuda, about 30 miles north.

Sleepy, tattered **St. John's,** the capital, has seen better days. It's a large, neatly laid out town, 6 miles from the airport and less than a mile from Deep Water Harbour Terminal. Protected in the throat of a narrow bay, the town is full of cobblestoned sidewalks, weather-beaten wooden houses, corrugated iron roofs, and louvered Caribbean verandas. The streets were built wide to let the trade winds keep them cooler. The port is the focal point of commerce, industry, and government, as well as visitor shopping.

Frommer's Ratings: Antigua					
	Poor	Fair	Good	Excellent	Outstanding
Overall Experience				✓	
Shore Excursions			✓		
Activities Close to Port			✓		
Beaches & Water Sports					✓
Shopping		✓			
Dining/Bars			✓		

Frommer's Favorite Antigua Experiences

- **Cruise down Fig Tree Drive:** Twenty-some miles long, this route crosses the main mountain range of Antigua and is the island's most scenic drive (see "On Your Own: Beyond Walking Distance," below).
- **Take a four-wheel-drive island tour:** Drive down rainforest trails and make a stop at the beach. Sounds fun, huh? (See "Shore Excursions," below.)

COMING ASHORE   Only smaller ships anchor directly at English Harbour; everyone else reaches it via taxi or shore excursion from Deep Water Harbour Terminal in St. John's, the island's capital. Passengers landing in St. John's can head directly to the nearby duty-free shopping centers, Heritage Quay (pronounced *Key*) and Redcliffe Quay. You don't need a guide to walk around this sleepy town, which lies less than a mile from the pier. Credit-card phones are located on the dock.

CURRENCY   The **Eastern Caribbean dollar (EC$)** is used on these islands; however, you'll find that nearly all prices, except those in certain tiny restaurants, are given in U.S. dollars. The exchange rate is EC$2.70 to US$1 (EC$1 is worth about 37¢). It's always a good idea to ask if you're not sure. Unless otherwise specified, rates quoted in this section are given in U.S. dollars.

INFORMATION   Head to the **Antigua and Barbuda Department of Tourism** at Long and Thames streets in St. John's (☎ **268/462-0480**). Don't expect the staff here to tell you much more than the basics. Open Monday to Thursday from 8am to 4:30pm and Friday from 8am to 3pm.

LANGUAGE   The official language is English.

GETTING AROUND

BY TAXI   They meet every cruise ship. The one-way fare from the airport to English Harbour is an expensive $25 and up. The taxis don't have meters; although the government fixes the rates, it's always wise to negotiate the fare before getting in. One of the best ways to see Antigua is by private taxi, since the drivers are also guides. Most taxi tours cost $16 and up per hour.

BY BUS   Buses are cheap, but I don't recommend them for the average visitor. Most fares are $1.

BY RENTAL CAR   I don't recommend renting a car here because the roads are seriously potholed, local taxi drivers remove the signs (no kidding!), and driving is on the left.

SHORE EXCURSIONS

✪ **Four-Wheel-Drive Island Tour** ($62, 3 hours): A tour of the whole island via four-wheel drive will take you along rainforest trails and to the ruins of forts, sugar mills, and plantation houses, and is a great way to get a feel for Antigua. The tour includes a stop at the beach for some swimming.

Antigua

Nelson's Dockyard and Clarence House at English Harbour ($30–$60, 3 hours): This is the major excursion on the island. On the way, you get to view some of the island's lush countryside. That still leaves you plenty of time in the day for shopping or hitting the beach.

Catamaran Tour ($45, 3 hours): The boat takes you along coast of Antigua, making a stop for swimming and sunbathing.

A Cruise on the *Jolly Roger* ($60 adults, $30 children): Antigua's famous "pirate ship," the *Jolly Roger,* is one of the island's most popular attractions. You're taken for a fun-filled day of sightseeing and snorkeling, plus dancing on the poop deck (members of the crew teach passengers how to dance calypso) and lunch, with drinks and barbecued steak, chicken, or lobster.

TOURING THROUGH LOCAL OPERATORS

Jolly Roger **Cruise:** If your ship doesn't offer this excursion, you can book it independently. Call ☎ **268/462-2064** at least a day or two ahead to make a booking. The ship berths at Redcliffe Quay, within walking distance of the cruise ship docks in St. John's. The daily cruises depart at 9:30am and return at 3pm.

ON YOUR OWN: WITHIN WALKING DISTANCE

If you don't want to go to English Harbour, you can stay in St. John's to shop and explore. All of its minor attractions can be reached on foot from the cruise ship dock. The people in town may impress you, if not the town itself. They're helpful, have a sense of humor, and will guide you in the right direction if you've lost your way.

The **market** in the southern part of St. John's is colorful and interesting, especially on Saturday morning, when vendors are busy selling their fruits and vegetables and gossiping. The partially open-air market lies at the lower end of Market Street.

The Anglican **St. John's Cathedral,** between Long Street and Newgate Street at Church Lane, has had a disastrous history. Originally built in 1683, it was replaced in 1745 by a stone structure, which was destroyed by an earthquake in 1843. The present pitch-pine interior dates from 1847. The interior was being restored in 1973 when another earthquake badly damaged the twin towers. The towers and the southern section have since been restored.

The **Museum of Antigua and Barbuda,** at Market and Church streets (☎ 268/462-1469), traces the history of the nation from its geological birth to the present day. Housed in the old Court House building dating from 1750, exhibits include a wattle-and-daub house model, African-Caribbean pottery, and utilitarian objects of daily life. It's open Monday to Friday from 8:30am to 4pm, Saturday from 10am to 1pm. Admission is free.

The 3½-acre **Antigua and Barbuda Botanical Gardens,** at the corner of Nevis and Temple streets (☎ 268/462-1007), was established in 1893 in the Green Belt of the capital. As you enter, you can't miss the unfolding majesty of an 80-year-old ficus tree, contrasting sharply with the rolling lawns. The melodic sounds of tree frogs and birds emanate from the rainforest hollow, which is filled with trees draped with lianas. Ferns, tropical blossoms, herbal plants, dripping philodendrons, rare bromeliads, and a colorful carpet of flowers also await the visitor. Open daily from 9am to 6pm. Admission is by a minimum donation of $2.

ON YOUR OWN: BEYOND WALKING DISTANCE

One of the major attractions of the eastern Caribbean, **Nelson's Dockyard National Park** (☎ 268/460-1379) sits 11 miles southeast of St. John's on one of the world's safest harbors, and is open daily from 8am to 6pm. (Admission $5 per person to tour the dockyard; children under 13 free.) The centerpiece of the national park is the only existing example of a Georgian naval base. English ships used the harbor as a refuge from hurricanes as early as 1671, and Admiral Nelson made it his headquarters from 1784 to 1787. The dockyard played a leading role in the era of privateers, pirates, and great sea battles in the 18th century.

The restored dockyard is sometimes known as a Caribbean Williamsburg. Its colonial naval buildings stand now as they did when Nelson was here. Nelson never lived at **Admiral House** (☎ 268/463-1379), however, which was built in 1855 and has been turned into a museum of nautical memorabilia. Admission is $2.

The park itself is well worth exploring. It's filled with sandy beaches and tropical vegetation, including various species of cactus and mangroves that shelter a migrating colony of African cattle egrets. Nature trails (costing an additional $2.50) expose the vegetation and coastal scenery. You'll also find archeological sites that date back to before the Christian era. Tours of the dockyard last 15 to 20 minutes, but tours along nature trails can last anywhere from 30 minutes to 5 hours.

For an eagle's eye view of English Harbour, take a taxi up to the top of **Shirley Heights,** directly to the east of the dockyard. Still standing are Palladian arches, once part of a barracks. The **Block House** was put up as a stronghold in case of siege. The nearby Victorian cemetery contains an obelisk monument to the men of the 54th Regiment.

On a low hill overlooking Nelson's Dockyard, **Clarence House** (☎ 268/463-1026) was built by English stonemasons to accommodate Prince William Henry, who later became King William IV. The future monarch stayed here while in command of HMS

Pegasus in 1787. The house is at present the country home of the governor of Antigua and Barbuda, and is open to visitors when His Excellency is not in residence. A care-taker will show you through (it's customary to tip). You'll see many pieces of furniture on loan from the National Trust. Princess Margaret and Lord Snowdon stayed here on their honeymoon.

Take a taxi from English Harbour 2¹/₂ miles east to the **Dow's Hill Interpretation Center** (☎ **268/460-1053**), which offers a multimedia journey through six periods of the island's history. You'll learn about the Amerindian hunters, the British military, and the struggles connected with slavery. It's open 9am to 5pm daily, and admission, in-cluding the multimedia show, is $5 for adults, $2 for children under 16. A belvedere provides a panoramic view of the park, and a footpath leads to **Fort Barclay,** a fine specimen of old-time military engineering at the entrance to English Harbour. The path starts just outside the dockyard gate; the fort is about half a mile away.

In Brown's Bay Mill, near Freetown, the partially restored **Harmony Hall** (☎ **268/460-4120**) 1843 plantation house and sugar mill overlooks Nonsuch Bay, making it an ideal lunch stopover or shopping expedition. It displays Antigua's best selection of Caribbean arts and crafts, and in November hosts the annual Caribbean Craft Fair. Lunch, served daily from noon to 4pm, features Green Island lobster, flying fish, and other specialties. The place is special and worth the effort to reach it. Follow the signs along the road to Freetown and Half Moon Bay. You'll have to negotiate the fare for the 40-minute taxi ride from St. John's, which can range from $20 to $30.

On the way back to your cruise ship from English Harbour, ask your taxi driver to take you along the 20-some-mile circular route down ✪ **Fig Tree Drive,** across the main mountain range of Antigua. Although rough and very potholed in places, it's the island's most scenic drive. Some of the steep hillsides are so lush they evoke a rainforest. The drive passes through tropical settings and fishing villages along the southern coast. Nearly every hamlet has a little battered church and lots of goats and children running about. There are also the ruins of several old sugar mills. However, don't expect fig trees—*fig* is the Antiguan word for bananas.

SHOPPING

Most shops in St. John's are clustered on St. Mary's Street or High Street, lying within an easy walk of the cruise ship docks. There are many duty-free items for sale here, in-cluding English woolens and linens. You can also purchase Antiguan specialties, such as original pottery, local straw work, Antigua rum, hand-printed local designs on fab-rics, floppy foldable hats, and shell curios.

If you want an island-made **bead necklace,** don't bother to go shopping; just lie on any beach and a "bead lady" will find you.

Specialty shops worth exploring include **Caribelle Batik,** Redcliffe Street, for ba-tik and tie-dye items, silk dresses and separates, jewelry, and scarves; **Island Hopper,** Jardine Court, St. Mary's Street, for unusual T-shirts, spices, coffees, handcrafts, and casual wear; and **The Scent Shop,** Lower High Street, for crystal and perfumes (it's the island's oldest perfume shop).

Located at the cruise dock, **Heritage Quay,** Antigua's first shopping-and-entertainment center, is a multimillion-dollar complex featuring some 40 duty-free shops and a vendors' arcade where local artists and craftspeople display their wares. Shops feature artwork, china and crystal, Swiss-made watches, and a great selection of swimwear. Restaurants offer a range of cuisine and views of St. John's Harbour. A food court serves visitors who prefer local specialties in an informal setting.

Redcliffe Quay, near Heritage Quay, was a slave-trading quarter that filled up with grog shops and a variety of merchants after abolition. Now it has been redeveloped and

Port Tip: Beach Safety

It's unwise to have your fun in the sun at what appears to be a deserted beach. You could be the victim of a mugging. Also, readers increasingly complain of beach vendors hustling everything from jewelry to T-shirts. The beaches are open to all, so hotels can't restrain these bothersome peddlers.

contains a number of the most interesting shops in town, selling batiks and accessories, casual and dressy clothing, art, herbs, and spices, and black opal, imperial topaz, and other exotic gemstone jewelry designs by the well-known Hans Smit.

BEACHES

Antigua is beaches, beaches, and more beaches. Some are superior, and all are public. There's a lovely one at **Pigeon Point,** in Falmouth Harbour, about a 4-minute taxi ride from Admiral's Inn. The fine beach at **Dickenson Bay,** near the Rex Halcyon Cove Hotel, is a center for water sports; for a break, you can enjoy over-the-water meals and drinks on the hotel's Warri Pier.

There are more beaches at the Curtain Bluff resort, where long **Carlisle Beach** is set against a backdrop of coconut palms. **Morris Bay** attracts snorkelers. The beach at **Long Bay** is on the somewhat remote eastern coast, but most visitors consider it worth the effort. The famous **Half Moon Bay** attracts blue bloods to its mile-long stretch of sand. **Runaway Beach** is one of Antigua's most popular; its white sands make it worth fighting the crowds. **Five Islands** is actually a quartet of remote beaches with brown sands and coral reefs, located near the Hawksbill Hotel.

Taxis will take you from the cruise ship dock in St. John's to your choice of beach, but remember to make arrangements to be picked up at an agreed-upon time. A typical fare to Pigeon Point or Long Bay, both about 15 miles (25 minutes) from St. John's, is $20 per car. To Runaway, a distance of only 3 miles (5 minutes), the charge is $8 per car. For Five Islands, 6 miles or 10 minutes away, the fare is $12. Confirm all fares with the driver before setting out.

SPORTS

GOLF   The 18-hole, par-70 **Cedar Valley Golf Club,** Friar's Hill Road (☎ 268/462-0161), is 3 miles east of St. John's, a 5-minute, $12 taxi ride from the cruise dock. The island's largest golf course, with panoramic views of Antigua's northern coast, it was designed by the late Richard Aldridge to fit the contours of the area.

SCUBA DIVING   You can arrange a dive through **Dive Antigua,** at the Rex Halcyon Cove, Dickenson Bay (☎ 268/462-3483), Antigua's oldest and most experienced dive operation. It's located about a 10-minute or $6 taxi ride from the cruise ship dock.

WINDSURFING   Located at the Lord Nelson Beach Hotel on Dutchman's Bay, **Windsurfing Antigua** (☎ 268/462-9463) will accommodate beginners, intermediates, and "shredders" alike. It's about a $6 or 5-mile ride from the cruise ship dock.

GREAT LOCAL RESTAURANTS & BARS

Most cruise passengers dine either in St. John's or at nearby English Harbour or Shirley Heights. Reservations usually aren't needed for lunch unless it's a heavy cruise ship arrival day. In that case, call from the dock when you come ashore.

IN ST. JOHN'S   Big Banana Holding Company, on Redcliffe Quay (☎ 268/462-2621), serves the best pizza on the island in what used to be a slave quarters (you can get a great frothy coconut or banana crush, too, as well as overstuffed baked potatoes, fresh fruit salad, or conch salad); **Hemingway's,** on St. Mary's Street (☎ 268/462-2763), has an upper veranda and serves salads, sandwiches, burgers, sautéed filets of fish, pastries, ice cream, and an array of brightly colored tropical drinks.

AT ENGLISH HARBOUR   Admiral's Inn, in Nelson's Dockyard (☎ 268/460-1027), is housed in a 1788 building and features a menu that changes every day but usually features pumpkin soup and a choice of four or five main courses, such as local red snapper, grilled steak, or lobster. The service is agreeable and the setting heavy on atmosphere.

AT SHIRLEY HEIGHTS   Shirley Heights Lookout (☎ 268/460-1785) is the best alternative to the Admiral's Inn. In the 1790s, the building was the lookout station for unfriendly ships heading toward English Harbour; today, it offers such favorites as grilled lobster in lime butter and garlic-flavored shrimp. You can order less expensive hamburgers and sandwiches in the pub downstairs.

2 Aruba

Aruba, in the Dutch Leewards, is one of the most popular destinations in the Caribbean. Until its beaches were "discovered" in the 1970s, though, Aruba was an almost forgotten outpost of Holland, mostly valued for its oil refineries and salt factories. Aruba became a self-governed part of the Netherlands in 1986 and has its own royally appointed governor and an elected parliament. Today it's favored for the lunar landscapes of its desertlike terrain, spectacular beaches, constant sunshine, and gambling.

Just 6 miles at its widest point and 20 at its longest, Aruba is shaped more or less like a triangle; one side faces west and is home to the hotels and beaches, and along the southern side are the airport, capital city of Oranjestad, and an oil refinery. It's Aruba's northern half that is wild and woolly—a dry, windswept collage of cacti, rock, and the island's signature divi-divi trees.

The capital, **Oranjestad,** isn't a picture-postcard port, but it has glittering casinos, lots of shopping, and one of the Caribbean's finest stretches of beach. With only 17 inches of rainfall annually, Aruba is dry and sunny almost year-round, and trade winds keep it from becoming unbearably hot. The air is clean and exhilarating, like that of Palm Springs, California. Aruba also lies outside the path of hurricanes that batter islands to the north.

Its population of about 90,000 is culturally diverse, with roots in Holland, Portugal, Spain, Venezuela, India, Pakistan, and Africa.

Frommer's Favorite Aruba Experiences

- **Rent a Jeep or do a Jeep tour:** There's more to Aruba than a 7-mile strip of oceanfront high-rise hotels and wide white-sand beach, and this is the way to see it. (See "Shore Excursions" and "On Your Own: Touring by Rental Jeep," below.)
- **Take an *Atlantis* submarine trip:** A real submarine takes you down 150 feet to see the undersea world (see "Shore Excursions," below).

COMING ASHORE   Cruise ships arrive at the Aruba Port Authority, a modern terminal with a tourist information booth and the inevitable duty-free shops. From the pier it's just a 5-minute walk to the major shopping districts of downtown Oranjestad. If you opted not to take one of the shore excursions, you can make your way around on your own, allowing some time for Aruba's famous beach (just a 5- to 10-minute taxi ride away) in between luncheon stopovers and shopping.

CURRENCY   The currency is the **Aruba florin (AFl),** which is divided into 100 cents. Silver coins are in denominations of 5, 10, 25, and 50 cents and 1 and 2¹/₂

Frommer's Ratings: Aruba					
	Poor	Fair	Good	Excellent	Outstanding
Overall Experience					✓
Shore Excursions			✓		
Activities Close to Port				✓	
Beaches & Water Sports					✓
Shopping				✓	
Dining/Bars				✓	

florins. The 50-cent piece, the square "yotin," is Aruba's best-known coin. The exchange rate is 1.77 AFl to US$1 (1 AFl is worth about 56¢). Unless otherwise stated, prices quoted in this section are in U.S. dollars.

INFORMATION   For information, go to the **Aruba Tourism Authority,** 172 L.G. Smith Blvd., Oranjestad (☎ 297/8-21019). Open Monday to Saturday from 9am to 5pm.

LANGUAGE   The official language here is Dutch, but nearly everybody speaks English. The language of the street is often Papiamento, a patois. Spanish is also widely spoken.

GETTING AROUND

BY RENTAL CAR   It's easy to rent a car or four-wheel-drive vehicle and explore Aruba (I don't recommend renting a scooter or motorcycle, though, unless you plan on keeping to the paved roads only). You won't have much trouble finding your way around, but if you really want to explore Aruba's rough, moon-like hinterland, you need to rent a Jeep. The rental agencies are just outside the airport's main terminal. Try **Budget Rent-a-Car,** 1 Kolibristraat (☎ 800/472-3325 in the U.S., or 297/8-28600); **Hertz,** 142 L. G. Smith Blvd. (☎ 800/654-3001 in the U.S., or 297/8-24545); or **Avis,** 14 Kolibristraat (☎ 800/331-1084 in the U.S., or 297/8-23496).

BY TAXI   Taxis don't have meters, but fares are fixed. Tell the driver your destination and ask the fare before getting in. The main office is on Sands Street between the bowling center and Taco Bell. A **dispatch office** is located at Bosabao 41 (☎ 297/8-22116). A ride from the cruise terminal to most of the beach resorts, including those at Palm Beach, costs about $8 to $16 per car, plus a small tip. A maximum of five passengers is allowed. It's next to impossible to locate a taxi on some parts of the island, so when traveling to a remote area or restaurant, ask the taxi driver to pick you up at a certain time. Some English-speaking drivers are available as guides. A 1-hour tour (and you don't need much more than that) is offered at $35 per hour for a maximum of four passengers.

BY BUS   Aruba has excellent bus service, with regular daily service from 6am to midnight. The round-trip fare between the beach hotels and Oranjestad is about $2. Try to have exact change. Buses stop across the street from the cruise terminal on L. G. Smith Boulevard and will take you to any of the hotel resorts or the beaches along the West End.

SHORE EXCURSIONS

✪ **Four-Wheel-Drive Backcountry Aruba Tour** ($72, 6 hours): Just like the solo tour described above, but this version does the tour in a convoy of four-passenger sports utility vehicles (with you behind the wheel). A stop is made for lunch and some swimming. If you don't have the gumption to go it alone but you're still looking for some adventure, this is a great alternative.

Aruba

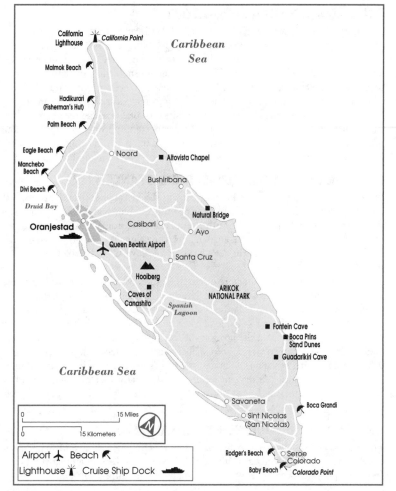

⭘ *Atlantis* **Submarine Journey** ($72 adults, $36 children 4 to 16; 2 hours): One of Aruba's most diverting pastimes, an underwater journey on the submarine *Atlantis* is a great opportunity for non-divers to witness firsthand the underwater life of a coral reef. Passengers submerge to about 150 feet without ever getting wet. The submarine departs from the Oranjestad harbor front every hour on the hour, Tuesday to Sunday from 10am to 2pm. Each tour includes a 25-minute transit by catamaran to Barcadera Reef, 2 miles southeast of Aruba, a site chosen for its huge variety of underwater flora and fauna. At the reef, participants transfer to the submarine for a 1-hour underwater tour and lecture. Book this through your cruise ship or make advance reservations with *Atlantis*. The company's offices are at Seaport Village Marina (opposite the Sonesta) in Oranjestad.

Aruba Bus Tour ($26, 3 hours): City and countryside air-conditioned bus tour takes passengers along part of Aruba's wild and woolly windward coastline, to the Natural Bridge (a rocky "bridge" cut by the sea and wind) and the Casibari rock formations, as well as along Aruba's bustling hotel strip.

TOURING WITH LOCAL OPERATORS

Catamaran Cruise/Snorkeling: De Palm Tours, L. G. Smith Blvd. 142, in Oranjestad
(☎ 297/8-24400), combines boat rides with snorkeling. For $40 per person, they'll
take you on a 1¹/₂-hour "fun cruise" aboard a catamaran, after which passengers stop
for 3 hours at the company's private De Palm Island for snorkeling. Lunch and an open
bar aboard are included in the price. If there are enough takers, the tour leaves daily at
10am and returns at 4pm, just in time to return to the cruise ship. De Palm also offers a 1-hour glass-bottomed-boat cruise that visits two coral reefs and the German shipwreck *Antilla*. The cruise costs about $18 per person and operates Tuesday and
Wednesday. (Many lines offer this tour in two separate parts; the cruise and snorkeling is one tour and the glass-bottomed boat ride to the *Antilla* is another.)

ON YOUR OWN: WITHIN WALKING DISTANCE

Bustling **Oranjestad,** the capital and port, attracts shoppers rather than sightseers. The
town has a very Caribbean flavor, with both Spanish and Dutch architecture. The main
thoroughfare, Lloyd G. (L. G.) Smith Boulevard, runs from the airport along the
waterfront and on to Palm Beach, changing its name along the way to J. E. Irausquin
Boulevard. Most visitors cross the road heading for **Caya G. F. Betico Croes,** where
they find the best shopping.

After a shopping trip, you might return to the harbor, where fishing boats and schooners, many from Venezuela, are moored. Nearly all newcomers to Aruba like to take a
picture of **Schooner Harbor.** Colorful boats are docked along the quay, and boatpeople
display their wares in open stalls. The local patois predominates. A little farther along, fresh
seafood is sold directly from the boats at the fish market. On the sea side, you'll find
Wilhelmina Park, named after Queen Wilhelmina of the Netherlands. A tropical garden has been planted here along the water, and there's a sculpture of the Queen Mother.

Aside from shopping, Aruba's major attraction is **Palm Beach,** among the finest
beaches in the Caribbean. Most of Aruba's high-rise hotels sit in a Las Vegas–style strip
along the pure white sand.

ON YOUR OWN: TOURING BY RENTAL JEEP

The best way to see all of Aruba and its intriguing terrain—a dry, windswept collage
of cacti, rock, and the island's signature divi-divi trees—is to ✪ **rent a four-wheel drive
Jeep.** You can rent a convertible Suzuki Samurai from the airport for about $60 to $70
per day, and share the expense with another couple to cut costs. Car-rental companies
will give you a map highlighting the best routes to reach the attractions.

Here's a good route to follow: Following the system of roads that circle the perimeter of the island, start your journey clockwise from the airport. Head back past the hotel
strip and on to the island's northwestern-most point. Here, the **California Lighthouse,**
named for a ship that wrecked in the area nearly a century ago, affords sweeping 360-
degree views of the island. (Tour the island counterclockwise and you'll hit the Lighthouse in time to watch the magnificent sunset melt into the sea.)

By the time you reach the Lighthouse, you've already entered Aruba's twilight zone.
From here on, your four-wheel-drive adventure will take you into the island's moonlike
terrain, past huge heaps of giant boulders and barren rocky coastlines. The smooth, well-
maintained road system that links together the hotel strip and Oranjestad transforms itself into a single band of rubble, and the calm, bright turquoise sea turns rough and rowdy.

Reaching the **Alto Vista Chapel,** about 5 miles or so from the Lighthouse, chances
are a thin film of red dust has already coated you and the Jeep. But don't let that stop
you from having a peek inside the quaint pale-yellow church that sits atop a small hill.
From its solitary perch, enjoy breathtaking views.

Farther along on the northern coast, you'll approach the hulking ruins of the **Bushiribana Gold Smelter** amid a desolate stretch of parched landscape. Don't bother stopping for a closer look at its graffitied walls, though; its impact is more powerful from a distance.

Just beyond it is the **Natural Bridge,** one of Aruba's most popular attractions. Over the centuries, the crashing ocean surf and whipping wind crafted this "bridge" out of the vulnerable coral rock. The **Thirst Aid Station** restaurant sits nearby, and with its campy colored lights and used-car-lot metallic fringes strung across the ceiling, you may find it to be an interesting site in itself (it's also one of the few places to grab a couple of cold drinks and a sandwich before hitting the road again).

Just before the Gold Smelter and Natural Bridge, keep a look out for **secluded beach coves.** While some are littered with plastic bottles and debris, just as many are pristine patches of paradise. Often just 50 to 100 feet from the road, the craggy coast opens up to random wedges of protected beach and shallow water, perfect for a dip.

Next, veer off towards the center of the island to check out the bizarre **Ayó and Casibari rock formations.** Somewhat of a mystery even to geologists, it's as though the random piles of massive boulders have been dropped from the sky. If you can handle the gusting winds, climb to the top of the mound for great views. Be sure to look for the ancient **Amerindian drawings** painted on the rocks at Ayó.

In the center of the island, **Hooiberg** is affectionately known as "The Haystack." It's Aruba's most outstanding landmark. On a clear day, you can see Venezuela from atop this 541-foot hill.

Farther east along the desolate northern coast is a series of caves punched into the cliffsides of the area's mesas. Have a look inside the graffiti-covered, bat-inhabited **Guadirikiri, Fontein, and Tunnel of Love caves;** rent flashlights for $6 apiece (there's no admission charge).

Heading southeast toward Aruba's behemoth oil refinery is **Baby Beach,** at the island's easternmost point. Like a great big bathtub, this shallow bowl of warm turquoise water is protected by an almost complete circle of rock, and is a great place for a peaceful dip after a sweaty day behind the wheel.

Before returning to the ship, in San Nicolas you might want to grab a cool drink at Aruba's most famous local dive, **Charlie's Bar and Restaurant** at Blvd. Veen Zeppenveldstraat 56 (Main Street). Charlie's dates from 1941 and qualifies through its decor and history as one of the most authentic and raffish bars in the West Indies. It's also perhaps the most overly decorated bar, sporting an array of memorabilia and local souvenirs.

SHOPPING

Aruba is a shopper's paradise. An easy walk from the cruise terminal, Oranjestad's half-mile-long **Caya G. F. Betico Croes** compresses six continents into one main, theme-park–like shopping street. While this is not technically a free port, the duty is only 3.3%, and there's no sales tax. You'll find the usual array of jewelry, liquor, Swiss watches, German and Japanese cameras, English bone china and porcelain, French perfume, British woolens, Indonesian specialties, Madeira embroidery, and Dutch, Swedish, and Danish silver and pewter. Delft blue pottery is an especially good buy, as are Edam and Gouda cheeses from Holland. Stamp collectors can purchase colorful and artistic issues at the post office in Oranjestad.

The **Alhambra Moonlight Shopping Center,** L. G. Smith Boulevard, next to the Alhambra Casino, blends international shops, outdoor marketplaces, cafes, and restaurants, and sells everything from fine jewelry, chocolates, and perfume to imported craft items, leather goods, clothing, and lingerie.

The Seaport Village/Seaport Market, overlooking Oranjestad's harbor, at L. G. Smith Blvd. 82, is Aruba's densest concentration of shopping options, with several bars and cafes, two casinos, and at least 200 purveyors of fashion, gift items, sporting goods, liquors, perfumes, and photographic supplies.

BEACHES

The western and southern shores, known as the Turquoise Coast, attract sun seekers to Aruba. An $8 taxi ride from the cruise terminal will get you to Palm Beach and Eagle Beach, the two best beaches on the island. The latter is closer to Oranjestad. Aruba's beaches are open to the public, so you can spread your towel anywhere along this 7-mile stretch of uninterrupted sugar-white sand, which also includes Manchebo Beach or Druid Bay Beach. But you will be charged for using the facilities at any of the hotels on this strip.

In total contrast to this leeward side, the northern, or windward, shore is rugged and wild.

SPORTS

GOLF   Aruba's long-awaited Tierra del Sol Golf Course (☎ 297/8-67800) opened in 1995. Designed by the Robert Trent Jones II Group, this 18-hole, par-71, 6,811-yard course is on the northwest coast, near the California Lighthouse. It was designed to combine the beauty of the island's indigenous flora, such as the swaying divi-divi tree, with lush greens. The course is managed by Hyatt Resorts Caribbean. Greens fees are $120 in winter, including golf cart, or $75 after 3pm. Off-season, the fees drop to $75, or $55 after 3pm. The course is open daily from 6am to 7pm.

SCUBA DIVING & SNORKELING   Scuba divers can explore stunning marine life, with endless varieties of coral, as well as tropical fish in infinite hues. At some points visibility is up to 90 feet. Most divers head for the German freighter *Antilla,* which was scuttled in the early years of World War II off the northwestern tip of Aruba, near Palm Beach. Red Sails Sports, Palm Beach (☎ 297/8-61603), is the island's best water-sports center, offering sailing, windsurfing, water-skiing, and scuba diving. The resort scuba-diving course is tailored for cruise ship passengers. Certified divers pay $36 and up for one-tank excursions.

WINDSURFING   Divi Winds Center, J. E. Irausquin Blvd. 41 (☎ 297/8-23300, ext. 623), near the Tamarind Aruba Beach Resort, is the island's windsurfing headquarters. Equipment rents for $15 per hour or $30 per half day, $50 all day. The resort is on the tranquil (Caribbean) side of the island, away from the fierce Atlantic waves. You can also arrange Sunfish lessons or rent snorkeling gear. The operation has another location at the Hyatt.

GAMBLING

Although cruise ships have their own casinos, you can also try your luck ashore at roulette, craps, blackjack, Caribbean stud poker, baccarat, and the ubiquitous one-armed bandits. Aruba's gaming establishments are second only to San Juan in the Caribbean. Most casinos here are open day and night, thus drawing both cruise ship passengers and land-based vacationers. They're mainly located in the big hotels on Palm Beach, an $8 to $12 taxi ride from the cruise terminal.

The casino at the Holiday Inn Aruba Beach Resort, L. G. Smith Blvd. 230 (☎ 297/8-67777), wins the prize for all-around gambling action. It keeps its doors open daily from 9am to 4am.

Closer to Oranjestad, the Crystal Casino at the Aruba Sonesta Resort & Casino at Seaport Village (☎ 297/8-36000) is open 24 hours. It evokes European casinos with its luxurious furnishings, ornate moldings, marble, brass, gold leaf, and crystal chandeliers.

Casino Masquerade, at the Radisson Aruba Caribbean Resort & Casino, J. E. Irausquin Blvd. 81 (☎ **297/8-66555**), is the newest casino in Aruba. Located in the center of the high-rise hotel area, it's open daily from 10am to 4am.

The **Casablanca Casino** occupies a large room adjacent to the lobby of the Wyndham Hotel and Resort, J. E. Irausquin Blvd. (☎ **297/8-64466**). **Casino Copacabana,** in the island's most spectacular hotel, Hyatt Regency Aruba, L. G. Smith Blvd. 85 (☎ **297/8-61234**), evokes France's Côte d'Azur. These two are open throughout the day, accommodating cruise ship passengers.

Outdrawing them all, however, is the **Royal Cabaña Casino,** at the La Caba a All-Suite Beach Resort & Casino, J. E. Irausquin Blvd. 250 (☎ **297/8-79000**), the third largest in the Bahamian-Caribbean region. It's known for its three-in-one operation, combining a restaurant, showcase cabaret theater, and nightclub. The casino, the largest on Aruba, has 33 tables and games plus 320 slot machines.

More than just a casino, the **Alhambra,** L. G. Smith Blvd. 47 (☎ **297/8-35000**), offers a collection of boutiques, along with an inner courtyard modeled after an 18th-century Dutch village. The desert setting of Aruba seems appropriate for this Moorish-style building, with its serpentine mahogany columns, repeating arches, and sea-green domes. The casino and its satellites are open daily from 10am until very late at night.

The **Aruba Palm Beach Resort & Casino,** J. E. Irausquin Blvd. 79 (☎ **297/8-23900**), opens its slots at 9am and its other games at 1pm. **Americana Aruba Beach Resort & Casino,** J. E. Irausquin Blvd. 83 (☎ **297/8-64500**), opens daily at noon for slots, blackjack, and roulette; however, other games aren't available until 8pm, when most cruise ships have departed.

GREAT LOCAL RESTAURANTS & BARS

If there are a lot of cruise ships in port, call from a pay phone in the cruise ship terminal to make a reservation. If there aren't many ships around, chances are you can just walk in. All restaurants listed are in Oranjestad.

Boonoonoonoos, Wilhelminastraat 18 (☎ **297/8-31888**), is in an old-fashioned Aruban house on the capital's main shopping street, and features dishes from throughout the Caribbean. ✪ **Chez Mathilde,** Havenstraat 23 (☎ **297/8-34968**), Oranjestad's French restaurant, is expensive, but most agree that it's worth the price, especially those who order the chef's bouillabaisse, made with more than a dozen different sea creatures. **The Paddock,** 13 L. G. Smith Blvd. (☎ **297/8-32334**), is a cafe and bistro with a Dutch aesthetic and ambience and a menu of sandwiches, salads, fish, and more. **The Waterfront Crabhouse,** Seaport Market, L. G. Smith Boulevard. (☎ **297/8-36767**), is a seafood restaurant set at the end of a shopping mall.

3 Barbados

No port of call in the southern Caribbean can compete with Barbados when it comes to diversions, attractions, and fine dining. But what really puts Barbados on world tourist maps are its seemingly endless stretches of pink-and-white sandy beaches, among the best in the entire Caribbean Basin.

This Atlantic outpost was one of the most staunchly loyal members of the British Commonwealth for over 300 years, and although it gained its independence in 1966, British-isms still remain—the accent is Brit, driving is on the left, and Queen Elizabeth is still officially the head of state.

Frommer's Ratings: Barbados					
	Poor	Fair	Good	Excellent	Outstanding
Overall Experience				✓	
Shore Excursions			✓		
Activities Close to Port			✓		
Beaches & Water Sports			✓		
Shopping			✓		
Dining/Bars			✓		

Originally operated on a plantation economy that made its aristocracy rich, the island is the most easterly in the Caribbean, floating in the mid-Atlantic like a great coral reef and ringed with beige-sand beaches. Cosmopolitan Barbados has the densest population of any island in the Caribbean, a sports tradition that avidly pursues cricket, and a loyal group of return visitors who appreciate its many stylish, medium-sized hotels. Overall, service is usually extremely good. Topography varies from rolling hills and savage waves on the eastern (Atlantic) coast to densely populated flatlands, rows of hotels and apartments, and sheltered beaches in the southwest.

The people in Barbados are called *Bajans,* and you'll see this term used everywhere.

Frommer's Favorite Barbados Experiences

- **Rent a car for a Barbados road trip:** Seventeenth-century churches, tropical flowers, snorkeling, great views, and more are just a rental car ride away (see "On Your Own: Beyond Walking Distance," below).
- **Visit Gun Hill Signal Station:** If you've got less time, hire a taxi or rent car, and go to Gun Hill for panoramic views of the island (see "On Your Own: Beyond Walking Distance," below).
- **Dive deep on a submarine**: Two 28- and 48-passenger sightseeing submarines make several dives daily from 9am to 6pm (see "Shore Excursions," below).

COMING ASHORE   The cruise ship pier, a short drive from Bridgetown, the capital, is one of the best docking facilities in the southern Caribbean. You can walk right into the modern cruise ship terminal, which has car rentals, taxi services, sightseeing tours, and a tourist information office, plus shops and scads of vendors (see "Shopping," below). You'll also find credit-card telephones, and phone cards and stamps for sale.

If you want to go into Bridgetown instead of the beach, you can take a hot, dusty walk of at least 30 minutes, or catch a taxi. The one-way fare ranges from $4 on up.

CURRENCY   The **Barbados dollar (BD$)** is the official currency, available in $100, $20, $10, and $5 notes and $1, 25¢, and 10¢ silver coins, plus 5¢ and 1¢ copper coins. The exchange rate is BD$1.98 to US$1 (BD$1 is worth about 51¢). Unless otherwise specified, prices in this section are given in U.S. dollars. Most stores take traveler's checks or U.S. dollars, so don't bother to convert them if you're here for only a day.

INFORMATION   The **Barbados Tourism Authority** is on Harbour Road (P.O. Box 242), Bridgetown, Barbados, W.I. (☎ 246/427-2623). Its cruise terminal office is always open when a cruise ship is in port.

LANGUAGE   English is spoken with an island lilt.

Barbados

Legend:
- Airport ✈
- Beach 🏖
- Church ⛪
- Lighthouse 🗼
- Cruise Ship Dock 🚢

North Point

Archer's Bay

River Bay

Stroud Bay

Cuckold Point

Harrison Point

ST. LUCY

Gay's Cove

Pico Teneriffe

Maycock's Bay

Fairfield

Coleton

Atlantic Ocean

Half Moon Fort

Six Men's Bay

Heywoods Beach

Morgan Lewis Beach

ST. PETER

Speightstown

Greenland

St. Andrew's Church

ST. ANDREW

Mullins Beach

Gibbs Beach

SCOTLAND

Turner's Hall Woods

Chalky Mount

Cattlewash

Tent Bay

Gold Coast

Lower Carlton

Bathsheba

ST. JAMES

ST. JOSEPH

Martin's Bay

Congor Rocks

Church Point

FOLKSTONE UNDERWATER PARK

Welchman Hall

Blackmans

ST. JOHN

Consett Bay

CULPEPPER ISLAND

Holetown

Paynes Bay

Sunset Crest

ST. THOMAS

Ragged Point Lighthouse

Lazaretto

Locust Hall

Three Houses

Kitridge Point

Prospect

Warrens

Bushy Park

Sandford

Bottom Bay

Paradise Beach

Brighton Beach

ST. MICHAEL

ST. GEORGE

ST. PHILIP

Long Bay

Black Rock

Marchfield

Beachy Head

Deep Water Harbour

Crane Beach

Queen's Park

CHRISTCHURCH

Bridgetown

Carlisle Bay

Needham's Point

Hastings

St. Lawrence

Tom Adams Hwy.

Grantley Adams International Airport

Rockley Beach

Worthing

Maxwell

Sandy Beach

Oistins

Long Bay

Casuarina Beach

Caribbean Sea

South Point

Silver Sands Beach

0   5 Miles

0   5 Kilometers

N

Caribbean Islands

Barbados

- Flower Forest of Barbados **3**
- Francia Plantation **5**
- Gun Hill Signal Station **6**
- Harrison's Cave **4**
- Sam Lord's Castle **7**
- St. James Church **1**
- Welchman Hall Gully **2**

GETTING AROUND

BY TAXI   They're not metered, but their rates are fixed by the government. They're identified by the letter *Z* on their license plates.

BY BUS   Blue-and-yellow **public buses** fan out from Bridgetown every 20 minutes or so onto the major routes; their destinations are marked on the front. Buses going south and east leave from Fairchild Street, and those going north and west depart from Lower Green and the Princess Alice Highway. Fares are BD$1.50 (75¢ U.S.) and exact change is required.

Privately owned **minibuses** run shorter distances and travel more frequently. These bright yellow buses display destinations on the bottom-left corner of the windshield. In Bridgetown, board at River Road, Temple Yard, and Probyn Street. Fare is BD$1.50 (75¢ U.S.).

BY RENTAL CAR   While it's a good way to see the island if you've got an adventurous streak and an easy-going attitude, before you decide to rent a car, keep in mind that driving is on the left side of the road and the signs are totally inadequate. There are several car rental agents at the cruise terminal (be sure you take a look at the car before signing on the dotted line).

SHORE EXCURSIONS

It's not easy to get around Barbados quickly and conveniently, so a shore excursion is a good idea here.

✪ **Submarine Trip** ($79, 2 hours): You no longer have to be an experienced diver to see what lives 150 feet below the surface of the sea around Barbados. All visitors can view the sea's wonders on air-conditioned submersibles that seat 28 to 48 passengers and make several dives daily from 9am to 6pm. Passengers are transported aboard a ferry boat from the waterfront in downtown Bridgetown to the submarine site, about a mile from the west coast of Barbados. The ride offers a view of the west coast of the island. The submarines have viewing ports, allowing you to see a rainbow of colors, tropical fish, plants, and even a shipwreck that lies upright and intact below the surface. The same company also offers cruises aboard an air-conditioned semisubmersible boat. These trips give you a snorkeler's view of the reef through large viewing windows without actually going under ($35 for adults, 2 hours).

Harrison's Cave ($33, 3 to 4 hours): Most cruise lines offer a tour to Harrison's Cave in the center of the island (see "On Your Own: Beyond Walking Distance," below, for details).

Barbados Highlights Bus Tour ($29, 3 hours): Tours take passengers by bus to Gun Hill Signal Station, St. John's Church and Sam Lord's Castle Resort (see "On Your Own: Beyond Walking Distance," below," for details).

TOURING THROUGH LOCAL OPERATORS

Island Tours/Eco Tours ($56 per person, 6 to 8 hours): Since most cruise lines don't really offer a comprehensive island tour, many passengers deal with one of the local tour companies. **Bajan Tours,** Glenayre, Locust Hall, St. George (☎ **246/437-9389**), offers an island tour that leaves between 8:30am and 9am, and returns to the ship before departure. It covers all the island's highlights. On Fridays, they conduct a heritage tour, focusing mainly on the island's major plantations and museums. On Tuesdays and Wednesdays, they offer an Eco Tour, which takes in the natural beauty of the island. Call ahead for information and to reserve a spot.

If you can afford it, **touring by taxi** is far more relaxing than the standardized bus tour. Nearly all Bajan taxi drivers are familiar with their island and like to show off their knowledge to visitors. The standard rate is about $17.50 per hour.

ON YOUR OWN: WITHIN WALKING DISTANCE

About the only thing you can walk to is the cruise terminal. The modern, pleasant complex has an array of duty-free shops and retail stores, plus many vendors selling arts and crafts, jewelry, liquor, china, crystal, electronics, perfume, and leather goods.

ON YOUR OWN: BEYOND WALKING DISTANCE

I don't recommend wasting too much time in Bridgetown—it's hot, dry, and dirty, and the honking horns of traffic jams only add to its woes. So unless you want to go shopping, you should spend your time exploring all the beauty the island has to offer.

Welchman Hall Gully, St. Thomas (Highway 2 from Bridgetown; ☎ 246/ 438-6671), is a lush tropical garden owned by the Barbados National Trust. The gully is 8 miles from the port and features some plants that were here when the English settlers landed in 1627. It can be reached by bus from the terminal.

All cruise ship excursions visit **Harrison's Cave,** Welchman Hall, St. Thomas (☎ 246/438-6640), Barbados's top tourist attraction. Here you can see a beautiful underground world from aboard an electric tram and trailer. If you'd like to go on your own, a taxi ride takes about 30 minutes and costs just under $20.

A mile from Harrison's Cave is the **Flower Forest,** Richmond Plantation, St. Joseph (☎ 246/433-8152). This old sugar plantation stands 850 feet above sea level near the western edge of the "Scotland district," in one of the most scenic parts of Barbados. The forest is 12 miles from the cruise terminal; one-way taxi fare is about $15.

A fine home still owned and occupied by descendants of the original owner, the **Francia Plantation,** St. George (☎ 246/429-0474), stands on a wooded hillside overlooking the St. George Valley. You can explore several rooms. The plantation lies about 20 miles from the port; one-way taxi fare is $20.

The **Gun Hill Signal Station,** Highway 4 (☎ 246/429-1358), one of two such stations owned and operated by the Barbados National Trust, is strategically placed on the highland of St. George and commands a panoramic view from east to west. Built in 1818, the station is 12 miles from the port; the one-way taxi ride costs $17.50.

Sam Lord's Castle Resort, Long Bay, St. Philip (☎ 246/423-7350), was built in 1820 by one of Barbados's most notorious scoundrels, Samuel Hall Lord. Legend says he made his money by luring ships onto the jagged, hard-to-detect rocks of Cobbler's Reef. You can explore the architecturally acclaimed centerpiece of this luxury resort, which has a private sandy beach. It's a $12 taxi ride from the cruise terminal.

TOURING BY RENTAL CAR

If you're patient with the lack of road signs, rent a car and spend the day exploring the island's interior. Worthwhile sites include the 17th-century **St. James' church** near Holetown, a humble yet awesome building made of limestone and surrounded by tropical poinsettia, frangi-pani, bougainvillea, and hibiscus plants. Next store is the **Folkestone Marine Park and Visitors Centre.** Tour the small museum there, and then head over to the adjacent beach and do some **snorkeling** (rentals are right there); just off shore are schools of brightly colored fish. Don't miss out on panoramic views of the island from the quaint **Gun Hill Signal Station** and check out the fascinating limestone caverns and the stalactites and stalagmites of **Harrison's Cave.** St. John's Church, built on a cliff 800 feet above the sea, is also not to be missed. Lunch along the way at beachside cafes along Barbados's Gold Coast, like the Fisherman's Pub and Beach Bar on Orange Street, in Speightown, and enjoy some fried fresh fish or curried chicken. Remember, driving is on the left and cars can be rented at the cruise terminal (ask to see the car first before paying).

SHOPPING

The **cruise terminal** contains an array of duty-free shops and retail stores, plus a plethora of vendors selling arts and crafts, jewelry, liquor, china, crystal, electronics, perfume, and leather goods. You'll find a wider selection and better prices in Bridgetown, however.

Good duty-free buys include cameras, watches, crystal, gold jewelry, bone china, cosmetics and perfumes, and liquor (including locally produced Barbados rum and liqueurs), along with tobacco products and British-made cashmere sweaters, tweeds, and sportswear. **Cave Shepherd,** Broad Street, Bridgetown, is the largest department store on Barbados and the best place to shop for tax-free merchandise.

Among Barbados handcrafts, **black-coral jewelry** is outstanding. Local clay potters turn out different products, some based on designs centuries old. Crafts include wall hangings made from grasses and dried flowers, straw mats, baskets, and bags with raffia embroidery. Bajan leatherwork includes handbags, belts, and sandals.

Some standout stores include **Articrafts,** Broad Street, Bridgetown, for Bajan arts and crafts, straw work, handbags, and bamboo items; **Best of Barbados,** in the Southern Palms, St. Lawrence Gap, Christ Church, which sells only products (coasters, mats, T-shirts, pottery, dolls and games, cookbooks, and other items) designed and/or made on Barbados; **Colours of De Caribbean,** the Waterfront Marina, Bridgetown, for tropical clothing, jewelry, and decorative objects; **Cotton Days,** Lower Bay Street, St. Michael, for casually elegant one-of-a-kind garments, suitable for cool nights and hot climes; **The Shell Gallery,** Carlton House, St. James, for the best collection of shells in the West Indies, featuring the shell art of Maureen Edghill, the finest artist in the field; and **Walker's Caribbean World,** St. Lawrence Gap, for many locally made items, as well as handcrafts from the Caribbean Basin.

BEACHES

Beaches on the island's western side—the luxury resort area called the **Gold Coast**—are far preferable to those on the surf-pounded Atlantic side. All Barbados beaches are open to the public, even those in front of the big resort hotels and private homes. The government requires that there be access to all beaches, via roads along the property line or through the hotel entrance.

ON THE WEST COAST (GOLD COAST)   Take your pick of the West Coast beaches, which are a 15-minute, $8 taxi ride from the cruise terminal. **Payne's Bay,** with access from the Coach House or the Bamboo Beach Bar, is a good beach for water sports, especially snorkeling. There's a parking area here. This beach can get rather crowded, but the beautiful bay makes it worth it. Directly south of Payne's Bay, at Fresh Water Bay, is a trio of fine beaches: **Brighton Beach, Brandon's Beach,** and **Paradise Beach.**

Church Point lies north of St. James Church, opening onto Heron Bay, site of the Colony Club Hotel. Although this beach can get crowded, it's one of the most scenic bays in Barbados, and the swimming is ideal. Retreat under some shade trees when you've had enough sun. You can also order drinks at the Colony Club's beach terrace.

Snorkelers in particular seek out the glassy blue waters by **Mullins Beach.** There are some shady areas. You can park on the main road. Order food and drink at the Mullins Beach Bar.

ON THE SOUTH COAST   Depending on traffic, South Coast beaches are usually easy to reach from the cruise terminal. Figure on an $8 taxi fare. **Sandy Beach,** reached from the parking lot on the Worthing main road, has tranquil waters opening onto a lagoon. This is a family favorite, with lots of screaming and yelling, especially on weekends. Food and drink are sold here.

Windsurfers are particularly fond of the trade winds that sweep across **Casuarina Beach,** even on the hottest summer days. Access is from Maxwell Coast Road, across the property of Casuarina Beach Hotel. This is one of the wider beaches on Barbados. The hotel has food and drink.

Silver Sands Beach is to the east of the town of Oistins, near the very southernmost point of Barbados, directly east of South Point Lighthouse and near the Silver Rock Hotel. This white sandy beach is a favorite with many Bajans, who probably want to keep it a secret from as many tourists as possible. (Tough luck, Bajans!) Windsurfing is good here, but not as good as at Casuarina Beach. You can buy drinks at Silver Rock Bar.

ON THE SOUTHEAST COAST   The southeast coast is known for its big waves, especially at **Crane Beach,** a white sandy stretch set against a backdrop of cliffs and palms. Prince Andrew owns a house overlooking this spectacular beach, and the Crane Beach Hotel towers above it from the cliffs. Crane Beach often appears in travel magazine articles about Barbados. It offers excellent body surfing, but this is ocean swimming, not the calm Caribbean, so be careful. At $17.50 from the cruise pier, the one-way taxi fare is relatively steep, so share a ride with some friends.

SPORTS

GOLF   The 18-hole championship golf course of the west coast **Sandy Lane Hotel,** St. James (☎ **246/432-1311**), is open to all. Greens fees are $135 in winter and $110 in summer for 18 holes, or $100 in winter and $80 in summer for nine holes. Carts and caddies are available. Make reservations the day before you arrive in Barbados or before you leave home. The course is a 20- to 25-minute taxi ride from the cruise terminal. The one-way fare is about $13.

HORSEBACK RIDING   Maintained by Swedish-born Elizabeth Roachford and her four daughters, **Caribbean International Riding Centre,** Cleland Plantation, Farley Hill, St. Andrew (☎ **246/422-7433**), offers riding for equestrians of all experience levels. The shortest ride is a 75-minute escorted trek through tropical forests, followed by a relaxing cool drink in the club room. The most scenic tour goes through the Gully Ride and continues out to a cliff with a panoramic view of almost the entire east coast of Barbados. Advance reservations are required. It's about a 20-minute or $10 taxi ride from the port.

SCUBA DIVING & SNORKELING   The clear waters off Barbados have a visibility of more than 100 feet most of the year, providing great views of lobsters, moray eels, sea fans, gorgonias, night anemones, octopuses, and more than 50 varieties of fish, as well as wrecks and coral. **The Dive Shop,** Pebbles Beach, Aquatic Gap, St. Michael (☎ **246/426-9947**), offers the best scuba diving on Barbados and also offers snorkeling trips. Sign up for scuba at a booth next to the dock. Visitors with reasonable swimming skills who have never dived before can also take a resort course. The Dive Shop provides transportation to and from the cruise terminal.

WINDSURFING   Experts say that Barbados windsurfing is as good as any this side of Hawaii. In fact, it's a very big business between November and April, when thousands of windsurfers from all over the world come here. **Silver Sands** is rated the best spot in the Caribbean for advanced windsurfing (skill rating five to six). **Barbados**

Windsurfing Club, at the Silver Sands Hotel in Christ Church (☎ 246/428-6001), gives lessons, and rents boards. To reach the center, take a taxi from the cruise terminal; it's a $10 one-way fare.

GREAT LOCAL RESTAURANTS & BARS

SOUTH OF BRIDGETOWN   Brown Sugar, Aquatic Gap, St. Michael (☎ 246/426-7684), is an alfresco restaurant in a turn-of-the-century bungalow. The chefs prepare some of the tastiest Bajan specialties on the island. Of the main dishes, Creole-broiled pepper chicken is popular, as are the stuffed crab backs.

ON THE SOUTH COAST   Sand Dollar, in the Bagshot House Hotel, St. Lawrence Coast Road, Christ Church (☎ 246/435-6956), offers well-prepared menu items such as well-seasoned peppersteak, Mount Gay ribs, brochettes of jerk shrimp, a succulent chicken with a honey rum sauce, and different versions of steak and lobster. **T.G.I. Boomers,** St. Lawrence Gap, Christ Church (4 miles south of Bridgetown along Highway 7 near Rockley Beach; ☎ 246/428-8439), offers seafood, steaks, and hamburgers. For lunch, try a daily Bajan special or a jumbo sandwich. A special 16-ounce daiquiri will put a glow on your afternoon. (All these restaurants are about an $8 one-way taxi ride from the cruise terminal.)

4 British Virgin Islands: Tortola & Virgin Gorda

With its small bays and hidden coves that were once havens for pirates, the British Virgin Islands are among the world's loveliest cruising grounds. This British colony has some 40 islands in the northeastern corner of the Caribbean about 60 miles east of Puerto Rico, most of them tiny rocks and cays. Only **Tortola, Virgin Gorda,** and **Jost Van Dyke** are of significant size. The other tiny islets have names like Fallen Jerusalem and Ginger. Norman Island is said to have been the prototype for Robert Louis Stevenson's *Treasure Island.* Blackbeard inspired the famous ditty by marooning 15 pirates and a bottle of rum on the rocky cay known as Deadman Bay. Yo ho ho.

Columbus came this way in 1493, but the British Virgins apparently made little impression on him. Although the Spanish and Dutch contested it, Tortola was officially annexed by the English in 1672. Today, these islands are a British colony, with their own elected government and a population of about 17,000.

The vegetation is varied and depends on the rainfall. In some parts, palms and mangos grow in profusion, whereas other places are arid and studded with cactus.

Many of the smaller cruise lines such as Seabourn, Windstar, and Windjammer Barefoot Cruises call at Tortola and the more scenic Virgin Gorda and Jost Van Dyke. Unlike the rigid programs at St. Thomas and other major docking ports, visits here are less structured, and each cruise line is free to pursue its own policy.

TORTOLA

Road Town, the colony's capital, sits about midway along the southern shore of 24-square-mile Tortola. Wickhams Cay, a 70-acre landfill development and marina, brought a massive yacht-chartering business to Road Town and transformed this sleepy village into a bustling center. If your ship isn't visiting Virgin Gorda but you want to, it's only a 12-mile trip from Tortola via boat, ferry, or launch.

The island's entire southern coast is characterized by rugged mountain peaks. On the northern coast are beautiful bays with white sandy beaches, banana trees, mangoes, and clusters of palms.

The British Virgin Islands

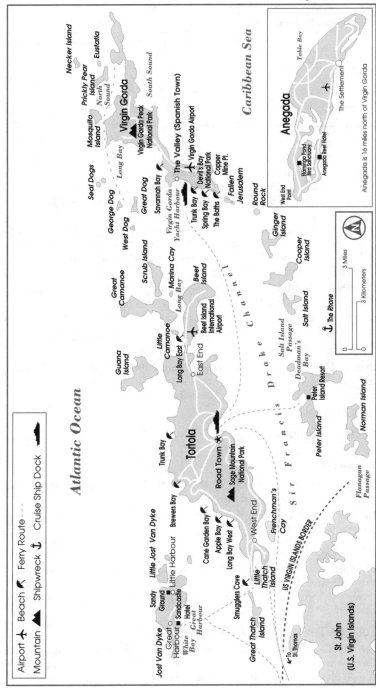

Airport ✈ Beach ➤ Ferry Route - - -
Mountain ▲ Shipwreck ⚓ Cruise Ship Dock ⚓

Atlantic Ocean

Necker Island
Eustatia
Prickly Pear Island
North Sound
South Sound
Mosquito Island
Virgin Gorda
Virgin Gorda Peak National Park
The Valley (Spanish Town)
Virgin Gorda Airport
Seal Dogs
Long Bay
George Dog
Great Dog
Savannah Bay
Virgin Gorda Yacht Harbour
Devil's Bay National Park
Copper Mine Pt.
Fallen Jerusalem
West Dog
Trunk Bay
Spring Bay
The Baths
Scrub Island
Marina Cay
Beef Island
Round Rock
Great Camanoe
Long Bay
Beef Island International Airport
Ginger Island
Little Camanoe
Long Bay East
East End
Cooper Island
Guana Island
Drake Channel
Salt Island
Salt Island Passage
The Rhone
Trunk Bay
Tortola
Road Town
Sage Mountain National Park
Deadman's Bay
Peter Island Resort
Sir Francis
Brewers Bay
Cane Garden Bay
Apple Bay
Long Bay West
West End
Frenchman's Cay
Peter Island
Norman Island
Little Jost Van Dyke
Little Harbour
Little Thatch Island
Smugglers Cove
Flanagan Passage
US VIRGIN ISLANDS BORDER
Sandy Ground
Sandcastle Hotel
Jost Van Dyke
Great Harbour
White Bay
Great Harbour
Great Thatch Island
To St. Thomas
St. John (U.S. Virgin Islands)

Anegada

Caribbean Sea

Table Bay
The Settlement
Flamingo Pond Bird Sanctuary
Anegada Reef Hotel
West End Point

Anegada is 16 miles north of Virgin Gorda

N

3 Miles
3 Kilometers
0
0

Frommer's Ratings: Tortola					
	Poor	Fair	Good	Excellent	Outstanding
Overall Experience				✓	
Shore Excursions			✓		
Activities Close to Port			✓		
Beaches & Water Sports			✓		
Shopping		✓			
Dining/Bars			✓		

Frommer's Favorite Tortola Experiences

- **Visit Bomba's Surfside Shack:** The oldest, most memorable bar on Tortola may not look like much, but it's the best party on the island (see "Great Local Restaurants & Bars," below).
- **Spend a day at Cane Garden Bay:** It's the best beach on the island, with palm trees, sand, and a great local restaurant for lunch and drinks (see "Beaches," below).
- **Take an island tour:** Open-air safari buses take you on a scenic journey around the island (see "Shore Excursions," below).

COMING ASHORE   Visiting cruise ships anchor at Wickhams Cay 1 in Road Town. You'll be brought ashore by tender. The pier, built in the mid-1990s, is a pleasant 5-minute walk to Main Street. You should have no trouble finding your way around town.

CURRENCY   The **U.S. dollar** is the legal currency, much to the surprise of arriving Britishers who find no one willing to accept their pounds.

INFORMATION   The **B.V.I. Tourist Board Office** (☎ 284/494-3134) is at the center of Road Town near the ferry dock south of Wickhams Cay 1. Pick up a copy of the *Welcome Tourist Guide.* Open Monday to Friday from 9am to 5pm.

LANGUAGE   English is spoken here.

GETTING AROUND

BY TAXI   Taxis meet every arriving cruise ship. To call a taxi in Road Town, dial ☎ **284/494-2322.**

BY BUS   **Scato's Bus Service** (☎ 284/494-5873) picks up passengers who hail it down. Fares for a trek across the island are $1 to $3.

BY RENTAL CAR   I don't recommend driving here, as the roads are bad and driving is on the left.

SHORE EXCURSIONS

✪ **Island Tour** ($29, 3 hours): Hop on an open-air safari bus and embark on a scenic journey around the island, enjoying some panoramic views and good photo ops, and ending with a stop at Cane Garden Bay Beach for swimming, sunbathing, and just plain old relaxing.

TOURING THROUGH LOCAL OPERATORS

Bus Tours/Snorkeling/Glass-Bottomed Boat Tours: Since the shore excursions here are very modest, you might consider calling **Travel Plan Tours,** Romasco Place, Wickham's Cay, Road Town (☎ 284/494-2872), which will take one to three people on a 3-hour guided tour of the island, a snorkeling excursion, or a glass-bottomed boat tour.

Taxi Tours: You can take a 2- to 3-hour taxi tour for about $45 for up to three people. For a taxi in Road Town, call ☎ **284/494-2322.**

ON YOUR OWN: WITHIN WALKING DISTANCE

About the only thing within walking distance are the handful of shops on Main and Upper Main streets in Road Town.

ON YOUR OWN: BEYOND WALKING DISTANCE

You have mainly nature to look at on Tortola. The big attraction is **Mount Sage National Park,** which rises to 1,780 feet and covers 92 acres. It was established in 1964 to protect the remnants of Tortola's original forests not burned or cleared during its plantation era. You can still find the traces of a primeval rainforest here. This is a great place to enjoy a picnic while overlooking neighboring islets and cays. Any taxi driver can take you to the mountain. Before going, stop at the tourist office (see above) and pick up a brochure with a map and an outline of the park's trails. The two main hikes are the Rain Forest Trail and the Mahogany Forest Trail.

SHOPPING

Shopping on Tortola is a minor activity compared to other Caribbean ports. Most stores are on Main Street in Road Town. Only British goods are imported without duty, and they are the best buys, especially English china. You'll also find West Indian art, terra-cotta pottery, wicker and rattan home furnishings, Mexican glassware, dhurrie rugs, baskets, and ceramics.

Some good shops to visit include **Caribbean Corner Spice House Co.,** in Soper's Hole, which has the finest selection of spices and herbs on the island, along with a selection of Cuban cigars, local handcrafts, and botanical skin-care products; **Pusser's Company Store,** Main Street, Road Town, for Pusser's rum, fine nautical artifacts, and a selection of Pusser's sports and travel clothing and upmarket gift items; and the **Sunny Caribbee Herb and Spice Company,** Main Street, Road Town, for Caribbean spices, seasonings, teas, condiments, and handcrafts. You can buy two world-famous specialties here: West Indian Hangover Cure and Arawak Love Potion.

BEACHES

Most of the beaches are a 20-minute taxi ride from the cruise dock. Figure on about $15 one way, but discuss it with the driver before setting out. You can also ask him to pick you up at a designated time.

The finest beach is at ✪ **Cane Garden Bay,** which compares favorably to the famous Magens Bay Beach on the north shore of St. Thomas. It's on the northwest side of the island, across the mountains from Road Town, but it's worth the effort to get there, and is so special you might take a taxi here in the morning and not head back to your cruise ship until departure time. With its palm-draped white sandy beach, this half-moon–shaped bay has as much South Seas charm as any place in the Caribbean. Plan to have lunch here at **Rhymer's** (☎ **284/495-4639**), where the chef will cook some conch or whelk, or perhaps some barbecue spareribs. The beach bar and restaurant is open daily from 8am to 9pm, serving breakfast, lunch, and dinner, with main courses ranging from $12 to $20. Ice and freshwater showers are available. Rhymer's rents towels, as well as Sunfish and windsurfers.

Surfers like **Apple Bay,** also on the northwest side. A hotel here called Sebastians caters to the surfing crowd that visits in January and February, but the beach is ideal year-round. **Brewers Bay,** site of a campground, is on the northwest shore near Cane Garden Bay. Both snorkelers and surfers come here. **Smugglers Cove** is at the extreme western end of Tortola, opposite the offshore island of Great Thatch and very close to St. John's in the U.S. Virgin Islands. Snorkelers also like this beach, sometimes known as Lower Belmont Bay.

Long Bay Beach is on Beef Island, east of Tortola and the site of the major airport. To get to this mile-long stretch of white sandy beach, cross the Queen Elizabeth Bridge, and then take a left on a dirt road before the airport. From Long Bay you'll have a good view of Little Camanoe, one of the rocky offshore islands around Tortola.

Marina Cay, off Tortola's East End, is known for its good snorkeling beach. I also recommend the beach at **Cooper Island,** across Drake's Channel. Underwater Safaris (see "Sports," below) leads snorkel expeditions to both sites.

SPORTS

HORSEBACK RIDING   Shadow's Ranch, Todman's Estate (☎ 284/494-2262), offers rides through Mount Sage National Park or down to the shores of Cane Garden Bay. Call for details Monday to Saturday from 9am to 4pm. They're located about 15 miles from the cruise dock; taxi fare is $12.

SCUBA DIVING   *Skin Diver* magazine has called the wreckage of the HMS *Rhône,* which sank in 1867 near the western point of Salt Island, the world's most fantastic shipwreck dive. It teems with marine life and coral formations, and was featured in the motion picture *The Deep. Chikuzen* is another intriguing dive site off Tortola, although it's no *Rhône.* It's a 270-foot steel-hulled refrigerator ship that sank off the island's east end in 1981. The hull, still intact under about 80 feet of water, is now home to a vast array of tropical fish, including yellowtail, barracuda, black-tip sharks, octopus, and drum fish. **Baskin in the Sun** (☎ 800/233-7938 in the U.S., or 284/494-2858), a PADI five-star facility on Tortola, is a good choice for divers. It has two different locations: at the Prospect Reef Resort, near Road Town, and at Soper's Hole, on Tortola's West End. Baskin's most popular trip is the supervised "Half-Day Scuba Diving," catering to beginners, but there are trips for more advanced levels as well. Daily excursions are scheduled to the HMS *Rhône,* as well as "Painted Walls" (an underwater canyon formed of brightly colored coral and sponges), and the "Indians" (four pinnacle rocks sticking out of the water, which divers follow 40 feet below the surface). **Underwater Safaris** (☎ 800/537-7032 in the U.S., or 809/494-3235) takes you to all the best sites. It offers a complete PADI and NAUI training facility, and is associated with The Moorings yacht charter company. Underwater Safaris' Road Town office is a 5-minute or $4 taxi ride from the docks.

GREAT LOCAL RESTAURANTS & BARS

On Cappoon's Bay, ✪ **Bomba's Surfside Shack** (☎ 284/495-4148) is the oldest, most memorable bar on Tortola, sitting on a 20-foot-wide strip of unpromising coastline near the West End. It's the "junk palace" of the island, covered with Day-Glo graffiti and laced with wire and rejected odds and ends of plywood, driftwood, and abandoned rubber tires. Despite its makeshift appearance, the shack's got a sound system that can get a great party going any time of the day. The Sunday and Wednesday night barbecue is $7 per person. Open daily from 10am to midnight (or later, depending on business).

Standing on the waterfront across from the ferry dock, **Pusser's Road Town Pub** (☎ 284/494-3897) serves Caribbean fare, English pub grub, and good pizzas. The drink to have here is the famous Pusser's Rum, the same blend of five West Indian rums that the Royal Navy served to its men for more than 300 years. Honestly, it's not the world's greatest rum, but sometimes you just have to do things for the experience. **Capriccio di Mare,** Waterfront Drive (☎ 284/494-5369), is the most authentic-looking Italian cafe in the Virgin Islands, serving fresh pastas with succulent sauces, well-stuffed sandwiches, and the best pizzas on the island. **Callaloo,** at the Prospect Reef Resort (☎ **284/494-3311**), sits within a very romantic setting if it's a balmy day and the tropical breezes are blowing. Begin with the conch fritters or shrimp cocktail, and don't pass on the house salad, which has a zesty papaya dressing. Main dishes include fresh fish. At **Pusser's Landing,** Frenchman's Cay, on the West End (☎ **284/495-4554**), you can enjoy grilled fish, such as mahi-mahi, West Indian roast chicken, or an English-inspired dish, like shepherd's pie. Try the mango soufflé for dessert.

VIRGIN GORDA

Instead of visiting Tortola, some small cruise ships put in at lovely Virgin Gorda, famous for its boulder-strewn beach known as **The Baths.** The second-largest island in the colony, it got its name ("Fat Virgin") from Christopher Columbus, who thought the mountain framing it looked like a protruding stomach. At 10 miles long and two miles wide, the island is about 12 miles east of Road Town, so it's easy to take a ferry or boat here if your ship only visits Tortola.

The island was a fairly desolate agricultural community until Little Dix Bay Hotel opened here in the early 1960s, following his success with Caneel Bay on St. John a decade earlier. Other major hotels followed, but the privacy and solitude he envisioned still reign supreme on Virgin Gorda.

Frommer's Favorite Virgin Gorda Experiences

- **Visit The Baths:** House-sized boulders and clear waters make for excellent swimming and snorkeling in a fabulous setting (see "Beaches," and "Shore Excursions," below).
- **Spend a beach day in Spring Bay or Trunk Bay:** Located near The Baths, Spring Bay has one of the best beaches on the island, with white sand, clear water, and good snorkeling. Trunk Bay, a wide sand beach that can be reached by boat or via a rough path from Spring Bay, is another good bet (see "Beaches," below).
- **Take an island tour:** Open-air safari buses do a good job of showing guests this beautiful island (see "Shore Excursions," below).

COMING ASHORE   Virgin Gorda doesn't have a pier or landing facilities to suit any of the large ships. Most vessels anchor and send small craft ashore. Many others dock beside the pier in Road Town on Tortola and then send tenders across the channel to Virgin Gorda.

CURRENCY   The **U.S. dollar** is the legal currency.

LANGUAGE   English.

GETTING AROUND

The best way to see the island is to call Andy Flax at the Fischers Cove Beach Hotel (☎ **284/495-5252**). He runs the **Virgin Gorda Tours Association,** which gives island

Frommer's Ratings: Virgin Gorda					
	Poor	Fair	Good	Excellent	Outstanding
Overall Experience					✓
Shore Excursions			✓		
Activities Close to Port				✓	
Beaches & Water Sports				✓	
Shopping		✓			
Dining/Bars			✓		

tours for about $20 per person. Tours leave twice daily. They will pick you up at the dock if you give them 24 hours' notice.

BY TAXI   Many taxi drivers await visitors disembarking from tenders and small boats at Spanish Town. They can take you to the baths and the beach.

SHORE EXCURSIONS

✪ **The Baths Excursion** ($38, 3 to 4 hours): All cruise lines stopping at the island offer this trip. (See "Beaches," below, for details.)

✪ **Island Tour** ($42, 3 to 4 hours): The open-air safari buses do a good job of showing guests this beautiful island. Going across the island via North Sound Road, you'll get views of the entire, erratically shaped island (Tortola and St. Thomas, too) and the sea from the base of 1,500-foot Gorda Peak as well as other elevated points along the way.

ON YOUR OWN

Whether close to the landing facilities or not, everything there is to do in Virgin Gorda is covered in the other sections of this review.

BEACHES

The major reason cruise ships come to Virgin Gorda is to visit ✪ **The Baths,** where house-sized boulders toppled over one another to form saltwater grottoes. The pools around The Baths are excellent for swimming and snorkeling (equipment can be rented on the beach), and it's a fun exercise to walk between and among the boulders, which in places are very cave like. There's a cafe just above the beach, for a quick snack or a cool drink before heading back to the ship.

Near The Baths is ✪ **Spring Bay,** one of the best of the island's beaches, with white sand, clear water, and good snorkeling. ✪ **Trunk Bay** is a wide sand beach that can be reached by boat or via a rough path from Spring Bay. **Savannah Bay** is a sandy stretch north of the yacht harbor, and **Mahoe Bay,** at the Mango Bay Resort, has a gently curving beach and vivid blue water.

Devil's Bay National Park can be reached by a trail from The Baths. The walk to the secluded coral-sand beach takes about 15 minutes through a natural setting of boulders and dry coastal vegetation.

SPORTS

WATER SPORTS   Kilbrides Underwater Tours, at the Bitter End Resort at North Sound (☎ **800/932-4286** in the U.S., or 809/495-9638), offers the best diving in the British Virgin Islands at 15 to 20 dive sites, including the wreck of the HMS *Rhône.* You can purchase a video of your dive.

GREAT LOCAL RESTAURANTS & BARS

At the end of the waterfront shopping plaza in Spanish Town, **Bath and Turtle Pub,** Virgin Gorda Yacht Harbour (☎ **284/495-5239**), is the island's most popular bar and pub. You can join the regulars over midmorning guava coladas or peach daiquiris. From its handful of indoor and courtyard tables, you can order fried fish fingers, nachos, very spicy chili, pizzas, Reubens or tuna melts, steak, lobster, and daily seafood specials such as conch fritters. **Chez Bamboo** (☎ **284/495-5963**) lies beside the main road, a short walk north of the Yacht Harbour at Spanish Town. Menu items include Carib-Creole specialties, many with a New Orleans flavor. **Teacher Ilma's** (☎ **284/495-5355**) serves dishes such as chicken, local goat, lobster, conch, pork, or your choice of grouper, snapper, tuna, dolphin, swordfish, or triggerfish.

5 Cozumel & Playa del Carmen

A very popular cruise port, the island of Cozumel has white-sand beaches and fabulous scuba diving, but its greatest draw is its proximity to the ancient Mayan ruins at Tulum and Chichén Itzá. Some ships also stop at nearby Playa del Carmen on the mainland of the Yucatán Peninsula, as it's easier to visit the ruins from there than from Cozumel. Generally, you can do tours to the ruins from either Cozumel or Playa del Carmen.

MAYAN RUINS ON THE MAINLAND

The largest and most fabled of the Yucatán ruins, **Chichén Itzá** was founded in A.D. 445 by the Mayans, and then inhabited by the conquering Toltecs of Central Mexico. Two centuries later, it was mysteriously abandoned. After lying dormant for two more centuries, the site was resettled and enjoyed prosperity again until the early 13th century, when it was once more relinquished to the surrounding jungle. The area covers 7 square miles, so you can see only a fraction of it on a day trip.

The best known of the ruins is the pyramid **Castillo of Kukulkán,** which is actually an astronomical clock designed to mark the vernal and autumnal equinoxes and the summer and winter solstices. A total of 365 steps, one for each day of the year, ascend to the top platform. During each equinox, light striking the pyramid gives the illusion of a giant snake slithering down the steps to join its gigantic stone head mounted at the base.

The government began restoration on the site in the 1920s. Today it houses a museum, a 250-seat restaurant, and a shop. Admission is included in shore excursions; otherwise, the site and museum cost $4 Monday to Saturday, and free on Sunday. Children under 12 are admitted free. Use of a video camera costs $4. It's open daily from 8am to 5pm.

Eighty miles south of Cancún, the walled city of **Tulum** is the single most visited Mayan ruin. It was the only Mayan city built on the coast and the only one inhabited when the Spanish conquistadors arrived in the 1500s. From here you can see wonderful panoramic views of the Caribbean. Tulum consists of 60 individual structures. As with Chichén Itzá, its most prominent feature is a pyramid topped with a temple to Kukulkán, the primary Mayan/Olmec god. Other important structures include the Temple of the Frescoes, the Temple of the Descending God, the House of Columns, and the House of the Cenote, which is a well. Entrance is included in shore excursions; otherwise, it's $3.50 Monday to Saturday, free on Sunday. Use of a video camera costs $4. The site is open daily from 8am to 5pm.

A 35-minute drive northwest of Tulum puts you at **Cobá,** site of one of the most important city-states in the Mayan empire. Cobá flourished from A.D. 400 to 1100, its population numbering perhaps as many as 40,000. Excavation work began in 1972, but archaeologists estimate that only 5% of this dead city has yet been uncovered. The site lies on four lakes. Its 81 primitive acres provide excellent exploration opportunities for the hiker. Cobá's pyramid, Nohoch Mul, is the tallest in the Yucatán. The price of admission is included in shore excursions; otherwise, it's $2 Monday to Saturday, free on Sunday, and free for children under 12. Each video camera carries an additional $4 charge. The site is open daily from 8am to 7pm. The location is 105 miles south of Cancún.

COZUMEL

The ancient Mayans who lived here for 12 centuries would be shocked by the million cruise passengers who now visit Cozumel each year. Their presence has greatly changed San Miguel, the only town, which now has fast-food eateries and a Hard Rock Café. However, development hasn't touched much of the island's natural beauty. Ashore (away from San Miguel) you will see abundant wildlife, including armadillos, brightly colored tropical birds, and lizards. Offshore, the government has set aside 20 miles of coral reefs as an underwater national park, including the stunning Palancar Reef, the world's second largest natural coral formation.

Frommer's Favorite Cozumel Experiences

- **Visit the Mayan ruins at Chichén Itzá or Tulum:** Chichén Itzá is the largest and most fabled of the Yucatán ruins—and you get to fly in a small plane to get there! Tulum is perched dramatically above the ocean, and tours there often includes a stop at the beautiful Xel-Ha Lagoon for some swimming (see "Mayan Ruins on the Mainland," above, and "Shore Excursions," below).
- **Rent a motorscooter:** You can easily see most of the island this way, including its wild and natural side (see "On Your Own: Beyond Walking Distance," below).
- **Sign up for a Jeep trek:** Explore Cozumel's jungles and sandy back roads caravan-style, and then stop at a beach for lunch and swimming (see "Shore Excursions," below).

COMING ASHORE   Ships arriving at Muelle Fiscal on Cozumel tender passengers directly to the heart of San Miguel. From the downtown pier, it's possible to walk to the shops, restaurants, and cafes. Other ships anchor off the well-accoutered international pier 4 miles from San Miguel (about a $4 taxi ride from town). The beaches are close to the international pier.

CURRENCY   The Mexican currency is the nuevo peso, or new peso. Its symbol is the "$" sign, but it's hardly the equivalent of the U.S. dollar. The exchange rate is $9.56 pesos to US$1 ($1 peso is worth about 10¢) The main tourist stores gladly accept U.S. dollars, credit cards, and traveler's checks, but if you want to change money, there are lots of banks within a block or so from the Muelle Fiscal pier.

INFORMATION   The **Tourism Office,** Plaza del Sol (☎ **987/2-0972**), distributes *Vacation Guide to Cozumel* and *Cozumel Island's Restaurant Guide;* both have island maps. Open Monday to Friday from 8am to 2:30pm.

LANGUAGE   Spanish is the tongue of the land, although English is spoken in most places that cater to tourists.

GETTING AROUND   The town of San Miguel is so small you can walk anywhere you want to go. Essentially, there's only one road in Cozumel—it starts at the northern tip of the island, hugs the western shoreline, and then loops around the southern tip and returns to the capital.

By Taxi   Taxi service is available 24 hours a day. Call ☎ **987/2-0236.** Cabs are relatively inexpensive, but since it's customary here to overcharge cruise ship passengers, settle on a fare before getting in. The average fare from San Miguel to most major resorts and beaches is about $8 and about $4 between the International terminal and downtown. More distant island rides cost $12 and up.

Frommer's Ratings: Cozumel					
	Poor	Fair	Good	Excellent	Outstanding
Overall Experience				✓	
Shore Excursions					✓
Activities Close to Port				✓	
Beaches & Water Sports		✓			
Shopping				✓	
Dining/Bars			✓		

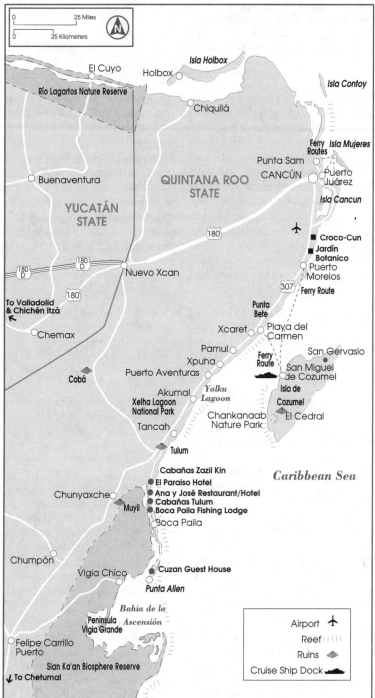

0 25 Miles
0 25 Kilometers

El Cuyo
Holbox
Isla Holbox
Isla Contoy
Río Lagartos Nature Reserve
Chiquilá

Ferry Routes *Isla Mujeres*
Punta Sam
CANCÚN
Puerto Juárez
Isla Cancun

Buenaventura

QUINTANA ROO STATE

YUCATÁN STATE

180

■ Croco-Cun
■ Jardín Botanico

180 D
180 D
180

Nuevo Xcan

Puerto Morelos
307 Ferry Route

To Valladolid & Chichén Itzá

Punta Bete

Chemax

Xcaret Playa del Carmen

Pamul
Xpuha
Puerto Aventuras

San Gervasio
Ferry Route
San Miguel de Cozumel

Cobá

Akumal *Yalku Lagoon*
Xelha Lagoon National Park
Tancah

Isla de Cozumel

Chankanaab Nature Park
El Cedral

Tulum

Caribbean Sea

Cabañas Zazil Kin
● El Paraiso Hotel
Chunyaxche
Muyil
● Ana y José Restaurant/Hotel
● Cabañas Tulum
● Boca Paila Fishing Lodge
Boca Paila

Chumpón

Vigia Chico
● Cuzan Guest House
Punta Allen

Bahia de la Ascensión

Peninsula Vigia Grande

Felipe Carrillo Puerto

Sian Ka'an Biosphere Reserve
↓ To Chetumal

Airport ✈
Reef ||||||
Ruins ≋
Cruise Ship Dock 🚢

Port Tip: Calling Home

You can make telephone calls in Cozumel from a phone center in the international pier or at the **Calling Station,** Avenida Rafael Melgar 27 (☎ **987/2-1417**), at the corner of Calle 3 in San Miguel, 3 blocks from Muelle Fiscal.

By Rental Car   If you want to drive yourself, four-wheel-drive vehicles or open-air Jeeps are the best rental choice. **Budget Rent-a-Car,** Avenida 5A at Calle 2 N. (☎ **800/527-0700** in the U.S., or 987/2-0903), 2 blocks from the pier at Muelle Fiscal, rents both. A four-door economy car rents for about $35 a day, with a Jeep Cherokee going for $45 and up.

By Moped   Mopeds are a popular means of getting about despite heavy traffic, hidden stop signs, potholed roads, and a high accident rate. The best and most convenient rentals are at **Auto Rent** (☎ **987/2-0844**) in the Hotel Ceiba, a block from the pier at Muelle Fiscal. The cost is about $28 per day. Mexican law requires helmets.

By Ferry   A number of passenger ferries link Cozumel with Playa del Carmen. The most comfortable are the two big speedboats and water-jet catamaran run by **Aviomar** (☎ **987/ 2-0477**). They operate Monday to Saturday from 8am to 8pm, Sunday from 9am to 1pm. The trip takes 45 minutes. All the ferries have ticket booths at the main pier. One-way fares range from $4 to $5 per person. You'll get a ferry schedule when you buy your ticket.

SHORE EXCURSIONS

It's easier to see the ruins at Chichén Itzá, Tulum, and Cobá from Playa del Carmen, since it's on the mainland and so closer to the ruin sites. Many ships, en route to Cozumel, pause in Playa del Carmen to drop off passengers who have signed for ruins tours. Then, after the tours, passengers either take a ferry back to the ship in Cozumel or, if the tour is by plane, get dropped off at the airport in Cozumel, near downtown. See "Mayan Ruins on the Mainland," above, for details about the ruins.

✪ **Chichén Itzá Excursion** ($184, 6 hours): Founded in A.D. 445, Chichén Itzá is the largest and most fabled of the Yucatán ruins—and you can even climb up its tallest pyramid for wonderful views of the ancient city, much of which is still covered in foliage and earth. You'll take a 45-minute flight each way on 10- to 20-seater aircraft. The flight there is almost as interesting as the ruins. This tour may leave from Playa del Carmen. (Note: It can get hot. Bring water.)

✪ **The Mayan Ruins of Tulum** ($66, 5 hours): Very worthwhile. The ruins of this walled city are all the more spectacular because they're located on a cliff, dramatically perched above the ocean. This tour often includes an hour or two stop at the Xel-Ha Lagoon, a beautiful and natural setting for swimming (in this case, the tour is 7 to 8 hours long and costs another $20 or so). The tour leaves from Playa del Carmen.

✪ **Jeep Trek** ($74, 5 to 6 hours): Hop in a jeep seating four and explore the natural side of Cozumel, its jungle mangroves and sandy back roads. Much of the route is off road, and the Jeeps travel in a convoy, with one of you driving. Included is a beach stop and picnic lunch.

Horseback-Riding Tours ($71, 3 to 4 hours): Worthwhile horseback riding tours are offered that take riders through ancient Mayan sites tucked away in Cozumel's tropical forest. Do the tour to see Cozumel's tropical forests and for the fun of riding a horse, not for the ruins—there are really no authentic ruins to speak of; most are reproductions. The tour includes a guide who discusses Mayan culture and customs while exploring the inside of a cave where the Mayans gathered for ceremonial meetings. A bus transports riders to a ranch, where the ride begins.

San Miguel de Cozumel

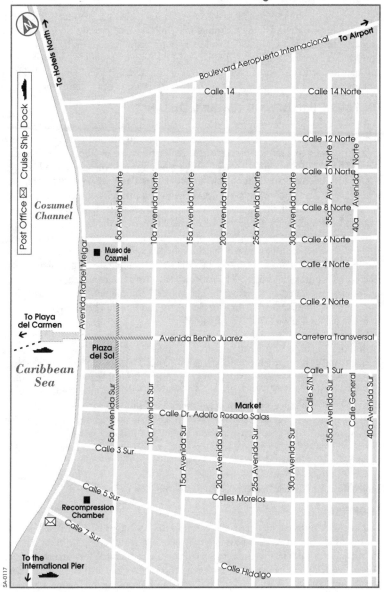

ON YOUR OWN: WITHIN WALKING DISTANCE

The classic grid layout makes getting around the town of San Miguel easy. Directly across from the docks, the main square—**Plaza del Sol** (also called *la plaza* or *el parque*)—is excellent for people watching. Avenida Rafael Melgar, the principal street along the waterfront, runs along the western shore of the island, site of the best resorts and beaches. Most of the shops and restaurants are on Rafael Melgar, although many well-stocked duty-free shops line the Malecón, the seaside promenade.

Only 3 blocks from Muelle Fiscal on Agenda Rafael Melgar between Calles 4 and 6 N., the **Museo de la Isla de Cozumel** (☎ 987/2-1434) has two floors of exhibits displayed in what was Cozumel's first luxury hotel. Exhibits start in the pre-Hispanic times and continue through the colonial era to the present. Included are many swords and nautical artifacts; one display showcases endangered species. The highlight is a reproduction of a Mayan house. Open daily from 10am to 6pm; admission is $1.75.

ON YOUR OWN: BEYOND WALKING DISTANCE

You can ✪ **rent a motorscooter** and zip around most of the island, including its wild and natural side. Stop for lunch at a beachside, open-air seafood restaurant for some grilled fish and a cool drink. Scooters can be rented from several outfits, including **Auto Rent** (☎ 987/2-0844) in the Hotel Ceiba, a block from the pier at Muelle Fiscal.

Outside of San Miguel is the **Chankanaab Nature Park,** where a saltwater lagoon, offshore reefs, and underwater caves have been turned into an archaeological park, botanical garden, and wildlife sanctuary. More than 10 countries have contributed seedlings and cuttings. Some 60 species of marine life occupy the lagoon, including sea turtles. Reproductions of Mayan dwellings are scattered throughout the park. There's also a wide white-sand beach with thatch umbrellas and a changing area with lockers and showers. Both scuba divers and snorkelers like examining the sunken ship offshore (there are four dive shops here). The park also has a restaurant and snack stand.

The park is located at Carretera Sur, kilometer 9 (no phone). It's open daily from 9am to 5pm. Admission is $7, free for children 9 and under. The 10-minute taxi ride from the pier at Muelle Fiscal costs about $5.

Mayan ruins on Cozumel are very minor compared to those on the mainland. **El Cedral** lies 2 miles inland at the turnoff at kilometer 17.5, east of Playa San Francisco. It's the island's oldest structure, with traces of original Mayan wall paintings. The Spanish tore much of it down, and the U.S. Army nearly finished the job when it built an airfield here in World War II. Little remains now except a Mayan arch and a few small ruins covered in heavy growth. Guides at the site will show you around for a fee.

Another meager ruin is at **San Gervasio,** reached by driving west across the island to the army airbase, and then turning right and continuing north 4 miles to San Gervasio. This was once a ceremonial center and capital of Cozumel. The Mayans dedicated the area to Ixchel, the fertility goddess. The ruins cost $3.50 to visit, plus $1 for entrance to the access road. Guides will show people what's left, including several broken columns and lintels, for $12. Open daily from 8am to 5pm.

SHOPPING

You can walk from the pier at Muelle Fiscal to the best shops in San Miguel. Because of the influx of cruise ship passengers, prices are relatively high here. **Agencia Publicaciones Gracia,** Avenida 5A, is Cozumel's best source for English-language books, guidebooks, newspapers, and magazines. It's a block from Muelle Fiscal. **Casablanca,** Avenida Rafael Melgar 33 (located in front of the international port), has a fine selection of Mexican jewelry and loose stones, plus a well-chosen collection of Mexican crafts. **Explora,** Avenida Rafael Melgar 49 (1½ blocks from Muelle Fiscal), is your best bet for women's casual clothing and attractive beachwear. **Gordon Gilchrist,** Studio 1, Avenida 25 S. 981 at Calle 15 S., produces Cozumel's finest etchings of local Mayan sites. **Rachat & Romero,** Avenida Rafael Melgar 101 has a wide variety of loose stones, which they can mount while you wait. **Ultra Femme,** Avenida Rafael Melgar 341 is one of the most important jewelers in Cozumel, and the exclusive distributor of Rolex watches on the Mexican Riviera. **Unicornio,** 5 Avenida Sur 2 (2 blocks from Muelle Fiscal), has Mexican handcrafts.

BEACHES

Cozumel's best powdery white-sand beach, **Playa San Francisco,** stretches for some 3 miles along the southwestern shoreline. It was once one of the most idyllic beaches in Mexico, but resort development is threatening to destroy its old character. You can rent equipment for water sports here, or have lunch at one of the many *palapa* restaurants and bars on the shoreline. The beach is a $4 taxi ride south of San Miguel's downtown pier. If you land at the international pier, you're practically at the beach already.

Many of your fellow cruisers have heard of the fine **Playa del Sol,** about a mile south of Playa del San Francisco, so it's likely to be overcrowded.

Playa Bonita (sometimes called Punta Chiqueros) is one of the least crowded beaches, but it lies on the east (windward) side of the island and is difficult to reach unless you rent a vehicle or throw yourself on the mercy of a taxi driver. It sits in a moon-shaped cove sheltered from the Caribbean Sea by an offshore reef. Waves are only moderate here, and the sand's powdery and the water's clear.

SPORTS

SCUBA DIVING Jacques Cousteau did much to extol the glory of Cozumel for scuba divers. Here he discovered black coral in profusion, plus hundreds of species of rainbow-hued tropical fish. Underwater visibility can reach 250 feet. All this gives Cozumel some of the best diving in the Caribbean. Cruisers might want to confine their adventures to the finest spot, Palancar Reef. Lying about a mile offshore, this fabulous water world features gigantic elephant-ear sponges and black and red coral, as well as deep caves, canyons, and tunnels. It's a favorite of divers from all over the world. The best scuba outfitter is **Aqua Safari,** Avenida Rafael Melgar at Calle 5, next to the Vista del Mar Hotel (☎ **987/2-0101**). Hours are daily from 8am to 2pm. A worthwhile competitor is **Diving Adventures,** Calle 51 Sur no. 2, near the corner of Avenida Rafael Melgar (☎ **987/2-3009**). Its prices and itineraries are equivalent.

SNORKELING Shallow reefs at Playa San Francisco or Chankanaab Bay are among the best spots. You'll see a world of sea creatures parading by, everything from parrotfish to conch. The best outfitter is **Cozumel Snorkeling Center,** Calle Primera Sur (☎ **987/2-0539**), which offers a 3-hour snorkeling tour, including all equipment and refreshments. They can also arrange parasailing here. Hours are Monday to Saturday from 8am to 1pm and from 4 to 8pm, Sunday from 8am to 1pm.

GREAT LOCAL RESTAURANTS & BARS

Right in front of the in-town cruise dock, ✪ **Café del Puerto,** Avenida Rafael Melgar 3, is a local favorite. The kitchen bridges the gap between Mexico and Europe with dishes like a superbly prepared mustard steak flambé, succulent lobster, and Yucatán chicken wrapped in banana leaves. Just north of the ferry pier, **Carlos 'n Charlie's,** Avenida Rafael Melgar 11, is Mexico's equivalent of the Hard Rock Café, but much wilder. Sawdust litters the floor (to sop up the beer), music blares, and tourists pound back yard-long glasses of beers like they're going out of style. Many a cruise passenger has stumbled back from Carlos 'n Charlies, clutching their yard-long glasses as though they were the Holy Grail—proof that they've been to Mexico. People come here for good times and the spicy, tasty ribs. You can dine surprisingly well on Yucatán specialties, and the best chicken and beef fajitas in Cozumel. The **Hard Rock Cozumel** itself, at Avenida Rafael Melgar 2A, serves the best juicy burgers in Cozumel, as well as grilled beef or chicken fajitas. A half block from the pier, **Las Palmeras,** Avenida Rafael Melgar, is ideal for casual eating. If you arrive in time, it serves one of the best breakfasts in town; for lunch, they offer tempting seafood dishes or Mexican specialties.

El Capi Navegante, Avenida 10A Sur 312 at Calles 3 and 4 (5 blocks from Muelle Fiscal), offers the freshest fish in San Miguel with a great lobster soufflé. **La Choza,** Calle Rosada Salas 198 at Avenida 10A Sur (2 blocks from the Muelle Fiscal pier), offers real local cooking that's a favorite of the town's savvy foodies.

PLAYA DEL CARMEN

Some cruise ships spend a day at Cozumel and then another at Playa del Carmen, but most drop off passengers here for tours to Tulum and Chichen Itza, and then head on to spend the day tied up at Cozumel.

The famed white-sand beach here was relatively untouched by tourists not many years ago, but today the pleasure-seeking hordes have replaced the Indian families who used to gather coconuts for copra. If you can tolerate the crowds, snorkeling is excellent over the offshore reefs. Turtle-watching is another local pastime.

Avenida Juárez in Playa del Carmen is the principal business zone for the Tulum-Cancún corridor. Part of Avenida 5 running parallel to the beach has been closed to traffic, forming a good promenade. Most visitors at some point head for **Rincón del Sol,** a tree-filled courtyard built in the colonial Mexican style. It has the best collection of handcraft shops in the area, some of which offer goods of excellent quality, not the junky souvenirs peddled elsewhere.

Frommer's Favorite Playa del Carmen Experiences

• **Have beer and nachos on the beach:** Hang out on the beach for great views of the anchored ships a mile or so out at sea and the tourists coming in off the tenders. A couple of casual beachside restaurants provide all the beer, quesadillas, and nachos you'll need.

• **Take a tour of Tulum or Chichén Itzá:** Both of the tours described in the Cozumel section are also offered here.

COMING ASHORE Some cruise ships dock at anchor or at the pier of Cozumel, and then send passengers over to Playa del Carmen by tender. Others dock at the new Puerto Calica Cruise Pier, which is 8 miles south of Playa del Carmen. Taxis meet each arriving ship, and drivers transport visitors into the center of Playa del Carmen.

CURRENCY Mexican peso. See info under "Cozumel," above.

LANGUAGE Spanish, although English is widely spoken.

GETTING AROUND

BY TAXI Taxis are readily available to take you anywhere, but you can walk to the center of town, to the beach, and to most major shops.

BY RENTAL CAR If you decide to rent a car for the day, try **National,** Hotel Molcas, 1A Avenida Sur 5A (☎ 987/3-0360), or **Dollar,** Hotel Diamond at Playacar

Frommer's Ratings: Playa del Carmen					
	Poor	Fair	Good	Excellent	Outstanding
Overall Experience				✓	
Shore Excursions					✓
Activities Close to Port			✓		
Beaches & Water Sports			✓		
Shopping		✓			
Dining/Bars			✓		

(☎ 987/3-0340). Cars at either agency usually come with unlimited mileage and most forms of insurance included, and rent for between $50 and $72 a day.

SHORE EXCURSIONS

Most visitors head for the Mayan ruins the moment they reach shore (see "Shore Excursions" in the Cozumel section, above).

Xcaret Ecological Park ($36 adults, $24 kids): Lying 4 miles south of Playa del Carmen on the coast, Xcaret (pronounced "Ish-car-*et*") is a 250-acre ecological theme park where many visitors spend their entire day. It's a great place. Mayan ruins are scattered about the lushly landscaped acres. Visitors can put on life jackets for an underwater river ride, which takes them through currents running throughout a series of caves. You can also snorkel through these flooded caves. There's also a botanical garden and a dive shop. Xcaret is open Monday to Saturday from 8:30am to 8:30pm, Sunday from 8am to 5pm. Buses from Playa del Carmen come here frequently; a taxi costs $4 one-way. Sign up for an organized excursion and a shuttle will transport guests between ship and park.

ON YOUR OWN: WITHIN WALKING DISTANCE

You can walk to the center of town, to the beach, and to the small shopping district.

ON YOUR OWN: BEYOND WALKING DISTANCE

Other than the beach, there's no major attraction in Playa del Carmen except Xcaret (see above). Even if you come independently of a tour, general admission is a steep $39 for adults, $24 for children 5 to 11 (free for kids 4 and under). For information, call ☎ 988/3-0654. Buses from Playa del Carmen come here frequently; a taxi costs $4 one-way.

GREAT LOCAL RESTAURANTS & BARS

El Chino, Calle 4 (Avenida 15; ☎ 987/3-0015), is a pristine restaurant known locally for its regional Yucatán specialties as well as standard dishes from throughout Mexico. ✪ **Máscaras,** Avenida Juárez (☎ 987/3-1053), serves great pastas, brick-oven pizzas, and other Italian dishes. The four-cheese pizza is justifiably the most popular. **El Tacolote,** Avenida Juárez (☎ 987/3-1363), specializes in fresh seafood and the best grilled meats in town, brought to your table fresh from the broiler on a charcoal pan to keep the food warm.

6 Curaçao

As you sail into the harbor of Willemstad, be sure to look for the quaint "floating bridge," the **Queen Emma pontoon bridge,** which swings aside to open the narrow channel. Bordering the harbor are those much-photographed, picture-postcard pastel rows of gabled Dutch houses. Welcome to Curaçao, the largest and most populous of the Netherlands Antilles, just 35 miles north of the Venezuelan coast.

Curaçao, in the Netherlands Antilles, was first discovered by the Spanish around 1499, but in 1634 the Dutch came and prospered. In 1915, when the Royal Dutch/Shell Company built one of the world's largest oil refineries to process crude from Venezuela, workers from 50 countries poured into the island. Today, Curaçao remains a melting pot, although it still retains a Dutch flavor. A tropical Holland in miniature, this island has the most interesting architecture in the West Indies. Its Dutch-colonial structures give Willemstad a storybook look, but the rest of this desert-like island seems like the American Southwest, with three-pronged cacti, spiny-leafed aloes, and divi-divi trees bent by trade winds.

Since much of this island's surface is an arid desert, its canny Dutch settlers ruled out farming and developed Curaçao into one of the Dutch Empire's busiest trading posts. Until the post–World War II collapse of the oil refineries, Curaçao was a thriving

Frommer's Ratings: Curaçao					
	Poor	Fair	Good	Excellent	Outstanding
Overall Experience				✓	
Shore Excursions			✓		
Activities Close to Port				✓	
Beaches & Water Sports		✓			
Shopping			✓		
Dining/Bars			✓		

mercantile society with a capital (Willemstad) that somewhat resembled Amsterdam and a population with a curious mixture of bloodlines (including African, Dutch, Venezuelan, and Pakistani). Tourism began to develop during the 1980s, and many new hotels have been built.

Frommer's Favorite Curaçao Experiences

- **Visiting Christoffel National Park:** Hike up the 1,230-foot-high St. Christoffelberg, passing cacti, iguanas, wild goats, many species of birds, and ancient Arawak paintings along the way. There's also 20 miles of roads, so you can see the park by car (see "On Your Own: Beyond Walking Distance," below).
- **Gazing into the mirrored waters of Hato Caves:** Stalagmites and stalactites are mirrored in a mystical underground lake in these caves, whose limestone formations were created by water seeping through the coral (see "On Your Own: Beyond Walking Distance," below).
- **Take the Hato Caves/Curaçao Liqueur Tour:** This is a neat combination. A short bus ride gets you to the caves, and then to a plantation house and the liqueur factory for a tour (see "Shore Excursions," below).

COMING ASHORE   Cruise ships dock at the terminal just beyond the Queen Emma pontoon bridge, which leads to the duty-free shopping sector and the famous floating market. You can call home from the terminal's phone office. It's a 6- to 10-minute walk from here to the center of Willemstad, or you can take a taxi from the stand. The town itself is easy to navigate on foot. Most of it can be explored in 2 or 3 hours, leaving plenty of time for beaches or water sports. Although the ship terminal has a duty-free shop, save your serious purchases for Willemstad.

CURRENCY   The official currency is the **Netherlands Antillean florin (NAf),** also called a guilder, which is divided into 100 cents. The exchange rate is 1.77 NAf to US$1 (1 NAf is worth about 56¢). Canadian and U.S. dollars are accepted for purchases, so there's no need to change money. Unless otherwise noted, prices in this section are given in U.S. dollars.

INFORMATION   For visitor information, go to the **Curaçao Tourist Board,** Pietermaai (☎ 599/9-4616000). Open Monday to Friday from 9am to 5pm.

LANGUAGE   Dutch, Spanish, and English are spoken on Curaçao, along with Papiamento, a patois that combines the three major tongues with Amerindian and African dialects.

GETTING AROUND

BY TAXI   Taxis don't have meters, so settle on a fare before getting in. Drivers are supposed to carry an official tariff sheet. Generally, there's no need to tip. The best place to get a taxi is on the Otrabands side of the floating bridge or call ☎ 599/9-8690747.

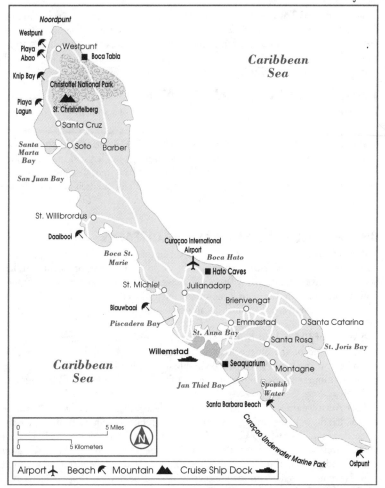

Noordpunt

Westpunt

Playa
Abao

Knip Bay

Playa
Lagun

Christoffel National Park

St. Christoffelberg

Santa
Marta
Bay

San Juan Bay

St. Willibrordus

Daaibooi

Boca St.
Marie

Westpunt

Boca Tabla

Santa Cruz

Soto   Barber

Piscadera Bay

Blauwbaai

St. Michiel

Julianadorp

Curaçao International
Airport

Boca Hato

Hato Caves

Brienvengat

Emmastad   Santa Catarina

St. Anna Bay   Santa Rosa

Willemstad   St. Joris Bay

Caribbean
Sea

Seaquarium   Montagne

Jan Thiel Bay   Spanish
Water

Santa Barbara Beach

Curaçao Underwater Marine Park   Ostpunt

Caribbean
Sea

0   5 Miles

0   5 Kilometers

N

Airport ✈ Beach 🏖 Mountain ▲▲ Cruise Ship Dock ⛴

A fleet of DAF yellow buses operates from Wilhelmina Plein, near the shopping center, and runs to most parts of Curaçao. You can hail a bus at any designated bus stop.

BY RENTAL CAR   Driving is on the right on paved roads. If you want to rent a car, try **Avis** (☎ **800/331-2112** or 599/9-681163), **Budget** (☎ **800/527-0700** or 599/9-683420), or **Hertz** (☎ **800/654-3001** or 599/9-868118).

SHORE EXCURSIONS

Many excursions aren't really worth the price here—you can easily see the town on your own and hop a taxi to the few attractions on the island outside of Willemsted (see "Touring Through Local Operators," below).

✪ **Hato Caves/Curaçao Liqueur Tour** ($30, 3 hours): After a short bus ride to the caves and a walking tour through the grottoes, stalactites, and petroglyphs, the tour takes passengers to an old plantation house for a look around, and then to Curaçao Liqueur Factory, where the popular liqueur is made from Laraha orange peels, for a tour and some sampling.

Countryside Bus Tour ($31, 2 to 3 hours): This excursion takes you via bus to sights like the Westpunt, Mt. Christoffel, the towering cacti, and the rolling hills topped by *landhuizen* (plantation houses) built more than 3 centuries ago. You'll also stop at a beach, the Curaçao Seaquarium, and Chobolobo, an old colonial mansion where the original Curaçao liqueur is still distilled.

TOURING THROUGH LOCAL OPERATORS

Taxi Tours: Up to four passengers can share the price of a tour by taxi, which costs about $30 per hour.

Island Tours: Taber Tours, Dokweg (☎ **599/9-7376637**), also offers several day or night excursions to points of interest. Its tour—through Willemstad, to the Curaçao Liqueur distillery, through the residential area and the Bloempot shopping center, and to the Curaçao Museum—costs $12.50 for adults, $6.25 for children under 12, including admission to the museum. That's a heckuva lot cheaper than the official excursions (see above).

ON YOUR OWN: WITHIN WALKING DISTANCE

Willemstad is the major attraction here, and you can see it on foot. After 10 years of restoration, the town's historic center and the island's natural harbor, Schottegat, have been inscribed on UNESCO's World Heritage List. Be sure and watch the Queen Emma pontoon bridge move (it is motorized and a "driver" actually drives it to the side of the harbor every so often so ships and boats can pass through the channel). It's really neat.

A **statue of Pedro Luis Brion** dominates the square known as Brionplein, at the Otrabanda end of the Queen Emma pontoon bridge. Born in Curaçao in 1782, Brion became the island's favorite son and best-known war hero. He was an admiral of the fleet under Simón Bolívar and fought for the independence of Venezuela and Colombia.

Fort Amsterdam, site of the Governor's Palace and the 1769 Dutch Reformed church, has the task of guarding the waterfront. The church still has a British cannonball embedded in it. The arches leading to the fort were tunneled under the official residence of the governor. A corner of the fort stands at the intersection of Breedestraat and Handelskade, the starting point for a plunge into the island's major shopping district.

A few minutes' walk from the pontoon bridge, at the north end of Handelskade, is the **Floating Market,** where scores of schooners tie up alongside the canal. Boats arrive here from Venezuela and Colombia, and other West Indian islands, to sell tropical fruits and vegetables, as well as handcrafts. The modern market under its vast concrete cap has not diminished the fun of watching the activity here. Either arrive early or stay late to view these marine merchants setting up or storing their wares.

Between the I. H. (Sha) Capriles Kade and Fort Amsterdam, at the corner of Columbusstraat and Hanchi Snog, is the **Mikve Israel-Emanuel Synagogue.** Dating from 1651, the Jewish congregation here is the oldest in the New World.

Next door, the **Jewish Cultural Historical Museum,** Kuiperstraat 26–28 (☎ **599/9-4611633**), is housed in two buildings dating from 1728. They were the rabbi's residence and the *mikvah,* or bath, for religious purification purposes.

You can walk from the Queen Emma pontoon bridge to the **Curaçao Museum,** Van Leeuwenhoekstraat (☎ **599/9-4626051**). The building, constructed in 1853 by the Royal Dutch Army as a military hospital, has been carefully restored and furnished with paintings, objets d'art, and antique furniture, and houses a large collection from the Caiquetio tribes. On the museum grounds is an art gallery for temporary exhibitions of both local and international art.

ON YOUR OWN: BEYOND WALKING DISTANCE

Cactus, bromeliads, rare orchids, iguanas, donkeys, wild goats, and many species of birds thrive in the 4,500-acre ✪ **Christoffel National Park,** located about a 45-minute taxi or car ride from the capital near the northwestern tip of Curaçao. The park rises from flat, arid countryside to 1,230-foot-high St. Christoffelberg, the tallest point in the Dutch Leewards. Along the way are ancient Arawak paintings and the Piedra di Monton, a rock heap piled by African slaves who cleared this former plantation. Legend says slaves could climb to the top of the rock pile, jump off, and fly back home across the Atlantic. If they had ever tasted a grain of salt, however, they would crash to their deaths. The park has 20 miles of one-way trail-like roads. The shortest is about 5 miles long, but takes about 40 minutes to drive because of its rough terrain. One of several hiking trails goes to the top of St. Christoffelberg. It takes about 1 1/2 hours to walk to the summit (come early in the morning before it gets hot). There's also a museum in an old storehouse left over from plantation days. Guided tours of the park are available. The park is open Monday to Saturday from 8am to 4pm and on Sunday from 6am to 3pm. Admission is $9 per person.

The **Curaçao Seaquarium,** off Dr. Martin Luther King Boulevard (☎ **599/ 9-4616666**), displays more than 400 species of fish, crabs, anemones, and other invertebrates, sponges, and coral. A rustic boardwalk connects the hexagonal buildings, which sit on a point near the site where the *Oranje Nassau* broke up on the rocks and sank in 1906. The Seaquarium also has Curaçao's only full-facility, white-sand, palm-shaded beach. In the "shark and animal encounter," divers, snorkelers, and experienced swimmers are able to feed, film, and photograph sharks, stingrays, lobsters, tarpons, parrotfish, and other marine life in a controlled environment. Nonswimmers can see the underwater life from a 46-foot semisubmersible observatory.

If you're here in the late afternoon, the semisubmersible **Seaworld Explorer** departs daily at 4:30pm on hour-long journeys. You'll see submerged offshore wrecks and rainbow-hued tropical fish swimming over coral reefs. Reserve a day in advance by calling ☎ **599/9-5604892.** Fares are $29 for adults, $19 for children 11 and under.

Stalagmites and stalactites are mirrored in a mystical underground lake in ✪ **Hato Caves,** F. D. Rooseveltweg (☎ **599/9-8680379**). Long ago, geological forces uplifted this limestone terrace, which was originally a coral reef. The limestone formations were created over thousands of years by water seeping through the coral. After crossing the lake, you enter two caverns known as "The Cathedral" and La Ventana, or "The Window." Displayed here are samples of ancient Indian petroglyphs. Professional local guides take visitors through the caves every hour. The caves are open daily from 10am to 4pm. Admission is $6.25 for adults, $4.75 for children 4 to 11 (free for kids 3 and under).

SHOPPING

Curaçao is a shopper's paradise, with some 200 stores lining such streets as Heerenstraat and Breedestraat in the 5-block district called the Punda. Many shops occupy the town's old Dutch houses. They also open for a few hours on Sunday and holidays if cruise ships are in port.

The island is famous for its 5-pound "wheelers" of Gouda or Edam cheese. Look for good buys in wooden shoes, French perfumes, Dutch Delft blue souvenirs, finely woven Italian silks, Japanese and German cameras, jewelry, silver, Swiss watches, linens, leather goods, liquor, and island-made rum and liqueurs, especially Curaçao liqueur, some of which has a distinctive blue color. Some stores also offer good buys on intricate lacework imported from everywhere between Portugal and China. If you're a street shopper and want something colorful, consider a carving or flamboyant painting from Haiti or the Dominican Republic. Both are hawked by street vendors at any of the main plazas.

Suggested shops include **Bamali,** Breedestraat 2, for Indonesian-influenced clothing (mostly for women); **Bert Knubben Black Koral Art Studio,** Dr. Martin Luther King Boulevard (in the Princess Beach Resort & Casino, for—you guessed it—black coral jewelry (Bert Knubben, a diver who has been harvesting corals for more than 35 years, was excepted from the Curaçao government's ban on collection of black coral); **Gandelman Jewelers,** Breedestraat 35, Punda, for a large selection of fine jewelry as well as Curaçaoan gold pieces; and **Curaçao Creations,** Schrijnwerkerstraat 14, for Curaçao handcrafts.

BEACHES

Curaçao's beaches are not as good as Aruba's 7-mile strip of sand, but it does have some 38 of them, ranging from hotel sand-patches to secluded coves. The sea water remains an almost-constant 76°F year-round, with good underwater visibility. The **Curaçao Seaquarium** has the island's only full-facility, white sand, palm-shaded beach, but you'll have to pay the full aquarium admission to get in (see "On Your Own: Beyond Walking Distance," above). The rest of the beaches on this island are public.

A good beach on the eastern side of the island is **Santa Barbara Beach,** on land owned by a mining company between the open sea and the island's primary water sports and recreational area, known as Spanish Water. You'll also find Table Mountain, a remarkable landmark, and an old phosphate mine. The natural beach has pure-white sand and calm water. A buoy line protects swimmers from boats, and there are rest rooms, changing rooms, a snack bar, and a terrace. You can rent water bicycles and small motorboats. Open daily from 8am to 6pm. The beach has access to the Curaçao Underwater Park.

Daaibooi is a good beach about 30 minutes from town, in the Willibrordus area on the west side of Curaçao. It's free, but there are no changing facilities.

Blauwbaai (Blue Bay) is the largest and most frequented beach on Curaçao, with enough white sand for everybody. Along with showers and changing facilities, there are plenty of shady places to retreat from the noonday sun. To reach it, take the road that goes past the Holiday Beach Hotel & Casino, heading in the direction of Juliandorp. Follow the sign that tells you to bear left for Blauwbaai and the fishing village of San Michiel.

Westpunt is known for its gigantic cliffs and the Sunday divers who jump from them into the ocean below. This public beach is on the northwestern tip of the island. **Knip Bay,** just south of Westpunt, has beautiful turquoise waters. On weekends, live music and dancing make the beach a lively place. Changing facilities and refreshments are available. **Playa Abao,** with crystal turquoise water, is situated at the northern tip of the island.

Taxi drivers waiting at the cruise dock will take you to any of the beaches at fares to be negotiated. You can also make arrangements to be picked up at a certain time and taken back to the cruise dock.

Warning: Beware of stepping on the hard spines of sea urchins, which are sometimes found in these waters. While not fatal, their spines can cause several days of real discomfort. For temporary first aid, try the local remedies of vinegar or lime juice.

SPORTS

SCUBA DIVING/SNORKELING/WATER SPORTS   You can see steep walls, at least two shallow wrecks, gardens of soft corals, and more than 30 species of hard corals at **Curaçao Underwater Park,** which stretches 12¹/₂ miles along Curaçao's southern coastline, from Princess Beach Resort & Casino to East Point, the island's southeasterly tip. The park has placed 16 mooring buoys at the best dive and snorkel sites, and a snorkel trail with underwater interpretive markers just east of the Princess Beach Resort & Casino. Access from shore is also possible at Santa Barbara Beach in Jan Thiel Bay. Spearfishing, anchoring in the coral, and taking anything from the reefs except photographs are strictly prohibited. **Seascape Dive and Watersports,** at the Curaçao Casino Resort, Piscadera Bay (☎ **599/9-4625000**), specializes in snorkeling and scuba-diving near reefs and underwater wrecks, and offers snorkeling excursions in the underwater park, water-skiing, Sunfish sail boats, and Jet-Ski rentals. It operates from a hexagonal kiosk set on stilts above the water, just offshore from the hotel's beach. Open from 8am to 5pm daily.

GREAT LOCAL RESTAURANTS & BARS

De Taveerne, Landhuis Groot Vavelaar, Silena (☎ **599/9-7370669**), is actually two restaurants: a French restaurant at street level and a less formal brasserie serving inexpensive international food on its second floor. If you're hot, dusty, and in a hurry, your best bet might be to order a platter of food in the brasserie. **Golden Star,** Socratesstraat 2 (at the corner of Dr. Hugenholtzweg and Dr. Maalweg, southeast of Willemstad; ☎ **599/9-4654795**), is the best place to go on the island for *criollo,* or local food. It's inland from the coast road leading southeast from St. Anna Bay, 8 minutes by taxi from the cruise dock. **La Pergola,** in the Waterfront Arches, Waterfort Straat (☎ **599/9-4613482**), is an Italian restaurant where the menu items change virtually every day. **Rijstaffel Restaurant Indonesia and Holland Club Bar,** Mercuriusstraat 13, Salinja (☎ **599/9-4612999**), is the best place on the island to sample the Indonesian *rijstaffel,* the traditional "rice table" with all the zesty side dishes. You must ask a taxi to take you to this villa in the suburbs near Salinja, near the Princess Beach Resort & Casino southeast of Willemstad.

7 Freeport/Lucaya

Bold and brassy Freeport/Lucaya on Grand Bahama Island is the second most popular tourist destination in the Bahamas. Its cosmopolitan glitz might be too much for some visitors, but there are alternatives to the glamour—sun, surf, and excellent golf, tennis, and water sports. Because the island is so big and relatively unsettled, there are plenty of places to get close to nature, or else you can gamble the day away or shop till you drop.

Frommer's Favorite Freeport/Lucaya Experiences

- **Catching a concert at Count Basie Square:** Right in the center of Port Lucaya, a vine-covered bandstand hosts the best live music on the island, performed nightly. And it's free (see "On Your Own: Beyond Walking Distance," below).
- **Visiting the Star Club:** Built in the 1940s, this place hosted many famous guests over the years, and is now the only 24-hour bar on the island (see "Great Local Restaurants & Bars," below).
- **Taking the Lucaya National Park Tour:** About 12 miles from Lucaya, the park has one of the loveliest, most secluded beaches on Grand Bahama (see "Shore Excursions," below).

Frommer's Ratings: Freeport/Lucaya

	Poor	Fair	Good	Excellent	Outstanding
Overall Experience					✓
Shore Excursions			✓		
Activities Close to Port				✓	
Beaches & Water Sports			✓		
Shopping				✓	
Dining/Bars			✓		

Freeport/Lucaya

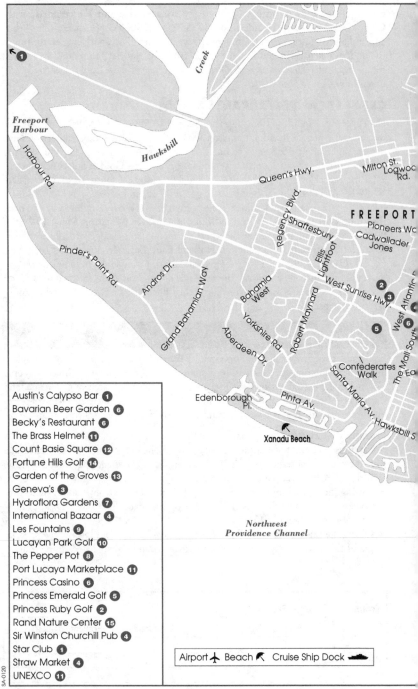

Austin's Calypso Bar ❶
Bavarian Beer Garden ❻
Becky's Restaurant ❻
The Brass Helmet ⓫
Count Basie Square ⓬
Fortune Hills Golf ⓮
Garden of the Groves ⓭
Geneva's ❸
Hydroflora Gardens ❼
International Bazaar ❹
Les Fountains ❾
Lucayan Park Golf ❿
The Pepper Pot ❽
Port Lucaya Marketplace ⓫
Princess Casino ❻
Princess Emerald Golf ❺
Princess Ruby Golf ❷
Rand Nature Center ⓯
Sir Winston Churchill Pub ❹
Star Club ❶
Straw Market ❹
UNEXCO ⓫

Airport ✈ Beach ⌅ Cruise Ship Dock ⛴

SA-0120

418

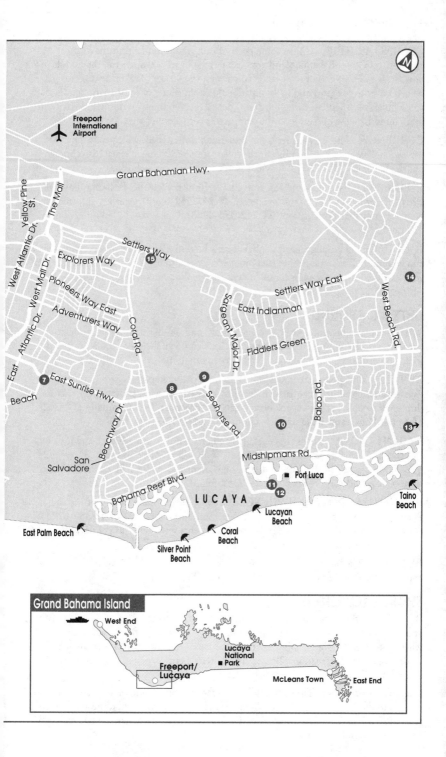

Freeport International Airport

Grand Bahamian Hwy.

Yellow Pine St.

The Mall

West Atlantic Dr.

Settlers Way

15

Explorers Way

West Mall Dr.

Pioneers Way East

Atlantic Dr.

Adventurers Way

Settlers Way East

East Indianman

Sargeant Major Dr.

Fiddlers Green

Coral Rd.

West Beach Rd.

14

East

7

East Sunrise Hwy.

8

9

Beach

Beachway Dr.

Seahorse Rd.

Balao Rd.

10

13

San Salvadore

Midshipmans Rd.

Port Luca

Bahama Reef Blvd.

LUCAYA

11

12

Taino Beach

East Palm Beach

Coral Beach

Lucayan Beach

Silver Point Beach

Grand Bahama Island

West End

Lucaya National Park

Freeport/ Lucaya

McLeans Town

East End

COMING ASHORE   Unlike some ports of call, where you land in the heart of everything, on Grand Bahama Island you're deposited in what cruisers call the middle of nowhere—the west end of the island. You'll want to take a $10 taxi ride (for two passengers) over to Freeport and its International Bazaar, center of most of the action. As you'll quickly learn after leaving the dreary port area, everything on this island is spread out. Grand Bahama doesn't have the compactness of Nassau.

CURRENCY   The legal tender is the **Bahamian dollar (B$),** which is on a par with the U.S. dollar. Both U.S. and Bahamian dollars are accepted on an equal basis throughout the Bahamas. Most large hotels and stores accept traveler's checks.

INFORMATION   Information is available from the **Grand Bahama Tourism Board,** International Bazaar in Freeport (☎ **242/352-6909**). Another information booth is located at Port Lucaya (☎ **242/373-8988**). Open 9am to 5:30pm Monday to Saturday.

LANGUAGE   The language of the Bahamas is English. Bahamians speak it with a lilt and with more British than American influence. They also pepper their colorful speech with words left from the indigenous Arawak tongue (like *cassava* and *guava*), as well as African words and phrases.

GETTING AROUND

You can explore the center of Freeport or Lucaya on foot, but if you want to make excursions into the West End or East End of the island, you'll either need a car or have to rely on taxis or the highly erratic public transportation.

BY TAXI   The government sets the taxi rates. The meter starts at $2, and 30¢ is charged for each additional quarter mile for two passengers. Most taxis wait at the cruise ship dock to pick up passengers, or you can call **Freeport Taxi Company** (☎ **242/ 352-6666**) or **Grand Bahama Taxi Union** (☎ **242/352-7101**).

BY RENTAL CAR   Roads are generally good on Grand Bahama Island, and it's easy to drive around. For car rentals, try **Avis** (☎ **800/331-2112** in the U.S., or 242/ 352-7666); **Hertz** (☎ **800/654-3001** in the U.S., or 242/352-9277); or the local **Star Rent-a-Car,** Old Airport Road (☎ **242/352-5953**).

BY MOTORSCOOTER OR BICYCLE   You can rent them at any of the major hotels such as **Princess Country Club,** West Sunrise Highway (☎ **242/352-6721**). A two-seater scooter requires a $100 deposit and rents for about $40 per day; bicycles require a $50 deposit and cost $12 for a half day, $20 for a full day.

BY BUS   Public bus service runs from the International Bazaar to downtown Freeport and from the Pub on the Mall to the Lucaya area. The typical fare is 75¢.

SHORE EXCURSIONS

Because most things to do here are in Freeport, the excursion offerings are weak and you can often manage better on your own. Many cruise ships tout a sightseeing trip where you spend about 30 minutes at the Garden of the Groves and then are led like cattle around the International Bazaar. This latter is better explored on your own. The 2¹/₂-hour trip costs about $18 per passenger.

Lucaya National Park Tour: Not all lines offer this, but if you see it offered, an excursion to the lush, 40-acre park on Sunrise Highway, is a worthwhile and relaxing afternoon. The park, about 12 miles from Lucaya, has one of the loveliest, most secluded beaches on Grand Bahama.

TOURING THROUGH LOCAL OPERATORS

Booze Cruise: Many lines offer booze cruises, but you can also arrange your own with **Superior Watersports** in Freeport (☎ 242/373-7863), which offers fun cruises on its *Bahama Mama,* a 72-foot catamaran with two semisubmersibles that dive 5 feet.

Swimming with Dolphins: You get to see porpoises up close with **The Dolphin Experience,** operated by the Underwater Explorers Society (UNEXSO), in Port Lucaya opposite Lucayan Beach Casino (☎ **800/992-3483** or 242/373-1250). UNEXSO conducts this unique dolphin/human familiarization program in which participants observe these intelligent, friendly animals close up and hear an interesting lecture by a member of the animal-care staff. This is not a swim-with-the-dolphins type of program, but all ages can step onto a shallow wading platform and interact with the animals. The dolphins are released daily to swim with scuba divers in the open ocean, however. The encounter on shore costs $36. An "Assistant Trainer" program is an all-day interactive experience in which a maximum of four people, aged 16 or older, can learn about dolphins and marine mammals in a behind-the-scenes experience. Participants help feed the animals and swim with them for a cost of $179. For $130, dolphins also swim out from Sanctuary Bay daily to interact with scuba divers from UNEXSO in an "open ocean" program.

ON YOUR OWN: WITHIN WALKING DISTANCE

There's nothing within walking distance; you have to head over to Freeport/Lucaya.

ON YOUR OWN: BEYOND WALKING DISTANCE

The prime attraction is the 11-acre **Garden of the Groves,** at the intersection of Midshipman Road and Magellan Drive (☎ 242/373-5668). Seven miles east of the International Bazaar, this scenic preserve of waterfalls and flowering shrubs has some 10,000 trees. The **Palmetto Café** (☎ 242/373-5668) serves snacks and drinks, and a Bahamian straw market sits at the entrance gate.

   Hydroflora Garden, on East Beach at Sunrise Highway (☎ 242/352-6052), is an artificially created botanical wonder, featuring 154 specimens of indigenous Bahamian plants. A special section is devoted to bush medicine.

   Filled with mangrove, pine, and palm trees, the 40-acre **Lucaya National Park,** Sunrise Highway (for information, contact Rand Nature Centre at ☎ 242/352-5438), is about 12 miles from Lucaya. The park contains one of the loveliest, most secluded beaches on Grand Bahama. A wooden path winding through the trees leads to this long, wide, dune-covered stretch. You can enter two caves, exposed when a portion of ground collapsed. The pools there are composed of 6 feet of freshwater atop a heavier layer of saltwater.

   Located 2 miles east of Freeport's center, the **Rand Nature Centre,** East Settlers Way (☎ 242/352-5438), is the regional headquarters of the Bahamas National Trust, a nonprofit conservation organization. Forest nature trails highlight native flora and bush medicine in this 100-acre pineland sanctuary. Wild birds abound. Other features include native animal displays, a replica of a Lucayan Indian village, an education center, and a gift shop.

   If your ship is in port late, head to ✪ **Count Basie Square** for one of the free nightly concerts. Count Basie had a grand home on Grand Bahama, and in the center of the waterfront restaurant and shopping complex of Port Lucaya there's a square named in his honor where a vine-covered bandstand hosts the best live music on the island, performed nightly. And it's free. Steel bands, small junkanoo groups, and even gospel singers from a local church are likely to perform here at night, their voices or music wafting across the 50-slip marina.

SHOPPING

There's no place for shopping in the Bahamas quite like the **International Bazaar,** at East Mall Drive and East Sunrise Highway. It's one of the world's most unusual shopping marts—Bahamian kitsch in poured concrete and plastic, 10 acres of born-to-shop theme park tastelessness—but in the nearly 100 shops, you're bound to find something that is both a discovery and a bargain. (Many items sold in the shops here could run about 40% less than in the United States, but don't count on it.) Displayed here are African handcrafts, Chinese jade, British china, Swiss watches, Irish linens, and Colombian emeralds—and that's just for starters. Continental cafes and dozens of shops loaded with merchandise await visitors. Buses marked INTERNATIONAL BAZAAR take you right to the much-photographed Toril Gate, a Japanese symbol of welcome.

The bazaar blends architecture from 25 countries into several theme areas: the Ginza in Tokyo for Asian goods; the Left Bank of Paris, or a reasonable facsimile, with sidewalk cafes where you can enjoy a café au lait and perhaps a pastry under shade trees; a Continental Pavilion for leather goods, jewelry, lingerie, and gifts at shops with names such as Love Boutique; India House for exotic goods such as taxi horns and silk saris; Africa for carvings or a colorful dashiki; and a Spanish section for Latin American and Iberian serapes and piñatas.

At the **Straw Market,** beside the International Bazaar, you'll find items with a special Bahamian touch—colorful baskets, hats, handbags, and place mats—all of which make good gifts and souvenirs of your trip.

The **Port Lucaya Marketplace** on Seahorse Road, the first of its kind in the Bahamas, was named after the original settlers of Grand Bahama. This is a shopping and dining complex set on 6 acres. Free entertainment, such as steel-drum bands and strolling musicians, adds to a festival atmosphere. The complex rose on the site of a former Bahamian straw market, but the craftspeople and their straw products are back in full force after having been temporarily dislodged. Full advantage is taken of the waterfront location. Many of the restaurants and shops overlook a 50-slip marina, home of a "fantasy" pirate ship featuring lunch and dinner/dancing cruises. A variety of charter vessels are also based at the Port Lucaya Marina, and dockage at the marina is available to visitors coming by boat to shop or dine. A boardwalk along the water makes it easy to watch the frolicking dolphins and join in other activities at the Underwater Explorers Society (UNEXSO).

Merchandise in the shops of Port Lucaya ranges from leather to lingerie to wind chimes. Traditional and contemporary fashions are featured for men, women, and children. Some of the better shops are **Coconits by Androsia,** an outlet of the famous batik house of Andros Island; **Jeweler's Warehouse,** a place for bargain hunters looking for good buys on discounted, close-out 14-karat gold and gemstone jewelry; the **UNEXSO Dive Shop,** selling swimsuits, wetsuits, underwater cameras, shades, hats, souvenirs, state-of-the-art diver's equipment, and computers; **Colombian Emeralds International,** offering a wide array of precious gemstone jewelry and one of the island's best watch collections; **Sea Treasures,** Spanish Section, with gold and silver jewelry inspired by the sea and handcrafted on the island; and **Bahamas Coin and Stamp Ltd.,** Arcade, specializing in Bahamian coin jewelry, ancient Roman coins, and relics from sunken Spanish galleons.

BEACHES

Grand Bahama has some 60 miles of white-sand beaches rimming the blue-green waters of the Atlantic. The mile-long **Xanadu Beach,** at the Xanadu Beach Resort, is the premier beach in the Freeport area. Most beaches are in the Lucaya area, site of the major resort hotels. The resort beaches, with a fairly active program of water sports, tend to be the most crowded in winter.

Other island beaches include **Taíno Beach,** lying to the east of Freeport, plus **Smith's Point** and **Fortune Beach,** the latter one of the finest on Grand Bahama. Another good beach, about a 20-minute ride east of Lucaya, is **Gold Rock Beach,** a favorite picnic spot with the locals, especially on weekends.

SPORTS

GENERAL WATER SPORTS   **Paradise Watersports,** at the Xanadu Beach Resort and Marina (☎ 242/352-2887), offers a variety of activities. With snorkeling trips, you cruise to a coral reef on a 48-foot catamaran. You can also rent paddleboats and go water-skiing, parasailing, or on a glass-bottomed boat ride.

GOLF   This island boasts more golf links than any other in the Bahamas. The courses are within 7 miles of one another, and you usually don't have to wait to play. All courses are open to the public year-round, and you can rent clubs from any of the pro shops on the island. Go on your own or sign up for an organized golf excursion if your ship offers them. **Fortune Hills Golf & Country Club,** Richmond Park, Lucaya (☎ 242/373-4500), was designed as an 18-hole course, but the back nine were never completed. You can replay the front nine for a total of 6,916 yards from the blue tees. Par is 72. The club is 5 miles east of Freeport. **Lucayan Park Golf & Country Club,** at Lucaya Beach (☎ 242/373-1066), is the best kept and most manicured course on Grand Bahama. The course was recently made over and is quite beautiful. It's known for its entrance and a hanging boulder sculpture. Greens are fast, and there are a couple of par-5 holes more than 500 yards long. Total distance from the blue tees is 6,824 yards, 6,488 from the white tees. Par is 72. Even if you're not a golfer, sample the food at the club restaurant. It offers everything from lavish champagne brunches to first-rate sea-food dishes. **Princess Emerald Course,** The Mall South (☎ 242/352-6721), is one of two courses owned and operated by the Bahamas Princess Resort & Casino. The Emerald Course was the site of the Bahamas National Open some years back. The course has plenty of trees along the fairways, as well as an abundance of water hazards and bunkers. The toughest hole is the ninth, a par 5 with 545 yards from the blue tees to the hole. The championship **Princess Ruby Course,** on West Sunrise Highway (☎ 242/352-6721), was designed by Joe Lee in 1968 and recently hosted the Michelin Long Drive competition. It's a total of 6,750 yards if played from the championship blue tees.

HORSEBACK RIDING   **Pinetree Stables,** North Beachway Drive, Freeport (☎ 242/373-3600), are the best in the Bahamas, superior to rivals on New Providence Island (Nassau). Pinetree offers trail rides to the beach Tuesday to Sunday at 9am, 10am, 11am, noon, and 2pm.

SCUBA DIVING & SNORKELING   One of the premier facilities for diving and snorkeling throughout the Bahamas and Caribbean is the **Underwater Explorers Society (UNEXSO),** at Lucaya Beach (☎ 242/373-1244). It has daily reef trips, shark dives, wreck dives, and night dives. This is also the only facility in the world where divers can swim alongside dolphins in the open ocean (see "Touring Through Local Operators," above). It offers a popular 3-hour learn-to-dive course every day as well as dives for the experienced. Snorkeling trips are also offered.

PARASAILING   **Clarion Atlantik Beach Resort,** on Royal Palm Way (☎ 242/373-1444), is the best center on the island for parasailing.

GAMBLING

Even though there are casinos aboard almost all ships, many passengers head immediately for a land-based casino once they hit shore. Most of the day life/nightlife in Freeport/Lucaya revolves around the **Princess Casino,** the Mall at West Sunrise

Highway (☎ 242/352-7811), a glittering, giant, Moroccan-style palace. It's open daily from 9am to 3am.

GREAT LOCAL RESTAURANTS & BARS

If you'd like to see what's left of the Bahamas "the way it was," head for the ✪ **Star Club,** on Bayshore Road (☎ 242/346-6207) in the West End. Built in the 1940s, it was the first hotel on Grand Bahama, and hosted many famous guests over the years. It's been a long time since any guests have checked in, but the place is still going strong as the only 24-hour bar on the island. Sometimes people leaving the casinos late at night come over here to eat grouper fingers, play pool, or listen to the taped music. The "club" is still run by the family of the late Austin Henry Grant Jr., a former Bahamian senator and West End legend. You can order Bahamian chicken in the bag, burgers, fish and chips, or "fresh sexy" conch prepared as chowder, fritters, and salads. But come here for the good times, not the food. You can also drop in next door at **Austin's Calypso Bar,** a real Grand Bahama dive if there ever was one. Austin Grant, the owner, will tell you about the good ol' days.

Geneva's, Kipling Lane, the Mall at West Sunrise Highway (☎ 242/352-5085), is another place where the food is the way it was before the hordes of tourists invaded. **Les Fountains,** East Sunrise Highway (☎ 242/373-9553), offers a great all-you-can-eat buffet as well as chicken, steak, and lobster, and dishes prepared at the jerk grill outside. **The Pepper Pot,** East Sunrise Highway at Coral Road (a 5-minute drive east of the International Bazaar, in a tiny shopping mall; ☎ 242/373-7655), serves take-out portions of the best carrot cake on the island, as well as a savory conch chowder, the standard fish and pork chops, chicken souse (an acquired taste), cracked conch, sandwiches and hamburgers, and an array of daily specials. **The Brass Helmet,** in the Port Lucaya Marketplace, directly above UNEXSO Dive Shop (☎ 242/373-2032), serves Bahamian staples, including cracked conch and grouper, plus an array of steaks, lobster, and a variety of pastas. **Becky's Restaurant,** at the International Bazaar, offers authentic Bahamian cuisine prepared in the time-tested style of the Out Islands.

Sir Winston Churchill Pub, East Mall (next to the Straw Market and the International Bazaar; ☎ 242/352-8866), is mainly a pizzeria, and also serves a selection of pastas, salads, and sandwiches. At the International Bazaar, the **Bavarian Beer Garden** features at least a dozen kinds of imported beer, recorded versions of oom-pah-pah music, such German fare as knockwurst, bockwurst, and sauerkraut, and a selection of pizzas.

8 Grand Cayman

Grand Cayman is the largest of the Cayman Islands, a British colony 480 miles due south of Miami (Cayman Brac and Little Cayman are the others). It's the top of an underwater mountain, whose side—known as the Cayman Wall—plummets straight down for 500 feet before becoming a steep slope that falls away for 6,000 feet to the ocean floor.

Despite its "grand" name, the place is only 22 miles long and 8 miles across at its widest point. Flat and prosperous, this tiny nation depends on Britain for its economic survival and attracts millionaire expatriates from all over because of its lenient tax and banking laws. Relatively unattractive, these islands are covered with scrubland and swamp, but boast more than their share of upscale, expensive private homes and condos. Until recently, Grand Cayman enjoyed one of the most closely knit social fabrics in the Caribbean, but with recent prosperity, some of it is beginning to unravel. More hotels have begun lining the sands of the nation's most famous sunspot, Seven Mile Beach, and the island attracts more than its share of scuba divers and snorkelers.

The Cayman Islands

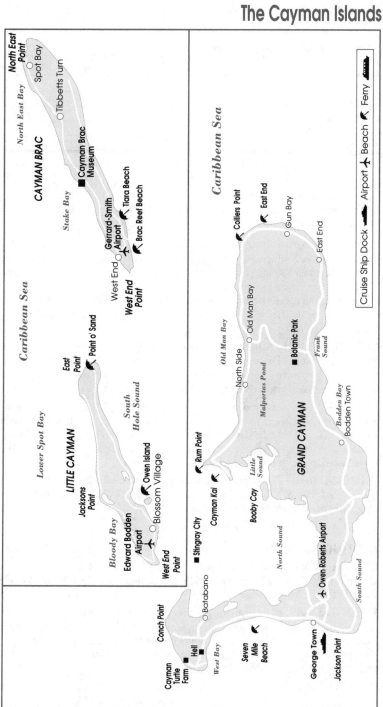

Cruise Ship Dock | Airport ✈ | Beach | Ferry

Caribbean Sea

CAYMAN BRAC

North East Point
Spot Bay
Tibbetts Turn
Cayman Brac Museum
Stake Bay
Gerrard-Smith Airport
Tiara Beach
Brac Reef Beach
West End
West End Point
North East Bay

LITTLE CAYMAN

Point o' Sand
East Point
South Hole Sound
Owen Island
Blossom Village
Jacksons Point
Edward Bodden Airport
West End Point
Bloody Bay
Lower Spot Bay

Caribbean Sea

GRAND CAYMAN

Colliers Point
East End
Gun Bay
East End
Old Man Bay
Old Man Bay
North Side
Botanic Park
Frank Sound
Malportas Pond
Bodden Bay
Bodden Town
Rum Point
Cayman Kai
Little Sound
Booby Cay
Stingray City
North Sound
South Sound
Owen Roberts Airport
Conch Point
Batabano
West Bay
Seven Mile Beach
George Town
Jackson Point
Cayman Turtle Farm
Hell

Frommer's Ratings: Grand Cayman					
	Poor	Fair	Good	Excellent	Outstanding
Overall Experience					✓
Shore Excursions					✓
Activities Close to Port				✓	
Beaches & Water Sports					✓
Shopping				✓	
Dining/Bars			✓		

Grand Cayman is also popular because of its laid-back civility (so civil that ships aren't allowed to visit on Sundays). **George Town** is the colony's capital and its commercial hub.

Frommer's Favorite Grand Cayman Experiences

- **Swimming with stingrays:** At Stingray City, you can hop into the water with dozens of these weird-looking but gentle sea creatures, which swim right into your arms, like dogs (see "Shore Excursions," below).
- **Taking in the scene on Seven Mile Beach:** Grand Cayman's famed stretch of sand is known for its array of water sports and its translucent aquamarine waters (see "Beaches," below).

COMING ASHORE   Cruise ships anchor off Georgetown and ferry their passengers to a pier on Harbour Drive. Located in the heart of the shopping district, the landing point couldn't be more convenient. There's a tourist information booth at the pier, and taxis line up to meet cruise ship passengers.

CURRENCY   The legal tender is the **Cayman Islands dollar (CI).** The exchange rate is CI.83 to US$1 (CI1 is worth about $1.20) Canadian, U.S., and British currencies are accepted throughout the Cayman Islands. Many restaurants quote prices in Cayman Islands dollars, which can lead you to think that food is cheaper than it is. Unless otherwise noted, prices in this section are given in U.S. dollars.

INFORMATION   The **Department of Tourism** is in the Pavilion Building, Cricket Square (P.O. Box 67), George Town, Grand Cayman, B.W.I. (☎ **345/949-0623**). Open Monday to Friday from 9am to 5pm.

LANGUAGE   English is the official language of the islands.

GETTING AROUND

BY TAXI   Taxi fares are fixed; typical one-way fares range from $11.50 to $20. **Cayman Cab Team** (☎ **345/947-4491**) and **Holiday Inn Taxi Stand** (☎ **345/945-4491**) offer 24-hour service.

BY RENTAL CAR   The roads are good by Caribbean standards, so driving around is relatively easy, as long as you remember to drive on the left side of the road. Reserve a car in advance with **Cico Avis** (☎ **800/331-1084** in the U.S., or 345/949-2468), **Budget** (☎ **800/527-0700** in the U.S., or 345/949-5605), or **Ace Hertz** (☎ **800/654-3131** in the U.S., or 345/949-7861).

BY MOTORSCOOTERS   The terrain is relatively flat, so motorcycles and bicycles are another way to get around. **Soto Scooters Ltd.,** Seven Mile Beach (☎ **345/945-4652**), at Coconut Place, offers Honda Elite scooters for about $30 daily, and bicycles for $15 daily.

SHORE EXCURSIONS

Nearly all the shore excursions here are underwater adventures, which you can book on your own or through your cruise ship.

✪ **Stingray City** ($38, 2 to 3 hours): The waters off Grand Cayman are home to Stingray City, one of the world's most unusual underwater attractions. Set in the very shallow, sun-flooded waters of North Sound, about 2 miles east of the island's northwestern tip, the site was discovered in the mid-1980s when local fishermen cleaned their catch and dumped the offal overboard. They noticed scores of stingrays (which usually eat marine crabs) feeding on the debris, a phenomenon that quickly attracted local divers and marine zoologists. Today, between 30 and 50 relatively tame stingrays hover in the waters around the site for their daily handouts from hordes (often hundreds of cruise passengers at a time) of snorkelers. *Tip:* Stingrays are terribly gentle creatures, but they possess viciously barbed stingers capable of inflicting painful damage to anyone mistreating them. Never try to grab one by the tail. As long as you don't, you can feed and pet these velvet-skinned creatures without incident.

Stingray City/Island Tour ($48, 3 hours): Stingray City is usually offered along with a short island tour, taking visitors to the Cayman Turtle Farm for 30 minutes or so as well as to the interesting rock formations (and T-shirt shops) of a town called Hell.

Atlantis **Submarine Excursion** ($74, 1½ hours): A 45-minute ride in the submarine *Atlantis XI* is usually offered. The "Atlantis Expedition" dive visits the Cayman Wall; the "Atlantis Discovery" lasts 40 minutes and introduces viewers to the marine life of the Caymans.

Seaworld Explorer Cruise ($33, 1 hour): A glass-bottomed boat takes you over tropical fish, stunning coral reefs, and even the remains of sunken ships.

TOURING THROUGH LOCAL OPERATORS

Stingray City: If the tours on your ship get booked, about half a dozen entrepreneurs lead expeditions to Stingray City, and there are usually a few tour agents waiting around the terminal in George Town. One well-known outfit is **Treasure Island Divers** (☎ **800/822-7552** or 345/949-4456), which charges snorkelers $25.

Taxi Tours: If you want to see the island, you can grab a taxi in port and take a tour. Taxis should cost about $40/hour and can hold up to five people, and a 3-hour tour covers all the sights in a leisurely fashion. Make sure to stop in the town called Hell and send a postcard home.

ON YOUR OWN: WITHIN WALKING DISTANCE

In George Town, **Cayman Islands National Museum,** Harbour Drive (☎ **345/ 949-8368**), is housed in a veranda-fronted building that once served as the island's courthouse and is very worthwhile. Exhibits include Caymanian artifacts collected by Ira Thompson (beginning in the 1930s), and other items portraying the natural, social, and cultural history of the Caymans. There's a gift shop, theater, and cafe (a $5 donation is requested).

ON YOUR OWN: BEYOND WALKING DISTANCE

The only green sea turtle farm of its kind in the world, **Cayman Turtle Farm,** Northwest Point (☎ **345/949-3894**), is the island's most popular land-based tourist attraction. Once a multitude of turtles lived in the waters surrounding the Cayman Islands, but today these creatures are an endangered species. The turtle farm's purpose is twofold: to provide the local market with edible turtle meat and to replenish the waters with hatchlings and yearling turtles. You can look into 100 circular concrete tanks containing turtles ranging in size from 6 ounces to 600 pounds, or sample turtle dishes at a snack bar and restaurant.

On 60 acres of rugged wooded land, **Queen Elizabeth II Botanical Park,** off Frank Sound Road, North Side (☎ **345/947-9462**), offers visitors a 1-hour walk along an 8-mile trail through wetlands, swamps, dry thicket, and mahogany trees. You might spot hickatees (the freshwater turtles found only on the Caymans and in Cuba), the rare Grand Cayman parrot, or the anole lizard with a cobalt-blue throat pouch. There are six rest stations along the trail, plus a visitor center and a canteen. There's also a heritage garden, a floral garden, and a lake.

The **Mastic Trail,** west of Frank Sound Road (☎ **345/949-1996**), is a restored 200-year-old footpath through a two-million-year-old woodland area in the heart of the island. Named for the majestic mastic tree, the trail showcases the reserve's natural attractions, including a native mangrove swamp, traditional agriculture, and an ancient woodland area. You can follow the 2-mile trail on your own, but I recommend taking a guided tour. The 3-hour guided tours, limited to eight participants, are offered Monday to Saturday. Reservations are required. Tours cost $25 CI ($31.25) per person. Participants should wear comfortable, sturdy shoes and carry water and insect repellent. The trail, adjacent to the Botanical Park, is about a 45-minute drive from George Town.

SHOPPING

There's duty-free shopping here for silver, china, crystal, Irish linens, British woolen goods, and such local crafts as black-coral jewelry, but I've found most prices to be similar to those in the U.S. Don't purchase turtle products, since they cannot be brought into the United States or most other Western nations.

Some standout shops include **Artifacts Ltd.,** Harbour Drive (on the harborfront, across from the landing dock), for back issues of some of Cayman stamps; **Black Coral and...,** Fort Street, for the stunning black-coral creations of internationally acclaimed sculptor Bernard K. Passman; **The Jewelry Centre,** Fort Street, one of the largest jewelry stores in the Caymans; and the **Kennedy Gallery,** West Shore Centre, specializing in watercolors by local artists.

BEACHES

Grand Cayman's ✪ **Seven Mile Beach,** which begins north of George Town, an easy taxi ride from the cruise dock, has sparkling white sands with a backdrop of Australian pines. The beach is really about 5¹/₂ miles long, but the label of "seven mile" has stuck. It's lined with condominiums and plush resorts, and is known for its array of water sports and its translucent aquamarine waters. The average water temperature is a balmy 80°F.

SPORTS

FISHING & GENERAL WATER SPORTS   Red Sail Sports (☎ **800/255-6425** in the U.S., or 345/947-5966) has its headquarters in a gaily painted wooden house beside the beach at the Hyatt Regency Grand Cayman on West Bay Road. Its half-day deep-sea fishing excursions for up to eight people depart daily at 7am and 1pm in search of tuna, marlin, and wahoo. Red Sail offers parasailing, water-skiing, and scuba diving for beginners as well as more advanced divers. In addition, it has one of the best-designed sailing catamarans in the Caribbean, berthed in a canal a short walk from the water sports center. There's a daily sail from 10am to 2pm to Stingray City, with snorkeling equipment and lunch included in the price.

GOLF   The major course on Grand Cayman is at the **Britannia Golf Club,** next to the Hyatt Regency on West Bay Road (☎ **345/949-8020**). The course was designed by Jack Nicklaus and is unique in that it incorporates three different courses in one: a 9-hole championship layout, an 18-hole executive set-up, and an 18-hole Cayman course. Non-guests of the club can reserve no more than 24 hours in advance.

SCUBA DIVING & SNORKELING   Coral reefs and other formations encircling the island are filled with marine life. It's easy to dive close to shore, so boats aren't necessary, but plenty of boats and scuba facilities are available, as well as many dive shops renting scuba gear to certified divers. The best dive operation is **Bob Soto's Diving Ltd.,** P.O. Box 1801, Grand Cayman, B.W.I. (☎ **800/262-7686** or 809/949-2022 for reservations, or 345/949-2022), with full-service dive shops at Treasure Island, the SCUBA Centre on North Church Street, and Soto's Coconut in the Coconut Place Shopping Centre. There are full-day resort courses as well as dives for experienced people daily on the west, north, and south walls, plus shore diving from the SCUBA Centre. The staff is helpful and highly professional.

GREAT LOCAL RESTAURANTS & BARS

Cracked Conch by the Sea, West Bay Road (near Turtle Bay Farm; ☎ **345/945-5217**), serves some of the island's freshest seafood, including a succulent turtle steak and the inevitable conch, plus an array of meat dishes, including beef, jerk pork and spicy combinations of chicken. The **Crow's Nest Restaurant,** South Sound (on the southwesternmost tip of the island, a 4-minute drive from George Town; ☎ **345/949-9366**), is one of those places that evokes the Caribbean "the way it used to be." There's no pretense here—you get good, honest Caribbean cookery, including grilled seafood, at great prices. Many dishes are spicy, especially their signature appetizer, fiery coconut shrimp.

The **Hog Sty Bay Café and Pub,** North Church Street (near the beginning of West Bay Road; ☎ **345/949-6163**), enjoys a loyal clientele, and is divided into an amusingly decorated pub and a Caribbean-inspired dining room open to a view of the harbor. In the pub, you can order such British staples as fish and chips or cottage pie. **Island Taste,** South Church Street (☎ **345/949-4945**), caters more to large appetites than to picky gourmets, and offers great value for the money. Most of the menu is devoted to seafood dishes, such as dolphin, turtle steak, and spiny lobster. **Ottmar's Restaurant and Lounge,** West Bay Road (side entrance of Grand Pavilion Hotel; ☎ **345/945-5879**), is one of the island's top restaurants, offering such dishes as Bavarian cucumber soup, bouillabaisse, French pepper steak, and Wiener schnitzel. Our favorite is chicken Trinidad, stuffed with grapes, nuts, and apples rolled in coconut flakes, sautéed golden brown, and served in orange-butter sauce.

9 Grenada

The southernmost nation of the Windward Islands, Grenada (Gre-*nay*-dah) is one of the lushest in the Caribbean. Called the "Spice Island," its extravagant fertility—a result of the gentle climate and volcanic soil—produces more spices than anywhere else in the world: cloves, cinnamon, mace, cocoa, tonka beans, ginger, and a third of the world's supply of nutmeg. There's a lot of very appealing local color, particularly since the political troubles of the 1980s seem to have ended. The beaches are white and sandy, and the populace (a mixture of English expatriates and islanders of African descent) is friendly. Once a British Crown Colony but now independent, the island nation also incorporates two smaller islands: Carriacou and Petit Martinique, neither of which has many tourist facilities.

St. George's, the country's capital, is one of the most colorful ports in the West Indies. Nearly landlocked in the deep crater of a long-dead volcano, and flanked by old forts, it reminds many visitors of Portofino, Italy. Here you'll see some of the most charming Georgian colonial buildings in the Caribbean. Frangipani and flamboyant trees add even more color.

Criss-crossed by nature trails, Grenada's interior is a jungle of palms, oleander, bougainvillea, purple and red hibiscus, crimson anthurium, bananas, breadfruit, birdsong, ferns, and palms. The island's lush tropical scenery and natural bounty attract visitors who want to snorkel, sail, fish, or loll the day away on the 2-mile-long, white-sand **Grand Anse Beach,** one of the best in the Caribbean.

Frommer's Favorite Grenada Experiences

- **Picnicking at Annandale Falls:** A 50-foot cascade is the perfect backdrop for a picnic among tropical flora—and you can swim in the falls afterward (see "On Your Own: Beyond Walking Distance," below).
- **Dining at Betty Mascoll's Morne Fendue:** At a plantation house built the same year she was born, Mrs. Mascoll and her veteran staff serve the most authentic local food on the island (see "Great Local Restaurants & Bars," below).
- **Visiting Levera National Park:** With beaches, coral reefs, a mangrove swamp, a lake, and a bird sanctuary, this is a paradise for hikers, swimmers, and snorkelers alike (see "On Your Own: Beyond Walking Distance," below).
- **Taking the rainforest and Grand Etang Lake tour:** Take a bus to an extinct volcanic crater some 1,900 feet above sea level. On the way, drive through rainforests and stop at a spice estate (see "Shore Excursions," below).

COMING ASHORE   Ships either dock at a pier right in St. George's or anchor in the much-photographed harbor and send their passengers to the pier by tender. A tourist information center at the pier dispenses island data. Pier telephones take major credit cards, or you can buy Island Phone Cards at the tourist information desk. The Carenage (St. George's main street) is only a short walk away from the pier; a taxi into the center of town costs about $3. To get to Grand Anse, you can take a regular taxi or a water taxi (see "Getting Around," below).

CURRENCY   The official currency is the **Eastern Caribbean dollar (EC$).** The exchange rate is EC$2.70 to US$1 (EC$1 is worth about 37¢). Always determine which dollars—EC or U.S.—you're talking about when discussing a price.

INFORMATION   Go to the **Grenada Board of Tourism,** on The Carenage in St. George's (☎ 473/440-2279), for maps and general information. Open Monday to Friday from 8am to 4pm.

LANGUAGE   English is commonly spoken on this island. Creole English, a mixture of African, English, and French, is spoken informally by the majority.

GETTING AROUND
St. George's can easily be explored on foot, although parts of the town are steep as it rises up from the harbor.

Frommer's Ratings: Grenada					
	Poor	Fair	Good	Excellent	Outstanding
Overall Experience					✓
Shore Excursions			✓		
Activities Close to Port				✓	
Beaches & Water Sports			✓		
Shopping			✓		
Dining/Bars			✓		

Grenada

BY TAXI   Taxi fares are set by the government. Most cruisers take a cab from the pier to somewhere near St. George's. You can also tap most taxi drivers as a guide for a day's sightseeing. The charge is about $15 per hour, but be sure to negotiate a price before setting out.

BY MINIVAN   Minivans charge EC$1 to EC$6 (40¢ to $2.20), and the most popular run is between St. George's and Grand Anse Beach. Most minivans depart from Market Square or from the Esplanade area of St. George's.

BY WATER TAXI   An ideal way to get around the harbor and to Grand Anse Beach. (The round-trip fare to the beach is $4.) A water taxi can take you from one end of The Carenage to the other for another $2.

BY RENTAL CAR   I don't recommend driving here.

SHORE EXCURSIONS

Because of Grenada's lush landscape, I recommend spending at least 3 hours touring its interior, one of the most scenic in the West Indies.

✪ **Rainforest/Grand Etang Lake Tour** ($37, 3 hours): This is worthwhile and a great way to experience Grenada's lush interior. Via bus, you travel past the red-tiled roofs of St. George's en route to the bright blue Grand Etang Lake within an extinct volcanic crater some 1,900 feet above sea level. On the way, you drive through rainforests and stop at a spice estate. Some tours include a visit to the Annandale Falls.

Island Bus Tour ($32, 3 hours): Typical scenic island tours take you through the highlights of the interior and along the coast, including Grand Anse Beach. You get to see the most luxuriant part of Grenada's rainforest, a nutmeg-processing station, a sugar factory, and many small hamlets along the way. Many cruise lines also book you on a tour ($27, 2 hours) that explores St. George's historical sites and forts before taking you to some of the island's natural highlights, including a private garden where some 500 species of island plants and flowers are cultivated.

Party Cruises ($28 without snorkeling gear and $37 with gear, 3 to 4 hours): Party cruises are popular here, with no shortage of rum and reggae music. Two large party boats, the *Rhum Runner* and *Rhum Runner II,* designed for 120 and 250 passengers, operate out of St. George's harbor, making three trips daily. The cost includes snorkeling stops at reefs and beaches along the way.

ON YOUR OWN: WITHIN WALKING DISTANCE

In St. George's, you can visit the **Grenada National Museum,** at the corner of Young and Monckton streets (☎ 473/440-3725), set in the foundations of an old French army barracks and prison built in 1704. This small but interesting museum houses finds from archeological digs, including ancient petroglyphs, plus a rum still, native fauna, and memorabilia depicting Grenada's history, including the island's first telegraph. There are also two bathtubs worth seeing—the wooden barrel used by the fort's prisoners and the carved marble tub used by Joséphine Bonaparte during her adolescence on Martinique. The most comprehensive exhibit illuminates the native culture of Grenada. The museum is open Monday to Friday and admission is $2.

ON YOUR OWN: BEYOND WALKING DISTANCE

You can take a taxi up Richmond Hill to **Fort Frederick,** which the French began in 1779. The British, having retaken the island in 1783 under provision of the Treaty of Versailles, completed the fort in 1791. From its battlements you have a panoramic view of the harbor and the yacht marina.

Don't miss the mountains northeast of St. George's. After a 15-minute drive, you reach ✪ **Annandale Falls,** a tropical wonderland where a 50-foot-high cascade drops into a basin. The overall beauty is almost Tahitian. You can have a picnic surrounded by liana vines, elephant ears, and other tropical flora and spices. **Annandale Falls Centre** offers gift items, handcrafts, and samples of the indigenous spices of Grenada. Nearby, an improved trail leads to the falls, where you can enjoy a refreshing swim. Swimmers can use the changing cubicles at the falls at no cost. The center is open daily from 8am to 4pm.

Opened in 1994, 450-acre park ✪ **Levera National Park** has several white sandy beaches for swimming and snorkeling, although the surf is rough. Offshore are coral reefs and seagrass beds. Inland, the park contains a mangrove swamp, a lake, and a bird sanctuary—perhaps you'll see a rare tropical parrot. It's a hiker's paradise. The interpretation center (☎ 473/442-1018) is open Monday to Friday from 8am to 4pm, Saturday from 10am to 4pm, and Sunday from 9am to 5pm. The park, about 15 miles from the harbor, can be reached by taxi, bus, or water taxi.

SHOPPING

The local stores sell luxury-item imports, mainly from England, at prices that are not quite duty-free. This is no grand Caribbean merchandise mart, so if you're cruising on to such islands as Aruba, Sint Maarten, or St. Thomas, you might want to postpone serious purchases. On the other hand, you can find some fine local handcrafts, gifts, and art here.

Spice vendors besiege you wherever you go. The spices here are fresher and better than any you're likely to find in your local supermarket, so nearly everybody comes home with a hand-woven basket of local spices. The Grenadians use every part of the nutmeg: They make the outer fruit into either a tasty liqueur or a rich jam, and ground the orange membrane around the nut into a different spice called mace. **Arawak Islands,** Upper Belmont Road, is a celebration of the best scents produced on an island that's legendary for spices. Look for at least nine different fragrances distilled from such island plants as frangipani, wild lilies, cinnamon, nutmeg, and cloves. You'll also find an all-natural insect repellent that some clients insist is the most effective (and safest) they're ever used.

Some worthwhile shops include **Art Fabrik,** Young Street, for batik shirts, shifts, shorts, skirts, T-shirts, and the like; **Creation Arts & Crafts,** The Carenage, for off-island handicrafts (from Venezuela, Sint Maarten, and Cuba); **Sea Change Bookstore,** The Carenage, for recent British and American newspapers; **Spice Island Perfumes,** The Carenage, for perfumes made from the natural extracts of local herbs and spices; and **Tikal,** Young Street, for handcrafts from Grenada and around the world.

BEACHES

Grenada's ✪ **Grand Anse Beach,** with its 2 miles of sugar-white sands, is one of the best beaches in the Caribbean. From the port, it's about a 10-minute, $10 taxi ride, although you can also take a water taxi from the pier for only $4 round-trip.

SPORTS

GOLF   The **Grenada Golf Course and Country Club,** Woodlands (☎ 473/444-4128), has a nine-hole course, with views of the Caribbean Sea and the Atlantic. It's open Monday to Saturday from 8am to sunset and on Sunday from 8am to 1:30pm.

SCUBA DIVING & SNORKELING   Grenada offers an underwater world rich in submarine gardens, exotic fish, and coral formations. Visibility is often up to 120 feet. Off the coast is the wreck of the nearly 600-foot ocean liner *Bianca C.* Novice divers should stick to the west coast; the more experienced might search out the sights along the rougher Atlantic side. **Daddy Vic's Watersports,** directly on the beach in the Grenada Renaissance, Grand Anse Beach (☎ 473/444-4371, ext. 638), is the premier scuba diving outfit. It also offers snorkeling trips, as well as windsurfer and Sunfish rentals, parasailing, and water-skiing. It can arrange to pick you up at the pier in a courtesy bus and bring you back to the cruise ship later. Canadian-run **Grand Anse Aquatics,** at Coyaba Beach Resort on Grand Anse Beach (☎ 473/444-4129), gives Daddy Vic's serious competition, offering both scuba diving and snorkeling jaunts to reefs and shipwrecks teaming with marine life. Diving instruction is available. (*Warning:* Grenada doesn't have a decompression chamber. In the event of an emergency, divers must be taken to the facilities on Barbados.)

GREAT LOCAL RESTAURANTS & BARS

Your last chance to enjoy food from old-time island recipes, many now fading from cultural memory, is at ✪ **Betty Mascoll's Morne Fendue,** at St. Patrick's (☎ 473/442-9330), 25 miles north of St. George's. This plantation house was built in 1912 of chiseled river rocks held together by a mixture of lime and molasses. Mrs. Mascoll was born that same year and has lived here ever since, continuing her long tradition of hospitality. You dine as an upper-class family did in the 1920s. Lunch is likely to include a yam-and-sweet-potato casserole or curried chicken with lots of island-grown spices. The most famous dish is Betty's legendary pepperpot stew, which includes pork and oxtail, tenderized by the juice of grated cassava. Mrs. Mascoll and her loyal, veteran staff need time to prepare, so it's imperative to call ahead. They serve a fixed-price lunch for EC$45 ($16.45) Monday to Saturday from 12:30 to 3pm.

Mamma's, Lagoon Road (☎ 473/440-1459), captures the authentic taste of Grenada. Meals include such dishes as callaloo soup with coconut cream, shredded cold crab with lime juice, freshwater crayfish, fried conch, and rotis made of curry and yellow chickpeas. **The Nutmeg,** The Carenage (located right on the harbor over the Sea Change Shop; ☎ 473/440-2539), is a hangout for the yachting set and a favorite with expatriates and visitors. The lobster Thermidor is the best in town.

Pierone, The Carenage (at the extreme northern end; ☎ 473/440-9747), is best suited for a midday pick-me-up, with or without alcohol, partly because of the cool breezes that blow in off the port. Menu items include such West Indian dishes as lambi (conch) chowder, sandwiches, and the most popular dish on the menu, lobster pando, a form of ragoût. **Rudolf's,** The Carenage (☎ 473/440-2241), serves the best steaks in the capital. Conch is prepared in several different ways, as are shrimp and octopus. Flying fish and dolphin deserve the most praise.

10 Guadeloupe

Part of the French West Indies, Butterfly-shaped Guadeloupe is actually two distinctly different volcanic islands separated by a narrow saltwater strait, the Rivière Salée. **Grande-Terre,** the eastern island, is typical of the charming Antilles, with rolling hills and sugar plantations. The western island, **Basse-Terre,** is rugged and mountainous, dominated by the active 4,800-foot volcano La Soufrière. Basse-Terre's mountains are covered with tropical forests, and the island is ringed by beautiful beaches. The surf pounds hard against its east-facing Atlantic coast, but calmer seas rule on the leeward bathing beaches.

Guadeloupe isn't as sophisticated or cosmopolitan as the two outlying islands over which it hold administrative authority (St. Barthélemy and the French section of St. Martin), but there's a lot of natural beauty in this department of mainland France. The islands have a relatively low population density, with only 340,000 people living here, mostly along the coast. Bananas grown on plantations are the main crop. The islands are ideal for scenic drives and Creole color, offering an insight into the French colonial world.

Guadeloupe's charm is not readily apparent when your ship arrives at **Pointe-à-Pitre,** the capital. This rather tacky port doesn't have the old-world charm of Fort-de-France on Martinique. The rather narrow streets are jammed during the day with crowds, creating a permanent traffic jam.

Frommer's Favorite Guadeloupe Experiences
- **Checking out the petroglyphs at Roches Gravées:** Near the pier in Trois Rivières are the Roches Gravées ("Carved Rocks"), onto which the island's original inhabitants, the Arawaks, carved petroglyphs of humans and animals. They most likely date from A.D. 300 or 400 (see "Basse-Terre," below).

Frommer's Ratings: Guadeloupe					
	Poor	Fair	Good	Excellent	Outstanding
Overall Experience				✓	
Shore Excursions			✓		
Activities Close to Port			✓		
Beaches & Water Sports			✓		
Shopping			✓		
Dining/Bars			✓		

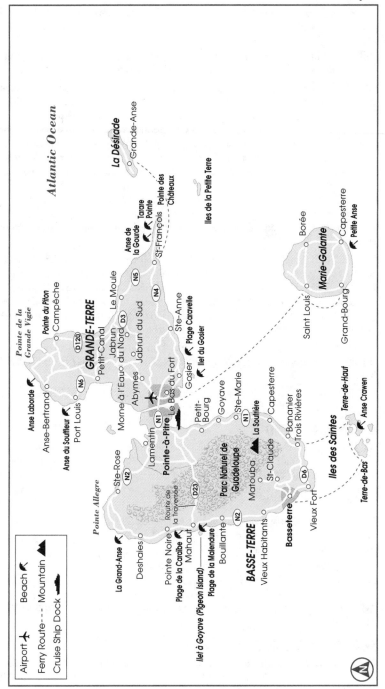

Atlantic Ocean

Pointe de la Grande Vigie

Pointe du Piton

Campêche

GRANDE-TERRE

Petit-Canal

D120

N6

Anse-Bertrand

Anse du Souffleur

Anse Laborde

Port Louis

Jabrun du Nord

Jabrun du Sud

Le Moule

N5

N4

D3

Morne à l'Eau

Abymes

Ste-Anne

Gosier

Plage Caravelle

Ilet du Gosier

St-François

Anse de la Gourde

Tarare

Pointe

Pointe des Châteaux

La Désirade

Grande-Anse

Iles de la Petite Terre

Le Bas du Fort

N1

Pointe-à-Pitre

Lamentin

Petit-Bourg

Goyave

Ste-Marie

N1

La Soufrière

Capesterre

Bananier

Trois Rivières

Ste-Rose

N2

Pointe Allegre

Deshaies

Pointe Noire

Plage de la Caraïbe

Ilet à Goyave (Pigeon Island)

Mahaut

Plage de la Malendure

Route de la Traversée

D23

Parc Naturel de Guadeloupe

Matouba

St-Claude

Bouillante

N2

Basseterre

Vieux Habitants

D6

Vieux Fort

BASSE-TERRE

La Grand-Anse

Saint Louis

Marie-Galante

Borée

Grand-Bourg

Capesterre

Petite Anse

Iles des Saintes

Terre-de-Haut

Anse Crawen

Terre-de-Bas

Airport ✈   Beach ✔
Ferry Route --- Mountain ▲
Cruise Ship Dock

- **Driving up a volcano:** La Soufrière rises to a height of some 4,800 feet, flanked by banana plantations and lush foliage. You can drive to 3,300 feet, and then hike right to the volcano's mouth (see "Basse-Terre," below).
- **Taking a jungle-hiking excursion:** Take a short hike through the jungle, and then have a dip at Carbet Falls (see "Shore Excursions," below).

COMING ASHORE   Cruise ships dock right in the commercial center of Pointe-à-Pitre at Centre St-Jean-Perse, a $20 million project that has transformed the port's waterfront, once a bastion of old warehouses. Named for a 20th-century poet and Nobel Laureate who was born just a few blocks away, this modern center is designed in a contemporary French Caribbean style, which blends well with the town's traditional architecture. Surrounded by small tropical gardens, it offers an array of duty-free shops selling Guadeloupean rum and French perfume. It's located near several open-air markets and small shops.

You'll find phones at Centre St-Jean-Pearse. Outlets labeled *Telecart en Vente Ici* sell *Telecartes*, prepaid discount phone cards that can be used in booths marked "Telecom." Phone connections are difficult in Guadeloupe, especially if you don't speak French, and expensive as well.

CURRENCY   Unlike most other parts of the Caribbean, the Yankee dollar isn't widely accepted here. Some shops take U.S. dollars, but the official monetary unit is the **French franc (F).** The exchange rate is 6.29F to US$1 (1F is worth about 16¢). Most restaurants quote prices in French francs; however, shops in and around the cruise dock generally have prices in both French francs and U.S. dollars. There's a bank at the Centre St-Jean-Pearse where you can convert your dollars to francs.

INFORMATION   The **Office Départmental du Tourisme** is located on Square de la Banque 5, in Pointe-à-Pitre (☎ **0590/82-09-30**). Open Monday to Friday 9am to 5pm.

LANGUAGE   The official language is French, and Creole is the unofficial second language. English is spoken only in the major tourist centers, rarely in the countryside.

GETTING AROUND

BY TAXI   You'll find taxis at the cruise dock. The taxi drivers charge whatever they can, although technically the government regulates fares. Always agree on the price before getting in. Call ☎ **0590/82-99-88** for a radio-dispatched cab. If you're traveling with people or can put together a party, it's possible to sightsee by taxi. Fares are negotiable.

BY BUS   Buses link almost every hamlet to Pointe-à-Pitre, and these jitney vans going to Basse-Terre leave from the Gare Routière de Bergevin. Those heading to other parts of Grande-Terre depart the Gare Routière de Mortenol.

BY RENTAL CAR   The road all the way around Basse-Terre makes for one of the loveliest drives in the Caribbean. Driving is on the right side of the road and is relatively easy. Reserve a car in advance from **Hertz** (☎ **800/654-3001** or 0590/21-09-35), **Avis** (☎ **800/331-2112** or 0590/21-13-54), or **Budget** (☎ **800/527-0700** or 0590/21-13-48).

SHORE EXCURSIONS

✪ **Jungle-Hiking Excursion** ($40, 4 hours): An excursion to the south side of Basse-Terre allows you to see the island's lush banana plantations and rainforests before doing a 30-minute jungle hike to reach the pictuesque Carbet Falls, where you're free to take a dip.

Island Tour ($30, 3 hours): Most cruise ships offer an island tour visiting both Grande-Terre and Basse-Terre. The tour includes a walk through the national park and a visit to a rum factory.

ON YOUR OWN: WITHIN WALKING DISTANCE

Saint-John Perse once wrote about the fine time sailors had when Pointe-à-Pitre was a stopover on the famous route du Rhum. But those days are long gone, and today you might not want to linger in town, where the only point of interest is shopping. It's best to visit Pointe-à-Pitre in the morning, when the **covered market** at the corner of rue Frébault and rue Thiers is at its liveliest.

The town center is **Place de la Victoire,** a park shaded by palm trees and poincianas. Here you'll see some old sandbox trees said to have been planted by Victor Hughes, a mulatto who organized a revolutionary army of both whites and blacks and established a dictatorship just before the Napoleonic era. The British kicked Hughes out after they defeated Napoleon and briefly took over Guadeloupe. A guillotine that Hughes kept busy stood here until modern times, but it's gone now.

A DRIVING TOUR

Here's a driving tour that touches on the best sights of Grande-Terre and Basse-Terre.

GRANDE-TERRE

From town, head to the "South Riviera," which runs along the coast from Pointe-à-Pitre to Pointe des Châteaux at the eastern end of Grande-Terre. At the tourist complex of **Bas du Fort,** 2 miles east of Pointe-à-Pitre near Gosier, you'll come to the **Aquarium de la Guadeloupe,** Place Créole, Marina Gosier (☎ 0590/90-92-38), one of the three most important aquariums of France and the largest and most modern in the Caribbean. The aquarium is home to tropical fish, coral, underwater plants, huge sharks, and other sea creatures. The exhibits are all clearly labeled. It's located just off the main highway near Bas-du-Fort Marina. Open daily from 9am to 7pm.

Some of the biggest and most important resorts of Guadeloupe are found at **Gosier,** with its nearly 5 miles of beach stretching east from Pointe-à-Pitre. Most shore excursions stop at **Fort Fleur-d'Epée,** which dates from the 18th century. Its dungeons and battlements are testaments to the ferocious fighting between the French and British armies seeking to control the island in 1794. The well-preserved ruins command the crown of a hill. From here you'll have good views over the bay of Pointe-à-Pitre, and on a clear day you can see the neighboring offshore islands of Marie-Galante and Iles des Saintes.

Seven miles east of St-François is **Pointe des Chêteaux,** the easternmost tip of Grande-Terre, where the Atlantic meets the Caribbean. You'll hear the waves crashing all around you, and see a cliff sculpted by the sea into castle-like formations. The view from here is panoramic. At the top is a cross put there in the 19th century.

You might want to walk to **Pointe des Colibris,** the extreme end of Guadeloupe. From here you'll have a view of the northeastern sector of the island, and of La Désirade to the east, an island that looks like a huge vessel at anchor. Among the coved beaches found here, **Plage de Tarare** is a nude beach.

You can use the N5 as an alternative route from St-François back to Pointe-à-Pitre from Pointe des Châteaux. After 9 miles, you reach the village of **Le Moule,** which was founded at the end of the 17th century, long before Pointe-à-Pitre. It used to be a major shipping port for sugar, though now it's just a tiny coastal fishing village. Le Moule never regained its importance after a hurricane devastated it and many other villages in 1928. However, a holiday center is now being developed along its 10-mile crescent-shaped beach.

Musée Edgar Clerc de Préhistoire Amérindienne le Moule (Edgar Clerc Museum at Le Moule), Parc de la Rosette, Le Moule (☎ **0590/23-57-57**), is devoted exclusively to the Arawak and Carib tribes in the Caribbean. It's one of the largest museums of its kind, containing relics gathered from throughout the Caribbean archipelago. Set 3 miles from Le Moule toward Campêche, the museum is open Tuesday to Sunday from 8:50am to 4:50pm. Admission costs 10F ($1.65) per person.

BASSE-TERRE

You can explore Basse-Terre's coast via the N1 from Pointe-à-Pitre. After a mile and a half, the Pont de la Gabarre crosses the Rivière Salée, the narrow strait separating Grande-Terre from Basse-Terre. For the next 4 miles the road runs straight through sugarcane fields. Turn right on the N2 toward **Baie Mahault.** (Don't confuse this with the town of Mahault, which is on Basse-Terre's western coast.) Leaving Baie Mahault, head northwest to Lamentin, a village settled by corsairs at the beginning of the 18th century. Here you'll see some colonial mansions scattered about.

From Lamentin, drive 6^1/$_2$ miles to **Ste-Rose,** where you can find several good beaches. On your left, a small road leads to **Sofaia,** from which you have a panoramic view over the coast and forest preserve. The locals claim that a sulfur spring here has curative powers.

A few miles farther along the N2 is Pointe Allègre, the northernmost point of Basse-Terre. At **Clugny Beach,** you'll be at the site where the first settlers landed on Guadeloupe. A couple of miles more brings you to **Grand Anse,** one of the best beaches in Guadeloupe. It's very large, still secluded, and sheltered by many tropical trees.

Snorkeling and fishing are popular pastimes at **Deshaies.** The narrow road winds up and down and has a corniche look to it. The blue sea is underneath, and above you can see green mountains studded with colorful hamlets.

Nine miles from Deshaies, **Pointe Noire** comes into view. Its name comes from black volcanic rocks. Look for the odd polychrome cenotaph in town.

You reach Mahaut 4 miles from Pointe Noire. On your left begins the **route de la Traversée,** the Transcoastal Highway. I recommend going this way, to pass through the scenic wonders of **Parc Naturel de Guadeloupe.** Taking up 74,100 acres, or about one-fifth of Guadeloupe, this huge tract of mountains, tropical forests, and panoramic scenery is home to a variety of animals, including titi (a raccoon adopted as the island's official mascot) and such birds as the wood pigeon, turtledove, and thrush. Small exhibition huts are scattered throughout the park, providing information on the volcano and the forest, as well as coffee, sugarcane, and rum. The Parc Naturel has no gates, no opening or closing hours, and no admission fee.

The big attraction of the park (and of Basse-Terre) is the famous sulfur-puffing ✪ **La Soufrière volcano.** The appearance of ashes, mud, billowing smoke, and earthquake-like tremors in 1975 proved that this old beast is still active. Rising to a height of some 4,800 feet, it's flanked by banana plantations and lush foliage. You can drive from Basse-Terre to the suburb of St-Claude, 4 miles up the mountainside at an elevation of 1,900 feet. St-Claude has an elegant reputation, with a perfect climate and tropical gardens. From here, you can drive up the narrow, winding road the Guadeloupeans say leads to hell—that is, the summit of La Soufrière. The road ends at a parking area at La Savane à Mulets, at an altitude of 3,300 feet. You can touch the ground in the parking lot and feel its heat. Hikers can climb right to the mouth of the volcano. Steam emerges from fumaroles and sulfurous fumes from the volcano's "burps."

From the park, the main road descends toward Versailles, a hamlet about 5 miles from Pointe-à-Pitre.

Heading south on the N2, you can continue along winding roads to the town of **Basse-Terre,** Guadeloupe's seat of government. Founded in 1634, it's the oldest town on the island. The town suffered heavy destruction at the hands of British troops in 1691 and again in 1702. It was also the center of fierce fighting during the French Revolution, when explosive tensions gripped Guadeloupe. Although there's not much to see here now other than a 17th-century cathedral and Fort St-Charles, it still has its charms. The market squares are shaded by tamarind and palm trees.

The country along the eastern coast of Basse-Terre is richer and greener than elsewhere on the island. Here near the pier in Trois-Rivières are the ✪ **Roches Gravées** ("Carved Rocks"), onto which the island's original inhabitants, the Arawaks, carved petroglyphs of humans and animals. They most likely date from A.D. 300 or 400. You'll also see specimens of plants, including cocoa, pimiento, and banana, that the Arawaks cultivated long before the Europeans set foot on Guadeloupe.

North of Trois-Rivières, in the town square of ✪ **Ste-Marie,** 4¹⁄₂ miles past Capesterre, you can stop and see the statue of Guadeloupe's first tourist: Christopher Columbus. He anchored a quarter of a mile from Ste-Marie on November 4, 1493, on his second voyage, and wrote in his journal, "We arrived, seeing ahead of us a large mountain which seemed to want to rise up to the sky, in the middle of which was a peak higher than all the rest of the mountains from which flowed a living stream." When Caribs started shooting arrows at him, however, he quickly departed.

SHOPPING

I suggest you skip a shopping tour of Pointe-à-Pitre if you're going on to Martinique, as you'll find far more merchandise there.

Your best buys here are anything French, sometimes cheaper than you can find them in the U.S. and Canada—perfumes from Chanel, silk scarves from Hermés, cosmetics from Dior, crystal from Lalique and Baccarat. Many eager shopkeepers stay open longer than usual and even on weekends when cruise ships are in port. If you buy luxury goods (such as perfumes) with foreign currency and show your passport, you can take your purchase with you, but if you buy any alcohol, the merchant delivers your purchase directly to the pier.

If you're adventurous, you might want to seek some **local goods** in little shops along the back streets of Pointe-à-Pitre. Considered collector's items are the straw hats, or *salacos,* made in Les Saintes islands. They look something like Chinese coolie hats and are usually well designed, often made of split bamboo. Native doudou dolls are also popular gift items.

Open-air stalls surround the **covered market** (*Marché Couvert*) at the corner of rue Frébault and rue Thiers. In madras turbans, local Creole women make deals over their strings of fire-red pimientos. The bright fabrics they wear compete with the rich tones of the oranges, papayas, bananas, mangoes, and pineapples for sale. The sounds of African-accented French fill the air.

Distillerie Bellevue, Rue Bellevue Damoiseau, dispenses the "essence of the island": *rhum agricole,* a pure rum fermented from sugarcane juice. Savvy locals say it's the only rum you can drink without suffering the devastation of a rum hangover the next morning. Once this liquor was available in great abundance, but now only two distilleries still process it. You can taste before purchasing.

Some of the best places for French goods include **Phoenicia,** 8 Rue Frébault, for French perfumes and imported cosmetics; **Rosébleu,** 5 Rue Frébault, for Pointe-à-Pitre's biggest stock of French crystal, jewelry, perfumes, gifts, and fashion accessories; **Soph't,** Immeuble Lesseps, Centre St-Jean Perse, for French lingerie; and **Vendôme,** 8–10 Rue Frébault, for imported fashions for both men and women, as well as a large selection of gifts and perfumes.

BEACHES

There is a plenitude of natural beaches dotting the island, from the surf-brushed dark strands of western Basse-Terre to the long stretches of white sand encircling Grande-Terre.

Outstanding beaches include **Caravele Beach,** a long, reef-protected stretch of sand outside Ste-Anne, about 9 miles from Gosier, the site of many leading resorts. Hotels welcome non-guests, but charge for changing facilities, beach chairs, and towels. Palm-studded ✪ **Grande Anse,** on Basse-Terre, is north of Deshaies on the northwest coast.

Sunday is family day at the beach here. Public beaches are generally free, but some charge for parking. Unlike hotel beaches, they have few facilities. Topless sunbathing is common at hotels, less so on village beaches. Nudist beaches include **Ilet du Gosier,** off Gosier, and **Plage de Tarare,** near the eastern tip of Grande-Terre at Pointe des Châteaux, also the site of many local restaurants.

SPORTS

GOLF   Guadeloupe's only course is the well-known **Golf de St-François** (☎ **0590/ 88-41-87**) at St-François, opposite the Hôtel Méridien about 22 miles east of Raizet Airport. The course runs alongside an 800-acre lagoon where windsurfing, water-skiing, and sailing prevail. The 6,755-yard, par-71 course designed by Robert Trent Jones, Sr., is challenging, with water traps on six holes, massive bunkers, prevailing trade winds, and a particularly fiendish 400-yard, par-4 ninth hole. The par-5 sixth is the toughest hole on the course; its 450 yards must be negotiated into the constant easterly winds.

SCUBA DIVING   Divers are drawn to the waters off Guadeloupe, which lack underwater currents and are relatively calm. There's also the **Cousteau Underwater Reserve,** a park with many attractive dive sites in which the underwater environment is rigidly protected. Jacques Cousteau described the waters off Guadeloupe's Pigeon Island as "one of the world's 10 best diving spots." During a typical dive, sergeant majors become visible at a depth of 30 feet, spiny sea urchins and green parrotfish at 60 feet, and magnificent stands of finger, black, brain, and star coral come into view at a depth of 80 feet. Despite damage caused by 1995 hurricanes, it's still one of the most desirable dive sites in the French-speaking world. **Centre International de la Plongée (C.I.P.),** B.P. 4, Lieu-Dit Poirier, Malendure Plage, 97125 Pigeon, Bouillante, Guadeloupe, F.W.I. (☎ **0590/98-81-72**), is the island's most professional dive operation, located at the edge of the Cousteau Underwater Reserve. Dive boats depart three times a day, catering to both certified divers and first-time divers seeking a resort course.

WINDSURFING & WATER-SKIING   Head for **Sport Away** (Nathalie Simon), Plage de St-François, St-François (☎ **0590/88-72-04**).

GREAT LOCAL RESTAURANTS & BARS

Volcanic, tropically forested Guadeloupe is fabled for female Creole chefs operating simple little bistros, sometimes in their own homes.

ON GRANDE-TERRE   **Restaurant Sucré-Salé,** Boulevard Le Gitimus (☎ **0590/ 21-22-55**), is very popular at lunchtime, serving a delectable menu that includes an impressive medley of grilled fish. At the far eastern end of Gosier village, en route to Ste-Anne, **Chez Violetta,** Perinette Gosier (☎ **0590-84-10-34**), is the most formally decorated of all the island's Creole restaurants. Try stuffed crabs, cod fritters, or classic *boudin* (blood sausage). The chef also makes a fine conch ragoût that's best when served with home-grown hot chilis.

ON BASSE-TERRE   **Chez Paul de Matouba,** beside the banks of the small Rivière Rouge (☎ **0590-80-29-20**), is the best choice if you've decided to visit La Soufrière.

The cooking is Creole, and crayfish dishes are the specialty. In winter, the restaurant may be filled with the tour-bus crowd. On the waterfront near the center of Ste-Rose, **Restaurant Clara** (☎ **0590-28-72-99**) combines fine French dining with authentic, spicy Creole cooking. Specialties at lunch may include *ouassous* (freshwater crayfish), brochette of swordfish, or sea-urchin omelets. In Port Louis, **Le Poisson d'Or,** Rue Sadi-Carnot 2 (☎ **0590/22-88-63**), shelters a mixture of local residents and French visitors. Despite the simple setting, the food is well prepared and satisfying. Try the stuffed crabs, the boudin of conch or fish, or octopus fricassee. **Chez Loulouse,** Malendure Plage (☎ **0590/98-70-34**), offers house-style Caribbean lobster, spicy versions of conch, octopus, and savory *colombos* (curries) of chicken or pork. Many guests like to sip rum punch on the panoramic veranda, although the dining room is a quieter oasis.

11 Jamaica

A favorite of North American honeymooners, Jamaica is a mountainous island rising from the sea 90 miles south of Cuba and about 100 miles west of Haiti. It's the third largest of the Caribbean islands, with some 4,400 square miles of predominantly green terrain, a mountain ridge peaking at 7,400 feet above sea level, and, on the north coast, many beautiful white-sand beaches rimming the clear blue sea.

One of the most densely populated nations in the Caribbean, with a vivid sense of its own identity, Jamaica has a history rooted in the plantation economy and some of the most turbulent and impassioned politics in the western hemisphere. It's one of the most successful black democracies in the world. The island is large enough to allow the more or less peaceful coexistence of all kinds of people within its beach-lined borders, from expatriate English aristocrats to devout Rastafarians.

Most cruise ships dock at **Ocho Rios** on the lush northern coast, although others are increasingly going to the city of **Montego Bay** ("Mo Bay"), 67 miles to the west. Both ports offer comparable attractions and some of the same shopping possibilities. Don't try to do both ports in 1 day, however, since the 4-hour round-trip ride leaves time for only superficial visits to each.

CURRENCY   The unit of currency is the **Jamaican dollar,** designated by the same symbol as the U.S. dollar ($). For clarity, I use the symbol **J$** to denote prices in Jamaican dollars. There is no fixed rate of exchange. The exchange rate is J$38.80 to US$1 (J$1 is worth about 3¢). Visitors can pay in U.S. dollars, but *be careful!* Always find out if a price is being quoted in Jamaican or U.S. dollars.

INFORMATION   In Ocho Rios, you'll find tourist board offices at the Ocean Village Shopping Centre in Ocho Rios (☎ **876/974-2582**); open Monday to Friday from 9am to 5pm. In Montego Bay, it's at Cornwall Beach, St. James (☎ **876/952-4425**). It's open Monday to Friday from 9am to 5pm.

LANGUAGE   The official language is English, but most Jamaicans speak a richly nuanced patois that's primarily derived from English but includes elements of African, Spanish, Arawak, French, Chinese, Portuguese, and East Indian languages.

OCHO RIOS

Once a small banana and fishing port, Ocho Rios is now Jamaica's cruise-ship capital. The bay is dominated on one side by a bauxite-loading terminal and on the other by resort hotels with palm tree–fringed beaches.

Although the Ocho Rios area has some of the Caribbean's most fabled resorts, the town itself is not much to see, but there are a few outdoor local markets (just be careful of pickpockets and aggressive hawkers) within walking distance, and Dunn's River

Frommer's Ratings: Ocho Rios					
	Poor	Fair	Good	Excellent	Outstanding
Overall Experience				✓	
Shore Excursions					✓
Activities Close to Port				✓	
Beaches & Water Sports			✓		
Shopping		✓			
Dining/Bars			✓		

is just a 5-minute taxi ride away. At the terminal is an information desk, bathrooms, and an army of official taxis ready to take you where you want to go.

Frommer's Favorite Ocho Rios Experiences

- **Tubing on the White River:** The River Tubing Safari excursion offered by most cruise lines is just a downright fantastic experience (see "Shore Excursions," below).
- **Riding horseback through the surf:** An excursion by horseback goes along the beach and through the surf to a lovely cove (see "Shore Excursions," below).
- **Riding a mountain bike to Dunn's River Falls:** This excursion takes you to the top of a mountain, where you hop on your mountain bike and soar downhill to the falls (see "Shore Excursions," below).

COMING ASHORE   Most cruise ships dock at the port of Ocho Rios, near Dunn's River Falls. Only a mile away is one of the most important shopping areas, Ocean Village Shopping Centre. Vendors are particularly aggressive in Ocho Rios. Don't expect to shop in the markets without a lot of hassle and a lot of very pushy hawking of merchandise, some of which is likely to be *ganja,* locally grown marijuana. (Remember, although it may be readily available, it's still illegal.)

GETTING AROUND

BY TAXI   Taxis are your best means of transport, but always agree on a fare before you get in. Rates are charged per taxi, not per person. You can also negotiate a price for a taxi to take you around to see the sights. Taxis licensed by the government display red Public Passenger Vehicle (PPV) plates. All others are gypsy cabs, which you should avoid.

BY RENTAL CAR   I don't recommend renting a car here.

SHORE EXCURSIONS

Dunn's River Falls Tour ($44, 4 hours): These falls cascade 600 feet to the beach and are the most visited attraction in Jamaica, which means they're hopelessly overcrowded when a lot of cruise ships are in port. Tourists are allowed to climb the falls, and it's a ball to slip and slide your way up with the hundreds of others, forming a human chain of sorts. Don't forget your waterproof camera and your aqua socks (most lines rent you aqua socks for an extra $5). This tour also visits Shaw Park Botanical Gardens, Fern Gully, and other local attractions, with time allocated for shopping. Wear a bathing suit under your clothes.

✪ **River Tubing Safari** ($59, 6 hours): This is one of the best excursions I've ever taken. After a scenic 30-minute or so van ride deep into the pristine jungles of Jamaica, the group of 20 or so passengers and a couple of guides get into the White River, sit back into big black inner tubes (they have wooden boards covering the bottom so your butt doesn't scrape the bottom of the river or any rocks you may run into), and begin

Jamaica

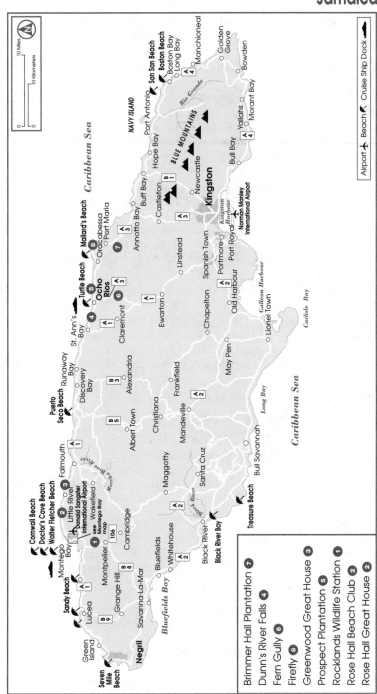

Brimmer Hall Plantation **7**
Dunn's River Falls **4**
Fern Gully **6**
Firefly **8**
Greenwood Great House **3**
Prospect Plantation **5**
Rocklands Wildlife Station **1**
Rose Hall Beach Club **1**
Rose Hall Great House **2**

Airport ✈ Beach 🏖 Cruise Ship Dock ⚓

the 3-mile glide downriver, passing by gorgeous, towering bamboo trees and other lush foliage. It's sometimes peaceful and sometimes exhilarating—especially when you hit the rapids!

✪ **Chukka Cove Horseback-Riding Excursion** ($76, 3 to 4 hours): Riders will love this trip, where you head along the beach and take your horse bareback into the surf for a thrilling ride through this beautiful cove.

✪ **Dunn's River Falls Mountain-Biking Trek** ($62, 4 hours): After you're driven up to the summit of 1,500-foot-high Murphy Hill, above Ocho Rios, hop on your mountain bike, strap on your helmet, and enjoy a mostly downhill ride through the natural limestone and ferns, passing the eight springs that form Dunn's River Falls. Once at the bottom, you'll have time to climb the falls before heading back to the ship.

Countryside/Plantation Bus Tour ($56, 4 hours): This tour includes a drive through the Jamaican countryside to Brimmer Hall Plantation, a working plantation property with a Great House and tropical crops, such as bananas and pimiento. On the way back, you pass the estates once occupied by Noel Coward and Ian Fleming. Often a stop at Dunn's River Falls is tacked on to the end of the tour. Another variation on this tour ($38, 4 to 5 hours) stops at the Prospect Plantation instead of Brimmer Hall.

Snorkeling Excursion ($31, 2 hours): A coral reef near the cruise pier is one of the best places in the area for snorkeling, with panoramic underwater visibility. You can also take a 1-hour cruise on a glass-bottomed boat for a look at underwater Jamaica.

Martha Brae River Rafting ($50, 5 hours): This tour, in 30-foot, two-seat bamboo rafts, is traditionally one of the most heavily booked tours from both Ocho Rios or Montego Bay. However, most people find it disappointing. I'd recommend the tubing and bicycling excursions instead, which I think are much better and more interesting choices.

ON YOUR OWN: WITHIN WALKING DISTANCE

Aside from some markets (see "Shopping," below), there's little to do close to the docks.

ON YOUR OWN: BEYOND WALKING DISTANCE

South of Ocho Rios, **Fern Gully** was originally a riverbed. Today, the main A3 road winds up some 700 feet through a rainforest filled with wild ferns, hardwood trees, and lianas. For the botanist, there are hundreds of varieties of ferns, and for the less plant-minded, roadside stands sell fruits and vegetables, carved-wood souvenirs, and basketwork. The road runs for about 4 miles.

Near Lydford, southwest of Ocho Rios, are the remains of **Edinburgh Castle.** This was the lair of one of Jamaica's most infamous murderers, a Scot named Lewis Hutchinson who used to shoot passersby and toss their bodies into a deep pit. The authorities got wind of his activities, and although he tried to escape by canoe, he was captured by the navy and hanged. Rather proud of his achievements (evidence of at least 43 murders was found), he left £100 and instructions for a memorial to be built. It never was, but the 1763 castle ruins remain. To get to Lydford, take the A3 south until you reach a small intersection directly north of Walkers Wood, and then follow the signposts west.

If you're here on a Thursday, the 1817 **Brimmer Hall Estate,** Port Maria, St. Mary's (☎ 876/974-2244), 21 miles east of Ocho Rios, is an ideal place to spend part of the day. Brimmer Hall is a working plantation where you're driven around in a tractor-drawn jitney to see the tropical fruit trees and coffee plants. Knowledgeable guides tell you about the processes necessary to produce the fine fruits of the island. Afterward, you can relax beside the pool and sample a wide variety of drinks, including an interesting

Ocho Rios

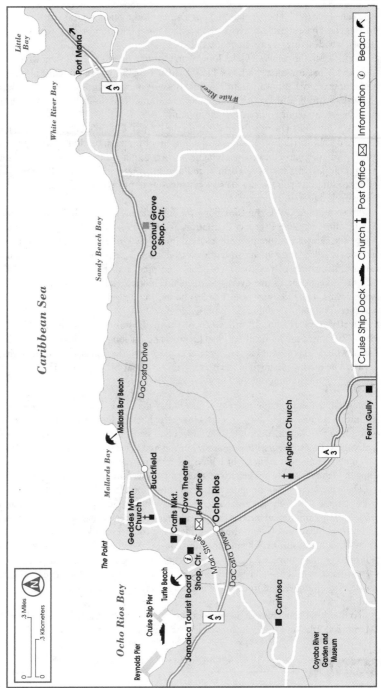

Caribbean Sea

Little Bay

White River Bay

White River

Port Maria

A 3

Sandy Beach Bay

Coconut Grove Shop. Ctr.

DaCosta Drive

Mallards Bay Beach

Mallards Bay

The Point

Buckfield

Geddes Mem. Church

Crafts Mkt.

Cove Theatre

Post Office

Ocho Rios

Anglican Church

A 3

Fern Gully

Ocho Rios Bay

Reynolds Pier

Cruise Ship Pier

Turtle Beach

Jamaica Tourist Board

Shop. Ctr.

Main Street

DaCosta Drive

A 3

Cariñosa

Coyaba River Garden and Museum

N

.3 Miles

.3 Kilometers

Cruise Ship Dock | Church | Post Office | Information | Beach one called "Wow!" The Plantation Tour Eating House offers typical Jamaican dishes for lunch. There's also a souvenir shop with a good selection of ceramics, art, straw goods, woodcarvings, rums, liqueurs, and cigars.

A mile from the center of Ocho Rios, at an elevation of 420 feet, **Coyaba River Garden and Museum,** Shaw Park Road (☎ 876/974-6235), was built on the grounds of the former Shaw Park plantation. The Spanish-style museum displays artifacts from the Arawak, Spanish, and English settlements in the area. The gardens are filled with native flora, a cut-stone courtyard, and fountains.

At the 600-foot **Dunn's River Falls,** on the A3 (☎ 876/974-2857), you can relax on the beach, splash in the waters at the bottom of the falls, or climb with a guide to the top and drop into the cool pools higher up between the cascades of water. The beach restaurant provides snacks and drinks, and dressing rooms are available. If you're planning to climb the falls, wear aqua socks or sneakers to protect your feet from the sharp rocks and to prevent slipping.

Three miles east of Ocho Rios along the A3, adjoining the 18-hole Prospect Mini Golf Course, working **Prospect Plantation** (☎ 876/994-1058) is often a shore excursion stop. On your leisurely ride by covered jitney you'll readily see why this section of Jamaica is called "the garden parish of the island." You'll see pimiento (allspice), banana, cassava, sugarcane, coffee, cocoa, coconut, pineapple, and the famous leucaena "Tree of Life," plus Jamaica's first hydro-electric plant. Horseback riding is available on three scenic trails. The rides vary from 1 to 2¼ hours; you'll need to book a horse 1 hour in advance.

Firefly, Grants Pen, 20 miles east of Ocho Rios above Oracabessa (☎ 876/997-7201), was the home of Sir Noel Coward and his longtime companion, Graham Payn, who, as executor of Coward's estate, donated it to the Jamaica National Heritage Trust. The recently restored house is as it was on the day Sir Noel died in 1973.

SHOPPING

In general, the shopping is better at Montego Bay than here, but if you're not going to Montego, wander the Ocho Rios **crafts markets.** Literally hundreds of Jamaicans pour into Ocho Rios hoping to peddle something, often something homemade, to cruise ship passengers. Prepare yourself for aggressive selling and fierce haggling. Every vendor asks too much for an item at first, which gives them the leeway to negotiate the price. Shopping in Ocho Rios may not be the most fun you've ever had. You might want to skip it.

There are seven main shopping plazas, including the **Ocho Rios Craft Park,** a complex of some 150 stalls. An eager seller will weave a hat or a basket while you wait, or you can buy from the mixture of ready-made hats, hampers, handbags, place mats, and lampshades. **Coconut Grove Shopping Plaza** is a collection of low-slung shops linked by walkways and shrubs. The merchandise consists mainly of local craft items. **Island Plaza** shopping complex is right in the heart of Ocho Rios. You can find some of the best Jamaican art here—all paintings by local artists. You can also purchase local handmade crafts (be prepared to do some haggling), carvings, ceramics, even kitchenware, and the inevitable T-shirts.

To find local handcrafts or art without the hassle of the markets, head for **Beautiful Memories,** 9 Island Plaza, which has a limited but representative sampling of Jamaican

---

Port Tip

Some so-called **duty-free prices** are indeed lower than stateside prices, but then the Jamaican government hits you with a 10% "General Consumption Tax."

art, as well as local crafts, pottery, woodwork, and hand-embroidered items. I generally ignore hotel gift shops, but the **Jamaica Inn Gift Shop** in the Jamaica Inn, Main Street, is better than most, selling everything from Blue Mountain coffee to Walkers Wood products, and even guava jelly and jerk seasoning. If you're lucky, you'll find marmalade from an old family recipe, plus Upton Pimento Dram, a unique liqueur flavored with Jamaican allspice.

If you'd like to flee the hustle and bustle of the Ocho Rios bazaars, take a taxi to **Harmony Hall,** Tower Isle, on the A3, 4 miles east of Ocho Rios. One of Jamaica's Great Houses, the restored house is now a gallery selling paintings and other works by Jamaican artists. The arts and crafts here are high-quality—not the usual junky assortment you might find at the beach.

BEACHES

Many visitors to Ocho Rios head for the beach. The most overcrowded is **Mallards Beach,** shared by hotel guests and cruise ship passengers. Locals may steer you to the good and less-crowded **Turtle Beach,** southwest of Mallards.

SPORTS

GOLF   **Super Club's Runaway Golf Course,** at Runaway Beach near Ocho Rios on the north coast (☎ 876/973-2561), is one of the better courses in the area, although it's nowhere near the courses at Montego Bay. Cruise ship passengers should call ahead and book playing times. The charge is $58 for 18 holes in winter. Players can rent carts and clubs. **Sandals Golf & Country Club,** at Ocho Rios (☎ 876/975-0119), is also open to the public. The course lies about 700 feet above sea level. To get there from the center of Ocho Rios, travel along the main bypass for 2 miles until Mile End Road; turn right at the Texaco station there, and drive for 5 miles.

GREAT LOCAL RESTAURANTS & BARS

Double V Jerk Centre, 109 Main St. (3 min. east of the town center; ☎ 876/ 974-5998), serves up the best jerk pork and chicken in town. Don't expect anything fancy. Just come for platters of meat. **Almond Tree Restaurant,** 87 Main St., in the Hibiscus Lodge Hotel (3 blocks from the Ocho Rios Mall; ☎ 876/974-2813), is a two-tiered patio restaurant overlooking the Caribbean, with a tree growing through its roof. Lobster Thermidor is the most delectable item on the menu. **Evita's Italian Restaurant,** Eden Bower Road (5 min. south of Ocho Rios; ☎ 876/974-2333), is the premier Italian restaurant in Ocho Rios, serving pastas and excellent fish dishes—especially the snapper stuffed with crabmeat and the lobster and scampi in a buttery white cream sauce. **Little Pub Restaurant,** 59 Main St. (☎ 876/974-2324), is an indoor-outdoor pub serving such items as grilled kingfish, stewed snapper, barbecued chicken, and the inevitable and overpriced lobster. The cooking is competent and the atmosphere very casual. **Parkway Restaurant,** 60 DaCosta Dr. (☎ 876/974-2667), couldn't be plainer or less pretentious, but it's always packed. Hungry diners are fed Jamaican-style chicken, curried goat, sirloin steak, fillet of red snapper, and to top it off, banana cream pie. Lobster and fresh fish are usually featured also. The food is straightforward, honest, and affordable.

When you're seated at the beautifully laid tables at the **Plantation Inn Restaurant,** in the Plantation Inn, Main Street (☎ 876/974-5601), you'll think you've arrived at Tara in *Gone With the Wind.* Jamaican specialties help spice up the continental cuisine in this romantic restaurant. **Ruins Restaurant, Gift Shop, and Boutique,** Turtle River, DaCosta Drive (☎ 876/974-2442), is in a dramatic setting, next to a waterfall and among the ruins of a sugar mill.

MONTEGO BAY

Montego Bay is sometimes less of a hassle than the port at Ocho Rios, and has better beaches, shopping, and restaurants, as well as some of the best golf courses in the Caribbean, superior even to those on Puerto Rico and the Bahamas. Like Ocho Rios, Montego Bay has its crime, traffic, and annoyance, but there's much more to see and do here.

There's little of interest in the town of Montego Bay itself except shopping, although the good stuff in the environs is easily reached by taxi or shore excursion. Getting around from place to place is one of the major difficulties here, as it is in Barbados. Whatever you want to visit seems to be in yet another direction.

Frommer's Favorite Montego Bay Experiences

In addition to these, my favorite shore excursions from Ocho Rios are also offered from Montego Bay.

- **Visiting Rocklands Wildlife Station:** This is the place to go if you want to have a Jamaican doctor bird perch on your finger or feed small doves and finches from your hand (see "On Your Own: Beyond Walking Distance," below).
- **Spend a day at the Rose Hall Beach Club:** With a secluded beach, crystal-clear water, a full restaurant, two beach bars, live entertainment, and more, it's well worth the $8 admission (see "Beaches," below).

COMING ASHORE   Montego Bay has a modern cruise dock with lots of conveniences, including duty-free stores, telephones, tourist information, and plenty of taxis to meet all ships.

GETTING AROUND

BY TAXI   If you don't book a shore excursion, a **taxi** is the way to get around. See "Getting Around" under "Ocho Rios," above, for taxi information, as the same conditions apply to Mo Bay.

BY MOTORSCOOTER   **Montego Honda/Bike Rentals,** 21 Gloucester Ave. (☎ **876/952-4984**), rents Hondas for $35 a day, plus a $300 deposit.

SHORE EXCURSIONS

Also see "Shore Excursions" under "Ocho Rios," above.

Croydon Plantation Tour ($55, 4 to 5 hours): Twenty-five miles from Montego Bay, the plantation can be visited on a half-day tour on Tuesday, Wednesday, and Friday. Included in the price are round-trip transportation from the dock, a tour of the plantation, a tasting of varieties of pineapple and other tropical fruits in season, and a barbecued chicken lunch.

Frommer's Ratings: Montego Bay					
	Poor	Fair	Good	Excellent	Outstanding
Overall Experience				✓	
Shore Excursions					✓
Activities Close to Port				✓	
Beaches & Water Sports			✓		
Shopping			✓		
Dining/Bars			✓		

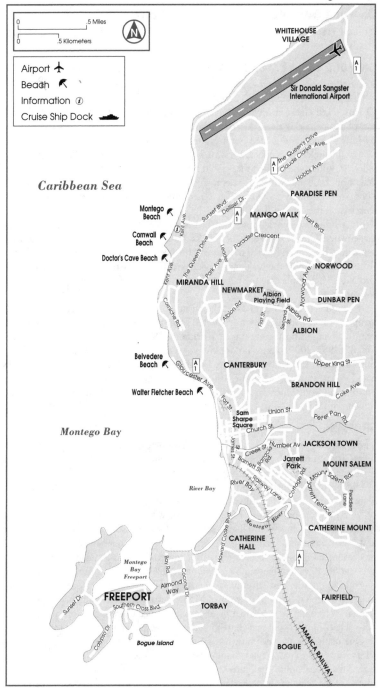

0 | .5 Miles
0 | .5 Kilometers

N

Airport ✈
Beach 🏄
Information ⓘ
Cruise Ship Dock 🚢

Caribbean Sea

WHITEHOUSE VILLAGE

A1

Sir Donald Sangster International Airport

The Queen's Drive
Claude Clarke Ave.
Hobbs Ave.

PARADISE PEN

A1

Sunset Blvd.
Delisser Dr.

Montego Beach 🏄

MANGO WALK

Hart Blvd

Cornwall Beach 🏄

Paradise Crescent

Doctor's Cave Beach 🏄

Kent Ave.

The Queen's Drive

Leader

Park Ave.

NORWOOD

Norwood Ave.

MIRANDA HILL

NEWMARKET

Albion Playing Field

DUNBAR PEN

Corniche Rd.

Albion Rd.

First St.

Second St.

Albion Rd.

ALBION

Belvedere Beach 🏄

Gloucester Ave.

A1

CANTERBURY

Upper King St.

BRANDON HILL

Coke Ave.

Walter Fletcher Beach 🏄

Fort St.

Sam Sharpe Square

Union St.

Church St.

Peter Pan Rd.

Montego Bay

James St.

Creek St.

Barnett St.

Barracks Rd.

Humber Av

JACKSON TOWN

Jarrett Park

MOUNT SALEM

Railway Lane

Cottage Rd.

Mount Salem Rd.

Peddlers Lane

River Bay

River Bay

Jarrett Terrace

CATHERINE MOUNT

Montego River

Montego Bay Freeport

Bay Rd.

Coconut Dr.

Howard Cooke Blvd.

CATHERINE HALL

A1

FREEPORT

Almond Way

Sunset Dr.

Southern Cross Blvd.

TORBAY

FAIRFIELD

Calypso Dr.

Bogue Island

BOGUE

JAMAICA RAILWAY

449

ON YOUR OWN: WITHIN WALKING DISTANCE

Nothing really. You'll have to take a taxi to the town for shopping or sign up for an excursion.

ON YOUR OWN: BEYOND WALKING DISTANCE

These attractions can be reached by taxi from the cruise dock.

Charging a steep admission, the most famous Great House in Jamaica is the legendary ☼ **Rose Hall Great House,** Rose Hall Highway (☎ 876/953-2323), located 9 miles east of Montego Bay along the coast road. The house was built about two centuries ago by John Palmer, and gained notoriety from the doings of "Infamous Annie" Palmer, wife of the builder's grandnephew, who supposedly dabbled in witchcraft and took slaves as lovers, killing them when they bored her. Annie also was said to have murdered several of her husbands while they slept, and eventually suffered the same fate herself. The house, now privately owned by U.S.-based philanthropists, has been restored. **Annie's Pub** sits on the ground floor.

On a hillside perch 14 miles east of Montego Bay and 7 miles west of Falmouth, **Greenwood Great House,** on the A1 (☎ 876/953-1077), is even more interesting to some than Rose Hall. Erected in the early 19th century, the Georgian-style building was from 1780 to 1800 the residence of Richard Barrett, a relative of Elizabeth Barrett Browning. On display are the family's library, portraits of the family, and rare musical instruments.

It's a unique experience to have a Jamaican doctor bird perch on your finger to drink syrup, or to feed small doves and finches from your hand, or simply to watch dozens of birds flying in for the evening at **Rocklands Wildlife Station,** Anchovy, St. James (☎ 876/952-2009). Lisa Salmon, known as the "Bird Lady of Anchovy," established this sanctuary. It's perfect for nature lovers and bird watchers, but don't take children 5 and under, as they tend to worry the birds. Rocklands is about a mile outside Anchovy on the road from Montego Bay. It's open daily from 2:30 to 5pm, and charges an admission of J$300 ($8.55).

SHOPPING

The main shopping areas are at **Montego Freeport,** within easy walking distance of the pier; **City Centre** (where most of the duty-free shops are, aside from those at the large hotels); and **Holiday Village Shopping Centre.**

Old Fort Craft Park, a shopping complex with 180 vendors licensed by the Jamaica Tourist Board, fronts Howard Cooke Boulevard up from Gloucester Avenue in the heart of Montego Bay, on the site of Fort Montego. With a varied assortment of handcrafts, this is browsing country. You'll see a selection of wall hangings, handwoven straw items, and hand-carved wood sculptures, and you can even get your hair braided. Vendors can be extremely aggressive, so be prepared for some major hassles, as well as some serious negotiation. Persistent bargaining on your part will lead to substantial discounts.

You can find the best selection of handmade Jamaican souvenirs at the **Crafts Market,** near Harbour Street in downtown Montego Bay. Straw hats and bags, wooden platters, straw baskets, musical instruments, beads, carved objects, and toys are all available here. That "jipijapa" hat will come in handy if you're going to be out in the island sun.

One of the newest and most intriguing places for shopping is a mall, **Half Moon Plaza,** set on the coastal road about 8 miles east of the commercial center of Montego Bay. This upscale mini-mall caters to the shopping and gastronomic needs of residents of one of the region's most elegant hotels, the Half Moon Club. Also on the premises are a bank and about 25 shops arranged around a central courtyard and purveying a wide choice of carefully selected merchandise.

Ambiente Art Gallery, 9 Fort St., stocks local artwork. At Blue Mountain Gems Workshop, at the Holiday Village Shopping Centre, you can take a tour of the work-shops to see the process from raw stone to the finished product available for purchase later. Caribatik Island Fabrics, Rock Wharf on the Luminous Lagoon, Falmouth (2 miles east of Falmouth on the north coast road), is the private living and work domain of Keith Chandler, who creates a full range of batik fabrics, scarves, garments, and wall hangings, some patterned after such themes as Jamaica's "doctor bird." Klass Kraft Leather Sandals, 44 Fort St., offers sandals and leather accessories made on location by a team of Jamaican craftspeople. All sandals cost less than $35. Things Jamaican, 44 Fort St., stocks Jamaican rums and liqueurs, jerk products, sculpture, handwoven Jamaican baskets, and more.

BEACHES

Cornwall Beach is a long stretch of white sand beach with dressing cabanas. Daily admission is $2 for adults, $1 for children. A bar and cafeteria offer refreshment. Hours are 9am to 5pm daily.

Doctor's Cave Beach, on Gloucester Avenue across from the Doctor's Cave Beach Hotel, helped launch Mo Bay as a resort in the 1940s. Admission to the beach is $2 for adults, half price for children up to 12. Dressing rooms, chairs, umbrellas, and rafts are available from 8:30am to 5pm daily.

One of the premier beaches of Jamaica, Walter Fletcher Beach in the heart of Mo Bay is noted for its tranquil waters, which make it a particular favorite for families with children. Changing rooms are available, and lifeguards are on duty. There's also a restaurant for lunch. The beach is open daily from 9am to 5pm, with an admission of $1 for adults, half price for children.

You may want to skip the public beaches and head for the ✪ Rose Hall Beach Club (☎ 876/953-2323), lying on the main road 11 miles east of Montego Bay. It sits on half a mile of secure, secluded, white sandy beach, by crystal-clear water. The club offers a full restaurant, two beach bars, a covered pavilion, an open-air dance area, showers, restrooms, and changing facilities, plus beach volleyball courts, various beach games, and a full water sports activities program. There's also live entertainment. Admission fees are $8 for adults, $5 for children. The club is open daily from 10am to 6pm.

SPORTS

GOLF Wyndham Rose Hall Golf & Beach Resort, Rose Hall (☎ 876/953-2650), has a noted course with an unusual and challenging seaside and mountain layout. The 300-foot-high 13th tee offers a rare panoramic view of the sea and the roof of the hotel, and the 15th green is next to a 40-foot waterfall, once featured in a James Bond movie. A fully stocked pro shop, a clubhouse, and a professional staff are among the amenities.

The excellent, regal course at the Tryall (☎ 876/956-5660), 12 miles from Montego Bay, has often been the site of major golf tournaments, including the Jamaica Classic Annual and the Johnnie Walker Tournament.

Half Moon, at Rose Hall (☎ 876/953-2560), features a championship course—designed by Robert Trent Jones, Sr.—that opened in 1961. The course has manicured and diversely shaped greens.

Ironshore Golf & Country Club, Ironshore, St. James, Montego Bay (☎ 876/953-2800), a well-known, par-72, 18-hole golf course is privately owned, but open to the public.

HORSEBACK RIDING The best horseback riding is offered by the helpful staff at the Rocky Point Riding Stables, at the Half Moon Club, Rose Hall, Montego Bay

(☎ 876/953-2286). The stables, built in the colonial Caribbean style in 1992, are the most beautiful in Jamaica.

RAFTING   Mountain Valley Rafting, 31 Gloucester Ave. (☎ 876/956-0020), offers excursions on the Great River. They depart from the Lethe Plantation, about 10 miles south of Montego Bay. Bamboo rafts are designed for two, with a raised dais to sit on. In some cases, a small child can accompany two adults on the same raft, although caution should be exercised. Ask about pickup by taxi at the end of the run. A half-day experience includes transportation to and from the pier, an hour's rafting, lunch, a garden tour of the Lethe property, and a taste of Jamaican liqueur.

WATER SPORTS   Seaworld Resorts Ltd., Cariblue Hotel, Rose Hall Main Road (☎ 876/953-2180), operates **scuba diving** as well as deep-sea fishing jaunts, plus many other water sports, including sailing and windsurfing. Its scuba dives go to offshore coral reefs that are among the most spectacular in the Caribbean. There are three PADI-certified dive guides, one dive boat, and all the necessary equipment for inexperienced or certified divers.

GREAT LOCAL RESTAURANTS & BARS

The **Pork Pit,** 27 Gloucester Ave., near Walter Fletcher Beach (☎ 876/952-1046), is the best place to go for the famous Jamaican jerk pork and jerk chicken. Many beachgoers come over here for a big lunch. Picnic tables encircle the building, and everything is open-air and informal. Order half a pound of jerk meat with a baked yam or baked potato and a bottle of Red Stripe beer. Prices are very reasonable.

The **Georgian House,** 2 Orange St. (☎ 876/952-0632), brings grand cuisine and an elegant setting to the heart of town. The lunch menu is primarily Jamaican. **The Native Restaurant,** Gloucester Ave. (☎ 876/979-2769), continues to win converts with such appetizers as jerk reggae chicken, ackee and saltfish (an acquired taste), smoked marlin, and steamed fish. Boonoonoonoos, billed as "A Taste of Jamaica," is a big platter with a little bit of everything, including meats and several kinds of fish and vegetables. **Pier 1,** Howard Cooke Boulevard (☎ 876/952-2452), features—among other dishes—fresh lobster, Jamaican soups such as conch chowder or red pea, the juiciest hamburgers in town, and an excellent steak sandwich with mushrooms.

12 Key West

No other port of call offers such a sweeping choice of fine dining, easy-to-reach attractions, street entertainment, and roguish bars as does this heavy-drinking, fun-loving town at the very end of the fabled Florida Keys. It's America's southernmost city at Mile Marker 0, where U.S. Route 1 begins, but it feels more like a colorful Caribbean outpost.

You have only a day, so flee the busy cruise docks and touristy Duval Street for a walk through hidden and more secluded byways, such as Olivia or William streets. Or you might want to spend your day playing golf or going diving or snorkeling.

Frommer's Ratings: Key West					
	Poor	Fair	Good	Excellent	Outstanding
Overall Experience				✓	
Shore Excursions				✓	
Activities Close to Port					✓
Beaches & Water Sports		✓			
Shopping			✓		
Dining/Bars				✓	

Key West

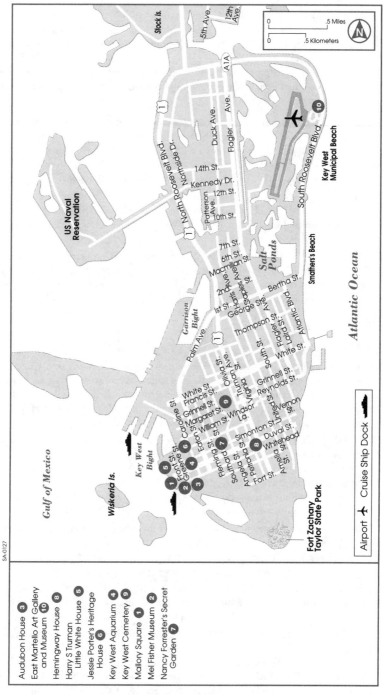

Key West

Gulf of Mexico

Wiskeria Is.

US Naval Reservation

Stock Is.

Atlantic Ocean

Key West Municipal Beach

Smather's Beach

Salt Ponds

Garrison Bight

Key West Bight

Fort Zachary Taylor State Park

Airport ✈ Cruise Ship Dock ⬛

Audubon House ③
East Martello Art Gallery and Museum ⑩
Hemingway House ⑧
Harry S Truman Little White House ⑤
Jessie Porter's Heritage House ⑥
Key West Aquarium ④
Key West Cemetery ⑨
Mallory Square ①
Mel Fisher Museum ②
Nancy Forrester's Secret Garden ⑦

SA-0127

453

Frommer's Favorite Key West Experiences

- **Viewing the sunset from Mallory Dock:** More than just a sunset, it's a daily carnival. If your ship is in port late enough, don't miss it (see "On Your Own: Within Walking Distance," below).
- **Taking a catamaran party cruise:** The popular Fury catamarans take passengers snorkeling and then back to shore, with music, booze, and a good time (see "Shore Excursions," below).

COMING ASHORE   Ships dock at Mallory Square, Old Town's most important plaza, or at nearby Truman Annex, a 5-minute stroll away. Both are on the Gulf of Mexico side of the island. Except for esoteric pockets, virtually everything is at your doorstep, including the two main arteries, Duval Street and Whitehead Street, each filled with shops, bars, restaurants, and the town's most important attractions.

CURRENCY   Obviously, U.S. dollars are used here. You can change other major currencies at First State Bank, 1201 Simonton St. (☎ 305/296-8535), open Monday to Friday from 9am to 3pm. On Friday, it reopens from 4 to 6pm. There's a 2% to 4% exchange fee.

INFORMATION   The Greater Key West Chamber of Commerce, 402 Wall St. (☎ 305/294-5988), lies near the cruise ship docks. This helpful agency answers questions about local activities, distributes free maps, and assists in arranging tours and fishing trips. Ask for *Pelican Path,* a free walking guide that documents the history and architecture of Old Town, and *Solares Hill's Walking and Biking Guide to Old Key West,* which contains eight walking tours.

GETTING AROUND

The island is only 4 miles long and 2 miles wide, so getting around is easy. Hundreds of people who live here own bicycles instead of cars. The most popular sights, including the Hemingway House and the Harry S Truman Little White House, are within walking distance of the cruise docks, so you're hardly dependent on public transportation unless you want to go to the beaches on the island's Atlantic side.

BY MOTORSCOOTER OR BICYCLE   One of the largest and best places to rent a bicycle or motorbike is **Keys Moped and Scooter Rental,** 523 Truman Ave., about a block off Duval Street (☎ 305/294-0399). Cruise ship passengers might opt for a 3-hour motorscooter rental for $12, or all day for $14. One-speed, big-wheeled "beach-cruiser" bicycles with soft seats and big baskets for toting beachwear rent for $4 for 8 hours. The outlet is open daily throughout the year from 9am to 6pm.

BY BUS   The cheapest way to see the island is by bus, which costs only 75¢ for adults, and 35¢ for senior citizens and children 6 years and older (kids 5 and under ride free).

BY RENTAL CAR   Walking or cycling is better than renting a car here, but if you do rent, try **Hertz,** 3491 S. Roosevelt Blvd. (☎ 800/654-3131 or 305/294-1039), **Tropical Rent-a-Car,** 1300 Duval St. (☎ 305/294-8136), or **Enterprise Rent-a-Car,** 3031 N. Roosevelt Blvd. (☎ 800/325-8007 or 305/292-0222). If you're visiting in winter, make reservations at least a week in advance.

BY TAXI   Island taxis operate around the clock, but are small and not suited for sightseeing tours. They will, however, take you to the beach and arrange to pick you up at a certain time. You can call one of four different services: **Florida Keys Taxi** (☎ 305/294-2227), **Maxi-Taxi Sun Cab System** (☎ 305/294-2222), **Pink Cabs** (☎ 305/296-6666), or **Island Transportation Services** (☎ 305/296-1800). Prices are uniform; the meter starts at $1.40, and adds 35¢ per quarter mile.

BY TRAM   The tram/trolley car tours are the best way to see Key West in a short time. In fact, the **Conch Tour Train** is Key West's most famous tourist attraction. It's a narrated 90-minute tour, going up and down all the most interesting streets and commenting on 60 local sites, giving you lots of lore about the town. The depot is located at Mallory Square near the cruise ship docks. Trains depart every 30 minutes. The trip is nonstop, unlike tours on the Old Town Trolley (see below), which allow you to get on and off. Departures are daily from 9am to 4:30pm and cost $15 for adults, $7 for children ages 4 to 12 (3 and under free). Call ☎ **305/294-5161** for more information.

Old Town Trolley is less popular than the Conch Tour Train, but appeals to visitors who want more flexibility. It lets you get off and explore a particular attraction, and then reboard another of its trains later. Professional guides spin tall tales about Key West as you ride. The trolleys operate 7 days a week from 9am to 4:30pm, with departures every 30 minutes at convenient spots throughout town. You can board the trolley near the cruise docks (look for signposts). Call ☎ **305/296-6688** for more information. Tours cost $16 for adults, $7 for children ages 4 to 12, free for children under 4.

SHORE EXCURSIONS

In Key West, it's definitely not necessary to take an organized excursion since everything is so accessible by foot or tram. If you like the services of a guide, most lines offer walking tours. Also, the trams and trolleys have running narratives going about Key West history and culture.

✪ **Catamaran Party Cruises** ($38, 3 hours): The popular Fury catamarans take passenger to a reef for some snorkeling and then finish the trip back to shore with music, booze, and a good time.

TOURING THROUGH LOCAL OPERATORS

Glass-Bottomed Boat Tours: The *MV Discovery* (☎ **305/293-0099**), a 78-foot motor craft, has 20 large viewing windows (angled at 45 degrees) set below the water line. Passengers can view reef life from the safety and comfort of below deck. It departs from Land's End Village & Marina at the western end of Margaret Street, a 6-block walk from the cruise ship docks. Two-hour morning tours depart daily at 9:30am in the off-season, daily at 10:30am December through April. The cost is $18.

ON YOUR OWN: WITHIN WALKING DISTANCE

If the lines aren't too long, you'll want to see the Harry S Truman Little White House and the Hemingway House, but don't feel obligated. If you want to see and capture the real-life mood and charm of Key West in a short time, leave the most-visited attractions to your fellow cruise ship passengers and head for the ones below marked with a star. All the sights below are an easy walk from the docks.

Audubon House, 205 Whitehead St. at Greene Street (☎ **305/294-2116**), is dedicated to the 1832 Key West sojourn of the famous naturalist John James Audubon. The ornithologist didn't live in this three-story building, but it's filled with his engravings. The main reason to visit is to see how wealthy sailors lived in Key West in the 19th century, and the lush tropical gardens surrounding the house are worth the price of admission.

Harry S Truman Little White House, 111 Front St. (☎ **305/294-9911**), the president's former vacation home, is part of the 103-acre Truman Annex near the cruise ship docks. The small house, which takes less than an hour to visit, affords a glimpse of a president at play.

There may be long lines at the **Hemingway House,** 907 Whitehead St. (☎ **305/ 294-1575**), where "Papa" lived with his second wife, Pauline. Here, in the studio annex, Hemingway wrote *For Whom the Bell Tolls* and *A Farewell to Arms*, among others. Hemingway had some 50 polydactyl (many-toed) cats, whose descendants still live on the grounds.

Jessie Porter Newton, known as "Miss Jessie" to her friends, was the grande dame of Key West. She invited the celebrities of her day to her house, including Tennessee Williams and her girlhood friend Gloria Swanson, as well as family friend Robert Frost, who stayed in a cottage out back. Today, you can cross her once hallowed grounds, look at the antique-filled rooms, and inspect her mementos and her exotic treasures collected by six generations of the Porter family at ✪ **Jessie Porter's Heritage House and Robert Frost Cottage,** 410 Caroline St. (☎ **305/296-3575**).

On the waterfront at Mallory Square, the **Key West Aquarium,** 1 Whitehead St. (☎ **305/296-2051**), in operation since 1932, was the first tourist attraction built in the Florida Keys. The aquarium's special feature is a "touch tank," where you can feel a horseshoe crab, sea squirt, sea urchin, starfish, and, of course, a conch, the town's mascot and symbol. It's worth taking a tour, as the guides are both knowledgeable and entertaining, and you'll get to pet a shark, if that's your idea of a good time.

The ✪ **Key West Cemetery** (☎ **305/296-2175**), 21 prime acres in the heart of the historic district, is the island's foremost offbeat attraction. The main entrance is at Margaret Street and Passover Lane. Stone-encased caskets rest on top of the earth because graves dug into the ground would hit the water table. There's also a touch of humor here: One gravestone proclaims "I Told You I Was Sick" and another says, "At Least I Know Where He Is Sleeping Tonight."

Treasure hunter Mel Fisher wears heavy gold necklaces, which he likes to say are worth a king's ransom. He isn't exaggerating. After long and risky dives, Fisher and his associates plucked more than $400 million in gold and silver from the shipwrecked Spanish galleons *Santa Margarita* and *Nuestra Señora de Atocha,* which were lost on hurricane-tossed seas some 350 years ago. Now this extraordinary long-lost Spanish jewelry, doubloons, and silver and gold bullion are displayed at the ✪ **Mel Fisher Maritime Heritage Society Museum,** 200 Greene St. (☎ **305/294-2633**), a true treasure trove near the docks.

Nancy Forrester's Secret Garden, 1 Free School Lane, off Simonton between Southard and Fleming streets (☎ **305/294-0015**), is the most lavish and verdant garden in town. Some 130 to 150 species of palms, palmettos, climbing vines, and ground covers are planted here, creating a blanket of lush, tropical magic. It's a 20-minute walk from the docks, near Key West's highest point, Solares Hill. Pick up a sandwich at a deli and picnic at tables in the garden.

If your ship leaves late enough, you can take in a unique local celebration: ✪ **viewing the sunset from Mallory Dock.** Sunset-watching is good fun all over the world, but in Key West it's been turned into a carnival-like, almost pagan celebration—a "blazing festival of joy," some call it. People from all over the world begin to crowd Mallory Square even before the sun starts to fall, bringing the place alive with entertainment—everything from a string band to a unicyclist wriggling free of a straitjacket. A juggler might delight the crowd with a machete and a flaming stick. The main entertainment, however, is that massive fireball falling out of view, which is always greeted with hysterical applause.

ON YOUR OWN: BEYOND WALKING DISTANCE
Nothin'. That's the beauty of Key West: Everything worthwhile is accessible by foot.

SHOPPING
Shopping by cruise ship passengers has become a local joke in Key West. Within a 12-block radius of Old Town, you'll find mostly tawdry and outrageously overpriced

merchandise—but if you're in the market for some Key West kitsch, this is the neighborhood for you.

Among the less-kitschy alternatives, a few stand out much farther along Duval Street, the main drag leading to the Atlantic, and on hidden back streets. You can reach all these stores from the cruise ship docks in a 15-to-20-minute stroll.

Cavanaugh's, 520 Front St., is a treasure trove of merchandise from all over the world—it's like wandering through the souks in the dusty back alleys of the Arab world. **Haitian Art Company,** 600 Frances St., claims to inventory the largest collection of Haitian paintings in the United States. Prices range from $15 to $5,000. **Key West Aloe, Inc.,** 524 Front St. or 540 Greene St., is aloe, aloe, and more aloe; the shop's inventory includes shaving cream, aftershave lotion, sunburn ointments, and fragrances for men and women based on such tropical essences as hibiscus, frangipani, and white ginger. **Key West Hand Print Fashions and Fabrics,** 201 Simonton St., sells bold, tropical prints—handprinted scarves with coordinated handbags and rack after rack of busily patterned sundresses and cocktail dresses that will make you look jaunty on the deck of an ocean liner. **Key West Island Bookstore,** 513 Fleming St., is well stocked in books on Key West and has Florida's largest collection of works by and about Hemingway. In the rear is a rare-book section where you may want to browse, if not buy. **Michael,** 400C Duval St., stocks coins from sunken wrecks and the Middle East, mounted in various settings.

BEACHES

Beaches are not too compelling here. Most are manmade, often with imported Bahamian or mainland Florida sand. Those mentioned below are free and open to the public daily from 7am to 11pm. There are few facilities, except locals hawking beach umbrellas, food, and drinks.

Fort Zachary Taylor State Beach is the best and the closest to the cruise ship docks, a 12-minute walk away. This 51-acre manmade beach is adjacent to the ruins of Fort Taylor, once known as Fort Forgotten because it was buried under tons of sand. The beach is fine for sunbathing and picnicking and is suitable for snorkeling, but rocks make it difficult to swim. To get there, go through the gates leading into Truman Annex. Watering holes near one end of the beach include the raffish Green Parrot Bar and a booze-and-burger joint, Gato Gordo.

Higgs Memorial Beach lies a 25-minute walk from the harbor near the end of White Street, one of the main east-west arteries. You'll find lots of sand, picnic tables sheltered from the sun, and fewer of your fellow cruise ship passengers. **Smathers Beach,** named in honor of one of Florida's most colorful former senators, is the longest (about 1 1/2 miles), most isolated, and least accessorized beach in town. Unfortunately it's a $9 one-way taxi ride from the cruise docks. The beach borders South Roosevelt Boulevard. There's no shade here.

In the 1950s, **Southernmost Beach** drew Tennessee Williams, but today it's more likely to fill up with visitors from the lackluster motels nearby. Except for a nearby restaurant, facilities are nonexistent. The beach lies at the foot of Duval Street on the Atlantic side, across the island from the cruise ship docks. It takes about 20 minutes to walk there along Duval Street from the docks. The beach boasts some white sand, but is not good for swimming. Nevertheless, it's one of the island's most frequented.

SPORTS

FISHING   As Hemingway, an avid fisherman, would attest, the waters off the Florida Keys are some of the world's finest fishing grounds. You can follow in his wake aboard the 40-foot *Linda D III* and *Linda D IV* (☎ **800/299-9798** in the U.S., or 305/296-9798), which offer the best deep-sea fishing here. Arrangements should be made a week or so before you are due in port.

GOLF   Redesigned in 1982 by architect Rees Jones, the **Key West Resort Golf Course,** 6450 E. Junior College Rd. (☎ **305/294-5232**), lies 6 miles from the cruise docks, near the southern tip of neighboring Stock Island. It features a challenging terrain of coral rock, sand traps, mangrove swamp, and pines. The course is a 10- to 15-minute, $15 taxi ride from the dock each way.

KAYAKING   If your ship gets in early, you can take a 3¹/₂-hour kayak tour through ✪ **Florida Keys Back Country Adventures,** 6810 Front St., Stock Island (☎ **305/ 296-0362**). Tours depart daily at 9am from Cudjoe Marina; the company will send a minivan for up to six passengers, if notified in advance. The shallow waters the tours visit, from 12 to 36 inches deep, are home to endless fish, stingrays, spiny lobsters, and crustaceans. You'll also see abundant bird life, especially hawks, bald eagles, and ospreys. There's no time for snorkeling during the half-day tour, but you can always dip into the cool waters whenever you come across a clean, sandy bottom.

SCUBA DIVING   The largest dive outfitter is **Captain's Corner,** 0 Duval Street, opposite the Pier House Hotel a block from the dock (☎ **305/296-8865**). The five-star PADI operation has 11 instructors, a 60-foot dive boat (used by Timothy "James Bond" Dalton during the filming of *License to Kill*), and a well-trained staff. To reach the departure point, make a left along the docks, and then walk for about a block to the northern tip of Duval Street.

SNORKELING   The *Reef Chief* (☎ **305/292-1345**) is a 65-foot, two-masted wooden schooner built in the 1970s and modeled on the forms made popular in the Chesapeake Bay during the 19th century. The 3¹/₂-hour snorkeling jaunts are closely synchronized with the arrival and departures of cruise ships, departing daily at 9am, 10:30am, or 2:30pm. The craft moors at the Safe Harbor Marina on Stock Island, a 15-minute, $12 one-way taxi ride from the docks. *Reef Chief* always drops anchor for around 90 minutes above reefs teeming with aquatic life. The shoals you visit are less crowded than those visited by boats berthed closer to the cruise docks.

GREAT LOCAL RESTAURANTS

All the restaurants listed below are within an easy 5- to 15-minute walk of the docks. Several "raw bars" near the dock area offer seafood, including oysters and clams, although the king here is conch—served grilled, ground in burgers, made into a chowder, fried in batter as fritters, or served raw in a conch salad.

Even if you don't have lunch, at least sample the local favorites: a slice of Key lime pie with a Cuban coffee. The pie's unique flavor is achieved from the juice and minced rind of the local, piquant Key lime.

Cruise ship passengers on a return visit to Key West often ask for "The Rose Tattoo," a historic old restaurant named for the Tennessee Williams film partially shot on the island. The restaurant is now the **Bagatelle,** 115 Duval St., at Front Street (☎ **305/ 296-6609**), one of Key West's finest. Look for daily specials or stick to the chef's better dishes, such as conch ceviche (thinly sliced raw conch marinated in lime juice and herbs). **Blue Heaven,** 729 Thomas St. (☎ **305/296-8666**), is a dive that serves some of the best food in town. Some of its finest food is fresh local fish, most often grouper or red snapper, and the hot and spicy jerk chicken is as fine as that served in Jamaica. **Camille's,** 703¹/₂ Duval St., between Angela and Petronia streets (☎ **305/296-4811**), is an unpretentious, hip cafe that serves the best breakfast in town and has the best lunch value. Try a sandwich made from the catch of the day served on fresh bread. Its Key lime pie is the island's best. **El Siboney,** 900 Catherine St. (☎ **305/296-4184**), is the place for time-tested Cuban favorites like *ropa vieja*, roast pork with garlic and tart sour oranges, and paella Valenciana (minimum of two).

Half Shell Raw Bar, Land's End Marina, foot of Margaret Street (☎ **305/ 294-7496**), is Key West's original raw bar, offering fresh fish, oysters, and shrimp direct from its own fish market. To be honest, though, I prefer the food at **Turtle Kraals Wildlife Bar & Grill,** Land's End Village, foot of Margaret Street (☎ **305/294-2640**). Try the tender Florida lobster, spicy conch chowder, or perfectly cooked fresh fish (often dolphin with pineapple salsa or baked stuffed grouper with mango crabmeat stuffing).

Pepe's Café & Steak House, 806 Caroline St., between William and Margaret streets (☎ **305/294-7192**), is the oldest eating house in the Florida Keys, established in 1909. Diners eat under slow-moving paddle fans at tables or dark pine booths with high backs. Cruise ship passengers enjoy the "in between" menu served daily from noon to 4:30pm. You get to choose from zesty homemade chili, perfectly baked oysters, fish sandwiches, and Pepe's deservedly famous steak sandwiches. **Siam House,** 829 Simonton St., parallel to Duval Street (☎ **305/292-0302**), just a 12-minute walk from the cruise docks, serves first-class Thai food, including crispy fish, a whole red snapper fast-fried and served with a sauce flavored with tamarind, garlic, and red peppers.

If something cool would go down better than a full meal, check out **Flamingo Crossing,** 1105 Duval St., at Virginia Street (☎ **305/296-6124**), which serves the best ice cream in the Florida Keys.

GREAT LOCAL BARS

Key West is a bar town. Most places recommended below offer fast food to go with their drinks. The food isn't the best on the island, but usually arrives shortly after you order it, which suits most rushed cruise ship passengers just fine.

Heavily patronized by cruise ship passengers, **Captain Tony's Saloon,** 428 Green St. (☎ **305/294-1838**), is the oldest active bar in Florida, and has it ever grown tacky. The 1851 building was the original Sloppy Joe's, a rough and tumble fisherman's saloon. Hemingway drank here from 1933 to 1937, and Jimmy Buffett got his start here before opening his own bar and going on to musical glory. The name refers to Capt. Tony Tarracino, a former Key West mayor and rugged man of the sea who owned the place until 1988.

Sloppy Joe's, 201 Duval St. (☎ **305/294-5717**), is the most touristy bar in Key West, visited by almost all cruise ship passengers, even those who don't normally go to bars. It aggressively plays up its association with Hemingway, although the bar stood on Greene Street back then (see Captain Tony's, above). Marine flags decorate the ceiling, and its ambience and decor evoke a Havana bar from the 1930s.

Jimmy Buffett's Margaritaville, 500 Duval St. (☎ **305/292-1435**), is the third most popular Key West bar with cruise ship passengers, after Captain Tony's and Sloppy Joe's. Buffett is the hometown boy done good, and his cafe, naturally, is decorated with pictures of himself. And, yes, it sells T-shirts and Margaritaville memorabilia in a shop off the dining room. His margaritas are without competition, but then they'd have to be, wouldn't they?

Open-air and very laid-back, the **Hog's Breath Saloon,** 400 Front St. (☎ **305/ 296-HOGG**), near the cruise docks, has been a Key West tradition since 1976. Drinking is a sport here, especially among the fishermen who come in after a day chasing the big one. Live entertainment is offered from 1pm to 2am.

For a real local hangout within an easy walk of the cruise ship docks, head to ✪ **Schooner Wharf,** 202 William St., Key West Bight (☎ **305/292-9520**), the most robust and hard-drinking bar in Key West, drawing primarily a young crowd, many of whom cater to the tourist industry or work on the town's fleet of fishing boats.

When the sunset crowds at Mallory Square get you down, retreat to **Sunset Pier Bar & Grill,** 0 Duval St. (behind the Ocean Key House; ☎ **305/295-7040**). You can still see everything, but you don't have to put up with the hassle. Tropical drinks, including a Sunset Pier margarita, are the bartender's specialties. Longtime favorite **Havana Docks Bar & Sunset Deck,** The Pier House, 1 Duval St. (☎ **305/296-4600**), rivals Sunset Pier Bar & Grill as the best barside sunset-watching spot. Live local island music toasts the setting sun.

13 Martinique

One of the most exotic French-speaking destinations in the Caribbean, Martinique was the site of a settlement demolished by volcanic activity (St. Pierre, now only a pale shadow of a once-thriving city). Like Guadeloupe and St. Barts, Martinique is legally and culturally French, although many Creole customs and traditions continue to flourish. The Creole cuisine is full of flavor and flair, and the island has lots of tropical charm.

When you arrive at **Fort-de-France,** Martinique's capital, you would never guess that this is one of the most beautiful islands in the Caribbean, but past the port are miles of white-sand beaches along an irregular coastline.

Martinique, about 50 miles at its longest and 21 miles at its widest, is mountainous, especially in the rain-forested northern region where the volcano **Mount Pelée** rises to a height of 4,656 feet. Hibiscus, poinsettias, bougainvillea, and coconut palms grow in lush profusion, and fruit—breadfruit, mangoes, pineapples, avocados, bananas, papayas, and custard apples—fairly drips from the trees.

Frommer's Favorite Martinique Experiences
- **Touring St-Pierre, site of a volcano eruption:** Mount Pelée erupted in 1902, killing 30,000 people. Today, you can see ruins of the church, the theater, and some other buildings, and tour a volcano museum (see "Sights Beyond Walking Distance," below).
- **Visiting the village of Trois-Ilets**: Tour where Joséphine, the wife of Napoleon I, was born in 1763. There's part of her home, a museum, and a botanical garden (see "Sights Beyond Walking Distance," below).

COMING ASHORE The Maritime Terminal is in a dreary commercial district of Fort-de-France, about a mile east of the center. Taxi drivers have a monopoly on transportation here and will charge $10 to make the trip (or more if they think they can get away with it). Many passengers make the usually hot and humid walk to downtown. If you walk, keep to the left after leaving the dock. This will take you to Place de la Savane, the heart of Fort-de-France.

At the pier you'll find a less-than-helpful tourist information office, a telephone, and a duty-free shop that is best skipped. Save purchases for the town center unless you're getting right back on the ship.

Frommer's Ratings: Martinique

	Poor	Fair	Good	Excellent	Outstanding
Overall Experience					✓
Shore Excursions			✓		
Activities Close to Port			✓		
Beaches & Water Sports				✓	
Shopping			✓		
Dining/Bars			✓		

Atlantic
Ocean

Martinique
Passage

Macouba

Grand' Rivière

Basse-Pointe

Leyritz   N1   Le Lorrain

Mt. Pelée

Ajoupa-Bouillon

Le Marigot

Le Prêcheur

N1

Morne Rouge

Ste-Marie

Tartane

Caravelle
Nature Preserve

St-Pierre

Morne des Esses

Caravelle Peninsula

Musée Gaugin

Trinité

Le Carbet   N2

N3

Gros-Morne

Balata

Bellefontaine

N4

Carbet Peak

St-Joseph

Case-Pilote

N1

Schoelcher

N1   Lamentin

Le François

Fort-de-France

Lamentin
International
Airport

Pointe du Bout

Mt. Vauclin   N6

Anse Mitan

N5

Anse-à-l'Ane

Vauclin

Les Trois-Ilets   D7

Grande Anse

Anses-d'Arlets

D7

Rivière-Pilote

D37   Le Diamant

Le Marin

Diamant Beach

Ste-Luce   D18A

Cap Chevalier

Diamond Rock

Ste-Anne

Les Salines

Petrified Forest

Pointe des Salines

St. Lucia Channel

Caribbean
Sea

Cruise Ship Dock   Airport   Beach   Mountain

Placing long distance calls in Martinique is just as difficult and frustrating as it is in Guadeloupe. Avoid calling home unless there's an emergency.

In some cases your cruise line may anchor in the Baie des Flamands. If so, passengers are transported by tender to the waterfront of Fort-de-France, thus putting you right in the heart of the city. The tourist office lies across the street from the landing dock in a building with an Air France logo.

CURRENCY   The **French franc (F)** is the legal tender here. The exchange rate is 6.29F to US$1 (1F is worth about 16¢). If you're going off on your own or plan to visit the countryside, you might want to exchange some money. A money-exchange service, **Change Caraibes** (☎ **0596/60-28-40**), is at rue Ernest-Deproge 4. It's open Monday to Friday from 7:30am to noon and 2:30 to 4pm.

INFORMATION   The **Office Départmental du Tourisme** (tourist office) is on boulevard Alfassa in Fort-de-France, across the waterfront boulevard from the harbor (☎ **0596/63-79-60**). It's open Monday to Friday 8am to 5pm and Saturday 8am to noon.

LANGUAGE   French is the official language. The local Creole patois uses words borrowed from French, English, Spanish, and African languages. English is occasionally spoken in the major hotels, restaurants, and tourist organizations, but don't count on driving around the countryside and asking for directions in English.

GETTING AROUND

BY TAXI   Travel by taxi is popular but expensive. Most of the cabs aren't metered, so you have to agree on the price of the ride before getting in. Night fares, in effect from 8pm to 6am, come with a 40% surcharge. For a radio taxi, call ☎ **0596/63-63-62.** If you want to rent a taxi for the day, it's better to have a party of at least three or four people to keep costs down. Based on the size of the car, expect to pay 700F ($112) to 850F ($136) and up for a 5-hour tour, depending on the itinerary you negotiate with the driver.

BY BUS   There are two types of buses operating on Martinique. Regular buses, called *grand busses,* hold about 40 passengers and cost 5F to 8F (80¢ to $1.30) to go anywhere within the city limits of Fort-de-France. *Taxis collectifs,* used to travel beyond the city limits, are privately owned minivans that traverse the island and bear the sign TC. Traveling in one of them is for the adventurous tourist—they are crowded and uncomfortable. A simple one-way fare is 30F ($4.80) from Fort-de-France to Ste-Anne. *Taxis collectifs* depart from the heart of Fort-de-France, at the parking lot of Pointe Simon.

BY RENTAL CAR   The scattered nature of Martinique's geography makes renting a car especially tempting. Call **Avis,** rue Ernest-Deproge 4 (☎ **800/331-1212** in the U.S., or 0596/51-17-70); **Budget,** rue Félix-Eboué 12 (☎ **800/527-0700** in the U.S., or 0596/63-69-00); or **Hertz,** rue Ernest-Deproge 24, at Lamentin Airport (☎ **800/ 654-3001** or 0596/60-64-64). Most car-rental rates are about $60 a day, including unlimited mileage. Prices are usually lower if you reserve a car from North America at least 2 business days before your arrival. You'll also be hit with a 9.5% value-added tax (VAT). Collision-damage waivers (CDWs) are an excellent idea in a country where the populace drives somewhat recklessly.

BY FERRY   The least expensive way to go between quai d'Esnambuc in Fort-de-France and Pointe du Bout, the main tourist zone, is by ferry (*vedette*). They usually run every day from 6am to midnight. The one-way fare is 32F ($5.10) per passenger. Schedules are printed in the free visitor's guide *Choubouloute,* which is distributed by the tourist office. However, if the weather is bad and/or the seas are rough, all ferry-boat services may be canceled.

A smaller ferryboat runs between Fort-de-France and Anse Mitan and Anse-à-l'Ane, across the bay, home to many two- and three-star hotels and several modest and unassuming Creole restaurants. The boat departs daily at 30-minute intervals between 6am and 6:30pm from quai d'Esnambuc in Fort-de-France. The trip takes about 15 minutes. The fare is 15F ($2.40) per passenger each way.

BY MOTORSCOOTER OR BICYCLE   Both can be rented from **Funny,** rue Ernest-Deproge 80, in Fort-de-France (☎ **0596/63-33-05**).

SHORE EXCURSIONS

In addition to the island tour below, most ships offer a snorkeling trip and a booze cruise.

✪ **Island Tour** ($42, 4 hours): There are many variations on this tour, but in some form you'll find the Pompeii of Martinique tour (see Mount Pelée in "Sights Beyond Walking Distance," below). It's one of the most intriguing shore excursions in the Caribbean. You're taken through the lush countryside to St-Pierre, where Mount Pelée killed 30,000 people in 1902.

ON YOUR OWN: WITHIN WALKING DISTANCE

Once past Fort-de-France's disappointing port, you'll find the town to be a mélange of New Orleans and the French Riviera. Iron grillwork balconies overflowing with flowers are commonplace here. Narrow streets climb up to houses on the steep hills. Almost a third of the island's year-round population of 360,000 lives in the capital, so it's not a small town.

At the center of the town lies **La Savane,** a broad garden with many palms and mangoes bordered by shops and cafes. In the middle of this grand square stands a statue of Joséphine, "é Napoleon's little Creole," carved in white marble by Vital Debray. The graceful statue looks toward Trois-Ilets, where she was born.

St. Louis Roman Catholic Cathedral, on rue Victor-Schoelcher, was built in 1875. The religious centerpiece of the island, it's an extraordinary iron building, which someone once likened to a Catholic railway station. A number of the island's former governors are buried beneath the choir loft.

A statue in front of the Palais de Justice portrays the island's second main historical figure (after Joséphine), Victor Schoelcher, who worked to free the slaves more than a century ago—you'll see his name a lot in Martinique. The **Bibliothèque Schoelcher,** rue de la Liberté 21, also honors this popular hero. This elaborate structure was first displayed at the Paris Exposition in 1889. The Romanesque portal in red and blue, the Egyptian lotus-petal columns, and even the turquoise tiles were taken apart and reassembled piece by piece here. It's open every day but Sunday.

Guarding the port is **Fort St-Louis,** built in the Vauban style on a rocky promontory. In addition, **Fort Tartenson** and **Fort Desaix** stand on hills overlooking the port as well.

Musée Départemental de la Martinique, rue de la Liberté 9, is the one place on Martinique that preserves its pre-Columbian past, with relics left from the early settlers, the Arawaks and the Caribs. The museum faces La Savane and is open Monday to Friday 8:30am to 5pm, and Saturday 9am to noon. Admission is 15F ($2.50) for adults, 10F ($1.65) for students, and 5F (85¢) for children.

SIGHTS BEYOND WALKING DISTANCE

Sacré-Coeur de Balata Cathedral, overlooking Fort-de-France at Balata, is a copy of the basilica looking down from Montmartre on Paris—and this one is just as incongruous, maybe more so. To get there, take the route de la Trace (Route N3). Balata is 6 miles north of Fort-de-France.

A few minutes' taxi ride from Fort-de-France on Route N3, the **Jardin de Balata** (Balata Garden) is a tropical botanical park created by Jean-Phillippe Thoze on land near his grandmother's house. He has restored the house, furnishing it with antiques and engravings depicting life in other days, and with bouquets and baskets of fruit renewed daily. The garden contains a profusion of flowers, shrubs, and trees. Balata is open daily. Admission is 35F ($5.85) for adults, 15F ($2.50) for children 7 to 12, and free for children under 6.

The major goal of all shore excursions, **St-Pierre** was the cultural and economic capital of Martinique until May 7, 1902. That very morning, locals read in their daily newspaper that "Montagne Pelée does not present any more risk to the population than Vesuvius does to the Neapolitans." Then at 8am, the southwest side of **Mount Pelée** exploded in fire and lava. By 8:02am, all but one of St-Pierre's 30,000 inhabitants were dead.

St-Pierre never recovered its past splendor. Ruins of the church, the theater, and some other buildings can be seen along the coast.

One of the best ways to get an overview of St-Pierre is to ride a rubber-wheeled "train," the **CV Paris Express,** which departs from the Musée Volcanologique (see below). Tours cost 50F ($8.35) for adults, and 25F ($4.20) for children, and run Monday through Friday from 10:30am to 1pm and 2:30 to 7pm. In theory, tours depart about once an hour, but actually they leave only when there are enough people to justify a trip.

Musée Volcanologique, rue Victor-Hugo, St-Pierre, was created by American volcanologist Franck Alvard Perret, who turned the museum over to the city in 1933. In pictures and relics excavated from the debris, you can trace the story of what happened to St-Pierre. Dug from the lava is a clock that stopped at the exact moment the volcano erupted. The museum is open daily from 9am to 5pm. Admission is 15F ($2.50), free for children 7 and under.

An idyllic excursion north of Fort-de-France is to **Le Carbet,** where Columbus landed in 1502 and the first French settlers arrived in 1635. The painter Paul Gauguin lived here for 4 months in 1887 before going on to do his most famous work on Tahiti. The landscape looks pretty much as it did when Gauguin depicted the beach in his *Bord de Mer.* **Centre d'Art Musée Paul-Gauguin,** Anse Turin, housed in a five-room building near the beach, commemorates the French artist's stay with books, prints, letters, and other memorabilia. Of special interest are fa ence mosaics made of pieces of colored volcanic rock excavated from nearby archaeological digs. There are also changing exhibits of works by local artists. The museum is open daily from 9am to 5:30pm. Admission is 15F ($2.50) for adults and students, 5F (85¢) for children under 8.

If you're driving yourself around or taking a taxi tour, you will find no better goal than **Hotel Plantation de Leyritz** near Basse-Pointe (☎ **0596/78-53-92**), one of the best restored plantations on Martinique and a good place for an authentic (and expensive) Creole lunch. It occupies the site of a plantation established around 1700 by Bordeaux-born Michel de Leyritz. Sprawled over flat, partially wooded terrain a half-hour's drive from the nearest beach (Anse à Zerot, in Sainte-Marie), it was the site of the "swimming pool summit meeting" in 1974 between Presidents Gerald Ford and Valéry Giscard d'Estaing. Part of the acreage still functions as a working banana plantation. The resort includes 16 acres of tropical gardens. At the core is a stone-sided 18th-century Great House.

Marie-Josèphe-Rose Tascher de la Pagerié was born in the charming little village of **Trois-Ilets** in 1763. As Joséphine, she was to become the wife of Napoleon I and empress of France from 1804 to 1809. She'd been previously married to Alexandre de Beauharnais, who had actually wanted to wed either of her two more attractive sisters.

Six years older than Napoleon, she pretended that she'd lost her birth certificate so he wouldn't find out her true age. Although many historians call her ruthless and selfish, she is still revered by some on Martinique as uncommonly gracious. Others, however, blame Napoleon's "reinvention" of slavery on her influence.

To reach her birthplace in Trois-Ilets (pronounced Twaz-ee-*lay*), take a taxi from the pier through lush countryside 20 miles south of Fort-de-France. In la Pagerié, a small museum, **Musée de la Pagerié** (☎ **0596/68-33-06**), sits in the former estate kitchen (the plantation house was destroyed in a hurricane) and displays mementos relating to Joséphine. You'll see a passionate love letter from Napoleon, along with her childhood bed. Here in this room Joséphine gossiped with her slaves and played the guitar. Still remaining are the partially restored ruins of the Pagerié sugar mill and the church where she was christened (the latter is in the village itself). A botanical garden, the **Parc des Floralies,** is adjacent to the golf course Golf de l'Impératrice Joséphine (see "Sports," below).

SHOPPING

Your best buys on Martinique are **French luxury imports,** such as perfumes, fashions, Vuitton luggage, Lalique crystal, or Limoges dinnerware. Sometimes prices are as much as 30% to 40% below those in the United States, but don't count on it. Some luxury goods—including jewelry—are subject to a value-added tax as high as 14%.

If you pay in dollars, store owners supposedly give you a 20% discount; however, their exchange rates are almost invariably far less favorable than those offered by the local banks, so your real savings is only 5% to 11%. Actually, you're better off shopping in the smaller stores, where prices are 8% to 12% less on comparable items, and paying in francs.

The main shopping street in Fort-de-France is **rue Victor-Hugo.** The other two leading shopping streets are **rue Schoelcher** and **rue St-Louis.**

Facing the tourist office and alongside **quai d'Esnambuc** is an open market where you can purchase local handcrafts and souvenirs, many of them tacky. Far more interesting is the display of vegetables and fruit—quite a show—at the open-air stalls along **rue Isambert.** Gourmet chefs can find all sorts of spices in the open-air markets, and such goodies as tinned pâté or canned quail in the local *supermarchés.*

Shops on every street sell bolts of the ubiquitous, colorful, and inexpensive local fabric, *madras.* So-called haute couture and resort wear are sold in many boutiques dotting downtown Fort-de-France.

Cadet-Daniel, rue Antoine-Siger 72, competes with **Roger Albert,** rue Victor-Hugo 7–9, to offer the best buys in French china and crystal. Before buying, do some comparison shopping.

Centre des Métieres d'Art, rue Ernest-Deproge, adjacent to the tourist office, is the best and most visible arts and crafts store in Martinique. You'll find both valuable and worthless local handmade artifacts for sale, including bamboo, ceramics, painted fabrics, and patchwork quilts suitable for hanging. The owner of **La Belle Matadore,** Immeuble Vermeil-Marina, Pointe du Bout (midway between the La Pagerié Hôtel and the Méridien Hotel), has carefully researched the history and traditions of the island's jewelry, and virtually all the merchandise sold here derives from models developed during slave days by the *matadores* (prostitutes), midwives, and slaves.

Martinique rum is considered by aficionados to be the world's finest (Hemingway, in *A Moveable Feast,* lauded it as the perfect antidote to a rainy day), and **La Case à Rhum,** in the Galerie Marchande, rue de la Liberté 5, offers all the brands. Bottles range in price from 42F ($7) for ordinary rum to 5,400F ($901.80) for a connoisseur's delight—a bottle of rum distilled by the Bally Company in 1924 in the nearby hamlet of Carbet. They offer samples in small cups to prospective buyers.

Set on the Route de Lamentin, midway between Fort-de-France and the Lamentin airport, **La Galleria** is, by anyone's estimate, the most upscale and elegant shopping complex on Martinique. On the premises are more than 60 different vendors, from France and the Caribbean. There's also a handful of cafes and restaurants, as well as an outlet or two selling the pastries and sweets for which Martinique is known.

BEACHES

The beaches south of Fort-de-France are white and sandy, but those to the north are mostly gray sand. Outstanding in the south is the 1 1/2-mile **Plage des Salines,** near Ste-Anne, with palm trees and a long stretch of white sand, and the 2 1/2-mile **Diamant,** with the landmark Diamond Rock offshore. Swimming on the Atlantic coast is for experts only, except at **Cap Chevalier** and **Presqu'ile de la Caravelle Nature Preserve.**

Pointe du Bout is a narrow peninsula across the bay from Fort-de-France, accessible by ferry (see "Getting Around"). It's the most lavish resort area of Martinique, with at least four of the island's largest hotels, an impressive marina, a golf course, about a dozen tennis courts, swimming pools, facilities for horseback riding and all kinds of water sports, a handful of restaurants, a gambling casino, and boutiques. The area's clean white-sand beaches were created by developers. The sandy beaches to the south at **Anse Mitan** have always been there welcoming visitors, however, including many snorkelers.

SPORTS

GOLF   The famous golf course designer Robert Trent Jones, Sr. visited Martinique and left behind the 18-hole **Golf de l'Impératrice-Joséphine** at Trois-Ilets (☎ 0596/68-32-81), a 5-minute, 1-mile taxi ride from the leading resort area of Pointe du Bout and about 18 miles from Fort-de-France. The only golf course on Martinique, it unfolds its greens from the birthplace of Empress Joséphine, across rolling hills with scenic vistas down to the sea. There's a pro shop, a bar, a restaurant, and three tennis courts.

HIKING   Personnel of the **Parc Naturel Régional de la Martinique** organize inexpensive guided excursions for small groups of tourists year-round. Contact them at the Excollège Agricole de Tivoli, B.P. 437, 97200 Fort-de-France (☎ 0596/64-42-59). This should be done 2 or 3 days before your cruise ship arrives in Martinique. **Presqu'ile de la Caravelle Nature Preserve,** a well-protected peninsula jutting into the Atlantic Ocean, has safe beaches and well-marked trails through tropical wetlands to the ruins of historic Château Debuc.

HORSEBACK RIDING   **Ranch Jack,** Morne Habitué, Trois-Ilets (☎ 0596/68-37-69), offers morning horseback rides for both experienced and novice riders. The daily promenades pass through the beaches and fields of Martinique, and the leaders offer a running commentary of the history, fauna, and botany of the island. Call Ranch Jack for transportation arrangements to and from the cruise dock.

SCUBA DIVING & SNORKELING   Divers come here to explore the Diamond Rock caves and walls and the ships sunk at St-Pierre during the 1902 volcanic eruption. Snorkeling equipment is also available at dive centers. Across the bay from Fort-de-France, in the Hotel Méridien, **Espace Plongée** (☎ 0596/66-00-00) is a major scuba center and the best in Pointe du Bout. They welcome anyone who shows up. Dive trips leave from the Méridien Hotel's pier. Prices include equipment rental, transportation, guide, and drinks on board. Dives are conducted twice daily. Full-day charters can be arranged. Cruise ship passengers should opt for the morning dives, as afternoon dives may not allow enough time to get back to the ship. The dive shop on the Méridien's beach stocks everything from weight belts and tanks to partial wetsuits and underwater cameras.

WINDSURFING Windsurfing is the most popular sport in the French West Indies. Equipment and lessons are available at all resort water-sports facilities, especially the **Hotel Méridien,** Pointe du Bout (☎ **0596/66-00-00**).

GREAT LOCAL RESTAURANTS & BARS
IN FORT-DE-FRANCE **À La Bonne Viande,** 11 rue Lamartine (☎ **0596/ 63-56-93**), is an atmospheric, charming restaurant in the center of town, serving specialties that include tournedos Rossini with foie gras and T-bones with béarnaise sauce. **Le Planteur,** 1 rue de la Liberté (on the southern edge of La Savane, right in the heart of town; ☎ **0596/63-17-45**), serves fresh and flavorful menu items such as cassoulet of minced conch.

AT POINTE DU BOUT **Pignon sur Mer,** Anse-à-l'Ane (a 12-minute drive from Pointe du Bout; ☎ **0596/68-38-37**), is a simple, unpretentious Creole restaurant serving island-inspired dishes that might include *delices du Pignon,* a platter of shellfish, or whatever grilled fish or shellfish was hauled in that day. **La Villa Créole,** Anse Mitan (☎ **0596/66-05-53**), is a 3- or 4-minute drive from the hotels of Pointe du Bout, and serves reasonably priced set-price menus that offer a selection of such staples as *accras de morue* (beignets of codfish); *boudin creole* (blood sausage); and *un féroce* (a local form of pâté concocted from fresh avocados, pulverized codfish, and manioc flour).

ON THE NORTH COAST: TWO "MAMA" CHEFS Like Guadeloupe, Martinique is famous for its female Creole chefs. If you opted for a taxi tour or a rented car, you can seek out two of the best of these Martinique "mamas" on the north coast.

Chez Mally Edjam, Rte. de la Côte Atlantique, Basse-Pointe (36 miles from Fort-de-France; ☎ **0596/78-51-18**), operates from a modest house beside the main road in the center of town. Grandmotherly Mally Edjam (assisted to an ever-increasing degree by her younger, France-born friend, Martine Hugé) is usually busy in the kitchen turning out her Creole delicacies, like stuffed land crab with a hot seasoning and a classic *colombo de porc* (the Creole version of pork curry).

Yva Chez Vava, Boulevard de Gaulle (west of Basse-Pointe; ☎ **0596/55-72-72**), is a combination private home and restaurant, representing the hard labor of three generations of Creole women. It was established in 1979 by a well-remembered, long-departed matron, Vava, whose daughter, Yva, is now assisted by her own daughter, Rosy. Local family recipes are the mainstay of this modest bistro, infused with a simple country-inn style. À la carte menu items include Creole soup, lobster, and various *colombos* or curries. Local delicacies have changed little since the days of Joséphine and her sugar fortune, and include *z'habitants* (crayfish), *vivaneau* (red snapper), *tazard* (kingfish), and *accras de morue* (cod fritters).

14 Nassau
Nassau is the capital of the Bahamas, and it has that nation's best shopping, best entertainment, and best beaches. It's big. It's bold. It's one of the busiest cruise ship ports in the world. It's got the old, it's got the new, there's probably something borrowed here, and there's a whole heckuva lot of blue seas. One million visitors a year make their way onto its shores to enjoy its bounty.

With its adjoining **Cable Beach** and **Paradise Island** (linked by bridge to the city), Nassau has luxury resorts set on powdery-soft beaches; all the water sports, golf, and tennis you could want; and so much duty-free shopping that its stores outdraw its museums. Yet historic Nassau hasn't lost its British colonial charms—it just boasts up-to-date tourist facilities to complement them.

Nassau

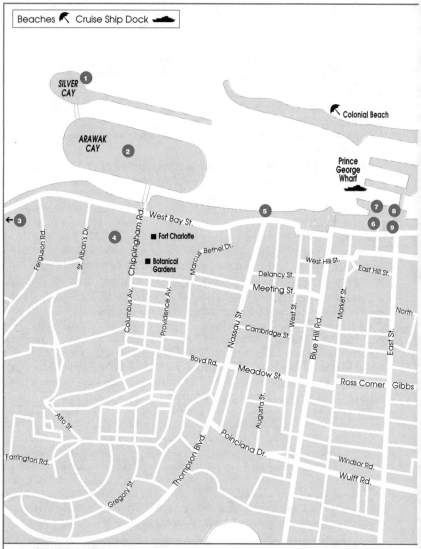

Beaches 🏄 Cruise Ship Dock ⛴

SILVER CAY ①

ARAWAK CAY ②

Colonial Beach 🏄

Prince George Wharf ⛴

← ③

④ ■ Fort Charlotte
   ■ Botanical Gardens

West Bay St.

Chippingham Rd.

Ferguson Rd.

St. Alban's Dr.

Columbus Av.

Providence Av.

Marcus Bethel Dr.

⑤

⑥ ⑦
⑧ ⑨

West Hill St.   East Hill St.

Delancy St.

Meeting St.

West St.

Nassau St.

Cambridge St.

Blue Hill Rd.

Market St.

North

Boyd Rd.

Meadow St.

Alto St.

Augusta St.

Ross Corner   Gibbs

East St.

Farrington Rd.

Thompson Blvd.

Poinciana Dr.

Gregory St.

Windsor Rd.

Wulff Rd.

SA-0129

Arawak Cay ②
Ardastra Gardens ④
Cable Beach ③
Cable Beach Golf ③
The Cloister ⑫
Crystal Cay ①
Crystal Palace Casino ⑤
Fort Fincastle ⑩
Hairbraider's Centre ⑨

Junkanoo Expo ⑧
Nassau International Bazaar ⑦
Paradise Island Casino ⑪
Paradise Island Golf ⑬
Potter's Cay ⑭
Prince George Plaza ⑥
Rawson Square ⑥
The Retreat ⑮
Straw Market ⑨

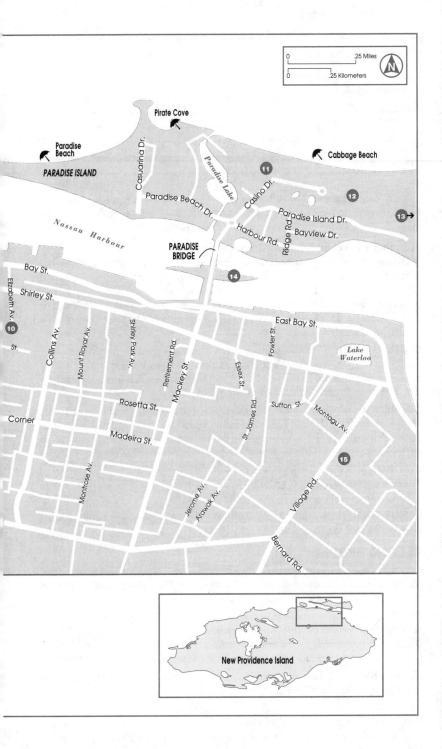

Pirate Cove

Paradise Beach

Cabbage Beach

PARADISE ISLAND

Casuarina Dr.

Paradise Lake

Paradise Beach Dr.

Casino Dr.

11

12

Paradise Island Dr.

13 →

Ridge Rd.

Bayview Dr.

Nassau Harbour

Harbour Rd.

PARADISE
BRIDGE

14

Bay St.

Shirley St.

Elizabeth Av.

10

St.

Collins Av.

Mount Royal Av.

Shirley Park Av.

Retirement Rd.

Mackey St.

East Bay St.

Fowler St.

*Lake
Waterloo*

Essex St.

Rosetta St.

Sutton St.

Montagu Av.

Corner

Madeira St.

St. James Rd.

15

Montrose Av.

Jerome Av.

Arawak Av.

Village Rd.

Bernard Rd.

0 .25 Miles

0 .25 Kilometers

New Providence Island

Frommer's Ratings: Nassau					
	Poor	Fair	Good	Excellent	Outstanding
Overall Experience				✓	
Shore Excursions			✓		
Activities Close to Port				✓	
Beaches & Water Sports			✓		
Shopping				✓	
Dining/Bars			✓		

Many people come on 3- to 4-day cruises leaving from Miami, Fort Lauderdale, and Port Canaveral. In recent years, the government has spent millions of dollars increasing its facilities, so now about a dozen cruise ships can pull into dock at one time.

Frommer's Favorite Nassau Experiences

- **Dining on fresh conch at Arawak Cay:** The small man-made island across West Bay Street is the place to go for the freshest stuff, washed down with coconut milk laced with gin (see "Great Local Restaurants & Bars," below).
- **Getting your hair braided:** For a new look, get your hair braided in the local style at the Hairbraider's Centre on Prince George Dock (see "On Your Own: Within Walking Distance," below).

COMING ASHORE   Cruise ships dock near Rawson Square, the very center of the city and its main shopping area. The Straw Market, at Market Plaza, is nearby, as is the main shopping artery of Bay Street. The Nassau International Bazaar is at the intersection of Woodes Rogers Walk and Charlotte Street.

CURRENCY   The legal tender is the **Bahamian dollar (B$1),** which is on a par with the U.S. dollar. Both U.S. and Bahamian dollars are accepted on an equal basis throughout the Bahamas. There is no restriction on the amount of foreign currency tourists can bring into the country. Most large hotels and stores accept traveler's checks.

INFORMATION   You can get help from the Information Desk at the **Ministry of Tourism's** office, Bay Street (☎ 242/356-7591), open Monday to Friday from 9am to 5pm. A smaller information booth can be found at Rawson Square near the dock.

LANGUAGE   The language of the Bahamas is English, spoken with a lilt that has more British in it than American.

GETTING AROUND

Unless you rent a horse and carriage, the only way to really see Old Nassau is on foot. All the major attractions and the principal stores are within walking distance. You can even walk to Cable Beach or Paradise Island.

BY TAXI   Taxis are practical, at least for longer island trips, and are required to have working meters, so you probably won't be cheated. The official fare is $2 at flag fall and 30¢ for each quarter mile for the first two passengers; additional passengers pay $2. Five-passenger cabs can be hired for $23 to $25 per hour. For a radio taxi, call ☎ 242/323-5111.

BY MINIBUS   The least expensive means of transport is by the medium-size buses called **jitneys.** The fare is 75¢; exact change is required.

BY FERRY   Ferries run from the end of Casuarina Drive on Paradise Island across the harbor to Rawson Square for $2 per person. These "water taxis" operate during the day at 20-minute intervals between Paradise Island and Prince George Wharf. The one-way fare is $2 per person.

BY HORSE-DRAWN CARRIAGE   The elegant, traditional way to see Nassau is in a horse-drawn surrey, the kind with the fringe on top. Negotiate with the driver and agree on the price before you get in. The average charge for a tour is $5 per person. The maximum load is three adults plus one or two children under the age of 12. The surreys are available daily from 9am to 4:30pm, except when horses are rested—usually from 1 to 3pm May through October, and from 1 to 2pm November through April. You'll find the surreys at Rawson Square, off Bay Street.

BY MOTORSCOOTER   Motorscooters have become a favorite mode of transportation. For a rental, contact **Ursa Investment,** Prince George Wharf (☎ **242/ 326-8329**). Mopeds cost about $20 per hour or $50 for a full day.

BY RENTAL CAR   If you want to rent a car, try **Avis** (☎ **800/331-1212** in the U.S., or 242/326-6380), **Budget** (☎ **800/527-0070** in the U.S., or 242/377-7405), and **Hertz** (☎ **800/654-3131** in the U.S., or 242/377-8684), and remember to drive on the left, British-style.

SHORE EXCURSIONS

There's a lot you can do on your own in Nassau, and it's easy to get around by taxi and on foot. Your ship will probably offer several organized island tours, as well as snorkeling and a range of water-born sightseeing tours via glass-bottomed boat and submarine and/ or booze cruises aboard a catamaran. Here are some of the best ones.

Heart of Nassau and Ardastra Gardens ($24, 2^1/$_2$ hours): You're taken along Bay Street, the main shopping district, and later treated to the famous marching flamingo review in the gardens. Other stops include the Queen's Staircase and Fort Charlotte.

Fort Fincastle Tour ($18, 2 hours): This tour takes you to a great view, the Queen's Staircase, and some of the most beautiful homes of Nassau, then across the bridge to view the highlights of Paradise Island, including the Cloisters and its side gardens.

Crystal Cay Tour ($25, 3 hours): The country's most popular attraction has a network of aquariums, an Underwater Observation Tower, landscaped park areas, lounges, and a restaurant. (*Note:* It's almost as easy to go on your own.)

TOURING WITH LOCAL OPERATORS

Goombay Guided Walking Tours: These free tours, arranged by the Ministry of Tourism (☎ **242/326-9772**), leave from the Tourist Information Booth on Rawson Square. Make an advance reservation, as schedules can vary. Usually the tours leave the booth at 10am and again at 2pm, except on Thursday and Sunday afternoon. These tours last for about 45 minutes and include descriptions of some of the city's most venerable buildings, with commentaries on the history, customs, and traditions of Nassau.

Walking Around Underwater: Hartley's Undersea Walk, East Bay Street (☎ **242/ 393-8234**), takes you on a 3^1/$_2$-hour cruise on the yacht *Pied Piper*. At one point you don a breathing helmet and spend about 20 minutes walking along the ocean bottom through a "garden" of tropical fish, sponges, and other undersea life. Entire families can make this walk. You don't even have to be able to swim. Trips are operated Tuesday to Saturday at 9:30am and 1:30pm.

Day Cruises: Nassau Cruises Ltd., at the Paradise Island Bridge (☎ **242/363-3577**), maintains a trio of three-deck motorized yachts, *Calypso I, Calypso IV,* and *The Islander*. These are the most luxurious of the day cruisers, and their trips to uninhabited Blue Lagoon Island are reason enough to take them. The yachts depart from a point just west of the toll booth at the Paradise Island Bridge. Daytime trips leave every day for the secluded beaches of Blue Lagoon Island, a 4-mile sail east of Paradise Island. The day sails leave at 10am and 11:30am and come back from the island at 1:30pm, 3pm, and

4:30pm. The day pass is $20 for adults and $10 for children, and pays for the boat ride only. The all-inclusive day pass is $50 for adults and $25 for children (3 to 12), and covers transportation, the boat ride, lunch, two daiquiris for adults, and all non-motorized water sports.

ON YOUR OWN: WITHIN WALKING DISTANCE

The best way to see some of the major public buildings of Nassau is to take a walk, which gives you not only an overview of the historical monuments, but a feel for the city and its history. Later you can concentrate on specific outlying sights, notably Ardastra Gardens and Coral Island Bahamas.

Begin your stroll around Nassau at **Rawson Square** in the center, home of the Straw Market stalls. I also enjoy the native market on the waterfront, a short walk through the Straw Market. This is where Bahamian fishermen unload a variety of fish and produce—crates of mangoes, oranges, tomatoes, and limes, plus lots of crimson-lipped conch. For a look, it's best to go any Monday to Saturday morning before noon.

You'll be aggressively solicited to have your hair braided in the local style at the ✪ **Hairbraider's Centre,** Prince George Dock. The government sponsors this open-air pavilion where all sorts of braiding experts gather. If you're looking for a new look, here's your chance.

Potter's Cay, under the Paradise Island Bridge, provides a chance to observe local life as nowhere else. Sloops from the Out Islands pull in here, bringing their fresh catch along with plenty of conch. Freshly grown herbs and vegetables are also sold here, along with plenty of limes (the Bahamians' preferred seasoning for fish) and tropical fruits, such as *paw-paw* (papaya), pineapple (usually from Eleuthera), and bananas. Little stalls sell conch in several forms: raw, marinated in lime juice, as spicy deep-fried fritters, and in conch salad and conch soup.

The Cloister, in front of the Ocean Club, Ocean Club Drive, Paradise Island (☎ 242/363-3000), is a real 14th-century cloister, built in France by Augustinian monks and reassembled here stone by stone. Huntington Hartford, the A&P stores heir, purchased the cloister from the estate of William Randolph Hearst at San Simeon in California, but the dismantled parts arrived unlabeled and unnumbered on Paradise Island. The deconstructed cloister baffled the experts until artist and sculptor Jean Castre-Manne set about to reassemble it. It took him 2 years, and what you see today presumably bears some similarity to the original. The gardens, extending over the rise to Nassau Harbour, are filled with tropical flowers and classic statuary.

Crystal Cay marine park, on Silver Cay just off West Bay Street, between downtown Nassau and Cable Beach (☎ 242/328-1036), has a network of aquariums, landscaped park areas, lounges, a gift shop, and a restaurant, but its outstanding feature is the Underwater Observation Tower. You descend a spiral staircase to a depth of 20 feet below the surface of the water, where you view coral reefs and abundant sea life in their natural habitat. The tower rises 100 feet above the water to two viewing decks. Graceful stingrays, endangered sea turtles, and Caribbean sharks swim in Shark Tank, which has both an overhead viewing deck and a below-water viewing area. Nature trails with lush tropical foliage, waterfalls, exotic trees, and wildlife further enhance this setting. You can get here via a scenic 10-minute ferry ride from the Prince George Dock.

Fort Fincastle, Elizabeth Avenue (☎ 242/322-2442), which can be reached by climbing the Queen's Staircase, was constructed in 1793 by Lord Dunmore, the royal governor. From here you can take an elevator ride to the top and walk on an observation floor (a 126-foot-high water tower and lighthouse) for a view of the harbor. Although the ruins of the fort can hardly compete with the view, you can walk around on your own or take a guided tour. You don't have to ask for a guide, since very assertive young men wait to show you around. Frankly, there isn't that much to see except some old cannons.

It's quite likely you'll miss the Junkanoo parade beginning at 2am on Boxing Day, December 26, but you can relive the Bahamian Junkanoo carnival at the **Junkanoo Expo,** Prince George Wharf (☎ 242/356-2731), in the old Customs Warehouse. All the glitter and glory of Mardi Gras comes alive in this museum, with its fantasy costumes used for the holiday bacchanal.

ON YOUR OWN: BEYOND WALKING DISTANCE

A flock of pink flamingos parading in formation is the main attraction at the lush, 5-acre ✪ **Ardastra Gardens,** Chippingham Road (near Fort Charlotte, about a mile west of downtown Nassau; ☎ 242/323-5806). These Marching Flamingos have been trained to obey the drillmaster's oral orders with long-legged precision and discipline. They perform daily at 11am, 2pm, and 4pm. Other exotic wildlife to be seen here are very tame boa constrictors, kinkajous (honey bears) from Central and South America, green-winged macaws, peafowl, blue-and-gold macaws, capuchin monkeys, and more. You can get a good look at the flora of the gardens by walking along the sign-posted paths, as many of the more interesting and exotic trees bear identification plaques. Guided tours of the gardens and the aviary are given Monday to Saturday at 10:15am and 3:15pm.

A true oasis in Nassau, the 11 acres of unspoiled gardens at **The Retreat,** Village Road (☎ 242/393-1317), are even more intriguing than the Botanical Gardens. They are home to about 200 species of exotic palm trees, as well as the headquarters for the Bahamas National Trust. Half-hour tours of the acres are given Tuesday to Thursday at noon.

GAMBLING

Many cruise ship passengers spend almost their entire time ashore at one of the casinos on Cable Beach or Paradise Island.

All gambling roads eventually lead to the extravagant **Paradise Island Casino,** in the Atlantis, Casino Drive (☎ 242/363-3000). For sheer gloss, glitter, and show-biz extravagance, this mammoth 30,000-square-foot casino, with adjacent attractions, is the place to go. It's the only casino on Paradise Island, and is superior to the Crystal Palace Casino. No visit to the Bahamas would be complete without a promenade through the Bird Cage Walk, an assortment of restaurants, bars, and cabaret facilities. Doric columns, a battery of lights, and a mirrored ceiling vie with the British colonial decor in the enormous gaming room. Some 1,000 slot machines operate 24 hours a day, and from mid-morning until early the following morning the 59 gaming tables are all seriously busy.

The dazzling **Crystal Palace Casino,** West Bay Street, Cable Beach (☎ 242/327-6200)—the only one on New Providence Island—is run by Nassau Marriott Resort. Although some savvy gamblers claim you get better odds in Las Vegas, this 35,000-square-foot casino nevertheless stacks up well against all the major casinos of the Caribbean. The gaming room features 750 slot machines in true Las Vegas style, along with 69 gaming tables. An oval-shaped casino bar extends onto the gambling floor, and a Casino Lounge, with its bar and bandstand, offers live entertainment. Open Sunday to Thursday from 10am to 4am, Friday and Saturday 24 hours.

SHOPPING

In 1992, the Bahamas abolished import duties on 11 categories of luxury goods, including china, crystal, fine linens, jewelry, leather goods, photographic equipment, watches, fragrances, and other merchandise, but even though prices are duty-free, you can still end up spending more on an item in the Bahamas than you would back home. If you're contemplating buying a good Swiss watch or some expensive perfume, it's best to look in your hometown discount outlets before making serious purchases here. While the advertised 30% to 50% reductions off stateside prices might be true in some cases, they're not in most.

The principal shopping area is a stretch of **Bay Street,** the main drag, and its side streets. There are also shops in the hotel arcades. In lieu of street numbers along Bay Street, look for signs advertising the various stores.

The pleasant new **Nassau International Bazaar** is composed of some 30 shops selling goods from around the globe. The bazaar runs from Bay Street down to the waterfront near the Prince George Wharf. The alleyways here have been cobbled and storefronts are garreted, evoking the villages of old Europe. **Prince George Plaza,** Bay Street, can be crowded with cruise ship passengers. Many fine shops here sell Gucci and other quality merchandise. You can also patronize an open-air rooftop restaurant overlooking the street. The **Straw Market** in Straw Market Plaza on Bay Street seems to be on every shopper's itinerary. Even those who don't want to buy anything come here to look around. You can watch the Bahamian craftspeople weave and plait straw hats, handbags, dolls, place mats, and other items, including straw shopping bags.

If you've fallen under the junkanoo spell and want to take home some steel drums, stop by **Pyfroms,** Bay Street. If you'd rather listen than play, try **Cody's Music and Video Center,** East Bay Street, corner of Armstrong Street, which specializes in contemporary music of the Bahamas and the Caribbean. The father of owner Cody Carter was mentor to many of the country's first Goombay and junkanoo artists.

Pipe of Peace, Bay Street, between Charlotte and Parliament streets, is called the "world's most complete tobacconist." You can buy both Cuban and Jamaican cigars here. (However, the Cuban cigars can't legally be brought back to the United States.)

Stamp collectors should stop by the **Bahamas Post Office Philatelic Bureau,** in the General Post Office, at the top of Parliament Street on East Hill Street, for beautiful Bahamian stamps, while **Coin of the Realm,** Charlotte Street, just off Bay Street, is the place for coin collectors.

The **Bahamas Plait Market,** Wulff Road, and **The Plait Lady,** the Regarno Building, Victoria and Bay streets, are both good choices for 100% Bahamian-made products. Both are far superior to the Straw Market, where some of the items are imported from Asia. **Island Tings,** Bay Street between East Street and Elizabeth Avenue, and **Seagrape,** West Bay Street, both offer Bahamian arts and crafts, plus jewelry and other items. **The Girls from Brazil,** Bay Street, is the best outlet for swimwear in Nassau, and **Mademoiselle, Ltd.,** Bay Street at Frederick Street, specializes in all kinds of resort wear as well as locally made batik garments by Androsia.

BEACHES

On New Providence Island, sun lovers flock to **Cable Beach,** one of the best-equipped in the Caribbean, with all sorts of water sports and easy access to shops, casinos, bars, and restaurants. The area was named for the telegraph cable laid in 1892 from Jupiter, Florida, to the Bahamas. Cable Beach runs for some 4 miles and is incredibly varied. Waters can be rough and reefy, and then turn calm and clear. The beach is about 2 miles from the port and can be reached by taxi or bus no. 10.

Cable Beach is far superior to the meager one in town, the **Western Esplanade,** which sweeps westward from the British Colonial hotel, but Western Esplanade is closer and more convenient for those arriving in a cruise ship. It has rest rooms, changing facilities, and a snack bar.

Even Cable Beach buffs like **Paradise Beach** on Paradise Island. It's convenient to Nassau—all visitors have to do is walk or drive across the bridge or take a boat from the Prince George Wharf (see "Getting Around," above). Admission to the beach is $3 for adults, $1 for children, including use of a shower and locker. An extra $10 deposit is required for towels.

Paradise Island has a number of smaller beaches, including **Pirate's Cove Beach** and **Cabbage Beach,** both on the north shore. Bordered by·casuarinas, palms, and sea grapes, Cabbage Beach's broad sands stretch for at least 2 miles. It's likely to be crowded with guests of the island's megaresorts. Escapists find something approaching solitude on the northwestern end, accessible only by boat or foot.

SPORTS

GOLF   South Ocean Golf Course, Southwest Bay Road (☎ 242/362-4391), is the best course on New Providence Island and one of the best in the Bahamas. It's located 30 minutes from Nassau on the southwest edge of the island. This 18-hole, 6,706-yard, par-72 beauty has some first-rate holes with a backdrop of trees, shrubs, ravines, and undulating hills. The lofty elevation offers some panoramic water views. It's best to phone ahead in case there's a tournament scheduled. **Cable Beach Golf Course,** Cable Beach, West Bay Road (☎ 242/327-6000), is a spectacular 18-hole, 7,040-yard, par-72 championship golf course, although not as challenging as South Ocean, above. Under the management of Radisson Cable Beach Hotel, this course is often used by guests of the other nearby hotels. **Paradise Island Golf Club,** Paradise Island Drive (☎ 242/363-3925), is a superb 18-hole championship course at the east end of Paradise Island. The 14th hole of the 6,771-yard, par-72 course has the world's largest sand trap: The entire left side over the hole is white sand beach.

HORSEBACK RIDING   On the southwest shore, 2 miles from the Nassau Airport, **Happy Trails Stables, Coral Harbour (☎ 242/362-1820), offers a 1-hour, 20-minute horseback trail ride for $60 per person, including free round-trip transportation from your hotel. The weight limit for riders is 200 pounds. Children must be 8 or older. Reservations are required, especially during the holiday season.

SCUBA DIVING & SNORKELING   Bahama Divers, East Bay Street (☎ 242/393-5644), offers a half day of snorkeling at offshore reefs, and a half-day scuba trip with preliminary pool instruction for beginners. Participants receive free transportation to the boats. Children must be 8 or older to go snorkeling. Reservations are required, especially during the winter season. **Stuart Cove's Dive South Ocean,** Southwest Bay Street, South Ocean (☎ 800/879-9832 in the U.S., or 242/362-4171), is about 10 minutes from top dive sites, including the coral reefs, wrecks, and underwater airplane structure used in filming James Bond thrillers. The Porpoise Pen Reefs and steep sea walls are also on the diving agenda. All prices for boat dives include tanks, weights, and belts. A special feature is a series of shark-dive experiences. **Sea & Ski Ocean Sports,** at the Radisson Grand Resort on Paradise Island (☎ 242/363-3370), offers scuba diving and snorkeling.

WATER SPORTS   Sea Sports, at the Nassau Marriott Resort & Crystal Palace Casino on West Bay Street (☎ 242/327-6200), offers a full water-sports program. You can rent Hobie cats, Sunfish, windsurfers, or even a kayak. You can also go parasailing and water-skiing. **Sea & Ski Ocean Sports,** at the Radisson Grand Resort on Casino Dr. (☎ 242/363-3370), offers scuba diving and snorkeling trips, parasailing, and windsurfers.

GREAT LOCAL RESTAURANTS & BARS

✪ **ON ARAWAK CAY   You'll get all the conch you can possibly eat on Arawak Cay, a small manmade island across West Bay Street. The Bahamian government created the cay to store large tanks of freshwater, of which New Providence Island often runs out. You don't go here to see the water tanks, however, but to join the locals in sampling their favorite food. The conch is cracked before your eyes (not everybody's favorite attraction), and you're given some hot sauce to spice it up. The locals wash it down with their favorite drink, coconut milk laced with gin (an acquired taste, to say the least). This ritual is a local tradition, and you'll feel like a real Bahamian if you participate.

IN NASSAU Bahamian Kitchen, Trinity Place, off Market Street (next to Trinity Church; ☎ 242/325-0702), is one of the best places for good, down-home Bahamian food at modest prices. Specialties include lobster Bahamian style, fried red snapper, and curried chicken. **Café Kokomo,** in the garden of the Parliament Hotel, 18 Parliament St. (☎ 242/322-2836), serves well-prepared Bahamian seafood in a verdant setting. If you like your dining with a view, there's no better place than the second-floor, open-air terrace of the **Poop Deck,** Nassau Yacht Haven Marina, East Bay Street (☎ 242/393-8175), overlooking the harbor and Paradise Island.

Far removed from the well-trodden tourist path, the **Shoal Restaurant and Lounge,** Nassau Street (☎ 242/323-4400), is a steadfast local favorite and ranks near the top for authentic flavor.

Green Shutters Restaurant, 48 Parliament St. (2 blocks south of Rawson Square; ☎ 242/325-5702), is an English pub transplanted to the tropics. It offers three imported English beers along with pub grub favorites such as steak-and-kidney pie, bangers and mash, shepherd's pie, and fish-and-chips. **Gaylord's,** Dowdeswell Street at Bay Street (☎ 242/356-3004), is the only Indian restaurant in the country, and as such, is now a culinary staple of Nassau, serving a wide range of Punjabi, tandoori, and curried dishes. **Caribe Café Restaurant and Terrace,** in the British Colonial Beach Resort, 1 Bay St. (☎ 242/322-3301), serves the food your kids have been crying for, including beef burgers or freshly made salads.

AT CABLE BEACH Café Johnny Canoe, in the Nassau Beach Hotel, West Bay Street (☎ 242/327-3373), serves burgers, all kinds of steaks, seafood, and chicken dishes. The best items on the menu are blackened grouper and barbecued fish. **Tequila Pepe's,** in the Radisson Cable Beach Hotel, West Bay Street (☎ 242/327-6000), serves buffet-style Tex-Mex dishes: fajitas, tacos, burritos, tamales, and chimichangas.

ON PARADISE ISLAND The Cave, at the Atlantis, Casino Drive (☎ 242/363-3000), is a burger and salad joint located near the beach of the most lavish hotel and casino complex on Paradise island. It caters to the bathing suit and flip-flops crowd. To reach the place, you pass beneath a simulated rock-sided tunnel illuminated with flaming torches. **Seagrapes Restaurant,** in the Atlantis, Casino Drive (☎ 242/363-3000), serves buffet-style tropical food, including Cuban, Caribbean, and Cajun dishes.

15 Puerto Rico

The Commonwealth of Puerto Rico, under the jurisdiction of the United States, is home to over 3 million people whose primary language is Spanish. It's the most urbanized island of the Caribbean, with lots of traffic, glittering casinos, relatively high crime, and a more-or-less comfortable mix of Latin culture with imports from the U.S. mainland. The island's interior is filled with ancient volcanic mountains, and its coastline is ringed with sandy beaches. In addition to the main island, the Commonwealth includes a trio of small offshore islands: Culebra, Mona, and Vieques. Vieques has the most tourist facilities of the three.

San Juan, Puerto Rico's 16th-century capital, is the Caribbean's most historic port and has some 500 years of history, reflected in its restored Spanish colonial architecture. Its shopping is topped by St. Thomas and Sint Maarten, but overall its historic sights,

Puerto Rico

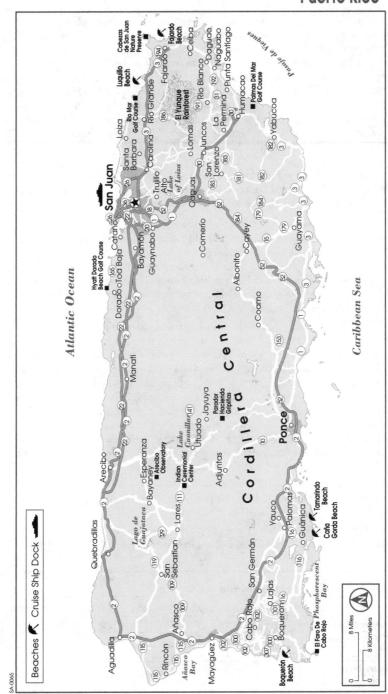

Beaches ↖ Cruise Ship Dock

Atlantic Ocean

Caribbean Sea

Pasaje de Vieques

San Juan

Cordillera Central

SA-0065

477

attractions, gambling, and diversions make it number-one in the Caribbean. You'll find some of the Caribbean's best restaurants and hotels here, as well, and it even has a glitzy beach strip, **the Condado.**

The Port of San Juan is the busiest ocean terminal in the West Indies, and second only to Miami for the North America cruise trade. Metropolitan San Juan includes the old walled city and the city center, which contains the Capitol building, on San Juan Island; Santurce, on a larger peninsula, reached by causeway bridges from San Juan Island (the lagoon front section here is called Miramar); Condado, the narrow peninsula that stretches from San Juan Island to Santurce; Hato Rey, the business center; Río Piedras, site of the University of Puerto Rico; and Bayamón, an industrial and residential quarter.

The Condado strip of beachfront hotels, restaurants, casinos, and nightclubs is separated from Miramar by a lagoon. Isla Verde, another resort area, is near the airport, which is separated from the rest of San Juan by an isthmus.

Frommer's Favorite San Juan Experiences

- **Taking a walking tour of 500-year-old Old San Juan:** Its cobblestoned, narrow streets and Spanish colonial architecture are stunning (see "Shore Excursions," and "On Your Own: A Walking Tour of Old San Juan," below).
- **Taking a hike through El Yunque Rain Forest:** The forest is home to 240 species of tropical trees, flowers, and wildlife, including millions of tiny coqui tree frogs (see "Shore Excursions," below).

COMING ASHORE Cruise ships dock on the historic south shore of Old San Juan, within the sheltered channel that was hotly contested by European powers during the island's early colonial days. Each of the piers are within a short walk of the Plaza de la Marina, the Wyndham Hotel, Old San Juan's main bus station, and most of the historic and commercial treasures of Old San Juan. During periods of heavy volume—usually Saturday and Sunday in midwinter, when as many as 10 cruise ships might dock in San Juan on the same day—additional, less convenient piers are activated. They include the Frontier Pier, at the western edge of the Condado, near the Caribe Hilton Hotel, and the Pan American Dock, in Isla Grande, across the San Antonio Channel from Old San Juan. Passengers berthing at either of these docks need some kind of motorized transit (usually a taxi or a van supplied by the cruise line as part of the shore excursion program) to get to the Old Town.

CURRENCY The **U.S. dollar** is the coin of the realm. Canadian currency is accepted by some big hotels in San Juan, but reluctantly.

INFORMATION For advice and maps, contact the **Tourist Information Center at La Casita,** Paseo de la Princesa near Pier 1 in Old San Juan (☎ 787/721-2400).

Frommer's Ratings: San Juan, Puerto Rico					
	Poor	Fair	Good	Excellent	Outstanding
Overall Experience					✓
Shore Excursions		✓			
Activities Close to Port					✓
Beaches & Water Sports			✓		
Shopping				✓	
Dining/Bars			✓		

LANGUAGE Most people in the tourist industry speak English, although Spanish is the native tongue.

GETTING AROUND

Driving is a hassle in congested San Juan. You can walk most of the Old Town on foot or take a free trolley. You can also take buses or taxis to the beaches in the Condado.

BY TAXI Taxis are operated by the Public Service Commission (PSC), and are metered in San Juan—or should be. The initial charge is $1, plus 10¢ for each one-tenth of a mile and 50¢ for every suitcase. A minimum fare is $3. Taxi companies are listed in the yellow pages of the phone book under "Taxis," or you can call the PSC (☎ 787/756-1919) to request information or report any irregularities.

BY TROLLEY When you tire of walking around Old San Juan, you can board one of its free trolleys. Departure points are the Marina and La Puntilla, but you can get on any place along the route. Relax and enjoy the sights as the trolleys rumble through the old and narrow streets.

BY BUS The Metropolitan Bus Authority operates buses in the greater San Juan area. Bus stops are marked by upright metal signs or yellow posts reading PARADA. Bus terminals in San Juan are in the dock area and at Plaza de Colón. A typical fare is 25¢ to 50¢. For route and schedule information, call ☎ 787/250-6064.

BY RENTAL CAR The major car-rental companies include **Avis** (☎ 800/331-1212 or 787/791-2500), **Budget** (☎ 800/527-0700 or 787/791-3685), and **Hertz** (☎ 800/654-3001 or 787/791-0840).

SHORE EXCURSIONS

In Old San Juan, there's really no need to bother with organized shore excursions, since it's easy enough to get around on your own. But if you prefer a guide to narrate or want to explore the island's El Yunque rainforest, an organized tour is a good idea.

San Juan City and Shopping Tour ($22, 3 hours): In Old San Juan you'll visit the massive El Morro Fortress built in 1539 and a few other sites. Then after some shopping, move on to the modern city of San Juan.

Juan Carlos and His Flamenco Rumba Show ($42, 1 hour): At the Club Tropicoro at the El San Juan Hotel and Casino, enjoy dance performances of the mambo, rumba, samba, conga, and flamenco.

El Yunque Rainforest and Bacardi Rum Tour ($32, 4 to 5 hours): By minibus, travel along the northeastern part of the island and take a short hike in the 28,000-acre El Yunque rainforest, home to hundreds of species of plants and animals. Afterward, tour the Bacardi Rum Plant, which produced something on the order of 100,000 gallons of the stuff daily. (And yes, you get free samples.)

TOURING THROUGH LOCAL OPERATORS

Rain Forest and Bacardi Rum Tour: If your ship doesn't offer it, Castillo Watersports & Tours, 2413 Calle Laurel, Punta La Marias, Santurce (☎ 787/791-6195 or 787/726-5752) has tours departing in the morning.

Ecotours: To explore some of Puerto Rico's hard-to-reach nature treasures, Tropix Wellness Tours (☎ 787/268-2173 or fax 787/268-1722) operates a series of ecotours. Four major tours explore the sea turtles' nesting sites in Culebra, the phosphorescent bay in Vieques, the Río Camuy cave system in Camuy, or the dry, desert-like forest in Guánica.

San Juan at a Glance

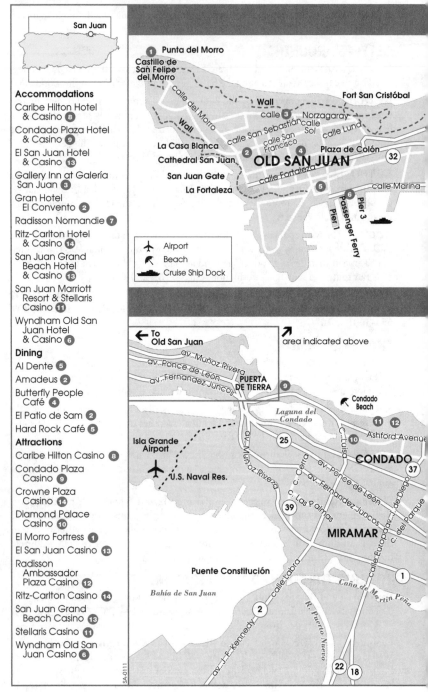

Accommodations

Caribe Hilton Hotel & Casino ❽

Condado Plaza Hotel & Casino ❾

El San Juan Hotel & Casino ❸

Gallery Inn at Galería San Juan ❸

Gran Hotel El Convento ❷

Radisson Normandie ❼

Ritz-Carlton Hotel & Casino ❿

San Juan Grand Beach Hotel & Casino ❸

San Juan Marriott Resort & Stellaris Casino ⓫

Wyndham Old San Juan Hotel & Casino ❻

Dining

Al Dente ❺

Amadeus ❷

Butterfly People Café ❹

El Patio de Sam ❷

Hard Rock Café ❺

Attractions

Caribe Hilton Casino ❽

Condado Plaza Casino ❾

Crowne Plaza Casino ⓮

Diamond Palace Casino ❿

El Morro Fortress ❶

El San Juan Casino ❸

Radisson Ambassador Plaza Casino ⓬

Ritz-Carlton Casino ⓮

San Juan Grand Beach Casino ❸

Stellaris Casino ⓫

Wyndham Old San Juan Casino ❻

SA-0111

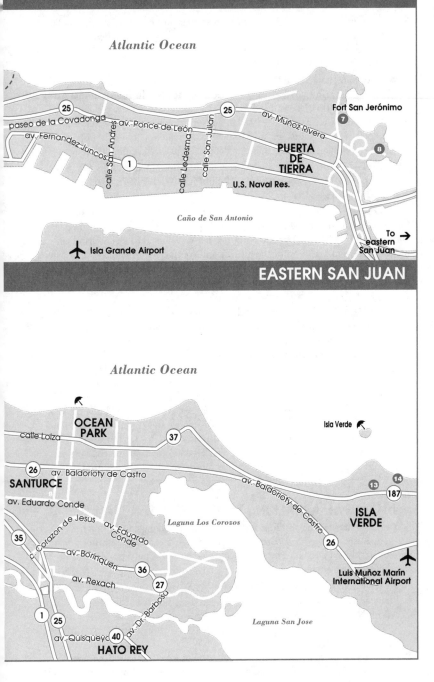

Atlantic Ocean

Fort San Jerónimo
7

8

25

25

av. Muñoz Rivera

paseo de la Covadonga

av.-Ponce-de-León

calle San Andrés

av. Fernandez Juncos

calle Ledesma

calle San Julián

**PUERTA
DE
TIERRA**

1

U.S. Naval Res.

Caño de San Antonio

✈ Isla Grande Airport

To →
eastern
San Juan

Atlantic Ocean

🏖

**OCEAN
PARK**

37

Isla Verde 🏖

calle Loíza

26

av. Baldorioty de Castro

SANTURCE

av.-Baldorioty-de-Castro

13

14

187

av. Eduardo Conde

35

av. Corazon de Jesus

av. Eduardo
Conde

Laguna Los Corozos

**ISLA
VERDE**

av. Borinquen

36

27

26

av. Rexach

av. Dr. Barbosa

✈

Luis Muñoz Marín
International Airport

1

25

Laguna San Jose

av. Quisqueya

40

HATO REY

481

San Juan as a Port of Embarkation

Since a number of cruise ships use San Juan as their port of embarkation and debarkation, you might have the opportunity to spend a night or two here before or after your cruise. If so, here's some information on planning your trip and some picks of the best hotels and nightlife.

Getting to San Juan & the Port

BY AIR　Visitors from overseas arrive at **Luis Muñoz Marín International Airport** (☎ 787/791-1014), situated on the city's easternmost side. It's about 7¹/₂ miles from the port. Taxis will be lined up outside the airport. The fixed fare is $8 to Isla Verde, $12 to Condado, and $16 to Old San Juan (including the port). The ride to the port takes about 30 minutes, depending on traffic conditions.

BY RENTAL CAR　The major car-rental companies include **Avis** (☎ 800/331-1212 or 787/791-2500), **Budget** (☎ 800/527-0700 or 787/791-3685), and **Hertz** (☎ 800/654-3131 or 787/791-0840).

THE DOCKS　Cruise ships in Puerto Rico dock on the historic south shore of Old San Juan, within the sheltered channel. As of this writing, there are eight piers within a short walk of the Plaza de la Marina, the Wyndham Hotel, Old San Juan's main bus station, and most of the historic and commercial treasures of Old San Juan. For information about the port, contact the **Port of San Juan,** P.O. 362829, San Juan, Puerto Rico 00936-2829 (☎ **787/723-2260**).

Accommodations

NEAR THE DOCKS　**Gran Hotel El Convento,** 100 Cristo St. (☎ **800/468-2779** or 787/723-9020), is Puerto Rico's most famous hotel; its third to fifth floors offer large rooms, many with views of the old town. **Wyndham Old San Juan Hotel & Casino,** 100 Brumbaugh St. (☎ 800/996-3426 or 787/721-5100), is right on the waterfront and the cruise docks. Bedrooms are tasteful and comfortable, and Old San Juan is at your doorstep. **Gallery Inn at Galería San Juan,** Calle Norzagaray 204–206 (☎ 787/722-1808), is a former 1700s Spanish aristocrat's home set on a hilltop with a sweeping view of the sea. It has comfortable and tasteful rooms (although lacking air-conditioning). There's also an on-site artists' studio here. The **Caribe Hilton,** Calle Los Rosales, Puerto de Tierra (☎ 800/HILTONS in the U.S. or Canada, or 787/721-0303), is near the old Fort San Jerónimo. You can walk to the 16th-century fort or spend the day on a tour of Old

ON YOUR OWN: A WALKING TOUR OF OLD SAN JUAN

The streets are narrow and teeming with traffic, but a walking tour through Old San Juan (in Spanish, *El Viejo San Juan*) is a stroll through 5 centuries of history. Within this 7-square-block landmark area in the city's westernmost part are many of Puerto Rico's chief historic attractions.

Begin your walk near the post office, amid the taxis, buses, and urban congestion of:

1. **Plaza de la Marina,** a sloping, many-angled plaza situated at the eastern edge of one of San Juan's showcase promenades—*el paseo de la Princesa.*

Walk westward along paseo de la Princesa, past heroic statues and manicured trees, until you reach:

2. **La Princesa,** the gray-and-white building on your right, which for centuries served as one of the most feared prisons in the Caribbean. Today it houses a museum and the offices of the Puerto Rico Tourism Company.

San Juan, and then come back and enjoy the beach and swimming cove. **Radisson Normandie,** Avenida Mu oz-Rivera at the corner of Calle Los Rosales (☎ 800/333-3333 in the U.S., or 787/729-2929) was built in the shape of the famous French ocean liner *Normandie,* and lies only 5 minutes from Old San Juan in a beachside setting.

IN CONDADO   In this area, filled with high-rise hotels, restaurants, and nightclubs, your best bets are the ✪ **Condado Plaza Hotel & Casino,** 999 Ashford Ave. (☎ 800/468-8588 in the U.S., or 787/721-1000), and the **San Juan Marriott Resort & Stellaris Casino,** 1309 Ashford Ave. (☎ 800/981-8546 in the U.S., or 787/722-7000).

IN ISLA VERDE   Closer to the airport than the other sections of San Juan, and right on the beach, your best bets are ✪ **El San Juan Hotel & Casino,** 6063 Isla Verde Ave. (☎ 800/468-2818 in the U.S., or 787/791-1000); **The Ritz-Carlton,** 6961 State Rd., no. 187 on Isla Verde (☎ 800/241-3333 in the U.S., or 787/253-1700); and **San Juan Grand Beach Hotel & Casino,** 187 Isla Verde Ave. (☎ 800/443-2009 in the U.S., or 787/791-6100).

San Juan After Dark

If you want to dance the night away, the **Babylon,** in the El San Juan Hotel & Casino, 6063 Isla Verde Ave. (☎ 787/791-1000), attracts a rich and beautiful crowd, as well as a gaggle of onlookers. For action in the Old Town, head for **Laser,** Calle del Cruz 251 (☎ 787/725-7581), near the corner of Calle Fortaleza. Salsa and merengue are often featured.

On the Condado, **Millennium,** in the Condado Plaza Hotel, 999 Ashford Ave. (☎ 787/722-1900), also draws disco devotees. It has a cigar bar on the side. If you just want a drink, **Fiesta Bar,** in the Condado Plaza Hotel & Casino, 999 Ashford Ave. (☎ 787/721-1000), attracts locals and visitors. **Palm Court,** in the El San Juan Hotel & Casino, 6063 Isla Verde Ave. (☎ 787/791-1000), is the most beautiful bar and dance spot on the island.

Stylish and comfortable, **Violeta's,** Calle Fortaleza 56 (☎ 787/723-6804), occupies the ground floor of a 200-year-old beamed house 2 blocks from the landmark Gran Hotel El Convento. An open courtyard in back provides additional seating. Margaritas are the drink of choice.

Continue walking westward to the base of the heroic fountain near the edge of the sea. Turn to your right and follow the seaside promenade as it parallels the edge of the:

3. City Walls, once part of one of the most impregnable fortresses in the New World and even today an engineering marvel. At the top of the walls you'll see balconied buildings that have served for centuries as hospitals and residences of the island's governors.

Continue walking between the sea and the base of the city walls until the walkway goes through the walls at the:

4. San Juan Gate, at Calle San Juan and Recinto del Oeste. This is actually more of a tunnel than a gate. Now that you're inside the once-dreaded fortification, turn immediately right and walk uphill along Calle Recinto del Oeste. The wrought-iron gates at the street's end lead to:

5. **La Fortaleza and Mansion Ejecutiva,** the centuries-old residence of the Puerto Rican governor, located on Calle La Fortaleza.

Now retrace your steps along Calle Recinto del Oeste, walking first downhill and then uphill for about a block until you reach a street called las Monjas. Fork left until you see a panoramic view and a contemporary statue marking the center of:

6. **Plazuela de la Rogativa,** the small plaza of the religious procession.

Continue your promenade westward, passing between a pair of urn-capped gateposts. You'll be walking parallel to the city walls. The boulevard will fork (bear to the right); continue climbing the steeply inclined cobble-covered ramp to its top. Walk westward across the field toward the neoclassical gateway of a fortress believed impregnable for centuries, the:

7. **Castillo de San Felipe del Morro ("El Morro"),** whose treasury and strategic position were the envy of both Europe and the Caribbean. Here, Spanish Puerto Rico struggled to defend itself against the navies of Great Britain, France, and Holland, as well as the hundreds of pirate ships that wreaked havoc throughout the colonial Caribbean. First built in 1540 and added to in 1787, the fortress walls were designed as part of a network of defenses that made San Juan *La Ciudad Murada* (the Walled City). The fortress sits grandly on a gently sloping, grassy hill, offering some excellent photo ops.

After your visit, with El Morro behind you, retrace your steps through the sunlit, treeless field to the point you stood at when you first sighted the fortress. Walk down the Calle del Morro past the:

8. **Antiguo Manicomio Insular,** originally built in 1854 as an insane asylum. It now houses the Puerto Rican Academy of Fine Arts. Further on, the stately neoclassical building (painted buff with fern-green trim) on your right is the:

9. **Asilo de Beneficencia** ("Home for the Poor"), which dates from the 1840s.

Continue walking uphill to the small, formal, sloping plaza at the street's top. On the righthand side, within a trio of buildings, is:

10. **La Casa Blanca,** built by the son-in-law of Juan Ponce de León to be the great explorer's island home (he never actually lived here, though). Today, this "White House" accommodates a small museum and has beautiful gardens.

Exit by the compound's front entrance and walk downhill, retracing your steps for a half block, and then head toward the massive and monumental tangerine-colored building on your right, the:

11. **Cuartel de Ballajá.** The military barracks of Ballajá evokes the most austere and massive monasteries of Old Spain. On the building's second floor is the **Museum of the Americas.**

After your visit, exit through the barracks's surprisingly narrow back (eastern) door, where you'll immediately spot one of the most dramatic modern plazas in Puerto Rico, the:

12. **Plaza del Quinto Centenario,** a terraced tribute to the European colonization of the New World, and one of the most elaborate and symbolic formal piazzas in Puerto Rico.

Now, walk a short block to the southeast to reach the ancient borders of the:

13. **Plaza de San José,** dominated by a heroic statue of Juan Ponce de León, cast from English cannon captured during a naval battle in 1797. Around the square's periphery are three important sites: the **Museo de Pablo Casals,** where exhibits honor the life and work of the Spanish-born cellist who adopted Puerto Rico as his final home; **Casa de los Contrafuertes** (House of the Buttresses); and **Iglesia de San José,** where the conquistador's coat-of-arms hangs above the altar. Established

Old San Juan Walking Tour

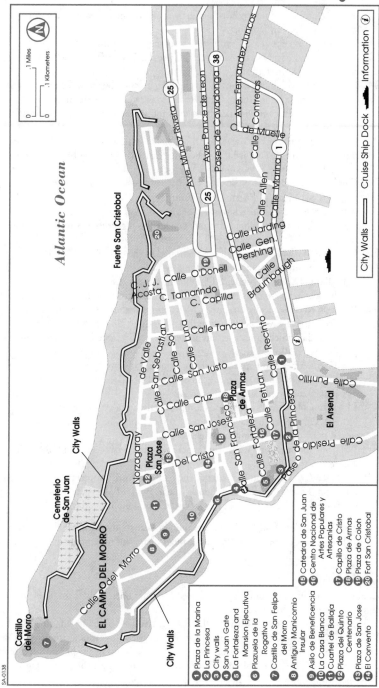

Atlantic Ocean

Castillo del Morro

Cemeterio de San Juan

City Walls

Fuerte San Cristobal

EL CAMPO DEL MORRO

Calle del Morro

City Walls

Calle J. J. Acosta
C. Tamarindo
C. Capilla
Calle O'Donell

Calle Harding
Calle Gen. Pershing
Calle Braumbaugh

Calle Allen
Calle Marina
Calle Contreras
C. de Muelle

Ave. Munoz Rivera
Ave. Ponce de Leon
Paseo de Covadonga
Ave. Fernandez Juncas

25
38
25
1

Calle Tanca
Calle San Justo
Calle San Sebastian
Calle Sol
Calle Luna
de Valle
Noizagaray
Plaza San Jose
Del Cristo
Calle Cruz
Calle San Jose
Calle San Francisco
Plaza de Armas
Calle Tetuan
Calle Fortaleza
Calle Recinto
Calle Puntilla
Calle Presidio
Paseo de la Princesa
El Arsenal

1 Plaza de la Marina
2 La Princesa
3 City walls
4 San Juan Gate
5 La Fortaleza and Mansion Ejecutiva
6 Plazuela de la Rogativa
7 Castillo de San Felipe del Morro
8 Antiguo Manicomio Insular
9 Asilo de Beneficencia
10 La Casa Blanca
11 Cuartel de Ballaja
12 Plaza del Quinto Centenario
13 Plaza de San Jose
14 El Convento
15 Catedral de San Juan
16 Centro Nacional de Artes Populares y Artesanias
17 Capillo de Cristo
18 Plaza de Armas
19 Plaza de Colon
20 Fort San Cristobal

City Walls ===== Cruise Ship Dock ▬ Information ⓘ

SA-0138

485

by the Dominicans in 1523, this church is one of the oldest places of Christian worship in the New World.

Exiting from the plaza's southwestern corner, walk downhill along one of the capital's oldest and best-known streets, **Calle del Cristo.** Two blocks later, at the corner of las Monjas, is:

14. El Convento, originally a convent in the 17th century, but now for many decades one of the few hotels in the old city. Recently restored, it's better than ever. Across the street from El Convento lies the island's most famous church and spiritual centerpiece, the:

15. Catedral de San Juan. Now walk 2 more blocks southward along Calle del Cristo, through one of the most attractive shopping districts in the Caribbean. After passing Calle La Fortaleza, look on your left for the:

16. Centro Nacional de Artes Populares y Artesanías, a popular arts and crafts center run by the Institute of Puerto Rican Culture.

Continue to the southernmost tip of Calle del Cristo (just a few steps away) to the wrought-iron gates that surround a chapel no bigger than a newspaper kiosk, the:

17. Capilla de Cristo. Its silver altar is dedicated to the "Christ of Miracles."

Retrace your steps about a block along the Calle del Cristo, walking north. Turn right along Calle La Fortaleza. One block later, go left onto Calle de San José, which leads to the site of the capital's most symmetrical and beautiful square, the:

18. Plaza de Armas, a broad and open plaza designed along Iberian lines during the 19th century. Two important buildings flanking this square are the neoclassic **Intendencia** (which houses certain offices of the U.S. State Department) and **San Juan's City Hall** (Alcaldía).

You can either end your tour here, or forge ahead to two important sites on the east side of Old San Juan. To continue, leave the square eastward along the Calle San Francisco. Eventually you'll come to:

19. Plaza de Colón, with its stone column topped with a statue of Christopher Columbus. On the south side of the square is the Tapía Theater, which has been restored to its original 19th-century elegance.

Then continue along Calle San Francisco to its intersection with Calle de Valle, and follow the signs to:

20. Fort San Cristóbal, built as part of the string of fortifications protecting one of Spain's most valuable colonies. Today, like its twin, El Morro, it is maintained by the National Park Service and can be visited throughout the day.

When you're through with this walking tour, be sure to just meander about Old San Juan's charming side streets; there are some quaint bars and restaurants that are perfect for a drink or some lunch.

GAMBLING

Casinos are one of the island's biggest draws. Most are open daily from noon to 4pm and again from 8pm to 4am.

The 18,500-square-foot **Casino at the Ritz-Carlton,** 6961 State Rd., no. 187, Isla Verde (☎ **787/253-1700**), is the largest in Puerto Rico. It combines the elegant decor of the 1940s with tropical fabrics and patterns. This is one of the plushest and most exclusive entertainment complexes in the Caribbean. You expect to see Joan Crawford arrive beautifully gowned and on the arm of Clark Gable.

The **San Juan Grand Beach Hotel & Casino,** 187 Isla Verde Avenue in Isla Verde (☎ **800/443-2009** in the U.S., or 787/791-6100), is a 10,000-square-foot gaming facility and an elegant rendezvous. One of its Murano chandeliers is longer than a bowling alley. The casino offers 207 slot machines, 16 blackjack tables, 3 dice tables, 4 roulette wheels, and a mini-baccarat table.

You can also try your luck at any of the following:

- **The Caribe Hilton,** Calle Los Rosales (☎ 787/721-0303)
- **The Wyndham Old San Juan Hotel & Casino,** 100 Brumbaugh St. (☎ 787/721-5100)
- **El San Juan Hotel and Casino,** 6063 Isla Verde Ave., Carolina (☎ 787/791-1000)
- **The Condado Plaza Hotel & Casino,** 999 Ashford Ave. (☎ 787/721-1000)
- **The Radisson Ambassador Plaza Hotel & Casino,** 1369 Ashford Ave. (☎ 787/721-7300)
- **The Diamond Palace Hotel & Casino,** 55 Condado Ave. (☎ 787/721-0810)
- **The Stellaris Casino** at the San Juan Marriott Resort, 1309 Ashford Ave. (☎ 787/722-7000)
- **The Crowne Plaza Hotel and Casino,** Route 187, km 1.5, Isla Verde (☎ 787/253-2929)

BEACHES

Beaches on Puerto Rico are open to the public, although you will be charged for use of *balneario* facilities, such as lockers and showers. Public beaches shut down on Mondays; if Monday is a holiday, the beaches are open for the holiday but closed the next day. Beach hours are from 9am to 5pm in winter, to 6pm in the off-season.

Bordering some of the Caribbean's finest resort hotels, the **Condado** and **Isla Verde** beaches are the most popular in town. Both are good for snorkeling, and have rental equipment for water sports. **Condado Beach** is the single most famous beach strip in the Caribbean, despite the fact it's not the best beach and can be crowded in winter. Its long bands of white sand border some of the Caribbean's finest resort hotels. Locals prefer to head east of El Condado to the beaches of **Isla Verde,** which are less rocky and better sheltered from the waves. You can reach the beaches of **Ocean Park** and **Park Barboa,** on San Juan's north shore, by bus.

Luquillo Beach, lying about 30 miles east of San Juan, is edged by a vast coconut grove. This crescent-shaped beach is not only the best in Puerto Rico, but one of the finest in the entire Caribbean. Coral reefs protect the crystal-clear lagoon from the fierce Atlantic. There are changing rooms, lockers, showers, and picnic facilities. However, the beach isn't as well-maintained as it used to be.

Dorado Beach, Cerromar Beach, and **Palmas del Mar** are the chief centers for those seeking the golf, tennis, and beach life. Sometimes they're overcrowded, especially on Saturday and Sunday, but at other times they're practically deserted. If you find a secluded beach, be careful. You'll have no way to protect yourself or your valuables.

SPORTS

BOATING   The **San Juan Bay Marina, ave. Fernández Juncos,** (☎ 787/721-8062) rents sailboats and powerboats. The 10-minute taxi ride here from the cruise docks should cost about $6.

DEEP-SEA FISHING   It's said in deep-sea fishing circles that **Capt. Mike Benitez,** who has chartered out of San Juan for more than 40 years, sets the standard by which to judge other captains. Benitez Fishing Charters can be contacted directly at P.O. Box 5141, Puerto de Tierra, San Juan, PR 00906 (☎ **787/723-2292** until 9pm). The captain offers a 45-foot air-conditioned deluxe Hateras, the *Sea Born.* Fishing tours for parties of up to six cost around $450 for a half-day excursion, and $750 for a full day, with beverages and all equipment included. In the waters just off Palmas del Mar, the resort complex on the southeast coast of Puerto Rico, **Capt. Bill Burleson,** P.O. Box 8270,

Humacao, PR 00792 (☎ **787/850-7442**), operates charters on his fully customized 46-foot sport-fisherman, *Karolette*. Burleson prefers to take fishing groups to Grappler Banks, 18 nautical miles away. It costs $500 for a maximum of six people for 4 hours, $675 for 6 hours, and $900 for 9 hours. He also offers snorkeling expeditions to Isla de Vieques and other locations at $85 per person for up to 5 hours.

GOLF   Puerto Rico may be a golfer's dream, but you'll need to sign up for the ship's excursion or rent a car to reach the major courses, which lie 45 minutes to 1 1/2 hours from San Juan. With 72 holes, the **Hyatt Resorts Puerto Rico at Dorado** (☎ **787/ 796-1234**) offers the greatest concentration of golf in the Caribbean, including the 18-hole Robert Trent Jones, Sr. courses at the Hyatt Regency Cerromar and the Hyatt Dorado Beach, and the par-72 East course at Dorado Beach, with the famous par-5, 5,540-yard 14th hole. The **Golf Club,** at Palmas del Mar in Humacao (☎ **787/ 852-6000,** ext. 54), is 45 miles east of San Juan. The par-72, 6,803-yard course was designed by Gary Player. **Rio Mar Golf Course,** at Palmer (☎ **787/888-8815**), is a 45-minute drive from San Juan along Route 187, on the northeast coast. The greens fees at this 6,145-yard course are less expensive after 2pm.

SCUBA DIVING   Puerto Rico offers excellent diving, but most of it is not within easy reach of San Juan. **Caribe Aquatic Adventures,** P.O. Box 9024278, San Juan Station, San Juan, PR 00902 (☎ **787/724-1882**), will take you to sites in San Juan. Its dive shop is located in the rear lobby of the Radisson Normandie Hotel.

WINDSURFING, JET-SKIING & SNORKELING   The best place for windsurfing and snorkeling on the island's north shore is along the well-maintained beachfront of the Hyatt Dorado Beach Hotel, near the 10th hole of the hotel's famous east golf course. Here, **Penfield Island Adventures** (☎ **787/796-1234,** ext. 3768, or 787/796-2188) offers 90-minute windsurfing lessons and board rentals. Boards designed specifically for beginners and children are available. The school benefits from the north shore's strong, steady winds and an experienced crew of instructors. There's also a 2-hour kayaking/ snorkeling trip, departing daily at 9:15am and 11:45am. You can also rent Waverunners (Jet Skis) and Sunfish sail boats.

SHOPPING

U.S. citizens don't pay duty on items bought in Puerto Rico and brought back to the mainland United States. You can find great bargains in San Juan; prices are often lower than those in St. Thomas. The streets of the **Old Town,** such as Calle San Francisco and Calle del Cristo, are the major venues. Most stores in Old San Juan are closed on Sunday. Native handcrafts can be good buys, including *santos* (hand-carved wooden religious figures), needlework, straw work, ceramics, hammocks, guayabera shirts for men, papier-mâché fruit and vegetables, and paintings and sculptures by Puerto Rican artists.

The biggest and most up-to-date shopping plaza in the Caribbean Basin is **Plaza Las Americas,** which lies in the financial district of Hato Rey, right off the Las Americas Expressway. The complex, with its fountains and advanced architecture, has more than 200 shops, most of them upmarket.

El Alcazar, Calle San José 103, is the largest emporium of antique furniture, silver, and art objects in the Caribbean. The best way to sift through the massive inventory is to begin at the address listed above, on Calle San José between Calle Luna and Calle Sol, and ask the owners, Sharon and Robert Bartos, to guide you to the other three buildings, all stuffed with important art and antiques.

Set in a 200-year-old colonial building, **Puerto Rican Arts & Crafts,** Calle Fortaleza 204, is one of the premier outlets on the island for authentic handcrafts. Of particular

---

Shopping Tip: San Juan Outlets

At **London Fog,** Calle del Cristo 156, and **Polo Ralph Lauren Factory Store,** Calle del Cristo 201, you can get the famous raincoats and the famous fashions at prices that are often 30% to 40% less than on the U.S. mainland.

---

interest are papier-mâché carnival masks from the town of Ponce; their grotesque and colorful features were designed to chase away evil spirits.

José E. Alegria & Associates, Calle del Cristo 152–154, is half antique shop, half an old-fashioned arcade lined with gift shops and boutiques. **Galería Botello,** Calle del Cristo 208, is a living tribute to the late Angel Botello, one of Puerto Rico's most outstanding artists. Once his home, today the space displays his paintings and sculptures, and also offers a large collection of Puerto Rican antique santos. **Haitian Souvenirs,** Calle San Francisco 206, specializes in Haitian art and artifacts. Its walls are covered with primitive Haitian landscapes, portraits, and crowd scenes, most costing from $35 to $350.

GREAT LOCAL BARS & RESTAURANTS IN OLD SAN JUAN

Al Dente, Calle Recinto Sur 309 (☎ 787/723-7303), is a relaxed, trattoria-like place serving reasonably priced dishes like brochettes of fresh tuna laced with pepper and Mediterranean herbs. ✪ **Amadeus,** Calle San Sebastián 106 (across from the Iglesia de San José; ☎ 787/722-8635), offers Caribbean cuisine with a nouvelle twist. **Butterfly People Café,** Calle Fortaleza 152 (☎ 787/723-2432), serves tropical and light European fare made with fresh ingredients. **El Patio de Sam,** Calle San Sebastián 102 (across from the Iglesia de San José; ☎ 787/723-1149), is a popular gathering spot for American expatriates, newspeople, and shopkeepers. It's known for having the best burgers in San Juan. Speaking of burgers, the **Hard Rock Café** is at Calle Recinto Sur 253 (☎ 787/724-7625).

La Bombonera, Calle San Francisco 259 (☎ 787/722-0658), offers exceptional food at affordable prices. For decades a rendezvous for the island's literati and Old San Juan families, the food is authentically Puerto Rican, homemade, and inexpensive. **La Mallorquina,** Calle San Justo 207 (☎ 787/722-3261), was founded in 1848, and its chef specializes in the most typical Puerto Rican rice dish: *asopao.* You can have it with either chicken, shrimp, or lobster and shrimp. The Nuevo Latino cuisine at ✪ **Parrot Club,** 363 Calle Fortaleza (☎ 787/725-7370), blends traditional Puerto Rican cookery with Spanish, Taíno, and African influences.

16 St. Barthélemy

Part of the French West Indies, lying 15 miles from Sint Maarten, St. Barthélemy (also called St. Barts or St. Barths) is a small, hilly island with a population of 3,500 people of European and African descent who live on 13 square miles of verdant and dramatically hilly terrain bordered by pleasant white-sand beaches. St. Barts is sophistication in the tropics, an expensive and exclusive stamping ground of the rich and famous, with a distinctive seafaring tradition and a decidedly French flavor—chic, rich, and very Parisian, with a touch of Normandy and even Sweden in its personality. It's quite the European playground, disguised as a Caribbean island.

Forget such things as historical sights or ambitious water sports here. Come instead for white sandy beaches, fine French cuisine, and relaxation in ultimate comfort. Only small cruise ships can visit this little French pocket of posh.

Frommer's Ratings: St. Barts					
	Poor	Fair	Good	Excellent	Outstanding
Overall Experience				✓	
Shore Excursions			✓		
Activities Close to Port				✓	
Beaches & Water Sports				✓	
Shopping				✓	
Dining/Bars			✓		

The island's capital and only town is **Gustavia,** named after a Swedish king. Set in a sheltered harbor, it looks like a little dollhouse-scale port.

Frommer's Favorite St. Barts Experiences

- **Hanging out at the Le Select cafe:** The most popular gathering place in Gustavia is *the* place to get a taste of local life (see "Great Local Restaurants & Bars," below).
- **Heading to the beaches:** There are several utterly gorgeous ones on St. Barts (see "Beaches," below).

COMING ASHORE   Cruise ships anchor right off Gustavia; tenders then ferry passengers to the heart of town. There are usually shaded refreshment stands on shore. A short walk will get you into Gustavia's restaurant and shopping district.

CURRENCY   The official monetary unit is the **French franc (F),** but most stores and restaurants prefer U.S. dollars. The exchange rate is 6.29F to US$1 (1F is worth about 16¢). I've used this rate to convert currency throughout this section.

INFORMATION   Go to the **Office du Tourisme** in the Town Hall, quai du Général-de-Gaulle, in Gustavia (☎ **0590/27-87-27**). Open Monday to Friday 9am to 5pm.

LANGUAGE   St. Barts is technically part of France, so the official language is French. However, nearly everyone speaks English.

GETTING AROUND

BY TAXI   Taxis meet all cruise ships and aren't very expensive, since no destination is all that far. Dial ☎ **0590/27-66-31** for taxi service. The fare is 25F ($4) for rides up to 5 minutes; each additional 3 minutes is another 20F ($3.20).

BY MINI-MOKE OR SAMURAI   If you're a confident driver, renting one of these open-sided Mini-Mokes and manual-transmission Suzuki Samurais is great fun and the only way to zip around the jagged (and picturesque) hills of this 8-square-mile island in style. It'll cost about $40 a day. Try **Budget** (☎ **800/527-0700** or 0590-27-66-30); **Hertz** (☎ **800/654-3001**), which operates through a local dealership, Henry's Car Rental; and **Avis** (☎ **800/331-1084** or 0590-27-71-43), whose local name is St. Barts Centre-Auto.

BY MOTORSCOOTER   You can rent motorbikes and scooters from **Rent Some Fun,** rue Gambetta in Gustavia (☎ **0590-27-70-59**). The approximately $30 daily rental fee covers both bike and helmet; a $200 deposit is required.

SHORE EXCURSIONS

Many passengers prefer to spend their time ashore walking around and exploring Gustavia, which should take no more than 2 hours.

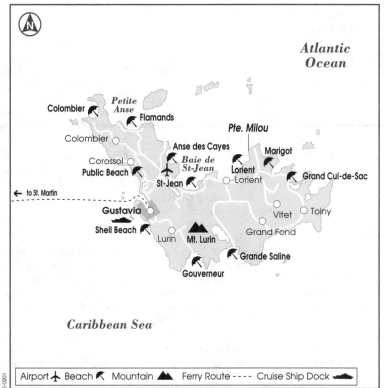

Airport ✈ Beach ★ Mountain ▲▲ Ferry Route - - - - Cruise Ship Dock ⛴

Minibus Island Tour ($25, 1¹/₂ hours): The duration is so short because there are almost no attractions other than the island's natural beauty and beaches. The minibus goes through the port, and then past the village of St-Jean to an overlook in Salinos, where you can take in the view. On the windward side of the island, you'll notice the different architecture required to withstand the heavy breezes. Next you'll head to Grand Cul-de-Sac for a view of the lagoon, and then have a brief stop at La Savone. You'll be brought back to the ship via Corossol, a tiny fishing village where the locals make straw from lantana palms.

ON YOUR OWN

All the big attractions—beaches, shopping, and people-watching—are covered elsewhere in this section.

SHOPPING

You don't pay any duty on St. Barts, so it's a good place to buy liquor and French perfumes at some of the lowest prices in the Caribbean. In fact, perfume and champagne are cheaper here than in metropolitan France. You'll also find good buys in sportswear, crystal, porcelain, watches, and other luxuries. The only trouble is that selections here are limited.

If you're in the market for island crafts, try to find those convertible-brim, fine straw hats St. Bartians like to wear. *Vogue* once featured them in its fashion pages. There are also some interesting block-printed cotton resort clothes on the island.

La Boutique Couleur des Îles, rue du Général-de-Gaulle 8, sells shirts and blouses for about $30 to $50 with hand-embroidered references to the flora and fauna of St. Barts. Laurent Eiffel, rue du Général de Gaulle, sells imitations of designer items that usually cost 10 times as much. Look for belts, bags, and accessories modeled after Versace, Prada, Hermés, Gucci, and Chanel. St. Barts Style, rue Lafayette, near the corner of rue du Port, stocks brightly hued beachwear by Jams World and Vicidomine. Le Comptoir du Cigare, rue du Général-de-Gaulle 6, caters to the villa-and-yacht crowd. Its cigars hail from Cuba and the Dominican Republic; connoisseur-quality rums come from Martinique, Cuba, and Haiti. (Remember that Cuban cigars cannot legally be brought into the United States, so you must smoke them abroad.)

Diamond Genesis/Kornérupine, rue du Général-de-Gaulle 12, Les Suites du Roi-Oskar-II, is one of the few shops on the island where jewelry is handcrafted on the premises—and sells for between $20 and $60,000. La Maison de Free Mousse, Carré d'Or, quai de la République, is the most unusual gift shop on St. Barts, with wood carvings and handcrafts from throughout Europe, Asia, and South America.

BEACHES

There are 14 white-sand beaches on St. Barts. My favorites (Gouverneur, Saline, Marigot, and Colombier) are pretty secluded, but few beaches here are ever crowded, even during winter. All are public and free, and easily accessible by taxi from the cruise pier. You can also make arrangements to be picked up at a scheduled time. Nude bathing is officially prohibited, but topless sunbathing is quite common.

Gouverneur on the south is gorgeous and offers some waves, but wear lots of sunscreen—there's no shade. Get there by driving or taking a taxi through Gustavia and up to Lurin. Turn at the Sante Fe Restaurant (see "Great Local Restaurants & Bars," below), and head down a narrow road. To get to the beach Saline, to the east of Gouverneur, drive up the road from the commercial center in St-Jean. A short walk over the sand dune and you're there. Like Gouverneur, it offers some waves but no shade.

Marigot, also on the north shore, is narrow but good for swimming and snorkeling. Colombier is difficult to get to, but well worth the effort for swimmers and snorkelers. You'll have to take a boat or a rugged goat path from Petite Anse past Flamands, a 30-minute walk. You can pack a lunch and eat in the shade.

The most famous beach is St-Jean, which is actually two beaches divided by the Eden Rock promontory. It offers water sports, beach restaurants, and a few hotels, as well as some shady areas. Flamands, to the west, is a very wide beach with a few small hotels and some lantana palms.

If you want a beach with hotels, restaurants, and water sports, the Grand Cul-de-Sac area on the northeast shore fits the bill. There's a narrow beach here protected by a reef.

SPORTS

SCUBA DIVING   Marine Service, quai du Yacht-Club in Gustavia (☎ 0590/27-70-34), operates from a one-story building on the water at the edge of a marina, across the harbor from the more congested part of Gustavia. The outfit is familiar with at least 15 unusual dive sites scattered at various points offshore, including The Grouper, a remote reef west of St. Barts, close to the uninhabited cay known as Ile Forchue. Almost as important are the reefs near Roche Rouge, off the opposite (i.e., eastern) edge of St. Barts. The island has only one relatively safe wreck dive, to the rusting hulk of *Kayali,* a trawler that sank offshore in 1994. It's recommended only for experienced divers. A *baptème* (baptism, or resort course) that includes two open-water dives for people who are strong swimmers but inexperienced divers, costs 650F ($108.55).

WATER-SKIING   Marine Service (see above) can also arrange water-skiing, offered daily from 9am to 1pm and again from 4:40pm to sundown. Because of the shape of the coastline, skiers must remain at least 80 yards from shore on the windward side of the island and 110 yards off the leeward side.

WINDSURFING   Try St. Barth Wind School near the Tom Beach Hotel on Plage de St-Jean. It's open daily from 9am to 5pm.

GREAT LOCAL RESTAURANTS & BARS

IN GUSTAVIA   The most popular gathering place in Gustavia is ✪ **Le Select,** rue de la France (☎ **0590/27-86-87**), apparently named after its more famous granddaddy in the Montparnasse section of Paris. It's utterly simple. A game of dominoes might be under way as you walk in. Tables are placed outside on the gravel in an open-air cafe garden near the port. The outdoor grill promises a "cheeseburger in Paradise." Jimmy Buffett might show up here, or perhaps Mick Jagger. The place is open Monday to Saturday from 10am to 11pm. The locals like it a lot, and outsiders are welcomed, but not necessarily embraced until they get to know you a bit. If you want to spread a rumor and have it travel fast across the island, start it here.

   L'Iguane, Carré d'Or, quai de la République (☎ **0590/27-88-46**), offers an international menu that includes sushi, American breakfasts, and California-style sandwiches and salads. **Wall House Restaurant,** La Pointe (adjacent to the public library and municipal museum), Gustavia (☎ **0590/27-71-83**), offers unpretentious, sunlit lunches featuring burgers, simple grills, salads, and sandwiches. Dinners are more elaborate.

AT MORNE LURIN   Santa Fe Restaurant, Morne Lurin (☎ **0590/27-61-04**), is a burger house and sports bar that's carved out a niche for itself among the island's English-speaking clientele. It features wide-screen TVs that present American sports events.

IN GRANDE SALINE   Le Tamarin, Plage de Saline (☎ **0590/27-72-12**), is an informal bistro isolated amid rocky hills and forests east of Gustavia. Menu items are mostly light, including gazpacho, a *pavé* of Cajun-style tuna with Creole sauce and baby vegetables, and chicken roasted with lemon and ginger.

IN GRAND CUL-DE-SAC   Lunching at **Club Lafayette,** Grand Cul-de-Sac (☎ **0590/27-62-51**), located in a cove on the eastern end of the island, is like taking a meal at your own private, very expensive beach club. The menu includes such items as warm foie gras served with apples, and one of the best meal-sized lobster salads on the island. **West Indies Café,** in El Sereno Beach Hotel, Grand Cul-de-Sac, 4 miles east of Gustavia (☎ **0590/27-64-80**), incorporates aspects of a Parisian cabaret with simple but well-prepared meals such as fish tartare, eggplant mousse, grilled lobster, and grilled tuna and snapper.

17 St. Croix

Even though seven different flags have flown over St. Croix and it's now part of the U.S. Virgin Islands, it's the nearly 2¹/₂ centuries of Danish influence that still permeates the island and its architecture.

   St. Croix boasts some of the best beaches in the Virgin Islands. At the east end of the island (which, incidentally, is the easternmost possession of the United States), the terrain is rocky and arid. The west end is lusher, with a rainforest of mango and mahogany, tree ferns, and dangling lianas. Rolling hills and upland pastures characterize the area lying between the two extremes. African tulips are just one of the species of flowers that add a splash of color to the landscape, which is dotted with stately towers that once supported grinding mills. The island covers 84 square miles.

Frommer's Ratings: St. Croix					
	Poor	Fair	Good	Excellent	Outstanding
Overall Experience				✓	
Shore Excursions				✓	
Activities Close to Port				✓	
Beaches & Water Sports				✓	
Shopping					✓
Dining/Bars			✓		

St. Croix now competes with St. Thomas for the Yankee cruise ship dollar. Although it gets nowhere near the number of visitors, St. Croix is more tranquil and less congested than its smaller sibling. The major attraction here is **Buck Island National Park,** a national offshore treasure.

Although large cruise ships moor at **Frederiksted,** most of the action is in **Christiansted,** located on a coral-bound bay about midway along the north shore and featuring more sights and better restaurants and shopping. The town is being handsomely restored, and the entire harborfront area is a national historic site.

Frommer's Favorite St. Croix Experiences
• **Visiting the Salt River Bay National Historical Park and Ecological Preserve:** The only spot where Columbus landed in what is now U.S. territory includes the site of the original Carib village Columbus explored, plus the largest mangrove forest in the Virgin Islands and an underwater canyon that attracts scuba divers (see "On Your Own: Beyond Walking Distance," below).
• **Visiting the lush St. George Village Botanical Garden:** Built around the ruins of a 19th-century sugarcane workers' village, it's a veritable Eden of tropical trees, shrubs, vines, and flowers (see "On Your Own: Beyond Walking Distance," below).
• **Biking along the coast of St. Croix:** On this tour, you pass through Frederiksted, then past ruins and through forests and rolling grasslands (see "Shore Excursions," below).

COMING ASHORE   Only cruise ships with fewer than 200 passengers can land directly at the dock at Christiansted. Others moor at a 1,500-foot pier at Frederiksted, a sleepy town that springs to life only when the ships arrive. Both piers have information centers and telephones.

I suggest you spend as little time as possible in Frederiksted and head immediately for Christiansted, some 17 miles away. It's easy to explore either Frederiksted or Christiansted on foot (the only way, really), although you might want to consider one of the shore excursions outlined below to see more of the island, especially its underwater treasures.

CURRENCY   The **U.S. dollar** is the official currency.

INFORMATION   The **U.S. Virgin Islands Division of Tourism** has offices in Christiansted at Queen Cross Street (☎ 340/773-0495), and at the Customs House Building, Strand Street in Frederiksted (☎ 340/772-0357). Open Monday to Friday from 9am to 5pm.

LANGUAGE   English is spoken here.

GETTING AROUND
BY TAXI   Taxis are unmetered, so agree on the rate before you get in. The **St. Croix Taxicab Association** (☎ 340/778-1088) offers door-to-door service. Taxi tours are a great way to explore the island. For one or two passengers, the cost is about $30 for 2

St. Croix

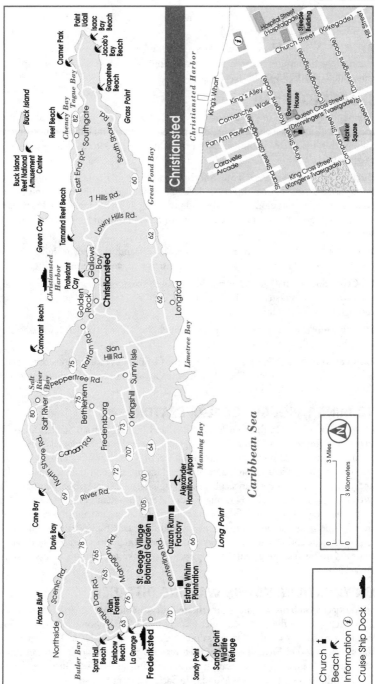

Christiansted

Caribbean Sea

Church ✝
Beach ◣
Information *i*
Cruise Ship Dock

hours or $40 for 3 hours. I don't recommend renting a car. It costs $20 to take a taxi from Christiansted to Frederiksted.

BY BUS   Air-conditioned buses run daily between Christiansted and Frederiksted about every 40 minutes between 5:30am and 9pm. The fare is $1. For more information, call ☎ **340/778-0898.**

SHORE EXCURSIONS

Although it's possible to get around St. Croix on your own, you'll find some of the most varied organized shore excursions in the Caribbean, including snorkeling and sailing trips, island tours, golf, island tours, catamaran party tours, hikes, and bicycle excursions.

Buck Island National Park Tour/Snorkeling ($46, 4 to 5 hours): The premier tour in St. Croix takes you to a tropical underwater wonderland of blue water and colorful coral reefs. Transportation is provided from the pier at Frederiksted to Christiansted, where a boat takes you over to Buck Island. An experienced guide provides snorkel lessons.

Island Tour ($28, 3 ¹/₂): For a taste of the whole island, this tour includes a visit to the Whim Great House sugar plantation, Christiansted, and other major sites.

St. Croix Bike Tour ($38, 3 hours): Bike along the coast of St. Croix, passing through the town of Frederiksted before heading out on the Northside Road, past ruins and through forests and rolling grasslands.

Hiking Tour ($25, 2 to 3 hours): Hike through the 225-acre Butler Bay preserve and enjoy bird watching and a good hearty walk.

Golf at Carambola ($74 to $105): One of the Caribbean's most famous courses is another excursion destination. The line will probably offer an excursion here, or you can do it on your own (see "Sports," below).

TOURING THROUGH LOCAL OPERATORS

Horseback Tour: On this tour, run by Paul and Jill's Equestrian Stables, Sprat Hall Plantation, Route 58 (☎ **340/772-2880**), you'll pass ruins of abandoned 18th-century plantations and sugar mills and climb the hills of St. Croix's western end. Tour guides give running commentaries on island fauna and history and on riding techniques. Paul and Jill's is the only equestrian stable in the Virgin Islands. The stables, owned by Paul Wojcie and his wife, Jill Hurd (a daughter of the establishment's original founders), are set on the sprawling grounds of the island's oldest plantation, and are known throughout the Caribbean for the quality of the horses and the scenic trail rides through the forests. Beginners and experienced riders alike are welcome. The afternoon tours are often too late for returning cruise ship passengers. Make reservations at least a day in advance.

ON YOUR OWN: WITHIN WALKING DISTANCE

If you decide to hang around **Frederiksted,** begin your tour at russet-colored **Fort Frederick,** next to the cruise ship pier (☎ **340/772-2021**). Some historians claim it was the first fort to sound a foreign salute to the U.S. flag, in 1776. The structure, at the northern end of Frederiksted, has been restored to its 1840 look. You can explore the courtyard and stables, and examine an exhibit area in what was once the Garrison Room. Admission is free. Open Monday to Saturday from 8am to 5pm.

In **Christiansted,** begin your visit at the **visitors' bureau** (☎ **340/773-0495**), a yellow building with a cedar-capped roof near the harborfront. It was built as the Old Scalehouse in 1856 to replace a similar, older structure that burned down. In its heyday, all taxable goods leaving and entering the harbor were weighed here. The scales could once accurately weigh barrels of sugar and molasses weighing up to 1,600 pounds.

Another major attraction is the **Steeple Building** (☎ 340/773-1460) or Church of Lord God of Sabaoth, which was completed in 1753 as St. Croix's first Lutheran church. It, too, stands near the harborfront; get there via Hospital Street. The building was deconsecrated in 1831, and has served at various times as a bakery, a hospital, and a school. Admission is $2, which also includes admission to Fort Christiansvaern (see below). Open daily 8am to 5pm.

Overlooking the harbor, **Fort Christiansvaern** (☎ 340/773-1460) is the best preserved colonial fortification in the Virgin Islands. The National Park Service maintains the fort as a historic monument. Its original star-shaped design was at the vanguard of the most advanced military planning of its era. Open Monday to Thursday 8am to 5pm, Friday and Saturday 9am to 5pm. Admission is included in the ticket to the Steeple Building (see above).

ON YOUR OWN: BEYOND WALKING DISTANCE

The only known site where Columbus landed in what is now U.S. territory was at Salt River, on the island's northern shore. To mark the 500th anniversary of his arrival, President George Bush signed a bill creating the 912-acre ✪ **Salt River Bay National Historical Park and Ecological Preserve.** The land mass includes the site of the original Carib village explored by Columbus and his men, along with the only ceremonial ball court ever discovered in the Lesser Antilles.

At the Carib settlement, the men of Columbus liberated several Taíno women and children held as slaves. On the way back to their vessels, the Spaniards faced a canoe filled with hostile Caribs, armed with poison arrows. One Spanish soldier was killed, and perhaps six Caribs were either slain or captured. This is the first documented case of hostility between invading Europeans and the Native Americans. Sailing away, Columbus named this part of St. Croix "Cape of the Arrows."

The park today is in a natural state. It has the largest mangrove forest in the Virgin Islands, sheltering many endangered animals and plants, plus an underwater canyon attracting scuba divers from around the world. The St. Croix Environmental Association, 3 Arawak Building, Gallows Bay, conducts tours of the area. Call them at ☎ 340/773-1989 for details.

Just north of Centerline Road, 4 miles east of Frederiksted at Estate St. George, lies the ✪ **St. George Village Botanical Garden of St. Croix** (☎ 340/692-2874), a veritable Eden of tropical trees, shrubs, vines, and flowers. Built around the ruins of a 19th-century sugarcane workers' village, the garden is a feast for the eye and the camera—from the entrance drive bordered by royal palms and bougainvillea to the towering kapok and tamarind trees. Restoration of the ruins is a continuing project, but two sets of workers' cottages provide space for a gift shop, rest rooms, a kitchen, and an office. Self-guided walking tour maps are available at the entrance to the Great Hall. Admission is $5 for adults, $1 for children 12 and under. From November to May hours are daily from 9am to 5pm; from June to October, Tuesday to Saturday from 9am to 4pm.

The **Cruzan Rum Factory,** West Airport Road, Route 64 (☎ 340/692-2280), distills the famous Virgin Islands rum, which residents consider to be the finest in the world. Guided tours depart from the visitors' pavilion; call for reservations and information.

The **Estate Whim Plantation Museum,** Centerline Road (about 2 miles east of Frederiksted; ☎ 340/772-0598), restored by the St. Croix Landmarks Society, is unique among the many old sugar plantations dotting the island. It's composed of only three rooms. Some say the house resembles a luxurious European château. Its 3-foot-thick walls are made of stone, coral, and molasses. Also on the museum's premises is a woodworking shop, the estate's original kitchen, a museum store, a servant's quarters, and tools from the 18th century. The ruins include remains of the plantation's sugar-processing plant, complete with a restored windmill.

SHOPPING

Americans get a break here, since they can bring home $1,200 worth of merchandise from the U.S. Virgin Islands without paying duty, as opposed to a paltry $400 from most other Caribbean ports. And liquor here is duty-free.

A major redevelopment of the waterfront at Christiansted, following the hurricanes of 1995, was **King's Alley Complex,** a pink-sided compound filled with the densest concentration of shopping options on St. Croix.

Worthwhile specialty shops include **Skirt Tails,** Pam Am Pavilion, one of the most colorful and popular boutiques on the island, specializing in hand-painted batiks for both men and women; **The White House,** King's Alley Walk, which stocks women's clothing ranging from dressy to casual and breezy—but all, everything, in white; **Elegant Illusions Copy Jewelry,** 55 King St., which sells credible copies of the baroque and antique jewelry your great-grandmother might have worn, priced from $9 to $1,000; **Larimar,** The Boardwalk/King's Walk, which specializes in larimar—a pale-blue pectolyte prized for its sky-blue color—in various gold settings; **Estate Mount Washington Antiques,** 2 Estate Mount Washington, which is the best treasure trove of colonial West Indian furniture and "flotsam" in the Virgin Islands; **Folk Art Traders,** 1B Queen Cross St., which deals in Caribbean art and folk-art treasures, such as carnival masks, pottery, ceramics, original paintings, and hand-wrought jewelry; and **Many Hands,** in the Pan Am Pavilion, Strand Street, which sells Virgin Islands handcrafts, spices and teas, handmade jewelry, and more.

The Royal Poinciana, 1111 Strand St., looks like an antique apothecary, but is actually the most interesting gift shop on St. Croix. You'll find such Caribbean-inspired items as hot sauces ("fire water"), seasoning blends for gumbos, island herbal teas, Antillean coffees, and a scented array of soaps, toiletries, lotions, and shampoos.

BEACHES

Beaches are the biggest attraction on St. Croix. The drawback is that getting to them from Christiansted or Frederiksted isn't always easy. Taxis will take you, but they can be expensive. In Christiansted, take a ferry to the **Hotel on the Cay,** a palm-shaded island in the harbor.

Most convenient for passengers arriving at Frederiksted is **Sandy Point,** the largest beach in all the U.S. Virgin Islands. Its waters are shallow and calm, perfect for swimming.

Cramer Park, at the northeastern end of the island, is a special public park operated by the Department of Agriculture. Lined with sea grape trees, the beach has a picnic area, a restaurant, and a bar.

I highly recommend **Cane Bay** and **Davis Bay.** They're both the type of beaches you'd expect to find on a Caribbean island—palms, white sand, and good swimming and snorkeling. Cane Bay attracts snorkelers and divers, with its rolling waves, coral gardens, and drop-off wall. It's near Route 80 on the north shore. Davis Beach draws bodysurfers. There are no changing facilities here. It's off the South Shore Road (Route 60), in the vicinity of the Carambola Beach Resort.

Windsurfers like **Reef Beach,** which opens onto Teague Bay along Route 82, East End Road, a half-hour ride from Christiansted. You can order food at Duggan's Reef. On Route 63, a short ride north of Frederiksted, **Rainbow Beach** invites with its white sand and ideal snorkeling conditions. **La Grange** is another good beach in the vicinity, also on Route 63, about 5 minutes north of Frederiksted. You can rent lounge chairs here, and there's a bar nearby.

At the **Cormorant Beach Club,** about 5 miles west of Christiansted, palm trees shade some 1,200 feet of white sands. A living reef lies just off the shore, making snorkeling ideal. **Grapetree Beach** offers a similar amount of clean white sand on the eastern tip of the island. Follow the South Shore Road (Route 60) to reach it. Water sports are popular here.

SPORTS

GOLF   St. Croix has the best golfing in the U.S. Virgins. In fact, guests staying on St. John's and St. Thomas often fly over for a day's round on the island's two 18-hole and one 9-hole golf courses. The **Carambola Golf Course,** on the northeast side of St. Croix (☎ 340/778-5638), was designed by Robert Trent Jones, Sr., who called it "the loveliest course I ever designed." The course, formerly the site of "Shell's Wonderful World of Golf," has been likened to a botanical garden. Golfing authorities consider its collection of par-3 holes to be the best in the tropics. Carambola's course record of 65 was set by Jim Levine in 1993. The **Buccaneer** (☎ 340/773-2100, ext. 738), 2 miles east of Christiansted, is a challenging 5,810-yard, 18-hole course with panoramic vistas. Players can knock the ball over rolling hills right to the edge of the Caribbean. A final course is the **Reef,** at Teague Bay on the east end of the island (☎ 340/773-8844), a 3,100-yard, nine-hole course. The longest hole is a 579-yard par 5.

SCUBA DIVING   Divers love St. Croix's sponge life, beautiful black-coral trees, and steep drop-offs near the shoreline. This island is home to the largest living reef in the Caribbean. Its fabled north shore wall begins in 25 to 30 feet of water and drops—sometimes almost straight down—to 13,200 feet. There are 22 moored diving sites. Favorites among them include the historic **Salt River Canyon,** the coral gardens of **Scotch Banks,** and **Eagle Ray,** filled with cruising rays. **Pavilions** is yet another good dive site, with a pristine virgin coral reef. The best site of all, however, is **Buck Island,** an underwater wonderland with a visibility of more than 100 feet and an underwater nature trail. All the minor and major agencies offer scuba and snorkeling tours to Buck Island. **Dive St. Croix,** 59 King's Wharf (☎ 800/523-DIVE in the U.S., or 340/773-2628; fax 340/773-7400), operates the 38-foot dive boat *Reliance.* The staff offers complete instruction, from beginners' courses through full certification. **V.I. Divers Ltd.,** in the Pan Am Pavilion on Christiansted's waterfront (☎ 800/544-5911 in the U.S., or 340/773-6045), is the oldest and one of the best dive operations on the island. *Rodales Scuba Diving* magazine rated its staff as among the top 10 worldwide. This full-service PADI five-star facility offers daily two-tank boat dives, as well as guided snorkeling trips to Green Cay.

WINDSURFING   The best place for windsurfing is the **St. Croix Water Sports Center** (☎ 340/773-7060), located on a small offshore island in Christiansted Harbor. It's part of the Hotel on the Cay. Besides windsurfing, you can sign up for parasailing and snorkeling.

GREAT LOCAL RESTAURANTS & BARS

IN CHRISTIANSTED   **Annabelle's Tea Room,** 51–ABC Company St. (☎ 340/773-3990), occupies a quiet courtyard and serves an assortment of sandwiches, salads, soups, and platters. **Harvey's,** 11B Company St. (☎ 340/773-3433), features the thoroughly zesty cooking of island matriarch Sarah Harvey. Main dishes are the type of food she was raised on: barbecue chicken, barbecue spareribs (barbecue is big here), boiled filet of snapper, and even lobster when they can get it. **Indies,** 55–56 Company St.

(☎ 340/692-9440), serves what may be the finest and freshest meal on St. Croix. The swordfish with fresh artichokes, shiitake mushrooms, and thyme has a savory flavor, as does the baked wahoo with lobster curry and fresh chutney and coconut.

Paradise Café, Queen Cross St. at 53B Company St. (across from Government House; ☎ 340/773-2985), serves New York deli–style sandwiches throughout the day—everything from a Reuben to a tuna melt. Of course, burgers are always featured. **St. Croix Chop House & Brew Pub,** King's Alley Walk (☎ 340/713-9820), boasts one of the best harbor views in Christiansted, and serves beer, burgers, and sandwiches at street level and a two-fisted menu upstairs that includes garlic-stuffed fillet steak and such fish as wahoo and marlin. **Tutto Bene,** 2 Company St. (☎ 340/773-5229), serves a full range of delectable pastas, plus fish, veggie frittatas, a chicken pesto sandwich, spinach lasagna, and more.

IN FREDERIKSTED   Le St. Tropez, Limetree Court, 67 King St. (☎ 340/772-3000), is the most popular bistro in Frederiksted, offering crêpes, quiches, soups, or salads at lunch in the sunlit courtyard. At night it's Mediterranean cuisine. **Pier 69,** 69 King St. (☎ 340/772-0069), looks like a combination of a 1950s living room and a nautical bar, and is a hangout for Christiansted's counterculture and a place for sandwiches and salads.

AROUND THE ISLAND   Duggan's Reef, East End Road, Teague Bay (☎ 340/773-9800), is the most popular restaurant on St. Croix. At lunch, a simple array of salads, crêpes, and sandwiches is offered. At dinner, specialties include Duggan's Caribbean lobster pasta and Irish whiskey lobster. **Sprat Hall Beach Restaurant,** Route 63 (1 mile north of Frederiksted; ☎ 340/772-5855), serves local dishes like conch chowder, pumpkin fritters, tannia soup, and the fried fish of the day. These local dishes have an authentic island flavor, perhaps more than anywhere else on St. Croix.

18 St. Kitts

This island, home to some 35,000 people, lies somewhat off the beaten tourist track and has an appealing small-scale charm. It was the first English settlement in the Leeward Islands, and its 68 square miles enjoyed one of the richest sugarcane economies of the plantation age. A lush, fertile island with a rainforest and waterfalls, it is crowned by the 3,792-foot Mount Liamuiga, a crater that, thankfully, has remained dormant (unlike the one at Montserrat). St. Kitts (also known as St. Christopher) retains a rich sense of British maritime history, and boasts Brimstone Hill, the Caribbean's most impressive fortress.

St. Kitts was given self-government in 1967, and, along with Nevis, to which it's tied politically, it became a state in association with Britain. In 1983, the Federation of St. Kitts and Nevis became a totally independent nation (although its looks like this alliance could be dissolved, as Nevis seems to favor becoming independent).

Frommer's Ratings: St. Kitts

	Poor	Fair	Good	Excellent	Outstanding
Overall Experience				✓	
Shore Excursions			✓		
Activities Close to Port			✓		
Beaches & Water Sports			✓		
Shopping		✓			
Dining/Bars			✓		

Airport ✈ Beach 𝄢 Cruise Ship Dock 🚢 Ferry Route --- Mountain ▲▲

Dieppe Bay
Sandy Bay
St. Paul's
Sadlers
Newton Ground
Hermitage Bay
Mount Liamuiga
Ottley's
Sandy Point Town
Brimstone Hill Fortress
Cayon
Keys
Atlantic Ocean
Half-Way Tree
Middle Island
Carib Rock Drawings
Old Road Town
St. Peter's
Challengers
Conaree Bay
Basseterre
North Frigate Bay
Frigate Bay
North Friar's Bay
Caribbean Sea
South Friar's Bay
Turtle Beach
Sand Bank Bay
Great Salt Pond
White House Bay
St. Anthony's Peak
Cockleshell Bay
Banana Bay
Nag's Head
to Nevis
0   5 Miles
0   5 Kilometers

St. Kitts is a delightful and relatively uncrowded island with beaches, shops, restaurants, and a capital, **Basseterre,** that looks like a Hollywood set for an 18th-century West Indies port. Although it's more active and lively than Nevis, its companion island 2¹/₂ miles across a strait, it still has a sleepy feel.

For the time being, at least, the bulk of the island's revenue still comes from sugar, not tourists. Cane fields climb the slopes of a volcanic mountain range, and you'll see ruins of old mills and plantation houses as you drive around the island. Any farmer will sell you a huge stalk of cane. To get the nectar-sweet juice, strip off the hard exterior and chew on the tasty reeds. It's best with ice and a little rum.

Frommer's Favorite St. Kitts Experiences

- **Hiking Mount Liamuiga:** The hike up this dormant volcano will take you through a rainforest and along deep ravines up to the rim of the crater at a cool 2,625 feet (see "On Your Own: Beyond Walking Distance," below).
- **Visiting the island's Sugar Factory and the Carib Beer Plant:** Anyone with a taste for rum will enjoy a trip to the Sugar Factory, where raw cane is processed into bulk sugar. At the beer plant, you get to sample a cold bottle at the end of the plant tour (see "On Your Own: Beyond Walking Distance," below).

COMING ASHORE   In April 1997, the government of St. Kitts and Nevis essentially replaced the older, drab-looking industrial piers that used to receive cruise ships by building Port Zante, a pier stretching from the center of Basseterre into deep waters offshore.

CURRENCY   The local currency is the **Eastern Caribbean dollar (EC$).** The exchange rate is EC$2.70 to US$1 (EC$1 is worth about 37¢). Many shops and restaurants quote prices in U.S. dollars. Always determine which currency locals are talking about. I have used U.S. dollar prices in this section.

INFORMATION   You can get local tourist information at the **St. Kitts/Nevis Department of Tourism,** Pelican Mall, Bay Road, in Basseterre (☎ **869/465-4040**). Open Monday to Friday from 9am to 5pm.

LANGUAGE   English is the language of the island.

GETTING AROUND

BY TAXI   Since most taxi drivers are also guides, this is the best means of getting around. Taxis aren't metered, so before heading out you must agree on the price, and ask if the rates quoted are in U.S. dollars or Eastern Caribbean dollars.

BY RENTAL CAR   I don't recommend renting a car.

SHORE EXCURSIONS

Choices for organized tours are limited, but expect a catamaran/snorkeling trip as well as island tours.

Brimstone Hill Tour ($28, 2$^1/_2$ hours): Visit this inspiring 17th-century citadel, which at some 800 feet above sea level, gives you a panoramic view of the coastline and the island. There's a museum, too.

Beach Horseback Ride ($38, 1 to 2 hours): Cruise ship passengers ride well-trained horses along the Atlantic coastline, where trade winds ensure a cool trip.

TOURS THROUGH LOCAL OPERATORS

Taxi Tours: Taxi drivers will take you on a 3-hour tour of the island for about $60. Lunch can also be arranged at one of the local inns. Good choices are **Golden Lemon** at Dieppe Bay (☎ **869/465-7260**) or **Rawlins Plantation,** Mount Pleasant (☎ **869/465-6221**).

ON YOUR OWN: WITHIN WALKING DISTANCE

Within walking distance of the pier, the charming town of Basseterre has typical British colonial architecture and some quaint buildings as well as shops and a market where the locals display fruits and flowers.

ON YOUR OWN: BEYOND WALKING DISTANCE

The **Brimstone Hill Fortress** (☎ **869/465-6211**), 9 miles west of Basseterre, is the major stop on any tour of St. Kitts. This historic monument, among the largest and best preserved in the Caribbean, is a complex of bastions, barracks, and other structures ingeniously adapted to the top and upper slopes of a steep, 800-foot hill.

The structure dates from 1690, when the British fortified the hill to help recapture Fort Charles below from the French. In 1782, an invading force of 8,000 French troops bombarded the fortress for a month before its small British garrison, supplemented by local militia, surrendered. When the British took the island back the next year, they proceeded to enlarge the fort into "The Gibraltar of the West Indies."

Today the fortress is the centerpiece of a national park featuring nature trails and a diverse range of plant and animal life, including green vervet monkeys. It's also a photographer's paradise, with views of mountains, fields, and the Caribbean Sea. On a clear day you can see six neighboring islands.

Visitors will enjoy the self-directed tours among the many ruined or restored structures, including the barrack rooms at Fort George. The gift shop sells prints of rare maps and paintings of the Caribbean. Admission is $5 for adults, $2.50 for children. The park is open daily from 9:30am to 5:30pm.

Mount Liamuiga, in the northwest of the island, was dubbed "Mount Misery" long ago. This dormant volcano sputtered its last gasp around 1692. Today, it's a major goal for hikers. A round-trip to the usually cloud-covered peak takes about 4 hours—2½ hours going up, 1½ coming down. Hikers usually make the ascent from Belmont Estate near St. Paul on the north end of St. Kitts. The trail winds through a rainforest and travels along deep ravines up to the rim of the crater at a cool 2,625 feet. Many hikers climb—or crawl—down a steep, slippery trail to a tiny lake in the caldera, some 400 feet below the rim.

You can reach the rim without a guide, but it's absolutely necessary to have one to go into the crater. **Greg's Safaris** (☎ **869/465-4121**) offers guided hikes to the crater for about $60 per person (a minimum of four hikers required), including breakfast and a picnic at the crater's rim. The same outfit also offers half-day rainforest explorations, also with a picnic, for $35 per person.

Anyone with a taste for rum will enjoy a trip to the **Sugar Factory,** where raw cane is processed into bulk sugar from February through July. The factory also produces a very light liqueur, CSR, which the locals use in a grapefruit drink they call "Ting."

You can also visit the **Carib Beer Plant,** an English lager brewery. If sales are any indication, Carib Beer is the best in the West Indies. You get to sample a cold bottle at the end of the plant tour. Reservations aren't required, but check with the tourist information office in Basseterre first to find out if the brewery is open.

SHOPPING

The best buys here are in local handcrafts, including baskets, coconut shells, and leather items made from goatskin. You can also find some decent values in clothing and fabrics, especially Sea Island cottons. Prices on some luxury goods can range from 25% to 30% below those on the North American mainland.

For one-stop shopping, head to **Pelican Shopping Mall,** which has some two dozen shops as well as banking services, a restaurant, and a philatelic bureau, where collectors can buy St. Kitts stamps and everyone else can mail letters. Little Switzerland and some major Caribbean retail outlets have branches here. Also check out the unusual merchandise in the shops on **Liverpool Row.** The shops along Fort Street are also worth browsing.

Rosemary Lane Antiques, 7 Rosemary Lane, stocks Kittitian, Caribbean, and international antiques, including furniture, paintings, silver, china and glass. **Lemonaid,** at the Golden Lemon Hotel, Dieppe Bay, specializes in local antiques, crafts, artwork, jewelry, and silverware. **The Palms,** in the Palms Arcade, Basseterre, specializes in island "things." You'll find handcrafts; larimar, sea opal, pottery, and amber jewelry; West Indies spices, teas, and perfumes; tropical clothes by Canadian designer John Warden; and Bali batiks by Kisha. **Cameron Gallery,** 10 N. Independence Sq., Basseterre, displays watercolors and prints by owner Rosey Cameron-Smith and some 10 to 15 other artists. **Kate Design,** Mount Pleasant, deals in paintings by English-born Kate Spencer. Her still lifes, portraits, and island scenes range in price from $200 to $3,000.

BEACHES

The narrow peninsula in the southeast contains the island's salt ponds and also boasts the best white-sand beaches. You'll find the best swimming at **Conaree Beach,** 3 miles from Basseterre; **Frigate Bay,** with its talcum-powder fine sand; the twin beaches of **Banana Bay** and **Cockleshell Bay,** at the southeast corner of the island; and **Friar's Bay,** a peninsula beach opening onto both the Atlantic and the Caribbean. All beaches, even those that border hotels, are open to the public. However, you must usually pay a fee to use a hotel's beach facilities.

SPORTS

GOLF The **Royal St. Kitts Golf Course,** Frigate Bay (☎ **869/465-8339**), is an 18-hole, par-72 championship course featuring seven beautiful ponds. It's bounded on the south by the Caribbean Sea and on the north by the Atlantic Ocean.

SCUBA DIVING & SNORKELING One of the best diving spots is **Nagshead,** at the south tip of St. Kitts. This is an excellent shallow-water dive for certified divers starting at 10 feet and extending to 70 feet. You'll see a variety of tropical fish, eaglerays, and lobster here. Another good site is **Booby Shoals,** between Cow 'n' Calf Rocks and Booby Island. Booby Shoals has abundant sea life, including nurse sharks, lobster, and stingrays. Dives here are up to 30 feet in depth, and are good for both certified and beginning divers. **Pro-Divers,** at Turtle Beach (☎ **869/465-3223**), arrangers scuba diving and snorkeling expeditions.

GREAT LOCAL RESTAURANTS & BARS

If you're looking for that unspoiled, casual beach restaurant, try **The Anchorage,** Frigate Bay (☎ **869/465-8235**), for a rum drink, hamburgers, or a dozen kinds of sandwiches along with fresh fish. **Ballahoo Restaurant,** The Circus, Fort Street, Basseterre (☎ **869/465-4197**), serves some of the best chili and baby back ribs in town. Seafood platters, such as chili shrimp or fresh lobster, are served with a coconut salad and rice. **Ocean Terrace Inn,** Fortlands (☎ **869/465-2754**), serves some of Basseterre's finest cuisine, along with one of the best views of the harbor. A meal might include tasty fish cakes, accompanied by breaded carrot slices, creamed spinach, a stuffed potato, johnnycake, a cornmeal dumpling, and a green banana in a lime-butter sauce, topped off by a tropical fruit pie and coffee. **Turtle Beach Bar & Grill,** near the Ocean Terrace Inn, on the Southeastern Peninsula (☎ **869/469-9086**), is an airy, sun-flooded restaurant set on the sands above Turtle Beach. Typical dishes might be stuffed broiled lobster, conch fritters, barbecued swordfish steak, prawn salads, and barbecued honey-mustard spareribs.

19 St. Lucia

In very recent years, St. Lucia (pronounced *Loo*-sha), second largest of the Windward Islands at about 240 square miles, has become one of the most popular destinations in the Caribbean, with some of the finest resorts. The heaviest development is concentrated in the northwest, between the capital of Castries and the northern end of the island, where there's a string of white-sand beaches.

Along with these beautiful beaches, an interior of relatively unspoiled green-mantled mountains, and two dramatic peaks (the Pitons), St. Lucia almost appears more South Pacific than Caribbean. In fact, it's got somewhat of a French and British heritage. Here you will find gentle valleys, banana plantations, a bubbling volcano, and fishing villages.

Frommer's Ratings: St. Lucia					
	Poor	Fair	Good	Excellent	Outstanding
Overall Experience				✓	
Shore Excursions				✓	
Activities Close to Port			✓		
Beaches & Water Sports				✓	
Shopping		✓			
Dining/Bars			✓		

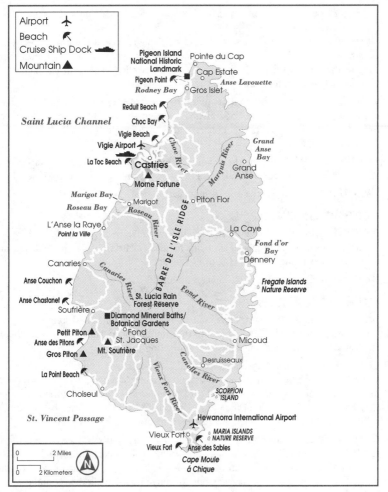

Castries, the capital, has grown up around an extinct volcanic crater that's now a large harbor surrounded by hills. Because of devastating fires, the town today has a look of newness, with glass-and-concrete buildings, but there's still an old-fashioned Saturday-morning market on Jeremy Street. The country women dress in traditional cotton head-dress to sell their luscious fruits and vegetables, while weather-beaten men sit close by playing *warrie,* a fast game played with pebbles on a carved board.

Frommer's Favorite St. Lucia Experiences

- **Riding a catamaran along the coast:** See the lush coast of St. Lucia and the mighty Pitons via catamaran, and then ride a minibus to visit a volcano, the Diamond Baths, and a sulfur springs (see "Shore Excursions," below).
- **Exploring a banana plantation:** They're St. Lucia's leading export (see "On Your Own: Beyond Walking Distance," below).

COMING ASHORE   Most cruise ships arrive at the fairly new pier at Pointe Seraphine, a short taxi ride from the center of Castries. Unlike piers on other islands, this one contains St. Lucia's best shopping. You'll find a money exchange, a small visitor information bureau, and a cable and wireless office. Phone cards are sold for use at specially labeled phones.

If Pointe Seraphine is too crowded, your ship might dock at the Elizabeth II pier. This facility is not geared to cruisers the way Point Seraphine is, but it's only a short walk to the center of Castries. Some smaller vessels, such as Seabourn's, anchor off Soufrière and carry you ashore by tender.

CURRENCY   The official monetary unit is the **Eastern Caribbean dollar (EC$)**. The exchange rate is EC$2.70 to US$1 (EC$1 is worth about 37¢). Most of the prices quoted in this section are in U.S. dollars, which are accepted by nearly all hotels, restaurants, and shops.

INFORMATION   The **St. Lucia Tourist Board** is at Point Seraphine in Castries (☎ 758/452-4094). Open Monday to Friday from 9am to 5pm.

LANGUAGE   English is the official language.

GETTING AROUND
BY TAXI   Most taxi drivers have been trained to serve as guides. Their cars are unmetered, but the government fixes tariffs for all standard trips. Be sure to determine if the driver is quoting a rate in U.S. or EC dollars.

BY RENTAL CAR   I don't recommend driving.

SHORE EXCURSIONS
Because of the difficult terrain, shore excursions are the best means of seeing this beautiful island in a day or less. In addition to the sampling below, most ships typically offer plantation tours, island bus tours, and snorkeling cruises.

✪ **Island Tour by Land and Sea** ($68 to $82, 8 hours): A picturesque journey from Castries via catamaran to the Piton peaks takes you along St. Lucia's verdant coast, docking at La Soufrière, where passengers board minibuses and visit La Soufrière volcano, the Diamond Baths (see "On Your Own: Beyond Walking Distance," below), and a sulfur springs. Lunch is included in a restaurant in Soufrière or on the boat.

✪ **Mountain Ridge Bike Tour** ($75, 3¹/₂ hours): From Castries, travel by bus to the top of Morne Fortune where your bike ride begins. You'll pedal through hilltop roads with dramatic views of the harbor on one side and a stunning mountain range on the other. The ride goes past banana plantations, through rural neighborhoods, and through lush valleys.

Morne Coubaril Plantation Tour ($46, 4 hours): By minibus, ride along the island's west coast, between the sea and the rainforest, with views of the Pitons. At the Morne Coubaril Estate, tour the working family plantation, and watch how coconuts, coffee, and cocoa are processed.

ON YOUR OWN: WITHIN WALKING DISTANCE
The principal streets of Castries are William Peter Boulevard and Bridge Street. A Roman Catholic cathedral stands on Columbus Square, which has a few restored buildings. **Government House** is a late Victorian structure.

Beyond Government House lies **Morne Fortune,** which means "Hill of Good Luck." Actually, no one's had much luck here, certainly not the French and British that battled for **Fort Charlotte.** The fort changed nationalities many times. You can visit the 18th-century barracks, complete with a military cemetery, a small museum, the Old Powder Magazine, and the "Four Apostles Battery"—four grim muzzle-loading cannons. The view of the harbor of Castries is panoramic. You can also see north to Pigeon Island or south to the Pitons. To reach Morne Fortune, head east on Bridge Street.

ON YOUR OWN: BEYOND WALKING DISTANCE

Bananas are St. Lucia's leading export, so if you're being taken around the island by a taxi driver, ask them to take you to one of the huge plantations. I suggest a look at one of the three biggest: the **Cul-de-Sac,** just north of Marigot Bay; **La Caya,** in Dennery on the east coast; and the **Roseau Estate,** south of Marigot Bay.

St. Lucia's first national park, **Pigeon Island National Landmark,** was originally an island. It's now joined to the northwest shore of the mainland by a causeway. Forty-four-acre Pigeon Island got its name from the red-neck pigeon, or ramier, which once made this island home. It's ideal for picnics and nature walks. Its Interpretation Centre is equipped with artifacts and a multimedia display of local history, ranging from the Amerindian occupation of A.D. 1000 to the Battle of Saints, when Admiral Rodney's fleet set out from Pigeon Island and defeated Admiral De Grasse in 1782.

On Pigeon Island's west coast are two white-sand beaches. There's also a restaurant, **Jambe de Bois** ("Leg of Wood"), named after a peg-legged pirate who once used the island as a hideout. The **Captain's Cellar Olde English Pub,** under the interpretive center, evokes an 18th-century English bar.

The park is open daily from 9am to 5pm. For more information, call the St. Lucia National Trust (☎ 758/452-5005). The best way to get here is to take a taxi and arrange to be picked up in time to return to the ship.

La Soufrière, a little fishing port and St. Lucia's second largest settlement, is dominated by the dramatic ✪ **Pitons,** two pointed peaks called Petit Piton and Gros Piton, which rise to 2,460 and 2,619 feet, respectively. Formed by lava and once actively volcanic, these mountains are now clothed in green vegetation. Their sheer rise from the sea makes them such visible landmarks that they've become the very symbol of St. Lucia. Waves crash around their bases.

Near the town of Soufrière lies the famous "drive-in" volcano, ✪ **La Soufrière,** a rocky lunar landscape of bubbling mud and craters seething with fuming sulfur. You literally ride into an old crater and walk between the sulfur springs and pools of hissing steam. The fumes are said to have medicinal properties. A local guide is usually waiting nearby; if you do hire a guide, agree—then doubly agree—on what the fee will be.

Nearby are the **Diamond Mineral Baths** (☎ 758/452-4759), surrounded by a tropical arboretum. They were constructed in 1784 by order of Louis XVI, whose doctors told him that these waters were similar in mineral content to the waters at Aix-les-Bains. Their purpose was to help French soldiers fighting in the West Indies recuperate. Later destroyed, they were rebuilt after World War II. The water's average temperature is 106°F. You'll also find another fine attraction here, a waterfall that changes colors (from yellow to black to green to gray) several times a day. For EC$7 ($2.60), you can bathe and benefit from the recuperative effects yourself.

SHOPPING

Many stores sell duty-free goods; they also deliver tobacco products and liquor to the cruise dock. You'll find some good but not remarkable buys in bone china, jewelry, perfume, watches, liquor, and crystal. Souvenir items include bags and mats, local pottery, and straw hats—again, nothing remarkable.

Built for cruise ship passengers, **Pointe Seraphine** has the best collection of shops on the island. You must present your cruise pass when making purchases here. Liquor and tobacco will be delivered to the ship.

Gablewoods Mall, on Gros Islet Highway, 2 miles north of Castries, contains three restaurants and one of the densest concentrations of stores on St. Lucia.

At **Caribelle Batik,** Howelton House, Old Victoria Road, The Morne, just a 5-minute taxi ride from Castries, you can watch St. Lucian artists creating intricate patterns and colors through the ancient art of batik. **Eudovic Art Studio,** Goodlands, Morne Fortune, sells wood carvings by Vincent Joseph Eudovic, a native of St. Lucia, and some of his pupils. Take a taxi from the cruise pier. **Choiseul Art & Craft Center,** La Fargue, Choiseul (southwest of Castries), is a government-funded retail outlet and training school that perpetuates the tradition of handmade Amerindian pottery and basketware. Some of the best basket weaving on the island is done here, using techniques practiced only in St. Lucia, St. Vincent, and Dominica. Look for place mats, handbags, woodcarvings (including bas-reliefs crafted from screw pine), and pottery.

BEACHES

If you don't take a shore excursion, you might want to spend your time on one of St. Lucia's famous beaches. I prefer the calmer shores along the western coast, since the rough surf on the windward Atlantic side makes swimming potentially dangerous.

Leading beaches include **Pigeon Island,** off the northern shore, with white sand and picnic facilities; **Vigie Beach,** north of Castries Harbour, with fine sands, often light beige in color; and **Reduit Beach,** with its fine brown sands, which lies between Choc Bay and Pigeon Point. For a novelty, you might try the black volcanic sand at Soufrière, whose beach is called **La Toc.**

Just north of Soufrière is that beach connoisseur's delight, **Anse Chastanet** (☎ 758/459-7000), with its white sands set at the foothills of lush, green mountains. While here, you might want to patronize the facilities of the Anse Chastanet Hotel.

All beaches are open to the public, even those along hotel properties, but you must pay to use a hotel's beach equipment.

SPORTS

HORSEBACK RIDING   You can go horseback riding at **Cas-En-Bas and Cap Estate Stables,** north of Castries. To make arrangements, call René Trim at ☎ 758/450-8273. Ask about a picnic trip to the Atlantic side of the island, with a barbecue lunch and drink included. Departures are at 8:30am, 10am, 2pm, and 4pm. Nonriders can also join the excursion; they are transported to the site in a van and pay half price.

SCUBA DIVING   In Soufrière, **Scuba St. Lucia,** in the Anse Chastanet Hotel (☎ 758/459-7000), at the southern end of Anse Chastanet's quarter-mile secluded beach, is a five-star PADI dive center. It offers great diving and comprehensive facilities. Some of the most spectacular coral reefs of St. Lucia—many only 10 to 20 feet below the surface—provide shelter for sea creatures just a short distance offshore. **Rosemond Trench Divers, Ltd.,** at the Marigot Beach Club, Marigot Bay (☎ 758/451-4761), will take both novices and experienced divers to shallow reefs or to some of the most challenging trenches in the Caribbean.

The best center for all **water sports** except diving is **St. Lucian Watersports,** on Reduit Beach at the Rex St. Lucian Hotel (☎ 758/452-8351).

GREAT LOCAL RESTAURANTS & BARS

IN CASTRIES   At the **Green Parrot,** Red Tape Lane, Morne Fortune (about 1½ miles east of the town center; ☎ 758/452-3399), there's an emphasis on St. Lucian specialties and home-grown produce. Try the christophine au gratin (a Caribbean squash with cheese) or the Creole soup made with callaloo and pumpkin. **Jimmie's,** Vigie Cove Marina (☎ 758/452-5142), is known for its fresh-fish menu and tasty Creole cookery. Constructed in the 19th century as a Great House, **San Antoine,** Morne Fortune (☎ 758/452-4660), lies up the Morne hill. You might begin with the classic callaloo soup, and then follow with fettuccine Alfredo, or perhaps fresh fish en papillote (baked in parchment). The view and ambience are more stunning than the cuisine.

AT MARIGOT BAY **Café Paradis,** at the Marigot Beach Club (take a ferry across Marigot Bay; ☎ 758/451-4974), is a culinary showplace, the proud domain of a French-trained chef who was eager to escape to the Caribbean. To reach the place, you'll have to take a ferryboat across Marigot Bay. It runs from the Moorings Marigot Bay Resort about every 10 minutes throughout the day and evening. **Hurricane Hole,** in the Moorings, Marigot Bay (☎ 758/451-4357), is the cozy restaurant of the Marigot Bay Resort, which charters yachts to clients from around the hemisphere. The menu is geared to surf-and-turf fans.

IN THE SOUFRIÈRE AREA **Chez Camilla Guest House & Restaurant,** 7 Bridge St. (1 block inland from the waterfront; ☎ 758/459-5379), which is the only really good place to eat in the village of Soufrière itself, serves sandwiches, cold salads, omelets, and burgers at lunch. **Dasheene Restaurant & Bar,** in the Ladera Resort, between Gros and Petit Piton (☎ 758/459-7323), serves the most refined and certainly the most creative cuisine in St. Lucia. The chef has a special flair for seafood pasta or marinated sirloin steak. Best bet is the catch of the day, likely to be kingfish or red snapper, grilled to perfection.

IN RODNEY BAY At **The Lime,** Rodney Bay, north of Reduit Beach (☎ 758/452-0761), is a casual local place specializing in stuffed crab backs and fish steak Creole, and it also serves shrimp, steaks, lamb and pork chops, and rotis (Caribbean burritos). **The Mortar & Pestle,** in the Harmony Marina Suites, Rodney Bay Lagoon (☎ 758/452-8711), offers indoor-outdoor dining with a view of the boats moored at the nearby marina. For something truly regional, try the Barbados souse, with marinated pieces of lean cooked pork, or the frogs' legs from Dominica.

20 Sint Maarten & St. Martin

Legend has it that a gin-drinking Dutchman and a wine-guzzling Frenchman walked around this island one day in 1648 to claim territory for their countries. The Frenchman covered the most ground, but the canny Dutchman got the more valuable real estate. Whether the story is true or not, this island, measuring only 37 square miles, is today the smallest territory in the world shared by two sovereign states. The Dutch side is known as Sint Maarten; the French side, St. Martin. Once you've cleared customs on either side, the only way you'll know you're crossing from Holland into France is by the "Bienvenue Française" signs marking the boundary. Coexistence between the two nations is very peaceful.

Most cruise ships land at **Philipsburg,** capital of the Dutch side, although smaller ships can maneuver into the harbor of **Marigot** on the French side. Don't come to either side to escape the crowds. The 100% duty-free shopping has turned the island into somewhat of a shopper's paradise (more so on the Dutch side), and Philipsburg especially is nearly always bustling with cruise ship passengers.

Although the boom was severely slowed by the hurricanes of 1995, the island quickly rebuilt, and today its 36 white-sand beaches remain unspoiled, if somewhat rearranged by Mother Nature, and the clear turquoise waters are as enticing as ever.

SINT MAARTEN

Founded in 1763 by Comdr. John Phillips, a Scot in Dutch employ, Sint Maarten's capital, Philipsburg, curves along the shores of Great Bay. The main thoroughfare is busy Front Street, which stretches for about a mile and is lined with stores selling international merchandise. More shops lie along the little lanes, known as *steegijes,* that connect Front Street with Back Street, another shoppers' mart.

Sint Maarten & St. Martin

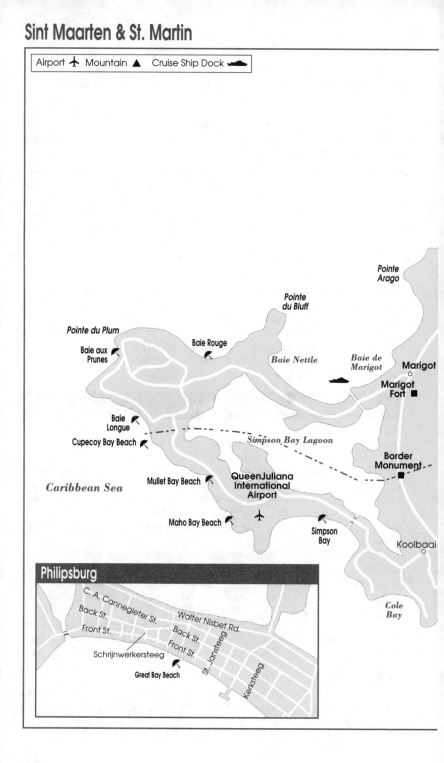

Airport ✈ Mountain ▲ Cruise Ship Dock ⛴

Pointe Arago

Pointe du Bluff

Pointe du Plum

Baie aux Prunes

Baie Rouge

Baie Nettle

Baie de Marigot

Marigot

Marigot Fort ■

Baie Longue

Cupecoy Bay Beach

Simpson Bay Lagoon

Border Monument ■

Caribbean Sea

Mullet Bay Beach

QueenJuliana International Airport

Maho Bay Beach

Simpson Bay

Koolbaai

Cole Bay

Philipsburg

C. A. Cannegieter St.

Back St.

Front St.

Walter Nisbet Rd.

Back St.

Front St.

St. Jansteeg

Schrijnwerkersteeg

Kerksteeg

Great Bay Beach

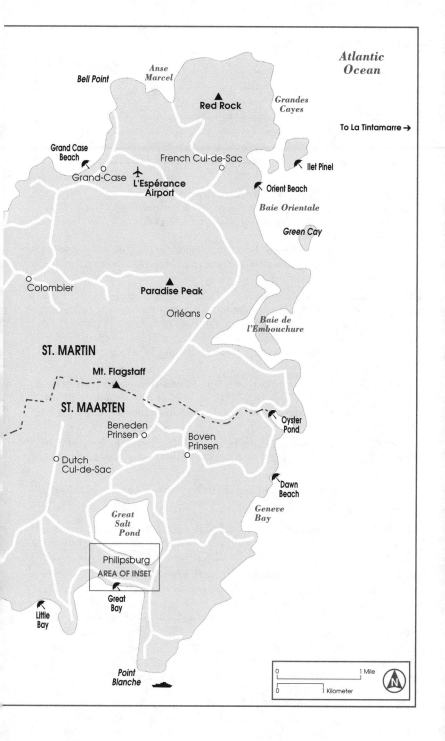

Atlantic
Ocean

Bell Point

Anse
Marcel

Red Rock

Grandes
Cayes

To La Tintamarre →

Grand Case
Beach

Grand-Case

French Cul-de-Sac

Ilet Pinel

L'Espérance
Airport

Orient Beach

Baie Orientale

Green Cay

Colombier

Paradise Peak

Orléans

Baie de
l'Embouchure

ST. MARTIN

Mt. Flagstaff

ST. MAARTEN

Oyster
Pond

Beneden
Prinsen

Boven
Prinsen

Dutch
Cul-de-Sac

Dawn
Beach

Geneve
Bay

Great
Salt
Pond

Philipsburg

AREA OF INSET

Little
Bay

Great
Bay

Point
Blanche

0	1 Mile
0	1 Kilometer

N

Frommer's Ratings: Sint Maarten					
	Poor	Fair	Good	Excellent	Outstanding
Overall Experience				✓	
Shore Excursions			✓		
Activities Close to Port				✓	
Beaches & Water Sports			✓		
Shopping					✓
Dining/Bars			✓		

Frommer's Favorite Sint Maarten Experiences

- **Joining the America's Cup sailing regatta:** What an opportunity! You get to race against actual former contenders of the famed America's Cup race (see "Shore Excursions," below).
- **Heading to the beach at Orient Bay:** On the French side, colorful open-air restaurants line this very European beach and its striped umbrellas (see "Shore Excursions," below).

COMING ASHORE   Most vessels land at Philipsburg, docking about a mile southwest of town at A. C. Wathey Pier at Point Blanche. Some passengers walk the distance, but taxis do await all cruise ships. There are almost no facilities at A. C. Wathey Pier except for a few phones. Passengers can use an AT&T credit card or call collect here. Some ships anchor in the mouth of the harbor, and then take passengers by tender to Little Pier in the heart of town.

CURRENCY   The legal tender in Dutch Sint Maarten is the **Netherlands Antilles guilder (NAf).** The exchange rate is 1.77 NAf to US$1 (1 NAf is worth about 56¢). However, U.S. dollars are also accepted here. Prices in this section are usually given in U.S. currency.

INFORMATION   Go to the **Tourist Information Bureau,** in the Imperial Building at 23 Walter Nisbeth Rd. (☎ 599/5-22337). Open Monday to Friday from 8am to noon and 1 to 5pm.

LANGUAGE   Although the official language is Dutch, most people also speak English.

GETTING AROUND

BY TAXI   Taxis are unmetered, but Dutch Sint Maarten law requires drivers to list fares to major destinations on the island. There are minimum fares for two passengers, and each additional passenger pays another $2. Call a cab at ☎ 599/5-54317.

MINIBUSES   The privately owned and operated minibuses are a reasonable way to get around, if you don't mind some inconveniences and possible overcrowding. They run daily from 7am to midnight and serve most major locations on Sint Maarten. Fares range from $1.15 to $2. The most popular run is from Philipsburg to Marigot on the French side.

BY RENTAL CAR   Rental cars are a practical way to see both the Dutch and the French sides of the island. **Budget** (☎ 800/527-0700 in the U.S., or 599/5-54030), **Hertz** (☎ 800/654-3131 in the U.S., or 599/5-54314), and **Avis** (☎ 800/331-1212 in the U.S., or 599/5-52847) all have agencies here. If you're calling in advance, you might try **Auto Europe** (☎ 800/223-5555). Rates begin at $45 per day with unlimited mileage for a subcompact car. Drive on the righthand side of the road on both sides of the island.

SHORE EXCURSIONS

The beaches and shopping are some of the biggest attractions here. Other typical excursions include snorkeling cruises and island tours.

♻ **America's Cup Sailing Regatta** ($71, 3 hours): Sail on one of the actual former contenders of the America's Cup race, and compete in an actual race. This is a hands-on tour where you'll be grinding winches, trimming sails, and ducking under booms. It's great fun.

Island Tour ($20, 3 hours): By minibus, you'll see both sides, stopping for panoramic views. There's usually a stopover in Marigot for sightseeing and shopping.

Pinel Island Snorkeling Tour ($29, 3 hours): After a scenic bus ride to Cul-de-Sac on the French side, take a tender to Pinel Island for snorkeling (equipment is included in the price).

Butterfly Farm and Marigot ($38, 3¹/₂ hours): After a scenic drive through both the French and Dutch sides of the island, visit a butterfly farm, where a guide points out the different species. End the tour with a short stop in Marigot.

Orient Bay Excursion ($43, 4 to 5 hours): You'll be driven to the beach in Orient Bay, with the driver narrating the sights along the way. Spend a couple of hours at this wide, colorful beach, often called "the French Riviera of the Caribbean." The excursion includes beach chairs and lunch.

ON YOUR OWN

This is a shopping/beaching/gambling kind of port, and all those attractions are covered in the other sections of this review.

GAMBLING

In the absence of natural wonders or man-made attractions, the biggest onshore lure for cruise ship passengers are the casinos on the Dutch side. They open anywhere between 11am and 1pm daily and operate into the wee hours of the night.

Most of the casinos are in the big hotels. **Casino Royale,** at the Maho Beach Hotel on Maho Bay (☎ **599/5-52115**), which opened in 1975, has 6 roulette wheels, 3 craps tables, 16 blackjack tables, and 3 Caribbean stud-poker tables. It also offers baccarat, minibaccarat, and more than 250 slot machines. There's no admission, and a snack buffet is complimentary.

Another popular casino is at the **Pelican Resort and Casino** on Simpson Bay (☎ **599/5-42503**), built to a Swiss design incorporating a panoramic view of the water. This Las Vegas–style casino has 2 craps tables, 3 roulette tables, 9 blackjack tables, 2 stud-poker tables, and 120 slot machines.

The Roman-themed **Coliseum Casino,** on Front Street in Philipsburg (☎ **599/ 5-32102**), tries hard to attract gaming enthusiasts, especially "high rollers," and has the highest table limits ($1,000 maximum) on Sint Maarten. Upon the management's approval, the Coliseum also offers credit lines for clients with a good credit rating at any U.S. casino. This casino features about 225 slot machines, 4 blackjack tables, 3 poker tables, and 2 roulette wheels.

SHOPPING

The main shopping area is in the center of Philipsburg. Most stores are on the two leading streets, **Front Street** (*Voorstraat* in Dutch), which is closer to the bay and **Back Street** (*Achterstraat*), which runs parallel to Front. You'll find all the usual suspects— Little Switzerland and a host of jewelry/gift/luxury item shops—as well as some standout local shops. In general, the price marked on the merchandise in the major retail outlets is what you're supposed to pay. At small, personally run shops, however, some polite bargaining might be in order.

Old Street Shopping Center, with entrances on Front Street and Back Street, features more than two dozen shops and boutiques, including branches of such famous stores as Colombian Emeralds. Dining facilities include the Philipsburg Grill and Ribs Co. and Pizza Hut.

The **Guavaberry Company,** 10 Front St., sells the rare "island folk liqueur" of Sint Maarten, which for centuries was made in private homes but is now available to everyone. Sold in square bottles, the liqueur is aged and has a fruity, woody, almost bittersweet flavor. It's made from rum that's given a unique flavor by rare local berries usually grown in the hills in the center of the island. You can blend it with coconut for a unique guavaberry colada or pour a splash into a glass of icy champagne. Don't confuse guavaberries with guavas—they're very different. Stop in at their shop and free-tasting house.

The **Shipwreck Shop,** Front Street, stocks West Indian hammocks, beach towels, sea salt, cane sugar, spices, baskets, handcrafts, jewelry, T-shirts, postcards, books, and much more.

BEACHES

Sint Maarten has 36 beautiful white-sand beaches, so it's comparatively easy to find one for yourself. But if it's too secluded, be careful: There have been reports of robberies on some remote beaches. Don't carry valuables to the beach.

You can often use the changing facilities at some of the bigger resorts for a small fee. Nudists should head for the French side, but the Dutch side is getting more liberal about such things.

On the west side of the island, **Mullet Bay Beach** is shaded by palm trees, but can get crowded on weekends. You can arrange water-sports equipment rentals through the Mullet Bay Resort.

Great Bay Beach is best if you'd like to stay near Front Street in Philipsburg. This mile-long beach is sandy, but since it borders the busy capital it may not be as clean as some of the more remote beaches. Immediately to the west, at the foot of Fort Amsterdam, **Little Bay Beach** looks like a Caribbean postcard, but it, too, can be overrun with visitors.

Stretching the length of Simpson Bay Village, white sand **Simpson Bay Beach,** is shaped like a half moon. It lies west of Philipsburg, just east of the airport. You can rent water-sports equipment here.

West of the airport, **Maho Bay Beach,** at the Maho Beach Hotel and Casino, is ideal in many ways, if you don't mind the planes passing overhead. Palms provide shade, and food and drink can be purchased at the hotel.

The sands are pearly white at **Oyster Pond Beach,** near the Oyster Pond Hotel northeast of Philipsburg. Bodysurfers like the rolling waves here. Nearby **Dawn Beach** is noted for its underwater tropical beauty, with reefs lying offshore.

Beyond the sprawling Mullet Beach Resort on the Dutch side, **Cupecoy Bay Beach** lies just north of the Dutch-French border on the western side of the island. It's a string of three white-sand beaches set against a backdrop of caves and sandstone cliffs that provide morning shade. The beach doesn't have facilities, but is nonetheless popular. One section of the beach is "clothing optional."

SPORTS

GOLF The **Mullet Bay Resort** (☎ 599/5-52801, ext. 1850) has an 18-hole course designed by Joseph Lee that's one of the most challenging in the Caribbean. Mullet Pond and Simpson Bay lagoon provide both beauty and hazards.

HORSEBACK RIDING   At **Crazy Acres,** Dr. J. H. Dela Fuente Street, Cole Bay (☎ 599/5-42793), riding expeditions invariably end on an isolated beach where horses and riders can enjoy a cool post-ride romp in the water. Two experienced escorts accompany a maximum of eight people on the 2¹/₂-hour outings. Riders of all experience levels are welcome. Wear a bathing suit under your riding clothes. Reservations should be made at least 2 days in advance.

SCUBA DIVING   Underwater visibility runs from 75 to 125 feet in the island's crystal-clear bays and countless coves. The biggest attraction for scuba divers is the 1801 British man-of-war HMS *Proselyte,* which came to a watery grave on a reef a mile off the coast. The PADI-instructed program at **Pelican Watersports,** Pelican Resort & Casino, Simpson Bay (☎ 599/5-42604), features the most knowledgeable guides on the island, each one familiar with Sint Maarten dive sites. Divers are taken out in custom-built 28- and 35-foot boats. Many say that this is the best reef diving in the Caribbean.

GREAT LOCAL RESTAURANTS & BARS

✪ **Cheri's Café,** 45 Cinnamon Grove, Shopping Centre, Maho Beach (☎ 599/5-53361), is the island's hot spot, once voted best bar in the West Indies by *Caribbean Travel and Life* readers. You can get really fresh grilled fish, 16-ounce steaks, and juicy burgers. Some come for the inexpensive food, others for the potent drinks.

Antoine's, 119 Front St., Philipsburg (☎ 599/5-22964), offers sophistication, style, and cuisine that's mainly old continental favorites, almost equally divided between meat and fish dishes. **Chesterfields,** Great Bay Marina, Philipsburg (☎ 599/5-23484), serves platters of fish, grilled steaks and other meats, sandwiches, and salads at lunchtime. **Crocodile Express Café,** Casino Balcony, at the Pelican Resort & Casino, Simpson Bay (☎ 599/5-42503, ext. 1127), serves hearty deli fare, including well-stuffed sandwiches. **Da Livio Ristorante,** 159 Front St. (at the bottom of Front Street), Philipsburg. (☎ 599/5-23363), is the finest Italian dining in Sint Maarten. A favorite dish is homemade manicotti della casa, filled with ricotta, spinach, and a zesty tomato sauce. **The Greenhouse,** Bobby's Marina (off Front Street), Philipsburg (☎ 599/5-22941), is a breezy, open-air restaurant serving lunches that include the catch of the day, a wide selection of burgers, and conch chowder.

ST. MARTIN

The St. Martin side of the island is decidedly French. The tricolor flies over Marigot's *gendarmerie;* towns have names like Colombier and Orléans; the streets are called "rue de la Whatever."

French St. Martin is governed from Guadeloupe and has direct representation in the French government in Paris. **Marigot,** the principal town in St. Martin, has none of Philipsburg's frenzied pace and cruise ship crowds. In fact, it looks like a French village transplanted to the Caribbean. Not only is there shopping, but some excellent French Creole restaurants as well.

Frommer's Favorite St. Martin Experiences

- **Joining the America's Cup Regatta or heading to Orient Bay:** Both these excursions listed under Sint Maarten, above, are also available on the French side.
- **Trekking up to the ramparts of Fort St. Louis:** It's a 10- or 15-minute walk from the heart of Marigot to the top, where you're treated to panoramic views of Marigot and beyond (see "On Your Own," below).
- **Having lunch at Madame Claude's Petit Club:** At the oldest restaurant in Marigot you can savor the rich flavors of the Creole and French cuisine served on the

Frommer's Ratings: St. Martin					
	Poor	Fair	Good	Excellent	Outstanding
Overall Experience				✓	
Shore Excursions			✓		
Activities Close to Port				✓	
Beaches & Water Sports				✓	
Shopping				✓	
Dining/Bars				✓	

restaurant's cozy, colorfully painted upstairs terrace (see "Great Local Restaurants & Bars," below).

COMING ASHORE   Medium-sized vessels can dock at the pier at Port-Royale, at the bottom of the Boulevard de France in the heart of Marigot. When you disembark, you'll see a rather lavish marina, the headquarters of the island's tourist office, and arcades of shops nearby. If a cruise ship is already at the pier, which can accommodate only one ship at a time, the second ship must anchor and send tenders ashore. Large ships generally dock on the Dutch side of the island, but if they call here, passengers must tender in.

CURRENCY   French St. Martin uses the **French franc (F),** although U.S. dollars seem to be preferred. The exchange rate is 6.29F to US$1 (1F is worth about 16¢). Canadians should convert their money into U.S. dollars, not into francs.

INFORMATION   The **Office du Tourisme** is at the Port de Marigot (☎ **0590/ 87-57-21**). Open Monday to Friday from 9am to 5pm.

LANGUAGE   Although the official language is French, most people also speak English.

GETTING AROUND

BY TAXI   Taxis are the most common means of transport. A **Taxi Service & Information Center** operates at the port of Marigot (☎ **0590/87-56-54**). It also books 2-hour sightseeing trips around the island. Always agree on the rate before getting into an unmetered cab.

BY RENTAL CAR   Rental cars are a practical way to see the island. **Budget** (☎ **800/ 527-0700** in the U.S., or 0590/87-38-22), **Hertz** (☎ **800/654-3001** in the U.S., or 0590/87-73-01), and **Avis** (☎ **800/331-1212** in the U.S., or 0590/87-50-60) all have agencies here. Rates begin at $35 per day with unlimited mileage. Drive on the righthand side of the road.

BY MINIVAN   Local drivers operate a diverse armada of privately owned minivans and minibuses. There's a departure every hour between Marigot and the Dutch side. Because it's sometimes difficult for a newcomer to identify the buses, it's best to ask a local.

SHORE EXCURSIONS

All the same excursion offered in Dutch Sint Maarten (see above) are also offered here.

ON YOUR OWN

All of Marigot's shopping is within walking distance, as well as several restaurants and cafes. Don't miss out on a short hike up to Fort St. Louis for lovely, panoramic views of much of the island.

Beyond walking distance, we're mostly talking beaches (see below).

BEACHES

Top rating on the French side goes to **Baie Longue,** a long, beautiful beach that's rarely overcrowded. Chic and very expensive La Samanna, a deluxe hotel, opens onto this beachfront, which is one of the few on the island that grew rather than diminished in size during the 1995 hurricanes. Unfortunately, the storms created unexpected holes offshore, which makes swimming here more hazardous than before. The beach lies to the north of Cupecoy Beach, by the Lowlands road.

If you continue north, you reach the approach to **Baie Rouge,** another long and popular stretch of sand and jagged coral. Snorkelers are drawn to the rock formations at both ends of this beach, many of which were exposed through erosion caused by the 1995 storms. There are no changing facilities, but that doesn't matter for some, who get their suntan *au naturel.*

Orient Beach is one of the Caribbean's most famous clothing-optional beaches. Colorful canvas umbrellas create a European feel, and there are charming beachside cafes for lunch.

On the north side of the island, to the west of Espérance airport, **Grand-Case Beach** is small but select. Despite the many tons of storm debris left in 1995 by the hurricanes, the sands are once again white and clean.

SHOPPING

Many day-trippers come over to Marigot just to look at the collection of French boutiques and shopping arcades. Because it's a duty-free port, the shopping here is some of the best in the Caribbean. Whether you're seeking jewelry, perfume, or St-Tropez bikinis, you'll find it in one of the boutiques along rue de la République and rue de la Liberté. There's a wide selection of **European merchandise,** much of it geared to the luxury trade. Crystal, perfumes, jewelry, and fashions are sometimes 25% to 50% less expensive than in the United States and Canada. You'll also find fine liqueurs, cognacs, and cigars.

Prices are often quoted in U.S. dollars, and salespeople frequently speak English. U.S. dollars, credit and charge cards, and traveler's checks are usually accepted.

At harbor side in Marigot, there's a frisky **morning market** with vendors selling spices, fruit, shells, and local handcrafts. Mornings are even more alive at **Port La Royale,** the bustling center of everything. Schooners unload produce from the neighboring islands, boats board guests for picnics on deserted beaches, and a brigantine sets out on a sightseeing sail. The owners of a dozen different little dining spots get ready for the lunch crowd. The largest shopping arcade on the French side is here, with many boutiques that often come and go rapidly.

Galerie Périgourdine, another cluster of boutiques, faces the post office. Here you might pick up some designer wear for both men and women, including items from the collection of Ted Lapidus.

Worthwhile specialty shops include **Gingerbread & Mahogany Gallery,** 4–14 Marina Royale (in a narrow alleyway at the marina), which deals in Haitian art by both "old masters" and talented amateurs; **Havane,** Port La Royale, which offers exclusive collections of French clothing for men, in both casual and high-fashion designs; **La Romana,** 12 rue de la République, which sells chic women's clothing, focusing on Italian styles; and **Oro de Sol Jewelers,** rue de la République, which stocks high-fashion jewelry studded with precious stones, plus gold watches by Cartier, Chopard, Ebel, Patek Philippe, and Bulgari.

Local artist **Roland Richardson,** a gifted impressionist painter known for his landscape, portraiture, and colorful still life paintings, has an art gallery on the waterfront.

SPORTS

GENERAL WATER SPORTS   Most of St. Martin's large beachfront hotels maintain facilities for Jet Skiing, water-skiing, and parasailing, often from makeshift kiosks on the beaches. Two independent operators that function from side-by-side positions on Orient Bay, close to the cluster of hotels near the Esmeralda Hotel, are **Kon Tiki Watersports** (☎ 0590/87-46-89) and **Bikini Beach Watersports** (☎ 0590/ 87-43-25). You can rent Jet Skis and go parasailing.

SCUBA DIVING   Scuba diving is excellent around French St. Martin, with reef, wreck, cave, and drift dives ranging from 20 to 70 feet. Dive sites include Ilet Pinel for shallow diving; Green Key, a barrier reef; Flat Island for sheltered coves and geologic faults; and Tintamarre, known for its shipwreck. The island's premier dive operation is **Marine Time,** whose offices are in the same building as L'Aventure, Chemin du Port, 97150 Marigot (☎ 0590/87-20-28). Operated by England-born Philip Baumann and his Mauritius-born colleague, Corine Mazurier, this outfit offers morning and afternoon dives in deep and shallow water, to wrecks and over reefs.

SNORKELING   The island's tiny coves and calm offshore waters make it a snorkeler's heaven. The waters off the northeastern shore are protected as a regional underwater nature reserve, **Reserve Sous-Marine Régionale.** This area includes Flat Island (also known as Tintamarre), Pinel Islet, Green Key, and Petite Clef. The use of harpoons and spears is strictly forbidden. Snorkeling can be enjoyed individually or on sailing trips. You can rent equipment at almost any hotel on the beach.

WINDSURFING   Because of prevailing winds and calmer, more protected waters, most windsurfers gravitate to the island's easternmost edge, most notably Coconut Grove Beach, Orient Beach, and, to a lesser extent, Dawn Beach. The best of the several outfits that specialize in windsurfing is **Tropical Wave,** Coconut Grove, Le Galion Beach, Baie de l'Embouchure (☎ 0590/87-37-25), set midway between Orient Beach and Oyster Pond, amid a sunblasted, scrub-covered, isolated landscape. The combination of wind and calm waters here is considered almost ideal.

GREAT LOCAL RESTAURANTS & BARS

Madame Claude herself is running the show at the ✪ **Petit Club,** the oldest restaurant in Marigot, located on the main street in the heart of town. Savor the rich flavors of the Creole and French cuisine—like spicy conch stew or fresh fish Creole style—served on the restaurant's cozy, colorfully painted upstairs terrace. **La Brasserie de Marigot,** rue du Général-de-Gaulle 11 (☎ 0590/87-94-43), is where the real French eat, a great choice for good food at good prices. Meals include pot-au-feu, duck breast with peaches, filet of beef with mushroom sauce, and even chicken on a spit and steak tartare. **La Maison sur le Port,** Boulevard de France (☎ 0590/87-56-38), is a grand, Parisian, and upscale choice, with cookery that's grounded firmly in France, but with Caribbean twists and flavors. At lunch, you can choose from a number of salads as well as fish and meat courses.

21 St. Thomas & St. John

Vacationers discovered St. Thomas right after World War II, and they've been flocking here in increasing numbers ever since. Today, the island is one of the busiest ports in the Caribbean, often hosting more than 10 cruise ships a day during the peak winter season. **Charlotte Amalie,** its capital, has become the Caribbean's major shopping center.

Tourism and U.S. government programs have raised the standard of living here to one of the highest in the Caribbean. The island, 12 miles long and 3 miles wide, is now

St. Thomas

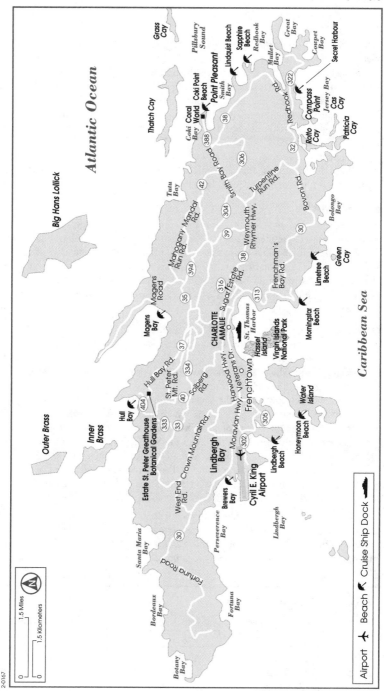

Atlantic Ocean

Caribbean Sea

Big Hans Lollick

Grass Cay

Thatch Cay

Pillsbury Sound

Lindquist Beach

Sapphire Beach

Redhook Bay

Great Bay

Coppet Bay

Secret Harbour

Coki Point Beach

Point Pleasant

Coki Coral Bay World

Smith Bay

Mullet Bay

322

Compass Point

Jersey Bay

Cas Cay

Redhook Rd.

38

Rolfo Cay

Patricia Cay

32

388

306

Smith Bay Road

Turpentine Run Rd.

Bovoni Rd.

Tutu Bay

42

304

Bolongo Bay

Mandal Run Rd.

Mahogany Run Rd.

39

Weymouth Rhymer Hwy.

38

30

Green Cay

394

Frenchman's Bay Rd.

Limetree Beach

35

316

313

Magens Road

Sugar Estate Rd.

Magens Bay

37

CHARLOTTE AMALIE

St. Thomas Harbor

Morningstar Beach

Hull Bay Rd.

334

St. Peter Mt. Rd.

Solberg Rd.

40

Hassel Island

Virgin Islands National Park

Hull Bay

404

Frenchtown

Water Island

333

Estate St. Peter Greathouse Botanical Gardens

33

Crown Mountain Rd.

Moravian Hwy, Harwood Hwy, Veterans Dr.

Honeymoon Beach

305

Lindbergh Bay

302

Lindbergh Beach

West End Rd.

Brewers Bay

Cyril E. King Airport

Lindbergh Bay

Santa Maria Bay

30

Perserverence Bay

Fortuna Road

Bordeaux Bay

Fortuna Bay

Botany Bay

Outer Brass

Inner Brass

Airport ✈ Beach ⬇ Cruise Ship Dock ⬇

1.5 Miles

1.5 Kilometers

0

0

2-0167

the most developed of the U.S. Virgins. Condominium apartments have grown up over the debris of bulldozed shacks.

In stark contrast to this busy scene, more than half of nearby St. John, the smallest of the U.S. Virgin Islands, is pristinely preserved in the gorgeous **Virgin Islands National Park.** The wildlife here is admired by ornithologists and zoologists around the world. A rocky coastline, forming crescent-shaped bays and white-sand beaches, rings the whole island. Panoramic views and ruins of 18th-century Danish plantations dot St. John's miles of serpentine hiking trails. Island guides can point out mysterious geometric petroglyphs incised into boulders and cliffs; of unknown age and origin, the figures have never been deciphered.

Most cruise ships dock in Charlotte Amalie on St. Thomas, but a few anchor directly off St. John. Many of those that stop only at St. Thomas offer excursions to St. John. If yours doesn't, it's easy to get to St. John on your own.

ST. THOMAS

With a population of some 50,000 and a large number of American expatriates and temporary sun-seekers in residence, tiny St. Thomas isn't exactly a tranquil tropical retreat. You won't have any beaches to yourself. Shops, bars, and restaurants (including a lot of fast-food joints) abound here, and most of the locals make their living by the tourist trade. Most native Virgin Islanders are the descendants of slaves brought from Africa. In fact, Charlotte Amalie was one of the major slave-trading centers in the Caribbean.

Frommer's Favorite St. Thomas Experiences

- **Biking around the island:** You'll get great views and a great workout, too (see "Shore Excursions," below).
- **Kayaking among the island's mangroves:** You'll learn about the local lagoon ecosystem and get some exercise, to boot (see "Shore Excursions," below).
- **Plunging 90 feet down in to the ocean:** On the *Atlantis* submarine, you'll enjoy a world of exotic marine life up close (see "Shore Excursions," below).
- **Visiting the colorful village of Frenchtown:** Have lunch in a village settled by French-speaking citizenry uprooted when the Swedes invaded and took over in St. Barts (see "On Your Own: Beyond Walking Distance," below).
- **Taking a nature walk:** The lush Estate St. Peter Greathouse Botanical Gardens has 200 varieties of plants and trees, plus a rainforest, an orchid jungle, a monkey habitat, and more (see "On Your Own: Beyond Walking Distance," below).

COMING ASHORE Most cruise ships anchor at Havensight Mall, at the eastern end of Charlotte Amalie harbor, 1 1/2 miles from the town center. The mall has a tourist information office, restaurants, a bookstore, a bank, a U.S. postal van, phones that accept long-distance credit cards, and a generous number of duty-free shops. Many people

Frommer's Ratings: St. Thomas					
	Poor	Fair	Good	Excellent	Outstanding
Overall Experience				✓	
Shore Excursions				✓	
Activities Close to Port				✓	
Beaches & Water Sports				✓	
Shopping					✓
Dining/Bars			✓		

make the long, hot walk to the center of Charlotte Amalie, but the road passes a housing development where some cruise passengers have been mugged in the past. Take a taxi for about $3 per person.

If Havensight Mall is clogged with cruise ships, your ship will dock at the Crown Point Marina, to the west of Charlotte Amalie. A taxi is your best bet—the 30-minute walk into Charlotte Amalie feels longer on a hot day, and isn't terribly picturesque. A taxi ride into town from Crown Point Marina costs about $4.

CURRENCY The U.S. dollar is the local currency.

INFORMATION The **U.S. Virgin Islands Division of Tourism** has offices at Tolbod Gade (☎ **340/774-8784**), open Monday to Friday from 8am to 5pm, and Saturday from 8am to noon. Here you can pick up *St. Thomas This Week,* which includes maps of St. Thomas and St. John. There's also an office at the Havensight Mall.

LANGUAGE It's English.

GETTING AROUND

BY TAXI Taxis are the chief means of transport here. They're unmetered, so agree with the driver on a fare before you get in. The official fare for sightseeing is $30 for two passengers for 2 hours; each additional passenger pays another $12. For 24-hour radio-dispatch service, call ☎ **340/774-7457.** Many taxis transport 8 to 12 passengers in vans to multiple destinations for a lower price.

BY BUS Comfortable and often air-conditioned, government-run Vitran buses serve Charlotte Amalie and the countryside as far away as Red Hook, a jumping-off point for St. John's. They run daily between 5am and 10:40pm. You rarely have to wait more than 30 minutes during the day. A one-way ride costs 75¢ within Charlotte Amalie, $1 to outer neighborhoods, and $3 for rides as far as Red Hook. For routes, stops, and schedules, call ☎ **340/774-5678.**

BY TAXI VAN Less structured and more erratic are "taxi vans," privately owned vans, minibuses, or open-sided trucks operated by local entrepreneurs. They make unscheduled stops along major traffic arteries and charge the same fares as the Vitran buses. If you look like you want to go somewhere, one will likely stop for you. They may or may not have their final destinations written on a cardboard sign displayed on the windshield.

BY RENTAL CAR I don't recommend renting a car here.

SHORE EXCURSIONS

In addition to the excursions below, there's plenty of organized snorkeling trips, booze cruises, and island tours offered in St.Thomas.

✪ **Island Mountain Bike Adventure** ($59, 3¹/₂ hours): For great views of the island and a decent bout of exercise, too, this bike tour starts after a short minivan ride to an elevated part of the island. With a few exceptions, most of the ride is downhill, but you'll definitely work up a sweat. The tour ends at a beach, where there's time for some swimming and relaxing.

✪ **Kayaking the Marine Sanctuary** ($59, 3¹/₂ hours): Kayak from the mouth of the marine sanctuary at Holmberg's Marina and spend nearly an hour paddling among the mangroves, while a naturalist explains the mangrove and lagoon ecosystem. At the middle, there's about half an hour to snorkel or walk along the coral beach at Bovoni Point before kayaking back to the starting point.

Island Tour by Minibus and Tram ($29, 3 hours): First drive along the impressive Skyline Drive for panoramic views of St. John's and the ship harbor, and then up to the 1,400-foot-high Mountain Top for awesome views of Magens Bay as well as the

British Virgin Islands. Then hop in the Paradise Point Tramway for a 15-minute ride to the top of Paradise Point, some 700 feet above the sea.

Atlantis Submarine Odyssey ($82, 2 hours): Descend about 90 feet into the ocean in this air-conditioned submarine for views of exotic fish and sealife.

Virgin Islands Seaplane Exploration ($104, 1¹/₂ hours): For great views of these islands, their beaches, old sugar plantations, and lush foliage, there's no better vantage point than from above.

TOURING THROUGH LOCAL OPERATORS

St. John's Yachting/Snorkeling Excursion: You can avoid the crowds by sailing aboard *Fantasy* (☎ 340/775-5652), which departs from the American Yacht Harbor at Red Hook at 9:30am daily. It sails to St. John and nearby islands, carrying a maximum of six passengers, for swimming, snorkeling, beachcombing, or trolling. Snorkel gear with expert instruction is provided, as is a champagne lunch. An underwater camera is also available. There are full-day and half-day tours.

ON YOUR OWN: WITHIN WALKING DISTANCE

The color and charm of a slightly seedy Caribbean waterfront come vividly to life in Charlotte Amalie. In days of yore, seafarers from all over the globe flocked to this old-world Danish town. Confederate sailors used the port during the Civil War.

The old warehouses once used for storing pirates' loot still stand and, for the most part, house today's shops. In fact, the main streets (called "Gades" here in honor of their Danish heritage) are now a virtual shopping mall and are usually packed with visitors. Sandwiched among the shops are a few historic buildings, most of which can be covered on foot in about 2 hours.

Before starting your tour, stop off in the so-called **Grand Hotel,** near Emancipation Park. No longer a hotel, it has a restaurant, bar, shops, and a visitor center. Also, from **Hotel 1829** a street farther up, there are views of the harbor below from its wood-paneled pub/restaurant, a great place for a drink or some lunch.

Stray behind the seafront shopping strip (Main Street) of Charlotte Amalie and you'll find pockets of 19th-century houses and, high on the steep sloping Crystal Gade, the truly charming, cozy, brick-and-stone **St. Thomas Synagogue,** built in 1833 by Sephardic Jews. There's a great view from here as well.

Dating from 1672, **Fort Christian** rises from the harbor to dominate the center of town. Named after the Danish king Christian V, the structure has been everything from a governor's residence to a jail. Many pirates were hanged in its courtyard. Some of the cells have been turned into the rather minor **Virgin Islands Museum,** displaying Native American artifacts of only the most passing interest. Admission is free. The fort is open Monday to Friday from 8am to 5pm.

Seven Arches Museum, Government Hill (☎ 340/774-9295), is a 2-century-old Danish house completely restored to its original condition and furnished with antiques. You can walk through the yellow ballast arches and visit the great room with its view of the busy harbor.

The Paradise Point Tramway (☎ 340/774-9809) affords visitors a dramatic view of Charlotte Amalie harbor at a peak height of 697 feet. The tramways transport customers from the Havensight area to Paradise Point, where riders disembark to visit shops and a popular restaurant and bar.

ON YOUR OWN: BEYOND WALKING DISTANCE

Coral World Marine Park & Underwater Observatory, 6450 Coki Point, off Route 38, 20 minutes from downtown Charlotte Amalie (☎ 340/775-1555), is the

Charlotte Amalie

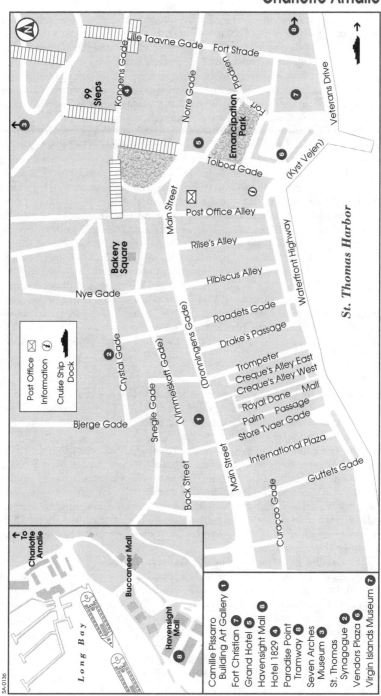

St. Thomas Harbor

99 Steps

Emancipation Park

Bakery Square

Long Bay

Buccaneer Mall

Havensight Mall

← To Charlotte Amalie

Streets:
Lille Taavne Gade
Fort Strade
Kongens Gade
Norre Gade
pladsen
Fort
Tolbod Gade
Veterans Drive
Main Street
Post Office Alley
Rlise's Alley
Hibiscus Alley
Nye Gade
Raadets Gade
Drake's Passage
Trompeter
Creque's Alley East
Creque's Alley West
Royal Dane Mall
Palm Passage
Store Tvaer Gade
International Plaza
Guttets Gade
Curaçao Gade
Crystal Gade
Snegle Gade
(Vimmelskaft Gade)
(Dronningens Gade)
Bjerge Gade
Back Street
Main Street
Waterfront Highway
(Kyst Vejen)

Legend:
⊠ Post Office
ⓘ Information
Cruise Ship Dock

Camille Pissarro Building Art Gallery ①
Fort Christian ⑦
Grand Hotel ⑤
Havensight Mall ⑧
Hotel 1829 ④
Paradise Point Tramway ⑧
Seven Arches Museum ③
St. Thomas Synagogue ②
Vendors Plaza ⑥
Virgin Islands Museum ⑦

SA-0136

number-one attraction in St. Thomas. The 3¹/₂-acre complex features a three-story underwater observation tower 100 feet offshore. Through windows you'll see sponges, fish, coral, and other underwater life in their natural state. In the Marine Gardens Aquarium, saltwater tanks display everything from sea horses to sea urchins. An 80,000-gallon reef tank features exotic Caribbean marine life. Another tank is devoted to sea predators, including circling sharks. The entrance is hidden behind a waterfall. The latest addition to the park is a semisubmarine that lets you enjoy the panoramic view and the underwater feeling of a submarine without truly submerging.

West of Charlotte Amalie, **Frenchtown** was settled by a French-speaking citizenry uprooted when the Swedes invaded and took over in St. Barts. They were known for wearing *cha-chas*, or straw hats. Many of the people who live here today are the direct descendants of those long-ago residents. This colorful fishing village contains several interesting restaurants and taverns. To get there, take a taxi down Veteran's Drive (Route 30) west and turn left at the sign to the Admirals Inn.

The lush **Estate St. Peter Greathouse Botanical Gardens,** at the corner of St. Peter Mountain Road (Route 40) and Barrett Hill Road (☎ **340/774-4999**), decorates 11 acres on the volcanic peaks of the island's northern rim. It's the creation of Howard Lawson DeWolfe, a Mayflower descendant who, with his wife, Sylvie, bought the estate in 1987 and set about transforming it into a tropical paradise. It's filled with self-guided nature walks that acquaint you with some 200 varieties of plants and trees, including an umbrella plant from Madagascar. There's also a rainforest, an orchid jungle, a monkey habitat, waterfalls, and reflecting ponds. From a panoramic deck you can see some 20 of the Virgin Islands. The house itself is worth a visit, its interior filled with local art. The complex is open daily from 9am to 5pm. Admission is $8 for adults, $4 for children.

SHOPPING

St. Thomas is famous for its shopping. As at St. Croix, American shoppers can bring home $1,200 worth of merchandise without paying duty. You'll sometimes find well-known brand names at savings of up to 40% off stateside prices—but you'll often have to plow through a lot of junk to find the bargains.

Many cruise ship passengers shop at the **Havensight Mall,** where they disembark, but the major shopping goes on along the harbor of Charlotte Amalie. **Main Street** (or Dronningens Gade, its old Danish name) is the main shopping area. Just north of Main Street is merchandise-loaded **Back Street,** or Vimmelskaft. Many shops are also spread along the **Waterfront Highway** (also called Kyst Vejen). Running between these major streets is a series of side streets, walkways, and alleys, all filled with shops. All the usual suspects sell all the usual jewelry, watches, perfume, gift items, etc., but there are a number of other interesting shops.

The **Camille Pissarro Building Art Gallery,** Caribbean Cultural Centre, 14 Dronningens Gade, is the house where the impressionist painter Pissarro was born on July 10, 1830. The art gallery is reached by climbing a flight of stairs. In three high-ceilinged and airy rooms, you'll see all the available Pissarro paintings relating to the islands. Many prints and note cards of local artists are available, too, as well as original batiks, alive in vibrant colors.

Street vendors ply their trades in a designated area called **Vendors Plaza,** at the corner of Veterans Drive and Tolbod Gade. Hundreds of them converge under oversize parasols there Monday to Saturday from 7:30am to 5:30pm, and on Sunday if a cruise ship is expected. Food vendors set up on sidewalks outside Vendors Plaza.

Just for fun, you'll want to have a peak in **Lover's Lane,** Raadets Gade 33 (beside Veteran's Drive, on the second floor), with its stock of provocative lingerie, inflatable men and women, massage aids of every conceivable type, the largest inventory of vibrators in the Virgin Islands, and all the lace, leather, or latex you'll ever need.

BEACHES

Instead of looking at the minor attractions or going shopping, many cruise ship passengers prefer to spend their time ashore on a beach. St. Thomas has some good ones, and you can reach them all relatively quickly in a taxi (arrange for the driver to return and pick you up at a designated time). If you're going to St. John, you may want to do your beaching there (see "Beaches," under St. John's, below).

All the beaches in the U.S. Virgin Islands are public, but some still charge a fee. Mind your belongings at the beach, as St. Thomas has pickpockets and thieves who target visitors.

THE NORTH SIDE   Lying across the mountains 3 miles north of the capital, **Magens Bay** was once hailed as one of the world's 10 most beautiful beaches, but its reputation has faded. Though still beautiful, it isn't as well-maintained as it should be and is often overcrowded, especially when many cruise ships are in port. It's less than a mile long and lies between two mountains. Admission is $1 for adults and 25¢ for children under 12. Changing facilities are available, and you can rent snorkeling gear and lounge chairs. There's no public transportation here, so take a taxi. The gates are open daily from 6am to 6pm (you'll need insect repellent after 4pm).

Located in the northeast near Coral World, **Coki Beach** is good, but it, too, becomes overcrowded when cruise ships are in port. Snorkelers come here often, as do pickpockets—protect your valuables. Lockers can be rented at Coral World, next door. An East End bus runs to Smith Bay and lets you off at the gate to Coral World and Coki.

Also on the north side is **Renaissance Grand Beach Resort,** one of the island's most beautiful beaches. It opens onto Smith Bay, right off Route 38, near Coral World. Many water sports are available here.

THE SOUTH SIDE   On the south side, **Morningstar** lies about 2 miles east of Charlotte Amalie at Marriott's Frenchman's Reef Beach Resort. You can wear your most daring swimwear here, and you can also rent sailboats, snorkeling equipment, and lounge chairs. The beach can be easily reached via a cliff-front elevator at the Marriott.

Limetree Beach, at the Bolongo Bay Beach Club, lures those who love a serene spread of sand. You can feed hibiscus blossoms to iguanas and rent snorkeling gear and lounge chairs. There's no public transportation, but it's easy to get here by taxi from Charlotte Amalie.

One of the most popular, **Brewer's Beach** lies in the southwest near the University of the Virgin Islands. It can be reached by the public bus marked FORTUNA heading west from Charlotte Amalie. **Lindberg Beach,** near the airport, also lies on the Fortuna bus route heading west from Charlotte Amalie.

THE EAST END   Small and special, **Secret Harbour** sits near a collection of condos. With its white sand and coconut palms, it's a veritable cliché of Caribbean charm. No public transportation stops here, but it's an easy taxi ride east of Charlotte Amalie heading toward Red Hook.

Sapphire Beach is one of the finest on St. Thomas, set against the backdrop of the Doubletree Sapphire Beach Resort & Marina complex, where you can lunch or order drinks. Windsurfers like this beach a lot. You can also rent snorkeling gear and lounge chairs here. A large reef lies close to the shore, and there are great views of offshore cays and St. John. To get to this beach, you can take the East End bus from Charlotte Amalie, going via Red Hook. Ask to be let off at the entrance to Sapphire Bay; it's not too far to walk from there to the water.

SPORTS

GOLF   Designed by Tom and George Fazio, **Mahogany Run** on the north shore, Mahogany Run Road (☎ 800/253-7103 or 340/777-6006), is one of the most beautiful courses in the West Indies. This 18-hole, par-70 course rises and drops like a roller coaster on its journey to the sea. Cliffs and crashing sea waves are the ultimate hazards at the 13th and 14th holes. The golf course is an $8 taxi ride from the cruise dock.

SCUBA DIVING & SNORKELING   The waters off the U.S. Virgin Islands are rated as one of the "most beautiful areas in the world" by *Skin Diver* magazine. Thirty spectacular reefs lie just off St. Thomas alone. **Dive In!,** in the Doubletree Sapphire Beach Resort & Marina, Smith Bay Road, Route 36 (☎ 800/524-2090), offers professional instruction, daily beach and boat dives, custom dive packages, underwater photography and videotapes, and snorkeling trips.

WINDSURFING   Check out the major resort beaches and at some public beaches, including Brewers Bay, Morningstar Beach, and Limetree Beach. **Renaissance Grand Beach Resort,** Smith Bay Road, Route 38 (☎ 340/775-1510), is the major hotel offering windsurfing.

GREAT LOCAL RESTAURANTS & BARS

IN CHARLOTTE AMALIE   **Beni Iguana's Sushi Bar,** in the Grand Hotel Court, Veteran's Drive (☎ 340/777-8744), is the only Japanese restaurant on St. Thomas. **Greenhouse,** Veterans Drive (☎ 340/774-7998), attracts cruise ship passengers with daily specialties, including much American fare and some Jamaican-inspired dishes. The **Hard Rock Café,** 5144 International Plaza (on the second floor of a pink-sided mall), the Waterfront, Queen's Quarter (☎ 340/777-5555), has the best burgers in town, but people mainly come for the good times. ✪ **Virgilio's,** 18 Dronningens Gade (entrance on a narrow alleyway running between Main and Back streets; ☎ 340/776-4920), is the best northern Italian restaurant in the Virgin Islands. The lobster ravioli here is the best there is.

IN FRENCHTOWN   At **Alexander's,** rue de St. Barthélemy (west of town; ☎ 340/776-4211), there's a heavy emphasis on seafood—the menu even includes conch schnitzel on occasion. Other dishes include a mouthwatering Wiener schnitzel and homemade pâté. ✪ **Craig & Sally's,** 22 Honduras (☎ 340/777-9949), serves dishes that, according to the owner, are not "for the faint of heart, but for the adventurous soul"—roast pork with clams, filet mignon with macadamia-nut sauce, and grilled swordfish with a sauce of fresh herbs and tomatoes.

ON THE NORTH COAST   **Eunice's Terrace,** 66–67 Smith Bay, Route 38 (just east of the Coral World turnoff; ☎ 340/775-3975), is one of the island's best-known West Indian restaurants, and oozes with local color. The place made news around the world on January 5, 1997, when Bill and Hillary Clinton showed up unexpectedly for lunch. Surrounded by secret service men, they shared a conch appetizer, then Mrs. Clinton went for the vegetable plate while the president opted for the catch of the day, which he reportedly loved.

ON SAPPHIRE BEACH   **Seagrape,** in the Doubletree Sapphire Beach Resort & Marina, Rte. 6, Smith Bay Rd. (☎ 340/775-6100), is counted among the finest dining rooms along the east coast of St. Thomas. The lunch menu includes the grilled catch of the day and freshly made salads.

NEAR THE SUB BASE   **Victor's New Hide Out,** 103 Sub Base, off Route 30 (☎ 340/776-9379), has some of the best local dishes on the island, but first you have to find it—this hilltop perch is truly a place to hide out. Take a taxi. Its dishes have sophisticated flair and zest, as opposed to the more down-home cookery found at Eunice's Terrace (see above).

ST. JOHN

St. John lies about 3 miles east of St. Thomas across Pillsbury Sound. The island, the smallest and least populated of the U.S. Virgins, is about 7 miles long and 3 miles wide, with a total land area of some 20 square miles. When held under Danish control, it was slated for big development, but a slave rebellion and a decline of the sugarcane plantations ended that idea. Since 1956, more than half its land mass, as well as its shoreline waters, have been set aside as the **Virgin Islands National Park.** Miles of winding hiking trails lead to panoramic views and the ruins of 18th-century Danish plantations. Mysterious geometric petroglyphs incised into boulders and cliffs can be pointed out by island guides; of unknown age and origin, the figures have never been deciphered. Since St. John is easy to reach from St. Thomas, many cruise ship passengers spend their entire day here.

Frommer's Favorite St. John Experiences

- **Touring the island in an open-air safari bus:** The views are spectacular from the island's coastal road, and you'll visit the ruins of a plantation and one of St. John's excellent beaches (see "Shore Excursions," below).
- **Beaching yourself in Trunk Bay:** Although it can get somewhat crowded, it's a gorgeous beach and there's some decent snorkeling, too (see "Beaches," below).

COMING ASHORE   Cruise ships cannot dock at either of the piers in St. John. Instead, they moor off the coast of Cruz Bay, sending in tenders to the National Park Service Dock, the larger of the two piers. Most cruise ships docking at St. Thomas offer shore excursions to St. John's pristine acres and beaches.

If your ship docks on St. Thomas and you don't take a shore excursion to St. John, you can get here from Charlotte Amalie by ferry. Ferries leave the Charlotte Amalie waterfront for St. John's Cruz Bay at 1- to 2-hour intervals, from 9am until the last departure around 5:30pm. The last boat leaves Cruz Bay for Charlotte Amalie at 3:45pm. The ride takes about 45 minutes and costs $7 each way. Call ☎ **340/ 776-6282** for more information.

Another ferry leaves from the Red Hook pier on St. Thomas's eastern tip more or less every half hour, starting at 6:30am. It's a 30-minute drive from Charlotte Amalie's port to the pier at Red Hook; the ferry trip to Cruz Bay on St. John takes another 20 minutes each way. The one-way fare is $3 for adults, $1 for children under 11. Schedules can change without notice, so call in advance (☎ **340/776-6282**). You can take a Vitran bus from a point near Market Square directly to Red Hook for $1 per person each way, or negotiate a price with a taxi driver.

Frommer's Ratings: St. John					
	Poor	Fair	Good	Excellent	Outstanding
Overall Experience				✓	
Shore Excursions			✓		
Activities Close to Port				✓	
Beaches & Water Sports				✓	
Shopping		✓			
Dining/Bars		✓			

GETTING AROUND

BY TAXI   The most popular way to get around is by surrey-style taxi. Typical fares from Cruz Bay are $3 to Trunk Bay, $3.50 to Cinnamon Bay, or $7 to Mahoe Bay. For more information, call ☎ **340/693-7530.**

BY RENTAL CAR   The extensive Virgin Islands National Park has kept the island's roads undeveloped and uncluttered, with some of the most panoramic vistas anywhere. Renting a vehicle is the best way to see these views, especially if you like to linger at particularly beautiful spots. Open-sided Jeep-like vehicles are the most fun of the limited rentals here. There's sometimes a shortage of cars during the busy midwinter season, so try to reserve early. Remember to drive on the left (even though steering wheels are on the left, too—go figure).

The two largest car-rental agencies are located on St. John: **Avis** (☎ **800/331-1212** or 340/776-6374) charges between $78 and $82 per day, and **Hertz** (☎ **800/654-3001** or 340/693-7580), $63 to $80 per day. Gasoline is seldom included in the price of a rental, and your car is likely to come with just enough fuel to get you to one of the island's two gas stations. Because of the distance between stations, it's never a good idea to drive around St. John with less than half a tank of gas.

BY BICYCLE   Bicycles are available for rent from the **Cinnamon Bay Watersports Center** on Cinnamon Bay Beach (☎ **340/776-6330**). St. John's steep hills and off-road trails can challenge the best of riders, but cyclists in search of more moderate rides can visit the ruins at Annaberg or the beaches at Maho, Francis, Leinster, or Watermelon Bay.

SHORE EXCURSIONS

Island Tour ($39, 4 to 5 hours): Since most ships tie up in St. Thomas, tours of St. John first require a ferry or tender ride to Cruz Bay on St. John. Then you board open-air safari buses for a tour that includes a stop at the ruins of a working plantation, the Annaberg Ruins, as well as a stop at a beach, like Trunk Bay. The views from the coastal road of the islands and sea beyond are spectacular.

TOURING THROUGH LOCAL OPERATORS

Taxi Tours: Taxi tours of about 2 hours cost from $30 for one or two passengers, or about $12 per person for three or more riders, and are one of the best ways of seeing St. John. Almost any taxi at Cruz Bay can take you on these tours, or you can call ☎ 340/693-7530.

ON YOUR OWN: WITHIN WALKING DISTANCE

Most cruise ship passengers dart through Cruz Bay, a cute little West Indian village with interesting bars, restaurants, boutiques, and pastel-painted houses. You can browse through **Wharfside Village,** a complex of courtyards, alleys, and shady patios with a mishmash of boutiques, restaurants, fast-food joints, and bars.

Located at the public library, **Elaine Ione Sprauve Museum** (☎ 340/776-6359) isn't big, but it does contain some local artifacts, and will teach you some of the history of the island. It's open Monday to Friday from 9am to 5pm. Admission is free.

ON YOUR OWN: BEYOND WALKING DISTANCE

Two-thirds of St. John is national park land. If you want to explore the **Virgin Islands National Park,** stop off first at the visitor center (☎ 340/776-6201), right on the dock at St. Cruz. Here you'll see some exhibits and learn more about what you can see and do in the park.

St. John

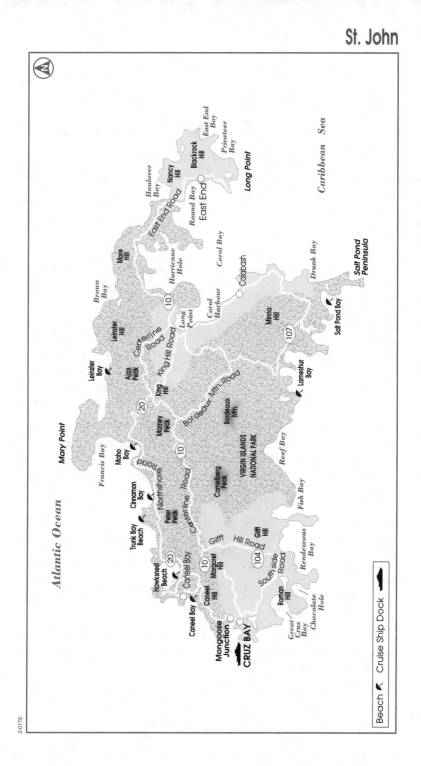

Atlantic Ocean

Caribbean Sea

Mary Point

East End Bay
Privateer Bay
Long Point
Blackrock Hill
Nancy Hill
Hawlover Bay
Round Bay
East End
Coral Bay
Drunk Bay
Salt Pond Peninsula
Mare Hill
Hurricane Hole
Coral Harbour
Calabash
Salt Pond Bay
Brown Bay
10
Long Point
Minna Hill
107
Leinster Hill
Centerline Road
King Hill Road
Leinster Bay
Alex Peak
Lameshur Bay
Francis Bay
20
King Hill
Bordeaux Mtn. Road
Bordeaux Mtn.
Maho Bay
Mamey Peak
10
Reef Bay
VIRGIN ISLANDS NATIONAL PARK
Northshore Road
Cinnamon Bay
Camelberg Peak
Fish Bay
Trunk Bay Beach
Peter Peak
Centerline Road
Gifft Hill
Hawksnest Beach
20
Caneel Bay
Gifft Hill Road
Rendezvous Bay
Margaret Hill
10
104
South Side Road
Caneel Bay
Caneel Hill
Roman Hill
Chocolate Hole
Mongoose Junction
CRUZ BAY
Great Cruz Bay

Beach ◄   Cruise Ship Dock

2-0175

529

Established in 1956, the park totals 12,624 acres, including submerged land and water adjacent to St. John. You can explore the park on the more than 20 miles of biking trails, or rent your own car, Jeep, or Mini-Moke. Make sure you drive on the left. If you want to hike, stop at the office of the park ranger, adjacent to the pier, to watch an 18-minute video about the park. Also pick up maps and instructions before setting out on any of the clearly marked hiking trails. You can take a taxi for about $5 to the starting point of whatever trail you select.

Within the park, try to see the **Annaberg Ruins,** Leinster Bay Road, where the Danes founded a thriving plantation and sugar mill in 1718. You'll find tidal pools, forest lands, hilltops, wild scenery, and the ruins of several Danish plantations. It's located off North Shore Road east of Trunk Bay on the north shore. On certain days of the week (dates vary), guided walks of the area are given by park rangers. Check with the park's visitor center.

SHOPPING

Compared to St. Thomas, there's not a lot of shopping on St. John, but the boutiques and shops at Cruz Bay are generally more interesting. Most of them are clustered at **Mongoose Junction,** in a woodsy area beside the roadway, about a 5-minute walk from the ferry dock.

IN MONGOOSE JUNCTION   Bamboula has an unusual and appealing collection of gifts from the Caribbean, Haiti, India, Indonesia, and Central Africa. **The Canvas Factory** produces its own handmade, rugged, and colorful canvas bags. **Donald Schnell Studio** deals in handmade pottery, sculpture, and blown glass. The **Fabric Mill** features silk-screened and batik fabrics from around the world. **R and I Patton Goldsmithing** has a large selection of island-designed jewelry in sterling silver, gold, and precious stones.

IN CRUZ BAY   As you wait at Cruz Bay for the ferry back to St. Thomas, you can browse through the shops of Wharfside Village. **Pusser's of the West Indies** is located here, offering a large collection of classically designed, old-world travel and adventure clothing, along with unusual accessories—as well as Pusser's famous rum, of course. A good, cheap gift item is packets of Pusser's coasters, which have the recipe for that classic Caribbean rum specialty—the Painkiller—on the back.

BEACHES

For a true beach-lover, missing the great white sweep of **Trunk Bay** would be like touring Europe and skipping Paris. Trouble is, the word is out. This gorgeous beach is usually overcrowded, and there are pickpockets lurking about. The beach has lifeguards and offers rentals, such as snorkeling gear. The underwater trail near the shore attracts beginning snorkelers in particular. Both taxis and "safari buses" to Trunk Bay meet the ferry as it docks at Cruz Bay.

Caneel Bay, the stamping ground of the rich and famous, has seven perfect beaches on its 170 acres—but only one open to the public. That's **Hawksnest Beach,** a little gem of white sand beloved by St. Johnians. The beach is a bit narrow and windy, but beautiful, as filmmakers long ago discovered. Close to the road you'll find barbecue grills. Safari buses and taxis from Cruz Bay will take you along North Shore Road.

The campgrounds of **Cinnamon Bay** and **Maho Bay** have their own beaches, where forest rangers sometimes have to remind visitors to put their swimsuits back on. Snorkelers find good reefs here. Changing rooms and showers are available.

Salt Pond Bay is known to locals but often missed by visitors. The bay here is tranquil, but there are no facilities. The Ram Head Trail begins here and winds for a mile to a panoramic belvedere overlooking the bay.

SPORTS

HIKING   The network of trails in Virgin Islands National Park is the big thing here. The visitor center at Cruz Bay gives away free trail maps of the park. Since you don't have time to get lost—you don't want the ship to leave without you!—it's best to set out with someone who knows his or her way around. Both **Maho Bay** (☎ **340/ 776-6226**) and **Cinnamon Bay** (☎ **340/776-6330**) conduct nature walks.

KAYAKING & WINDSURFING   The most complete line of water sports available on St. John is offered at the **Cinnamon Bay Watersports Center** on Cinnamon Bay Beach (☎ **340/776-6330**). The windsurfing here is some of the best anywhere, for both the beginner and the expert. High-quality equipment is available for all levels, even for kids. Want to paddle to a secluded beach, explore a nearby island with an old Danish ruin, or be able to jump overboard anytime you like for snorkeling or splashing? Then try a sit-on-top kayak; one- and two-person kayaks are available for hourly rentals. You can also rent a 12- or 14-foot Hobie monohull sailboat.

SCUBA DIVING & SNORKELING   Ask about scuba packages at **Low Key Watersports,** Wharfside Village (☎ **800/835-7718** or 340/693-8999). All wreck dives are two-tank/two-location dives. Snorkel tours are also available. The center uses its own custom-built dive boats and also specializes in water sports gear, including masks, fins, snorkels, and dive skins. It can arrange day-sailing charters, kayaking tours, and deep-sea sport fishing. **Cruz Bay Watersports,** P.O. Box 252, Palm Plaza, St. John, U.S.V.I. 00831 (☎ **800/835-7730** or 340/776-6234), is a PADI and NAUI five-star diving center on St. John. Snorkel tours are available daily.

GREAT LOCAL RESTAURANTS & BARS

Pusser's, Wharfside Village, Cruz Bay (near the ferry dock; ☎ **340/693-8489**), is actually three bars, all serving the famous Pusser's rum and menu choices that include jerk tuna filet, jerk chicken with a tomato basil sauce over penne, and spaghetti with lobster cooked in rum, wine, lemon juice, and garlic. **The Fish Trap,** in the Raintree Inn, Cruz Bay (☎ **340/693-9994**), is known for its wide selection of fresh fish, but also caters to vegetarians and the burger crowd. The Italian food at ✪ **Paradiso,** Mongoose Junction (☎ **340/693-8899**), is the best on the island—the chicken Picante Willie— a spicy, creamy picante sauce over crispy chicken with linguini and ratatouille—was featured in *Bon Apétit.*

12 | Bermuda & the Panama Canal Route

After the Caribbean, the island nation of **Bermuda,** sitting out in the Atlantic roughly parallel to South Carolina (or Casablanca, if you're measuring from the east), is the other major cruise destination from the eastern seaboard. Most cruise ships bound for here depart from New York or Boston.

Transiting the **Panama Canal** is spectacular in itself, but on typical Canal itineraries you get more: on the eastern side, visits to the rain forests of Costa Rica, the Mayan ruins of Guatemala, and the Kuna culture of the San Blas Islands; on the western side, the beauty of the Mexican Riviera.

1 Bermuda

Although Bermuda was discovered by the Spanish in the early 16th century, it was the British who first settled here in 1609 when the *Sea Venture,* en route to Virginia's Jamestown colony, was wrecked on the island's reefs. No lives were lost, and the crew and passengers built two new ships and continued on to Virginia, but three crewmembers stayed behind and became the island's first permanent settlers. Bermuda became a crown colony in 1620 and remains one today. Still very British, the ubiquitous Bermuda shorts are worn by many, horse-drawn carriages trot about, driving is on the left, and the island is divided up into parishes. It's a genteel, sane, and orderly place and even prohibits rental cars and limits the number of regularly visiting cruise ships to six.

Not to say things aren't bustling during the week in **Hamilton** and **St. George's** when the ships are in town, but a calm and controlled atmosphere reigns as visitors fan out across the island. There are many powdery soft beaches easily accessible by taxi or motor scooter; **Horseshoe Bay** and **Elbow Beach** are popular and the many unnamed slivers of silky beach tucked into the jagged coastline are worth discovering. There are more **golf courses** per square mile than any other place in the world. For shoppers, Front and Queen Streets in Hamilton offer dozens of shops and department stores, most specializing in English items like porcelain, crystal, wool clothing, and linens. For history buffs, the nearly 300-year-old St. Peter's church and several museums are within walking distance of the pier in St. George's, and Fort St. Catherine is just about a mile away. The exhibits at the Maritime Museum, which is built into the ruins of Bermuda's oldest fort at the Royal Naval Dockyard, are impressive and varied.

Bermuda

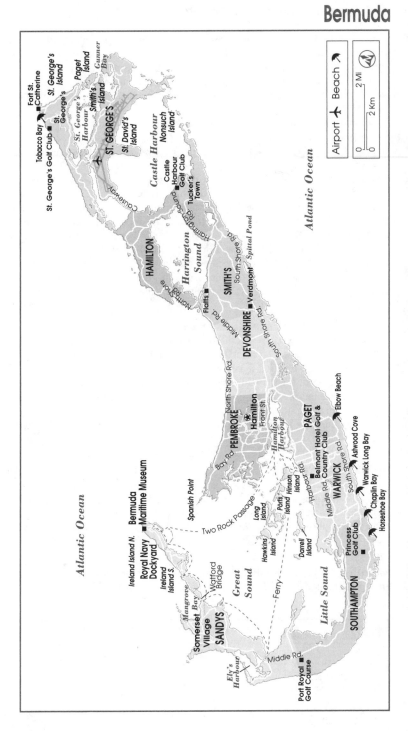

Airport ✈ Beach ⚐

0 ___ 2 Km
0 ___ 2 Mi

Atlantic Ocean

St. George's Island
Paget Island
Gunner Bay
Fort St. Catherine
Tobacco Bay ⚐
St. George's
St. George's Golf Club
St. George's Harbour
Smith's Island
ST. GEORGE'S
St. David's Island
Castle Harbour
Nonsuch Island
Castle Harbour Golf Club
Tucker's Town
Causeway

HAMILTON

Harrington Sound
Harrington Sound

North Shore Rd.

SMITH'S
South Shore Rd.
Verdmont ■
Spittal Pond

Flatts ■
DEVONSHIRE
Middle Rd.
South Shore Rd.

North Shore Rd.

Bay Rd.
PEMBROKE
Hamilton ✪
Front St.
Hamilton Harbour

PAGET
Belmont Hotel Golf & Country Club ■
Harbour Rd.
Hinson Island
Ports Island
Long Island
Darrell Island
Hawkins Island

Elbow Beach ⚐
Astwood Cove ⚐
Warwick Long Bay ⚐
WARWICK
Middle Rd.
South Shore Rd.
Chaplin Bay ⚐
Horseshoe Bay ⚐

Spanish Point

Two Rock Passage

Ireland Island N.
Bermuda Maritime Museum ■
Royal Navy Dockyard
Ireland Island S.

Great Sound

Ferry

Little Sound

Princess Golf Club ■
SOUTHAMPTON

Mangrove Bay
Watford Bridge
Somerset Village
SANDYS

Ely's Harbour
Middle Rd.
Port Royal Golf Course

Atlantic Ocean

Atlantic Ocean

533

Cruise ships have been sailing to Bermuda for over a century, making it one of the earliest cruise destinations. The Quebec Steamship Company, which eventually evolved into the Furness Bermuda Line, began its New York-to-Bermuda service in 1874 with the small steamers *Canima* and *Bermuda* and then added two new building, the *Orinoco* in 1881 and the *Trinidad* in 1893, plus the liner *Pretoria,* acquired from the Union Line in 1897.

Bermuda has carefully managed the number of cruise ships visiting to maintain a semblance of order and keep the island from getting overrun with too many tourists (and to protect its hotel trade). Today, the government allows six cruise ships—five on weekdays and the other on weekends—to visit the island on a regular basis during its season, late April through October, when the temperatures hover around 75°F and extended rainfall is rare. (For a listing of the ships, see below.)

Unlike most Caribbean itineraries, on which ships visit ports for a day at most, the majority of Bermuda-bound ships spend 3 whole days of a 7-night cruise at the island. Four ships ply the New York-to-Bermuda run, and a fifth sails from Boston, spending a day and a half at sea each way and the rest of the time tied up at Hamilton, St. George's, or the Royal Naval Dockyard. At press time, a sixth ship, the *Crown Dynasty* of Crown Cruise Line, the new premium sister line to Commodore Cruise Line, announced it would offer weekly sailings from Philadelphia in conjunction with Apple Vacations.

Frommer's Favorite Bermuda Experiences
- **Hopping a local ferry in Hamilton:** For a few bucks you get a scenic ride to the Royal Naval Dockyard on the island's far west end, where you can tour the historic fortress ruins and excellent museums.
- **Renting a motor scooter and touring the island independently:** Bermuda's roads are well maintained (but can get crowded at rush hour), the island is scenic, and its beaches are easy to find.
- **Having lunch at Waterloo House:** The elegant patio restaurant at the Waterloo House, within walking distance of the cruise ship docks in Hamilton, offers idyllic views of the boats and yachts in Hamilton Harbour.

SHIPS VISITING BERMUDA   For 2000, the six ships sailing regular Bermuda routes are Celebrity's *Zenith,* Princess's *Pacific Princess,* Royal Caribbean's *Nordic Empress,* and an as-yet-unnamed NCL ship, all sailing from New York; Norwegian's *Norwegian Majesty,* sailing from Boston; and Crown Cruise Line's *Crown Dynasty,* sailing from Philadelphia (Crown is a new venture of Commodore Cruise Line—see Commodore review for information). See cruise line reviews in chapters 6 through 9 for details on all ships and itineraries.

COMING ASHORE   Cruise ships tie up at three harbors in Bermuda; most are at the docks smack dab in the middle of Hamilton or St. George's in the east end, and

Frommer's Ratings: Bermuda					
	Poor	Fair	Good	Excellent	Outstanding
Overall Experience					✓
Shore Excursions			✓		
Activities Close to Port				✓	
Beaches & Water Sports					✓
Shopping					✓
Dining/Bars			✓		

less often at the Royal Naval Dockyard in the west end. Exploring, especially from Hamilton and St. George's, couldn't be easier as the ships pull right to the docks (no need to tender back and forth).

CURRENCY   The legal tender in Bermuda is the **Bermuda dollar (BD$)** and it's pegged to the U.S. dollar on an equal basis—BD$1 equals US$1. There's no need to exchange any U.S. money for Bermudian.

INFORMATION   Bermuda's **Visitor Service Bureau** has several branches, including at the ferry terminal in Hamilton (☎ 441/295-1480) and King's Square in St. George's (☎ 441/297-1642).

LANGUAGE   English is the official language.

GETTING AROUND

BY TAXI   Taxis are regulated by meter and are clean, new, and plentiful at all three cruise piers—but they're expensive! Expect to pay $4 for the first mile and $1.40 for each additional mile; fares go up 25% between 10pm and 6am as well as on Sundays and holidays. If you want to go touring, the hourly rates for a taxi are $37.50; the minimum is 3 hours. When a taxi has a blue flag on its hood (locals call it the "bonnet"), drivers are qualified to serve as tour guides (and they don't charge extra for the tour). There are several authorized taxi companies on the island, including **Radio Cab** (☎ 441/295-4141), **C.O.O.P** (☎ 441/292-4476), and **Sandys** (☎ 441/234-2344). Taxi fares add up and you can pay $20 or $30 before you know it; if you can, split a taxi (most are minivans) among four people.

BY BUS   Buses are a good option in Bermuda; they're cheap, clean, and go everywhere. Some, however, don't run on Sundays and holidays. Bermuda is divided into 14 zones of about 2 miles each. The regular cash fare for up to three zones is $2.50, or $4 for more than three zones. If you use tokens, these fares are 25¢ less. You must have exact change or tokens to use the buses. You can purchase tokens at the Central Bus Terminal on Washington Street in Hamilton. You can also purchase day passes. For more information on bus service, call ☎ 340/292-3854.

BY MOTORSCOOTER   A popular way to travel, there are motorscooters everywhere. Roads are well-maintained on Bermuda, but remember that driving is on the left. Rental fees are pretty standard across the island. Mopeds go for about $33 for the first day and $57 for 2 days; scooters go for about $42 for 1 day. You need a major credit card, and you must buy a one-time insurance policy costing $15. You can rent from **Astwood Cycles** (☎ 441/292-2245) along Front Street in Hamilton, adjacent to the cruise ship terminal; **Eve's Cycles** (☎ 441/236-6247), which sets up shop near the cruise terminal in Hamilton; or **Oleander Cycles** (☎ 441/295-0919) on Gorham Road in Hamilton.

BY FERRY   It's an interesting and efficient way to get around, and you get some sightseeing done in the process. The government-run ferries criss-cross Great Sound between Hamilton and Somerset (where the Royal Naval Dockyard is located), charging only $3.75 one way. Service also goes between Hamilton and Paget and Warwick, across the harbor. Buy tickets and get schedules at the Ferry Terminal (adjacent to the cruise ship docks) or Central Bus Terminal in Hamilton. Or call for information at ☎ 441/295-4506.

BY HORSE-DRAWN CARRIAGE   Before 1946, this was the only way to get around. Now it's a quaint way. Drivers congregate along Front Street in Hamilton, adjacent to the No. 1 cruise ship terminal. A single carriage accommodating one to four passengers and drawn by one horse costs $20 for 30 minutes. Another 30 minutes is another $20. For longer rides, the fee is negotiable. Unless you make special arrangements for a night ride, you aren't likely to find any carriages after 4:30pm. For more information, contact Terceira's Stables at ☎ **441/236-3014.**

BY RENTAL CAR   There are no rental cars permitted on the island.

SHORE EXCURSIONS

Bermuda is truly an island made for independent exploring, offering a great combination of history, beaches, and shopping. Take your pick. Hamilton and St. George's are conducive to walking tours, and the beaches and golf courses are easily accessible by taxi, bus, or motorscooter.

Guided Walking Tour of St. George's ($21, 1 hour): Learn about Bermuda's history, including its churches, art galleries, libraries, and private gardens.

West End Highlights ($40, 3 hours): This minibus tour takes you from Hamilton to the Royal Naval Dockyard; en route you'll sightsee and then explore the many exhibits at the Dockyard's museums.

Snorkeling Trip ($42, 3 hours): From Hamilton, board a boat and motor out to a snorkeling spot hear the West End as the captain talks to passengers about Bermuda history and customs. Then, after an hour or so of snorkeling, the fun begins: The music is turned on, the dancing starts, and the bar opens as the boat heads back to port.

Glass-Bottomed Boat Cruise ($26, 2 hours): See the coral reefs and colorful fish living in Bermuda's waters, then view one of Bermuda's famous shipwrecks and enjoy a rum swizzle from a fully stocked bar.

Golf Excursion (about $66 to $160, half-day): Well-known courses visited on these excursions include Mid Ocean Golf Club, among the best in world; Castle Harbour Golf Club; Riddells Bay Golf & Country Club, a veritable golfing institution built in 1922; Port Royal Golf Course; and St. George's Golf Club, Bermuda's newest course, designed by Robert Trent Jones. Excursions include tee times for 18 holes at one of these challenging courses as well as carts. A taxi to and from the courses may be extra and club rental is about $30 extra. The golf excursions are often sold directly through an onboard golf pro who organizes lessons on the ship too.

ON YOUR OWN: A WALKING TOUR OF HAMILTON

Hamilton has been the capital of Bermuda since 1815, when it replaced St. George's, and was once known as the "Show Window of the British Empire." Today, it's the economic hub of the island. Following is a walking tour that introduces you to all that's noteworthy in Hamilton.

Start at the harbor front at the:

1. **Visitors Service Bureau/Ferry Terminal.** Pick up some free maps and brochures of the island here.

From the bureau, you'll emerge onto **Front Street,** Hamilton's main street and shopping area. Before 1946, there were no cars here, but today its busy traffic includes small autos, buses, mopeds, bicycles, and horse-drawn carriages.

Walk directly south of the Ferry Terminal toward the water, taking a short side street between the Visitors Service Bureau and the large Bank of Bermuda. You'll come to:

2. **Albouy's Point,** a small grassy park with benches and trees that open onto a panoramic vista of the boat- and ship-filled slip. Nearby is the Royal Bermuda Yacht Club, an elite rendezvous for both the Bermudian and the American yachting set since the 1930s.

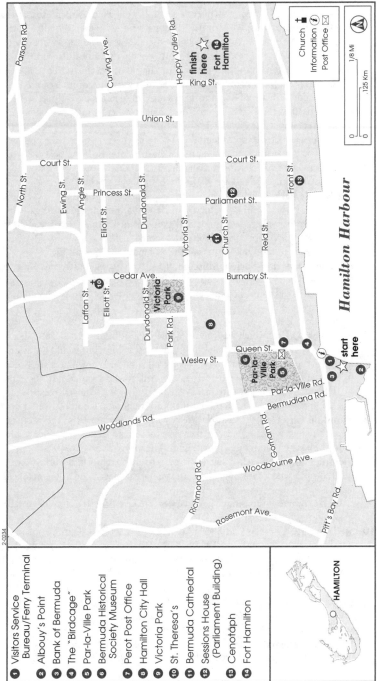

Hamilton Harbour

Church
Information
Post Office

finish here — Fort Hamilton

start here

1. Visitors Service Bureau/Ferry Terminal
2. Albouy's Point
3. Bank of Bermuda
4. The "Birdcage"
5. Par-la-Ville Park
6. Bermuda Historical Society Museum
7. Perot Post Office
8. Hamilton City Hall
9. Victoria Park
10. St. Theresa's
11. Bermuda Cathedral
12. Sessions House (Parliament Building)
13. Cenotaph
14. Fort Hamilton

HAMILTON

2-0234

After taking in the view, walk directly north, crossing Point Pleasant Road, to the:

3. Bank of Bermuda, open Monday through Friday 9:30am to 3pm. Here is Bermuda's most extensive coin collection—there's at least one sample of every coin minted in the U.K. since the reign of King James I in the early 17th century. You'll also see Bermuda's famous money, called "hog money." In use since the early 1600s, the hog coin is stamped on one side with the ill-fated *Sea Venture* and on the other side with a wild hog, the main source of food for the early settlers.

Now, head east along Front Street to the point where it intersects with Queen Street. Here is:

4. The Birdcage, the perch in the middle of the intersection from which police direct traffic. It's the most photographed sight in Bermuda. If the bobby directing traffic is a man, he'll likely be wearing Bermuda shorts.

Next, continue north along Queen Street until you reach:

5. Par-la-Ville Park, which was once a private garden attached to the townhouse of William B. Perot, the first postmaster of Bermuda, who designed the gardens in the 19th century. He collected rare and exotic plants from all over the globe, including the Indian rubber tree, which was seeded in 1847.

Also opening onto Queen Street at the entrance to the park is the:

6. Bermuda Historical Society Museum, 13 Queen Street, which is also the Bermuda library. Here you'll find curiosities, including cedar furniture, collections of antique silver and china, hog money, a 1775 letter from George Washington, and other things.

Next door is the:

7. Perot Post Office, which was run by William Perot from 1818 to 1862. It's said that he'd go down to collect mail from the clipper ships, but would put it under his top hat to maintain his dignity. As he strolled through town, he'd greet friends by tipping his hat, and thereby deliver the mail, too. He started printing stamps in 1848 and today they're extremely valuable (only 11 are known to exist).

Continue onto Queen Street, and then turn right onto Church Street to reach:

8. Hamilton City Hall, 17 Church Street, which dates from 1960 and is crowned by a white tower. The bronze weather vane on top is a replica of the *Sea Venture*.

In the back of Hamilton City Hall, opening onto Victoria Street, lies:

9. Victoria Park, a cool, refreshing 4-acre oasis frequented by office workers on their lunch break. It has a sunken garden, ornamental shrubbery, and a Victorian bandstand.

Cedar Avenue is the eastern boundary of Victoria Park. If you follow it north for 2 blocks, you'll reach:

10. St. Theresa's, a Roman Catholic cathedral that's open daily 8am to 7pm and for Sunday services. Dating from 1927, its architecture was inspired by the Spanish Mission style. It's one of a half-dozen Roman Catholic churches in Bermuda. Its gold-and-silver chalice was a gift from Pope Paul VI when he visited the island in 1986.

After seeing the cathedral, retrace your steps south along Cedar Avenue until you reach Victoria Street. Cedar now becomes Burnaby Street; continue south on this street until you come to Church Street and then turn left, until you see:

11. Bermuda Cathedral, or the Cathedral of the Most Holy Trinity as it is sometimes called. This neo-Gothic church is the seat of the Anglican Church of Bermuda.

When you leave the cathedral, continue east along Church Street to:

12. Sessions House (Parliament Building), on Parliament Street, between Reid and Church streets. It's open to the public Monday through Friday (9am to 12:30pm and 2 to 5pm). On Fridays you can see Bermuda's political process in action, with the speaker wearing a full wig and a black robe. Bermuda has the third oldest parliament in the world, after Iceland's and England's.

Continue walking south along Parliament Street until you approach Front Street, where you should turn left toward the:

13. Cenotaph, a memorial to Bermuda's dead in both world wars.

From here, continue east along Front Street until you reach King Street, and then head north to Happy Valley Road. Go right until you see the entrance (on your right) to:

14. Fort Hamilton, an imposing old fortress on the eastern outskirts of Hamilton. The Duke of Wellington ordered its construction to protect Hamilton Harbour. It offers panoramic views of the city and harbor, although with its moat and 18-ton guns, the fort was outdated before it was even completed.

ON YOUR OWN: A WALKING TOUR OF ST. GEORGE'S

St. George's was the second English town to be established in the new world, after Jamestown in Virginia. King's Square, also called Market Square or the King's Parade, is the center of life here, and it's just steps from where the cruise ships dock. From here you can begin the following walking tour, which takes you to all the major sights in this most quaint and historical of towns.

1. King's Square is about 200 years old, and it's not as historic as St. George's itself. This was formerly a marshy part of the harbor—at least when the shipwrecked passengers and crew of the *Sea Venture* first saw it. On the square, notice a replica of the pillory and stocks that were formerly used to punish criminals (and in many cases, the innocent).

From the square, head south across the small bridge to:

2. Ordnance Island, jutting into St. George's Harbour. The British once stored gunpowder and cannons here, but today the island houses the *Deliverance,* a replica of the vessel that carried the shipwrecked *Sea Venture* passengers on to Virginia. Alongside the ship is a ducking stool, a contraption used in 17th-century witch trials.

Retrace your steps across the bridge to King's Square. On the waterside stands the:

3. White Horse Tavern, a restaurant jutting out into St. George's Harbour (consider it for lunch or a drink). It was once the home of John Davenport, who came to Bermuda in 1815 to open a dry-goods store. Turns out Davenport was a bit of a miser: Upon his death, some 75,000 English pounds' worth of gold and silver were discovered stashed away in his cellar.

Across the square stands the:

4. Town Hall, the meeting place of the corporation governing St. George's. Inside, a multimedia audiovisual presentation is shown several times a day.

From King's Square, head east along King Street, cutting north on Bridge Street. There you'll come to the:

5. Bridge House, 1 Bridge Street. Constructed shortly after 1700, this was once the home of several governors of Bermuda. Furnished with 18th- and 19th-century antiques, it's now home to an art gallery and souvenir shop.

Return to King Street and continue east to the:

6. Old State House, which actually opens onto Princess Street, at the top of King Street. This is the oldest stone building in Bermuda, dating from 1620, and was once the home of the Bermuda Parliament.

Continue your stroll down Princess Street until you come to Duke of York Street and the entrance to:

7. Somers Gardens. The heart of Sir George Somers, the admiral of the *Sea Venture,* is buried there.

Walk through Somers Gardens and up the steps to the North Gate onto the Blockade Alley. If you look up the hill, you'll see what is known as the "the folly of St. George's," the:

8. Unfinished Cathedral, which was intended to replace St. Peter's (see below). Work began in 1874, but eventually came to an end; the church was beset by financial difficulties and a schism in the Anglican congregation.

After viewing the ruins, turn left onto Duke of Kent Street, which leads down to the:

9. St. George's Historical Society Museum, at the intersection of Featherbed Alley and Duke of Kent Street. An example of 18th-century architecture, the house has a collection of Bermudian historical artifacts and cedar furniture.

Around the corner on Featherbed Alley is the:

10. Featherbed Alley Printery, which has a working replica of the type of printing press invented by Johann Gutenberg in Germany in the 1450s.

Go up Featherbed Alley and straight onto Church Street. At the junction with Broad Lane, look to your right to see the:

11. Old Rectory, at the head of Broad Alley, behind St. Peter's Church. Now a private home administered by the National Trust, it was built in 1705 by a reformed pirate. It's open on Wednesdays only from noon to 5pm.

Next, go through the back of the churchyard entrance, opposite Broad Alley, to reach:

12. St. Peter's Church. The church's main entrance is on Duke of York Street. This is believed to be the oldest Anglican place of worship in the western hemisphere. In the churchyard, some headstones date back some 300 years. The present church was built in 1713.

Across the street is the:

13. Bermuda National Trust Museum. Once the Globe Hotel, headquarters of Major Norman Walker, the Confederate representative in Bermuda, today it houses relics from the island's involvement in the American Civil War (from Bermuda's perspective).

As you continue west along Duke of York Street, you'll reach **Barber's Lane,** which honors Joseph Hayne Rainey, a former slave from South Carolina who was a barber in St. George's before eventually returning to the States to be elected the first black member of the U.S. House of Representatives. Nearby is **Petticoat Lane,** also known as Silk Alley. The name dates from the 1834 emancipation, when two former slave women who'd always wanted silk petticoats like their former mistresses finally got some—and then paraded up and down the lane to show off their new finery.

Continue until you reach:

14. Tucker House, which opens onto Water Street. This was the former home of a prominent Bermudian family, and now houses an excellent collection of antiques.

Diagonally across from the Tucker House is the:

15. Carriage Museum, 22 Water St. Here are some of the most interesting carriages used in Bermuda until 1946, when the automobile arrived.

End your tour across the street at:

16. Somers Wharf, a multimillion-dollar waterfront restoration project that includes shops, restaurants, and taverns.

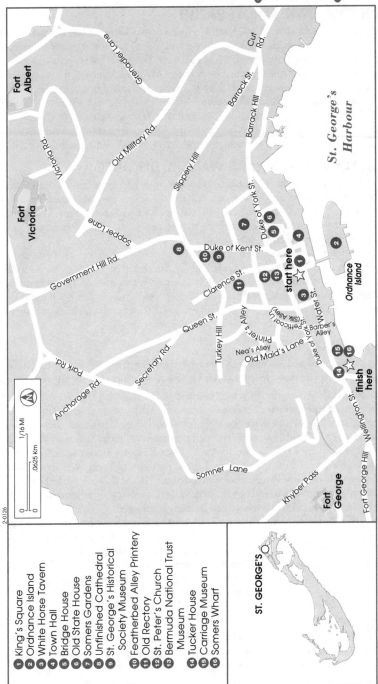

St. George's Harbour

Ordnance Island

start here

finish here

Fort Albert

Fort Victoria

Fort George

1/16 MI
.0625 Km

2-0126

1 King's Square
2 Ordnance Island
3 White Horse Tavern
4 Town Hall
5 Bridge House
6 Old State House
7 Somers Gardens
8 Unfinished Cathedral
9 St. George's Historical Society Museum
10 Featherbed Alley Printery
11 Old Rectory
12 St. Peter's Church
13 Bermuda National Trust Museum
14 Tucker House
15 Carriage Museum
16 Somers Wharf

ST. GEORGE'S

ON YOUR OWN: SANDYS PARISH

If your ship docks at the Royal Naval Dockyard on the west end, you can walk to the sprawling complex there. Constructed by convict labor, this 19th-century fortress was used by the British Navy until 1951 as a strategic dockyard. Today, it's a major tourist attraction and its centerpiece is the Bermuda Maritime Museum, the most important and extensive museum on the island. Exhibits are housed in six large halls within the complex, and the displays all relate to Bermuda's long connection with the sea, from Spanish exploration to 20th-century ocean liners. You can have a look at maps, ship models, and artifacts like gold bars, pottery, jewelry, and silver coins recovered from the 16th- and 17th-century shipwrecks, like the *Sea Venture*. A visit is a must.

ON YOUR OWN: BEYOND WALKING DISTANCE

A mile or two from King's Square in St. George's, overlooking the beach where the shipwrecked crew of the *Sea Venture* came ashore in 1609, is **Fort St. Catherine,** which you'll want to see. Completed in 1614 and reconstructed several times after, it was named for the patron saint of wheelwrights and carpenters. The fortress houses a museum, with several worthwhile exhibits.

The **Bermuda Railway Trail,** in Sandys Parish, stretches for 21 miles. It was created along the course of the old Bermuda Railway, which served the island from 1931 to 1948, until the automobile was introduced. Armed with a copy of the *Bermuda Railway Trail Guide,* available at the various visitors centers, you can set out on your own expedition via foot or bicycle (most of the moped/scooter rental agencies rent bicycles as well). Most of the trail winds along a car-free route.

SHOPPING

You'll get quality and lots of British items, but don't expect great deals. Nothing in Bermuda is cheap, but keep your eyes peeled for sales, especially at the department stores.

HAMILTON   Hamilton offers the best and widest shopping choices on the island. **Front and Queen streets** have dozens of shops and department stores, most specializing in English items such as porcelain, crystal, wool clothing, and linens. **Trimingham's** and **H.A. & E. Smith,** two popular department stores on Front Street, as well as other nearby boutiques, sell Waterford, Baccarat, Kosta-Boda, Orrefors, and Galway crystal vases, wine glasses, bowls, and curios; Lalique porcelain figurines; Wedgwood, Royal Doulton, Royal Copenhagen, Spode, Aynsley, and Royal Worcester fine bone china dinnerware, vases, bowls, and curios; Shetland, lamb's wool, and cashmere sweaters and skirts from Scotland and England; and Burberry's rainwear.

Archie Brown on Front Street and the **Scottish Wool Shop** on Queen Street specialize in sweaters, woolens, and tartans of all kinds. **A. S. Cooper & Sons** on Front Street is the island's oldest and largest china and glassware store—it has it all. The **Irish Linen Shop** on the corner of Queen and Front streets sells pure Irish linen tablecloths and hand towels. For antique prints, engravings, and magazine illustrations, check out **Pegasus,** across from the Hamilton Princess Hotel on Pitts Bay Road. Many other stores along and adjacent to Front Street sell clothing, arts and crafts, and souvenirs.

ST. GEORGE'S   You'll find many shops selling the same types of items as in Hamilton, including branches of famous Front Street stores. You'll find it all on **King's Square,** the **Somers Wharf** complex, and **Water Street.** But if you're a hardcore shopper, don't miss out on Hamilton, which is Bermuda's shopping mecca.

SPORTS

GOLF   Bermuda has more courses per square mile than any other place in the world. They're all easily accessible via taxi, and your ship will likely have organized excursions to them if you'd rather not go it alone. The following are all 18-hole courses. The par-70, 5,777-yard course at the **Belmont Hotel Golf & Country Club,** Warwick Parish (☎ **441/236-6400**), was designed in 1923 by Emmett Devereux, a Scotsman. It's been challenging golfers ever since, especially its par-5 11th hole, a severe dogleg left with a blind tee shot. **Castle Harbour Golf Club,** Hamilton Parish (☎ **441/298-6959**), is a par-71, 6,440-yard course designed by the noted golf architect Charles Banks and known for its challenging tee shots. This is one of the more expensive course to play on. The par-71, 6,565-yard **Port Royal Golf Course,** Southampton Parish (☎ **441/238-9430**), was designed by Robert Trent Jones and lies along an ocean terrain. It's a public course and ranks among the very best on the island—as a matter of fact, it's rated among the best in the *world.* Jack Nicklaus likes to play here. **Southampton Princess Golf Club,** Hamilton Parish (☎ **441/239-6952**), is a par-54, 2,684-yard course with elevated tees, strategically placed bunkers, and an array of water hazards to challenge even the most experienced golfers. **St. George's Golf Club,** St. George's Parish (☎ **441/297-8067**), is one of the island's newest and best. This par-62, 4,043-yard course, designed by Robert Trent Jones, is within walking distance of historic St. George's.

SCUBA DIVING   To see some of Bermuda's shipwrecks, **Blue Water Divers Co., Ltd.,** Robinson's Marina, Southampton (☎ **441/234-1034**) is Bermuda's oldest and largest full-service scuba-diving operation. All equipment is provided; reservations are necessary.

BEACHES

Bermuda is known for its beaches, and there are many powdery soft beaches (not really pink as they're touted—or maybe I'm just color-blind) easily accessible by taxi or motorscooter. **Horseshoe Bay** in Southampton Parish and **Elbow Beach** in Paget Parish are very popular and often crowded public beaches, and the many unnamed slivers of silky beach tucked into the jagged coastline are worth discovering. Hotel beaches are generally private. (Elbow Beach charges $4 for visitors; the adjacent Elbow Beach Hotel offers facilities and rentals. Horseshoe Bay is a free public beach and has a place to get snacks.)

Also consider these public beaches: **Astwood Cove** (Warwick Parish) is remote and rarely overcrowded—ditto for **Chaplin Bay** (Warwick and Southampton Parishes); **Warwick Long Bay** (Warwick Parish) is popular and set against a backdrop of scrubland and low grasses; and **Tobacco Bay Beach** (St. George's Parish), is popular and the most frequented beach on St. George's Island.

GREAT LOCAL RESTAURANTS & BARS

You don't go to Bermuda for its cuisine, but there are some tasty local specialties, such as fish chowder laced with rum and sherry peppers (yum!!) as well as spiny Bermuda lobster, mussel pie, and wahoo steak.

IN HAMILTON   Try the **Waterloo House,** Pitts Bay Road (☎ **441/295-4480**), at the elegant Relais Châteaux hotel, within walking distance of the ship docks. Lunch is served on the outdoor patio overlooking the colorful and idyllic harbor, and many snazzy-looking business people lunch here. The fish chowder is great. The **Lobster Pot & Boat House Bar,** 6 Bermudian Rd. (☎ **441/292-6898**), serves a great baked fish and lobster dish. The **Hog Penney,** 5 Burnaby Hill (☎ **441/292-2534**), is Bermuda's most famous pub and a great choice for lunch. With its dark paneled walls and classic pub ambience, you'll think you're in merry old England. The fresh fish and chips is a good choice, along with a cool pint of ale.

IN ST. GEORGE'S   Don't miss a meal at the **Black Horse Tavern,** 101 St. David's Road (☎ **441/297-1991**), for an authentic taste of Bermuda—or so the locals maintain.

Order curried conch stew or fish chowder, among many other options. The **White Horse Tavern,** King's Square (☎ **441/297-1838**), is the oldest in St. George's and a favorite casual hangout with tourists. There's a terrace with great views of the square and all the hubbub below. Have a beer and a burger.

2 The Panama Canal

The Panama Canal is an awesome feat of engineering and human effort. Constructed over many years, starting in 1880, it was completed in 1914 at the expense of thousands of lives, and the vast majority of the original structure and equipment is still in use. Transiting the Canal, which links the Atlantic Ocean with the Pacific, is a thrill for anyone even vaguely interested in engineering or history.

Transiting the canal takes one day, generally about 8 hours from start to finish, and it's a fascinating procedure (it often costs ships about $100,000 to pass through; the fee is based on a ship's weight). Your ship will line up in the morning, mostly with cargo ships, to await its turn through the canal. The route is about 50 miles long and includes passage through three main locks, which, through gravity alone, raise ships over Central America and down again on the other side. Between the locks, ships pass through artificially created lakes like the massive **Gatun Lake,** 85 feet above sea level.

While transiting, your ship will feature a running narration of history and facts about the canal by an expert on board for the day.

Cruises that include a canal crossing are generally 10 to 14 nights long, with popular routes between Florida and Acapulco, visiting a handful of Caribbean islands along the way as well as a few ports in Central America, including Panama's San Blas Islands, Costa Rica's Puerto Caldera, and Guatemala's Puerto Quetzal, in addition to other ports along the coast of Mexico.

SHIPS TRANSITING THE PANAMA CANAL   For 2000, 19 ships will be sailing itineraries that include transits of the Panama Canal: American Canadian Caribbean's *Grande Caribe,* Carnival's *Jubilee,* Celebrity's *Zenith,* Crystal's *Harmony* and *Symphony,* Cunard's *QE2,* Holland America's *Maasdam* and *Nieuw Amsterdam,* Mediterranean Shipping's *Melody,* Norwegian's *Norwegian Majesty,* Princess's *Crown Princess* and *Sun Princess,* Radisson's *Radisson Diamond* and *Seven Seas Navigator,* Regal's *Regal Empress,* Royal Caribbean's *Vision of the Seas,* Royal Olympic's *Stella Solaris,* Seabourn's *Seabourn Legend* and *Seabourn Pride.* See the cruise line reviews in chapters 6–9 for details.

PORTS ALONG THE CANAL ROUTE

The **San Blas Islands** are a beautiful archipelago and home to the Kuna Indians, whose women are well known for their colorful, hand-embroidered stitching. If you get a chance to go ashore, the women, dressed in their traditional *molas* (brightly and intricately embroidered blouses), sell all manner of embroidered molas in square blocks and strips. They make great pillow covers or wall hangings, and cost about $5 to $10 each. When your ship anchors offshore at the islands, be prepared for throngs of Kunas to emerge from the far-off distance, paddling their dugout canoes (a few have motors) up to the ship, where they will spend the entire day calling for money or anything else ship

Canal Trivia

A treaty signed between the United States and Panama in 1977 stipulated that canal operations would be passed from U.S. into Panamanian hands at the stroke of midnight on December 31, 1999, the start of the new millennium.

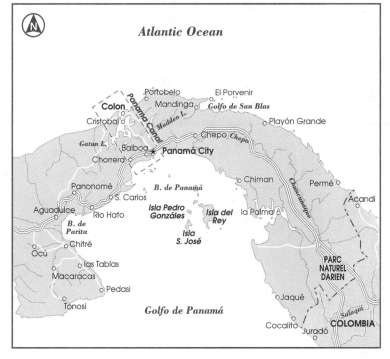

passengers toss overboard. The Kuna seem to enjoy diving overboard to retrieve fruit or coins thrown to them, but of course, it's a sad sight too, watching entire families so desperate and needy.

In **Costa Rica,** many ships call at Puerto Caldera on the Pacific side or Puerto Limón on the Atlantic side. While there's nothing to see from either cargo port, both are great jumping-off points for tours that all visiting ships offer of the country's lush, beautiful rainforests, which are alive with some 850 species of birds, 200 species of mammals, 9,000 species of flowering plants, and about 35,000 species of insects. After a scenic bus ride, tours will take you on a nature walk through the forest.

In **Guatemala,** most Panama Canal–bound ships call at Puerto Quetzal, on the Pacific Coast; a few may call at Santo Tomas on the Caribbean side. Both are used as gateways to Guatemala's spectacular Mayan ruins at Tikal. They're the country's most famous attractions and considered the most spectacular yet discovered anywhere in the world, with over 3,000 temples, pyramids, and other buildings of the ancient civilization nestled in thick jungle. Much of it is still uncovered. The setting is surreal. Some of the ruins date as far back as A.D. 300. Excursions here are neither cheap nor easy, but the journey is well worth the effort. A tour involves buses, walking, and a 1-hour flight; expect to pay about $350-plus. Excursions to the less-spectacular Mayan sites in Honduras are also offered from Puerto Quetzal, as are several overland tours of Guatemala's interior.

Part 4

Appendixes

With information on end-of-cruise concerns such as tipping, disembarking, and retrieving your luggage, plus sample daily activity calendars for all the lines and an index by ship name.

Appendix A: Cruise Price Comparisons

Figuring out the price of a cruise is rarely a simple task—it's like driving in some foreign place without a·map. Why? Because prices listed in the cruise lines' brochures are notoriously unreliable—they're what the lines would *like* to get for their cabins, but the prices you'll actually pay after cruise line and travel agent discounts will be anywhere from 10 to 50 percent less.

To give you an accurate look at what you can really expect to pay, I asked travel agency giant The Travel Company to provide the rates in the following pages, which represent the **actual discounted rates** consumers were paying through The Travel Company for late January 2000 sailings as this book went to press (June 1999). Other travel agencies may also be able to obtain similar rates. Remember that rates are always subject to the basic principles of supply and demand, so those listed here are meant as a guide only and are in no way etched in stone—the price you pay may be higher or even lower, depending on how far ahead you book, when you choose to travel, whether there are any special discounts being offered by the lines, and a slew of other factors.

The following pages offers prices for the following three basic types of accommodations:

- Lowest-category inside cabins (without windows)
- Lowest-category outside cabins (with windows)
- Lowest-category suites

Remember that cruise ships generally have several different categories of cabins within each of these three basic divisions, all priced differently, and that the prices I've listed represent the *lowest* categories for inside and outside cabins and suites. If you're interested in booking a roomier, higher-level cabin in any category, you'll find the price will be higher. In general, the cost of a top-level inside cabin will probably be very close to the rate for a low-level outside cabin, and the cost of a top-level outside may be very close to the rate for a low-level suite. See chapters 2 and 5 for more information on pricing and choosing your cabin.

To contact **The Travel Company,** call ☎ **800/242-9000** or visit their Website at **www.travelco.com.** All rates are cruise only; per person and based on double occupancy. Offers are capacity controlled and may be withdrawn by the cruise lines without notice. Fares reflected may vary depending on sailing date and are shown to provide the average level discount which can be obtained by booking through The Travel Company. Rates include port charges; government fees and taxes are additional. Other restrictions may apply.

Brochure Prices vs. Sample Actual Prices*					
Line	Ship	Itinerary (night/region)**	Lowest Inside (brochure/actual)	Lowest Outside (brochure/actual)	Lowest Suite (brochure/actual)
ACCL	Grande Caribe	11/PC	$2,151	$2,151	N/A
	Grande Mariner	11/C	$1,942	$1,942	N/A
	Niagara Prince	6/Bel	$1,038	$1,058	N/A
Cape Canaveral	Dolphin IV	2/C	$259/$199	$309/$269	$369/$339
		4/C	$469/$369	$549/$509	$669/$619
Carnival	Carnival Destiny	7/E or W	$1,629/$949	$1,879/$1,079	$2,779/$2,430
	Carnival Triumph	7/E or W	$1,629/$949	$1,879/$1,079	$2,779/$2,430
	Celebration	7/C	$1,329/$899	$1,579/$1,009	$2,679/$1,950
	Ecstasy	3/C	$689/$329	$779/$389	$1,039/$899
	Fantasy	3/C	$689/$329	$779/$389	$1,039/$899
	Fascination	7/E	$1,329/$799	$1,579/$909	$2,379/$1,950
	Imagination	4/W	$849/$449	$979/$509	$1,279/$979
	Inspiration	7/S	$1,329/$799	$1,579/$909	$2,379/$1,950
	Jubilee	10/E & S	$1,689/$995	$1,839/$1,104	$2,939/$2,650
	Paradise	7/E or W	$1,329/$899	$1,579/$1,009	$2,379/$1,950
	Sensation	7/E	$1,329/$799	$1,579/$909	$2,379/$1,950
	Tropicale	4/W	$849/$449	$979/$509	$1,379/$979
Celebrity	Century	7/E or W	$1,795/$899	$2,225/$1,049	$3,825/$3,210
	Galaxy	7/S	$1,795/$879	$2,225/$1,029	$3,825/$3,210
	Horizon	10/E & S	$2,345/$1,384	$2,745/$1,548	$4,195/$3,412
	Mercury	7/W	$1,795/$899	$2,225/$1,049	$3,825/$3,210
	Zenith	10/PC	$2,645/$1,499	$3,045/$1,999	$4,645/$3,412
		7/Ber	$1,995/$1,049	$2,445/$1,174	$4,195/$2,912
Clipper	Nantucket Clipper	7/E	N/A	$1,950/$1,352	N/A
	Yorktown Clipper	7/E	N/A	$1,950/$1,352	N/A
Club Med	Club Med II	7/C	N/A	$1,260/$960	N/A
Commodore	Enchanted Capri	2/W	$389/$299	$439/$369	$519/$464
		5/W	$975/$589	$1,095/$654	$1,300/$1,064
	Enchanted Isle	7/W	$1,250/$699	$1,500/$819	$1,840/$1,562
Costa	CostaRomantica	7/E or W	$1,099/$720	$1,529/$980	$2,729/$2,460
	CostaVictoria	7/E or W	$1,199/$720	$1,529/$980	$2,829/$2,460
Crystal	Crystal Harmony	11/PC	$4,030/$2,215	$4,410/$2,860	$6,210/$5,050
	Crystal Symphony	10/E	$4,595/$3,480	$4,785/$3,625	$7,995/$6,815

Line	Ship	Itinerary (night/region)**	Lowest Inside (brochure/actual)	Lowest Outside (brochure/actual)	Lowest Suite (brochure/actual)
Cunard	Caronia	14/PC	N/A	$3,930/$3,210	$9,950/$9,312
	QE2	7/E	$1,150/$909	$1,640/$1,132	$3,420/$3,133
Disney	Disney Magic	3/B	$619/$494	$1,184/$984	$1,894/$1,575
		4/B	$729/$579	$1,294/$1,069	$2,019/$1,865
		7/B & land	$1,199/$949	$1,874/$1,549	$2,925/$2,724
	Disney Wonder	3/B	$619/$494	$1,184/$984	$1,894/$1,575
		4/B	$729/$579	$1,294/$1,069	$2,019/$1,865
		7/B & land	$1,199/$949	$1,874/$1,549	$2,925/$2,724
Holland America	Maasdam	10/C	$2,599/$1,262	$2,989/$1,414	$5,889/$3,304
	Nieuw Amsterdam	14/S	$3,249/$1,599	$3,669/$1,804	$4,599/$3,015
	Noordam	10/PC	$2,369/$1,399	$2,869/$1,614	$3,649/$2,094
	Ryndam	7/W	$1,859/$969	$2,069/$1,174	$4,069/$2,340
	Veendam	7/E or W	$1,859/$969	$2,069/$1,174	$4,069/$2,340
	Westerdam	7/E	$1,579/$838	$1,819/$998	$3,799/$2,189
Mediterranean Shipping	Melody	12/E	$1,265/$920	$1,775/$1,040	$2,925/$1,870
Norwegian	Norway	7/E	$1,269/$669	$1,819/$1,119	$2,319/$1,647
	Norwegian Dream	7/S	$1,569/$1,049	$1,869/$1,149	$2,669/$1,499
	Norwegian Majesty	10/PC	$2,009/$1,319	$2,409/$1,629	$3,059/$1,828
		7/Ber	$1,889/$999	$2,139/$1,209	$3,339/$2,878
	Norwegian Sea	7/W	$1,569/$889	$1,869/$1,069	$2,619/$1,769
	Norwegian Wind	7/W	$1,569/$1,049	$1,869/$1,149	$2,669/$1,499
Premier	Big Red Boat	3/B	$599/$329	$709/$409	$849/$687
		4/B	$699/$389	$909/$487	$1,109/$917
	Rembrandt	7/E	$1,198/$799	$1,498/$917	$2,298/$1,978
	SeaBreeze	7/W	$1,198/$799	$1,498/$917	$2,298/$1,978
Princess	Crown Princess	10/PC	$2,968/$1,549	$3,268/$1,749	$4,518/$2,374
	Dawn Princess	7/S	$1,733/$949	$2,273/$1,248	$2,873/$1,549
	Grand Princess	7/E	$2,018/$1,089	$2,358/$1,289	$2,958/$1,599
	Pacific Princess	7/Ber	$1,918/$1,099	$2,258/$1,249	$3,222/$2,249
	Sea Princess	7/W	$1,733/$969	$2,273/$1,248	$2,873/$1,549
	Sun Princess	10/PC	$2,728/$1,499	$3,386/$1,999	$6,239/$2,374
Radisson	Radisson Diamond	6/E	N/A	$3,595/$1,795	$4,295/$2,195

Brochure Prices vs. Sample Actual Prices* (continued)

Line	Ship	Itinerary (nights/region)**	Lowest Inside (brochure/actual)	Lowest Outside (brochure/actual)	Lowest Suite (brochure/actual)
Regal	Regal Empress	7/W	$1,031/$599	$1,291/$699	$1,631/$1,449
Royal Caribbean	Enchantment of the Seas	7/E or W	$1,399/$949	$1,849/$1,199	$2,399/$1,878
	Grandeur of the Seas	7/E	$1,399/$949	$1,849/$1,199	$2,399/$1,878
	Legend of the Seas	14/PC	$3,149/$1,699	$3,699/$2,249	$4,449/$2,109
	Majesty of the Seas	7/W	$1,399/$899	$1,699/$999	$2,399/$1,878
	Monarch of the Seas	7/S	$1,399/$899	$1,699/$999	$2,399/$1,878
	Nordic Empress	3/W	$599/$419	$849/$509	$1,249/$1,019
		7/Ber	$1,499/$989	$1,899/$1,148	$3,299/$2,893
	Sovereign of the Seas	3/B	$599/$369	$849/$479	$1,249/$1,019
	Splendour of the Seas	10/W & S	$1,999/$1,329	$2,499/$1,549	$3,049/$2,109
	Vision of the Seas	10/PC	$2,199/$1,399	$3,099/$1,899	$4,049/$2,499
Royal Olympic	Stella Solaris	11/W	$2,765/$1,936	$3,755/$2,629	$4,690/$3,283
Seabourn	Seabourn Goddess I	5/E	N/A	$2,920/$2,628	$5,690/$5,121
	Seabourn Goddess II	5/E	N/A	$2,920/$2,628	$5,690/$5,121
	Seabourn Legend	7/E	N/A	N/A	$2,990/$2,691
	Seabourn Pride	7/E	N/A	N/A	$2,990/$2,691
Star Clippers	Star Clipper	7/E	$1,457/$960	$1,825/$1,170	$2,525/$2,102
Tall Ship Adventures	Sir Francis Drake	7/E	N/A	$995/$986	$1,395/$1,381
Windjammer	Amazing Grace	13/E & S	N/A	$1,450/$1,435	$3,050/$3,020
	Flying Cloud	6/E	N/A	$975/$860	$1,175/$980
	Legacy	6/E	N/A	$1,075/$860	$1,325/$980
	Mandalay	6/E	N/A	$975/$860	$1,175/$980
	Polynesia	6/E	N/A	$975/$860	$1,175/$980
	Yankee Clipper	6/E	N/A	$975/$860	$1,075/$980
Windstar	Wind Spirit	7/E	N/A	$3,880/$2,402	N/A
	Wind Star	7/Bel	N/A	$3,880/$2,402	N/A
	Wind Surf	7/E	N/A	$3,880/$2,402	N/A

** *Abbreviations used for itineraries: C = Caribbean, E = Eastern Caribbean, W = Western Caribbean, S = Southern Caribbean, B = Bahamas, Ber = Bermuda, Bel = Belize, PC = Panama Canal*

Appendix B: Sample Daily Calendars & Menus

In your average workaday life you do 1,001 little things every day. You walk the dog, recharge the cel phone, iron your suit, recharge the dog, walk the cel phone . . . it's overwhelming, really. That's why you're going on a cruise. Get away from it all for a while. Take it easy.

Or is it? Do you really intend to hole up in a deck chair, slathered with tanning oil, a floppy canvas hat perched on your head and a copy of the latest John Grisham propped on your tan line? Or are you planning to ditch that act as soon as you step aboard, pull out the Armani tux (or your newest Helmut Lang dress) and head out to sample the 1,001 excitements available aboard today's cruise ships. I can see you now, leaning beguilingly against the lounge bar. *Hello. Haven't seen you on this ship before* . . .

The decision is yours: You can do absolutely nothing or absolutely everything. Whatever your intention, there's a ship out there for you, and plenty where the onboard atmosphere changes depending on the time of day, giving you the broadest possible experience for your buck.

In this section I've reproduced sample daily activity calendars for nearly all the lines I've profiled and listed a representative selection of dinner main courses as well. Understand that this is a *sample:* Each day of your cruise will be different; some of the activities I've listed might not be scheduled during your trip, and many that I haven't listed probably will. Also note that some activities will actually take place more often than it says in these pages. For instance, a movie that I've listed at 2:30pm may also be showing at 6, 9, and 11pm. My intention here was simply to give you an idea of the kind of activities you might encounter in a typical day aboard a particular line.

A few of the smaller lines—American Canadian Caribbean, Tall Ship Adventures, and Windjammer—don't publish activity calendars at all. On these ships, it's the cruise itself, or the ports of call visited, that draws passengers in. Talent shows and Vegas-style entertainment are simply not part of the equation. I've included sample main courses for Windjammer and Tall Ship Adventures, but American Canadian's bootstrap ethos doesn't even allow this: On their ships, menus are posted on blackboards in the dining rooms during every meal. This in itself should give you some idea of the kind of line ACCL is.

So delve in. Imagine waking up in your stateroom and reaching down to grab the calendar that's been slipped under your door while you slept. The day stretches out before you like a vast, unexplored continent. You've only to step out on deck . . .

⊂ CAPE CANAVERAL
≈≈ C R U I S E   L I N E

DAY AT SEA

6:30am	Early bird coffee
7:30am	Shore Excursion Office opens for last-minute sale of all tours
8am	The pool opens
8am	*Dolphin IV* arrives in Freeport, The Bahamas
8am–8pm	Ping-Pong tables and shuffleboard courts are open
10am	Morning movie
12:30–2:30pm	The sounds of the islands
2pm	Ping-Pong tournament
2pm	Afternoon movie
2:30pm	Line dance—learn a new step
2:45pm	Trivia, trivia! Test your knowledge for fun and prizes
3–4pm	The sounds of the islands
3:30pm	Important disembarkation talk
3:30pm	All aboard! The *Dolphin* sails for Port Canaveral at 4pm
3:30–8pm	Beauty salon and massage therapy
4pm	Pool games—Fun in the sun with your cruise staff
4:30pm	Horse racing
5pm	Art auction at sea
5pm	The Casino and gift shop open
5pm	Trapshooting on the high seas
5pm	Tour of the Navigation Bridge
5–6pm	Formal portraits taken
5:30pm	First seating, Captain's Reception
7:30pm	Second seating, Captain's Reception
7:30–8:15pm	Live entertainment
8:45pm	First seating, Grand Farewell showtime. An evening of entertainment in the Rendezvous Lounge.
9:30pm–1:30am	Dance to the sounds of live music
10pm	Snowball jackpot bingo
10:30pm	Dance till the wee hours
10:45pm	Second seating, Grand Farewell showtime
11:30pm	The disco is the place to meet
Midnight	A night at the movies

Dining Hours: Breakfast Buffet 7–10am • Breakfast 7am, 8:15am • Buffet Lunch noon–2:30pm • Lunch noon–2pm • Coffee, Tea & Cookies 4–5pm • Dinner 6pm, 8:15pm • Buffet Magnifique midnight–1am

Dress for the Evening: Semiformal (jacket and tie requested for men)

DINNER MAIN COURSES

Filet of Tilapia • *sautéed in butter, fresh lemon juice, green peppercorn, and lime sauce*

Coq-au-Vin Chambertin • *tender young chicken braised in a robust sauce of red wine with pearl onions*

Veal Schnitzel Modena • *milk-fed veal dusted with Parmigiana, sautéed in butter, glazed with the chef's special sauce and served with fettuccine*

Roast Leg of Lamb • *leg of U.S. spring lamb marinated and roasted, served in its own juices*

Tenderloin of Beef Brillat-Savarin • *sliced center-cut of beef tenderloin, served with Béarnaise and Bordelaise sauces*

Exotic Vegetable Cannelloni with Roasted Red Pepper Coulis • *broccoli, snow peas, baby corn, mozzarella, and cottage cheese wrapped in a delicate egg crêpe*

DAY AT SEA

7am–8pm	Nautica Spa and Gym opens
8am	Slot machines open
8am	Beginners step aerobics
9am	Late seating for breakfast
9am–6pm	Shuffleboard available
9:30–10:30am	Library opens
10am	Aqua Aerobics
10am–late	Full Casino opens
10:30am–noon	Photo Gallery opens
1pm	Talent show registration
1pm	Ice-carving demonstration
1pm	The slot tournament!
2pm	Ping-Pong Tournament
2–2:30pm	Tour of the Bridge
2–5pm	Calypso music
2:30pm	Newlywed and Not-So-Newlywed Game
3pm	Cooking lesson and food-carving demonstration
3pm	Showing of a feature film
3:30pm	Jackpot bingo
4:30pm	Debarkation briefing by cruise director
4:45–5:45pm	Main seating, "Fun Ship" party—complimentary hors d'oeuvres, cocktail music

7:15–8:15pm	Late seating, "Fun Ship" party—complimentary hors d'oeuvres, cocktail music
8pm	Main seating, jackpot bingo—snowball game
8:30pm	Showtime for main seating
9:30pm–1:30am	Party music with live entertainer
9:30pm–1:30am	Rockin' the night away with live entertainer
9:30pm–1:30am	Visit the spinning piano bar
9:45pm–1:30am	Great music for listening and dancing with the live trio
10pm	Late seating, monster bingo
10pm	Disco opens
12:30am	Quiche & Salad Buffet
1:30am	Mini Buffet

Dining Hours: Coffee 6:30am • Breakfast 7:45am • Light Breakfast 8–10am • Salad Bar noon–2:30pm • Sunlovers Luncheon noon–2:30pm • Lunch noon, 1:30pm • Coffee, Tea, Ice Cream & Treats 4:45–5pm • American Dinner 6pm, 8:15pm • Pasta Buffet 12:30–1:30am • Mini Buffet 1:30–2am • Coffee, Tea, Bouillion available 24 hours

Dress for the Evening: Casual

DINNER MAIN COURSES

Broiled Chicken Breast • *with almonds, sugar snap peas, and new potatoes*

Grilled Jumbo Shrimp • *with mushroom risotto*

Baked Jumbo Shrimp • *with lemon butter*

Roast Tenderloin of Beef • *with Bordelaise sauce*

Veal Parmigiana • *sautéed and topped with tomato sauce and mozzarella*

Grilled Marinated Vegetables • *zucchini, eggplant, and yellow squash*

DAY IN PORT

8:30am	Walk a mile with your sports director
9am	The pools are open
9:30am	Bridge lesson
10am	*Galaxy* is scheduled to dock at the International Pier, Cozumel
10–11:30am	The library is open. Daily quiz is available.
10:30am	Movie time: (A current feature film)
10:30am	Staying aboard? The entertainment staff organizes indoor games

11am	Computers made easy—a beginner's seminar
11am	Celebrity Social House— Coffee talk with the entertainment staff
11:30am–3:30pm	Background music to tan by
2:30–3:30pm	The library is open
3pm	Afternoon bridge play
3:30pm	The "Intra" Net—A basic beginners seminar
3:30pm	Pool Volleyball Challenge with the entertainment staff
3:30pm	Golf lessons with pro
3:30–5pm	Music on deck with live band
4pm	Teatime. A string quartet brings you a relaxed mood.
4pm	Arts and crafts
4:15pm	Catholic mass
4:30pm	Dance class, ballroom style
4:30pm	Friends of Lois and Bill W. meet
4:30pm	Improve your swing with golf pro
5pm	Celebrity Lecture Series
5pm–1am	Tasty cigars available. Cigar rolling demonstrations.
5:15–6:15pm	Traditional Greek music
6pm	Movie Time: (A current feature film)
6:45pm	All aboard, please
7pm	*Galaxy* is scheduled to sail for Montego Bay, Jamaica
7:30–8pm	Melody Makers play for your musical enjoyment
7:45pm	Casanova's Country Music Jamboree
8pm	Mastermind Team Trivia
8:45pm	Main Seating, Celebrity Showtime
9:45pm–1am	Our musical duo entertains
9:45pm–1:30am	Hit Music with Melody Makers
10pm–late	Spicy disco DJ plays the beat
10:20pm	Live vaudeville entertainment
10:45pm	Late Seating, Celebrity Showtime
11pm–1am	Tex-Mex deck celebration—line dancin'

Dining Hours: Coffee & Tea 6:30–7:30am • Continental Breakfast 6:30–10am • Breakfast Buffet 7–10am • Breakfast 7:30am–8:45am • Late Breakfast 10–11:30am • Croissants, Danishes & Muffins available 10–noon • Buffet Luncheon noon–2:30pm • Hot Dogs & Hamburgers noon–2:30pm • Pastries 3–5pm • Pizza 3–7pm • Afternoon Tea 4–5pm • Dinner 6pm, 8:30pm • Pizza 10pm–1am • Buffet midnight

Dress for the Evening: Informal (Ladies: informal dress or pants and blouse. Gentlemen: jacket and tie)

DINNER MAIN COURSES

Yakutat Bay Halibut Steak • *broiled Halibut complemented by a beurre blanc, enhanced with preserved black beans*

Broiled Lobster Tail • *topped with green asparagus tips, presented with melted drawn butter*

Roast Glazed Northern Duckling • *slowly oven-roasted until tender and crisp, enhanced with apple and wild berries in a sweet sherry sauce*

Scaloppine di Vitello al Limone • *thin slices of milk-fed veal enhanced by a natural sauce with the delicate essence of lemon*

Prime Rib of Beef • *the finest cut of prime rib presented with baked Idaho potato, natural juice, and creamed horseradish*

Ziti Alla Gorgonzola • *cooked al dente and served in a creamy gorgonzola sauce with roasted garlic and sliced shiitake*

CLIPPER

DAY IN PORT

6am	Departure of the Nantucket Clipper en route to Road Town, Tortola
7:30am	Approximate arrival of the *Nantucket Clipper* in Road Town, Tortola
8am	Sage Mountain Park hike
8:30am, 9:30am, 1:45pm, 2:45pm	Departure of Peter Island snorkel excursions
9am, 2pm	Departure of Cane Garden Bay Beach buses
9:30am, 2:15pm	Departure of Tortola Island tours
5:45pm	Lecture Presentation
9pm	Enjoy music of the Caribbean performed by local band
9pm	Movie presentation: (A current feature film)

Dining Hours: Early-Bird Breakfast 7am • Breakfast 7:45–8:15am • Lunch 12:30pm • Dinner 7:15pm

Dress for the Evening: Casual

DINNER MAIN COURSES

Fresh Broiled Florida Lobster Tail • *stuffed with baby shrimp, blue crab, and fresh herbs, served with drawn butter and fresh lemon*

Boursin Chicken • *boneless skinless chicken breast stuffed with herbed boursin cheese, breaded, baked, and served with sauce veloute*

Fresh Pasta with a Wild Mushroom Cream Sauce

Grilled Mahimahi • *served moist with tropical fruit salsa garnished with lemon and lime*

Vegetable Lasagna • *fresh garden vegetables layered with a low-fat ricotta cheese and fresh lasagna noodles*

Club Med®

DAY IN PORT—ONBOARD SPORTS ACTIVITIES

8:30–9:30am	Fitness instructor available
9am	*Club Med 2* arrives in St. Martin
9am	Relaxation exercises
10am	First tender leaves for shore
10am	Body sculpting
10am–5pm	Waterskiing, sailing, and windsurfing at the Nautical Hall
11am	Meeting for certified scuba divers in the Nautical Hall
11:15am	Departure of scuba diving from the Nautical Hall
11:30am	Water aerobics in The Bahamas swimming pool
2pm	Snorkeling departure from the Nautical Hall
5pm	Low-impact aerobics
5–7pm	Fitness instructor available
5:30pm	Stretching flexibility
3am	Last tender leaves from shore

Dining Hours: Full Buffet & Menu Breakfast 7–10:30am • Continental Breakfast 10:30–11:30am • Lunch 12:30–2:30pm • Tea & Pastries 4–5:30pm • Dinner 7:30–9:30pm

Dress for the Evening: Casual

DINNER MAIN COURSES

Emincé of Chicken with Curry, Rice, and Exotic Fruits

Rissole of Salt Cod with a Lobster Mousseline

Tagliatelle Pasta with Smoked Salmon

Lamb Filet with Sage Juice and Celery Flan

Sirloin Steak with Pepper Sauce and Potatoes Alsacian Style

Filet of Bass with Balsamique Vinegar and Polenta Tassinoise Style

Commodore
CRUISE LINE

DAY AT SEA

7am	Catholic mass
8am	Interdenominational church service
9am	Shore excursion briefing and orientation talk
10am	Walk-a-Mile

10am	Brain teasers and crossword puzzles
10am	Horse racing at sea
10am–1pm	Photo Gallery opens for purchase of pictures
10:15am	Art animation auction at sea
10:30am	Catch the scent: A special perfume seminar
11am	Port and shopping briefing
11:30am	Massage demonstration
Noon–2pm	Out on deck with deck DJ
1pm	Trapshooting
1pm	Friends of Dr. Bob and Bill and Lois W.
2–3pm	Enchanted Isle Quartet performs for your listening pleasure
2:15pm	"Gem Stone" seminar
2:30pm	Snowball jackpot bingo
2:45pm	Wine and cheese tasting
3pm	Gaming lessons with your Casino staff
3pm	Service club meeting
3–4pm	Shore excursion manager will be available for inquiries
3:15pm	"Afternoon Madness" with your cruise director
5:15pm	First seating, Captain's welcome aboard cocktail party
7:30pm	Second seating, Captain's welcome aboard cocktail party
7:30–8:15pm	Piano player performs in our Intimate Lounge
7:45–8:30pm	Join live player at the piano for your listening pleasure
8:45pm	First seating for featured live entertainment
9:30pm	Piano player performs in our Intimate Lounge
9:45pm	Music under the stars with deck DJ
10pm	The Disco opens
10:30pm	Last seating for featured entertainment
11:15pm–midnight	Dance with the Enchanted Isle Quartet

Dining Hours: Breakfast Buffet 7–10am • Breakfast 7:30–9:30am • Lunch noon, 1:30pm • Buffet Lunch noon–2pm • Hamburgers & Hot Dogs noon–1:45pm • Afternoon Snacks 4–4:45pm • Dinner 6pm, 8:15pm • Italian buffet 11:30pm–12:30am

Dress for the Evening: Formal (jacket and tie requested for men)

DINNER MAIN COURSES

Surf & Turf, Commodore Style • *a filet mignon and broiled lobster tail served with drawn butter and saffron rice pilaf*

Linguini with Fruits of the Seas • *buttered noodles with baby shrimp, scallops, and crab meat in a light basil cream sauce*

Scaloppini à la Francaise • *dipped lightly into egg batter, sautéed to a golden brown, and served with buttered noodles*

Roast Prime Rib of Beef Au Jus • *served with stuffed baked potatoes*

DAY IN PORT

7:30am	The CostaVictoria is due to dock in St. Thomas, U.S.V.I.
8–9am	Port lecturer is available for maps and information
9–10am	Host hour: Meet cruise staff for a friendly chat
10am	Informal cards and games
3:30pm	Dance class
4pm	Foozeball with your cruise staff
5pm	Afternoon walkathon
5–6:30pm	Basketball fun
5:30pm	All on board
5:30pm	Sailaway celebration
5:30–6:30pm	Live duo entertains you
6pm	*CostaVictoria* sails to Serena Cay
6pm	Afternoon stretch
7:45pm	Bingo time
7:45pm	Honeymooners cocktail party
8:30pm–midnight	Italian-style entertainment
8:45pm	Showtime (featuring headliner)
8:45pm–1am	The Italian melodies of our live band
10:15pm	The great *CostaVictoria* pizza-throwing contest
10:45pm	Showtime (featuring headliner)
11pm	The Rockstar Disco opens
11:45pm–1:30am	Enjoy the melodies of our live duo

Dining Hours: Coffee & Croissants 6:30–7am • Breakfast 7:30am, 8:45am • Breakfast Buffet 7–10am • Croissants 10–11:30am • Lunch 11:30am–1:45pm • Lunch Buffet noon–2:30pm • Lunch Grill noon–2:30pm • Afternoon Tea 4–5pm • Pizza 3–8pm, 9:30pm–1am • Dinner 6:15pm, 8:30pm • Ice Cream 10pm–midnight • Late-Night Buffet 8pm–12:30am

Dress for the Evening: Casual

DINNER MAIN COURSES

Ravioli alla Piemontese • *ricotta cheese ravioli tossed in a hearty meat and tomato sauce and served with Italian Parmesan*

Filetto di Salmone Fresco • *broiled steak of fresh Pacific salmon served with dill mousseline*

Coda di Aragosta • *broiled Caribbean lobster tail with drawn butter*

Filetto di Manzo alla Rossini • *grilled tenderloin of beef with Madeira mushroom sauce, goose liver pâté, and potato croquettes*

Scaloppina al Limone con Agrumi • *tender escalope of veal in a lemon sauce presented with citrus wedges and served with château potatoes*

DAY AT SEA

8am	Fitness class
9am	Walk-a-Thon
9am	Friends of Bill W. meet fellow guests
10am	Fitness center orientation
10am	Golf clinic
10:15am	Spa demonstration
10:30am	Bridge players meet
10:30am	Dance class
10:30am	Crystal enrichment series (lectures)
11:30am	Progressive jackpot bingo
11:45am	Pianist entertains
1pm	Art auction
1:30pm	Crystal enrichment series (lectures)
2pm	Singles get-together
2:30pm	Mixed doubles Ping-Pong tournament
2:30pm	Arts & crafts demonstration
2:30pm	Golfers meet for tips and putting
2:30pm	Movie matinee
3pm	Complimentary dance class
3pm	Fitness class
3pm	Fine art auction
3:30pm	Traditional English tea
3:45pm	Progressive jackpot bingo
4pm	Fitness class
5:30pm	Captain's cocktail party
5:45pm	Pianist entertains
7:45pm	More piano entertainment
8:30pm	A feature film presentation
9pm	Dancing begins
9:30pm	More piano entertainment
10pm	DJ spins dance hits for late-night disco
11:30pm	Karaoke Sing-Along

Dining Hours: Early-Risers Breakfast 7–9am • Late-Risers Breakfast 10:30am • Lunch noon–1:30pm • First Dinner Seating 6:30pm • Second Dinner Seating 8:30pm

Dress for the Evening: Formal (Ladies: evening gown or formal cocktail dress. Men: Tuxedo or dark business suit)

DINNER MAIN COURSES

Broiled Fresh Alaskan King Crab Legs • *in half shell, served with drawn butter, green asparagus, pilaf rice*

Sauteed Veal Medallions Provence • *with homemade mushroom ravioli, tomato confit, and sautéed leaf spinach*

Herb Marinated Grill Quail • *presented on braised green cabbage with port wine sauce and potato blinis*

Celery and Sweet Potato Piccata • *with spaghetti, tomato sauce, and broccoli florets*

Baked Suprême of Wild Pheasant with Potato Crust • *with black currant sauce, caramelized apple slices, champagne sauerkraut, and gallettes of sweet corn*

CUNARD

DAY IN PORT

8am	Gym Guidance
9am	*Sea Goddess I* anchors off Jost Van Dyke, British Virgin Islands
10:30am	Zodiac service to the beach will be established and operate on a continuous basis throughout the day
Noon	Caviar and champagne are served in the surf
12:30pm	BBQ lunch *Sea Goddess*–style is served on the beach
5pm	Last zodiac departs from shore
5pm	Body toning
5:30pm	Private consultations
6pm	*Sea Goddess I* sails for St. Thomas, U.S. Virgin Islands
7pm	The Main Salon is open for cocktails and dancing
7:30pm	The Captain's Reception, in the Main Salon
10pm	The Main Salon is open for coffee, after-dinner drinks, and dancing
10pm	The Piano Bar is open
10pm	The Casino is open for blackjack
10:30pm	Live music in the Piano Bar

Dining Hours: Early-Risers Coffee 7–8am • À La Carte Breakfast 8–10am • Breakfast 8–11am • Lunch 12:30–2pm • Afternoon Tea 5–6pm • Dinner 8–10pm

Dress for the Evening: Jacket and tie are requested after 7pm

DINNER MAIN COURSES

Gratinated Filet of Monkfish • *served on a bed of leaf spinach*

Herb Marinated Veal Scallopini • *with sautéed Chanterelles and risotto "Napoletana"*

Grilled Baby Lamb Chops • *with mango-mint chutney*

Fresh Steamed Maine Lobster • *with spicy tomato-olive ragoût and wild rice*

Grilled Mignon of Beef Tenderloin "Madagascar" and Pommes Pont Neuf

To support Disney's premise that it provides a vacation experience tailored to adults, children, and families, the line produces not one, not two, but *seven* different daily activities calendars, directed at the following groups: ages 3–5, ages 6–8, ages 9–10, ages 11–12, teens, families, and adults. The following is a sample. Also, as passengers on Disney's ships dine in a different restaurant every night, we've provided sample dinner main courses from two of the onboard eateries.

DAY AT SEA—FAMILY

8–9am	Goofy's Family Fitness
9:30–10:30am	Shore Talk
1:30–3pm	Mickey 200: Design, build, and race your own vegetable race car
1:30–2pm	Poolside games
9:30–11:30pm	Nautical Mystery Tour: While trying to solve this mystery, you will decipher clues that lead your family all over the ship

DAY AT SEA—ADULT

9–11am	Adult activity time (activities vary)
11–12:30pm	Adult activity time (activities vary)
12:15–1:15pm	Bingo
3:30–4:30pm	Wine tasting
5–8pm	Adult activity time (activities vary)
Midnight–1am	Bingo
12:45–1:45am	Charade of Stars karaoke

DAY AT SEA—AGES 6–8

8:30–9am	Sign-in
9–9:30am	Activities in the Club and Lab
9:30–10:30am	Eggsperiments: Children experiment with one of the engineering marvels of our world: the egg
10:30–11am	Activities
11am–noon	Lunch
Noon–1pm	Activities in the Lab
1–2pm	Animation Antics: Children are introduced to simple animation techniques and put their new skills to work drawing Mickey Mouse

2–3:30pm	Activities on the Sports Deck and in the Lab
3:30–4pm	Snack in the Lab
4–5pm	Escape from Hook!: Peter Pan is celebrating his birthday and he's invited his young friends to disguise themselves and attend. They must make sure that Hook doesn't invade the festivities or beware!
5–6:30pm	Activities in the Club
6:30–7:30pm	Child dinner
7:30–9pm	Activities in the Club
9–10pm	The Eyes Have It!: Children peek at the science behind vision, and make their own 3D glasses to take with them
10–10:30pm	Snack
11pm–12:30am	Activities in the Club

DAY AT SEA—TEENS

10:30–11:30am	Shooting Stars: Teens form crews; select roles as directors, actors, techs, or costumers; and make silver screen history, then attend an onboard premier screening
3:30–4pm	ESPN Sports Challenge
4–5pm	Comedy Hour
10–11:30pm	The Glow Jam: Sports that are as much fun to watch as they are to play, using a glowing array of sports equipment
Midnight–1am	Carpe Notta: In the spirit of the Dead Poets Society, teens can meet on deck to light the lamp of knowledge, express themselves, and talk about the topics of the day

Dining Hours: Unavailable at press time.

Dress for the Evening: Informal

DINNER MAIN COURSES—LUMIÉRE'S RESTAURANT

Les Fruits de Mer • *lobster, prawns, scallops, mussels, and Atlantic rockfish poached with vegetable julienne in a delicate tarragon sauce, served with rice pilaf*

Poussin Rôti • *whole game hen with rosemary and thyme, served with gratin potatoes, pesto French green beans, and glazed carrots*

Jarret d'Agneau Braisé • *lamb shank braised with vegetables and red wine, with roasted onion mashed potatoes, flageolet beans, and ratatouille*

Ravioli aux Champignons "Maurice" • *mushroom and ricotta cheese ravioli on a bed of tender vegetables with a black bean essence*

Filet de Vivaneau • *oven-baked fresh Gulf snapper on a bed of spinach fettucini tossed with saffron beurre blanc and vegetable brunoise, garnished with tomato Provencale*

Filet de Boeuf au Poivre "Gaston" • *sliced tenderloin of beef with green peppercorn sauce, roasted onion mashed potatoes, and ratatouille*

DINNER MAIN COURSES—ANIMATOR'S PALATE

Under the Sea • *mustard and herb-crust baked salmon filet with red skin mashed potatoes in a Zinfandel glaze*

Pasta Pinocchio • *rigatoni sautéed with garlic, crushed plum tomatoes, white wine, leeks, and Calamata olives in a basil leaf cream*

Chicken Timon • *roasted chicken breast with simmered mushrooms, tomatoes, and spinach with multicolored gnocchi*

Animator's Choice • *Parmesan-and-herb crusted veal cutlets on artichoke and sun-dried tomato risotto*

Moufasa's Pride • *grilled beef tenderloin with a Cheddar cheese corn cake, roasted vegetables, port wine balsamic jus, and yellow pepper coulis*

DAY IN PORT

7am	The *Maasdam* is scheduled to anchor at George Town, Grand Cayman
7am–7pm	Fitness instructors are available for assistance
7am–7pm	Thirty-minute workout
7am–9pm	Ocean Spa and Jacuzzis are open
8–8:30am	Walk-a-mile with our fitness instructor
8–9:30am	Port lecturer answers your questions
8:45am	Low-impact aerobics
9am–6pm	Sports equipment is available
9:45am	Women's golf putting tournament
10:30–11am	Lemonade is served on the outside decks
1:30pm	Deck quoits tournament with the cruise staff
2pm	Informal bridge or cards get-together
3:15pm	Team trivia with the cruise staff
3:30–4pm	Iced tea is served on the outside decks
3:30–4pm	Afternoon tea is served
3:45pm	Open Ping-Pong with the cruise staff
4–4:30pm	Walk-a-mile with our fitness instructor
4:30pm	Snowball cash bingo
4:30pm	Friends of Bill W. meet
4:30pm	Volleyball with the cruise staff
4:45pm	Stretch and relax
5:30pm	All aboard! The last tender leaves from the shore
7:30pm	Art auction
8:30pm	Showtime in the Rembrandt Lounge
9:45pm	Evening team trivia
10:15pm	Showtime in the Rembrandt Lounge

11:15pm	Karaoke time
12:30am	DJ dance music

Dining Hours: Continental Breakfast 6:30–10:30am • Breakfast 7–10am • Lunch 11:30am–2pm • Hamburgers & Hot Dogs 11:30am–5pm • Stir-Fry & Taco Bar 11:30am–2:30pm • Ice Cream 11:30am–2:30pm, 4–5pm, 11:15pm–12:15am • Pizza 4–5pm • Dinner 6pm, 8:15pm • Caribbean Late-Night Snack 11:15pm–12:15am

Dress for the Evening: Elegantly Casual (Women: dress or blouse and slacks. Gentlemen: jacket required, tie optional)

DINNER MAIN COURSES

Seafood Linguini with Lobster Sauce • *selected seafood garnished with asparagus and broccoli*

Broiled Petit Filet Mignon Bella Bella • *topped with crabmeat and Béarnaise sauce and served with dauphinoise potatoes, asparagus tips, and carrot vichy*

Veal Scaloppini au Citron • *served with lemon-infused natural sauce and capers, sautéed Spaetzle with Gruyère cheese and cauliflower Du Barry*

Roasted Duckling à l'Orange • *with orange and Grand Marnier sauce, potato croquettes, red cabbage, and snow peas*

Red Snapper Filet Vera Cruz • *baked in its own juice, garnished with bell peppers, tomato, onions, olives, and served with snow peas and Spanish rice*

Stir-Fried Vegetables Over Fried Tofu • *served in a flour tortilla basket on a bed of basmati rice laced with black bean sauce*

MEDITERRANEAN SHIPPING CRUISES

DAY AT SEA

9am	Morning walk; good-morning announcement from the bridge
9:15am	Gymnastics and stretching at the Calypso Pool
10am	Compulsory emergency lifeboat training drill in the cinema, Deck 4
10:30am	Paint your own T-shirts at the Riviera Terrace
11am	Cooking demonstration with Michele, Riviera Terrace
11am	Games in the swimming pool
11am	The Crazy Dance with the Entertainment Team at the Junkanoo Lounge
11:25am	Aperitif Game at the Riviera Terrace
11:30am	Aerobics with the Paris Paris Ballet
3pm	Card tournaments "Scala 40"
3:45pm	Belly dancing lessons with Georgia at the Calypso Pool

4–4:45pm	Tea, cakes, and music at the Sunrise Terrace
4:15pm	South American Dance with the Paris Paris Ballet
4:45pm	The Grand Slam (a great new team game) begins at the Junkanoo Lounge
7pm	Casino opens
9:15pm	Movie time in the cinema
10pm	Disco opens, Deck 6
11:45pm	Buffet flambé on Deck 7, beside the Calypso Pool

Dining Hours: Breakfast (Open Seating) 7–10am • Lunch (Open Seating) noon–2:30pm • First Dinner Seating 6:30pm • Second Dinner Seating 8:30pm

Dress for the Evening: Casual

DINNER MAIN COURSES

Cream chicken • *with royal pastry*

Baked lobster in oven • *with pilaf rice*

Casserole of vegetables • *gratinated with Fontina cheese*

Scottadito of lamb • *with balsamic vinegar served with Pont-neuf potatoes*

Sautéed veal scallop • *with fresh tomatoes and rocket salad*

NORWEGIAN
CRUISE LINE

DAY AT SEA

8:30–9am	Morning stretch with your Sports Afloat staff
8:45–9:45am	The library is open
9am	Walk a Mile with a Smile with your cruise director's staff
9am	Take the trivia challenge and pick up today's quiz
9am	Cashier's window opens in Casino Royale (slots remain open from last night)
9am	Intermediate Step with your Sports Afloat staff
9am–6pm	Ping-Pong, golf driving, basketball, and shuffleboard equipment available
9:30am	Voice from the Bridge: Captain's morning address
10am	Make-up boat drill
10am–noon	Morning drink special: Bloody Marys, Screwdrivers, and Mimosas
10:30am	Cooking demonstration with our chef de cuisine
10:30am	Craft Corner with your cruise director's staff
11am–12:45pm	DJ plays your favorite island tunes

11:30am	Napkin folding—come and learn how to spice up your tables
11:30am–2pm	Connoisseur's Corner: Join your wine steward and talk wine
Noon	Casino Royale opens for your gambling pleasure
12:45pm	Friends of Bill W. meet
12:45pm	Pool games
1pm	Service club meeting: Lions, Kiwanis, etc.
1pm	Vigorous 1-mile walk with cruise director
1–1:30pm	Fresh fruit smoothie tasting with your bar staff
2pm	Step aerobics with your Sports Afloat staff
2–3pm	Gaming lessons begin: blackjack, dice, and Caribbean stud poker
2:15pm	Port and shopping talk
2:30–5:30pm	DJ plays your favorite island sounds
2:45pm	Honeymooner's champagne party
3pm	Giant jackpot bingo
3pm	Perfume seminar: Come sample our "Scentsational" perfumes
3pm	Belly Buster with your Sports Afloat staff
3–4pm	The Library is open
3:15pm	Art auction extravaganza
3:30pm	Snorkeling demonstration with your Dive-In instructors
3:30pm	Wine tasting
3:45pm	Basketball free throw contest
4:30pm	Bridge play available with your fellow passengers
5–6pm	Enjoy piano melodies
5–6pm	Enjoy great music and dancing with our musical duo
5–6pm	Captain's party for main seating
5–6:15pm	Special invitation: professional studio portraits
7–8pm	Captain's party for late seating
7–8:45pm	Special invitation: professional studio portraits
7:15–9pm	Our musical duo plays all your favorites
7:30–8:30pm	Enjoy piano melodies
9pm, 10:30pm	Featured entertainment
9:45pm	Enjoy the sounds of our musical duo
10pm–12:30am	Entertainer plays your favorite tunes at the piano
10pm–close	DJ plays the hits you want to hear
11:15pm	Singles party
11:45pm	Late-night comedy
Midnight–1am	Chocoholic extravaganza

Dining Hours: Continental Breakfast 6:30–10:30am • Breakfast Buffet 7:30–10am • Breakfast 8–10am • Lunch noon, 1:30pm • Sandwich Bar noon–5pm • Ice Cream 2–4:30pm • Dinner 6pm, 8:30pm • Le Bistro Dining 6–10:30pm • Chocoholic Extravaganza midnight–1am • Coffee & Tea available 24 hours

Dress for the Evening: Formal (Women: formal gown or cocktail dress. Men: tuxedo or jacket and tie)

DINNER MAIN COURSES

Ravioli di Riocotta in Salsa di Zucca • *ravioli stuffed with ricotta cheese, sweet pumpkin sauce*

Broiled Filet of Flounder • *with steamed red beets, foamy green pea sauce, boiled potatoes*

Veal Piccata Maître d'Hôtel • *sautéed medallions of veal with mushrooms, asparagus, glazed with Béarnaise sauce, Milanese risotto*

Roast Prime Rib of Kansas Beef • *with creamed horseradish, baked Idaho potatoes, natural juice*

Jumbo Shrimps with Lobster Basil Sauce • *served with angelhair pasta*

⚓ PREMIER CRUISES

DAY AT SEA

6am–11pm	Exercise Room open
8am	Golf Academy open. Teaching pro available for lessons
8am	Walk a mile with your fitness director
8am	Movie: (Current feature film)
8am–8:30pm	Steiners Beauty and Fitness/Massage Salon open
8am–10pm	Pools and Jacuzzis open
8:30am	Interdenominational service
3pm	Movie: (Current feature film)
3–6pm	Foot and ankle massage
3:15pm	Family cash snowball bingo
3:30–4:45pm	Art auction at sea
4pm	Trapshooting
5–6pm	Main seating, Captain's Champagne Reception
6pm	Movie: (Current feature film)
6pm	Virtual reality—step inside the game
6–8pm	Fitness/wellness evaluations
7–8:15pm	Late seating, Captain's Champagne Reception
7:30–8:30pm	Join DJ and dance to Big Band and Ballroom Music
8pm–midnight	Shooting Star Photo Gallery open for photos and videos
8:30pm	Main seating, preshow music with the orchestra

8:15–10pm	Get steamed with "Steamer"! Sit back, relax, and enjoy great music
9pm	Movie: (Current feature film)
9:15pm	Port Lucaya talk with your lecturer
9:30pm	Poker game starts
9:30pm–midnight	Party under the stars with our musical group
9:45pm	Family cash bingo
10–11pm	Join staff for "Name That Tune"!
10pm–1am	Party in the Lucky Star Lounge
10pm	Karaoke showtime
10pm	Join DJ; let's jam to the music, back when it was still rock 'n' roll
10:15pm	Late seating, preshow music with the "Excalibur Orchestra"
Midnight	Movie: (Current feature film)

Dining Hours: Early-Risers Coffee & Danish 6–7:30am • Buffet Breakfast 7:30–10:30am • Breakfast 7:30am, 8:45am • Buffet Lunch noon–2pm • Lunch noon, 1:30pm • Ice Cream 2–5pm • Afternoon Tea 4:15–5:15pm • Dinner 6pm, 8:15pm • Late-Night Snacks 9:30–10:30pm • Pizza Time 11:30pm–12:30am • Gala Buffet 12:30–1:30am

Dress for the Evening: Formal (Casual following dinner)

DINNER MAIN COURSES

Catch of the Day • *your waiter will explain*

Fettuccine Alfredo • *with the classic Italian creamy dressing*

Lobster Newburg • *morsels of lobster in a cream sauce with English mustard, served in a puff pastry shell*

Suprême of Chicken • *poached skinless chicken breast with champagne sauce*

Roast Prime Rib of Aged Kansas Choice Beef • *cooked to perfection and served with its natural juice and creamy horseradish*

P R I N C E S S ® 〰.

DAY AT SEA

8am	Brain-Waves quiz
8am–noon	Princess Links is open
9am	Fine jewelry sale
9–9:20am	Walk-a-mile
9–10am	Men's doubles shuffleboard tournament
9–10am	Women's doubles Ping-Pong get-together
9–11am	Tour of the Commanding Bridge
9:30–9:50am	Morning stretch

9:30–10:30am	Snorkeling demonstration
10–10:30am	Talent show sign-up and rehearsal
10–10:30am	Cards and games with the cruise staff
10–10:45am	Morning quiz with the cruise staff
10–10:45am	Hi/Lo aerobics
10–10:45am	Paddle tennis tournament
10–10:45am	Culinary demonstration
10–11am	Fruit- and vegetable-carving demonstration
10am–noon	The Library is open
10:15am	Captain's Circle scavenger hunt
10:30–11am	Life equipment workout
10:30–11:30am	Scrabble and backgammon tournament
10:45–11am	Minimize your middle
11am–noon	Line dance class
11:15am–noon	Jackpot bingo
11:30am–noon	Singles mingles. Those traveling alone are invited to meet the cruise staff for champagne and introductions.
11:30am–12:15pm	Aerobics circuit
11:30am–2pm	Lunchtime melodies
11:45am–12:15pm	Aquafit
2–2:30pm	Fun in the sun pool games. Crazy aquatic antics with the cruise staff.
2–4pm	Celebrity photo opportunity—an invitation to meet Mr. Gavin McLeod, Captain Stubing of *The Love Boat*
2–4pm	The Library is open
2–6pm	Prince Links is open
2:30–3:15pm	Water volleyball
2:30–3:15pm	Newlywed and Not-So-Newlywed Game show
2:30–3:30pm	Friends of Dr. Bob and Bill W. meeting
2:30–4pm	Nonhost bridge play
3–3:30pm	Collector's seminar—Lladró, the number-one collectible in the world
3:15–4pm	Dice horse racing and horse auction
3:30–4pm	Basketball shoot-out
3:30–4:15pm	Step class
3:30–4:30pm	Outburst: the hilarious and outrageous game hosted by your cruise staff
3:30–4:30pm	Afternoon tea
4–4:45pm	Bonanza bingo
4:30–5pm	Firm and fabulous health and fitness class
5–8:30pm	Early evening music and dancing with our musical duo
5:15–5:45pm	Walk-a-mile

5:30–6:30pm	Latin American–style dancing
5:30–8pm	Predinner music for your listening pleasure
5:45–6:30pm	Enjoy a predinner dance
7:45–8:30pm	Enjoy a predinner dance
8pm	Evening cards and games
8pm–late	Dance with music by our musical duo
8pm–late	Blackjack, roulette, craps, stud poker, slots in the Casino
8:15pm	Princess Theatre presents "Mystique"— A mysterious undersea adventure
8:15pm	The Vista Lounge presents live entertainment
8:30pm–midnight	Piano melodies in the Atrium Lounge
9pm–late	DJ spins the Top 40 sounds
9:15pm–late	Music, hilarity, and a touch of class with our live performer
10:15pm	"Mystique"—A mysterious undersea adventure
10:30pm	Karaoke
10:30pm	Evening cards and games
11:45pm	Cabaret spotlight

Dress for the Evening: Casual

DINNER MAIN COURSES

Ravioli con Salsa di Funghi Porcini • *meat-filled pasta squares in a creamy mushroom sauce*

Alaskan Halibut and Saffron Mayonnaise • *sautéed fish with beans, bell pepper boats, and crusty new potatoes*

Broiled Lobster Tail • *on a shell with drawn lemon butter and rice pilaf*

Royal Pheasant in Pan Juices • *oven roasted with Brussels sprouts, mushrooms, and Parisienne potatoes*

Beef Wellington • *puff-pastry wrapped tenderloin in a black truffle Madeira sauce with baby vegetables and Duchess potatoes*

RADISSON SEVEN SEAS
CRUISES

DAY IN PORT

7:30am	Stretch and walk
8am	Today's trivia and crossword
9am	Fitness at sea—aerobics
9am	Snorkel and scuba instruction in the pool
9:30am	Fitness at sea—gym instruction
10am	Fitness at sea—sit and be fit

11am	Interdenominational worship service will be held in The Club
Noon	The *Radisson Diamond* will arrive in St. Kitts
3–5pm	Hot snacks and afternoon tea are served in The Grill
6:30pm	Captain requests the pleasure of your company for his Welcome Aboard Cocktail Party in the Windows Lounge
6:30–7:30pm	Cocktail time with our piano player
7–9:30pm	Dinner is served in The Grand Dining Room
9:30pm	All Aboard as the *Radisson Diamond* prepares to sail for St. Barts
9:45pm	Dance to the music of our live band
10:15pm	The Gordeno Connection in Jazz Rock Café
10:30pm	Late-nighters join our piano entertainer in The Club
After the Show	Continue dancing to the music of our live band in the Windows Lounge
11:15pm	Disco with DJ in the Windows Lounge

Dining Hours: Early-Risers Coffee 6:30–7:30am • Buffet Breakfast 7:30–9:30am • Breakfast 8–10am • Late-Risers Coffee 9:30–11am • Lunch Buffet 11:30am–2pm • Lunch 12:30–2pm • Hot Snacks & Afternoon Tea 3–5pm • Dinner 7–9:30pm

Dress for the Evening: Formal

DINNER MAIN COURSES

Pacific Salmon • *herb roasted, with Pinot Noir sauce*

Grilled Swordfish • *with tomato basil beurre blanc*

Grilled Gulf Shrimp • *with black bean compote, avocado, and tomato relish*

Pan-Roasted Chicken Breast • *with walnut and smoked ham compote, apple Riesling sauce*

Sautéed Breast of Duckling • *with peach pecan chutney*

Pan-Roasted Pheasant • *with wild rice copote, white Zinfandel thyme sauce*

Grilled New York Strip Steak • *with horseradish and pistachio butter*

Grilled Veal Chop • *with brandied wild mushrooms*

DAY AT SEA

8:30am–noon	Eye-opener at the Pool Bar
9–10am	The Library is open
9:15am	Financial lecture
9:30am	Morning movie: (Current feature film)
9:30am	Ping-Pong tournament and shuffleboard open play

10:15am	Vegetable-carving demonstration
10:15am	Horse racing shipboard style
11am	Debarkation talk with your cruise director
1pm	Passenger talent show sign-up
1–2pm	Music by the pool
1:30–2pm	Passengers wishing to visit the Navigation Bridge may do so at this time
2pm	Crazy Legs contest with the cruise staff
2:15pm	Skeetshooting with our staff
2:55pm	Drawing for raffle
3–3:30pm	The Library is open
3pm	Family Feud with the cruise staff
3:45pm	Giant jackpot bonanza bingo
4:30pm	Friends of Bill W. meet in the Library
4:30pm	Afternoon showtime with live entertainment
5–6pm	Cocktail music on deck with our piano player
5:15pm	Passenger talent show
5:30pm	Evening movie: (Current feature film)
7:30–8:30pm	Our piano player performs at the Piano Bar
7:30–8:30pm	Happy hour
7:45pm	Final jackpot bingo
8:45pm	First seating, featured attraction
9:45pm	Final high-seas horse racing
10pm	Showtime in the Mermaid Lounge
10:30pm	Second seating, featured attraction

Dining Hours: Early-Bird Coffee 6:30am • Breakfast 7:30am, 8:45am • Continental Breakfast 8–10am • Buffet Lunch noon–1:30pm • Lunch noon, 1:30pm • Pizza noon–4pm • Ice Cream & Cookies 4–4:45pm • Dinner 6pm, 8:30pm • International Buffet 11:30pm–1:30am

Dress for the Evening: Informal (Please, no shorts in the Dining Room)

DINNER MAIN COURSES

Poached Alaskan Salmon • *tender salmon filet garnished with a julienne of fresh vegetables and lemon dill butter*

Roast Prime Ribs of Beef • *served au jus with Yorkshire pudding*

Grilled Rosemary Chicken • *marinated in lemon with rosemary and herbs, served with grilled tomato*

Loin of Pork Piquant • *sliced roasted pork loin with olive oil, garlic, and white wine sauce*

Ravioli Amatriciana • *pasta sautéed with tomatoes, onions, crumbled bacon, and dusted with Pecorino Romano cheese*

Melanzane Ripiene, all Fiorentina • *battered eggplant slices filled with ricotta cheese, served over spinach with a fresh basil tomato sauce*

ROYAL ⚓ CARIBBEAN.

DAY IN PORT

8am	The *Majesty of the Seas* is due to anchor off George Town, Grand Cayman
8am	Sunrise stretch class
8–10am	Sign up for Saturday's guest talent show
8:30am	Tender tickets are available from the cruise staff commencing at 8:30am in the Blue Skies Lounge
9:15am	Fun fitness (all levels: fun, light, low-impact)
10–11am	Daily trivia
10am	Cards and board games available all day
1:30–2:30pm	Sail-away music with "Cruise Control"
2:30pm	Last tender leaves from shoreside
2:30pm	Horse racing at the pool—"The Grand Majesty Derby"
2:45pm	Belly-flop competition
3pm	De-stress clinic
3:15pm–3am	Casino Royale open
3:30–4pm	Preview: Park West art auction at sea
3:30–7pm	Shopping time—Boutiques of the Centrum are now open
3:30pm	Cozumel port and shopping talk
3:45pm	Five-minute makeover
4pm	Ice-carving demonstration
4–5pm	Step aerobics
4–6pm	Auction: Park West art auction at sea
4:15–5:30pm	Bingorama No. 4
4:15–6pm	Music by our steel band, "Cruise Control"
5–5:30pm	Legs, tums, and buns workout
5–5:30pm	Country line dancing
5–6pm	Friends of Bill W. meeting
5:30–8:30pm	Margarita madness
7:30–8:30pm	Karaoke night
7:45–8:45pm	Join live entertainer for all your favorite musical requests and fun
9–10pm	Main seating for featured entertainment
9pm–1am	Cigar aficionados! Enjoy a quiet moment with good friends, a fine cognac, and a first class cigar
10–11pm	Dance music featuring our swing band
10pm–12:30am	Join our featured entertainer for all your favorite musical requests and fun

10pm–12:30am	Country-western barn dance
10:30pm	Stargazing
10:30pm–3am	Dancing to the top discs
10:45–11:45pm	Second seating for featured entertainment
11:15pm–12:15am	Dance music featuring our swing band
11:30–2am	Disco inferno
12:30–1:30am	Blue Note jazz

Dining Hours: Early-Bird Coffee 6:30–7am • Breakfast 7–9am • Continental Breakfast 7–10am • Late-Risers Breakfast 7–10am • Luncheon 12:30–2:30pm • Snack Luncheon 2–4pm • Afternoon Snack Service 4–5pm • Dinner 6:15pm, 8:30pm • Italian Galley Buffet 11:45pm–1am • Late-Night Snack 1–6am

Dress for the Evening: Casual or Country-Western

DINNER MAIN COURSES

Ravioli Filled with Ricotta • *topped with crisp vegetables and tomato sauce*

Pan-Seared Filet of Salmon • *served with asparagus tips, wild mushrooms, peanut ginger sauce, sautéed garden vegetables*

Deviled Crab Del Rey • *blue crab meat sautéed with red and green bell peppers, accompanied by fried rice*

Roast Chinese Duck • *with spiced hoisin sauce, fried rice, stir-fried vegetables*

Grilled Medallions of Veal • *garnished with sautéed portobello mushrooms, served with garlic mashed potatoes*

Roast Prime Rib of Beef • *natural jus with au gratin potato and sautéed garden vegetables*

 *Royal Olympic Cruises*

DAY AT SEA

7am	Early bird coffee
7:20am	Deck walk
8am	Catholic liturgy in the Theater
8:30am–12:30pm	The Hospitality Desk opens for information in the Solaris Foyer
8:45am	Sit and be fit
9–10am	The Library is open
9–9:30am	"Today with Your Cruise Director"
9:30am	Team trivia
9:30am	Video presentation
9:45–11am	Gym consultations and advice
10:30am	Destinations enhancement lecture: "Historical Role of the Caribbean"

10:30am	Movie presentations: (Current feature film)
11:30am	Jackpot bingo
11:30am	Bridge lecture
11:45am–12:30pm	Musical cocktails in the Solaris Piano Bar
12:30–1:30pm	Music on deck for your pleasure
1:45pm	Duplicate and rubber play in the Card Room
2pm	Lecture: "The Health Puzzle—Putting the Pieces Together"
2pm	The Hospitality Desk reopens for information
2:30pm	Dance class
3pm	Movie presentations: (Current feature film)
3pm	Arts and crafts project
3:45pm	"Rhythm and Motion in the Ocean"—upper and lower body toning with rhythmic movements
4–4:30pm	The Library is open
4:30pm	Deck walk
5pm	"Awesome Abdominals with Back Conditioning and Stretching"
6pm	Video presentation: (Current feature film)
6:30–7:30pm	Music for dancing in the Solaris Lounge
6:30–7:30pm	Musical happy hour with our live trio
6:45–7:30pm	Musical entertainment in the Grill Bar
9–9:45pm	Continuous music for your dancing and listening pleasure with the Starlight Orchestra
10pm	Featured entertainment
10:30pm	Movie presentation: (Current feature film)
11pm	Music begins and goes until the wee hours
11pm	The Taverna Night Club cranks up with a beat and DJ
11–11:45pm	Continuous music with our live trio and the Starlight Orchestra
11pm–midnight	Light night snack buffet

Dining Hours: Early-Risers Coffee & Danish 6:30–7:30am • Breakfast Buffet & À la Carte 7:30–9:30am • Breakfast Buffet 8:30–10am • Hot Bouillion Served 11am • Luncheon 12:30pm • Luncheon Buffet 12:30–2pm • Afternoon Tea 4–5pm • Dinner 7:30 • Light Night Snacks 11pm–midnight

Dress for the Evening: Formal

DINNER MAIN COURSES

Rock Lobster Mediterranean style

Medallions of Veal • *with forest mushrooms*

Roast Duckling à la Bigarade • *with orange sauce*

Roast Prime Tenderloin of Beef • *with Bordelaise sauce*

Smoked Turkey Breast • *with seasonal fruits*

FIRST-DAY ACTIVITIES

3pm	Embarkation begins. Welcome aboard.
3–10pm	Port talk on St. Barts and Antigua, broadcast on Suite TV channel 7
4:30pm	All ashore who's going ashore. Those sailing should be aboard by this time.
4:30pm	Compulsory lifeboat mustering for all guests
4:45pm	Join the family on deck as the captain prepares to depart. Enjoy the music of our live quartet as we sail away.
6:30pm	Enjoy the piano stylings of our featured player during cocktails
6:45pm	Who's Who! Cruise director welcomes you to the Portofino Bar and introduces our travel manager, cruise consultant, staff managers, and entertainers.
9pm	Join gamblers for blackjack and slot machine action
9:30pm	Coffee and liqueurs served to the sounds of the live quartet for your listening and dancing pleasure throughout the evening
10:15pm	Musical fun quiz. Staff members ask the musical questions. Your team could be sipping the prize champagne tonight.

Dining Hours: Dinner 7:30–9:30pm

Dress for the Evening: Casual (jacket for men) after 6pm

DINNER MAIN COURSES

Sautéed Norwegian Salmon • *with sour cream and chive sauce*

Broiled Maine Lobster • *in champagne butter sauce*

Loin of Lamb • *with eggplant and prosciutto baked in phylo dough*

Roast Prime Rib of Beef • *in natural gravy*

Grilled Veal Chop • *with mango slice and watercress purée*

STAR CLIPPERS

DAY IN PORT

8–8:30am	Morning fitness on the Tropical Deck
10am	The Captain will introduce his officers and staff on the Tropical deck
10:30am–noon	Sports team hands out snorkeling gear on the Sports Deck
11am	Meeting for certified and noncertified divers in the Library
Noon	"Discover Scuba" theory lessons. If you are interested in trying scuba diving, you should attend this class in the Library.
1pm	*Star Clipper* drops anchor off Hillsborough. A tender service to the island will begin and leave every half hour from the ship.
4pm	"Discover Scuba" practical class in the aft deck pool
4:30pm	Last tender from the beach. Beautiful night sail to Grenada.
5pm	Storytime with captain on the Sundeck. Information talk on Grenada.
7–8:30pm	Cocktail hour—Come and join us in the Piano Bar for one of our special early evening cocktails
10pm	Music quiz in the Piano Bar

Dining Hours: Continental Breakfast 6:30–10am • Buffet Breakfast 8–10am • Luncheon Buffet noon–4pm • Hors d'Oeuvres 5–6pm • Dinner 7:30–9:30pm • Late-Night Snacks 11:30pm–12:30am

Dress for the Evening: Casual

DINNER MAIN COURSES

Filet of Turbot • *with lobster sauce*

Roast Duckling • *with grapes and Curaçao sauce*

(Chef's specials are also available each evening)

Tall Ship Adventures doesn't publish daily activity calendars. See the line review in chapter 9 for a description of shipboard life.

DINNER MAIN COURSES

Mahimahi • *with scalloped potatoes and mixed vegetables*

BBQ Chicken and Pork Chops • *with rice and peas*

Steak • *with oven-browned potatoes and glazed carrots*

Curry Shrimp • *with white rice and peas and carrots*

BBQ Steak/Fish • *with cauliflower cheese bake and corn on the cob*

Turkey and Dressing • *with mashed potatoes and gravy and mixed vegetables*

Broiled Lobster Tails • *with creamed noodles and mixed vegetables*

Windjammer Barefoot Cruises doesn't publish daily activity calendars. See the line review in chapter 9 for a description of shipboard life.

DINNER MAIN COURSES

Curried Beef

Grilled Wahoo

Garlic Roast Pork with Guava Sauce

Linguini Bolognese

Prime Ribs

Cornish Game Hens

Coconut Fried Shrimp

WINDSTAR® CRUISES
A HOLLAND AMERICA LINE COMPANY

DAY IN PORT

6am–midnight	Fitness room and sauna open
7:30am	Sports store is open. Stop by and get your snorkeling gear.
8am	Daily quiz is available at the Reception
8am	*Wind Star* will anchor off Isle des Saintes. Tender service will begin after arrival and run every 30 minutes.
8:15am, 10:30am	Divers meet on deck 2 aft for your dive
1:30–4pm	Sports Platform open. Join staff for swmming, windsurfing, sailing, water skiing, kayaking, and banana boat rides.
2:30pm	Bridge get-together in the Library
4:30pm	All aboard. The last tender departs from Isle des Saintes.
4:30pm	Meet in the lounge for an informal talk on marine conservation
5pm	*Wind Star* sails for Pigeon Island, St. Lucia
6–7pm	Join gamblers in the Casino
6:30–8pm	Cocktails in the lounge with music by our duo. Join chefs for caviar and smoked salmon.
7:15pm	Your host will be in the lounge for a briefing on your day tomorrow in Pigeon Island, St. Lucia
9:30pm	Dance to the upbeat sounds of our musical duo
9:30pm	Join gamblers in the Casino for blackjack and poker

Dining Hours: Continental Breakfast 6–10am • Breakfast 7:30–9:30am • Lunch 12:30–2pm • Tea 4–5pm • Dinner 7:30–9:15pm

Dress for the Evening: Casual (Please, no shorts, jeans, or tennis shoes in the restaurant)

DINNER MAIN COURSES

Grilled Filet of Fresh Swordfish • *with French lentils and apple smoked bacon*

Roasted Young Chicken • *with creamy polenta, artichokes, and crispy Parmesan chips*

Broiled Tenderloin of Beef • *with roasted shallot ravioli, sautéed mushrooms, and a garlic sauce*

Veal Osso Buco • *served with vegetables and pasta*

Homemade Garlic Gnocchi • *with pancetta, aparagus, and sun-dried tomatoes*

Appendix C:
Wrapping Up Your Cruise—
Debarkation Concerns

Hardly anybody likes to get off the ship at the end of their cruise, but it's part of the deal. To make matters easier, here's a discussion of a few matters you'll have to take care of before heading back to home sweet home.

1 Tipping

Like waiters and waitresses in the U.S., the cruise industry pays its staff low wages, with the understanding that the bulk of their salaries will come from tips. No matter which cabin you occupied or what price you paid for it, if service is satisfactory, you'll be expected to tip a recommended amount (of course, you can always tip more), which comes to about $70 per person (adult or child) for a weeklong cruise. Only some upscale ships, including Radisson's *Radisson Diamond,* forbid tipping altogether.

Tipping is so formally integrated into the cruise experience that it's almost ritualistic, and cruise lines aren't shy about reminding you. Each line has clear **guidelines for gratuities,** which are usually printed in the daily schedule or announced toward the end of the cruise. Likewise, cabin stewards usually leave **little white envelopes** (marked for cabin attendants, dining stewards, and waiters) along with suggested tipping percentages and amounts where you'll be sure not to miss them. Other lines, usually the small, offbeat lines like Windjammer Barefoot Cruises, prefer that a single tip be delivered to a central source; the pooled funds are then equitably distributed to the crew.

Even on lines like Holland America and Windstar, which promote their "tipping not required" policies, tipping really is expected and the policy is more a way to be diplomatic than to discourage tipping. Granted, if you received truly lousy service, reflect that in the tip you leave as you would at a restaurant shoreside.

Suggested tipping amounts vary slightly with the line and its degree of luxury. As a rule of thumb, however, each passenger should expect to tip about $3.50 per person per day for the **cabin steward** and the **dining room waiter** and about $2 for the dining room **busboy.** (As a generous tipper and one-time waitress, if service has been good, I generally throw in another $5 or $10 for each at the end of the week, but this of course is not necessary.) Like at any good hotel, feel free to distribute additional tips to anyone else who made your life particularly pleasant during your time on board.

Wine stewards and **bartenders** are usually rewarded with a 15% surcharge that's added onto a bill every time you sign it; of course, you may want to tip more if you're a barfly. Some lines suggest you tip the **maître d'** about $5 per person for the week and slip another couple of bucks to the **chief housekeeper;** it's your choice (if I've never even met these people, I don't feel obligated to tip them). Some maître d's will appreciate a discreet tip if they've gone to the trouble of reassigning you to a new table at dinner; some will not accept tips for this.

Tip **masseurs and masseuses, hair stylists,** and **manicurists** immediately after they work on you; 15% is standard. Tips can be paid in cash or charged to your onboard account (and the Steiner spa and salon people will do this for you unless you indicate otherwise; don't feel pressured into giving a tip if your treatment was not satisfactory).

WHEN DO YOU DISTRIBUTE YOUR TIPS?

It's good form to tip your dining stewards during the cruise's final dinner, instead of waiting until breakfast the next morning, when stewards might be assigned other stations or be unavailable. Incidentally, you are expected to tip your waiter and busboy for each night of your cruise, even if you did not dine in the main restaurant an evening or two.

SPECIAL TIPPING SITUATIONS

In case you didn't know, tipping the captain or one of the captain's officers is a no-no (they're on full salary, and are—or are expected to be—above all that). If you found someone among the staff to be outstandingly able and helpful, be sure to say so on the **comment card** that's left in your cabin toward the end of your cruise. If you're feeling especially ambitious and kindhearted, write a brief letter praising this person's performance and send it to the cruise line's director of passenger services.

2 Disembarking

You knew it would finally get to this.

It's a good idea to begin packing before dinner of the final night aboard, and be sure to fill out the **luggage tags** given to you, which might be color-coded, and attach them securely to each piece (if you need more than they leave for you, there are always extras at the purser's desk). You'll be requested to leave your luggage outside your cabin door before you retire for the cruise's final night (by midnight or so), and in the wee hours a crew of deckhands will pick it up and spirit it away. The luggage will be tossed into big rolling carts (like the airlines use) somewhere below deck, and at disembarkation, you'll find your baggage waiting for you at the terminal, organized by the colored or numbered tags you attached to it.

If you've neglected to place any baggage outside your door before the designated deadline, you'll have to lug it off the ship yourself. If you leave something behind, the cruise line might eventually return it to you (if it's ever turned in, of course), but not without a prolonged hassle.

Cruise Tip: Don't Pack Your Booze

Don't pack newly purchased bottles of liquor in the luggage you leave out for the crew to carry off the ship, thinking it's only going 100 yards between your cabin and the terminal before you see it again. A friend absently-mindedly did this and the next morning found her bag sitting in the terminal in a pool of rum. Big mess!

Ships normally arrive in port on the final day of the cruise between 6 and 8am, and need at least 90 minutes to unload baggage and complete dockage formalities. That means no one disembarks much before 9am, and it can sometimes take until 10 before you're allowed to leave the ship.

When disembarkation is announced, get ready for the chaos. No matter how you slice it, departures just aren't graceful, and are, frankly, a blunt return to reality. The staff is distracted and busily preparing for the new group of passengers boarding a few hours later (the friendly bartender you chatted with every night or the perky social hostess may not have much time for you now); the crew has only about 5 hours to prepare the ship for the next departure.

Since guests are generally asked to vacate their cabins by about 8am so stewards can begin cleaning them for the arriving guests, pooped people by the hundreds, surrounded by their bags, fill virtually every available inch of every public area (stairs and floors not excluded), waiting to hear the numbers they've been assigned so they can finally depart. Remember, **patience is a virtue.**

It's no surprise that this whole process goes much more smoothly on smaller ships with fewer passengers.

Disembarking through the cruise ship terminal is the equivalent of departing from an international flight. You need to claim your luggage and then pass through customs before exiting the terminal. This normally entails handing the immigration officer your filled-out customs declaration form as you breeze past, without even coming to a full stop. There are generally **porters** available in the terminals, but you might have to haul your luggage through customs before you can get to them. It's customary to pay them at least $1 per bag. Alternatively, there may be **wheeled carts** available (for free or no more than $1.50 each) to help you push your possessions out the door.

3 Customs

Customs officers are most interested in expensive, big-ticket items like cameras, jewelry, china, or silverware. They don't care much about your souvenir items unless you've bought so many that they couldn't possibly be intended for your personal use, or they're concealing illegal substances.

U.S. CUSTOMS

The U.S. government generously allows U.S. citizens $1,200 worth of duty-free imports every 30 days from the U.S. Virgin Islands; those who exceed their exemption are taxed at a 5% rate, rather than the normal 10%. The limit is $400 for your regular international destinations such as the French islands of Guadeloupe and Martinique. The limit is $600 if you return directly from the following islands and countries: Antigua and Barbuda, Aruba, the Bahamas, Barbados, Belize, Costa Rica, Dominica, the Dominican Republic, Grenada, Guatemala, Haiti, Honduras, Jamaica, Montserrat, the Netherland Antilles (Curaçao, Bonaire, Sint Maarten, Saba, and St. Eustatius), Panama, St. Kitts and Nevis, St. Lucia, St. Vincent and the Grenadines, Trinidad and Tobago, and the British Virgin Islands. If, for instance, your cruise stops in the U.S. Virgin Islands and the Bahamas, your total limit is $1,200 and no more than $600 of that amount can be from the Bahamas. If you visit only Puerto Rico, you don't have to go through customs at all, since it's an American commonwealth.

U.S. citizens or returning residents at least 21 years of age who are traveling directly or indirectly from the U.S. Virgin Islands are allowed to bring in free of duty 1,000 cigarettes. Duty-free limitations on articles from other countries are generally 1 liter of alcohol, 200 cigarettes (one carton), and 100 cigars (not Cuban). Unsolicited gifts can be mailed to friends and relatives on the U.S. mainland at the rate of $200 per day from the U.S. Virgin Islands or $100 per day from other islands. Unsolicited gifts of any value can be mailed from Puerto Rico. Most meat or meat products, fruit, plants, vegetables, or plant-derived products will be seized by U.S. Customs agents unless they're accompanied by an import license from a U.S. government agency.

Joint Customs declarations are possible for members of a family traveling together. For instance, if you're a husband and wife with two children, your exemptions in the U.S. Virgin Islands become duty-free up to $4,800!

Collect receipts for all purchases made abroad. Sometimes merchants suggest making up a false receipt to undervalue your purchase, but be aware that you could be involved in a "sting" operation—the merchant might be an informer to U.S. Customs. You must also declare on your customs form all gifts received during your stay abroad.

I've found clearing customs in Florida to be a painless and speedy process, with customs officials rarely asking for anything more than your filled-out customs declaration form as they nod you through the door. Of course, better safe than sorry. It's prudent to carry proof that you purchased expensive cameras or jewelry on the U.S. mainland. If you purchased such an item during an earlier trip abroad, you should carry proof that you have previously paid customs duty on the item.

To be on the safe side, if you use any medication containing controlled substances or requiring injection, carry an original prescription or note from your doctor.

For more specifics, request the free *Know Before You Go* pamphlet from the U.S. Customs Service, P.O. Box 7407, Washington, DC 20044 (☎ **202/927-6724;** www.customs.ustreas.gov).

CANADIAN CUSTOMS

Canada allows its citizens a $500 exemption if they are out of the country for at least 7 days, and they are permitted to bring back duty-free 200 cigarettes, 200 grams of tobacco, 40 Imperial ounces of liquor, and 50 cigars. In addition, they are allowed to mail gifts valued at $60 (Canadian) or less to Canada from abroad, provided the gifts are unsolicited and aren't alcohol or tobacco. It's a good idea to enclose a gift card and write on the package: "Unsolicited gift, under $60 value." All valuables, such as expensive cameras you already own, should be declared with their serial numbers on the Y-38 Form before departure from Canada.

For more information, write for the *I Declare* booklet, issued by **Revenue Canada,** 2265 St. Laurent Blvd., Ottawa, ON, KIG 4K3, or call them at (☎ **800/461-9999** or 613/993-0534.

BRITISH CUSTOMS

If you return from the Caribbean either directly to the United Kingdom or arrive via a port in another European Community (EC) country where you and your baggage did not pass through Customs controls, you must go through U.K. Customs and declare any goods in excess of the allowances. These are 200 cigarettes, 100 cigarillos, 50 cigars, or 250 grams of tobacco; 2 liters of still table wine and 1 liter of spirits or strong liqueurs (over 22% alcohol by volume), or 2 liters of fortified or sparkling wine or other liqueurs; 60cc/ml of perfume; 250cc/ml of toilet water; and £145 worth of all other goods, including gifts and souvenirs. (No one under 17 years of age is entitled to a tobacco or alcohol allowance.) Only go through the green "nothing to declare" line if you're sure you have no more than the Customs allowances and no prohibited or restricted goods.

For further information, contact **HM Customs and Excise Office,** Dorset House, Stamford Street, London SE1 9PY (☎ **0171/202-4227**).

Appendix D: Airline & Chain Hotel Toll-Free Numbers & Web Sites

AIRLINES

Air Canada
☎ 800/776-3000
www.aircanada.ca

American Airlines
☎ 800/433-7300
www.americanair.com

America West Airlines
☎ 800/235-9292
www.americawest.com

British Airways
☎ 800/247-9297
☎ 0345/222-111 in Britain
www.british-airways.com

Canadian Airlines International
☎ 800/426-7000
www.cdnair.ca

Continental Airlines
☎ 800/525-0280
www.flycontinental.com

Delta Air Lines
☎ 800/221-1212
www.delta-air.com

Kiwi International Air Lines
☎ 800/538-5494
www.jetkiwi.com

Midway Airlines
☎ 800/446-4392

Northwest Airlines
☎ 800/225-2525
www.nwa.com

Tower Air
☎ 800/34-TOWER (800/348-6937)
www.towerair.com

Trans World Airlines (TWA)
☎ 800/221-2000
www.twa.com

United Airlines
☎ 800/241-6522
www.ual.com

US Airways
☎ 800/428-4322
www.usair.com

Virgin Atlantic Airways
☎ 800/862-8621 in continental U.S.
☎ 0293/747-747 in Britain
www.fly.virgin.com

MAJOR HOTEL & MOTEL CHAINS

Best Western International
☎ 800/528-1234
www.bestwestern.com

Clarion Hotels
☎ 800/CLARION
www.hotelchoice.com/cgi-bin/res/webres?clarion.html

Comfort Inns
☎ 800/228-5150
www.hotelchoice.com/cgi-bin/res/webres?comfort.html

Courtyard by Marriott
☎ 800/321-2211
www.courtyard.com

Days Inn
☎ 800/325-2525
www.daysinn.com

Doubletree Hotels
☎ 800/222-TREE
www.doubletreehotels.com

Econo Lodges
☎ 800/55-ECONO
www.hotelchoice.com/cgi-bin/res/
    webres?econo.html

Fairfield Inn by Marriott
☎ 800/228-2800
www.fairfieldinn.com

Hampton Inn
☎ 800/HAMPTON
www.hampton-inn.com

Hilton Hotels
☎ 800/HILTONS
www.hilton.com

Holiday Inn
☎ 800/HOLIDAY
www.holiday-inn.com

Howard Johnson
☎ 800/654-2000
www.hojo.com/hojo.html

Hyatt Hotels & Resorts
☎ 800/228-9000
www.hyatt.com

ITT Sheraton
☎ 800/325-3535
www.sheraton.com

La Quinta Motor Inns
☎ 800/531-5900
www.laquinta.com

Marriott Hotels
800/228-9290
www.marriott.com

Motel 6
☎ 800/4-MOTEL6 (800/466-8536)

Quality Inns
☎ 800/228-5151
www.hotelchoice.com/cgi-bin/res/
    webres?quality.html

Radisson Hotels International
☎ 800/333-3333
www.radisson.com

Ramada Inns
☎ 800/2-RAMADA
www.ramada.com

Red Carpet Inns
☎ 800/251-1962

Red Lion Hotels & Inns
☎ 800/547-8010
www.travelweb.com

Red Roof Inns
☎ 800/843-7663
www.redroof.com

Residence Inn by Marriott
☎ 800/331-3131
www.residenceinn.com

Rodeway Inns
☎ 800/228-2000
www.hotelchoice.com/cgi-bin/res/
    webres?rodeway.html

Super 8 Motels
☎ 800/800-8000
www.super8motels.com

Travelodge
☎ 800/255-3050

Vagabond Inns
☎ 800/522-1555
www.vagabondinns.com

Wyndham Hotels and Resorts
☎ 800/822-4200 in Continental U.S.
    and Canada
www.wyndham.com

Frommer's Online Directory

By Michael Shapiro

Michael Shapiro is the author of *Internet Travel Planning*
(The Globe Pequot Press).

Frommer's Online Directory is a new feature designed to help you take advantage of the Internet to better plan your trip. Part 1 lists general Internet resources that can make any trip easier, such as sites for booking airline tickets. In Part 2 you'll find some top online cruise sites, including those of the cruise lines themselves and of agencies like the Centers for Disease Control (which monitors cleanliness of cruise ships), plus others that offer cruise deals, listings of cruise-oriented travel agents, and commentary by your fellow cruisers. Part 3 includes sites for Caribbean destinations and leading cruise lines, organized by island. Please keep in mind that this is not a comprehensive list, but rather a discriminating selection to get you started. We've awarded stars to the best sites, which are earned, not paid for (unlike some Web-site rankings that are based on payment).

1 Top Travel-Planning Web Sites

Among the most popular travel sites are online travel agencies. The top agencies, including **Expedia, Preview Travel,** and **Travelocity,** offer an array of tools that are valuable even if you don't book online. You can check flight schedules, cruise packages, hotel availability, or even get paged if your flight is delayed.

While online agencies have come a long way over the past few years, they don't always yield the best price. Unlike a travel agent, for example, they're unlikely to tell you that you can save money by flying a day earlier or a day later. On the other hand, if you're looking for a bargain fare, you might find something online that an agent wouldn't take the time to dig up. Because airline commissions have been cut, a travel agent might not find it worthwhile to spend half an hour trying to find you the best deal. On the Net, you can be your own agent and take all the time you want.

Online booking sites aren't the only places to book airline tickets. All **major airlines** have their own Web sites and often offer incentives, such as bonus frequent flyer miles or Net-only discounts, for buying online. These incentives have helped airlines capture the majority of the online booking market. According to Jupiter Communications, online agencies such as Travelocity booked about 80% of tickets purchased online in 1996, but by 2000, airline sites (such as the United

Net Security

Far more people look online than book online, partly because they fear putting their credit cards through on the Net. Although secure encryption has made this fear less justified, there's no reason why you can't find a flight online and then book it by calling a toll-free number or contacting your travel agent. To be sure you're in secure mode when you book online, look for a little icon of a key (in Netscape) or a padlock (Internet Explorer) at the bottom of your Web browser.

Airlines site, www.ual.com) were projected to own more than 60% of the online market, with online agencies' share of the pie dwindling each year.

Note: See Appendix D, "Airline & Chain Hotel Toll-Free Numbers & Web Sites," for toll-free numbers and Web addresses for airlines and hotels.

WHEN SHOULD YOU BOOK ONLINE?

Online booking is not for everyone. If you prefer to let others handle your travel arrangements, one call to an experienced travel agent should suffice. But if you want to know as much as possible about your options, the Net is a good place to start, especially for bargain hunters. Hundreds of thousands of people have embraced online booking for airline tickets, but far fewer feel comfortable booking cruises online, because choosing a cruise is much more involved than booking an airline ticket.

The most compelling reason to use online booking is to take advantage of last-minute specials, such as last-minute cruise deals or Internet-only airfares that must be purchased online. Another advantage is that you can cash in on incentives for booking online, such as rebates or bonus frequent flyer miles. Online booking works best for flights within North America—for international tickets, it's usually cheaper and easier to use a travel agent or consolidator.

LEADING BOOKING SITES

Below are listings for the top travel booking sites. The starred selections are the most useful and best designed sites.

Cheap Tickets. www.cheaptickets.com
Essentials: Discounted rates on domestic and international airline tickets and hotel rooms.

Sometimes discounters such as Cheap Tickets have exclusive deals that aren't available through mainstream channels. Registration at Cheap Tickets requires entering a credit card number before getting started, which is one reason many people elect to call the company's toll-free number rather than book online. One of the most frustrating things about the Cheap Tickets site is that it will offer fare quotes for a route, and later show this fare is not valid for your dates of travel (other Web sites, such as Preview Travel, consider your dates of travel before showing what fares are available). Despite its problems, Cheap Tickets can be worth the effort because its fares can be lower than those offered by its competitors.

✪ **Expedia. expedia.com**
Essentials: Domestic and international flight hotel and rental car booking, late-breaking travel news, destination features and commentary from travel experts, and deals on cruises and vacation packages. Free registration is required for booking.

Expedia's Cruise Outlet (**www.expcruiseoutlet.com**) recently listed some cruise specials on its home page, such as a 4-day Baja cruise for $349. But when I tried its

---

Take a Look at the Frommer's Site!

Of course, we're a little biased, but we highly recommend Arthur Frommer's Budget Travel Online (**www.frommers.com**) as an excellent travel-planning resource that's especially valuable for finding cruise deals, plus indispensable travel tips, reviews, monthly vacation giveaways, and online booking. Best Cruise Bargains (**www.frommers.com/hottest/cruise**) includes the latest specials on cruises around the world.

Subscribe to Arthur Frommer's Daily Newsletter (**www.frommers.com/ newsletters**) to get the latest travel bargains and inside travel secrets in your mailbox every day. You'll read daily headlines and articles from the dean of travel himself, highlighting last-minute deals on airfares, accommodations, cruises, and package vacations. You'll also find great travel advice by checking our Tip of the Day or Hot Spot of the Month.

Search our Destinations archive (**www.frommers.com/destinations**) of more than 200 domestic and international destinations for great places to stay, tips for traveling there, and what to do while you're there. Once you've researched your trip, you might try our online reservation system (**www.frommers.com/ booktravelnow**) to book your dream vacation at affordable prices.

---

search engine, where you enter your destination, travel dates, and budget, Expedia twice coughed up a blank page. This has the potential to be a valuable planning tool, but at press time it wasn't much to write home about.

On the other hand, Expedia makes it easy to handle flight, hotel, and car booking on one itinerary, so it's a good place for one-stop shopping. Expedia's hotel search offers crisp, zoomable maps to pinpoint most properties—particularly valuable if you're booking a pre-cruise stay in a port of call and want a hotel close to the docks. Another option allows you to click on the camera icon to see images of hotel rooms and facilities. Like many online databases, though, Expedia focuses on the major chains, such as Hilton and Hyatt, so don't expect to find too many one-of-a-kind resorts or B&Bs here.

Once you're registered (it's necessary to do this only once from each computer you use), you can start booking with the Roundtrip Fare Finder box on the home page, which expedites the process. After selecting a flight, you can hold it until midnight the following day or purchase online. If you think you might do better through a travel agent, you'll have time to try to get a lower price.

Preview Travel. www.previewtravel.com
Essentials: Domestic and international flight, hotel and rental car booking; Travel Newswire lists fare sales; and deals on cruises and vacation packages. Free (one-time) registration is required for booking. Express booking for members, although at press time this feature was buried below the fold on Preview's reservation page.

Preview features the most inviting interface for booking trips, but the wealth of graphics can make the site somewhat slow to load. Use Farefinder to quickly find the lowest current fares on flights to dozens of major cities. Carfinder offers a similar service for rental cars, but you can search only airport locations, not city pick-up sites. To see the lowest fare for your itinerary, enter the dates and times for your route and see what Preview comes up with. The site's Best Fare Finder feature searches for the best deal on your itinerary, and then checks flights that are a bit later or earlier to see if it

---

Note to AOL Users

You can book flights, hotels, rental cars, and cruises on AOL at keyword: Travel. The booking software is provided by Preview Travel and is similar to Preview on the Web. Use the AOL "Travelers Advantage" program to earn a 5% rebate on flights, hotel rooms, and car rentals.

---

might be cheaper to fly at a different time. While these searches have become quite sophisticated, they still occasionally overlook deals that might be uncovered by a top-notch travel agent. If you have the time, see what you can find online and then call an agent to see if you can get a better price.

With Preview's Fare Alert feature, you can set fares for up to three routes and you'll get e-mail notices when the fare drops below your target amount. For example, you could tell Preview to alert you when the fare from New York to Miami drops below $200. If it does, you'll get an e-mail message telling you the current fare.

Priceline.com. www.priceline.com
Essentials: Launched in 1998 with a $10 million ad campaign featuring William Shatner, Priceline lets you "name your price" for domestic and international airline tickets.

Here's how it works: You select a route and dates, guarantee with a credit card, and make a bid for what you're willing to pay. If one of the airlines in Priceline's database has a fare that's lower than your bid, your credit card is automatically charged for a ticket. The downside? You can't say when you want to fly—you have to accept any flight leaving between 6am and 10pm, and you may have to make a stopover. Also, no frequent flyer miles are awarded, and tickets are nonrefundable and can't be exchanged for another flight. So if your plans change, you're out of luck. Priceline can be good for travelers who have to take off on short notice (and who are thus unable to qualify for advance purchase discounts), but this isn't usually the case if you're booking a flight to get to your cruise. If you do use the service, be sure to shop around first—if you overbid, you're required to purchase the ticket and Priceline pockets the difference.

Travelocity. www.travelocity.com
Essentials: Domestic and international flight, hotel, and rental car booking; and deals on cruises and vacation packages. Travel Headlines spotlights latest bargain airfares. Free (one-time) registration is required for booking.

Travelocity almost got it right. Its Express Booking feature enables travelers to complete the booking process more quickly than at Expedia or Preview, but Travelocity gums up the works with a page called "Featured Airlines." Big placards of several featured airlines compete for your attention—if you want to see the fares for all available airlines, click the much smaller box at the bottom of the page labeled "Book a Flight."

Some have worried that Travelocity, which is owned by American Airlines' parent company, AMR, directs bookings to American. This doesn't seem to be the case; I've booked there dozens of times and have always been directed to the cheapest listed flight, for example, on Tower or ATA. But this "Featured Airlines" page seems to be Travelocity's way of trying to cash in with ads and incentives for booking certain airlines: You get 1,500 bonus frequent flyer miles if you book through United's site, for example, but the site doesn't tell you about other airlines that might be cheaper. If the United flight costs $150 more than the best deal on another airline, it's not worth spending the extra money for a relatively small number of bonus miles.

On the plus side, Travelocity has some leading-edge techie tools for modern travelers. Fare Watcher is an "intelligent agent" that keeps you informed of the best fares offered for the city pairs (round-trips) of your choice. Whenever the fare changes by $25 or more, Fare Watcher alerts you by e-mail. Through Flight Paging (which makes sense only if you own an alphanumeric pager with national access that can receive e-mail), Travelocity's paging system can alert you if your flight is delayed.

FINDING LODGINGS ONLINE

While the services above offer hotel booking, it can be better to use a site devoted primarily to lodging because you might find properties that aren't listed on more general online travel agencies. Some lodging sites specialize in a particular type of accommodation, such as bed-and-breakfast inns, which you won't find on the more mainstream booking services. Other services, such as TravelWeb, offer weekend deals on major chain properties, which cater to business travelers and have more empty rooms on weekends.

All Hotels on the Web. www.all-hotels.com
Okay, so this site doesn't include all the hotels on the Web, but it does have tens of thousands of listings throughout the world. Bear in mind that each hotel listed has paid a small fee of $25 and up for placement, so it's not an objective list, but more like a book of online brochures.

Hotel Reservations Network. www.180096hotel.com
Bargain room rates at hotels in more than two dozen U.S. and international cities. The cool thing is that HRN books blocks of rooms in advance, so sometimes it has discounted rooms at hotels that are "sold out." Select a city, enter your dates, and you'll get a list of best prices for a selection of hotels. Descriptions include an image of the property and a locator map; to book online, click the "Book Now" button. HRN is notable for some deep discounts, even in cities where hotel rooms are expensive. The toll-free number is printed all over this site; call it if you want more options than are listed online.

Places to Stay. www.placestostay.com
Mostly one-of-a-kind places in the U.S. and abroad that you might not find in other directories, with a focus on resort accommodations. Again, listing is selective—this isn't a comprehensive directory, but can give you a sense of what's available at different destinations.

✪ TravelWeb. www.travelweb.com
TravelWeb lists more than 16,000 hotels worldwide, focusing on chains such as Hyatt and Hilton, and you can book almost 90% of them online. TravelWeb's Click-It Weekends, updated each Monday, offers weekend deals at many leading hotel chains. TravelWeb is the online home for Pegasus Systems, which provides transaction processing systems for the hotel industry.

LAST-MINUTE DEALS & OTHER ONLINE BARGAINS

Just as airlines have taken to the Net to offer last-minute bargains, cruise companies are coming online with similar deals. Several sites, such as Arthur Frommer's Budget Travel Online, collect late-breaking cruise deals, and some, including 1travel.com, will e-mail these to you each week.

Most airline deals are announced on Tuesday or Wednesday and are valid for travel the following weekend, but some can be booked weeks or months in advance. You can sign up for weekly e-mail alerts at airlines' sites (for airline's Web site addresses, see Appendix E) or check sites such as WebFlyer (see below) that compile lists of these bargains. To make it easier, visit a site (see below) that rounds up all the deals and sends them in one convenient weekly e-mail. But last-minute deals aren't the only online bargains; other sites can help you find value even if you can't wait until the eleventh hour.

✪ 1travel.com. www.1travel.com
Deals on domestic and international flights, cruises, hotels, and all-inclusive resorts such as Club Med. 1travel.com's Saving Alert compiles last-minute air deals so you don't have to scroll through multiple e-mail alerts. A feature called "Drive a little using low-fare airlines" helps map out strategies for using alternative airports to find lower fares. Farebeater searches a database that includes published fares, consolidator bargains, and special deals exclusive to 1travel.com. *Note:* The travel agencies listed by 1travel.com have paid for placement.

BestFares. www.bestfares.com
Budget seeker Tom Parsons lists some great bargains on airfares, hotels, rental cars, and cruises, but the site is poorly organized. News Desk is a long list of hundreds of bargains but they're not broken down into cities or even countries, so it's not easy trying to find what you're looking for. If you have time to wade through it, you might find a good deal. Some material is available only to paid subscribers.

Go4less.com. www.go4less.com
Specializing in last-minute cruise and package deals, Go4less has some eye-popping offers, such as off-peak Caribbean cruises for under $100 per day. The site has a clean design but the bargains aren't organized by destination. You can avoid sifting through all this material by using the Search box and entering vacation type, destination, month, and price.

Moment's Notice. www.moments-notice.com
As the name suggests, Moment's Notice specializes in last-minute vacation and cruise deals. You can browse for free, but if you want to purchase a trip, you have to join Moment's Notice, which costs $25.

Smarter Living. www.smarterliving.com
Best known for its e-mail dispatch of weekend deals on 20 airlines, Smarter Living also keeps you posted about last-minute bargains on everything from Windjammer Cruises to flights to Iceland.

✪ WebFlyer. www.webflyer.com
WebFlyer is the ultimate online resource for frequent flyers and also has an excellent listing of last-minute air deals. Click on "Deal Watch" for a round-up of weekend deals on flights, hotels, and rental cars from domestic and international suppliers.

Late-Night Bookings

While most people learn about last-minute air deals from e-mail dispatches, it can be best to find out precisely when these offers become available and check airlines' Web sites at this time. To find out when deals become available, check the pages devoted to these deals on airlines' Web pages. Because these deals are limited, they can vanish within hours, sometimes even minutes, so it pays to log on as soon as they're available. An example: Southwest's specials are posted at 12:01am Tuesdays (Central time). So if you're looking for a cheap flight, stay up late and check Southwest's site at that time to grab the best new deals.

TRAVELER'S TOOLKIT

Veteran travelers usually carry some essential items to make their trips easier. Following is a selection of online tools to smooth your journey.

ATM Locators. Visa: www.visa.com/pd/atm.
Mastercard: www.mastercard.com/atm.
Find ATMs in hundreds of cities in the U.S. and around the world. Both include maps for some locations and both list airport ATM locations, some with maps. Remarkably, MasterCard lists ATMs on all seven continents (there's even one at Antarctica's McMurdo Station). *Tip:* You'll usually get a better exchange rate using ATMs than exchanging traveler's checks at banks.

Intellicast. www.intellicast.com
Weather forecasts for all 50 states and cities around the world. Note that temperatures are in Celsius for many international destinations.

✪ MapQuest. www.mapquest.com
Specializing in U.S. maps, MapQuest enables you to zoom in on a destination, calculate step-by-step driving directions between any two U.S. points, and locate restaurants, hotels, and other attractions on maps.

Net Café Guide. www.netcafeguide.com/mapindex.htm
Locate Internet cafes at hundreds of locations around the globe. Catch up on your e-mail, log onto the Web, and stay in touch with the home front, usually for just a few dollars per hour—as opposed to the up to $15 *per minute* you'll pay to call home from a ship at sea.

Tourism Offices Worldwide Directory. www.towd.com
An extensive listing of tourism offices, some with links to these offices' Web sites.

Trip.com: Airport Maps and Flight Status. www.trip.com
Mostly a business travel site where you can find out when an airborne flight is scheduled to arrive, the site also has a "Guides and Tools" function that allows you to peruse airport maps for more than 40 domestic cities.

Universal Currency Converter. www.xe.net/currency
See what your dollar or pound is worth in more than a hundred other countries. (Even though you'll rarely have to convert money at any Caribbean ports, it pays to know what the rate is—if only for perspective.)

U.S. Customs Service Traveler Information. www.customs.gov/travel/travel.htm
Wondering what you're allowed to bring in to the U.S.? Check at this thorough site, which includes maximum allowance and duty fees.

2 Leading Web Sites for Cruise Planning

The first section below includes some of the best Web sites dedicated specifically to cruises. The next section has the Web addresses of the cruise lines evaluated in this book, and the final section has the leading Web sites for about two dozen Caribbean cruise destinations, from Aruba to the Virgin Islands.

TOP CRUISE SITES

When it comes to planning a cruise, information is power. Using Web sites devoted to cruises can augment the information in this book. You can find some late-breaking deals, read cruise reviews from other travelers, and comparison shop with one click of your mouse. While travel agents are also an excellent resource, they can sometimes be influenced by incentives to book a certain number of cruises with a particular line. So get online, see what's out there, and then, armed with information from this book and the Net, seek the advice of a knowledgeable agent.

Caribbean Cruise and Travel Magazine.
  www.visitorinfo.com/caribbean/travel.htm
A nice collection of travel features on Caribbean cruising, lodging, and sightseeing. When your cruise is over, you can submit your story for consideration.

CDC Vessel Sanitation Program.
  www.cdc.gov/nceh/programs/sanit/vsp/scores/scores.htm
Twice each year, the CDC (Centers for Disease Control) rates sanitary conditions aboard all ships that have foreign itineraries and carry 13 or more passengers. Access this link for the latest test results.

✪ **Cruise Critic. www.cruisecritic.com or AOL keyword Cruise Critic**
This well-known site offers tons of reader reviews.

✪ **Cruise Lines International Association (CLIA). www.cruising.org**
CLIA, the cruise industry's marketing arm, maintains a Web site that lists CLIA-affiliated travel agencies and more.

Cruise News. www.cruise-news.com
News on seasonal and themed cruises and information about upcoming launches of new ships. You'll also find links to agents who specialize in selling cruise vacations.

Cruise News Daily. www.reply.net/clients/cruise/news.html
A matter-of-fact daily update on cruise news, such as delays on a cruise line unveiling a new ship, or special deals on off-peak cruises. You can sign up for a weekly e-mail dispatch or check the Web site daily for news items.

✪ **CruiseOpinion.com. www.cruiseopinion.com**
The most valuable part of CruiseOpinion.com is the section of passenger reviews. Most people who comment include their age, occupation, and number of cruises they've taken, and some add their e-mail address so you can send follow-up questions. This site is a fine example of travelers getting online to help one another.

Cruise Travel. www.travel.org/CruiseTravel
The Web site of this cruise-lovers' cruise magazine offers in-depth, well-researched articles on ships and all facets of cruising.

Cruise Week News. www.cruise-week.com
A concise roundup of the week's cruise news is posted each Wednesday. You can also have this dispatch delivered via e-mail.

Dialysis at Sea Cruises. www.dialysis-at-sea.com
"Dialysis doesn't take a vacation—but you can," says this Web site. Learn about cruises in the Caribbean and other destinations, all on ships outfitted to care for dialysis patients. Also see ADA Vacations Plus (**www.vacations-plus.com**).

Internet Cruise Travel Network. www.cruisetravel.com
This is an online cruise agency where you can check prices and look for special deals. It has far too many unnecessary images, which makes surfing slow here. In many cases, you can't find prices online but have to call a toll-free number for the latest deals.

Porthole. www.porthole.com
The Web site of this cruise magazine offers light feature articles on cruising and a great list of cruise links.

Sealetter. www.sealetter.com
This well-stocked Web site, managed by a husband-and-wife travel agent team, features lots of reader ship reviews, cruise tips, and loads of great cruise links.

Steiner Leisure. www.steinerleisure.com
Steiner runs most of the onboard spas in the cruise industry. Via its site, you can get a preview of the spa treatments you'll find aboard ship.

CRUISE LINE WEB SITES

Many of the leading cruise line sites offer similar features. Just about all of them include sailing schedules and itineraries, price estimates, ship descriptions, and destination information. Some offer last-minute specials for people who can book just a week or two ahead. At press time, we hadn't seen many other discounts for buying direct through cruise line Web sites, but these discounts are inevitable, so keep checking online.

American Canadian Caribbean Line	www.accl-smallships.com
Cape Canaveral Cruise Line	www.capecanaveralcruise.com
Carnival Cruise Lines	www.carnival.com
Celebrity Cruises	www.celebrity-cruises.com
Clipper Cruise Line	www.clippercruise.com
Commodore Cruise Line	www.commodorecruise.com
Costa Cruise Lines	www.costacruises.com
Crystal Cruises	www.crystalcruises.com
Cunard	www.cunardline.com
Disney Cruise Line	www.disneycruise.com
Holland America Line	www.hollandamerica.com
Mediterranean Shipping Cruises	crucerosmsc-arg.com
Norwegian Cruise Line	www.ncl.com
Premier Cruises	www.premiercruises.com
Princess Cruises	www.princess.com
Radisson Seven Seas Cruises	www.rssc.com
Regal Cruises	www.regalcruises.com
Royal Caribbean International	www.rccl.com
Royal Olympic Cruises	www.royalolympiccruises.com
Seabourn Cruise Line	www.seabourn.com
Star Clippers	www.star-clippers.com
Tall Ship Adventures	www.tallshipadventures.com
Windjammer Barefoot Cruises, Ltd.	www.windjammer.com
Windstar Cruises	www.windstarcruises.com

3 Caribbean Destinations

Most of the sites listed below cater more to land-based travelers who will be spending significant time on the islands and require lodging, but on-the-go cruise passengers may still find them useful to get a virtual idea of what awaits them at the ports of call. Also, some offer detailed information on dive sites for you scuba divers, and info on nightlife that's valuable if your ship will be in port late.

GENERAL REGIONAL SITES

Calabash Skyviews. www.skyviews.com
About 20 islands are covered here, and for each you'll find solid information on sightseeing, getting around (including driving tours), beaches, and shopping. Also included are links to tour operators and outfitters.

Caribbean Online. www.caribbean-on-line.com
A general interest guide to the Caribbean that can help you find tour operators, golf courses, sailing trips, and more. You'll also find advice on getting there, lodging, dining and shopping.

Caribbean Travel Planner. caribbeantravel.com
A general introduction, including maps, hotel listings, activities, and more.

The Civilized Explorer: Caribbean. www.cieux.com/trinfo3.html
A healthy collection of links for more than two dozen Caribbean destinations. Consider this site a port of embarkation rather than a destination in itself.

✪ Interknowledge: The Caribbean. www.interknowledge.com/indx02.htm
About a dozen destinations are covered here, mostly with official tourism bureau information. But don't let that discourage you—there's advice here on golfing, fishing, beaches, and points of interest. You'll also find a calendar of events.

Island Connoisseur: Caribbean SuperSite. caribbeansupersite.com
Use the pull-down menu on the home page to choose one of more than two dozen Caribbean destinations. Some of the general information is pretty thin, but you'll find a nice collection of links to Web sites featuring everything from dining to travelogues.

TravelFacts. www.travelfacts.com
Use the pull-down menu to select your destination and you'll find extensive listings for sightseeing, tours, dining, lodging, shopping, and more. Some of the navigation is clunky; for example, at press time, instead of listing all the essential information for a restaurant on one page, you had to click on separate links for details, contact info, etc.

Turqoise Net. www.turq.com
A bare-bones guide to some of the islands, with information on lodging and dining, but it does have links to some properties' own Web sites, which can be useful. You'll also find links to tourism offices, news from the Caribbean, maps, weather, and a photo album.

Yahoo Travel: Caribbean. travel.yahoo.com/Destinations/caribbean
Links, links, and more links. In a very simple format, Yahoo list sites for each Caribbean island and has categories for dining, lodging, and activities, as well as getting around, sports and outdoors, and general guides.

PORT-SPECIFIC SITES
ANTIGUA

✪ Antigua and Barbuda. www.antigua-barbuda.org
An extensive, well-designed, and informative guide from the Antigua & Barbuda Department of Tourism. The site covers about 20 subjects from Carnival to transportation.

Antigua Nice Ltd. www.antiguanice.com
A generic but useful guide to activities, dining, and lodging, with links to some companies' own Web sites.

Antigua Today. AntiguaToday.com
This collection of Antigua Web pages includes more than 400 referrals to hotels, restaurants, and other sites in Antigua.

ARUBA

Aruba Experience. www.aruba-experience.com
Tips for dining, shopping, and nightlife from the pages of this free tourist magazine.

✪ Visit Aruba. www.visitaruba.com
This Web site really gets it. Rather than trying to imitate a guide book, Visit Aruba offers features that complement this print guide. You'll find a news desk listing the latest happenings, trip reports from other travelers, a map of diving locations, even local recipes.

Welcome to Aruba. www.aruba.com
An updated events calendar plus listings for shopping, dining, lodging, and activities. Use the links and e-mail addresses here to get in touch with tour operators and outfitters.

BARBADOS

Barbados Tourism Encyclopedia. barbados.org
Information on events, special vacation package discounts, and advice on dining and lodging from the Barbados Tourism Authority. You'll also find maps, sightseeing tours, and shopping tips.

✪ Fun Barbados. funbarbados.com
This site lives up to its name: After you spend a few minutes hear you'll be itching to get to the islands. There's extensive information, from the basics (shopping, lodging, dining) to the more esoteric (biking, gardens, caves).

BRITISH VIRGIN ISLANDS

British Virgin Islands. www.bviwelcome.com
There's nothing spectacular about this site, but it has solid information on dining, lodging, and, best of all, activities. Click on "At Sea" and use the pull-down menu to choose from scuba, kayaking, or other water sports.

✪ Scuba Mom's BVI Resort Reviews. www.scubamom.com/bvi
Lynn McKamey (a.k.a. ScubaMom) offers extensive personal reviews of resorts and dive spots around the British Virgin Islands. You'll also find lots of pictures and maps, which can make pages slow to load, but they're worth the wait.

Ultimate BVI. www.ultimatebvi.com
While you'll find advice on dining, lodging, and shopping information here, most useful are the sections on diving and boating, with information on charters and e-mail links that enable you to contact the proprietors. One really annoying aspect of this site is that it launches a new browser window (which slows down surfing) when you click on some links.

Welcome to the British Virgin Islands. www.britishvirginislands.com
A well-designed but not very extensive guide to some of BVI's hotels, restaurants, and shops. Most useful are the sections on boating and water sports, where you can explore your options and use e-mail to connect with outfitters before you go.

COZUMEL

✪ Cozumel.net. www.cozumel.net
This site is a cut above the typical dining/lodging/activities sites. Click on "Fun Things to Do" for outfitters for scuba diving, snorkeling, deep sea fishing, and land-based adventures like mountain biking and camping.

✪ Isla Cozumel.net. www.islacozumel.net
Although this site is made up primarily of online brochures from dive shops, restaurants, and hotels, the listings are extensive and informative. You can comparison shop among dozens of dive shops, places to shop, and land-based adventures.

Viva Cozumel. viva-cozumel.com
With weather forecasts, links to dive shops, and listings for restaurants and hotels, this site can come in handy—just don't expect objectivity, as the businesses pay for space to advertise their wares.

CURAÇAO

✪ **Curacao.com. www.curacao.com**
With a seemingly endless supply of links, this site can help you find a beach, restaurant, or club for some late-night festivities. Curacao.com is well organized and has extensive sections on culture, tours, and events.

Curacao Official Tourism Site. www.curacao.org
If you can get past the hideous design, you might find some serviceable information on dining, lodging, diving, and other activities.

FREEPORT/LUCAYA & NASSAU

The Bahamas Guide. www.thebahamasguide.com
An island-by-island guide to water sports, dining, lodging, and shopping. Bear in mind that this guide lists only selected business (most likely those that pay for placement). Some of the listings, such as the one for The Lucayan resort, have links to the property's own Web site (**www.thelucayan.com**).

✪ **Bahamasnet. www.bahamasnet.com**
A well-organized site with sections on dining, hotels, activities, shopping, and more. Most of the listings have links to pages on the Bahamasnet site, pages that are presumably paid for.

✪ **Bahamas On-line. www.bahamas-on-line.com**
An easy-to-use directory for finding restaurants, lodging, dive shops, and more. Some listings link to outside Web sites; for example, the listing for Small Hope Bay Lodge links to that resort's home page (**www.SmallHope.com**).

Grand Bahama Island. www.grand-bahama.com
This guide from the Grand Bahama Island Tourism Board includes advice on what to do, where to stay, and what parks to visit. You'll also find a calendar of events and an e-mail link you can use to contact the board if you have any questions.

GRAND CAYMAN

Cayman Islands. www.caymanislands.ky
Find out about the Batabano Carnival or get up to speed on the Cayman Islands International Fishing Tournament. This site, from the Cayman Islands Department of Tourism, smartly features upcoming happenings on its home page, while also offering advice on dining, lodging, and shopping.

✪ **Cayman Web World. cayman.com.ky**
Cayman Web World does a fine job highlighting the Caymans' attractions and has advice for dining, lodging, and shopping.

GRENADA

Grenada. www.travelgrenada.com
From sights and tours to spices and recipes, this site captures the flavor of Grenada and can help you get the most from your trip. You'll find sections on shopping, water sports, cruises, lodging, and weddings.

Grenada: The Spice of the Caribbean. www.grenada.org
This site, from the Grenada Board of Tourism, includes basic visitor information.

GUADELOUPE

Antilles Info Tourisme: Guadeloupe.
    www.antilles-info-tourisme.com/guadeloupe/p2-in-gb.htm
Enjoy a virtual sightseeing tour or stock up on ideas for how to spend your time while in Guadeloupe. You'll also find basics on dining, lodging, nightlife, and even some

local recipes. This colorful site is illuminated with nice photography and captures the essence of the "butterfly island."

Guadeloupe: The Civilized Island. www.cieux.com/gdlp.html
While this is not the best-organized site, it has lots of nice photos, ideas for climbing a volcano, and insider advice.

JAMAICA

Discover Jamaica. www.discoverjamaica.com
Although this is a pretty generic site, you can find solid descriptions of Jamaica's regions, including dining, lodging, and activities.

✪ **Jamaica Tourist. www.jamaicans.com/tourist/index.htm**
An insider's guide to the island written from a Jamaican's perspective.

Jamaica Tourist Board. www.jamaicatravel.com
This official site does a nice job of providing detailed information.

KEY WEST

Discover: Key West. key-west.com
A well-rounded guide to Key West, including an events calendar and extensive listings for attractions, sightseeing, and art galleries.

Gay Key West Travel Guide. www.gaykeywestfl.com
A guide to gay-friendly lodgings, restaurants, and clubs.

MARTINIQUE

**Martinique (from See Caribbean).
   www.see-caribbean.com/martinique/index.html**
A pretty thin site, but it does have some nice images.

Tourist Martinique. www.touristmartinique.com
A decent general introduction to Martinique.

NASSAU

See "Freeport/Lucaya & Nassau," above.

PUERTO RICO

Escape to Puerto Rico. escape.topuertorico.com
This is an all-in-one site that will give you an idea of what to do even if you have just a little time in San Juan.

Welcome to Puerto Rico. Welcome.toPuertoRico.org
This site can help you get oriented and offers ideas for how to spend your time in Puerto Rico.

ST. BARTS

St. Barth's Online. www.st-barths.com/guide.html
While many people come to St. Barts simply to lie around, there's lots to do, if you're up for it. Among the categories on this site: The Place, The People, Beaches, and Cultural Events. There's also tips for getting around, lodging, dining, and shopping.

ST. KITTS

✪ **Accenting St. Kitts and Nevis. www.stkitts-nevis.com**
Whether your interest is golfing, fishing, boating, or just about anything else, you'll likely find some information here to help you plan your time on the island. You'll also find tips for dining, lodging, and nightlife.

St. Kitts and Nevis Explorer. **www.chrisevelyn.com/St.Kitts-Nevis/home.htm**
This is a personal guide with virtual tours and advice on attractions and lodging, but beware: It can be very slow to load.

ST. LUCIA

St. Lucia Hotel and Tourism Association. **www.stluciatravel.com.lc**
This is a boosterish guide, but may give you some ideas for things to do.

St. Lucia Tourist Board. **www.stlucia.org**
Official information from the local tourism authority.

SINT MAARTEN/ST. MARTIN

Mr. St. Martin. **www.mrstm.com**
The self-proclaimed authority for St. Martin, this site is a place to find a hotel or restaurant, chat online with others about St. Martin/Sint Maarten, or check the weather.

St. Maarten St. Martin. **www.St-Maarten-St-Martin.com**
From the scenic images of beaches and virtual reality panoramas to solid nuts-and-bolts advice for getting around, this site will whet your appetite for a visit to the island.

U.S. VIRGIN ISLANDS (ST. THOMAS, ST. JOHN & ST. CROIX)

America's Caribbean Paradise: U.S. Virgin Islands Tourist Guide. **www.usvi.net**
This site includes a photographic tour of the three main islands, as well as updates on nightlife and festivals.

United States Virgin Islands. **www.virginisles.com**
This extensive guide is a bit boosterish, but valuable for its extensive coverage of what to see and do.

Index by Ship Name

FROMMER'S® COMPLETE TRAVEL GUIDES

FROMMER'S® DOLLAR-A-DAY GUIDES

Australia from $50 a Day
California from $60 a Day
Caribbean from $70 a Day
England from $70 a Day
Europe from $60 a Day
Florida from $60 a Day

Hawaii from $70 a Day
Ireland from $50 a Day
Israel from $45 a Day
Italy from $70 a Day
London from $85 a Day
New York from $80 a Day

New Zealand from $50 a Day
Paris from $85 a Day
San Francisco from $60 a Day
Washington, D.C.,
 from $60 a Day

FROMMER'S® PORTABLE GUIDES

Acapulco, Ixtapa &
 Zihuatanejo
Alaska Cruises & Ports of Call
Bahamas
Baja & Los Cabos
Berlin
California Wine Country
Charleston & Savannah
Chicago

Dublin
Hawaii: The Big Island
Las Vegas
London
Maine Coast
Maui
New Orleans
New York City
Paris

Puerto Vallarta, Manzanillo
 & Guadalajara
San Diego
San Francisco
Sydney
Tampa & St. Petersburg
Venice
Washington, D.C.

FROMMER'S® NATIONAL PARK GUIDES

Family Vacations in the
 National Parks
Grand Canyon

National Parks of the
 American West
Rocky Mountain

Yellowstone & Grand Teton
Yosemite & Sequoia/
 Kings Canyon
Zion & Bryce Canyon

FROMMER'S® GREAT OUTDOOR GUIDES

New England
Northern California

Southern California & Baja
Washington & Oregon

FROMMER'S® MEMORABLE WALKS

Chicago
London

New York
Paris

San Francisco
Washington D.C.

FROMMER'S® IRREVERENT GUIDES

Amsterdam
Boston
Chicago
Las Vegas

London
Los Angeles
Manhattan

New Orleans
Paris
San Francisco

Seattle & Portland
Vancouver
Walt Disney World
Washington, D.C.

FROMMER'S® BEST-LOVED DRIVING TOURS

America
Britain
California

Florida
France
Germany

Ireland
Italy
New England

Scotland
Spain
Western Europe

THE UNOFFICIAL GUIDES®

SPECIAL-INTEREST TITLES

WHEREVER YOU TRAVEL, *H*ELP IS NEVER FAR AWAY.

From planning your trip to providing travel assistance along the way, American Express® Travel Service Offices are always there to help you do more.

Caribbean

BAHAMAS
Playtours (R)
303 Shirley St.
Nassau
(242) 322-2931

BARBADOS
Barbados International Travel Service
Horizon House
McGregor St.
(246) 431-2423

BRITISH VIRGIN ISLANDS
Travel Plan Ltd. (R)
Romasco Place
Road Town
Tortola
(284) 494-6239

U.S. VIRGIN ISLANDS
Southerland Tours (R)
Chandlers Wharf
Gallows Bay
St. Croix
(340) 773-9500

CAYMAN ISLANDS
Cayman Travel Services, Ltd. (R)
Shedden Rd., Elizabethan Sq.
George Town
Grand Cayman
(345) 949-8755/5400

JAMAICA
Grace Kennedy Travel Ltd. (R)
19-21 Knutsford Blvd.
Kingston 5
(876) 929-6290

MARTINIQUE
Roger Albert Voyages (R)
7 Rue Victor Hugo
Fort de France
(596) 71-71-71/71-42-20

PUERTO RICO
Travel Network (R)
1035 Ashford Ave.
Condado Area
San Juan
(787) 725-0960

ST. KITTS
Kantours (R)
Liverpool Row
Basseterre
(869) 465-2098

ST. MAARTEN
S.E.L. Maduro & Sons, (W.I.) Inc. (R)
Emmaplein Bldg. One
Philipsburg
(599)(5) 22678

Travel

www.americanexpress.com/travel

American Express Travel Service Offices are found in central locations throughout the Caribbean.